Beyond Yellow English

OXFORD STUDIES IN SOCIOLINGUISTICS

General Editors
Nikolas Coupland
Adam Jaworski
Cardiff University

Recently Published in the Series:

Beyond Yellow English

*Toward a Linguistic Anthropology
of Asian Pacific America*

Edited by
Angela Reyes
Adrienne Lo

OXFORD
UNIVERSITY PRESS

2009

Oxford University Press, Inc., publishes works that further
Oxford University's objective of excellence
in research, scholarship, and education.

Oxford New York
Auckland   Cape Town   Dar es Salaam   Hong Kong   Karachi
Kuala Lumpur   Madrid   Melbourne   Mexico City   Nairobi
New Delhi   Shanghai   Taipei   Toronto

With offices in
Argentina   Austria   Brazil   Chile   Czech Republic   France   Greece
Guatemala   Hungary   Italy   Japan   Poland   Portugal   Singapore
South Korea   Switzerland   Thailand   Turkey   Ukraine   Vietnam

Published by Oxford University Press, Inc.
198 Madison Avenue, New York, New York 10016

www.oup.com

Oxford is a registered trademark of Oxford University Press

Library of Congress Cataloging-in-Publication Data
Beyond yellow English : toward a linguistic anthropology of Asian Pacific America / edited by Angela Reyes,
Adrienne Lo.
p. cm. — (Oxford studies in sociolinguistics)
Includes bibliographical references and index.
ISBN 978-0-19-532735-9; 978-0-19-532736-6 (pbk.)
1. Sociolinguistics—United States. 2. Asian Americans—Languages. 3. Asian Americans—Ethnic identity.
4. Asian Americans and mass media. 5. Language and education—United States. I. Reyes, Angela, 1970– II. Lo,
Adrienne.
P40.45.U5B49 2008
306.4408995'073—dc22   2008006542

9 8 7 6 5 4 3 2 1
Printed in the United States of America
on acid-free paper

To S. D. and R. B.

CREDITS

Chapter 2 is a revised version of Bucholtz, Mary. 2004. Styles and stereotypes: The linguistic negotiation of identity among Laotian American youth. *Pragmatics* 14:127–148.

Chapter 3 is a revised version of Reyes, Angela. 2004. Asian American stereotypes as circulating resource. *Pragmatics* 14:173–192.

Chapter 4 is a revised version of Lo, Adrienne. 2004. Evidentiality and morality in a Korean heritage language school. *Pragmatics* 14:235–256.

Chapter 8 is reprinted from Kang, M. Agnes. 2004. Constructing ethnic identity through discourse: Self-categorization among Korean American camp counselors. *Pragmatics* 14:217–233.

Chapter 14 is reprinted from Duranti, Alessandro and Jennifer F. Reynolds. 2000. Phonological and cultural innovations in the speech of Samoans in southern California. *Estudios de Sociolingüística* 1:93–110.

Chapter 16 is reprinted from Chun, Elaine. 2004. Ideologies of legitimate mockery: Margaret Cho's revoicings of Mock Asian. *Pragmatics* 14:263–289.

Chapter 17 is reprinted from Labrador, Roderick N. 2004. "We can laugh at ourselves": Hawai'i ethnic humor, Local identity and the myth of multiculturalism. *Pragmatics* 14:291–316.

Chapter 18 is reprinted from Shankar, Shalini. 2004. Reel to real: Desi teens' linguistic engagements with Bollywood. *Pragmatics* 14:317–335.

Chapter 20 is reprinted from Hinton, Leanne. 1999. Trading tongues: Loss of heritage languages in the United States. *English Today* 15:21–30.

Chapter 21 is a revised version of Talmy, Steven. 2004. Forever FOB: The cultural production of ESL in a high school. *Pragmatics* 14:149–172.

Chapter 22 is a revised version of He, Agnes. 2004. Identity construction in Chinese heritage language classes. *Pragmatics* 14:199–216.

CONTENTS

CONTRIBUTORS

Asif Agha is professor of anthropology and chair of the Department of Anthropology at the University of Pennsylvania. His research interests include linguistics, anthropology, semiotics; language structure and function, language typology and universals; social theory; language and social relations; discourse analysis; metaphor and tropes, register and style; communicative practices in the media; Sino-Tibetan and Indo-Aryan linguistics. He is the author of *Language and Social Relations* (2007).

Niko Besnier is professor of cultural anthropology at the University of Amsterdam. His research has focused on identity formation in the context of globalization and transnationalism, with particular reference to gender, sexuality, interaction, and ideology, and he has conducted fieldwork in two Pacific Island locations, Tonga and Tuvalu. His forthcoming book is titled *Gossip and the Everyday Production of Inequality*.

Mary Bucholtz is professor of linguistics at the University of California, Santa Barbara. Her research investigates the relationship between language and identity, especially with respect to gender, ethnicity, and youth; she has carried out research on language and whiteness, the linguistic appropriation of African American Vernacular English, and the linguistic construction of Latino immigrant youth identities, among other topics. Bucholtz has edited several books on language and gender and has published numerous articles on language and identity.

Elaine W. Chun is an assistant professor of linguistics in the English Department at the University of South Carolina. She conducts research among Asian American youths in multiethnic high schools in the United States. Her work examines practices of "borrowing" linguistic resources across community boundaries, specifically as these practices relate to ideologies of language, humor, race, class, and gender. Her most recent work uses methods of ethnography and discourse analysis to investigate stylized mocking performances of gendered and racialized stereotypes at a high school in Texas. She has also published on the use of stereotypical forms of African American English by Korean American male youths.

Christianne Collantes has an Honors BA degree in English literature and women's studies from the University of Toronto. She will be attending McMaster's MA program in globalization, with a focus on Filipino youth culture, "Third World" feminism, and race and globalization.

Valerie Damasco is a graduate student in adult education and community development at the University of Toronto. She has an Honors BS degree in psychology and sociology. Her research focuses on the life histories of nurses from the Philippines who migrated to Canada in the 1960s. She is currently co-officer of Research and Publications and on the Standing Committee on Education and Training for the Community Alliance for Social Justice in Toronto, Ontario, Canada, and an active member of the Philippine Women Centre of Ontario under the National Alliance of Philippine Women in Canada.

Angela F. De Ocampo has an Honors BA degree in social and cultural anthropology and French as a Second Language from the University of Toronto.

Alessandro Duranti is professor of anthropology at UCLA and the director of the Center for Language, Interaction and Culture (CLIC). His main areas of research are political discourse, agency and intentionality, orality and literacy, the history of linguistic anthropology, and jazz aesthetics. He has carried out fieldwork in (Western) Samoa and the United States. His books include *From Grammar to Politics: Linguistic Anthropology in a Western Samoan Village* (1994), *Linguistic Anthropology* (1997), *Linguistic Anthropology: A Reader* (2001), and *A Companion to Linguistic Anthropology* (2004).

Monina Febria holds an Honors BA degree in international studies and political science from the University of Toronto. She is currently working for the Ontario Council of Agencies Serving Immigrants (OCASI), a provincial advocacy body seeking equality and access for immigrants and refugees in all aspects of Canadian life. She is the co-organizer of a Toronto-based book club named "Pinay," which focuses on North American literature written by various Asian American and Asian Canadian authors.

Susan Gal is Mae and Sidney G. Metzl Distinguished Service Professor of Anthropology and Linguistics at the University of Chicago. She is the author of *Language Shift* (1979), coauthor of *The Politics of Gender after Socialism* (2000), and coeditor of several volumes, including *Languages and Publics: The Making of Authority* (2001). Gal has written on multilingualism and language change, and the politics of language. One of her current projects explores the global circulation and transformation of emotionally charged political terms such as "transparency," "truth," and "democratic speech"; another project concerns the semiotics of linguistic differentiation.

Agnes Weiyun He is associate professor of applied linguistics and Asian studies at the State University of New York-Stony Brook. She is the author of *Reconstructing Institutions: Language Use in Academic Counseling Encounters* (1998), coeditor of *Talking and Testing: Discourse Approaches to the Assessment of Oral Proficiency* (1998), primary editor of *Chinese as a Heritage Language: Fostering Rooted World Citizenry* (2008), as well as author of more than twenty research articles. Her work has been funded by the Spencer Foundation, the National Academy of Education, and the U.S. Department of Education.

Jane H. Hill is Regents' Professor in the Departments of Anthropology and Linguistics at the University of Arizona. She is a specialist on Native American languages, focusing on the Uto-Aztecan family, with fieldwork on Cupeño, Tohono O'odham, and Nahuatl. Her interests include language contact and multilingualism in the U.S. Southwest and Mexico, and in the way popular ideas about these phenomena shape the uses of language in communities in those regions, especially in the construction of white racist culture. She is the author of more than 100 books and articles. Hill has served as president of the Society for Linguistic Anthropology and as president of the American Anthropological Association. She is a Fellow of the American Association for the Advancement of Science and a Member of the American Academy of Arts and Sciences.

Leanne Hinton is professor emeritus of the Linguistics Department at the University of California at Berkeley, where she was director of the Survey of California and Other Indian Languages. Her books include *Havasupai Songs: A Linguistic Perspective* (1984), *Flutes of Fire: Essays on California Indian Languages* (1994), *The Green Book of Language Revitalization in Practice* (with Ken Hale, 2001), and *How to Keep Your Language Alive* (2002). She has written hundreds of articles on Native American languages and concentrates especially on language revitalization for endangered Native American languages. She was awarded the Lannan Foundation's Cultural Freedom Award in 2006.

M. Agnes Kang is assistant professor in the School of English at the University of Hong Kong. Her research focuses on the areas of discourse and ethnic identity, interactional sociolinguistics, and, more recently, on social interaction in the medical context. She is currently working on a project examining the interactional means by which social actions are accomplished in prenatal genetic counseling sessions in Hong Kong. Her articles have appeared in the *Journal of Sociolinguistics*, *Pragmatics*, and *Text*.

Wendy L. Klein is a postdoctoral scholar in linguistic and cultural anthropology at the Center on the Everyday Lives of Families (CELF), an interdisciplinary research center at the University of California, Los Angeles. Her research examines Indian immigrant family life in the United States, marital communication, and child socialization into notions of responsibility and ethnic and religious identification.

Roderick N. Labrador is the director of Gaining Early Awareness and Readiness for Undergraduate Programs (GEAR UP) at the University of Hawai'i at Manoa. He earned his doctorate in sociocultural anthropology from the University of California, Los Angeles.

Adrienne Lo is assistant professor in the Department of Educational Psychology at the University of Illinois at Urbana-Champaign. Her research interests include heritage language learning, the discursive production of race, and the socialization of morality and emotion in Korean American educational institutions. She is currently working on a project on the transnational lives of Korean "early study abroad" students.

Bonnie McElhinny is associate professor of anthropology and of women and gender studies at the University of Toronto. Her research focuses on language, gender, and political economy. A recent research project funded by the Canadian Social Sciences and Humanities Research Council investigates North American interventions into Filipino child-rearing practices, and Filipino responses to these, throughout the twentieth and early twenty-first centuries. Two articles based on this research appear in recent issues of *American Anthropologist* and *Anthropologie et Sociétés*. She is the founding coeditor of *Gender and Language* (2006), and editor of the book *Words, Worlds and Material Girls: Language, Gender, Globalization* (2007).

Emi Morita is assistant professor in the Department of Japanese Studies at the National University of Singapore. Her research interests include conversation analysis, interactional linguistics, and language socialization. Using naturalistic conversational data to examine how particular Japanese lexical items are deployed in talk-in-interaction, her analyses explore the ways in which micro-level conversational concerns are tied to macro-level social organization.

Joseph Sung-Yul Park is assistant professor in the Department of English Language and Literature at the National University of Singapore. His research interests include language and globalization, language ideology, and interactional linguistics. Through his recent work, he has been exploring the role of global English in identity construction within Asian contexts, with a particular focus on South Korea. He is the author of the forthcoming book, *The Local Construction of a Global Language: Ideologies of English in South Korea*.

Angela Reyes is associate professor of linguistics in the English Department at Hunter College, City University of New York. Her research focuses on discourse, ethnicity, style, and Asian American identity. She is the author of *Language, Identity, and Stereotype Among Southeast Asian American Youth: The Other Asian* (2007). She is currently carrying out a research study on Asian American cram schools in New York City.

Jennifer F. Reynolds is assistant professor of anthropology at the University of South Carolina. She is a linguistic and cultural anthropologist, with topical specializations in language socialization, performance, language ideology, transnational migration, and the anthropology of childhood. She has worked in a range of multilingual communities—Samoans in Los Angeles, Kaqchikel Mayas in Guatemala, Western Mono Indians in California, and Mexican immigrant children in Chicago. Most of her research addresses the question of how children and youths' quotidian discourse practices reflect, challenge, and at times reconstitute societal discourses on childhood and development, race and ethnicity, and immigration.

Jason Salonga is a graduate student in structural engineering at the University of Toronto. He has a BA degree in visual arts and BESc degree in civil engineering from the University of Western Ontario. He has been a performer and choreographer in many Filipino cultural groups including Magdaragat Philippines Inc., Folklorico Filipino Canada, and the Western Ontario Organization of Filipinos.

Shalini Shankar is assistant professor in the Department of Anthropology and the Asian American Studies Program at Northwestern University. Her book, *Desi Land: Teen Culture, Class, and Success in Silicon Valley* (2008), analyzes how language use, material culture, and media inform broader dynamics of class, race, and community for Desi teens. Her current research examines intersections of language use, race, and diaspora in the development and production of Asian American advertising.

Juyoung Song is a graduate of the Language, Literacy, and Culture program at The Ohio State University. Her dissertation is an ethnography of Korean-English bilingual children's language socialization, with a focus on their negotiation of ideologies and identity in a bilingual setting. Her research interests include language socialization, interlanguage and cross-cultural pragmatics, language and identity in online communication, and second language teacher education.

Asuka Suzuki is a PhD candidate in the Department of East Asian Languages and Literatures at the University of Hawai'i at Mānoa. Her primary research interests include conversation analysis, linguistic anthropology, and Japanese pedagogy. Drawing on a conversation analytic approach, her current research focuses on examining social interactions involving first and/or second language speakers of Japanese.

Steven Talmy is assistant professor of teaching English as a second language in the Department of Language and Literacy Education, University of British Columbia. His research interests include the negotiation of multilingual identities in schools, K–12 ESL, critical analyses of discourse, and the sociology of ESL education.

Bonnie Urciuoli is professor of anthropology at Hamilton College in Clinton, New York. She has done research on language contact situations and the manifestation of class and race prejudice in language, publications on which include *Exposing Prejudice: Puerto Rican Experiences of Language, Race and Class* (1996). Her current research examines the multi-sited production and representation of "diversity" in U.S. liberal arts education. Her recent publications address the semiotics of educational and corporate discourses of "diversity" and "skills," and the relation of the neoliberalization of higher education to the perception of student and worker selves.

Shirley Yeung is completing her master's degree in sociocultural anthropology at the University of Toronto. Her current research focuses on the relationship between postcolonial nationalism, Philippine literature, and the *Sikolohiyang Pilipino* (Philippine Psychology) movement. Her broader interests include studying the role of science and the arts in national politics, epistemology, and the anthropology of religion. She holds a fellowship from the Social Sciences and Humanities Research Council.

Beyond Yellow English

Introduction

On Yellow English and Other Perilous Terms

Adrienne Lo and Angela Reyes

The nearly 12 million individuals who classified themselves as of Asian or Pacific Islander heritage in the 2000 U.S. Census represent one of the fastest growing groups in the United States. The Asian Pacific American (APA) population has grown eightfold since 1970, and APAs now constitute approximately 4 percent of the total U.S. population. Yet the linguistic practices of this group remain relatively understudied. In descriptions of ethnic and regional dialects across the United States, for example, Asian Pacific Americans are notably absent (Metcalf 2000; Wolfram and Schilling-Estes 2006; Wolfram and Ward 2006). And only a handful of monographs have been devoted to the language practices of APAs (Fu 1995; Reyes 2007; Shin 2005), in comparison with the robust literature on the language practices of African Americans, U.S. Latinos, and Native Americans. Since work on APA language practices in fact dates from the earliest days of linguistic anthropology and sociolinguistics (e.g., Ervin-Tripp 1964; Gumperz 1982; Kuo 1974; Reinecke and Tokimasa 1934; Spencer 1950), why is there so little research in this area? In this introduction, we offer some possible explanations for this lacuna, review some of the research trends in this area, and discuss what a reinvigorated program of research on APAs might add to the study of language, culture, and identity.

What Is "Asian Pacific America"?

Like most scholars in Asian American studies, we recognize that terms like "Asian Pacific American," "Asian American," "Southeast Asian American," and so forth, are highly controversial.[1] Not only do such terms lump together individuals from a wide range of ethnic, linguistic, and national origins, they also foreground ethnicity and race above other, perhaps more relevant, social categories like sexuality, class, age, nation, place of residence, or institution. As Joseph Sung-Yul Park's chapter points out, participants may not identify themselves as "Asian American" or "Asian" or even "American." In some cases, other racialized categories, such as the African American gangster or the white nerd may provide the overarching framework that APAs situate themselves within (Bucholtz, this volume). Even in contexts where categories such as "Pacific Islander" do seem to be prominent local classifications, these categories are often interwoven with other ones, such as class, nation, and language proficiency, as Steven Talmy's chapter shows. Moreover, the indexical meaning of terms like "Sikh," "Japanese," "Korean," "American," and "Asian" is often fraught with contention, as the chapters by M. Agnes Kang, Wendy L. Klein, Park, Angela Reyes, Juyoung Song, and Asuka Suzuki demonstrate. Rather than taking these terms as empirical descriptions, the chapters in this book examine the local specificity of such terms, how different participants orient to such categories in interaction, and how such orientations may change over time.

Though it is prominently displayed in the title of our volume, the term "Asian Pacific America" is not a label that we are necessarily committed to. We recognize the inherent problems in using such a term, in light of its connection to racial hegemony and essentialization. The reason we (and many other scholars in Asian American studies) continue to use these words is that they point to a racializing discourse that has a profound impact on the ways that APAs are situated on a racial and ethnolinguistic landscape. While we certainly recognize the absurdity of grouping the huge diversity of individuals that are classified under the APA umbrella together, the fact remains that APAs are often seen as a single group according to widely circulating American ideologies of race (see, e.g., the U.S. Census). Moreover, the very language that we use to talk about who is APA or not reveals culturally salient ideologies about who is a prototypical "Asian American" and who is not.[2] Whether we like it or not, the term "Asian Pacific American" is not only an enduring category but one that sheds light on social processes that are of immense importance and consequence to individuals, groups, and society. For those who willingly claim the term, it can have enormous social and political utility. For those who are forced inside its parameters, it can be confining and oppressive. While we do not necessarily embrace the term or its essentializing ramifications, we recognize that we must live with it for the time being.

Another term that is prominently displayed in the title, "yellow" (a discussion of "Yellow English" to follow), is also not unproblematic.[3] Like other color labels that have become emblematic of racial groups, such as "black" and "white," the term "yellow" has been the cause of much controversy in its use to symbolize (East) Asian phenotype. Though this term has a history as an ethnic epithet, it also has a history as a reclaimed and celebrated term by Asian American individuals and groups. "Yellow

Power," for example, is the name of a social movement that began in the 1970s by Asian American activists. Similar to the political movements of African Americans, women, and other disenfranchised groups, the Yellow Power Movement fought for equal rights and for the end of discrimination in American society. In addition, several books by Asian American authors reclaim "yellow" in their titles, for example, scholarly work such as *Yellow: Race in America Beyond Black and White* (2003) by Frank Wu, and literary work such as *Yellow* (2001) by Don Lee, and *Yell-Oh Girls* (2001), a collection of young Asian American women writers edited by Vickie Nam. Our choice to use the term "yellow" both points to the unavoidable ways in which APAs have been racialized in the United States, and nods to the efforts of those who have reclaimed and redefined the term.

Invisibility of Asian Pacific Americans in Language Research

Relative to other racial and ethnic groups in the U.S., Asian Pacific Americans have received comparatively little attention from scholars in linguistic anthropology and sociolinguistics. Whereas the language practices of African Americans have been of abiding interest to linguistic anthropologists, sociolinguists, and dialectologists since the 1970s (e.g., Baugh 1983; Kochman 1981; Labov 1972; Mitchell-Kernan 1972; Morgan 2002), and significant bodies of work on Latinos (e.g., Bailey 2002; Fought 2003; Penfield and Ornstein-Galicia 1985; Zentella 1997) and Native Americans (e.g., Basso 1979; Kroskrity 1993; Leap 1993; Philips 1983) form a long-standing tradition, linguistic anthropological work on APAs outside of Hawai'i has yet to receive the same kind of sustained scholarly attention as other racial and ethnic groups in the United States.[4] Although scholars working in Canada, the United Kingdom, and Australia have produced key monographs on the language practices of second- and third-generation Asians in those countries (Li 2002; Nishimura 1997; Rampton 1995; Tuc 2003; Wei 1994), here in the United States we still lack such major book-length treatments on APAs outside of Hawai'i (see, e.g., Reyes 2007; Shin 2005 for exceptions). Given that APAs constitute one of the fastest growing segments of the U.S. population,[5] why have they not garnered more attention from scholars? We offer a few reasons for why Asian Pacific Americans have been relatively absent from research on language practices in the United States.

Sociolinguistic Models of Distinctiveness: The Plight of Yellow English

First, research that has attempted to delineate the contours of "Yellow English" (Kim 1975) (along the lines of "Black English") has not been very productive. That is, efforts to find a variety of ethnically or racially distinctive APA English have generally been unsuccessful. Researchers have found, instead, that the forms of English spoken by APAs are often not recognizable as indexing a particular ethnic or racial group across a speech community (Hanna 1997; Lindemann 2003). As Mary Bucholtz (this volume) notes, current paradigms of language and ethnicity are not very applicable to the APA case because distinctiveness-centered models, which are widely used in sociolinguistics, fail when confronted with the speech practices of APAs. Given the inability of APAs to fit such models, the process of "erasure" (Gal and Irvine 1995) may aptly describe how Asian American discursive practices have been erased, or at least ignored, given that their absence bolsters the ideology that group *x* speaks language *x*, a distinguishable speech variety from language *y* spoken by group *y*.

As Elaine Kim observed (1975), stereotypic representations of Asians in the media, which are linked to stock characters like the wise sage or bumbling incompetent, still have a profound impact on the ways that the English spoken by APAs is viewed (see Chun, Labrador, this volume). Labeling this "Yellow English"—which more recent scholarship describes as "Mock Asian" (see Chun, this volume)—Kim calls our attention to the all too common stylizations of Asian (American) speech as a type of foreign accent. Similar to the Latino case, the English spoken by APAs is often interpreted in terms of an accent or interference from another language, rather than as evidence of dialectal features of English (Lippi-Green 1997). Yet, when Asian Americans are identified as sounding "Asian American," what is salient about their English does not seem to be linked to a particular native or heritage language (Hanna 1997; Spencer 1950). Even in cases where heritage language interference is detected, researchers find that these features are not retained across subsequent generations (e.g., Mendoza-Denton and Iwai 1993; Wolfram, Christian, and Hatfield 1986).

As it stands, then, the most salient widely circulating speech style associated with APAs is this highly performative foreign accent called Yellow English or Mock Asian, which is still prominent in the popular media (Lee 2006). This is not to suggest that other widely or locally circulating APA varieties do not exist (see Labrador, this volume, as well as the ways that specific ethnic groups like Indian Americans are racialized through media performances of "brown voice" [Davé 2005]), but that the interaction between local ideologies of language and identity and widely circulating ones is mediated through stereotypes that circulate across contexts (Reyes 2007). This volume thus attempts to move "beyond Yellow English" to consider the complex ways that Mock Asian as well as other styles of speech are utilized by APA speakers in the performance of aspects of identity. It also moves beyond the distinctiveness paradigm in sociolinguistics to suggest that an ethnic dialect is not necessary in the performance of an ethnic identity. In fact, by focusing on the use of speech varieties (e.g., African American English; see Bucholtz, Reyes, this volume), speech practices (e.g., codeswitching; see Duranti and Reynolds Morita, Song, this volume), and speech genres (e.g., narrative; see Hinton, Klein, McElhinny et al., this volume), the chapters in this volume reveal not only the complicated ways in which ethnicity can be performed but also how other aspects of identity may emerge with more relevance in any given interaction.

Racializing Discourses in the United States: Forever Foreigner and Honorary White

Another main reason why APAs have been overlooked in language research has to do with how APAs have been uniquely racialized by pervading U.S. discourses in ways that have shaped both popular as well as scholarly perspectives. As Mia Tuan

(1998) notes, APAs tend to be pigeonholed as either "forever foreigners" or "honorary whites." The "forever foreigner" viewpoint is reflected by the fact that research on APAs to date has tended to foreground issues related to bilingualism, such as heritage language maintenance, codeswitching, the impact of speakers' heritage languages on their English, and accent perception.[6] Although U.S.-born Asian Americans who are native speakers of English are the fastest growing segment of the Asian Pacific American population (Ong and Leung 2003) and approximately 60 percent of APAs rate themselves as speaking English well according to the 2000 U.S. Census, work on English as a primary medium of communication is still dwarfed by research that highlights bilingual issues.[7]

The "forever foreigner" aspect also results in APAs being situated in relation to "real" native speakers in their home countries, rather than in relation to the American context. Some researchers of heritage languages, for example, look at APA language practices from an explicitly comparative deficit perspective by emphasizing the ways in which APAs' heritage language practices fall short of "authentic" native speakers in Asia and the Pacific. Moreover, it is not uncommon for researchers to look at APAs living in the United States as though they were monolingual (and monocultural) speakers of their heritage languages. Thus, we find scholars who look at the acquisition or functional grammar of Asian and Pacific Islander languages using Asian Pacific American subjects with little attention paid to their multilingual or multicultural context. While this is seen as perfectly acceptable, it is difficult to imagine a parallel case in which a scholar wanting to study the acquisition or use of French would choose all of their subjects from Parisian émigrés in New York, as though living in the United States would not make their language practices fundamentally different from those of French speakers living in France. Although this treatment of immigrants may not be particular to APAs (witness corresponding treatments of Latinos, for example), the image of APAs as living in cloistered ethnic enclaves, somehow separate and apart from the rest of American society, legitimates scholars' depiction of Asian Pacific *Americans* as the repositories of some fundamentally unchanging "Asian" (or "Samoan," etc.) essence (Ong and Nonini 1997).

The "forever foreigner" image coexists alongside a contradictory "honorary white" viewpoint, which is equally problematic in that it assumes all APAs assimilate to some idea of the white middle-class mainstream in a way that erases their racial status. This perspective argues that APAs simply exemplify another case of the American "melting pot" and over a generation or two become equivalent to "white" mainstream English speakers. This stereotype ignores both the well-documented examples of racism that greets APAs in communities that are suddenly "flooded" by them[8] as well as the ways in which many APAs may not be assimilating to middle-class white norms of spoken English (see Bucholtz, Reyes, this volume; Zhou and Bankston 1998).

This racial positioning thus leads to three simultaneous trends. First, APAs are often situated as non-English-speaking foreigners in ways that erase their membership in American society. At the same time, second- and later-generation APAs are seen as linguistically and culturally assimilated to middle-class white norms. Last, APAs are often positioned by scholars as well as by members of their ethnic communities as "inauthentic" speakers of heritage languages, evaluated by the *deficiency* of their linguistic practice when measured against "real" native speakers.

Previous Research on Asian Pacific American Linguistic Practices

Early sociolinguistic research on mainland APAs includes Robert Spencer's (1950) article in *American Speech* on the English of Japanese American *nisei* (second generation). Based on his research in internment camps, this work outlines several linguistic and paralinguistic features of the speech of Japanese Americans. Spencer points out that the distinctive patterns of English that he observed are not so much the product of a "foreign accent" as they are reflective of the social isolation that many *nisei* faced. Several studies have found that participants do not seem to be able to identify either first- or second-generation APAs as APA based exclusively on listening to tape recordings of their English (Hanna 1997; Lindemann 2003). The experimental methods used in these elicitation studies have not generally been successful in disentangling the complex issues surrounding the English that APAs speak. These include: (1) In what situations and with whom do APAs speak a version of English that is different from Mainstream American English?; (2) What are the features of this English?; (3) Is this variety identifiable as indexing a particular ethnic or racial identity?; and (4) If so, who recognizes it as such?

Another body of work examining APA linguistic practices is codeswitching. One of the earliest studies is Susan Ervin-Tripp's (1964) article on the speech of Japanese war brides married to American servicemen that appeared in the special issue of the *American Anthropologist* edited by John Gumperz and Dell Hymes. Ervin-Tripp examined the ways in which Japanese American women invoke different topics when speaking in English or Japanese to American or Japanese interlocutors. Work on codeswitching continues to be one of the more productive areas of inquiry, with bodies of work on codeswitching among Vietnamese Americans (Kleifgen 2001), Korean Americans (Ha 1995; Kang 2003; Lo 1999; Shin and Milroy 2000; Yoon 1992), Japanese Americans (Kozasa 2000), and Japanese Canadians (Nishimura 1997).

Issues in heritage language learning, literacy, and second language learning among APAs are also growing fields of research. In particular, the heritage language learning of Chinese Americans, Korean Americans, and Japanese Americans has received much attention in recent years (e.g., He and Xiao, 2008; Kondo-Brown 2006; Kondo-Brown and Brown 2007; Lee and Shin, forthcoming). Literacy practices have been documented among Hmong Americans (Weinstein-Shr 1993), Khmer Americans (Hardman 1998; Needham 2003; Skilton-Sylvester 2002), Laotian Americans (Fu 1995), native Hawaiians (Au 1980), Samoan Americans (Duranti, Ochs, and Ta'ase 1995), Korean Americans (Scarcella and Chin 1993), Japanese Americans (Miller 2004), Filipino Canadians (Li 2000), and Chinese Canadians (Li 2002, 2006). Finally, there is an abundance of work in second language studies examining English language learning among Asian immigrants in several locales, including the mainland United States (e.g., Chiang and Schmida 1999; Hakuta 1975; Harklau 1994), Hawai'i (e.g., Schmidt 1983), and Canada (e.g., Duff, Wong, and Early 2002; Pon, Goldstein, and Schecter 2003).

Organization of the Volume

By taking a discourse approach to examine how APA identities are locally constituted in conjunction with ideologies of race and ethnicity, we seek to problematize essentialist approaches that equate APA identity with speaking either a heritage language or an ethnically marked form of English. Instead, the chapters in this book look at how such identities take shape as they locally emerge in interaction. This focus on the situated unfoldings of identity reveals how interactants position themselves relative to others and to the discourses that circulate through mass media, institutions, and everyday contexts.

Though each chapter in this volume focuses on individuals who get categorized or categorize themselves under the larger APA umbrella, the chapters are also quite diverse in several regards. Authors deal with a range of different data sets: classroom interaction (He, Lo, Talmy), casual conversation (Duranti and Reynolds, Morita, Park, Reyes, Shankar, Song), interviews (Bucholtz, Klein, McElhinny et al.), autobiographies (Hinton), public performances (Chun, Labrador), and large meetings (Kang, Suzuki). In doing so, several chapters problematize the public/private distinction, revealing how publicly circulating discourses get taken up even in private settings (e.g., Klein, Shankar). There is a diversity of research methodologies, including variations of narrative analysis (e.g., McElhinny et al.), conversation analysis (e.g., He), and sociolinguistic and linguistic anthropological methods of discourse analysis (e.g., Bucholtz).

The book is divided into five parts. Each part contains three or four chapters followed by a commentary. The volume could have been organized in multiple ways given each chapter's ability to highlight different relationships across the collection. The groupings we created underscore issues that we hope will be of particular theoretical interest to sociolinguists and linguistic anthropologists.

Part I, "Interactional Positionings of Selves and Identities," focuses on the ways in which individuals interactionally position themselves in microlevel interaction. Each of the three chapters illustrates how this locally traceable process relies on the invocation of widely circulating categories, particularly those of race, ethnicity, and linguistic form. Mary Bucholtz's chapter describes how two Laotian American teenagers position themselves with relation to the "model-minority nerd" and the more recent "gangster" stereotype of Asian Americans. By using the locally available resources of African American English and youth slang, these girls find ways to position themselves between the school's binary black/white dichotomy, showing how APAs can carve out a distinct social space even in the absence of an ethnically distinctive dialect of English. Angela Reyes's chapter reveals the complex ways that Southeast Asian American teenagers at a youth center orient to both locally and widely circulating stereotypes about Asians. Reyes shows that teens can both resist as well as embrace stereotypes as resources for identity making. Adrienne Lo's chapter looks at how a Korean American teacher's use of evidential marking interactionally positions her students as opposing moral types. In each of these chapter, participants' identities as, for example, "model minority" or "Asian" or "morally suspect" are not natural categories, but indexically emergent in ways that link them to particular ideologies and practices.

Part II, "Discursive Constitutions of Groups and Communities," highlights the multifaceted ways in which APAs orient themselves with respect to particular types of communities. Bonnie McElhinny et al. examine how discontinuities are accounted for in Filipino Canadian immigrants' life stories about work choices. In these narratives, coherence and agency take different shape than in white middle-class narratives. Wendy L. Klein's chapter on Punjabi Sikh families in Los Angeles focuses on how members of different generations articulate their understanding of what it means to wear a *dastaar* or turban. She argues that ideological perspectives on the significance and practice of wearing a turban are variable and reflect historically situated processes of identification. Both M. Agnes Kang and Asuka Suzuki show how cleavages of identity operate even within what might be considered a single ethnic community. Kang's chapter examines how participants at a Korean American camp carefully situate themselves within a field of oppositions, locally producing categorical distinctions among participants as "Korean," "American," and "Korean American," and locating self and others in these discursively constituted groups. Suzuki traces how interactants reformulate generational, regional, and practice-based categories of Japanese and Japanese American identity in Hawai'i across turns. The chapters in this section illustrate how the establishment of groups, group practices, and group membership is emergent in conjunction with the identification of relevant contextual factors that come to bear on speakers and interactions.

Part III, "Languages in Contact," centers on issues of linguistic change and innovation in contexts where two or more codes meet and mix. Using the concept of indexical order, Emi Morita's chapter examines how the insertion of the English *me* in Japanese utterances emerged historically with different meanings in different Japanese and Japanese American communities. Joseph Sung-Yul Park explores how Korean international students in the United States orient themselves in relation to categories of identity through their recontextualization of language ideologies about who is and is not a legitimate speaker of English. Juyoung Song looks at the multifaceted strategies that bilingual Korean American children undertake to avoid using Korean address terms. Focusing on moments of bilingual creativity, Song's chapter complicates code boundaries by revealing instances where children create hybrid and bivalent forms (Woolard 1998). In the chapter by Alessandro Duranti and Jennifer F. Reynolds, phonological innovations in the speech of Samoan Americans are identified through the analysis of codeswitching data, revealing implications for cultural innovations among this community of speakers. While much previous research on Asian American language use deals with codeswitching, this group of chapters brings a renewed rigor, incorporating linguistic anthropological concepts to reveal complex indexical processes when two or more languages are in play.

Part IV, "Linguistic Practices in Media Contexts," contains three chapters that focus on the circulation of discourses of language and identity in mass communication. While Elaine W. Chun analyzes the complex indexical and ideological values of a Korean American comedian's performances of "Mock Asian," Roderick N. Labrador reveals how having a distinctively foreign "accent" is a central stigmatizing feature in the racist depiction of Filipinos in the discourse of local comedians in Hawai'i. Both Chun's and Labrador's chapters explore ideologies of humor and race that license second- and later-generation comedians and their audiences to instantiate a hierarchy of differentiation (Bucholtz and Hall 2004) by mocking the linguistic practices of those with a foreign accent. Shalini Shankar's chapter highlights the ways in which Bollywood films[9] serve as an empowering resource for Desi youth, providing them with frameworks for understanding their own lives. In each chapter, contextually bound media practices in which individuals engage profoundly influence the production and interpretation of APA identities.

Part V, "Educational Institutions and Language Acquisition," examines school settings in which APA identities are produced in relation to language learning. Leanne Hinton analyzes narratives of Asian American college students, who consistently identify matters of heritage language loss and English language acquisition as key issues in their identity development. Steven Talmy's chapter reveals how differentiating oneself from more newly arrived FOBs[10] is a key social practice for immigrant youth in a Hawai'i high school who use Pidgin to underscore both the long history of their childhood socialization in Hawai'i and their affiliation as "Local." Agnes Weiyun He's chapter demonstrates how teachers and students in a Chinese heritage language classroom negotiate the use of two different Chinese writing systems, which disrupts and recreates the ongoing emergence of authority in the classroom. These chapters reveal how educational settings in which issues of language learning are underscored become crucial sites in which APA identities are shaped.

Future Research

We hope that this volume will be an important first step toward a reinvigorated program of research on APAs and language. In putting this volume together, we attempted to secure broad coverage of various ethnic groups, regions, and sociocultural contexts, but given the highly selective focus of current research, we were not able to include many aspects of the APA experience. In addition to the many different ethnic groups (including mixed-race APAs) who are underrepresented, we would have liked to redirect attention beyond the immigrant and second generation to examine third- and later-generation APAs, who are nearly entirely absent from current research paradigms. We need more work outside of the usual focus on urban areas, on arenas in which APA identity may not necessarily be graspable in the ways that we have tended to look for it.

Although the chapters in this volume tend to take an ethnicity- or race-based approach to APA identity, we wish to emphasize that coverage of specific ethnic groups can never provide a complete picture of APA language use. These subgroups are also fractured: a chapter on Chinese Americans cannot in any way be representative of all Chinese Americans since ethnicity is not necessarily a unifying characteristic across speakers. As mentioned earlier, sometimes other factors like class (Labrador, this volume), gender (Chun, Labrador, this volume), sexuality (Manalansan 1995), institutional roles (He, Lo, Talmy, this volume), generation, age, language, and so forth, may in fact be more salient in a particular local context. As a number of the chapters demonstrate, intraethnic othering (Pyke and Dang 2003) is often quite powerful, revealing the fissures within what might otherwise be considered a 'single' ethnic group (see Kang, Labrador, Suzuki, this volume).

We highlight the following directions for future research in this area. First, we need more work which takes a comparative racialization perspective to examine how APA identity is the result of complex processes of definition in relation to other racialized groups (Kim 1999; Molina 2006). Second, greater attention to the transnational context of APA lives, and the ways that language ideologies get transformed and recontextualized is important (see Duranti and Reynolds, Morita, Park, Song, this volume). Last, we hope that our volume will help to spur work that attempts to integrate close attention to the particularities of interaction with the wider discourses that frame APA identity.

This volume developed from two sessions at the American Anthropological Association annual meetings in 2002 and 2003, and a special issue of Pragmatics *14 (2/3) in 2004. We would like to thank the following people for their encouragement of this work over the past several years: Mary Bucholtz, Barbara Johnstone, Bonnie McElhinny, Kent Ono, John Rickford, Andrew Wong, and Ana Celia Zentella. Thanks also to Mi-Suk Seo, Tomomi Kumai, Hyojin Jenna Chi, and Robin Conley for their editorial assistance. Preparation of this chapter, which represents the equal work of both authors, was supported by grants from the University of Illinois Research Board and the Woodrow Wilson National Fellowship Foundation. Selected portions of this chapter are taken from Angela Reyes and Adrienne Lo (2004) "Language, identity and relationality in Asian Pacific America: An introduction" in* Pragmatics *14(2/3):115–125.*

NOTES

1. See Davé et al. (2000), Hirabayashi and Alquizola (2001), Kauanui (2005), Nomura (2003), and Wright and Spickard (2002) among others for discussions of the politics of the problematics of which groups have been central or peripheral to Asian American studies.

2. The normative "Asian American" subject, who is marked in terms of ethnicity, class, and generation, is revealed through the ways that the term appears in conjunction with or in contrast to other terms (e.g., Asian *and* Pacific Islander American, South Asian American vs. [East] Asian American, etc.).

3. The very choice of "Yellow" here, as opposed to "Brown," which is the color that many APAs identify with instead, points to the ways that this kind of racializing discourse takes those who are considered "Yellow" (e.g., Chinese, Japanese, etc.) as "core" members of a category that also includes those who might be considered "Brown" (e.g., Filipino Americans, Indian Americans, etc.) (Prashad 2000; Rondilla 2002).

4. Research on Hawai'i Creole and the politics of language in Hawai'i has been robust (e.g., Reinecke 1969; Romaine 1999, 2002; Sato 1985, 1991).

5. Between 1990 and 2000, the APA population in the United States increased 72 percent. The total U.S. population growth during that time was 13 percent. According to the latest census projections, the number of APAs is expected to reach 33 million by 2050.

6. See, e.g., Ching and Kung (1997), Jo (2001), Li (1982), Sridhar (1988), and Tse (1996).

7. See Bailey (1997), Chun (2001), Hanna (1997), Kang (2003), Kang and Lo (2004), Mendoza-Denton and Iwai (1993), Reyes (2007), Ryoo (2005), and Yamaguchi (2005) for exceptions.

8. See Crawford (1992, 1–11, 136–147) for discussions of linguistic racism in Monterey Park, Calif., and Lowell, Mass.

9. Bollywood films are films produced in Bombay (Mumbai), India.

10. FOB is an acronym of "Fresh Off the Boat," a derogatory label for an unacculturated Asian immigrant newly arrived to the United States.

REFERENCES

Au, Kathryn Hu-Pei. 1980. Participation structures in a reading lesson with Hawaiian children: Analysis of a culturally appropriate instructional event. *Anthropology and Education Quarterly* 11:91–115. .

Bailey, Benjamin H. 1997. Communication of respect in interethnic service encounters. *Language in Society* 26:327–356.

————. 2002. *Language, race, and negotiation of identity: A study of Dominican Americans.* The new Americans. New York: LFB Scholarly Publishing.

Basso, Keith H. 1979. *Portraits of "The Whiteman": Linguistic play and cultural symbols among the western Apache.* Cambridge; New York: Cambridge University Press.

Baugh, John. 1983. *Black street speech: Its history, structure, and survival.* Texas linguistics series. Austin: University of Texas Press.

Bucholtz, Mary, and Kira Hall. 2004. Language and identity. In *A companion to linguistic anthropology,* ed. Alessandro Duranti, 369–394. Malden, Mass.: Blackwell.

Chiang, Yuet-Sim D., and Mary Schmida. 1999. Language identity and language ownership: Linguistic conflicts of first-year university writing students. In *Generation 1.5 meets college composition: Issues in the teaching of writing to U.S.-educated learners of ESL,* ed. Linda Harklau, Kay M. Losey, and Meryl Siegal, 81–96. Mahwah, N.J.: Lawrence Erlbaum.

Ching, Marvin K. L., and Hsiang-te Kung. 1997. Ethnic identity, Americanization, and survival of the mother tongue: The first- vs. the second-generation Chinese of professionals in Memphis. In *Language variety in the South revisited,* ed. Cynthia Bernstein, Thomas Nunnally, and Robin Sabino, 163–170. Tuscaloosa and London: University of Alabama Press.

Chun, Elaine. 2001. The construction of White, Black, and Korean American identities through African American Vernacular English. *Journal of Linguistic Anthropology* 11:52–64.

Crawford, James. 1992. *Hold your tongue: Bilingualism and the politics of English only.* Reading, Mass.: Addison-Wesley.

Davé, Shilpa. 2005. Apu's brown voice: Cultural inflection and South Asian accents. In *East Main Street: Asian American popular culture,* ed. Shilpa Davé, LeiLani Nishime, and Tasha G. Oren, 313–336. New York: New York University Press.

Davé, Shilpa, Pawan Dhingra, Sunaina Maira, Partha Mazumdar, Lavina Dhingra Shankar, Jaideep Singh, and Rajini Srikanth. 2000. De-privileging positions: Indian Americans, South Asian Americans, and the politics of Asian American studies. *Journal of Asian American Studies* 3:67–100.

Duff, Patsy, Ping Wong, and Margaret Early. 2002. Learning language for work and life: The linguistic socialization of immigrant Canadians seeking careers in healthcare. *Modern Language Journal* 86:397–422.

Duranti, Alessandro, Elinor Ochs, and Elia K. Ta'ase. 1995. Change and tradition in literacy instruction in a Samoan American community. *Educational Foundations* 9:57–74.

Ervin-Tripp, Susan. 1964. An analysis of the interaction of language, topic, and listener. *American Anthropologist* 66:86–102.

Fought, Carmen. 2003. *Chicano English in context.* New York: Palgrave Macmillan.

Fu, Danling. 1995. *My trouble is my English: Asian students and the American dream.* Portsmouth, N.H.: Boynton/Cook: Heinemann.

Gal, Susan, and Judith Irvine. 1995. The boundaries of languages and disciplines: How ideologies construct difference. *Social Research* 62:967–1001.

Gumperz, John. 1982. Fact and inference in courtroom testimony. In *Language and social identity,* ed. John Gumperz, 163–194. Cambridge: Cambridge University Press.

Ha, Francis Inki. 1995. Shame in Asian and Western cultures. *American Behavioral Scientist* 38:1114–1131.

Hakuta, Kenji. 1975. Learning to speak a second language: What exactly does the child learn? In *Developmental psycholinguistics: Theory and applications*, ed. Daniel P. Dato, 193–207. Washington, D.C.: Georgetown University Press.

Hanna, David B. 1997. Do I sound "Asian" to you?: Linguistic markers of Asian American identity. In *Penn Working Papers in Linguistics*, ed. Alexis Dimitriadis, Laura Siegel, Clarissa Surek-Clark, and Alexander Williams, 4:141–153. Philadelphia: University of Pennsylvania Department of Linguistics.

Hardman, Joel. 1998. Literacy and bilingualism in a Cambodian community in the USA. In *Literacy development in a multilingual context: Cross-cultural perspectives*, ed. Aydin Yèucesan Durgunoglu and Ludo Verhoeven, 51–81. Mahwah, N.J.: Lawrence Erlbaum.

Harklau, Linda. 1994. ESL versus mainstream classes: Contrasting L2 learning environments. *TESOL Quarterly* 28:241–272.

He, Agnes Weiyun, and Yun Xiao, ed. 2008. *Chinese as a heritage language: Fostering rooted world citizenry*. National Foreign Language Resource Center. University of Hawai'i at Manoa. Honolulu: University of Hawai'i Press.

Hirabayashi, Lane Ryo, and Marilyn Caballero Alquizola. 2001. Whither the Asian American subject? In *Color-line to borderlands: The matrix of American ethnic studies*, ed. Johnnella E. Butler, 169–202. Seattle: University of Washington Press.

Jo, Hye-young. 2001. 'Heritage' language learning and ethnic identity: Korean Americans' struggle with language authorities. *Language, Culture and Curriculum* 14:26–41.

Kang, M. Agnes. 2003. Negotiating conflict within the constraints of social hierarchies in Korean American discourse. *Journal of Sociolinguistics* 7:299–320.

Kang, M. Agnes, and Adrienne Lo. 2004. Two ways of articulating heterogeneity in Korean-American narratives of ethnic identity. *Journal of Asian American Studies* 7:93–116.

Kauanui, J. Kēhaulani. 2005. Asian American studies and the 'Pacific question.' In *Asian American studies after critical mass*, ed. Kent A. Ono, 123–143. Malden, Mass.: Blackwell.

Kim, Claire Jean. 1999. The racial triangulation of Asian Americans. *Politics and Society* 27:105–138.

Kim, Elaine. 1975. Yellow English. *Asian American Review* 2:44–63.

Kleifgen, Jo Anne. 2001. Assembling talk: Social alignments in the workplace. *Research on Language and Social Interaction* 34:279–308.

Kochman, Thomas. 1981. *Black and white styles in conflict*. Chicago: University of Chicago Press.

Kondo-Brown, Kimi, ed. 2006. *Heritage language development: Focus on East Asian immigrants*. Amsterdam; Philadelphia: John Benjamins.

Kondo-Brown, Kimi, and James Dean Brown, ed. 2007. *Teaching Chinese, Japanese, and Korean heritage language students: Curriculum needs, materials, and assessments*. Mahwah, N.J.: Lawrence Erlbaum.

Kozasa, Tomoko. 2000. Code-switching in Japanese/English: A study of Japanese-American WWII Veterans. In *Japanese/Korean linguistics*, ed. Mineharu Nakayama and Charles J. Quinn, Jr., 9:209–222. Stanford, Calif.: Center for the Study of Language and Information.

Kroskrity, Paul V. 1993. *Language, history, and identity: Ethnolinguistic studies of the Arizona Tewa*. Tucson: University of Arizona Press.

Kuo, Eddie C. Y. 1974. Bilingual pattern of a Chinese immigrant group in the United States. *Anthropological Linguistics* 16:128–140.

Labov, William. 1972. *Language in the inner city: Studies in the Black English vernacular*. Philadelphia: University of Pennsylvania Press.

Leap, William. 1993. *American Indian English*. Salt Lake City: University of Utah Press.

Lee, Don. 2001. *Yellow*. New York: W. W. Norton.

Lee, Jin Sook, and Sarah J. Shin, ed. Forthcoming. *Korean as a heritage language*. A special issue of *Heritage Language Journal* 6.

Lee, Jung-Eun Janie. 2006. *Representations of Asian speech in Hollywood films*. Department of Linguistics, University of California at Santa Barbara.

Li, Guofang. 2000. Family literacy and cultural identity: An ethnographic study of a Filipino family in Canada. *McGill Journal of Education* 35:9–29.

———. 2002. *East is east, west is west?: Home literacy, culture, and schooling*. New York: Peter Lang.

———. 2006. *Battles of literacy and culture: Teaching and learning in a new social order*. Albany: State University of New York Press.

Li, Wen Lang. 1982. The language shift of Chinese Americans. *International Journal of the Sociology of Language* 38:109–124.

Lindemann, Stephanie. 2003. Koreans, Chinese or Indians? Attitudes and ideologies about non-native English speakers in the United States. *Journal of Sociolinguistics* 7:348–364.

Lippi-Green, Rosina. 1997. *English with an accent: Language, ideology, and discrimination in the United States*. London; New York: Routledge.

Lo, Adrienne. 1999. Codeswitching, speech community membership, and the construction of ethnic identity. *Journal of Sociolinguistics* 3:461–479.

Manalansan, Martin F. 1995. "Performing" Filipino gay experiences: Linguistic strategies in a transnational context. In *Beyond the lavender lexicon: Authenticity, imagination, and appropriation in lesbian and gay languages*, ed. William Leap, 249–266. Amsterdam: Gordon and Breach.

Mendoza-Denton, Norma, and Melissa Iwai. 1993. "They speak more Caucasian": Generational differences in the speech of Japanese-Americans. In *Proceedings of the First Annual Symposium about Language and Society—Austin*, ed. Robin Queen and Rusty Barrett, 58–67. Austin: University of Texas.

Metcalf, Allan A. 2000. *How we talk: American regional English today*. Boston: Houghton Mifflin.

Miller, Laura. 2004. Consuming Japanese print media in Chicago. In *Ethnolinguistic Chicago: Language and literacy in the city's neighborhoods*, ed. Marcia Farr, 357–380. Mahwah, N.J.: Lawrence Erlbaum.

Mitchell-Kernan, Claudia L. 1972. Signifying and marking: Two Afro-American speech acts. In *Directions in sociolinguistics*, ed. John J. Gumperz and Dell Hymes, 161–179. New York: Blackwell.

Molina, Natalia. 2006. *Fit to be citizens?: Public health and race in Los Angeles, 1879–1939*. Berkeley and Los Angeles: University of California Press.

Morgan, Marcyliena H. 2002. *Language, discourse and power in African American culture*. Studies in the social and cultural foundations of language, no. 20. Cambridge; New York: Cambridge University Press.

Nam, Vickie, ed. 2001. *Yell-oh girls: Emerging voices explore culture, identity, and growing up Asian American*. New York: Harper Paperbacks.

Needham, Susan. 2003. "This is active learning": Theories of language, learning, and social relations in the transmission of Khmer literacy. *Anthropology and Education Quarterly* 34:27–49.

Nishimura, Miwa. 1997. *Japanese/English code-switching: Syntax and pragmatics*. Berkeley insights in linguistics and semiotics 24. New York: Peter Lang.

Nomura, Gail M. 2003. Introduction: On our terms: Definitions and context. In *Asian/Pacific Islander American women: A historical anthology*, ed. Shirley Hune and Gail M. Nomura, 16–23. New York: New York University Press.

Ong, Aihwa, and Donald Nonini. 1997. *Ungrounded empires: The cultural politics of modern Chinese transnationalism*. New York: Routledge.

Ong, Paul, and Loh-Sze Leung. 2003. Demographics. In *The new face of Asian Pacific America: Numbers, diversity, and change in the twenty-first century,* ed. Eric Yo Ping Lai and Dennis Arguelles, 7–16. San Francisco: AsianWeek.

Penfield, Joyce, and Jacob L. Ornstein-Galicia. 1985. *Chicano English: An ethnic contact dialect.* Amsterdam; Philadelphia: John Benjamins.

Philips, Susan Urmston. 1983. *The invisible culture: Communication in classroom and community on the Warm Springs Indian reservation.* New York: Longman.

Pon, Gordon, Tara Goldstein, and Sandra R. Schecter. 2003. Interrupted silences: The contemporary education of Hong Kong-born Chinese Canadians. In *Language socialization in bilingual and multilingual societies,* ed. Robert Bayley and Sandra R. Schecter, 114–127. Clevedon, United Kingdom: Multilingual Matters.

Prashad, Vijay. 2000. *The karma of brown folk.* Minneapolis: University of Minnesota Press.

Pyke, Karen, and Tran Dang. 2003. "FOB" and "whitewashed": Identity and internalized racism among second generation Asian Americans. *Qualitative Sociology* 26:147–172.

Rampton, Ben. 1995. *Crossing: Language and ethnicity among adolescents.* New York: Longman.

Reinecke, John E. 1969. *Language and dialect in Hawaii: A sociolinguistic history to 1935.* Honolulu: University of Hawaii Press.

Reinecke, John E., and Aiko Tokimasa. 1934. The English Dialect of Hawaii. *American Speech* 9:122–131.

Reyes, Angela. 2007. *Language, identity, and stereotype among Southeast Asian American youth: The other Asian.* Mahwah, N.J.: Lawrence Erlbaum.

Romaine, Suzanne. 1999. Changing attitudes towards Hawai'i Creole English: Fo' get one good job, you gotta know ho fo; talk like one haole. In *Creole genesis, attitudes and discourse,* ed. John Rickford and Suzanne Romaine, 287–301. Amsterdam: John Benjamins.

———. 2002. Signs of identity, signs of discord: Glottal goofs and the green grocer's glottal in debates on Hawaiian orthography. *Journal of Linguistic Anthropology* 12:189–224.

Rondilla, Joanne L. 2002. The Filipino question in Asia and the Pacific: Rethinking regional origins in diaspora. In *Pacific diaspora: Island peoples in the United States and across the Pacific,* ed. Paul Spickard, Joanne L. Rondilla, and Debbie Hippolite Wright, 56–66. Honolulu: University of Hawai'i Press.

Ryoo, Hye-Kyung. 2005. Achieving friendly interactions: A study of service encounters between Korean shopkeepers and African American customers. *Discourse and Society* 16:79–105.

Sato, Charlene J. 1991. Sociolinguistic variation and language attitudes in Hawaii. In *English around the world: Sociolinguistic perspectives,* ed. Jenny Cheshire, 647–663. Cambridge: Cambridge University Press.

Scarcella, Robin, and Kusup Chin. 1993. *Literacy practices in two Korean-American communities.* Research Report 8. Santa Cruz, Calif.: National Center for Research on Cultural Diversity and Second Language Learning.

Schmidt, Richard. 1983. Interaction, acculturation, and the acquisition of communicative competence: A case study of an adult. In *Sociolinguistics and language acquisition,* ed. Nessa Wolfson and Elliott Judd, 137–174. Rowley, Mass.: Newbury House.

Shin, Sarah J. 2005. *Developing in two languages: Korean children in America.* Clevedon, United Kingdom: Multilingual Matters.

Shin, Sarah J., and Lesley Milroy. 2000. Conversational codeswitching among Korean-English bilingual children. *International Journal of Bilingualism* 4:351–383.

Skilton-Sylvester, Ellen. 2002. Literate at home but not at school: A Cambodian girl's journey from playwright to struggling writer. In *School's out! Bridging out-of-school literacies with classroom practice,* ed. Glynda A. Hull and Katherine Schultz, 61–90. New York: Teachers College Press.

Spencer, Robert F. 1950. Japanese-American language behavior [Dec.]. *American Speech* 25:241–252.

Sridhar, Kamal K. 1988. Language maintenance and language shift among Asian-Indians: Kannadigas in the New York area. *International Journal of Sociology of Language* 69:73–87.

Tse, Lucy. 1996. Language brokering in linguistic minority communities: The case of Chinese- and Vietnamese-American students. *Bilingual Research Journal* 20:485–498.

Tuan, Mia. 1998. *Forever foreigners or honorary whites?: The Asian ethnic experience today.* New Brunswick, N.J.: Rutgers University Press.

Tuc, Ho-Dac. 2003. *Vietnamese-English bilingualism: Patterns of code-switching.* London; New York: Routledge Curzon.

Wei, Li. 1994. *Three generations, two languages, one family: Language choice and language shift in a Chinese community in Britain.* Multilingual matters 104. Clevedon; Philadelphia: Multilingual Matters.

Weinstein-Shr, Gail. 1993. Literacy and social process: A community in transition. In *Cross-cultural approaches to literacy,* ed. Brian Street, 272–293. Cambridge: Cambridge University Press.

Wolfram, Walt, Donna Christian, and Deborah Hatfield. 1986. The English of adolescent and young adult Vietnamese refugees in the United States. *World Englishes* 5:47–60.

Wolfram, Walt, and Natalie Schilling-Estes. 2006. *American English: Dialects and variation.* Malden, Mass.; Oxford: Blackwell.

Wolfram, Walt, and Ben Ward. 2006. *American voices: How dialects differ from coast to coast.* Malden, Mass.; Oxford: Blackwell.

Woolard, Kathryn A. 1998. Simultaneity and bivalency as strategies in bilingualism. *Journal of Linguistic Anthropology* 8:3–29.

Wright, Debbie Hippolite, and Paul Spickard. 2002. Pacific Islander Americans and Asian American identity. In *Contemporary Asian American communities: Intersections and divergences,* ed. Linda Trinh Võ and Rick Bonus, 105–119. Philadelphia: Temple University Press.

Wu, Frank. 2003. *Yellow: Race in America beyond black and white.* New York: Basic Books.

Yamaguchi, Masataka. 2005. Discursive representation and enactment of national identities: The case of Generation 1.5 Japanese. *Discourse and Society* 16:269–299.

Yoon, Keumsil Kim. 1992. New perspective on intrasentential code-switching: A study of Korean-English switching. *Applied Psycholinguistics* 13:433–449.

Zentella, Ana Celia. 1997. *Growing up bilingual: Puerto Rican children in New York.* Malden, Mass.: Blackwell.

Zhou, Min, and Carl L. Bankston. 1998. *Growing up American: How Vietnamese children adapt to life in the United States.* New York: Russell Sage Foundation.

I

Interactional Positionings
of Selves and Identities

2

Styles and Stereotypes

Laotian American Girls' Linguistic Negotiation of Identity

Mary Bucholtz

Within the last two decades, an outpouring of research on East, South, and Southeast Asian immigrants to the United States and their descendants has documented the diverse experiences of the extremely varied groups assigned to the category of "Asian American." Until recently, linguistic contributions to this scholarly undertaking primarily tended to be from the perspective either of applied linguistics or of the sociology of language, with the emphasis on acquisition of English by the immigrant generation on the one hand, and maintenance and shift of the heritage language by the second generation and later generations on the other. Despite the utility of such research, what these studies often leave out is a careful consideration of language and identity, and particularly how English may become a semiotic resource for establishing new forms of identity within the racial landscape of the United States. For Asian Americans, who in the U.S. context are racialized as nonwhite, this identity project is complicated by the need to navigate the hegemonic U.S. model of race as a dichotomy between blackness and whiteness, a view that may still hold ideological sway even in local contexts in which the available racialized positions are far more complex, such as many parts of California. Thus the construction of local Asian American identities through linguistic and other semiotic resources often emerges in relation to powerful racial ideologies of dichotomous difference. At the same time, Asian Americans are also the targets of widely circulating cultural stereotypes that serve to delimit and define the racialized category to which they have been assigned. This chapter considers the different ways in which some Asian American youth in California use local varieties of English to negotiate ideologies of race and Asianness in the production of identity.

Research on contemporary cultural ideologies associated with Asian Americans has focused primarily on the stereotype of the model minority. In this stereotype, Asian immigrants are portrayed as hard-working entrepreneurs who achieve middle-class status without the benefit of government assistance due to the high value their culture—conceived in the singular in this stereotype—places on assiduous effort. By the same token, Asian American youth, the children and grandchildren of these immigrants, are often represented as mild-mannered and socially incompetent nerds with a knack for math and science whose academic success owes nothing to affirmative-action policies. Though grounded in a (more or less) positive rather than negative misrepresentation of a racialized group, the model-minority myth has been shown to promote racism both because it creates an ideological expectation that minorities can and should advance socioeconomically without assistance—a belief that is damaging to Asian and non-Asian immigrants alike—and because it ignores the fact that many Asian Americans do not fit the stereotype (Chan 1991; Wu 2001). In particular, the notion of Asian Americans as a model minority focuses on a relatively small group of middle-class Asian Americans, primarily of East and South Asian descent, to the exclusion of other Asian immigrants, especially many of those from Southeast Asia, who do not bring with them the economic and educational advantages that enable social mobility in the United States. With respect to youth, Lee (1994) points out that this ideology misses the fact that some students of Asian heritage are not academically oriented and others may not achieve academic success despite their efforts. Moreover, the supposed positive valorization of Asian Americans carries a negative social subtext. According to the stereotype, Asian Americans' intelligence and industriousness is counterbalanced by social ineptitude. The model-minority stereotype relegates Asian American youth to social marginality: smart but uncool (see also Lee 1994).

For many Southeast Asian Americans, however, the model-minority stereotype is less often invoked than is a second cultural ideology that draws on much more familiar negative attitudes of the majority toward minority groups. This ideology positions Southeast Asian Americans as problematic immigrants who are dependent on government assistance and are the sources of an array of social ills. Young people in particular are the targets of a moral panic concerning the rise of Southeast Asian American youth gangs in the 1990s (e.g., Joe 1994; Song et al. 1992; Vigil and Yun 1990). Through these contrasting ideologies, a two-tiered racialized hierarchy of Asian Americans has developed in U.S. racial discourse. While a racial status of "honorary whiteness" is conferred—albeit ambivalently and partially—upon some middle-class Asian Americans (Tuan 1999), working-class East and Southeast Asian Americans are often subject to the same kind of racial profiling and problematizing as are working-class African Americans and Latinos (see also Lee 2005).

This chapter examines how two Southeast Asian American girls in a multiracial high school in California, both refugees from Laos, navigated these two contrasting racial ideologies imposed on Southeast Asian Americans by using locally available linguistic and other semiotic resources. Taking different pathways through the local racial terrain, the girls both participated in and refused the binary terms of racializing discourse in the United States. The constraints on identity imposed by the stereotypes were both reinforced by and reinforcing of local racial ideologies in which language was mapped onto race in a binary fashion. Each girl's style was produced linguistically through a positive or negative orientation to the linguistic resources of African American Vernacular English (AAVE) and youth slang. Given the authority of African American youth styles in shaping youth cultures in California and elsewhere, each girl's linguistic practices affiliated her with one or the other pole of this dichotomy. However, these teenagers also maintained linguistic and cultural styles apart from either of the two locally dominant racialized groups. In this way, the girls' differently constituted identities as Laotian American negotiated rather than capitulated to the school's black/white racial dichotomy.

Laotian Americans: The Formation of an Ethnic Category

Laotians are among the most recent Asian immigrants to the United States, having come as refugees along with Vietnamese and Cambodians between the 1970s and the 1990s following the overthrow of the U.S.-backed anticommunist governments of their home countries. Laotians are a minority among these immigrants: Approximately 21 percent of Southeast Asian refugees to the United States are from Laos, about half of whom are from highland ethnic groups such as Hmong; the largest group of refugees, roughly 66 percent, is Vietnamese. Many Laotian refugees spent time in United Nations-funded refugee processing centers in Thailand before being allowed to enter the United States.

Laotian Americans are not a single ethnic group but comprise the lowland Tai-Kadai groups (the largest grouping), the Austroasiatic groups in the foothills, and the Tibeto-Burman highland groups—including Hmong, Iu Mien, Lahu, and others. Because of its diversity, small size, and dispersal across the United States, the Laotian American group is less visible than its Vietnamese and Cambodian counterparts. Through secondary migration and other factors, many Laotians (like other Southeast Asian refugees) settled in California, particularly in San Diego and Orange County, the Central Valley, and the San Francisco Bay Area. Compared with East and South Asian Americans and even with some other Southeast Asian American groups, Laotian Americans suffer a number of economic and social disadvantages: Laotian youth have some of the highest rates of high-school dropouts, incarceration, and teen pregnancy among Asian immigrant groups (Rumbaut 2005), and their families are among the most impoverished and least educated of Asian immigrants (Ngo and Lee 2007; Portes and Rumbaut 2001; Rumbaut 1995). These facts run counter to the model-minority stereotype, touted by researchers and the media alike to account for the academic success of Southeast Asian immigrant groups, including many Laotians, despite social and economic disadvantages (e.g., Caplan, Whitmore, and Choy 1989; cf. Zhou and Xiong 2005).

As this brief overview suggests, the labels *Asian American*, *Southeast Asian American*, and *Laotian American* erase a great deal of internal diversity.[1] Their homogenizing force not only eradicates differences in experience and situation but belies the range of ethnic options (Waters 1990) available to those who are so labeled. In making sense of how race and ethnicity inflect individuals' identities, then, it is necessary to look beyond group labels imposed from outside and to examine how identity is forged through socially meaningful practices. Foremost among these is language, as the most semiotically complex human activity. Through their use of language, individuals and groups may deliberately claim or repudiate a given identity, or assign or withhold an identity with respect to someone else. This self-aware display of identity, or *identity performance*, foregrounds the agentive dimension of the construction of self and other. Alternatively, language users may establish an identity by drawing on particular linguistic structures in largely nonreflective ways based on long-standing habit. This habitual enactment of identity, or *identity practice*, highlights the less deliberate dimension of identity construction. While linguistic practice and performance are both at work in the construction of different kinds of Laotian American identity, I focus here on linguistic practice, which has been examined less often than linguistic performance in the emergent body of linguistic scholarship on Asian American identity.

Language, Style, and Asian American Identity

The use of linguistic structures to index social positioning has been termed *style* (Eckert 2000; Eckert and Rickford 2001). As an indexical process, style both creates and exploits sociolinguistic stereotypes (Ochs 1992; see also Agha 2007). The question of style is especially central in the study of youth, who, within the institutional structure of the educational system, often elaborate the semiotic distinctions that organize social divisions in the larger society. In addition, style offers an entry point into the study of Asian American language and identity, an area of research that presents difficulties for traditional sociolinguistic approaches to language and ethnicity. These approaches, which are centrally concerned with the linguistic distinctiveness of ethnic groups, are ill equipped to account for situations in which speakers' language use is not ethnically distinctive. Considering linguistic practice and performance as style enables researchers to recognize how speakers may creatively draw on the existing resources of other social groups for their own identity work.

As research on Asian American language use demonstrates, distinctiveness-centered models of language and ethnicity that, despite serious problems, have been widely used for the study of other ethnic groups within the United States fail outright when confronted with Asian Americans' speech practices, especially but not only those of the English-speaking second generation. Inspired by studies of ethnic varieties of American English, such as AAVE and Chicano English, some researchers have investigated the question of whether Asian American speech communities likewise have developed their own varieties of English. Although a few studies have found small differences in some Asian Americans' speech compared with European Americans (e.g., Hanna 1997; Mendoza-Denton and Iwai 1993), it is generally recognized that the tremendous cultural, linguistic, and economic diversity of Asian Americans precludes the formation of a distinctive and uniform "Asian American English." Typically, it appears that middle-class Asian Americans acquire the phonological and grammatical form of Standard English associated with their geographic region within the United States, unlike many middle-class African

Americans and Latinos, whose Standard English may also include some phonological elements associated with their ethnic communities. Given the smaller numbers of Asian Americans compared to African Americans and Latinos, and at least some Asian Americans' relatively greater access to the middle class, it is unsurprising that many native-born middle-class Asian Americans would speak more or less like their European American counterparts. Little attention has been paid, however, to working-class Asian Americans' language. Research on Latinos' English language use has demonstrated that Standard English is not the only available target for speakers in the first and second immigrant generations (Goldstein 1987; Wolfram 1973; Zentella 1997); both New York Puerto Ricans and California Chicanos have been found to draw on AAVE in addition to their own ethnic group's variety of English as part of their linguistic repertoires. It is plausible that working-class Asian Americans who may or may not have an ethnically distinctive English variety of their own might similarly draw on linguistic resources from other ethnic groups with whom they have contact, but this possibility has not been widely explored (but see Reyes 2005).[2]

Even if the variety of English spoken by Asian Americans is not structurally distinctive from that of other ethnic groups, it may nonetheless serve as a resource for constructing social identity. This point is underscored by Norma Mendoza-Denton and Melissa Iwai (1993), who note, in an analysis of Japanese American and European American girls' phonology, that young people's linguistic practice is not determined by ethnicity; teenagers with similar demographic backgrounds may speak differently due to different orientations to youth-cultural styles (see also Bucholtz 2002; Mendoza-Denton 1999). Such style-based identities are often shaped by ethnicity, insofar as certain styles are available to some ethnic groups but not others. This is particularly the case with AAVE, which has become increasingly used emblematically as a cross-ethnic marker of youth identity among young people of color; European Americans' use of AAVE is generally more likely to be met with suspicion or ridicule from both ingroup and outgroup members (Bucholtz 1997; Cutler 2003), unless speakers have credentials within the local speech community (Sweetland 2002).

Because Asian Americans are widely considered to lack a distinctive variety of English and because they are often viewed by non-Asian Americans as primarily defined by the immigrant experience, even after several generations in the United States (Tuan 1999), research on Asian American communities' language use has been largely focused on educational and macrosociological issues regarding second language acquisition and heritage language shift, with much less discussion of the ways in which social identities may be intertwined with linguistic practice. Only recently has scholarship on Asian American language use turned to the question of identity (e.g., Kang and Lo 2004; Reyes 2007; for a parallel development in England, see Rampton 1995), particularly regarding the intersection of race and ethnicity with gender. Those studies that have begun to emerge in recent years offer an innovative point of departure for scholarly analysis by focusing centrally on how speakers linguistically negotiate widespread racialized and gendered ideologies about Asians and Asian Americans. Scholars have begun to document the ways in which, through the appropriation of the dialects, languages, and styles of other groups, Asian Americans may align with other ethnoracial categories, especially African Americans (Chun

2001; Reyes 2005) and/or may enter into dialogue with gender ideologies within and about Asian American communities (Chun, this volume; Lo 1999). Much of this research examines various kinds of identity performance, in which linguistic styles and their concomitant stereotypes of race and/or gender are used deliberately and artfully to produce identity effects and to counter as well as produce cultural ideologies (see also Lee 2006). In addition to this valuable perspective, it is important to understand how habitual and less fully purposeful productions of language and linguistic ideologies constitute identity practice, a more routinized form of identity work.

The connection between practice and performance as different techniques for producing identity is built into the view of identity that Kira Hall and I have formulated (Bucholtz and Hall 2004, 2005). In this approach, identity is understood as a set of relational and emergent social outcomes of ideologically shaped discourse, via both practice and performance. Styles, as well as other linguistic resources, may be put to use to establish these relations between social groups or individuals. Of particular relevance in the context of the analysis below are two identity relations: *adequation*, or the ideological creation of an interactionally sufficient but necessarily incomplete similarity between social groups or individuals; and *distinction*, or the ideological production of social difference (cf. Irvine 2001). These relations differ from the notion of distinctiveness that has influenced traditional sociolinguistic scholarship, because what counts as difference (or sameness) is determined not by researchers but in the first instance by cultural members. Much of the research cited above demonstrates how adequation and distinction emerge as the effects of deliberate identity performance; the present chapter focuses instead on how these identity relations may be produced through habitual linguistic practice, via the variety of English a speaker uses every day.

Local Identities

The data for this article come from a year-long ethnographic sociolinguistic study of a multiracial high school in the San Francisco Bay Area, which I call Bay City High School. The school was a harbinger of California's shifting racial demographics in that at the time of the study (1995–1996), as now, it had no racial majority; unlike the state as a whole, however, in which whites and Latinos are the largest populations, the two largest racialized groups at Bay City High were European Americans and African Americans. Asian Americans (excluding Pacific Islanders, who were a small group at the school) constituted 10 percent of the student body, a figure roughly equivalent to the number of Latinos in the school's population. Within this group, there was tremendous diversity based on country of heritage, immigrant generation, social class, and youth cultural style.

My research at this school concentrated on European Americans' linguistic practices in a context in which, unlike most other parts of the United States, they were not a racial majority. However, I had opportunities to study Asian American teenagers as well in classrooms, on the school grounds where I was a participant-observer, and within predominantly European American friendship groups. Most of the students in such groups were middle-class, native-born, and of East Asian backgrounds, while working-class Asian American students, who were largely immigrants of Southeast Asian descent, tended to cluster in homogeneous groupings.[3] Unlike their middle-class counterparts, who were often the only Asian members of their friendship groups, these Southeast Asian American students were highly visible as a distinctive group in part because of their recognizable clothing styles, influenced by but usually slightly different from the baggy hip-hop style associated with African American youth fashion,[4] and in part because during lunch and before and after school they congregated around a low wall in the middle of the schoolyard, an area to which one European American student gave the racially charged (and ethnically inaccurate) label "The Great Wall of China."

In light of the school's demographics, a robust racial ideology had developed within Bay City High whereby race was organized in binary terms of black and white, which were positioned as polar opposites. Students who belonged to neither of these racialized groupings were either ideologically invisible to the dominant groups or were perceived as more or less like one group or the other. Thus although many Latino, Native American, and Asian American students at the school operated largely outside of this dichotomy, outsiders often understood them as "acting black" or "acting white." The social archetypes of these two polar categories were the African American gangster, on the one hand, and the European American nerd, on the other. The gangster was often invoked by middle-class European American (and some Asian American) students as a menacing, violent, but "cool" (i.e., culturally authoritative) figure who was racially associated with blackness and linguistically associated with AAVE, and especially with the use of African American youth slang (Bucholtz 1999a). The nerd was invoked by students of all races as a hapless, uncool, but intelligent figure who was racially associated with whiteness and linguistically associated with Standard English, and especially with a lexically formal, hyper-articulated, and structurally conservative superstandard variety of English (Bucholtz 2001). These archetypes were also tied to social-class positioning, with the gangster understood as working-class and the nerd as middle-class (regardless of the varying socioeconomic statuses of particular individuals who claimed or were assigned either of these identities).

Despite similar life experiences and socioeconomic backgrounds, the two Laotian American girls discussed in this chapter chose different routes through this racially polarized stylistic landscape. Nikki and Ada both came to California in childhood as refugees; both their families were working-class. Yet the differences in their identities are clear even from the choice each girl made regarding her pseudonym in this study.[5] Both girls had Laotian names but opted for non-Laotian pseudonyms for the study, but the girl who adopted a gangster style and identity selected the cute and trendy name *Nikki*, while the girl who affiliated with a nerdy friendship group asked to be called by the more old-fashioned name *Ada* (with the spelling pronunciation ['ædə], a characteristic nerdy practice because of the privileging of written language among nerds; see Bucholtz 1996). The linguistic data for both girls come from informal ethnographic interviews, although their linguistic practices were also confirmed through participant-observation of their interactions in class and among their friends.

"Nikki: When You in a Gang... You Have a Little Clique"

Nikki was a fifteen-year-old sophomore from Laos who arrived in California around the age of five. At the time of the study she was a former member of a girl gang affiliated with the Crips, which, along with the Bloods, is one of the two major black gangs in California. Originally founded by African Americans in Los Angeles, both the Crips and the Bloods now have Latino, Asian American, Pacific Islander, and other affiliate gangs, and both gangs have also spread to Northern California and other states. Nikki had recently chosen to be "jumped out" of her gang (that is, ritually beaten to symbolize the end of her membership) because of parental pressure, but she still hung out with her gangster friends and her boyfriend, who belonged to the male counterpart of her gang, and she maintained numerous gang practices, habitually wearing blue bandannas and clothing (the symbolic color of the Crips) and using her gang names (including "Tiny" for her small size and "Puff" for her heavy marijuana use). In other ways her baggy, oversized style of dress resembled that of many African American, Latino, and Asian American students at the high school (as well as a few European Americans; see Bucholtz 1997) who were influenced by hip-hop, the dominant musical and cultural form for most students of color.

A fluent bilingual in English and Lao, Nikki was an outgoing student who readily joked with other students of many different ethnic groups and youth styles in the classroom. In fact, gang membership encouraged cross-racial friendship ties to an extent that was often rare for students who did not participate in gangs: Nikki was on friendly terms with members of Mexican American and African American Crips-affiliated youth gangs both within the school and outside of it, although due to her small size and bubbly personality she was sometimes teased by these other students for her gang identification. As an ex-gang member, she was also able to maintain friendly relations with members of the Bloods, the Crips' archrival gang.

I carried out part of my fieldwork in a yearlong health course in which Nikki was a student, and for this reason she frequently treated our interaction as a chance to display to an adult her good judgment about behaviors negatively sanctioned in the class, such as drinking, smoking, and stealing. Even so, her language did not mark the interview as formal; rather, it was very colloquial, with elements of nonstandard grammar and phonology throughout.

In example (1), Nikki responds to my question about whether there are any benefits associated with being in a gang; earlier in the interview she has described the problems with gang membership:[6]

(1)

1	Nikki:	and it's like,
2		when you in a gang,
3		right,
4		(.) you have a little clique,=
5		=your own clique,=
6		=right.
7	Mary:	<low volume> {Right.}

```
 8  Nikki:     .h
 9             And,
10             let's say,
11             <voice creak> I have funk with this Mexican girl,
12             and she claim different colors,
13             I claim blue,
14  Mary:      Um [hm.    ]
15  Nikki:        [and she] claim red.
16             And that's Bloo:d and Crip.
17             (.) <tongue click> (.) So they're,
18             <voice creak> against each other,
19             and then,
20             she would try: to like have funk with me by,
21             .h bringing her partners up,
22             because she don't want to fight me,
23             like she's afraid,
24             or some[thing.  ]
25  Mary:            [Ri:ght.]
26  Nikki:     So:,
27             it's like backup,=
28             your friend would back you up,
29             you know,
30             and be there for you.
```

In this example, Nikki makes clear the importance of gangs in guaranteeing support for their members in threatening situations; she noted in the same interaction that one of her gang friends had vowed to continue to look out for Nikki even though she had left the gang. Thus although Nikki was no longer an official member, she remained closely tied to her former gang both in her social networks and in her social identity.

Nikki's social identity was also evident in her speech style. As noted above, the stereotype of the gangster style at Bay City High School was associated with African American youth culture and language. It should be underscored, however, that this association rested on ideology rather than on any real connection between African Americans and gangs. While some black students at the school, like those of other ethnoracial groups, did belong to gangs, gang membership was by no means restricted to African Americans nor was it a major part of the school's black youth culture. Nevertheless, African American youth language and style heavily influenced the stylistic practices of youth gangs (as well as other youth) of all races and ethnicities at Bay City High, because of its cultural authority as an urban style and its close association with hip-hop, an important cultural form for many urban-identified youth, including those in gangs.

Example (2) illustrates some of the linguistic practices that contributed to Nikki's style. In this example she describes to me how her parents confronted her about her gang membership during a discussion about whether she planned to attend college:

(2)

1	Nikki:	\<creaky voice\> {I-}
2		I was all telling them,
3		"I don't have much ski:lls,"
4		you know,
5		and they was like,=
6		="No:,
7		if you stop whatever you doing,"=
8		=I was like,
9		"What am I doing,"
10		and then she knows too.
11		(She's) like,
12		"I know what you be doing,"
13		you know,
14		".h bad things,"
15		right.
16		I was like,
17		"(.) O:↑kay!"
18	Mary:	@ @ @=
19	Nikki:	=And then,=
20	Mary:	=Wow.
21	Nikki:	Yeah,
22		and then I was like,
23		"All right,
24		Mom,
25		to make you happy,"=
26		because,
27		.h I could see like the expression?
28		in her face?=
29	Mary:	=Mm:.=
30	Nikki:	=Like she's so sad,
31	Mary:	[Mm.]
32	Nikki:	[.h:] No,
33		I just felt like,
34		"Oh,
35		it's all my fault,"

As both examples (1) and (2) indicate, Nikki's language was extensively influenced by AAVE grammar (as well as AAVE phonology, which is not noted in the transcript). However, like many European American users of AAVE features, Nikki could not be mistaken for a fluent AAVE speaker. Her speech included several grammatical characteristics of nonnative English not illustrated above, such as use of a singular verb form with a plural subject (e.g., *they goes to, um, Parkville*) and the use of idiosyncratic pluralization (e.g., *I told them, like, I have schools*). Neither of these structures is typical of AAVE as spoken in California. In addition, several aspects of her pronunciation were considerably different from AAVE phonology, particularly vowel quality.

But where European American teenagers who appropriate elements of AAVE in their everyday speech tend to adopt primarily phonological and lexical features and perhaps a few emblematic grammatical structures (Bucholtz 1999a; Cutler 1999), Nikki's use of AAVE features was much more far-ranging, encompassing a number of different aspects of the dialect's grammar. Some elements of her AAVE use were not distinctive to that variety but rather were general features of nonstandard American English, such as multiple negation, the use of *ain't*, and the regularization of third-person singular verbal morphology (example 1, line 22: *because she don't want to fight me*; example 2, lines 5–6: *and they was like, "No:"*). Yet in addition to these grammatical structures, Nikki made use of other patterns that have a far more restricted distribution across varieties of American English, including some structures that are largely distinctive to AAVE among U.S. varieties of English, such as zero marking of the third-person singular in present-tense verbs (example 1, lines 13 and 15: *I claim blue,...and she claim red*), habitual *be* (example 2, lines 11–12: *(She's) like, "I know what you be doing"*), and zero copula (example 1, lines 2 and 4: *when you in a gang,...you have a little clique"*). Moreover, her pronunciation included phonological patterns that are characteristic of AAVE, such as consonant cluster simplification, postvocalic /r/ deletion, and fortition of voiced interdental fricatives; additionally, the pronunciation of *all right* as [a:jʔt] (example 2, line 23) is typical of the speech of many African American teenagers (Reyes 2005). Nikki's use of AAVE remained at the level of individual features rather than the acquisition of the complete linguistic system and hence would not count as fluency in the variety, yet the range and use of AAVE features were much more deeply embedded into her everyday linguistic practice than for most European American users of AAVE at Bay City High.

Perhaps even more than her use of elements of AAVE phonology and grammar, it was Nikki's use of African American youth slang that marked her orientation to the local authority of African American youth culture (see also Reyes 2005). Many of the slang terms Nikki used had associations with gang life, due to the influence of African American youth culture on gang styles as well as on other youth styles, as noted above. Among the terms of this type that she used during our interaction are *partners* (pronounced ['paʔtnəz]; see example 1, line 21) 'friends, fellow gang members,' *jump out* 'ritually beat a gang member to symbolically end their gang affiliation,' *dog* 'insult,' *head* 'gang member,' *box* 'fight,' and *O.G.* (an abbreviation for *original gangster*) 'well-known or prototypical gang member.' However, many other terms came from African American youth language and culture more generally, such as *kick it* 'hang out,' *player* 'sexually promiscuous person,' *ride* 'car,' and *clown* 'mock.' Nikki's linguistic style, coupled with her baggy style of dress, was thus clearly influenced by elements of African American youth culture.

Nikki's use of the linguistic and other stylistic resources of African American youth, however, did not index her membership in a specifically African American youth culture, but rather functioned as a cross-racial and cross-ethnic urban youth style that was relevant to her identity as a (former) gang member. In this way Nikki's habitual identity practices established a relation of adequation with black youth that allowed her to interact successfully with other urban-identified teenagers of diverse races and ethnicities and to align herself with the generalized authority of African American youth culture while maintaining her own ethnic identity separate from other groups. Indeed, her primary friendships were not with African Americans but with other Laotian Americans, particularly gang members, who did not attend Bay City High School and lived in surrounding urban working-class communities.

In addition to her friendship with these urban-oriented teenagers, Nikki also had other Laotian American friends at Bay City High who did not share her orientation to African American youth culture. These she called her "goodie friends." In describing one such friend, Pouy, to me, she remarked, "She's nice, you know, even though she's a little boring." In example (3) I ask Nikki why Pouy is boring, and she responds:

(3)

1	Mary:	Why is she boring?
2	Nikki:	Huh?=
3		=.h like,
4		I mea:n,
5		she like study gi:rl,
6	Mary:	[Uh huh.]
7	Nikki:	[all she] do is like s:tudy,
8		talk abou-
9		.h like every time I talk to her,
10		she like,
11		<tongue click>
12		<smiling quality> {"let's go} study,"
13		and sometime I'm sick and tired,
14		but then,
15		I try: not to?
16		[you know?]
17	Mary:	[Mhm.]

Pouy was, in a word, nerdy: She was more interested in school than in participating in the activities of youth culture. Throughout the conversation, Nikki made clear the tension she experienced between hanging out with her cool gangster friends and with her boring but well-behaved school friends. As she remarked, a bit wistfully, of Pouy, "She could make me be a good girl, you know?" Yet her own allegiance, as displayed symbolically in her language and other semiotic resources, was to coolness as transmitted through African American youth culture.

Ada: "And That's When We Start to Split"

Like Nikki, Ada perceived gang participation and orientation to school as mutually exclusive pursuits, and like Nikki's "goodie friend" Pouy, she decided in favor of school. To Ada, the perpetuation of the model-minority stereotype was far less harmful than the very immediate dangers of gang culture. She was seventeen and a junior at the time of the study. She had been in the United States since the age of nine, having lived in a Thai refugee camp for two years as well as in the Philippines before immigrating to the United States. During this period she experienced a great deal of physical and emotional hardship, falling seriously ill twice and being exposed to the hazards of refugee camp life, from fire to murder.

Ada's best friend since her arrival in the United States was Bob, a middle-class European American girl who at the time of my study was a member of a small friendship network of nerdy girls (see Bucholtz 1999b). These girls embraced nerdiness as an alternative to the coolness and trendiness of the various forms of youth culture at the school. Instead of coolness, they placed high value on intelligence and humor, and they marked their rejection of coolness in many ways, including avoiding the slang and colloquial or nonstandard English used by their cooler peers. Ada was a peripheral member of this group, largely via her friendship with Bob. She deliberately chose not to befriend other Laotian American students, whom she considered "negative" in part because of their interest in joining gangs. She had several Asian American friends, whom she had met in English as a Second Language class, but they were of Chinese and Vietnamese backgrounds.

Although Ada was peripheral to Bob's friendship group at the time of the study, she had been affiliated with the group since elementary school, when she and Bob befriended two of the other members after being abandoned by their close friend Tina for a trendier set of friends. In example (4) she recounts the story of Tina's departure from Bob and Ada's group (a version of which I also heard from Bob):

(4)

1	Ada:	But then from then on,
2		me:,
3		Bob and Tina always be in s-
4		same class,
5		till,
6		fourth grade.
7	Mary:	Mm.
8	Ada:	And that's when we start to split. (1.3)
9		A:nd like Tina went,
10		hang around with,
11		like,
12		.h (0.6) uh:,
13		↑cool friend I guess,
14		I don't know how to say it,

When I asked Ada to explain why Tina left her friendship group, she elaborated (example 5):

(5)

| 1 | Ada: | Our personality is like, |
| 2 | | totally different from Tina's.= |

```
3  Mary:    =[Mm.]
4  Ada:     =[Tina] like,
5           to dress like those fancy clo:thes,
6           expensive stuff,
```

Most of the nerdy girls I spoke to dated their dawning recognition of social hier-archy to the period around fourth grade, a time when the heterosexual marketplace emerges as the structuring force of preadolescent life (Eckert 2002). Nerd girls delib-erately rejected the sharp gender differentiation that began to take place as part of the shift to adolescence, developing an alternative femininity that allowed them to be disinterested in the trappings of coolness, from fashion to language (Bucholtz 1996, 1999b, 2001, 2002, 2007). All the girls in Ada's group, including Ada herself, wore loose T-shirts and jeans, eschewing both the form-fitting style of popular European American girls and the extremely baggy style of girls who participated in urban-oriented youth styles originating in hip-hop. Also like the other girls in her group, Ada avoided slang, producing not a single slang term throughout our entire interview. Ada's nonuse of slang could have been due less to purposeful avoidance than to her relative lack of access to this symbolic resource, both as a nonnative speaker and as a participant in friendship groups in which slang was not used. In either case, in not pursuing slang as a desirable stylistic commodity as cool teenagers did, Ada signaled her nonparticipation in trendy youth culture. In this way she clearly distinguished herself from cool teenagers like Nikki.

Ada likewise aimed at a different variety of English than did Nikki. Having arrived in the United States more recently, Ada spoke a much less nativelike English, both in phonology and in grammar. Like Nikki, her phonology included pronunciations, such as extensive consonant cluster simplification and the deletion of final consonants, that are also found in AAVE (as well as many that are not). Also like Nikki, she used a num-ber of grammatical forms that at least superficially are structurally similar to features of AAVE, such as zero copula and habitual *be* (example 4, lines 1–4: *But then from then on, me:, Bob and Tina always be in s- same class*). But while Nikki's linguistic practices were associated with AAVE due to her engagement in cultural practices influ-enced by African American youth culture, Ada's divergent cultural practices pointed to a different interpretation of very similar linguistic forms. With little contact with AAVE speakers (even indirectly through other Southeast Asian Americans like Nikki who did have such contact), it is unlikely that Ada's use of these forms was due to the influence of AAVE. Moreover, her grammar was strikingly nonnative, rather than nonstandard like Nikki's. In lines 3 and 4 of example (4) above, she omits the determiner, a frequent pattern among nonnative speakers but rare in nonstandard varieties of English. Ada also had less than full control of complex English grammatical structures such as the conditional, as illustrated by (6), in which she discusses her best friend in Laos, whom she has not kept in touch with because she is not literate in Lao:

(6)

```
1  Ada:    That could have be,=
2          =because,
```

```
3              if I know it,
4              then I would have write and,
5              communicate with her sti:ll.
6              But I [ca:n't.]
7    Mary:     [Right.]
```

Yet this is not to say that Ada, as a less fluent speaker of English, was unable to use language semiotically as part of her speech style. For example, not all of her phonological patterns can be attributed solely to her status as a nonnative speaker. Postvocalic /r/ deletion or vocalization was one of the most salient characteristics of AAVE at Bay City High School, even among nonspeakers of the variety, and thus was often adopted by students like Nikki who claimed some affiliation to African American youth culture. By contrast, postvocalic /l/ deletion or vocalization, which is also characteristic of AAVE, was much less salient as a social marker, and was less often and less systematically taken up by non-African American students. Like many nonnative speakers who shared her linguistic background, Ada frequently deleted or vocalized postvocalic /l/; however, she tended not to do the same with postvocalic /r/, despite the fact that the latter process is characteristic of the nonnative English spoken by many Southeast Asian Americans. This practice aligned her linguistically with the /r/-ful pronunciation of her European American friendship group and against the /r/-less pronunciation of many urban-identified cool students, while she retained deletion of postvocalic /l/, a less socially marked pronunciation. Indeed, simply by aiming for Standard English rather than another variety as a language learner, Ada semiotically marked her social identity as different from students like Nikki.

Ada's nonnative use of English made her a frequent target of humor in her friendship group of nerdy European American girls, all of whom were native speakers of Standard English. She noted in our interview that her eating style too was a source of humor for these girls, ranging from how she peeled an orange to how she used a fork. In these and other ways Ada felt alienated from the rest of the group despite her friendship with them. In particular, her commitment to school and to her responsibilities at home separated her from these middle-class girls, who were equally serious students but whose educational advantages as native speakers and economic advantages as the children of professional parents meant that they could spend more time in leisure activities rather than studying or doing chores (examples 7 and 8):

(7)

```
1    Ada:      Oka:y,
2              I don't like to talk that much?
3    Mary:     Mm.
4    Ada:      I like to be on my own,
5              mostly,
6              when we eat lunch.
7              They just keep on ta:lking or giggling,
8              but I'm still eating and,
9              reading and doing my other,
```

```
10                homew[ork?]
11   Mary:             [Mm.]
```

(8)

```
 1   Ada:      Usually they watch like,
 2             those s- sho:w?
 3             like television show,
 4             they a:ll watch together,
 5             .h like,
 6             and then they ta:lk about it the next day,
 7             and I didn't f—
 8             I didn't have time watching the sho:w,=
 9             =because I was,
10             .h doing dishes:,
11             baby sit,
12             and doing homework,
13             [so,   ]
14   Mary:     [Right.]
15   Ada:      (0.9) <creaky> {I:} guess I feel left out that part,=
16   Mary:     =[Mhm.  ]
17   Ada:      =[because] I didn't,
18             (really) watch the show,
19             so I can't [communicate]=
20   Mary:                [Right.    ]
21   Ada:                            =with them that much.
```

Thus Ada, though associated with this group of white middle-class nerd girls, did not wholly enter into their community of practice, which was structured around verbal play and the display of intelligence, both arenas in which she was at a disadvantage as a nonfluent speaker of English. Rather, she entered into an alliance of convenience, partly because of her friendship with Bob and partly as a defense against the pressure to join a gang that she would be likely to experience if she hung out with other Laotian Americans at Bay City High. Relationally, Ada's linguistic and stylistic practices did not so much establish her similarity to the nerd girls in this group as create distance between herself and other Laotian Americans who participated in gangs. That is, Ada's language use established a relation of distinction from girls like Nikki more than one of adequation with Bob and her friends.

Divergent Styles of Laotian American Identity Practice

While Nikki's and Ada's ways of speaking frequently contained structural similarities, the two speech styles did not have the same semiotic value. Both girls used some linguistic forms that on their face could be interpreted either as features of AAVE or as characteristics of nonnative English. In contrast with Ada, Nikki's use of AAVE-like structures was extensive and also included general nonstandard English structures such as multiple negation, which Ada's speech lacked. In addition, Nikki's use of clearly nonnative forms was rare, while Ada regularly produced nonnative phonological and grammatical structures.

The fact that some aspects of Nikki's phonology and grammar were also characteristic of nonnative English, especially among first-generation Southeast Asian Americans, may argue against the claim that her speech was influenced by AAVE. The resemblance between structures produced by nonnative speakers and some parts of the AAVE grammatical system may be a matter of simple coincidence. However, it is precisely the ambiguity of the linguistic status of such forms that makes them available for different semiotic effects. Such ambiguity of linguistic forms shared by more than one language or variety has been termed *bivalency* by Kathryn Woolard, which she defines as the "simultaneous membership of an element in more than one linguistic system" (1998, 6; see also Errington 1998). Drawing on bilinguals' use of the closely related and structurally similar languages Castilian and Catalan, Woolard demonstrates that bivalent forms may be strategically exploited for particular rhetorical effects. Although her emphasis is on the highlighting of bivalency as part of identity performances, she notes that bivalent forms may not always be used strategically. That is, when a speaker of language A uses what is considered to other speakers of language A a form that is bivalent between languages A and B, it is often heard as unambiguously A, not B, because the social distinctions indexed by these two languages are not at issue. In such situations these forms may be part of identity work, but as part of habitual identity practices rather than deliberate performances.

The same is likely to be true even when, as here, what is at issue is not the exploitation of two linguistic systems but the use of certain elements of the larger grammatical system of AAVE, on the one hand, and definitionally unsystematic nonnative English, on the other. In Nikki's case, her fluency in English and her cultural affiliation with African American-influenced forms of youth culture together suggest that bivalent forms in her speech were heard by other teenagers as borrowed from AAVE. Ada's speech also contained some AAVE-like elements, but her nonfluency in English, coupled with her rejection of gang culture and her association with European American nerds, rendered these forms hearable as nonnative rather than AAVE-influenced. This analysis is supported by the fact that while other students teased Nikki for her alignment with gang style, they teased Ada for her nonnative speech and behavior. Thus members of the school were more likely to hear similar linguistic structures as the nonstandard English associated with cool and culturally authoritative youth in one instance, and as the nonnative English associated with uncool and socially marginalized teenagers in the other.

The styles with which Nikki and Ada aligned and disaligned simultaneously engaged and negotiated the ethnic stereotypes imposed on Asian Americans. Both girls felt the force of the model-minority stereotype, and both experienced the pull of gang membership that is widely experienced by Southeast Asian American youth. Their stylistic choices partly acquiesced to and partly refuted the stereotypes directed at them as Laotian Americans, but they did so in contrasting ways. At the same time, Ada's participation in nerdy social networks and Nikki's involvement with youth gangs both offered a significant challenge to normative gender ideologies. While each girl chose a different route through gender, they both rejected hegemonic American femininity. Through her informal gang affiliation, Nikki could display a physical and emotional toughness that was not part of dominant feminine youth styles at the school (see also Mendoza-Denton 2008), and through nerdy styles of dress and talk Ada could avoid the cuteness and sexualization that trendy girls embraced (Bucholtz 1999b). At the same time, in navigating the stereotypes directed at them as Southeast Asian Americans, both Nikki and Ada took up identity positions that in some ways reinforced the black/white racial divide of Bay City High School, by using language and other resources to develop cultural styles that were locally racialized as proto-typically black or white. Thus Asian Americans at the school could not wholly transcend the ideology of a black/white dichotomy even as their identity practices and performances challenged the binary terms in which race was cast.

Conclusion

This chapter provides one example of the diversity of Asian American language and identity despite the sharp ideological constraints imposed by the dominant racial and ethnic stereotypes of Southeast Asian Americans as either model-minority nerds or dangerous gangsters. The two Laotian American girls whose language and identities are the focus of the analysis here appear on the surface to be very similar in background, yet their stylistic identity practices display their different choices in relation to these stereotypes, with Ada positioning herself primarily within the first and Nikki positioning herself primarily within the second. To be sure, such choices are not the only ones available to working-class immigrant Asian American students, but it is extremely difficult for young people to circumvent stereotypes completely; even students like Ada, who are less interested in embracing a nerd identity than in avoiding a gangster identity, cannot avoid being classified by others as nerdy, by virtue of their nonparticipation in urban youth culture. This forced choice was less of a problem for many middle-class Asian Americans at Bay City High School who adopted youth cultural styles that were not directly associated with African American youth culture but were nevertheless considered cool. Such styles were less accessible to working-class immigrant Asian Americans, due to their linguistic and social marginalization from the typically middle-class, U.S.-born groups that embraced these styles.

Together with other semiotic resources, differences in the two girls' language, such as use or nonuse of youth slang or of individual features of AAVE, clearly signaled their different youth cultural styles. Likewise, the structural bivalency of certain elements of their speech was disambiguated in the context of their wider cultural practices. Forms that might bear some resemblance both to features of AAVE and to structures characteristic of nonnative English functioned semiotically as unambiguous indexes either of affiliation with urban youth culture (and gang culture as influenced by this broader cultural style), or of disaffiliation from youth culture. While Nikki's habitual language use constituted an identity practice that aligned or adequated her with the local urban youth culture in which African Americans held the highest cultural authority, Ada's own linguistic identity practices served primarily to disalign her from trendy youth culture and especially to create distinction between herself and participants in gang culture such as Nikki. Although neither girl was a native speaker of English, both girls' identities were linguistically produced neither in their native language nor in a shared, ethnically distinctive "Asian American English." Instead, both girls positioned themselves differentially in relation to locally available and semiotically powerful linguistic resources such as AAVE and youth slang to negotiate their identities.

Research on Asian Americans' language has often called attention to linguistic appropriation as a strategy for identity construction, perhaps because a distinctive linguistic variety is, as far as scholars have been able to determine, not available to Asian Americans in the same way as for African Americans or Latinos. It is for this reason that research on Asian Americans is likely to continue the ongoing challenge to traditional thinking about the relationship between language and identity, moving research away from the assumption that those who are classified as members of the same group will have a common language and a common identity. Despite the ideological force of stereotypes such as "model minorities" and "Asian gangsters," the vast diversity of Asian Americans as a panethnic category (and of ethnic subcategories such as Southeast Asian Americans and Laotian Americans) along every axis of comparison renders impossible the goal of mapping language onto groups without closely examining the social meanings of both in local contexts. The complexity of Asian Americans' identity practices and performances thus demands richer and more contextually nuanced theorizing of the relationship between language and identity.

An earlier version of this chapter was presented at the panel "Relationality: Constructing the Self against the Other in Asian Pacific America" organized by Adrienne Lo and Angela Reyes at the 2003 American Anthropological Association meeting in Chicago and published as Bucholtz (2004). I am grateful to Adrienne and Angie for inviting me to participate in the panel, for their enthusiasm for this project, and for their patience during its gestation. Thanks are also due to Susan Gal for extremely useful feedback on the oral version and to Mara Henderson for transcription assistance. All remaining weaknesses are my own responsibility.

NOTES

1. Despite the limitations of these or any other category labels, as a deliberate act of coalition building the construction of a panethnicity across Asian (or Southeast Asian or Laotian) ethnic groups can have political advantages (Espiritu 1992). See also Reyes (this volume).

2. While it is likely that at least some Asian American groups may have developed an ethnic variety of English, such a phenomenon has not yet been documented by scholars.

3. South Asian American students were not a large population at the school; none were members of any of the friendship groups I studied.

4. For example, many Southeast Asian American students wore baggier jeans than other students, and unlike other groups they ironed their pants and stapled or taped the cuffs under.

5. In addition to the speakers' names, I have changed all other identifying names and details in the transcripts and ethnographic descriptions.

6. Transcription Conventions

Each line represents a single intonation unit.

.	end of intonation unit; falling intonation
,	end of intonation unit; fall-rise intonation
?	end of intonation unit; rising intonation
!	raised pitch and volume throughout the intonation unit
↑	pitch accent
—	self-interruption; break in the intonation unit
-	self-interruption; break in the word, sound abruptly cut off
:	length
=	latching; no pause between intonation units
underline	emphatic stress; increased amplitude; careful articulation of a segment
(.)	pause of 0.5 seconds or less
(n.n)	pause of greater than 0.5 seconds, length indicated numerically
@	laughter; each token marks one pulse
.h	inbreath
[ ]	overlapping speech
< >	transcriber comment; nonvocal noise
{ }	stretch of talk to which transcriber comment applies
" "	reported speech or thought

REFERENCES

Agha, Asif. 2007. *Language and social relations.* Cambridge: Cambridge University Press.
Bucholtz, Mary. 1996. Geek the girl: Language, femininity, and female nerds. In *Gender and belief systems: Proceedings of the fourth Berkeley Women and Language Conference,* ed. Natasha Warner et al., 119–131. Berkeley: Berkeley Women and Language Group.
———. 1997. *Borrowed blackness: African American Vernacular English and European American youth identities.* PhD diss., University of California, Berkeley, Department of Linguistics.
———. 1999a. You da man: Narrating the racial other in the linguistic production of white masculinity. *Journal of Sociolinguistics* 3:443–460.
———. 1999b. "Why be normal?": Language and identity practices in a community of nerd girls. *Language in Society* 28:203–223.
———. 2001. The whiteness of nerds: Superstandard English and racial markedness. *Journal of Linguistic Anthropology* 11:84–100.
———. 2002. From "sex differences" to gender variation in sociolinguistics. In *Papers from NWAV 30. University of Pennsylvania Working Papers in Linguistics* 8, ed. Daniel Ezra Johnson and Tara Sanchez, 33–45. Philadelphia: University of Pennsylvania.
———. 2004. Styles and stereotypes: The linguistic negotiation of identity among Laotian American youth. *Pragmatics* 14(2–3):127–147.
———. 2007. Shop talk: Branding, consumption, and gender in American middle-class youth interaction. In *Words, worlds, and material girls: Language, gender, globalized economy,* ed. Bonnie McElhinny, 371–402. Berlin: Mouton de Gruyter.
Bucholtz, Mary, and Kira Hall. 2004. Language and identity. In *A companion to linguistic anthropology,* ed. Alessandro Duranti, 369–394. Oxford: Blackwell.

————. 2005. Identity and interaction: A sociocultural linguistic approach. *Discourse Studies* 7(4-5):585–614.

Caplan, Nathan, John K. Whitmore, and Marcella H. Choy. 1989. *The boat people and achievement in America: A study of family life, hard work and cultural values.* Ann Arbor: University of Michigan Press.

Chan, Sucheng. 1991. *Asian Americans: An interpretive history.* Boston: Twayne.

Chun, Elaine W. 2001. The construction of white, black, and Korean American identities through African American Vernacular English. *Journal of Linguistic Anthropology* 11:52–64.

Cutler, Cecelia A. 1999. Yorkville crossing: White teens, hip hop, and African American English. *Journal of Sociolinguistics* 3:428–442.

————. 2003. "Keepin' it real": White hip-hoppers' discourses of language, race, and authenticity. *Journal of Linguistic Anthropology* 13:211–233.

Eckert, Penelope. 2000. *Language variation as social practice.* Oxford: Blackwell.

————. 2002. Demystifying sexuality and desire. In *Language and sexuality: Contesting meaning in theory and practice*, ed. Kathryn Campbell-Kibler, Robert J. Podesva, Sarah J. Roberts, and Andrew Wong, 99–110. Stanford, CA.: CSLI Publications.

Eckert, Penelope, and John R. Rickford, eds. 2001. *Style and sociolinguistic variation.* Cambridge: Cambridge University Press.

Errington, Joseph. 1998. *Shifting languages: Interaction and identity in Javanese Indonesia.* Cambridge: Cambridge University Press.

Espiritu, Yen Le. 1992. *Asian American panethnicity: Bridging institutions and identities.* Philadelphia: Temple University Press.

Goldstein, Lynn M. 1987. Standard English: The only target for nonnative speakers of English? *TESOL Quarterly* 21:417–436.

Green, Lisa. 2002. *African American English: A linguistic introduction.* Cambridge: Cambridge University Press.

Hanna, David B. 1997. Do I sound "Asian" to you?: Linguistic markers of Asian American identity. *Penn Working Papers in Linguistics* 4(2):141–153.

Irvine, Judith T. 2001. "Style" as distinctiveness: The culture and ideology of linguistic differentiation. In *Style and sociolinguistic variation*, ed. Penelope Eckert and John R. Rickford, 21–43. Cambridge: Cambridge University Press.

Joe, K. A. 1994. Myths and realities of Asian gangs on the West Coast. *Humanity and Society* 18:3–18.

Kang, Agnes M., and Adrienne Lo. 2004. Two ways of articulating heterogeneity in Korean American narratives of ethnic identity. *Journal of Asian American Studies* 7:93–116.

Lee, Jung-Eun Janie. 2006. Representations of Asian speech in Hollywood films. Unpublished master's thesis, Department of Linguistics, University of California, Santa Barbara.

Lee, Stacey J. 1994. Behind the model-minority stereotype: Voices of high-achieving and low-achieving Asian American students. *Anthropology and Education Quarterly* 25:413–429.

————. 2005. Up against whiteness: Race, school, and immigrant youth. New York: Teachers College Press.

Lo, Adrienne. 1999. Codeswitching, speech community membership, and the construction of ethnic identity. *Journal of Sociolinguistics* 3:461–479.

Mendoza-Denton, Norma. 1999. Fighting words: Latina girls, gangs, and language attitudes. In *Speaking Chicana: Voice, power, and identity*, ed. D. Letticia Galindo and María Dolores Gonzales, 39–56. Tucson: University of Arizona Press.

———. 2008. *Homegirls: Language and cultural practice among Latina youth gangs.* Malden, Mass.: Blackwell.

Mendoza-Denton, Norma Catalina, and Melissa Iwai. 1993. "They speak more Caucasian": Generational differences in the speech of Japanese-Americans. In *SALSA 1: Proceedings of the first annual Symposium about Language and Society—Austin (Texas Linguistic Forum 33)*, ed. Robin Queen and Rusty Barrett, 58–67. Austin: University of Texas, Department of Linguistics.

Ngo, Bic, and Stacey J. Lee. 2007. Complicating the image of model minority success: A review of Southeast Asian American education. *Review of Educational Research* 77(4):415–453.

Ochs, Elinor. 1992. Indexing gender. In *Rethinking context: Language as an interactive phenomenon*, ed. Alessandro Duranti and Charles Goodwin, 335–358. Cambridge: Cambridge University Press.

Portes, Alejandro, and Rubén G. Rumbaut. 2001. *Legacies: The story of the immigrant second generation.* Berkeley: University of California Press.

Rampton, Ben. 1995. *Crossing: Language and ethnicity among adolescents.* London: Longman.

Reyes, Angela. 2005. Appropriation of African American slang by Asian American youth. *Journal of Sociolinguistics* 9(4):509–532.

———. 2007. *Language, identity, and stereotype among Southeast Asian American youth: The other Asian.* Mahwah, N.J.: Lawrence Erlbaum Associates.

Rumbaut, Rubén G. 1995. Vietnamese, Laotian, and Cambodian Americans. In *Asian Americans: Contemporary trends and issues*, ed. Pyong Gap Min, 232–270. Thousand Oaks, Calif.: Sage.

———. 2005. Turning points in the transition to adulthood: Determinants of educational attainment, incarceration, and early childbearing among children of immigrants. *Ethnic and Racial Studies* 28(6):1041–1086.

Shah, Bindi. 2007. Being young, female and Laotian: Ethnicity as social capital at the intersection of gender, generation, "race" and age. *Ethnic and Racial Studies* 30(1):28–50.

Song, John Huey-Long, John Dombrink, and Gil Geis. 1992. Lost in the melting pot: Asian youth gangs in the United States. *Gang Journal* 1:1–12.

Sweetland, Julie. 2002. Unexpected but authentic use of an ethnically-marked dialect. *Journal of Sociolinguistics* 6:514–536.

Tuan, Mia. 1999. *Forever foreigners or honorary whites?: The Asian ethnic experience today.* New Brunswick, N.J.: Rutgers University Press.

Vigil, James Diego, and Steve Yun. 1990. Vietnamese youth gangs in Southern California. In *Gangs in America*, ed. C. Ronald Huff, 146–162. Newbury Park, Calif.: Sage.

Waters, Mary C. 1990. *Ethnic options: Choosing identities in America.* Berkeley: University of California Press.

Wolfram, Walter A. 1973. *Sociolinguistic aspects of assimilation: Puerto Rican English in East Harlem.* Washington, D.C.: Center for Applied Linguistics.

Woolard, Kathryn A. 1998. Simultaneity and bivalency as strategies in bilingualism. *Journal of Linguistic Anthropology* 8:3–29.

Wu, Frank. 2001. *Yellow: Race beyond black and white.* New York: Basic Books.

Zentella, Ana Celia. 1997. *Growing up bilingual: Puerto Rican children in New York.* Malden, Mass.: Blackwell.

Zhou, Min, and Yang Sao Xiong. 2005. The multifaceted American experiences of the children of Asian immigrants: Lessons for segmented assimilation. *Ethnic and Racial Studies* 28(6):1119–1152.

3

Asian American Stereotypes as Circulating Resource

Angela Reyes

Perhaps one of the most interesting things about stereotypes is not whether they are true or false, but rather that individuals *need* them to move about the world. Walter Lippmann (1922), the first scholar to bring the topic of stereotypes to the social science table, refers to them as "pictures in the heads" of individuals looking out into their social world. He argues that we interact directly not with objective reality but with the representations we have created about that reality. To know that the substance in front of you is water, for example, is to already know that water is represented by the features: +liquid, +transparent, and so on. (Otherwise, every time you encounter water you would have no idea what it is.) A description of such features can be called a stereotype, defined by Hilary Putnam (1975) as

> a standardized description of features of the kind that are typical, or "normal," or at any rate stereotypical. The central features of the stereotype generally are criteria—features which in normal situations constitute ways of recognizing if a thing belongs to the kind or, at least, necessary conditions (or probabilistic necessary conditions) for membership in the kind. (Putnam 1975, 230)

Along this line of reasoning, stereotypes are simply typical features; at best, they are approximate descriptors that may or may not always be accurate or reliable. As such, if you are confronted with a substance that is +liquid but −transparent (because, perhaps, of a cloudy chemical treatment), you may still be able to recognize this substance as water since +liquid is a required condition, but +transparent is a typical, not necessary, feature. Stereotypes, then, can be quite useful as we interact with objects and people in our daily lives.

Yet the folk perception of stereotypes in the United States is that they are essentializing, largely negative, ideas held by people and used to judge or oppress other people. This notion has also been taken up by several researchers in Asian American Studies (e.g., Hamamoto 1994; R. Lee 1999; S. Lee 1996; Marchetti 1993). Jessica Hagedorn (1994), noting that stereotypes of Asian Americans in mainstream media can be multiple and conflicting, argues that Asian American men are depicted as sexless, villainous, and gentle, while Asian American women are portrayed as exotic, evil, and submissive—what filmmaker Renee Tajima calls the dragon lady/lotus blossom dichotomy. Yet perhaps most research has been in response to the prevalent portrayal of Asian Americans as the "model minority." Although the model minority stereotype explicitly emerged in the 1960s, some scholars argue that it had its origins in the cold war. At that time, Asian Americans were depicted as a successful case of ethnic assimilation in order to help contain what Robert Lee calls "the red menace of communism, the black menace of racial integration, and the white menace of homosexuality" (R. Lee 1999, 10). As the model minority stereotype later emerged explicitly during the civil rights movement in the 1960s, scholars argued that the myth of the Asian American success story was used not only to set a standard for how minorities should behave but also to silence the accusations of racial injustice by communities of color (S. Lee 1996). Thus, the model minority myth upholds the American ideologies of meritocracy and individualism, diverts attention away from racial inequality, sustains whites in the racial hierarchy, and pits minority groups against one another.

While such studies are extremely important in understanding the social impact of stereotypes and the consequences for Asian Americans in particular, there has been little work on stereotypes outside of this rather limited scope of research. Indeed some stereotypes may be hurtful toward individuals, but these same individuals can also reappropriate such stereotypes as a *resource* for accomplishing new social actions. This process is not unlike the reappropriation of ethnic epithets, such as "nigger" by African Americans (Kennedy 2002) and "chink" by Asian Americans (Reyes 2007), as solidarity terms under certain interactional conditions. Just as these practices can be controversial and confusing, particularly to those outside of the relevant ethnic grouping, the reappropriation of stereotypes can strike similar debates as to how previously pejorative and homogenizing representations of groups can take on new positive meanings. Using this idea of stereotype as resource, this chapter is interested in how people reappropriate stereotypes of their ethnic grouping as a means through which to position themselves and others in socially meaningful ways, accomplish new social actions and, in effect, assign new meanings to stereotypes.

Drawing on theories and methods in linguistic anthropology, this chapter examines the ways in which circulating stereotypes of Asian Americans emerge as resources in conversations among Asian Americans. Specifically, this chapter analyzes two video-recorded interactions at a videomaking project in Philadelphia's Chinatown to trace how Asian American teen participants invoke Asian American stereotypes, orient to them in various ways, and reappropriate them to: (1) position the self and other relative to stereotypes; (2) construct stereotyping as an oppressive practice to resist or as an interactional resource to celebrate; and (3) bring about interactional effects from widely circulating stereotypes (e.g., Asian store owner) that are different from those from locally circulating typifications (e.g., Asian mini-van driver), what I call "widespread typifications" and "local typifications," respectively. The relationships among these actions reveal how they rely on one another for their meaningfulness. Positioning the self and other, for example, is part and parcel of how stereotypes are used to resist oppression and celebrate identities. Likewise, the interactional effects of widespread and local typifications rely on whether these specific typifications are used to resist or celebrate. By interrogating the very notion of stereotype as a performative resource, this chapter illustrates how Asian American stereotypes can be creatively reappropriated by Asian American teens to accomplish meaningful, interrelated social actions.

Metapragmatic Stereotypes

Previous work on stereotypes has largely been the domain of social psychology. Social psychologists recognize that stereotypes are not simply mental phenomena, but consensually shared in a society (Stangor and Schaller 1996). Research in this area has asserted that stereotypes not only help individuals organize and simplify their environment, they also fulfill social functions (Leyens, Yzerbyt, and Schadron 1994). There have been attempts to categorize these functions of out-group stereo-typing (Tajfel 1981), and to delineate levels of analysis ranging from individual representations in the mind to collective representations shared by members of a "cultural group" (Stangor and Schaller 1996). Using data primarily from experiments and questionnaires, the individual approach is concerned with the meaning of stereotypes to individuals, while the sociocultural approach is concerned with the transmission of stereotypes and their societal consensus. Such quantitative measures are of some use, but fail to account for *functions* of stereotypes beyond static rules, stereotypes of the *self* and how people reappropriate them for meaningful action, and the level of *interaction* by focusing either too narrowly on the individual or too broadly on society.

This is not to say that social psychologists have completely overlooked the importance of analyzing language in stereotype research. Anne Maass and Luigi Arcuri (1996) recognize that "stereotypes are closely—if not inseparably—linked to language" (220). And since any instance of stereotyping uses as its vehicle language or other semiotic modalities, they also suggest that "our knowledge of stereotypes will remain incomplete without an analysis of the language" (Maass and Arcuri 1996, 220). Although there has been some discourse analytic research on stereotypes that comes out of a social psychology tradition (Giles 1977; van Dijk 1987; van Langenhove and Harré 1994), there is still a heavy reliance on analyzing decontextualized language, such as counting the number of ethnic slurs in a dictionary (e.g., Stangor and Schaller 1996).

Stereotype research in linguistic anthropology (e.g., Agha 1998), philosophy (e.g., Putnam 1975), sociolinguistics (e.g., Le Page and Tabouret-Keller 1985), and linguistic ethnography (e.g., Tusting, Crawshaw, and Callen 2002) takes into account important philosophical, ethnographic, and discourse perspectives that are overlooked by social psychologists. In this chapter, I draw primarily on theories and methods in linguistic anthropology to argue that stereotypes function *metapragmatically* (Silverstein 1993; Agha 1998) to enable interactants to perform social actions. Asif Agha (1998, 2004), building on Putnam (1975) and Michael Silverstein (1976, 1993), argues that "[s]ince our ideas about others are ideas ABOUT pragmatic phenomena, they are in principle metapragmatic constructs. In particular, such ideas are METAPRAGMATIC STEREOTYPES ABOUT PRAGMATIC PHENOMENA" (Agha 1998, 151). By definition, metapragmatic phenomena must take as their object pragmatic signs (Silverstein 1993). A pragmatic sign is any behaviorally deployable concomitant of action, such as owning a store, driving a car, having a visible skin color, or employing some distinctive type of speech. Metapragmatic stereotypes mediate between two pragmatic orders. Not only do metapragmatic stereotypes *construe* pragmatic behavior, such as recognizing and reifying a particular behavior as rigidly linked to social categories of persons, they also *enable* pragmatic behavior, making such metapragmatic stereotypes "reportable, discussable, open to dispute; they can be invoked as social standards, or institutionalized as such; they allow (and sometimes require) conscious strategies of self-presentation; they serve as models for some individuals, counter-models for others" (Agha 1998, 152). In other words, as metapragmatic stereotypes travel from interaction to interaction, they enable interactants to generate pragmatic behavior, such as arguing, celebrating, or denying someone a taxi ride because of the color of his or her skin. Metapragmatic stereotypes, then, circulate as models that we can invoke to perform social actions.

Situating Stereotypes

Sociolinguists and linguistic anthropologists have long recognized that interactions do not occur in vacuums, isolated from and uninfluenced by their surrounds. Rather, interactions are situated in particular settings and guided by particular contextual aspects that influence how discourse unfolds. The following interactions are no exception. The teens are voluntarily participating in a videomaking project at an Asian American community arts organization after school. They are drawn to this particular program and institution for several reasons—an interest in video, art, or activism; or because they want to be with their friends; meet new people; or be among those racially or ethnically similar, to name just a few. It is important to consider that the videomaking project occurs in a distinctly—and explicitly—Asian American institution, which may influence the types of interactions that are produced in it. It is equally important to consider the ways in which these interactions unfold as guided by the particular activity that the teens are engaged in. The next three sections describe the institution and the particular circumstances surrounding each of the two interactions that serve as the data for this paper.

An Asian American Teen Videomaking Project

The setting for this study is an Asian American teen videomaking project at the Asian Arts Initiative,[1] a community arts organization located near Philadelphia's

Chinatown. Like many other community arts organizations, the Asian Arts Initiative is grounded in the belief that political activism through the arts can lead to social change. Paul E. Willis (1990) states that "[t]hough subordinated and often marginalized, the many strands of the community arts movement ... share the continuing concern to democratize the arts and make them more a part of common experience" (Willis 1990, 4). By offering several programs for Asian American adult and youth constituencies, the Asian Arts Initiative fosters a sense that art belongs to everyday people and can help build a collective political and cultural voice for underrepresented populations.

This chapter is part of a four-year ethnographic and discourse analytic study of the Asian American teen videomaking project at the Asian Arts Initiative (see Reyes 2007). This project, which engages a new group of about fifteen teens each year, meets weekly from February to June. Teens, with the help of adult artists and volunteers, critically discuss issues relevant to their lives and communities, create a script based out of these discussions, then shoot and edit a fifteen-minute video that reflects their real-life experiences and perspectives. These videos are then screened at conferences and in classrooms. Having families that emigrated from Cambodia, Vietnam, or Laos, the teens are assigned to or assign themselves to the not unproblematic ethnic grouping of Southeast Asian American (see Bucholtz, this volume). Depending on the interactional circumstances, teens will use different "tactics of subjectivity" (Bucholtz and Hall 2004) to racially or ethnically self-identify. When teens identify as Asian or Asian American, they are exemplifying the process of *adequation* to foreground a similarity of identity based on a racial grouping. However, when teens identify by ethnicity alone, for example, Vietnamese or Cambodian, they are, in part, drawing on the process of *distinction* to highlight differences among Asian ethnic groups. There are several teens who identify as "mixed," which typically means that they are multiethnic, but it can also mean that they identify as one ethnicity although their families came from an area that was primarily another ethnicity, for example, ethnic Chinese from Cambodia. Most of the teens would be identified as second generation or "1.5 generation" (Rumbaut and Ima 1988), meaning they were born in another country but emigrated to the United States as young children. Many emigrated from refugee camps and processing centers in Thailand or the Philippines to poor urban neighborhoods in Philadelphia. Over the years I have been a volunteer and coordinator of the videomaking project, and also a staff member of the Asian Arts Initiative. Data collection methods include participant observation, field notes, interviews, and audio- and video-recording of interactions at project sessions and video screenings.[2]

Although the participants in this study and I oftentimes use "Asian American" to describe the institution as well as the participants, I do not wish to present this label as unproblematic. As a pan-ethnic unifying marker in theory, "Asian American" can also be understood as one of divisiveness in practice. Although it can be a strategic label for political mobilization, many note that "Asian American" has been commonly understood as representing only Chinese and Japanese Americans (Espiritu 1992, 50–51), thus excluding Southeast Asian Americans, like those in this study. Not only are labels such as "Asian American" exclusionary, they can also be gravely misleading. As Lisa Lowe (1996) argues, "important contradictions exist between an exclusively Asian American cultural nationalist construction of identity and the material heterogeneity of the Asian American constituency, particularly class, gender, and national-origin differences among peoples of Asian descent in the United States" (Lowe 1996, 38). Despite the ways in which the diversity among Asian ethnic groups complicates a unified formation of Asian American identity, the teens in this study commonly identify as Asian or Asian American, thus participating in the local construction of this unifying, yet homogenizing, label.

A Brainstorming Activity

This first interaction I present occurred during a project session in February 2001. This session was early in the project year, and used to help explore possible themes for the video. Teens and adult artists and volunteers were divided into four small groups. Each small group had a private area and was given a large piece of paper upon which to draw a large head in the center. After drawing the head, each group had to choose from a list of five statements. The following interaction is from one of the small groups, which consisted of two Cambodian-Chinese American boys, Moeun and Dan, and one Cambodian-Vietnamese-Chinese American girl, Anh, who were joined by the scriptwriting artist, Didi, an Indian American woman, as well as a project volunteer, Kelly, a Vietnamese American woman.[3] All five were sitting in a circle around the piece of paper. They chose the statement "I feel different." When Anh was about to write on the inside of the head "mean," which teens claimed is something that their siblings think of them, Didi stopped her and said, "no, this [pointing to the inside of the head] is what you really are and this [pointing to the outside of the head] is what people think." Didi's directions made the activity particularly conducive to eliciting stereotypes as it involved an explicit distinction between what others think of the teens and what the teens think of themselves.

The following transcript begins with Moeun, who offers a suggestion for something to write on the outside of the head.

(1) "Put owns a Chinese restaurant"[4]

	Moeun:	oh (.) put owns a Chinese restaurant
56	Anh:	((turns lips down, wrinkles forehead downward))
	Didi:	o::h ok[ay(.) yeah that's a good idea heh heh
58	Moeun:	[heh heh
	Anh:	owns a store? ((picks up marker))
60	Moeun:	yeah
	Didi:	yeah
62	Anh:	I own a s- my parents own a store ((leans in to write on paper, with lips still turned down and
64		forehead wrinkled downward))
	Moeun:	cause- Asian peop- cause like [Asian people=
66	Kelly:	[stereotypes
	Moeun:	=yea:::h
68	Dan:	they always got to own something

```
      Moeun:      yea::h
70    Kelly:      grocery store heh heh
      Anh:        yeah I own a grocery store ((turns lips down,
72                wrinkles forehead downward))
      Moeun:      my parents too heh heh
74    Anh:        ((turns lips up))
      Dan:        drives minivan
76    Moeun:      heh heh
      Anh:        o:h [yeah heh ((gazes at Moeun, points to Dan))
78    Moeun:          [hell yeah hell [yeah if you don't drive=
      Didi:                          [heh heh
80    Moeun:      =one you ain't Asian ((gazes at Anh, points to
                  Dan)) (1.9) drives minivan (4.6) heh heh
82    Anh:        my brother drives (psycho) people to work every
                  mo(hh)rning
84    Moeun:      heh heh
```

About a minute later, Olive, another project volunteer, came into the room. She was curious about why they had "minivan" written down. "That's a stereotype?" she asked. Moeun replied, "That's what people think." Anh clarified, "They think we drive minivans." Anh then paused and in a contemplative voice uttered, "But we do." Dan replied, "They shouldn't think that though."

A Scriptwriting Activity

This next interaction occurred at a scriptwriting session about one month later in March 2001. The teen scriptwriters were one Chinese American girl, Sara; one Chinese-Burmese (ethnic Chinese from Burma/Myanmar) American girl, Cindy; one Cambodian-Chinese American girl, Enoy; one Lao American boy, Rod; and one Haitian American girl, Jill, who is the only non-Asian participant in the videomaking project. The scriptwriting artist, Didi, an Indian American woman from the previous interaction, also appears here. They are writing the first scene of the script for the video they will be shooting in a few months. In the interaction I analyze here, the scriptwriters are trying to decide what one of the main characters in the video is going to say to his sister in the first scene, which takes place on a basketball court after school. They want the teenage boy, who is Chinese American, to call his sister to him, so the scriptwriters are thinking of reasons why he would need to do that.

The activity of scriptwriting, like the activity described in the previous section, can also be conducive to invoking stereotypes. Storytelling conventions and prior media representations of Asian Americans can function to restrict possibilities when developing characters in a script. As Didi, an experienced filmmaker, has said about scriptwriting, "The first lines that come to your mind are usually stereotypes." This interaction is no exception to her observation, but it is unlike the previous interaction in at least two ways. First, this scriptwriting activity is not asking for explicit distinctions between what others think about the teens and what the teens think about themselves. There is no specific discussion of whether the proposed reason for the boy calling his sister should or should not be a stereotypical idea about Asian Americans. Second, as opposed to the previous activity in which what the teens discussed was mainly for their own benefit, the writing of a script for a video that is going to be viewed by audiences might influence the kind of material that participants would want to include. Although the teens might not necessarily be wholly attuned to the potential consequences of their representations, the Asian Arts Initiative as a community organization is particularly sensitive to issues of representation. Thus the potential reproduction of stereotypes is carefully monitored.[5]

Before the interaction represented in the following transcript, Didi has asked the scriptwriters to come up with a line for the boy to say to his sister. Jill offers a suggestion.

(2) "Mom needs you at the store"

	Jill:	like mom [needs you at the- the store or=
86	Didi:	[I
	Jill:	=something (0.8)
88	Didi:	mom needs you at the store? or (0.7)
	Enoy:	I don't know (?)
90	Jill:	a lot of Chinese people do own a restaurant
	Sara:	no they're not [owning a restaurant they're=₁
92	Enoy:	[all right mom needs you to=₂
	Sara:	₁=**not** owning a restaurant
94	Enoy:	₂=watch- mom needs you to watch the store. they got to own something in their [life tell me=
96	Sara:	[no no
	Enoy:	=your parents don't own anything in their life
98		((waving pencil with quick downward motions in front of Sara's face))
100	Sara:	(?) in their life? they don't own anything <u>now</u>, they did [but-
102	Enoy:	[see see there you go ((waving pencil at Sara again, turns lips up, gazes at Jill))
104	Sara:	<u>but</u> that's <u>so:</u>- [that's so stereotypical you=
	Jill:	[it's what.
106	Sara:	=cannot do that no [way no ((slaps pencil=₁
	Enoy:	[heh heh yep all right=₂
108	Sara:	₁=down, puts hands under table))
	Enoy:	₂=((puts hands under table, then brings them
110		back up)) tell me tell me- um
	Sara:	no: ((puts hands palms facing out toward Enoy))
112	Enoy:	[they always- always no matter they got to own=
	Didi:	[what we have to do is-
114	Enoy:	=some kind of store
	Jill:	I know ((counting on fingers)) nail salon,
116		res[taurant, (???), hair salon
	Enoy:	[((gazing at Jill, counting on fingers))

118		hair salon al<u>ways</u> (.) there's no joke-
		Manhattan bagel (.) my <u>unc</u>le got a bagel store
120		what the hell is that? heh heh
	Rod:	[heh heh
122	Jill:	[heh heh
	Sara:	that's new that's new
124	Didi:	ok look it's really important-
	Enoy:	they comin' up man ((turns lips up, raises hand
126		palm up in front of Sara))
	Sara:	((places head face down on table))
128	Didi:	u::h
	Rod:	Asian bagel store ha ha

Identifying Stereotypes

Before analyzing how teens orient toward and reappropriate stereotypes, we must first identify what qualifies as a stereotype and if it is indeed invoked. As pointed out earlier, a stereotype can be fundamentally defined as a *typical feature of a kind* (Putnam 1975). The problem of identifying stereotypes engages two central questions: (1) what counts as typical? and (2) what counts as a typification? One way to discover what counts as typical from the participant perspective is to examine certain discursive features that index typicality, for example, adverbs such as "always." One way to discover what counts as a typification is to analyze two elements in an interaction: *reference* and *predication* (Wortham and Locher 1996); for the particular purposes of this chapter, this means relating some aspect of behavior (predication) to a particular social category of persons (reference).

In the following excerpts taken from the two full transcripts above, I use a triadic model to identify instances where reference (dotted), predication (dash), and what I call "typicality devices" (**bold**) together form stereotypes from the participant perspective. I will focus only on references that index Asian ethnic groups (often anaphorically through nonpronominal indexicals such as "they"), predications that describe behaviors of those references, and typicality devices that index these typifications as typical.

(3) Reference: "Chinese people"; predication: "do own a restaurant"; typicality device (plural quantifier): "a lot of"

| 90 | Jill: | **a lot of** Chinese people do own a restaurant |

(4) Reference: "Asian people" anaphorically indexed by "they"; predication: "own something"; typicality devices (adverb): "always," (aspect marker): "got to"

	Moeun:	cause- Asian peop- cause like [Asian people=
66	Kelly:	[stereotypes
	Moeun:	=yea:::h
68	Dan:	they **always got to** own something
	Moeun:	yea::h

(5) Reference: "Chinese people" (line 90) anaphorically indexed by "they"; predication: "own some kind of store"; typicality devices (adverb): "always," (phrasal adverb): "no matter," (aspect marker): "got to"

```
112   Enoy:     [they always- always no matter they got to own=
      Didi:     [what we have to do is-
114   Enoy:     =some kind of store
```

(6) Reference: "Asian people" (line 65) anaphorically indexed by "you"; predications: "don't drive one" ("minivan" line 75), "ain't Asian"; typicality device (conditional embedded clause): "if you don't…you ain't"

```
78   Moeun:    [hell yeah hell [yeah if you don't drive=
     Didi:                     [heh heh
80   Moeun:    =one you ain't Asian ((gazes at Anh, points to
               Dan)) (1.9) drives minivan (4.6) heh heh
```

The triadic model is not sufficient for identifying mainstream stereotypes but is necessary for identifying explicit stereotypes from the participant perspective.[6] In examples 3–5, the "Asian storeowner" is recognized as a stereotype from the perspective of participants in both interactions. But whether it is a stereotype relies on knowledge of its circulation beyond these two interactions. The image of the Asian storeowner does, in fact, circulate at the societal level, from representations of Asian storeowners in mainstream entertainment media, such as Apu on the *The Simpsons*, to news media portrayals of events, such as the 1992 Los Angeles riots, which highlighted the visibility of Korean shop owners (Sethi 1994). Thus, we can say that the Asian storeowner is, indeed, a stereotype, or what I call "widespread typification" because of its societal circulation. In example 6, on the other hand, teens from the first interaction seem to formulate what they interpret as a stereotype, that of the "Asian minivan driver." Yet since the image of the Asian minivan driver has a limited scope—as narrow as this particular interaction to as wide as perhaps Asian American communities in the Philadelphia area—I do not define it as a stereotype, but as a "local typification."

In addition to this triadic model, denotationally explicit metapragmatic signs (Silverstein 1993) (**bold**) and their subsequent uptake (dotted) are another way to discover how participants identify stereotypes.

(7) Denotationally explicit metapragmatic sign: "stereotypes"; uptake: "yea:::h"

```
     Moeun:    cause- Asian peop- cause like [Asian people=
66   Kelly:                                  [stereotypes
     Moeun:    =yea:::h
```

(8) Denotationally explicit metapragmatic sign: "stereotypical"; uptake: "heh heh yep"

```
104   Sara:    but that's so:- [that's so stereotypical you=
      Jill:                    [it's what.
```

106   Sara: =cannot do that no [way no ((slaps pencil=₁
      Enoy: [heh heh yep all right=₂

With the Asian storeowner identified by participants and myself as a stereotype that is invoked in both interactions, I will now examine how the teens orient toward this stereotype and reappropriate it for meaningful effects.

Positioning the Self and Other Relative to Stereotypes

One thing that the teens do with stereotypes is use them to position themselves and others in socially meaningful ways. There are two kinds of positioning at issue here: (1) teens positioning themselves and others as inhabiting the stereotype; and (2) teens positioning themselves with respect to one another. The first issue is concerned with the relationship between the "denotational text" and "interactional text" (Silverstein 1993), that is, with how the events discussed in the denotational text (i.e., stereotypes) relate to the participants in the interactional text (i.e., the teens). "Interactional positioning" (Gergen and Kaye 1992; Wortham 2001), which is primarily concerned with how the interactants are positioning themselves with respect to one another in the interactional text, can be operationalized to explore the second issue. The fact that the Asian American teens invoke an Asian American stereotype foregrounds the potential for inhabiting this stereotype since the teens, though ethnically diverse, do draw on the process of adequation to identify as Asian or Asian American.

In the following excerpts, both Anh and Sara are the first to position themselves as inhabiting the Asian storeowner stereotype by admitting that their families own or have owned stores. In order to inhabit a stereotype, I argue, one must locate herself or be located as a member of both the reference (in this case, "Asian") and the predication (in this case, "owns store"). Since Anh and Sara both identify or are identified as "Asian," they are indeed members of the reference; in the following excerpts, they become members of the predication as well. Whereas Anh willingly inhabits the stereotype, Sara is almost forced by Enoy who demands from her, "[tell me] your parents don't own anything in their life" (lines 95–97).

(9) Anh inhabits the stereotype

62   Anh: I own a s- my parents own a store ((leans in to
               write on paper, with lips still turned down and
64   forehead wrinkled downward))

(10) Sara inhabits the stereotype

100   Sara: (?) in their life? they don't own anything now,
               they did [but-

As Anh and Sara inhabit the stereotype, they also resist the stereotype. To signal resistance, Anh uses mostly paralinguistic cues, while Sara uses both paralinguistic and linguistic ones. Through her use of facial expressions, such as frowning and wrinkling her forehead downward (lines 56, 63–64 and 71–72), Anh displays resistance and perhaps irritation toward Moeun's suggestion to write "owns a Chinese restaurant" (line 55) on the piece of paper. Sara, on the other hand, uses some gestures, such as slapping her pencil down (line 106), but mostly uses denotationally explicit responses to resist scripting the Asian storeowner stereotype, for example, "they're not [owning a restaurant]" (lines 91 and 91–93), "you cannot do that" (lines 104–106), and "no (way)" (lines 106 and 110). By performing these moves of resistance, Anh and Sara are also interactionally positioning themselves in opposition to others, particularly Moeun and Enoy, who support the relevance of the stereotype in their respective interactions.

As Anh and Sara display resistance, the other interactants use the stereotype as a resource for creating relationships with one another as they interactionally position themselves as unified in support of the stereotype. In the first interaction, Didi ratifies Moeun's contribution, "owns a Chinese restaurant," with "o::h okay yeah that's a good idea" (line 57). Kelly and Dan also align with Moeun by laughing with him and providing supporting information that "owns a Chinese restaurant" is appropriate to write on the outside of the head. When Moeun says, "cause Asian people like" (line 65), both Kelly and Dan collaborate with Moeun in the typifying of Asians; Kelly says, "stereotypes" (line 66) and "grocery store" (line 70), and Dan says, "they always got to own something" (line 68). In the second interaction, after Jill suggests a line for the script, "like mom needs you at the store" (line 85), Enoy positions herself with respect to Jill as she agrees with her contribution, "all right …mom needs you to watch the store" (lines 92–94). In addition, Enoy and Jill, in one instance, jointly count types of stores that Asians own, "nail salon, restaurant … hair salon" (lines 115–118). Moeun, Didi, Kelly, and Dan, in the first interaction, and Enoy and Jill, in the second interaction, perform clear discursive patterns as they align in terms of assessments (Goodwin and Goodwin 1992)—joint laughter, cooperative completion of sentences, collaborative typification of Asians—that interactionally position them as aligned with one another, but aligned against Anh and Sara, respectively.

Anh and Sara's resistance breaks, however, when Moeun and Enoy co-inhabit the stereotype with them. This illustrates how interactional positions are momentary and may shift under certain interactional conditions.

(11) Moeun co-inhabits the stereotype

73   Moeun: my parents too heh heh

(12) Enoy co-inhabits the stereotype

       Enoy: [((gazing at Jill, counting on fingers))
118   hair salon al<u>ways</u> (.) there's no joke-
                   Manhattan bagel (.) my <u>un</u>cle got a bagel store
120   what the hell is that? heh heh

When Moeun co-inhabits the stereotype by admitting that his parents also own a store, Anh's resistance breaks. Anh seems pleased as she begins to smile (line 74), a facial signal new for her in this interaction. When Dan says, "drives minivan" (line 75), as another example of what others think of them, Moeun and Anh immediately align with each other. This is illustrated by their mutual eye gaze (lines 77 and 80), simultaneous pointing toward Dan (lines 77 and 80–81), and verbal agreement ("yeah" in lines 77 and 78). Erving Goffman (1963), Charles Goodwin (1981), and others argue that "gaze is not simply a means of obtaining information, the receiving end of a communication system, but is itself a social act" (Goodwin 1981, 92). As Anh and Moeun gaze at each other, they are doing more than communicating; they are accomplishing a mutual orientation toward the invocation of Asians driving minivans. Anh admits that her brother drives a minivan, but does so with more humor and less resistance than when she inhabited the Asian storeowner stereotype; laughter breaks through Anh's words as she says, "my brother drives (psycho) people to work every mo (hh) rning" (lines 82–83). Although owning a minivan may not seem to the outsider to relate to the topic of employment, it achieves such local meaning in this interaction. Anh's brother picks up Southeast Asian American workers on certain corners in South Philadelphia and drives them to work in the blueberry fields, garment factories, and other sweatshop labor. For this group of teens, owning a minivan is a narrowly circulating local typification that indexes low-income employment.

When Enoy co-inhabits the stereotype by admitting "my uncle got a bagel store" (lines 118–119), Sara's resistance also breaks. Rod and Jill join Enoy in laughter (lines 121–122) as the comic value of her inhabiting this stereotype may rely on the fact that her uncle owns a bagel store and not a Chinese restaurant, which has been listed as a typical occupation. Then, just as Anh's alignment shifted in the previous interaction after someone co-inhabited the stereotype with her, Sara's alignment begins to shift as well. Sara ratifies Enoy's statement by uttering, "that's new that's new" (line 123), amid the laughter. Seemingly pleased that she was able to break Sara's resistance a little, Enoy smiles, raises her hand in front of Sara's face and says, "they comin' up man" (lines 125–126). Finally, Sara, perhaps signaling that she has finally given up, places her head face down on the table (line 127).

Stereotypes as Oppressive Practice versus Celebratory Resource

In addition to reappropriating stereotypes in order to position themselves and others in socially meaningful ways, the teens also construct stereotyping as an oppressive practice to resist or as an interactional resource to celebrate. When stereotyping is characterized as oppressive practice, it seems an obvious resource for resisting mainstream homogenizing representations of Asians, as well as resisting attempts by participants within an interaction to homogenize Asian people. It is perhaps seen as acceptable to stereotype one's own ethnicity, because a person is assumed to know more about her own ethnicity or because she is seen as not being able to oppress her own (see Chun, this volume). Yet as revealed by their anger and resistance, Anh and Sara interpret others in the interaction as perpetuating stereotypes that serve to oppress Asian people. Anh constructs a stereotype as oppressive through its characterization of perpetuating only "false" things about Asians, but displays confusion when stereotypes have elements of "truth." For example, when Olive asked the teens why they had "minivan" written down on their paper, Anh said, "they think we drive minivans," then in a contemplative voice uttered, "but we do." Anh appears to have a moment of confusion. She recognizes that "they" think the teens drive minivans, but she also notes that it is "true" for her and so is in the moment trying to figure out if "true" characterizations of behavior qualify as stereotypes. Unlike Anh, Sara seems to argue that regardless if a stereotype is "true" or "false," it is still "stereotypical" (line 104) and thus oppressive and homogenizing.

When stereotypes are characterized as celebratory resource, they become resources for building social relationships and resources with which to identify. As explained above, Moeun and Dan and Jill and Enoy construct alliances that defend the relevance of a stereotype in their respective interactions. In addition, the teens collaboratively build stereotypes in ways that make them more accessible as resources with which to self- and other-identify. They do this by broadening a predication or reference (**bold**) so that it better applies to their experiences.

(13) Predication broadens from "owns a Chinese restaurant" to "owns a store"

	Moeun:	oh (.) put **owns a Chinese restaurant**
56	Anh:	((turns lips down, wrinkles forehead downward))
	Didi:	o::h ok[ay(.) yeah that's a good idea heh heh
58	Moeun:	[heh heh
	Anh:	**owns a store**? ((picks up marker))
60	Moeun:	yeah
	Didi:	yeah

(14) Reference broadens from "Chinese" to "Asian"

90	Jill:	a lot of **Chinese** people do own a restaurant
...		
129	Rod:	**Asian** bagel store ha ha

As these excerpts reveal, predications and references can broaden so as to become increasingly more applicable to interactants. After Moeun says, "put owns a Chinese restaurant" (line 55), Anh goes out of her way to make sure that Moeun also means "store" (line 59). By broadening the predication, Anh is able to construct the stereotype as applicable to her since her family owns a store, not a restaurant. In the second interaction, as the ethnicity of the characters in the script is explicitly "Chinese," Jill typifies only Chinese people when she says, "a lot of Chinese people do own a restaurant" (line 90). But then Enoy applies this stereotype to her own experience by mentioning that her uncle, who is ethnically mixed, owns a bagel store (line 119). Rod says, "Asian bagel store" (line 129), which reveals that this stereotype has indeed widened to apply to Asians, not just to Chinese people. These stereotypes, then, are formulated to be maximally applicable and available to the teens as meaningful resources to form relationships and resources with which to identify.

Interactional Effects of Widespread Stereotypes versus Local Typifications

When a "widespread typification" (e.g., Asian storeowner stereotype) is invoked in these two interactions, it brings about different interactional alignments and effects than those from a "local typification" (e.g., Asian minivan driver). A circulatory account of how stereotypes are formed and maintained can partly explain this. A typification of behavior, for example, "all Asians own stores," circulates as it travels through "discursive chains" (Agha 2003), that is, travels as a speaker tells this message to a hearer who in turn becomes a speaker who tells it to another hearer and so on. If a typification does not travel through discursive chains or only at a scale that reaches a limited number of people, it remains a local typification. Only after a typification has circulated widely in discursive chains at the societal level can it develop into a stereotype or widespread typification. Such widespread typification is indeed fragile and maintained only through continuous streams of discursive chains. Otherwise, a stereotype can fade if discursive chains break, they become filled with counter-messages, or their speakers and hearers die out.[7] It is important to note that these speakers and hearers need not be individuals, but can be vehicles through which material signs circulate. For example, stereotypes can circulate through various popular media, such as film, television, magazines, and newspapers, which can perpetuate the distribution of value regarding Asian Americans. Importantly, this process is not neutral since those who have the power to control these signs and sign vehicles play a crucial role in the political economy of texts (Bauman and Briggs 1990; Gal 1989; Irvine 1989).

In both interactions, widespread stereotypes and local typifications emerge in succession and bring about different kinds of alignments. Anh and Sara, who display resistance toward the widely circulating Asian storeowner stereotype, radically shift their alignment after stereotypes are co-inhabited and after local typifications, "drives minivan" (line 75) and "got a bagel store"[8] (line 119), are added in next-turn behavior. Both of these less indexically rigid local typifications (dotted) are contextualized with comic value by the subsequent laughter (**bold**).

(15) Laughter after local typification: "drives minivan"

	Dan:	drives minivan
76	Moeun:	**heh heh**
	Anh:	o:h [yeah heh ((gazes at Moeun, points to Dan))
78	Moeun:	[hell yeah hell [yeah if you don't drive=
	Didi:	**[heh heh**
80	Moeun:	=one you ain't Asian ((gazes at Anh, points to Dan)) (1.9) drives minivan (4.6) **heh heh**

(16) Laughter after local typification: "got a bagel store"

	Enoy:	[((gazing at Jill, counting on fingers))
118		hair salon al<u>ways</u> (.) there's no joke-

		Manhattan bagel (.) my <u>uncle</u> <u>got a bagel store</u>
120		what the hell is that? **heh heh**
	Rod:	[**heh heh**
122	Jill:	[**heh heh**

These local typifications are critical in breaking the interactional frame (Goffman 1974) from serious resistance to comic event, which results in Anh's compliance and Sara's surrender. As noted earlier, Anh and Sara interpret the Asian storeowner stereotype, which is dispersed throughout society by media corporations, as oppressive and homogenizing; local typifications, on the other hand, may be seen as novel, innocuous, and not in need of active resistance as they circulate locally in interactions with friends and provoke laughter. Constructing a common identity as they index in-group knowledge, these local typifications function to create a sense of community by distinguishing between those who know this local "fact" about Asian Americans from outsiders who do not. The teens display no problem with a local typification perhaps because it is within their control; communities outside of their own are unaware of it and thus cannot use it against them as they go about the world. If "Asian minivan driver" began to circulate widely in societal speech chain networks, it might no longer generate laughter among participants because it would no longer function to index in-group knowledge. Instead, the image of the Asian minivan driver would become another stereotype to contend with, yet also another stereotype to reappropriate as an interactional resource.

Conclusion

This chapter examined the ways in which metapragmatic stereotypes are circulating resources that can be creatively recontextualized in interaction. Analyzing video-recorded interaction, I examined the ways in which participants at an Asian American teen videomaking project invoked the widely circulating stereotype of the Asian storeowner, oriented toward it in radically different ways, and reappropriated it to various interactional effects. Specifically, teens employed stereotypes to position themselves and others in relation to stereotypes or in relation to one another; resist oppressive practices, form social relationships, or celebrate a means of identifying; and bring about different interactional alignments between stereotypes and local typifications. Oftentimes interactionally achieved identities were temporary and shifted according to how the discursive processes above unfolded and related to one another. This illustrates how stereotypes and identities can become active and mutually informing processes. Whether teens use stereotypes to resist others and homogenizing representations of Asian Americans or to celebrate a common identity together in opposition to others, the teens reveal how stereotypes can be incorporated into people's lives to various effects, and sought out as a means of identifying and imagining oneself, others, and connections between individuals and groups.

Still, as with the reappropriation of ethnic epithets, the Asian American teens who draw on Asian American stereotypes at the videomaking project raise compelling issues regarding the nature and circulation of stereotypes on a wider scale. Of course, the teen-created grassroots videos have very limited circulation and the teens themselves are not in influential positions to control signs and sign vehicles at the societal level. Yet by celebrating stereotypes or identifying with them, are the teens somehow participating in homogenizing their own communities, uncritically perpetuating sweeping stereotypes of Asian American behavior? Or are the teens, as emerging videographers, reclaiming historically pejorative typifications to create a more critical Asian American political production, whether deliberately or not. Indeed, the teens straddle at least two possible representations of Asian America: (1) a *homogeneous* Asian America, which conforms to wider mainstream discourses that lumps all Asian Americans together and essentializes them as, for example, storeowners; and (2) a *heterogeneous* Asian America, which is aligned with Yen Le Espiritu's (1992) and Lowe's (1996) conceptualization of a shifting, evolving, and richly diverse sociopolitically constructed racial category.

I am grateful to Elaine Chun and Adrienne Lo for providing me with insightful and detailed feedback on earlier versions of this chapter. I also thank Eiichiro Azuma, Sue Gal, Agnes He, and Grace Kao for their comments on the oral version of this chapter. All remaining weaknesses are my own. For generous funding support for this research, I thank the Ford Foundation and the Language in Education Division, Graduate School of Education at the University of Pennsylvania.

NOTES

1. The Asian Arts Initiative has requested that the name of the organization not be changed in publications resulting from this research.

2. This chapter analyzes interactions at project sessions, but see Angela Reyes (2002) for an analysis of a screening discussion where stereotypes about culture are invoked.

3. All names used for participants in this chapter are pseudonyms.

4. Transcription conventions are adapted from Marjorie Goodwin (1990):

word	(underline) utterance stress
word?	(question mark) rising intonation
word.	(period) falling intonation
word,	(comma) falling-rising intonation
word-	(dash) abrupt breaks or stops/
wo:rd	(colon) elongated vowel or consonant
wo(hh)rd	(hh) laughter breaking into utterance
(.)	(period in parentheses) a pause under 0.5 seconds
(0.5)	(number in parentheses) a silence measured 0.5 seconds and above
[word [word	(brackets) simultaneous talk by two or more speakers
word= =word	(equal sign) continuous talk
word=$_1$ $_1$=word	(equal sign with numeric subscript) continuous talk that latches by numeric subscript
(word)	(parentheses) doubtful transcription or conjecture
(?)	(question mark in parentheses) inaudible utterance(s)
...	(ellipsis) break in transcript; omitted lines
((word))	(double parentheses) transcriber comment

5. This is not to say that the Asian Arts Initiative does not allow stereotypes in the teen-created videos, but they do encourage critical discussion about why people produce them, why the teens might reproduce them, and what the repercussions of putting them in the videos might be.

6. The triadic model identifies only stereotypes that are explicitly presented as such by participants. Stereotypes that are invoked from utterances that do not employ typicality devices are outside the scope of this paper.

7. This does not mean, however, that stereotypes cannot resurrect. For instance, Gustav M. Gilbert (1951) found that in 1933, Princeton students thought that the Japanese were intelligent, industrious, and progressive, but in 1951, they saw the Japanese as sly and shrewd. Then in 1969, other researchers showed that the stereotypes had returned to what they were in 1933 (Leyens et al. 1994). This example reveals the cyclical nature of stereotypes as dictated by historical events, such as the Japanese defeating the Russians in 1904, World War II, and Japan's emerging presence in the global market in the 1960s.

8. Owning a bagel store may not technically qualify as a local typification, since a bagel store is still a store and can fall under the Asian storeowner stereotype. However, the *atypical* ownership of a *bagel* store, as illustrated by Enoy's "what the hell is that?" (line 120), as opposed to the *typical* ownership of a "nail salon, restaurant...hair salon" (lines 115–116) is what I am arguing here.

REFERENCES

Agha, Asif. 1998. Stereotypes and registers of honorific language. *Language in Society* 27:151–193.
———. 2003. The social life of cultural value. *Language and Communication* 23:231–273.
———. 2004. Registers of language. In *Companion to linguistic anthropology*, ed. Alessandro Duranti, 23–45. Malden, Mass.: Blackwell.
Bauman, Richard, and Charles Briggs. 1990. Poetics and performance as critical perspectives on language and social life. *Annual Review of Anthropology* 19:59–88.
Bucholtz, Mary, and Kira Hall. 2004. Language and identity. In *Companion to linguistic anthropology*, ed. Alessandro Duranti, 369–394. Malden, Mass.: Blackwell.
Espiritu, Yen Le. 1992. *Asian American panethnicity: Bridging institutions and identities.* Philadelphia: Temple University Press.
Gal, Susan. 1989. Language and political economy. *Annual Review of Anthropology* 18:345–367.
Gergen, Kenneth, and John Kaye. 1992. Beyond narrative in the negotiation of therapeutic meaning. In *Therapy as social construction*, ed. Sheila McNamee and Kenneth Gergen, 166–185. London: Sage.
Gilbert, Gustav M. 1951. Stereotype persistence and change among college students. *Journal of Abnormal and Social Psychology* 46:245–254.
Giles, Michael W. 1977. Percent black and racial hostility: An old assumption re-examined. *Social Science Quarterly* 58:412–417.
Goffman, Erving. 1963. *Behavior in public places: Notes on the social organization of gatherings.* New York: Free Press.
———. 1974. *Frame analysis: An essay on the organization of experience.* New York: Harper and Row.
Goodwin, Charles. 1981. *Conversational organization.* New York: Academic Press.
Goodwin, Charles, and Marjorie H. Goodwin. 1992. Assessments and the construction of context. In *Rethinking context: Language as an interactive phenomenon*, ed. Alessandro Duranti and Charles Goodwin, 147–189. Cambridge: Cambridge University Press.

Goodwin, Marjorie H. 1990. *He-said she-said: Talk as social organization among black children*. Bloomington: Indiana University Press.

Hagedorn, Jessica. 1994. Asian American women in film: No joy, no luck. *Ms.*, January/ February, 74–79.

Hamamoto, Darrell Y. 1994. *Monitored peril: Asian Americans and the politics of TV representation*. Minneapolis: University of Minnesota Press.

Irvine, Judith T. 1989. When talk isn't cheap: Language and political economy. *American Ethnologist* 16:248–267.

Kennedy, Randall. 2002. *Nigger: The strange career of a troublesome word*. New York: Pantheon Books.

Lee, Robert. 1999. *Orientals: Asian Americans in popular culture*. Philadelphia: Temple University Press.

Lee, Stacey J. 1996. *Unraveling the "model minority" stereotype: Listening to Asian American youth*. New York: Teachers College Press.

Le Page, Robert B., and Andrée Tabouret-Keller. 1985. *Acts of identity: Creole-based approaches to language and ethnicity*. Cambridge: Cambridge University Press.

Leyens, Jacques-Philippe, Vincent Yzerbyt, and Georges Schadron. 1994. *Stereotypes and social cognition*. London: Sage Publications.

Lippmann, Walter. 1922. *Public opinion*. New York: Harcourt Brace.

Lowe, Lisa. 1996. *Immigrant acts: On Asian American cultural politics*. Durham, N.C.: Duke University Press.

Maass, Anne, and Luigi Arcuri. 1996. Language and stereotyping. In *Stereotypes and stereotyping*, ed. C. Neil Macrae, Charles Stangor, and Miles Hewstone, 193–226. New York: The Guildford Press.

Marchetti, Gina. 1993. *Romance and the "yellow peril": Race, sex, and discursive strategies in Hollywood fiction*. Berkeley: University of California Press.

Putnam, Hilary. 1975. *Mind, language and reality*. London: Cambridge University Press.

Reyes, Angela. 2002. "Are you losing your culture?": Poetics, indexicality, and Asian American identity. *Discourse Studies* 4:183-199.

———. 2007. *Language, identity, and stereotype among Southeast Asian American youth: The other Asian*. Mahwah, N.J.: Lawrence Erlbaum.

Rumbaut, Rubén, and Kenji Ima. 1988. *The adaptation of Southeast Asian refugee youth: A comparative study*. Final report to the Office of Resettlement. San Diego, Calif.: San Diego State University.

Sethi, Rita C. 1994. Smells like racism: A plan for mobilizing against anti-Asian bias. In *The state of Asian America: Activism and resistance in the 1990s*, ed. Karin Aguilar-San Juan, 235–250. Boston: South End Press.

Silverstein, Michael. 1976. Shifters, linguistic categories, and cultural description. In *Meaning in anthropology*, ed. Keith H. Basso and Henry A. Selby, 11–55. Albuquerque: University of New Mexico Press.

———. 1993. Metapragmatic discourse and metapragmatic function. In *Reflexive language: Reported speech and metapragmatics*, ed. John A. Lucy, 33–58. New York: Cambridge University Press.

Stangor, Charles, and Mark Schaller. 1996. Stereotypes as individual and collective representations. In *Stereotypes and stereotyping*, ed. C. Neil Macrae, Charles Stangor, and Miles Hewstone, 3–40. New York: The Guildford Press.

Tajfel, Henri. 1981. *Human groups and social categories*. Cambridge: Cambridge University Press.

Tusting, Karin, Robert Crawshaw, and Beth Callen. 2002. 'I know, 'cos I was there': How residence abroad students use personal experience to legitimate cultural generalizations. *Discourse and Society* 13:651–672.

van Dijk, Teun A. 1987. *Communicating racism: Ethnic prejudice in thought and talk.* Newbury Park, Calif.: Sage Publications.

van Lagenhove, Luk, and Rom Harré. 1994. Cultural stereotypes and positioning theory. *Journal for the Theory of Social Behavior* 24:359–372.

Willis, Paul E. 1990. *Common culture: Symbolic work at play in the everyday cultures of the young.* Boulder and San Francisco: Westview Press.

Wortham, Stanton. 2001. *Narratives in action.* New York: Teachers College Press.

Wortham, Stanton, and Michael Locher. 1996. Voicing on the news: An analytic technique for studying media bias. *Text* 16:557–585.

Evidentiality and Morality in a Korean Heritage Language School

Adrienne Lo

R esearch on Korean interaction has tended to concentrate on certain kinds of socially valued practices and relationships. While there is a long-standing history of research on honorifics, politeness, and indirectness (e.g., Dredge 1983; Park 1990; Sohn 1986a), ways in which Korean speakers are impolite, direct, and authoritarian have received comparatively little attention. However, what is polite and indirect has value in the Saussurean sense as such only in the ways in which it functions in a cultural system where impoliteness is equally important. In order to understand how social norms operate, we must also attend to cases in which their violation is socially meaningful (Garfinkel 1967).

One cultural norm that has been articulated in grammatical terms in previous research on Korean interaction is the propensity not to "directly" speculate on another person's thoughts, intentions, and sensations (Choi 1991; Kim 1978; Lee 1993; Sohn and Park 2003). As the philosopher Daniel Dennett (1996) has noted, the question of who has a mind is fundamentally a moral question. From a different standpoint, work in linguistic anthropology has considered the extent to which it is considered culturally appropriate to speculate about others' unspoken intentions or to guess at the contents of other persons' minds (Du Bois 1993; Duranti 1988, 1993a, 1993b; Ochs 1984, 1988; Rosaldo 1980). Drawing on these scholars' work, I argue in this chapter that the practice of "mind-reading" relates to moral evaluation.

Using Alessandro Duranti's (1994) concept of a "grammar of praising and blaming," I demonstrate that when a teacher at a Korean heritage language school is depicting students as morally exemplary, she situates her knowledge of their past intentions, sensations, and emotions as epistemically uncertain through evidential morphemes.

When she is depicting students as morally lacking, she uses bare forms of the verb that situate her knowledge of their past intentions, sensations, and emotions as more certain. Evidential marking thus serves as a resource for indexically constructing others as different kinds of moral beings and for constituting respect, power, and authority.

Subjectivity

The concept of subjectivity has been of increasing interest to linguists and linguistic anthropologists lately. Most linguists date this concept to Emile Benveniste, who described subjectivity in terms of the ability of speakers to view themselves as subjects: "Language is marked so deeply by the expression of subjectivity that one might ask if it could still function and be called language if it were constructed otherwise" (Benveniste 1971, 225). In his discussion of deictics and tense, Benveniste highlighted the role of personal pronouns. He argued that sentences with the subject "I" draw attention to the speaker's attitude while sentences with the subject "he" or "she" are more descriptive. In Benveniste's view, subjectivity was therefore a deictic relationship between speakers and their utterances.

Work on subjectivity has often drawn a contrast between "subjective" and "objective" utterances. John Lyons, for example, contrasts the following two sentences:

I remember switching off the light
I remember myself switching off the light. (Lyons 1982, 107)

In his interpretation, the second sentence foregrounds the "objective observing self" because the speaker is taking a distanced perspective on herself, while the first foregrounds a "subjective experiencing self" because it is more anchored in the speaker's own consciousness. According to Lyons, the distinction between these two perspectives is gradual, and can be thought of as a continuum between the "objective" component of language, which communicates propositions, and the "subjective" component, which points to the speaker's expression of her own thoughts and beliefs.

Ronald W. Langacker presents a diagram, represented in figure 4.1, to schematize these two viewpoints. In the "egocentric viewing arrangement," the speaker locates herself within the field of observation, as an observer of a particular object, while in the "optimal viewing arrangement" she does not. Describing the second situation, Langacker writes "S focuses his attention solely on O, to the point that conscious awareness of SELF either fades away entirely or is greatly diminished. What S observes, in other words, is *O*, not *S observing O*" (Langacker 1990, 121, emphasis in the original). Other scholars have used different names for these two contrasting frameworks. Shoichi Iwasaki (1993) employs the terms S-perspective versus O-perspective in his discussion of subjectivity in Japanese, while Senko K. Maynard contrasts the narrative internal position, where "one locates oneself internal to the scene" with the narrative external position, where "the language producer describes the event as an outside observer" (Maynard 1993, 51). In any case, the difference between the two frameworks is essentially a matter of deixis; in the egocentric/"subjective" framework, the deictic origo is the speaker, whereas in the

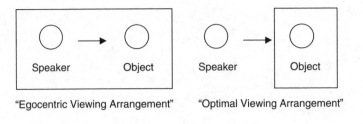

"Egocentric Viewing Arrangement"   "Optimal Viewing Arrangement"

Figure 4.1. "Egocentric" vs. "Optimal" Viewing Arrangements (Langacker 1985, 121)

optimal/"objective" framework the deictic origo is located outside of the speaker, in the person who is being spoken about (Agha 2002).

Evidentiality and Subjectivity

Evidential forms that mark epistemic stance are one of the resources through which subjectivity is indexed.[1] As a grammatical category, evidentiality refers to linguistic forms that relate either to the source of information for a proposition, for example (Bybee 1985), or "the expression of the speaker's attitude toward the situation his/her utterance describes" (Willett 1988, 52). Wallace Chafe (1986) calls the first one of these the "narrow sense" of evidentiality and the second one the "broad sense" while other scholars such as Talmy Givón discuss "evidentiary strength, evidentiary source, and evidentiary justification or knowledge" as interrelated aspects of a single phenomenon (Givón 1982, 25).

Scholars have highlighted the close relationship between subjectivity and evidentiality. Frank R. Palmer, for example, notes that epistemic forms of modality relating to inference and conclusion such as "Mary must have arrived" are "essentially subjective and performative" since they underscore the presence of the speaking subject (Palmer 1986, 33). Maynard argues that modal adverbs such as *as expected*, *probably*, and *certainly*, "do not directly modify verbs, but rather, express the speaking self's subjective, often emotional feelings and attitude toward and evaluation of what is to be stated" (Maynard 1993, 122). And work by Jose Sanders and Wilbert Spooren claims that Dutch modal verbs such as *blijken* 'apparently be' and *denken* 'think' express both a degree of subjectivity and degree of certainty of commitment, where subjectivity relates to the "foreground[ing] of the speaker's commitment to the validity of the proposition" (Sanders and Spooren 1996, 255).

Ilana Mushin (2001) posits that subjectivity is not in fact a dichotomous property, but rather a continuum. In her analysis, speakers' expressions of epistemological stance (which include, but are not limited to, the linguistic forms that come under the traditional label of "evidentiality") deictically project different degrees of subjectivity (see figure 4.2). While Mushin's taxonomy situates frameworks of epistemic stance as reflecting fundamentally cognitive, cross-linguistic "conceptual structures" rather than social positioning, her delineation of the links between the use or absence of evidentials and projections of subjectivity highlights the relationship between these two linguistic phenomena. Following Mushin's terminology, in this

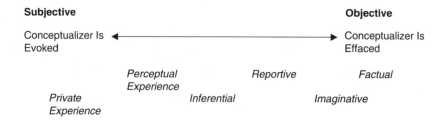

Figure 4.2. Relationship of Epistemological Stance to Subjectivity (Mushin 2001, 81).
Reprinted with permission of Elsevier

chapter I will use the term "subjective" to refer to those cases in which expressions
of epistemic stance locate the deictic origo in the speaker, and the term "objective" to
refer to those cases in which the deictic origo is located outside of the speaker.

Evidentiality as Social Resource

Scholars of formal and functional linguistics have primarily looked at evidentiality
as a grammaticalized category expressed in verbal morphology (e.g., Aikhenvald and
Dixon 2003; Chafe and Nichols 1986; Givón 1982; Willett 1988). As Barbara A. Fox
(2001) notes, much of this work, with the exception of Givón (1982, 1989) and Du
Bois (1986), treats evidentiality as pointing to the relationship between the speaker
and the outside world. Attempts to understand evidentiality as a resource that relates
interlocutors as social and moral beings have, however, received increased attention.
John B. Haviland (1989), for example, examines how Tzotzil "conversation as much
establishes a moral as a propositional universe of discourse" and argues that "evidentials can be about feelings and commitments as well as about truth" (Haviland
1989, 27). Jane H. Hill and Judith T. Irvine note that "ideas about responsibility and
agency index ideas about social persons, relationships, and groups" (Hill and Irvine
1993, 3) while Bambi B. Schieffelin (1996) investigates how speakers use evidentials
in Kaluli to establish themselves and texts as sources of authority. In recent years,
there has been more work on the social dimension of evidentiality in languages such
as English where evidentiality may not be encoded in obligatory verbal affixes but
is instead expressed through adverbs, periphrastic verb constructions, complement
clause constructions, and so forth (e.g., Atkinson 1999; Fox 2001; Raymond and
Heritage 2006).[2] This line of research foregrounds the ways in which evidentiality is
a resource that speakers use to construct social relationships with both their immediate interlocutors as well as with the people they are speaking about.

Speaking about Others' Thoughts,
Feelings, and Sensations

In this chapter, I will be looking at a claim that has been made in both the subjectivity literature as well as the literature on evidentiality. It is often argued that speakers in certain societies do not routinely overtly or explicitly represent the thoughts,

feelings, and sensations of other people. This has been claimed for languages from a number of different language families, including Japanese (Kamio 1995; Kuroda 1973), Korean (Kim 1978; Lee 1993), Samoan (Ochs 1988), and various indigenous languages spoken in both North and South America (e.g., Aikhenvald 2003, 149; de Reuse 2003, 93; McLendon 2003, 103–104). Speakers are said to use certain kinds of verb forms and evidential markers when speaking of their own thoughts, feelings, and sensations, but use different ones when speaking about other parties. While more contemporary treatments of grammar interpret violations of such norms in terms of a cultural dispreference for speculating about others' thoughts or in terms of the social positioning of interactants and their respective rights to claim knowledge of the item being discussed (e.g., Kamio 1995), others claim that such grammatical regularities reflect speakers' cognitive perspectives on others' minds.

Research on the Korean language by linguists claims that speakers routinely grammatically indicate their indirect access to other people's minds. This line of research argues that "objective" or "direct" statements about what another person is thinking, feeling, or intending are in fact ungrammatical in Korean. Hyo Sang Lee (1993), for example, claims that

> the informal ending -ô [e.g., the unmarked, bare form of the verb used in casual conversation] cannot be used to express other people's internal feelings or sensations, because the speaker does not have the authority over this kind of information. The informal ending -ô also cannot be used to describe the addressee's volitional activities...because it is the addressee who has the authority over the information conveyed, rather than the speaker.[3] (Lee 1993, 142)

In the following examples, statements about internal feelings, sensations, and activities with second- or third-person subjects that do not have evidential marking are classified as ungrammatical because the attribution of feeling or sensation is deictically centered outside of the speaker. One way to make these "objective" sentences grammatical, according to Lee, is to mark them with the particle -kwuna. Lee characterizes this particle, which attaches to the verb at the end of the sentence, as a marker of newly perceived unassimilated information. By deictically recentering the proposition, it marks a kind of perspective-taking, turning the ungrammatical "objective" statement with the bare form of the verb into a "subjective" noticing of new information that is anchored in the speaker's observation of the other person's apparent state (see table 4.1).

Similarly, Sung-Ock Sohn and Mee-Jeong Park argue that the indirect quotative marker -tay is used "when the speaker cannot read another's consciousness from his or her point of view" (Sohn and Park 2003, 109). In the following interaction, taken from a Bible study meeting, two Korean American women, H. and S., are talking about a pastor who is ill. Another woman, L., who is an overhearer to this conversation, asks if the pastor is sick using the indirect quotative marker -tay:

(1) "Is someone sick?" (Sohn and Park 2003, 109)

H.:   But why doesn't the church pray for (her)?
S.:   What prayer?
H.:   Well, if the pastor is sick people should pray for her once in a while.

L.:   *nwuka aphu-tay-yo?*
        someone sick-QT-POL
        'Is someone sick-TAY?'/'Did somebody say someone is sick?'

H.:   Oh, pastor Y. She had surgery and
L.:   Oh, I didn't know that.

TABLE 4.1. Deictic Recenterings

Ungrammatical, objective utterances about other people's feelings, sensations, and actions	Grammatical, subjective noticings about others' feelings, sensations, and actions
* *ne-nun chwu-e*[a] you TOP cold-INT 'You are cold'	*ne chwup-kwuna* you cold -UNASSIM '[I see] you are cold!'
* *cay-nun sulph-e* that child TOP sad-INT 'That child is sad'	*ne sulphu-kwuna* you sad - UNASSIM '[I see] you are sad!'
* *ne-nun ecay hakkyo-ey wa-ss-e* you TOP yesterday school-LOC come-PST-INT 'You came to school yesterday'	*ne ecay hakkyo wa-ss-kwuna* you yesterday school come-PST-UNASSIM '[I see] you came to school yesterday!'

From Lee (1993, 141–142, 148). (In Lee's original article, these examples were transcribed according to a mixed system of Yale and McCune-Reischauer romanization. I have transcribed and coded all of the excerpts in this article according to the Yale system, for the sake of consistency.)

[a]Native Korean speakers note that these sentences would be appropriate in cases where an interlocutor was contradicting an earlier assertion. For example, if someone were to deny being cold while visibly shivering, it would be acceptable to use the informal ending emphatically, for example, "You are cold!" Similarly, if a child denied going to school yesterday when in fact she did, an adult could say to her, "You did come to school yesterday" using the informal ending (E. Chun and J. Park, personal communication).

    In their discussion of this excerpt, Sohn and Park use Akio Kamio's (1997) model of the territory of information to analyze L.'s use of the quotative: "Note further that L. uses the short form [of the indirect quotative] instead of direct speech (i.e., the non-quotative form, *apha-yo*) to mark the inaccessibility of the information to the speaker. In other words, neither L. (speaker) nor S. (hearer) has access to the internal state of the person who is ill. Thus L. uses the hearsay *-tay* to frame the inaccessible territory of information" (Sohn and Park 2003, 109). In their analysis, the use of the quotative hearsay marker mitigates certainty because speakers are not supposed to be able to "read another's consciousness from his or her point of view" (Sohn and Park 2003, 109).[4] Here, the quotative form (*aphutayyo*) is deictically anchored to the speaker, whereas the direct bare form (*aphayo*), which projects "accessibility," is not. The use of the quotative thus frames the question about the pastor's illness as a "subjective" noticing, rather than an "objective" statement of fact. In her analysis of the acquisition of *-tay* by Korean-speaking infants, Soonja Choi likewise argues that "-TAY is also used when stating an emotional or physical state of a third person to which the speaker cannot get direct access"[5] (Choi 1991, 112). In both of these cases, native Korean speaker linguists understand the use of the quotative as a way of transforming an objective statement that claims access to another person's internal sensations, feelings, or thoughts into a subjective statement that marks one's distance and lack of access.

Lastly, linguists have claimed that Korean speakers do not make direct observations about a third party's emotions. Ki-Hong Kim writes:

> Emotion is said to be subjective; one can feel emotion only through one's own experience. … It is interesting to observe that in Korean it is ungrammatical to use emotion word [*sic*] with the second and third persons in the present tense. Emotion words used with the present tense are usually for the first person only. For instance, *ku salam-un kippu-ta* 'he is happy' is ungrammatical in Korean in normal context. The reason seems to be that emotions are subjective, therefore to express others' emotions seems unwarranted. However the sentence: *ce salam-un kippe-han-ta* 'that man is acting (looks) happy' is grammatical although the subject is in the third person because *kippe-han-ta* means 'acts/looks happy.' The sentence then is a simple observation by the speaker, rather than a categorical statement about the subject's emotion. (Kim 1978, 259)

Like the previous examples, the periphrastic construction serves to transform the "ungrammatical" objective statement about another's emotions into a "grammatical" subjective statement where the speaker's role as observer is demarcated.

According to these scholars, then, Korean grammar seems to encode the fact that speakers do not portray themselves as being able to read another adult's mind. Korean verbs that relate to someone's emotional or physical state or personal experience, they argue, are only used in the plain form in the first person when speaking about another adult. Claims about someone else's consciousness, thoughts, feelings, and sensations, these scholars claim, must be grammatically marked with periphrastic verb constructions or verbal suffixes that indicate the speaker's indirect observation of the third party's apparent state. In Langacker's terms, this would seem to indicate that when Korean speakers speak about the thoughts, feelings, or emotions of other people, they use "subjective" frameworks where the observer locates herself within the scene.

Reconstructing Actions and Feelings

In this chapter, I will discuss some apparent exceptions to these observations. I argue that the "objective" framework is not, in fact, unacceptable in Korean, but is culturally dispreferred. It is used to describe social types who are evaluated in the moment as morally inappropriate. Speakers' portrayals of access to another person's mind are thus indexical of social relations between interlocutors.

The narratives I examine are taken from interactions at a Korean heritage language school in California. This school, located in an ethnically mixed middle-class suburb, serves second-generation Korean Americans who generally have some degree of oral proficiency in Korean but have little background in reading and writing. Children attend two and a half hours of Korean language class and a half hour of enrichment classes in soccer, basketball, music, art, Korean drumming, tae kwon do, or Korean dance on Saturdays throughout the school year. The excerpts I will present were taken from a middle-level class of elementary school students ranging in age from eight to twelve. Their teacher was a Korean American woman in her thirties who immigrated to the United States three years before this class was recorded.

The first excerpt is taken from a class where the children have been misbehaving. Tardiness is a chronic issue in this class and this narrative contrasts two ways of walking into class late:

(3) "Some very nice behavior"[6]

| 1 | Teacher: | *kuliko*   *Cinsek-i-lang*   *Pyengsek-i-nun onul   nemwu* |
| | | and Jinsok-VOC-with Byungsok-VOC-TOP today   too much |

2
nemwu yeyppu-n mosup-ul   sensayng-nim-hanthey
too   pretty-RL appearance-ACC teacher-HT-DAT

3
po-ye-cwe-ss-e.
see/PAS give-PST-INT
'And today Jinsok and Byungsok showed the teacher some very very nice behavior.'

4
mwe-nya-ha-myen-un (.4) *ahop-si   samsipsam-pwun*
what-Q/PLN-do-if-RL   nine-hour thirty three-minutes

5
i-pwun   ccum-ey wa-ss-nuntey (.4)
two-minutes around-at come-PST-CIRCUM
'Because (.4) at around 9:33 or 9:32 they came, (.4)'

6
hekhekhekhek ilehkey ha-ko   wa-ss-e
huhhuhhuhuh like this do-CONN come-PST-INT
'(going) "huh huh huh huh" ((panting)), like this they came'

7
way kulay-ss-ul-kka.
why be so-PST-FUT/RL-Q/PRSUM
'Why were they like that?'

(.6)

8
way kulay-ss-ul-kka?
why be so-PST-FUT/RL-Q/PRSUM
'Why were they like that?'

| 9 | Students: | (   ) |

10	Teacher:	*e. (.2) cokum-ilato ppalli o-l-lyeko,*
		yes a little-even fast come-FUT/RL-in order to
		'Yes. (.2) In order to come even a little (more) quickly,'

(.2)

11   *sensayng-nim-hantey mianha-n   maum chinkwu-tul-hantey*
           teacher-HT-DAT   be sorry-RL feeling friends-PL-DAT

12   *mianha-n   maum-i   iss-ese   ttwie-o-n*
           be sorry-RL feeling-NOM be-CONN run-come-PST/RL

13   *kes   kath-ass-e.*
           thing seem-PST/INT
           'It seems that they were running because they felt sorry toward the teacher
           and sorry toward their friends.'

     (.2)

14   *tulewa-ss-nuntey   hekhekhekhek*
           come in-PST-CIRCUM ((panting sounds))
           'When they arrived, (they were going) "huh huh huh huh"'
           ((panting))

15   *ama   pwunmyenghi kulay-ss-ul-ke-ya.*
           probably certainly   be so-PST/FUT/RL-fact-be-INT
           'Probably, certainly, they must have been like (this)'

16   *emma na hakkyo nucu-myen an-tway-yo.*
           mom I   school be late-if   not-become-POL
           '"Mom, I can't be late for school."'

17   *halmeni   na ppalli ka-ya-tway-yo.*
           grandmother I   quickly go-must-become-POL
           '"Grandma, I really have to go."'

18   *kuntey yeki o-ta* ((points)) *po-nikka   cokum nuc-ess-e.*
           but   here come-while   see-because a little late-PST-INT.
           'Then as they came here ((points)) they realized they were a little late,'

19   *mak ttwi-ess-ul-ke-ya.*
           fully run-PST/FUT/RL-thing-be-INT
           'so they must have really run hard.'

20   ((Teacher closes eyes and pumps her arms, as if running))

21   *kuntey etten chinkwu-nun nuc-key   tulewa-ss-nuntey,*
           but   some friend-TOP late-ADV come in-PST-CIRCUM
           'But although some friends came in late,'

22   ((Teacher imitates slow, uncaring walk of other students, her eyes staring
           fixedly ahead))

23   *chinkwu-tul-hantey mianha-n   maum-to   eps-e.*
            friend-PL-DAT   be sorry-RL feeling-even not be-INT
            'They don't even feel sorry toward their friends.'

24   *sensayng-nim mianhay-yo   ha-nun   chinkwu-to eps-e.*
            teacher-HT   be sorry-POL say-PRS/RL friend-even not be-INT
            'None of these friends even say "Teacher, I'm sorry."'

25   *chenchenhi wa-ss-nuntey, (.2)   kwaynchanh-ci   mwe.*
            slowly   come-PST-CIRCUM be alright-COMM what
            'They came in slowly, (.2) "Well, it's OK, whatever."'

26   *ku-ke-nun   kwaynchanh-un ke-l-kka*
            that thing-TOP be alright-RL thing-FUT/RL-Q/PRSUM
            'Is that something that is OK?'

27   *kwaynchanh-ci   anh-un-ke-l-kka.*
            be alright-NOM not be-PRS/RL-thing- FUT/RL-Q/PRSUM
            'Is that something that is not OK?'

28   ((Teacher walks behind desk))

29   *ette-n   ke-l-kka-yo?*
            which-RL thing-PRS-PRSUM-POL
            'Which one is it?'

In this narrative, the teacher uses different kinds of evidential marking to talk about students she is praising versus those she is criticizing. When talking about the "good" Jinsok and Byungsok, she uses deductions and suppositions and positions her epistemic stance toward these students as relatively uncertain. She deictically locates her own presence as an observer, thereby employing a culturally preferred "subjective" framework. In contrast, she marks her epistemic stance toward the "bad" students as relatively certain. That is, she describes their actions, thoughts, and emotions using bare forms of the verb with no evidential marking, deictically centering her observations of their behavior as emanating from the students themselves (e.g., an "objective" framework). The contrast between these two forms of evidentiality shows how grammar helps to construct others as opposing types of moral beings.

In lines 11 through 12, for example, the teacher states "It seems that they were running because they felt sorry toward the teacher and sorry toward their friends." This statement is discursively marked as uncertain through the "*ttwieon kes kathasse*" ('it seems that they were running') construction. Here, her description of Jinsok and Byungsok's behavior is embedded within a grammaticalized form for indicating uncertainty consisting of a relativized past noun clause with the verb *katha* 'to seem, to be like.' In lines 18–19, the deductive nature of the teacher's expression, "Then as they came here they realized they were a little late, so they must have run really hard," is made evident through the *ess-ul-ke-ya* verb ending, where the embedding of the verb 'to run' within a past noun clause with the future relativizing infix *-ul* indicates presumption (Suh 1996). These markers of epistemic uncertainty, deduction, and presumption create a subjective framework, with the teacher as deictic origo.

When the teacher talks about how the bad students enter the classroom, however, her statement in line 25 does not have any evidential marking: "They came in slowly, and 'Well, it's OK, (.2) whatever.' " The deictic origo of the actions and projected affect is located within the students themselves. Moreover, these other students are not named. Instead, they are presented as social types ("some friends") and their behavior is typecast through the use of the generic present tense. The teacher thus positions herself as relatively more uncertain and distant from the students she is praising but relatively more certain toward the students whose behavior she is criticizing. The explicitly moral nature of her narrative can be seen in the ways that she invites students to evaluate the "bad" students' behavior as "OK" or "not OK" (lines 26–27) while juxtaposing their behavior against the exemplary Jinsok and Byungsok.

This contrast is also evident in the teacher's use of direct quotation. In the case of Jinsok and Byungsok, the quotes are set off with an explicit introductory frame that indicates that they are conjectures: "Probably, certainly, they must have been like (this)" (line 15), which reprises the *-ul ke* presumptive ending discussed above. In the case of the other students, the framing of the quote does not point to the teacher: "They came in slowly, (.2) 'Well, it's OK, whatever' " (line 25). In Erving Goffman's (1981) terms, the evidential marking and framing of line 13 distinguishes the teacher's voice as animator from the speech she conjectures Jinsok and Byungsok to have spoken earlier that morning. In line 25, however, she erases her own role as author, presenting the bad students' "words" as emanating directly from the students themselves, rather than in her interpretation of their demeanor.

Another aspect that contributes to the projection of an objective versus subjective framework is the teacher's differential characterization of their emotional states. Recall the earlier claims that Korean speakers do not speak directly of a third party's emotional state because "express[ing] others' emotions seems unwarranted" (Kim 1978, 259). In this case, however, when the teacher is negatively assessing students, she embeds her description within a matrix clause that uses a bare form of the verb ("They don't even feel sorry toward their friends" [line 23]). The positively assessed students' emotional state is deductively marked with the *-ul ke* ending: "It seems that they were running because they felt sorry toward the teacher and sorry toward their friends" (lines 12–13). While the same phrase, *mianhan maum*, or the feeling of being sorry is used for both the positively and the negatively evaluated students (lines 11, 12, and 23), the discursive embedding of this clause nevertheless reveals contrasting frameworks of subjectivity.

Evidential marking is therefore just one resource that the teacher uses to discursively construct Jinsok and Byungsok as agents who are morally responsible for their actions (Duranti 1994). They are given names, for example, while the bad students are only referred to with the indefinite "some students." In addition, her depiction of Jinsok and Byungsok uses verb forms that emphasize their agency. The first sentence of the narrative, which summarizes the main point of the story (Labov 1972), characterizes Jinsok and Byungsok's behavior with a benefactive form that discursively constructs their running as an action that was intentionally projected toward the teacher ("And today Jinsok and Byungsok showed the teacher some very very nice behavior"). In line 10 ("Yes. (.2) In order to come even a little (more) quickly,"), their entry into the classroom is depicted with the "intentive" verb ending -*lyeko* (Sohn 1999), which underscores the deliberateness of their actions. Indeed, students are asked to think about Jinsok and Byungsok's intentions in acting the way they did (lines 7–8), as their actions are portrayed as communicating emotions of regret toward their teacher and toward their fellow classmates (lines 11–12). This grammatical highlighting of Jinsok and Byungsok's actions constructs them as intentionally thoughtful agents who behave in ways that are cognizant of others' feelings and needs.

The evidential patterning in this narrative thus reveals how expressions of epistemic stance contribute to the creation of a certain kind of deictic field, which has consequences for the social and moral positioning of the interlocutors (Hanks 2005). By using prospective forms of the verb, explicitly deductive frames, and evidential uncertainty markers to describe the actions of the good students, the teacher marks a clear distinction between her subjectivity and that of the students. The epistemic stance of uncertainty in turn construes the "good" kids as social beings whose thoughts and minds are not readily apprehendable by others, as the norms of polite adult-adult conversation in Korean would predict. When talking about the "bad" students, the teacher effaces her presence as an observer. By using plain forms of the verb and minimal framing, the teacher creates a framework in which these typified students' actions, thoughts, and emotions are located as originating directly from their own bodies. This shifting of the deictic center from the teacher to the students indexes the relative power of the teacher over the students while construing them as persons who are less deserving of respect.

Reading Faces

In the next section, I show how the teacher uses a more objectifying evidential framework as she intensifies her negative assessment. This excerpt takes place less than a minute after the preceding one. The teacher tries to resume class and she asks students to read question number seven. No one responds to her request, and this leads to an extended narrative in which students are chastised for their inattention:

(4) "It's written all over their faces"

1   Teacher: *sensayng-nim-i   cikum mwe ilku-la-ko   hay-ss-e*
                teacher-HT-NOM now   what read-IMP-QT do-PST-Q/INT?
                'What did the teacher tell you to read just now?'

2   Students: *chil-pen*
                seven-number
                '(Question) number 7'

            (2.0)

3   Teacher: *colli-wun   salam*
                 be sleepy-PRS/RL people
                 '(Is there) anyone who is sleepy?'

                 (.4)

4   *kuman han-sikan-ccum ca-l-kka?*
                 stop   one hour-about sleep-FUT/RL-Q/PRSUM?
                 'Why don't we stop and just sleep for an hour?'

                 (.2)

5   *kongpwuha-ci   mal- ko?*
                 study-not do-NOML not-CONN
                 'Instead of studying?'

6   *etten chinkwu-nun co-n-ta,*
                 some friend-TOP   sleep-IN/DC/PLN
                 'Some friends are dozing off'

                 (.6)

7   *kuliko etten chinkwu-nun (.2) a onul   kkuthna-ko*
                 and   some friend-TOP   ah today finish-CONN

8   *mwe-ha-l-kka?*
                 what-do-FUT/RL-Q/ PRSUM
                 'And some friends (.2) (are like),
                 "Hmm, today what should I do after class?"'

9   *yakwucang-ka-l-kka?*
                 baseball field-go-FUT/RL-Q/PRSUM?
                 ' "Should I go to the baseball game?" '

10   *syophing-ka-l-kka?*
                 shopping-go-FUT/RL-PRSUM?
                 ' "Should I go shopping?" '

11   *ani-ya   ecekkey nay-ka   emma-hanthey kecismal-hay-ss-nuntey,*
                 no-be-INT yesterday I-NOM   mom-DAT   lie-say-PST-CIRCUM
                 ' "No, I lied to my mom yesterday." '

12   *a pay-ka   kophu-ntey, (.2) pipi-malyewu-ntey,*
                 ah stomach-NOM hungry-CIRCUM pee-feel an urge-CIRCUM
                 ' "Oh, I'm hungry. (.2) I want to pee." '

                 ((Students laugh))

13   *mak   ile-n   sayngkak-ha-n-ta.*
            continously like this-RL thought-do-IN/DC/PLN

14   *ette-n   chinkwu-nun.*
            some-RL friend-TOP
            'They keep thinking like this, some friends'

15   ((Teacher stands up straight))

            (.2)

16   *elkwul-ey ta sse-iss-e.*
            face-LOC all write-be-INT
            'It's written all over (their) faces.'

            (.2)

17   *kuliko etten chinkwu-nun*
            and   some friend-TOP
            'And some friends (are like)

18   *ah onul kongpwuha-ki-ka   nemwu silh-untey,*
            ah today study-NOML-NOM too dislike-CIRCUM
            "Oh today I really don't want to study"'

            (.2)

19   *nol-ko-man   siph-untey,*
            play-COMP-only want-CIRCUM.
            ' "I only want to play" '

20   *kulehkey sse-iss-nun chinkwu-to iss-ko.*
            like that   write-be-RL friend-also be-CONN
            'There are also friends who have that written
            (all over their faces).'

This narrative demonstrates how the act of projecting what is in another person's mind is related to the exercise of power and of moral evaluation (Foucault 1977). When speaking about the morally exemplary Jinsok and Byungsok in the first excerpt, the teacher portrays her knowledge of the boys' intentions as relatively distant through evidential marking. But when negatively assessing the bad students both in this narrative and in the one discussed earlier, the teacher situates herself as a kind of powerful panopticon who can see everything and peer directly into students' minds on the basis of their facial displays (Foucault 1977). She presents herself as having extended access to their private musings (e.g., lines 7–10 "Hmm, today, what should I do after class? Should I go to the baseball game? Should I go shopping?") and physical sensations that by definition can only be felt by the subject they originate from (e.g., line 12 "Oh, I'm hungry. I want to pee."). The series of direct quotations uses maximally objective bare forms to animate students' private thoughts. Moreover, these quotations are framed only by the repetition of the indefinite subject "*etten chinkwunun*" ('some friends') in lines 7 and 17, whereas the quotes attributed to the positively assessed Jinsok and Byungsok were framed with a full sentence and evidential markers that highlighted the fact that they were conjectured ("Probably, certainly, they must have been like this" [excerpt 3, line 15]). The use of the dispreferred objective framework animates students as morally wanting figures, who lie and are bored and disengaged from the task at hand.

In contrast with the earlier claims that Korean speakers routinely use evidentially uncertain forms to mark their limited access to others' subjectively experienced emotions, sensations, or consciousness, here the teacher foregrounds the obviousness of these thoughts and sensations, plainly "written" on their faces for all to see (line 16, line 20). By presenting students as people whose minds are easily read through their inappropriate actions and facial expressions, the teacher maximizes her authority over the students' subjectivities. This example illustrates how respect toward students is indexically constituted in the moment; the teacher expresses culturally preferred uncertain epistemic stances toward the "good" students, thus constituting them as worthy of respect, while indexing disrespect toward the "bad" students by marking her knowledge of their thoughts and sensations as certain. Evidential marking is therefore a means through which social asymmetries are produced; the teacher constitutes the bad children as children, and as not as social equals, in this exercise of subjectivity. As Foucault (1977) notes, this differential in the possession of and attribution of knowledge (e.g., the asymmetry of seeing-without-being-seen) is the very foundation of power.

Participation Frameworks as Dynamic Resources

In the preceding two excerpts, the teacher presents extended "readings" of students' thoughts, feelings, and sensations. Her depictions of students are not explicitly challenged by them; students do not say things like "No, that's not what I am thinking now," or "No, that's not what I meant when I walked into the classroom this morning." The frameworks that the teacher uses for these assessments, I argue, make these characterizations of students relatively more difficult for children to contest. The indefiniteness of the referent of "some friends" in both excerpts (4) and (5) makes any single child's contestation of the negative assessment potentially troublesome, while the very embeddedness of both the positive and negative assessments also does not afford students with a readily accessible interactional space from which to challenge these portrayals.

In fact, these kinds of narratives, in which the teacher purports to project exactly what children are/were thinking, feeling, and intending, tend to follow instances where the teacher uses participation frameworks where students *are* provided with an opportunity to either ratify or contest a particular moral ideology, and they explicitly defy the teacher. The following excerpt illustrates an earlier attempt in this class by the teacher to socialize promptness:

(5) 'If I came fifteen minutes late'

1   Teacher: *taum-cwu-ey sensayng-nim-i, (.2) sipo-pwun   cengto yeki nuc-key*
             next week-at teacher-HT-NOM   fifteen-minutes about here late-ADV

2   *tuleo-myen ette-l-kka.*
             enter-if   how-FUT/RL-Q/PRSUM
             'If I came here about fifteen minutes late next week, how would that be?'

             (2.0)

3   Student: (   )

4   Teacher: *e*
             'Mmm'

5   Student: **Fifty [push-ups**

6   Teacher: [*e*
             'Mmm'

7   Student: **Fifty push-ups**

8   Teacher: *e*
             'Mmm'

9   Student: **[Yeah**!

10   Student: **[Push-ups** (   )

11   Teacher: *e.   sensayng-nim-i   kulemyen* ((clears throat)) **nine forty-five**
             hmm teacher-HT-NOM then   **nine forty-five**

12   *ahop-si   sasip-o-pwun-ey   yeki o-l-kka-yo*
             nine-hour   forty-five-minutes-LOC here come-FUT/RL -Q/PRSUM-POL
             'Hmm. Shall I come here (late), at **9:45**, 9:45?'

13   Student: *ney*
             'Yes'

14   Student: [*ney*
             'Yes'

15   Teacher: [*cengmal?*
             'Really?'

In this excerpt, the teacher uses a transposed participation framework (Hanks 1990) to impress upon students the importance of coming to class on time. She asks them how they would feel if she came to class fifteen minutes late next week. When several boys in the class chime in with various cries to do push-ups, the teacher's utterance in lines 11–12 constructs these as non-aligning responses.[7] As she repeats her question: "Hmm. Shall I come here late, at **9:45**, 9:45?" The fact that the teacher here codeswitches into English, which is relatively rare for her, accentuates her efforts to make the lexical content of her utterance absolutely clear to the students. When other students respond "*ney*" or 'yes' in Korean, these are interpreted by the teacher as more inappropriate responses, as can be seen by the fact that she initiates repair in line 15 with the question "Really?" Through these repeated questions, the students are constructed as intransigent in their collective refusal to provide the "correct" answer to the teacher's question. When using a participation framework in which students are given an opportunity to demonstrate their (non) alignment with the teacher, the students and the teacher do not come to common agreement on the desirability and importance of being on time.

Conclusion

While earlier research in functional linguistics has claimed that Korean speakers routinely mark their access to others' thoughts and sensations as distant and uncertain, an interactional approach to evidential marking reveals that speakers use evidentials to evaluate others as kinds of moral beings. The cultural norm that speakers will use subjective, uncertain grammatical forms to talk about others' feelings, thoughts, and sensations is therefore not so much a rigid grammatical rule as it is a cultural expectation whose violation is itself a form of moral judgment and self- and other-positioning. Moreover, even in languages where evidentiality is not a highly grammaticalized class, speakers nonetheless use widely disparate grammatical forms together to form epistemically coherent kinds of frames in interaction.

Scholars of Korean interaction often focus on the socially valued ways in which speakers index politeness, respect, and social distance through expressions of epistemic uncertainty such as hedges, modal verbs, and negative questions (e.g., Dredge 1983; Park 1990; Sohn 1986a, 1986b). The literature in this area tends to look at such discursive resources as reflections of already existing social distances between people fixed through such attributes as age, institutional role, and generation. What I hope to have shown is that even in cases where age, generation, and social roles are highly asymmetric, speakers are nonetheless constantly evaluating and positioning one another as moral subjects through the dynamic means of language.

NOTES

1. A wide range of grammatical features have been analyzed as relating to subjectivity, including tense, subject marking, personal pronouns, switch-reference, adverbs, verbal structures, quotatives, sentence-final particles, and so forth (see Iwasaki 1993; Maynard 1993; and Scheibman 2002 for surveys of work on subjectivity in English and Japanese).

2. Research on the marking of evidentiality and epistemic stance in Korean interaction has focused on sentence-final particles and includes work that takes primarily a conversation

analytic perspective, as well as research that stems from a functional grammar tradition (e.g., Kim 2005; Kim and Suh 2004; Strauss 2005).

3. This *-ô* would be *-e* in Yale transcription.

4. A similar marking of "inaccessibility" using the indirect quotative in Japanese has been described by Satoko Suzuki (1998) as a kind of "psychological distancing" of the speaker from the information presented.

5. In the following interaction from Choi (1991), a two-year-old child uses the indirect quotative marker *-tay* to talk to her grandmother about a doll that is sick:

Child: *aphu-tay aka-ka*
                sick-QT   baby-NOM
                'The baby is sick-TAY'
Grandmother: *eti-ka   aph-e?*
                where-NOM sick-INT/Q
                'Where is (he) sick?'
Child: *yoki aka-ka...   cham aphu-tay aka-ka*
                here baby-NOM   quite sick-QT baby-NOM
                'The baby here...the baby is quite sick-TAY'

Choi's analysis of indirect versus direct experience echoes Sohn and Park (2003): "The suffix –TAY...indicates that the information does not come directly from the child's experience but indirectly from another source" (1991, 113). According to Choi, the importance of distinguishing the source of one's information in Korean is underscored by the fact that infants mark these kinds of distinctions in epistemic meaning before they use deontic modal forms.

6. Transcription conventions:

ACC:	accusative	ADV:	adverbial	CIRCUM:	circumstantial
COMM:	committal	COMP:	complementizer	CONN:	connective
DAT:	dative	DC:	declarative	FUT:	future
HT:	honorific title	IMP:	imperative	IN:	indicative
INT:	intimate speech level	LOC:	locative	NOM:	nominative
NOML:	nominalizer	PAS:	passive	PL:	plural
PLN:	plain speech level	POL:	polite speech level	PRESUM:	presumptive
PRS:	present	PST:	past tense/ perfect aspect	Q:	question
QT:	quotative	RL:	relativizer	TOP:	topic marker
VOC:	vocative				

(.4)	Pauses are given in tenths of a second.
Mak	Underlining indicates emphasis.
kuliko	Italics indicates speech in Korean.
9:45	Bold text indicates speech in English.
((panting))	Double parentheses enclose comments on the interaction.
=	Equal sign indicates latching.
[	Bracket indicates an onset of overlapping talk.
( )	Empty parentheses indicate speech that was unclear.
,	Commas indicate continuing intonation.
.	Periods indicate falling intonation.
?	Question marks indicate rising intonation.

7. It is likely that the teacher did not understand the English term "push-ups."

REFERENCES

Agha, Asif. 2002. Epistemic stance. In the *American Anthropological Association Anuual Conference*. New Orleans, La.

Aikhenvald, Alexandra Y. 2003. Evidentiality in Tariana. In *Studies in evidentiality*, ed. Alexandra Y. Aikhenvald and Robert M. W. Dixon, 131–164. Philadelphia: John Benjamins.

Aikhenvald, Alexandra Y., and Robert M. W. Dixon, ed. 2003. *Studies in evidentiality*. Philadelphia: John Benjamins.

Atkinson, Paul. 1999. Medical discourse, evidentiality and the construction of professional responsibility. In *Talk, work and institutional order*, ed. Srikant Sarangi and Celia Roberts, 75–107. Berlin: Mouton de Gruyter.

Benveniste, Emile. 1971. *Problems in general linguistics*. Coral Gables, Fla.: University of Miami Press.

Bybee, Joan L. 1985. *Morphology: A study of the relation between meaning and form*. Philadelphia: John Benjamins.

Chafe, Wallace. 1986. Evidentiality in English conversation and academic writing. In *Evidentiality: The linguistic coding of epistemology*, ed. Wallace Chafe and Johanna Nichols, 261–272. Norwood, N.J.: Ablex.

Chafe, Wallace, and Johanna Nichols, ed. 1986. *Evidentiality: The linguistic coding of epistemology*. Norwood, N.J.: Ablex.

Choi, Soonja. 1991. Early acquisition of epistemic meanings in Korean: A study of sentence-ending suffixes in the spontaneous speech of three children. *First Language* 11:93–119.

Dennett, Daniel Clement. 1996. *Kinds of minds: Toward an understanding of consciousness*. New York: Basic Books.

de Reuse, Wilhem J. 2003. Evidentiality in Western Apache (Athabaskan). In *Studies in evidentiality*, ed. Alexandra Y. Aikhenvald and Robert M. W. Dixon, 79–100. Philadelphia: John Benjamins.

Dredge, C. Paul. 1983. What is politeness in Korean speech? *Korean Linguistics* 3:21–32.

Du Bois, John. 1986. Self evidence and ritual speech. In *Evidentiality: The linguistic coding of epistemology*, ed. Wallace Chafe and Johanna Nichols, 313–336. Norwood, N.J.: Ablex.

———. 1993. Meaning without intention: Lessons from divination. In *Responsibility and evidence in oral discourse*, ed. Jane Hill and Judith T. Irvine, 48–71. Cambridge: Cambridge University Press.

Duranti, Alessandro. 1988. Intentions, language, and social action in a Samoan context. *Journal of Pragmatics* 12:13–33.

———. 1993a. Intentions, self, and responsibility: An essay in Samoan ethnopragmatics. In *Responsibility and evidence in oral discourse*, ed. Jane H. Hill and Judith T. Irvine, 24–47. Cambridge; New York: Cambridge University Press.

———. 1993b. Truth and intentionality: Towards an ethnographic critique. *Cultural Anthropology* 8:214–215.

———. 1994. *From grammar to politics: Linguistic anthropology in a western Samoan village*. Berkeley and Los Angeles: University of California Press.

Foucault, Michel. 1977. *Discipline and punish: The birth of the prison*. New York: Pantheon Books.

Fox, Barbara A. 2001. Evidentiality: Authority, responsibility, and entitlement in English conversation. *Journal of Linguistic Anthropology* 11:167–192.

Garfinkel, Harold. 1967. *Studies in ethnomethodology*. Englewood Cliffs, N.J.: Prentice-Hall.

Givón, Talmy. 1982. Evidentiality and epistemic space. *Studies in Language* 6:23–49.

———. 1989. *Mind, code, and context: Essays in pragmatics*. Hillsdale, N.J.: Lawrence Erlbaum.

Goffman, Erving. 1981. Footing. In *Forms of talk*, 124–159. Philadelphia: University of Pennsylvania.

Hanks, William F. 1990. *Referential practice: Language and lived space among the Maya*. Chicago: University of Chicago Press.

———. 2005. Explorations in the deictic field. *Current Anthropology* 46:191–220.

Haviland, John B. 1989. 'Sure, sure': Evidence and affect. *Text* 9:27–68.

Hill, Jane H., and Judith T. Irvine, ed. 1993. *Responsibility and evidence in oral discourse*. New York: Cambridge University Press.

Iwasaki, Shoichi. 1993. *Subjectivity in grammar and discourse: Theoretical considerations and a case study of Japanese spoken discourse*. Philadelphia: John Benjamins.

Kamio, Akio. 1995. Territory of information in English and Japanese and psychological utterances. *Journal of Pragmatics* 24:235–264.

———. 1997. Evidentiality and some discourse characteristics in Japanese. In *Directions in functional linguistics*, ed. Akio Kamio, 145–171. Amsterdam: John Benjamins.

Kim, Ki-Hong. 1978. Cultural and linguistic variables in the language of emotion of Americans and Koreans. In *Papers in Korean linguistics: Proceedings of the symposium on Korean linguistics*, ed. Chin-u Kim, Samuel Elmo Martin, Ho-min Sohn, and Seok C. Song, 259–267. Columbia, S.C.: Hornbeam Press.

Kim, Kyu-Hyun, and Kyung-Hee Suh. 2004. An analysis of Korean sentence-ending suffixes in caregiver-child interaction. *Ohak Yonku/Language Research* 40:923–950.

Kim, Mary Shin. 2005. Evidentiality in achieving entitlement, objectivity, and detachment in Korean conversation. *Discourse Studies* 7:87–108.

Kuroda, S.-Y. 1973. Where epistemology, style and grammar meet: A case study from the Japanese. In *A festschrift for Morris Halle*, ed. Paul Kiparsky and Stephen R. Anderson, 377–391. New York: Holt Rinehart and Winston.

Labov, William. 1972. *Language in the inner city: Studies in the Black English vernacular*. Philadelphia: University of Pennsylvania Press.

Langacker, Ronald W. 1985. Observations and speculations on subjectivity. In *Iconocity in syntax*, ed. John Haiman, 109–150. Amsterdam and Philadelphia: John Benjamins.

———. 1990. Subjectification. *Cognitive Linguistics* 1:5–38.

Lee, Hyo Sang. 1993. Cognitive constraints on expressing newly perceived information, with reference to epistemic modal suffixes in Korean. *Cognitive Linguistics* 4:135–167.

Lyons, John. 1982. Deixis and subjectivity: Loquor, ergo sum? In *Speech, place, and action: Studies in deixis and related topics*, ed. Robert J. Jarvella and Wolfgang Klein, 101–124. New York: John Wiley.

Maynard, Senko K. 1993. *Discourse modality: Subjectivity, emotion and voice in the Japanese language*. Philadelphia: John Benjamins.

McLendon, Sally. 2003. Evidentials in Eastern Pomo with a comparative survey of the category in other Pomoan languages. In *Studies in evidentiality*, ed. Alexandra Y. Aikhenvald and Robert M. W. Dixon, 101–129. Philadelphia: John Benjamins.

Mushin, Ilana. 2001. Japanese reportive evidentiality and the pragmatics of retelling. *Journal of Pragmatics* 33:1361–1390.

Ochs, Elinor. 1984. Clarification and culture. In *Georgetown University roundtable on languages and linguistics 1984*, ed. Deborah Schiffrin, 325–341. Washington, D.C.: Georgetown University Press.

———. 1988. *Culture and language development: Language acquisition and language socialization in a Samoan village*. New York: Cambridge University Press.

Palmer, Frank R. 1986. *Mood and modality*. Cambridge: Cambridge University Press.

Park, Mae-Ran. 1990. Conflict avoidance in social interaction: A sociolinguistic comparison of the Korean and Japanese honorific systems. In *Japanese/Korean Linguistics*, ed. Hajime Hoji, 111–128. Stanford, Calif.: Center for the Study of Language and Information.

Raymond, Geoffrey, and John Heritage. 2006. The epistemics of social relationships: Owning grandchildren. *Language in Society* 35:677–705.

Rosaldo, Michele. 1980. The things we do with words: Ilongot speech acts and speech act theory in philosophy. *Language in Society* 11:203–237.

Sanders, Jose, and Wilbert Spooren. 1996. Subjectivity and certainty in epistemic modality: A study of Dutch epistemic modifiers. *Cognitive Linguistics* 7:241–264.

Scheibman, Joanne. 2002. *Point of view and grammar: Structural patterns of subjectivity in American English conversation*. Studies in Discourse and Grammar 11. Philadelphia: John Benjamins.

Schieffelin, Bambi B. 1996. Creating evidence: Making sense of written words in Bosavi. In *Interaction and Grammar*, ed. Elinor Ochs, Emanuel A. Schegloff, and Sandra Thompson, 435–460. Cambridge: Cambridge University Press.

Sohn, Ho-Min. 1986a. Strategies of indirection in Korean. In *Linguistic expeditions*, 266–279. Seoul: Hanshin Publishing Company.

———. 1986b. Power and solidarity in the Korean language. In *Linguistic expeditions*, 389–410. Seoul: Hanshin Publishing Company.

———. 1999. *The Korean language*. Cambridge: Cambridge University Press.

Sohn, Sung-Ock, and Mee-Jeong Park. 2003. Indirect quotations in Korean conversations. In *Japanese/Korean Linguistics*, ed. Patricia Clancy, 105–118. Chicago: University of Chicago Press.

Strauss, Susan. 2005. Cognitive realization markers: A discourse-pragmatic study of the sentence ending particles *-kwun*, *-ney*, and *-tela*. *Language Sciences* 27:437–480.

Suh, Cheong-Soo. 1996. *Kwuke mwunpep [Korean grammar]*. Seoul: Hanyang University Press.

Suzuki, Satoko. 1998. *Tte* and *nante*: Markers of psychological distance in Japanese conversation. *Journal of Pragmatics* 29:429–462.

Willett, Thomas. 1988. A cross-linguistic survey of the grammaticization of evidentiality. *Studies in Language* 12:51–97.

On Using Semiotic Resources in a Racist World

A Commentary

Jane H. Hill

In reading the chapters by Mary Bucholtz, Angela Reyes, and Adrienne Lo I was struck by the attention that all of these authors give to the complexity of semiotic resources and their use, making us realize how much of the world we ignore when we operate with simplistic notions like "Asian." Bucholtz's young Laotian American women encounter what look at first like all-encompassing package deals—"gang girl" or "nerd girl"—that organize behavior from the width of their pants legs to the height of their vowels and shape every dimension of their lives, so that poor Nikki can't stay home and make her mother happy unless she endures being "jumped out" of her gang. However, Bucholtz emphasizes that alignments with these stylistic arrays need not be (and sometimes can't be) complete. Nikki uses just enough African American speech stereotypes to invoke "the generalized authority of African American youth culture," but not so many as to lose her place in the Laotian American community. And nerd-aligning Ada uses just enough Standard (and nerdly) postvocalic /r/ to demonstrate to other Laotian Americans that she does not plan to become a gang girl. And, even though Ada is blocked from full participation in the heavily verbal wit of the nerd-girl community of practice because of her nonnative English, she can still hang out with these girls and enjoy the protective coloration that their company provides. These cases are excellent object lessons in favor of the multidimensional theory of identity construction, differentiating between "adequation" (illustrated in Nikki's case) and "distinction" (seen in Ada's) that Bucholtz and her colleague Kira Hall (Bucholtz and Hall 2004) have proposed.

In Reyes's chapter, we don't encounter the kind of implicit enactment of alignments that Bucholtz has treated; rather, Reyes's young people use their consciousness of stereotypes metapragmatically. Threatening, widely known stereotypes like "owning a Chinese restaurant" require oppositional attention, while local stereotypes like "driving a minivan" can be used in kidding around to achieve interactional solidarity.

Lo's discussion moves into the realm of the kinds of resources that don't get noticed until a very good analyst comes along and shows us how they work. Like the other authors, Lo addresses a stereotype, in this case of Korean "indirection." An important tradition of analysis of the Korean language looks at grammaticalized markers that distinguish "subjective" distance from other persons, and inability to know their inner states, from "objective" statements of fact that are more like medical diagnoses than speculations about motives. Scholars in this tradition have claimed that "objective" usages about third parties are actually ungrammatical. Lo exploits the linguistic-anthropological insight that "grammar" is almost always tied somehow to social order (cf. Agha 2007), and that these links can be found in naturally occurring talk, to identify contexts when such usages are indeed grammatical, and highly pragmatically effective at that. So Korean evidential marking of various types turns out to be a flexible resource that is available for manipulation by speakers.

Being reminded of the complexity of semiotic resources, and the ways that they can be recruited and reshaped for pragmatic purposes through the active agency of actors and speakers, led me to think about the degree to which the properties of these resources might, indeed, constrain our agency. Lo's speaker, who is able to speak using markers of an objective stance about other people, is an adult teacher scolding the children who are her pupils. While those of us who teach school often wish that there were even more power differentials in this dyad, the teacher's power is considerable. At what point on the power-distance continuum would the sense of "ungrammaticality" of this kind of usage kick in for different kinds of Korean speakers? What I've called the stylistic "package deals" that Bucholtz discusses also raise this question. How much room is there to play with these complexes? Especially when elements of them such as gangsta clothing styles, or even the idea of AAVE itself, now that this has been co-opted by mass culture, may be shaped in market-making sites that are far from the streets and schoolyards where teenagers find spaces in which to make identities. And the kinds of stereotypes that Reyes's students work with are difficult to extract and insulate from the historical system of white racism that endows these with voicings and metapragmatic tendencies against which these young people must struggle. I think this is true even with very local propositions like the "Asians drive minivans" stereotype that Reyes thinks these students may have invented almost on the spot. I couldn't avoid noticing that this proposition articulates very well with racialized ideas about masculinity that are very much part of white racism and are shaped by marketers accordingly. Peculiarities in federal environmental regulations that favor "light trucks" have led car manufacturers to target men with campaigns to sell ever larger and ever more environmentally irresponsible sport-utility vehicles. One recent television advertisement specifically set up a "beige minivan" as the most embarrassing kind of car a white guy could drive—an embarrassment that could be avoided by buying the manufacturer's SUV.[1] A wonderful ongoing gag in the 1995 film *Get Shorty* had John Travolta, playing a charming mobster, driving a minivan because the rental agency was out of SUVs

(Travolta's deep masculine cool, of course, was adequate to this challenge to his identity). In this larger context, the idea that "Asians drive minivans" creates a new dimension in the iconic set of gender stereotypes that construct Asian males as effeminate and "unsexy," a useful Other against which whites can measure their masculinity.[2] Thus Asian men provide, along with African American and Latino men, a useful range of colored masculine Others against which white males can seek a "just right" masculine identity.

Let me develop this point about the larger system of white racism (since I'm writing on it for other reasons, it's what I'm thinking about now), to explore what kind of racializing system "Asians," with all their obvious diversity, fit into in the United States. In the 1990 U.S. Census, Asians were grouped together with "Pacific Islanders" in a single homogeneous group. But the designers of the 2000 U.S. Census responded to both scholarly and popular pressures for the recognition of diversity by an involuted taxonomy of "races" that recognizes six different kinds of Asians and three different kinds of Pacific Islanders, plus, of course, a "write-in" category and the notorious "mixed-race" option. Is this insistence on diversity the best way to get a purchase on what is going on with Asian American populations, on what they confront as they make their lives in the United States? Do we in fact see a huge diversity of experiences and outcomes, or does the system of white racism impose certain constraints that are felt right across the full spectrum of this diversity—and not only "Asian" diversity, but all the different ways of being black, or Latino, or Native American, or Arab American, or any kind of person of color?

My own view is that the elaborate taxonomies of the 2000 U.S. Census mystify a much simpler system: a single social division between whiteness and color that accounts for most of the ways that white racism plays out in the United States. This is a controversial position, not only because it de-emphasizes obvious diversity but also because it downplays what is sometimes called "black exceptionalism" (Espinoza and Harris 2000): the assertion that African Americans were uniquely damaged by the economic loss and social psychological degradations under slavery and Jim Crow[3] and that they are uniquely centered in white racist imagination as prototypical Others. There is much to recommend the concept of black exceptionalism. Almost certainly everyday white racism of the type that Davis (2000) has called "microaggression" is felt most acutely by working-class African Americans. Only African Americans are racialized by the "one-drop rule" (Harrison 1995, 60). The special status of African Americans is indicated by their uniquely low level of intermarriage with whites (Sanjek 1994).

While "black exceptionalism" is an important idea with much empirical support, a number of scholars have suggested that a more fundamental division between "whiteness" and "color," where blackness is perhaps centrally constitutive of a dimension of color, but not distinct from it, is both analytically and politically useful. Manning Marable (1995) pointed out that all people of color in the United States confront very similar structural contexts and have very similar experiences with racism, a circumstance that argues for the logic of political alliances across the diverse groups. Richard Delgado and Jean Stefancic (2000) report that museum collections of racial memorabilia show that, regardless of the minority group represented:

Each group is depicted, in virtually every epoch, in terms that can only be described as demeaning or worse. In addition, we found striking parallels among the stigma-pictures that society disseminated of the four groups [Mexicans, African Americans, Asians, and Native Americans]. The stock characters may have different names and appear at different times, but they bear remarkable likenesses and seem to serve similar purposes for the majority culture. (Delgado and Stefancic 2000, 226)

Carey McWilliams, surveying American minority groups in 1943, saw many historical and sociological connections among their experiences. For instance, McWilliams argues that the confrontation with Native Americans by the first colonists shaped the way that their descendants understood Africans brought as slaves. For the nineteenth century he shows that California politicians eager to crush the ambitions of Chinese immigrants worked closely with politicians from the Deep South who were building the edifice of Jim Crow segregation. He suggests that Mexican Americans in the U.S. Southwest simply filled for whites a political-economic and ideological site that elsewhere was occupied by African Americans, and were treated accordingly.

Even the limited data in this set of chapters make clear that Asians are very likely to experience life in the United States in terms of a whiteness versus color binary. For instance, Bucholtz reports that her Laotian high school students confront two choices in identity construction: alignment with "hyperwhite" nerds, or alignment with a gangster identity shaped around African American prototypes.

These structural and semiotic similarities in racial practices by whites, regardless of exactly who in the zone of "color" is the target, play out as common experiences of racism, where Asian Americans, regardless of subpopulation, share much with other racialized populations both historically and in contemporary struggles. For 100 years they were the targets of ferocious racializing immigration legislation that separated families and denied the most basic rights of membership in the American community even to people who had been here all their lives. This situation continues; Asians especially have been victims of the egregious Illegal Immigration Reform and Immigrant Responsibility Act of 1996 that permits deportation of permanent residents who are discovered to have committed felonies, even if these were juvenile mistakes long since absolved by years of law-abiding community membership. Asian Americans, like Native Americans and African Americans, have suffered the theft of their property, especially in the forced sales by the Japanese American community when they were removed to concentration camps from their homes on the West Coast during World War II. Asian Americans, like African Americans, Latinos, and American Indians, have been victims of racially based violence. The murders of Vincent Chin in Detroit in 1982 and of Yoshiro Hattori in Baton Rouge in 1992 are notorious because the white perpetrators either received very light prison sentences (in the case of the vicious murder of Vincent Chin, who was beaten to death with a baseball bat) or were let off without penalty (the shooter in the Hattori case). In the spring of 2004, when I wrote the first version of this discussion piece, the multi-national-origin Asian community of San Jose, California, was mourning, with fear and indignation, the death of Cau Bich Tran. Cau Bich Tran was a tiny twenty-five-year-old Vietnamese immigrant mother of two who was shot to death in her own home on July 13, 2003, by a San Jose police officer. A grand jury refused to indict the officer for what is widely considered in the local Asian community to have been an act of, if not flat-out murder, at best a manslaughter based in profound misjudgment rooted in racial stereotyping. The case so ruptured relationships between the community and the police that Asian women in San Jose were reluctant to call the police even when they were in danger (Anh Le, personal communication, March 9, 2004).

When new stereotypes about Asians appear, just as with stereotypes about other racialized groups, these have much more to do with white anxieties than with any cultural reality in the racialized population—and I think this is one reason the "mini-van" stereotype gets its purchase, because Reyes's Asian students were surely aware of these white anxieties. A much-discussed example is "Asian intelligence." As recently as 1974, when the U.S. Supreme Court ruled in *Lau v. Nichols* that bilingual education had to be provided for Chinese American students in San Francisco, the concern in California's Chinese American community was that schools were failing their children. Today's stereotype of the Asian academic superstar is thus not very old, and it has emerged along with the so-called "winner-take-all" economy, when whites, anxious about reduced social mobility, believe that admissions to "trophy" colleges and universities may give their children a crucial leg up in an increasingly frozen system of class and status. To quote a teenage character in a 2004 film (*The Perfect Score*), whites worry that high SAT scores[4] have been cornered by "Chinese girls who never watch television" (the burden of the film is that everybody else is better advised to cheat). But when whites act on this stereotype of Asian intelligence the result is often not preference, but discrimination. For instance, many in the California Asian community believe that new, post-affirmative action[5] criteria for admission to the University of California, which de-emphasize SAT scores, discriminate against Asians, who tend to do well on SAT tests. Since for many years the children of the community faced explicit quotas, they suspect that the motive for the de-emphasis on test results is to keep them from dominating university admissions (Izumi 2002).

In summary, Asian Americans, in spite of their reputation as the "model minority" that has produced many "honorary whites," have been the targets of exactly the same kinds of institutional and everyday racism that afflicts African Americans, Latinos, and Native Americans. These authors are able to use tools for microanalysis of discourse and conversation that shows that there is within this system space for appropriation and negotiation. There is not much wiggle room. But, given the world in which they live, in which choices about identities must be made within a constricting set of meanings, the creativity and grit that these chapters encounter among Asian youth, and their ingenuity in finding places where semiotic resources are flexible, do give one reason to hope.

NOTES

1. "SUV": Sport-utility vehicle. These vehicles (well-known examples include the Jeep Cherokee and the Ford Bronco) evade government standards for fuel economy by being classified as "light trucks," supposedly a category for working vehicles used in business, farming, and so forth. In fact, most SUVs are used for ordinary personal transportation on city streets.

2. My own response to the idea that Asian men aren't sexy is always "Three words: Chow Yun-Fat."

3. "Jim Crow" is the era of official racial segregation and white terrorism that endured from the 1870s until the 1960s in the United States.

4. The "SAT" is the Scholastic Aptitude Test. Scores on the SAT are an important factor restricting admission to many U.S. colleges and universities.

5. Affirmative action in admissions at the University of California was ended by amendment to the California State Constitution in 1996.

REFERENCES

Agha, Asif. 2007. *Language and social relations*. New York: Cambridge University Press.

Bucholtz, Mary, and Kira Hall. 2004. Language and identity. In *A companion to linguistic anthropology,* ed. Alessandro Duranti, 369–394. Oxford: Blackwell.

Davis, Peggy C. 2000. Law as microaggression. In *Critical race theory: The cutting edge,* ed. Richard Delgado and Jean Stefancic, 141–151. Philadelphia: Temple University Press.

Delgado, Richard, and Jean Stefancic. 2000. Images of the outsider in American law and culture. In *Critical race theory: The cutting edge,* ed. Richard Delgado and Jean Stefancic, 223–235. Philadelphia: Temple University Press.

Espinoza, Leslie, and Angela P. Harris. 2000. Embracing the tar baby: LatCrit theory and the sticky mess of race. In *Critical race theory: The cutting edge,* ed. Richard Delgado and Jean Stefancic, 440–447. Philadelphia: Temple University Press.

Harrison, Faye V. 1995. The persistent power of 'race' in the cultural and political economy of racism. *Annual Review of Anthropology* 24:47–74.

Izumi, Lance. 2002. University of California shuts out Asian achievers. http://www.bizjournals.com/sanfrancisco/stories/2002/09/02/editorial2.html.

Marable, Manning. 1995. *Beyond black and white: Transforming African-American politics.* London and New York: Verso.

McWilliams, Carey. 1943. *Brothers under the skin*. Boston: Little Brown and Company.

Robbins, Brian. 2004. *The perfect score,* 93 minutes. Hollywood: Paramount Pictures.

Sanjek, Roger. 1994. Intermarriage and the future of races in the United States. In *Race,* ed. Steven Gregory and Roger Sanjek, 103–130. New Brunswick, N.J.: Rutgers University Press.

Sonnenfeld, Barry. 1995. *Get shorty,* 105 minutes. Los Angeles: Jersey Films.

II

Discursive Constitutions of Groups and Communities

6

"Talk about Luck"

Coherence, Contingency, Character, and Class in the Life Stories of Filipino Canadians in Toronto

Bonnie McElhinny, Valerie Damasco, Shirley Yeung, Angela F. De Ocampo, Monina Febria, Christianne Collantes, and Jason Salonga

In *Life Stories: The Creation of Coherence*, Charlotte Linde argues that the creation of coherence is "a social obligation that must be fulfilled in order for the participants to appear as competent members of their culture" (1993, 16; see also Ginsburg 1989, 141). Her evidence for this claim is how middle-class professionals narrate their work lives against a norm that suggests that the "choice of profession is well-motivated, richly determined, and woven far back in time" (6).[1] Where speakers' work lives were seen as discontinuous, they felt compelled to account for this. Linde's analysis, however, does not seem to fully take into account the ways that some of the social privileges and status associated with being a middle-class speaker make coherent stories possible. "Coherence" thus remains the property of individuals or of individual stories. A more helpful perspective is to consider coherence and articulateness as "systematic outcomes of a set of relations among a group of persons bound in a social structure" (McDermott 1988, 38). In this view, articulateness and inarticulateness and coherence and incoherence "are not the properties of persons or of their utterances; they are the properties of situations that arrange for the differential availability of words and ways of appreciating words across persons in a community" (McDermott 1988, 6). Actions, including speech, can be understood as incoherent, contradictory, or poorly articulated, at best, or as deceptive or prevaricating, at worst, when judged from certain hegemonic positions.

One of the earliest analyses of Filipino interaction in North America, John Gumperz's (1982) analysis of the legal testimony of a Filipino-born physician, underlines this point. The physician was working in the emergency room of a U.S. naval hospital on the day that a child with severe burns was brought in for treatment. He treated the child for severe sunburn and sent her home. Later that day she died, and her burns were subsequently identified as child abuse. Her stepfather was convicted of manslaughter. The district attorney charged that the physician's testimony in the child abuse trial conflicted with testimony given to an FBI agent, and that he had perjured himself to cover up his own negligence. According to Gumperz, a key part of the defense attorney's argument was that the problem was cultural miscommunication. At least in part on the basis of expert sociolinguistic testimony, the physician was acquitted. Gumperz notes that "what counts as coherent in discourse depends on the range of interpretive options interactants recognize, on the frames of reference they adopt, and on how they use them to select among possible interpretations and eliminate sources of ambiguity" (1982, 178).[2]

In this chapter, we undertake a study of life stories told by Filipino Canadians, with particular attention paid to the ways in which they talk about their choice of profession, and with particular attention to what constitutes coherence for these speakers. For many immigrants to Canada, including Filipino Canadian immigrants, a discontinuous narrative about one's professional life is the norm. Indeed, one of the more pressing issues currently facing Canada is the fact that many professional immigrants do not end up working in the jobs for which they were trained; instead, they work at more menial jobs. "He is not working in his profession" was the formulation used by some Filipino Canadian speakers to flag both the work someone was trained to do and its continuing force for thinking about his identity, as well as the fact that that person might not be working in that job. These discontinuities, and the ways they shape the life chances of their Canadian-born children, are also often part of the ways second-generation Filipino Canadians tell the stories of their work lives. We begin by briefly reviewing the relevant literature on life histories and the methods we used for eliciting the life histories analyzed here. Then we offer a brief history of Filipinos in Canada, followed by an analysis of the life stories.

Life Histories: Theory and Methods

In this chapter, we are interested in life stories, that is, "narratively shaped fragments of more comprehensive life histories" (Ginsburg 1989, 133). This analytic positions itself at the intersection of the analysis of the "narratives of personal experience" in sociolinguistics (see Ochs and Capps 1996 for a helpful review) and the "life histories" studied in anthropology. Life stories are not just organized as tellable, plotted events (as narratives of personal experience often are) but are often also organized chronologically. They are not, however, the more comprehensive accounts long used as a key methodological tool in anthropology and sociology (Blackman 1992; Langness and Frank 1981; Espiritu 1995). We are particularly interested in fragments about people's work lives. In her influential study of similar fragments, Linde (1993) argues that the two key coherence principles of life stories are *causality* and *continuity*. Causality is demonstrated by portraying a chain of events that is a good reason for some particular event or sequence of events. She found that "establishing adequate causality for a choice of profession means establishing that good reasons exist for the speaker's choice of profession, or showing that, even if the reasons do not look good...somehow, they still can be seen as acceptable...correct and sufficient causality requires the narrator to establish that the protagonist exercised correct and sufficient *agency*" (Linde 1993, 127–128, emphasis added). In her middle-class sample, agency is often elaborated as something found within individuals themselves rather than in the interstices between people or in other kinds of complexly intertwined structures (compare Ahearn 2001 for a more dialogic approach to agency).

Middle-class speakers carefully steered a path through accounts that would have suggested the speaker accepted a deterministic way of understanding their life choices, and accounts that would have suggested that their lives had proceeded as entirely random. The effect was to suggest that their professional achievements were their individual achievements, in ways that obscured class, gender, and perhaps ethnic and citizenship privileges that made it possible to tell their stories in this way. *Character* was one of the most compelling causal explanations for choosing a profession or explaining success in it. For instance, in one story an editor talks about how she chose her field of work. She presents it as a natural evolution, based on her character traits: her nitpickiness, an interest in reading, her preference for correction versus creation. As Linde notes, the speaker's account contains material that suggests another way to structure the story, one that would show how her job opportunities were structured by family connections (her father knew publishers because he was a freelance writer, her husband was a writer/editor). These facts, however, are not presented as explanations for or causes of her career because an externally based account invites attribution to either accident or determinism. Crucially, the determinism here would be of a particularly non-meritocratic kind, which disguises certain kinds of privileges, linked to family, class, and/or ethnicity. One could also imagine speakers citing a lack of opportunity as something that structured their job choices, but this form of explanation was absent from the narratives of these middle-class speakers. Indeed, "[t]he belief that one is not subject to external limits of opportunity imposed by gender, social class, race, or ethnicity appears to be common to middle-class Americans of the post-war generation" (Linde 1993, 132). Where speakers do present such lack of opportunities as structuring job opportunities, they are often seen as being difficult, offering excuses, or failing to take personal responsibility for choices (see Reynolds and Taylor 2004, 205; Roberts, Davies, and Jupps 1992). Linde suggests that fate may be more likely to structure working-class narratives about people's lives, though this theme of class difference in life history narratives still remains under-studied over a decade later. In the case of immigrants, class, an analytic category closely tied to analyzing identities and relations within a national setting, may not even be fully adequate. Many Filipinos who migrate to Canada are middle-class professionals who find themselves working in jobs of lesser status, though migration often places them in a financially advantageous position vis-à-vis family and friends in the Philippines.

Of course, it is not only working-class and/or immigrant speakers who have to grapple with the dilemma of "inadequate causality" when they tell how they came to their current form of work. Linde notes that some of the speakers she interviewed used ways of talking about events that seemed *accidental* or *discontinuous*. She found that speakers tended to either show that something that seemed accidental or discontinuous really wasn't, or they showed that the accident or discontinuity wasn't a problem for them because of their talent for profiting from circumstances beyond their control ("when you get a lemon, you make lemonade"). What constitutes discontinuity is, of course, socially constructed, and therefore also potentially socially contested. Nonetheless, immigrants and the sons and daughters of immigrants may find themselves living lives that are understood as relatively less continuous, in ways that face them with narrative challenges of explaining the shape their lives take, as is evident in Cook-Gumperz and Gumperz's (1997) analysis of the ways that Pakistani applicants to a job training program in Britain are (mis)understood when they reconstruct past work experiences. Assumptions about what constitutes 'continuous' work experiences and 'adequate' explanations of interest in a particular job are at stake in such interviews.

In this chapter, we analyze portions of life stories told by five Filipino Canadians. These stories are drawn from a collection of twenty-five life histories elicited by members of our research collective. Four of the stories are told by adult immigrants and one by an adult child of immigrants. All of the interviews analyzed here were done by Filipino Canadian interviewers, most of which were in English, though sometimes interviewees also used Tagalog. Since the life histories analyzed below come from Filipinos who migrated to or were born in Canada at different moments, we offer a brief historical account that serves as context for our analysis, as we underline that these stories themselves contribute to the elaboration of the few available histories of Filipinos in Canada.

History of Filipinos in Canada

The migration of Filipinos to Canada has followed a pattern different from that of other immigrant groups. Filipino immigrants in Canada are predominantly recent immigrants (Kelly 2006). Less than 5 percent of the population arrived prior to 1970, and in 2001 over half of all Filipinos in Canada had arrived in just the previous ten years. Filipinos have tended to settle in Canada's urban centers, with the largest number living in Toronto (133,675 or 43.3 percent of Filipinos in Canada) (Kelly 2006, 13). Many of the rest have settled in Vancouver, Winnipeg, and Montreal. The recent increase in Filipino migration has three key explanations: (1) changes in Canadian immigration regulations in the 1960s that stressed educational qualifications and skill as the main conditions of admission regardless of country of origin (Aranas 1983, 83); (2) conditions of underdevelopment and poverty in the Philippines, which are experienced by worker-citizens as unemployment, underemployment, lack of educational and occupational opportunities, and low standards of living (Briones 1984; Eviota 1992; Philippine Women Centre 2001); and (3) the role American imperialism has played in constructing North America as an attractive goal for Filipinos (Choy 2003; Espiritu 2003).[3]

In the 1950s and 1960s, Filipinos who migrated to Canada were mostly professionals, including nurses, doctors, laboratory technicians, and office workers recruited to overcome the labor shortages in those fields. These workers entered

Canada as landed immigrants (i.e., permanent residents). This first wave of immigrants peaked in 1974 (Aranas 1983; Chen 1998; Cusipag and Buenafe 1993; Kelly 2006; Laquian 1973).

In the late 1970s, the age, gender, and occupational profile of the Filipino community changed. There was a higher proportion of clerical, manufacturing, and service workers, and the number of Filipino professionals declined, reaching its lowest point in the mid-1980s (Laquian 1973). With the addition of the family reunification category in 1978, many family members of the first wave of immigrants were sponsored, leading to a dramatic increase in the number of Filipino senior citizens (Aranas 1983; Bustamante 1984; Chen 1998).

During the 1980s many Filipinas entered Canada through the Foreign Domestic Movement (FDM), a program in which domestic workers were eligible to apply for landed immigrant status after two years of live-in service with a designated employer. Programs earlier in the twentieth century had recruited European domestics, but these domestics were given landed immigrant status upon arrival. As recruitment turned to the Caribbean in the mid-1950s and the Philippines in the 1980s, access to citizenship rights was more sharply curtailed. In 1992, the FDM was replaced by the Live-in Caregiver Program (LCP), a program in which eligibility criteria for entry to Canada became more restrictive than in the FDM, partly in the name of improving the quality of childcare in Canada (Bakan and Stasiulis 1997a). Close to 12 percent of all Philippine-born arrivals came under the LCP category between 1980 and 2001, and Filipinos overwhelmingly accounted for those recruited (25,846/32,474 or 79.6 percent of arrivals) (Kelly 2006). Filipino migration to Canada has thus taken on a distinctive gendered skew, with almost 60 percent of immigrants from the Philippines during this period being women (Kelly 2006, 11). Many professionals—nurses, midwives, graduate students in linguistics, office workers—now come to Canada through the LCP, hoping to find work in their own careers afterward.

The LCP is controversial: The distinctive intimacy of live-in caregiver work and the difficulties in monitoring the contract that governs it often lead to economic and sexual exploitation. The criteria it applies for access to citizenship are anomalous in light of how workers in other needed jobs are treated.[4] In addition, caregivers must leave their families behind, as they care for other people's families. Critiques of the LCP have been developed widely in the media, documentary films, and academic research (Arat-Koc 2001; Bakan and Stasiulis 1997a; Elvir 1997; England and Stiell 1997; Macklin 1994; Pratt 1999; Velasco 1997). Research critiquing state policies about the live-in caregiver program remains crucial for bringing to light economic exploitation and differentiated citizenship, but in recent years the overwhelming focus on this program as "the" issue confronting the Filipino community has perhaps had the inadvertent and ironic effect of representing the community largely as live-in caregivers. Even in many curricula devoted to gender studies, transnationalism, and social justice, Filipinos are solely represented by discussion of the LCP. Our life history research group was formed partly with the goal of developing a richer and broader picture of the issues currently facing Filipino Canadians, which includes but is not confined to domestic workers.

Discursive Analysis of Life Stories

Story 1: "This Is Really My Line"

A number of recent books have highlighted the role that American imperial intervention played in training health-care workers in the Philippines, as well as shaping the migration of professional health-care workers to the U.S. (Anderson 2006; Choy 2003). Catherine Ceniza Choy (2003) points out how the creation of an Americanized training hospital system in the Philippines established the professional and cultural preconditions that enabled Filipino nurses to work in North America. Work in North America came to be seen as a desirable experience, a prestigious path to professional mobility and a site at which nurses could elaborate their own cosmopolitan desires and identities through travel, material accumulation, marriage, and reconfigurations of family obligations. Choy points out that these programs were contradictory in that they promoted a sense of "independence" among participants, as they furthered racialized (post)colonial hierarchies between the Philippines and the United States, as well as within North American institutions (2003, 66, 70).

Marilou Santos (all names are pseudonyms) migrated to Canada in the 1960s to work in the field of nursing. In ways that are made possible by the centrality that nursing assumed as a possibility for advancement and migration in the Philippines, but in ways that are nonetheless styled as linked to her own temperament and personality, nursing became the career she desired to enter. Because her family could not afford to train her as a nurse, however, she settled for other medical careers: First she trained as a nursing attendant, and eventually became a midwife. Linde found that people often explained their current professions either with character traits or by offering accounts that related current tasks to early interests, thus suggesting that attitudes arising in childhood are intrinsic to the self. Marilou adopts both: She portrays nursing as a career that she liked from a young age, and something she loves doing.

> (1)
> I came from a family of ten children and there are so many of us that after I finished high school, I didn't know if I was going to college or not because money-wise, we had to see if we can afford it. And I am second to the oldest. **And I really wanted to go to nursing**. Like when I was in high school, I always say like- we are asked like, "What do you want to do when you finish high school?" and **I always used to say, "I want to be a nurse." You know how you already kind of have that in mind, what you want to do, what you want to be when you are young?**. ... So I started doing that [working in a hospital] and I said, **"Oh my, this is really my line, you know, I enjoy dealing with patients."**[5]

Because her family couldn't afford for Marilou to obtain a degree in nursing, she decided to take an exam for a government school in Manila that educated midwives. Students didn't have to pay tuition, though they did have to pay other expenses. From thousands of applicants, Marilou was among 140 chosen. After she graduated with honors, she was briefly employed—as most of the strongest midwifery graduates were—as a nanny for a wealthy family. She balked, however, at a job that consisted only of taking care of babies, briefly tried to set up an independent practice as a midwife, worked as a nursing aide, and eventually secured work as a midwife in a maternity hospital. Finally, in the mid-1960s she heard that midwives were being recruited to work in Canada as nursing aides.

Like Cherry Ruiz (whose story we discuss below), Marilou's story is strongly agentive. She portrays herself as proactively constructing career possibilities for herself. In talking about her application to work in Canada, she says, "I went and I got accepted and I worked there." Nonetheless, her story employs strategies that compel us to question the primacy of *the individual* in decision-making processes and as the locus of adequate causality in explaining the course of a career. In particular, she links her career choices to consulting her family about which career they could afford, and considering the ways that investment in her could mean failure to invest in her siblings. After graduating, she was urged by a physician to seek training as a nurse since she had such strong grades, but her parents told her that if she studied nursing, her sister would be denied the opportunity to train as a teacher. So, she didn't.

In the course of a lengthy interview, Marilou Santos repeatedly comes back to considering why she never became a nurse. At one point she includes a detailed explanation of a free course offered by the Canadian government to allow nursing aides from other countries to upgrade to be a nurse. She worries at this question throughout the interview, finally concluding

(2)
Oh yeah, that's right, you know what prevented me from doing that too? While I was in school, the government will subsidize my studies but I won't get money to send to the Philippines. That's what hindered me too from taking my nursing course because remember my goal here was to help out my family. And I said, if I go to school, that means, whatever money I'm sending home, will stop for a while until I'm finished. ...So that's why I did not go for it.

With this explanation found, she finally drops the question of why she didn't become a nurse. That is, she stops worrying about why her story didn't reach its "natural" conclusion, given her temperament, training, and opportunities. In Marilou's story, then, we see the portrayal of a highly agentive narrator who nonetheless invokes relationships with her natal family in explaining the choices that shaped her career.[6]

Story 2: "The Lady of the House"

Health-care professionals recruited in the 1960s work within structural and historical conditions that allow them to construct a story of their work-life that is both agentive and "coherent" like the speakers Linde studied. Live-in caregivers may be understood as health-care professionals in the Philippines where they are trained by nurses while wearing scrubs, but they are not so understood in Canada (McElhinny 2005). Furthermore, live-in caregivers were often professionals in the Philippines who themselves employed domestic workers. Because, for many, being a live-in caregiver is not an end in itself, but a means to an end, and because live-in work often represents a marked decrease in status, speakers like Carmen Abad sometimes distance themselves from the work in ways that accentuate the *discontinuities* between their former and current work. Rather than developing causal links between her work experiences, she highlights the *accidental* life events that shaped her career trajectory and choice of current profession.

Carmen describes in vivid detail the jobs she had at the University of the Philippines, one of the country's most prestigious universities, for nineteen years before she migrated to Canada. Although she grew up in a squatter community, she earned her undergraduate degree, and worked as a researcher at the Science Education Center, at the University's Information Office, and for the Office of the Secretariat. She emphasizes the research and writing skills she needed in each job, and her skill at meeting the competitive requirements for each of these jobs.

(3)
When you apply to a position in the University of the Philippines, from one office to another, we had to take examinations. And if you pass the examinations, then they'll accept you. So I passed the Science Education Center exam, I passed the Publications Office exam, and then I went to the Office of the Secretariat and they had an exam and I passed it. So (1-second pause) I got in there.

While the ways that many people tell stories about their work histories likely have implications for thinking about how job interviews might be conducted, Carmen's story is one of the few to explicitly report on her strategies for managing a work history that might be seen as less than ideal for her desired post. In discussing her embassy interview, her strategy is to actively disguise the parts of her earlier work life that she believes make her appear to be overly skilled for the position.

(4)
Tapos sabi naman sa akin ulit (and then he asked me again) "Are you sure? Are you sure you didn't attend university or colle::ge?"

"No (1-second pause), why:::::?" Sabi kong ganoon. (I said like that.) "No" sabi ko. (I said.) Sa isip isip ko, "Nako, baka- baka mahuli ako." (In my mind I was thinking, "Oh my, I might- I might get caught). "No. Why?"

So (1-second pause) the gentleman told me, "Okay, Mrs. Abad, you passed the interview stage" Kinamayan ako (he shook my hand) and he said, "You didn't go to university?"

Her story also suggests that even fluency in interview skills is grounds for suspicion, as she constructs her own educational qualifications as shining through her efforts to suppress them. These interview management strategies require the display of her skills at emotionally managing deskilling.

When Carmen describes her current job as a live-in caregiver, she downplays the fact that it is a job. Instead, she emphasizes her equitable relationship with her employer, a divorced working mother. She does not describe herself as a domestic worker but instead views herself in gender-coded terms as "the lady of the house."

(5)

And then, si Sarah, pag nag ano, pag nagpaparty (whenever she- whenever she hosts parties at her house), she will not say "oh this is my nanny- this is my- No.... "Oh Carmen, don't go yet, don't go yet." Sa isip isip ko, eh wala naman akong gagawin. (In my mind, I'm thinking, I'm not going to be doing anything anyway.) "Don't go yet, just meet my friends." **"Oh I want you to meet Carmen, the lady of the house. This is the mom and I am the father."**

In Carmen's story, we see the decoupling of agency, continuity, and adequate causality. Though she is portrayed as fully agentive throughout, her agency is displayed partly in constructing a believably discontinuous work history that will allow her to migrate to Canada. Although the metaphor of being "one of the family" has been critiqued by activists keen to highlight the inequities this masks (Bakan and Stasiulis 1997b), Carmen uses this metaphorical strategy to distance herself from a stigmatized and sometimes degrading job.

Story 3: "I Was Not Destined to Become a Priest"

In the stories we have seen so far, agency has loomed large, even if continuity and causality were styled differently than in stories told by Linde's middle-class speakers. In other stories, however, external structures figure much more significantly in the way people tell their stories. Luis Garcia is a fifty-six-year-old man who moved to Canada in 1979. He currently works in a payroll and accounting department, though he has also undertaken training for, or worked as, a priest, pilot, import-export executive, machine operator, mover, sales representative, computer-programmer, payroll clerk, and accountant. His account of his work life begins with immediate attention to the structural constraints on his earlier occupational choices. He and his family simply did not have the means to educate him for his chosen career in medicine, so he trained as a priest.

(6)

I was planning to take pre-med and become a doctor you know things like that and so I had to take my pre-medical exam and my mother said that we cannot afford that. ... Then that's when some of the priests and the Legion of Mary asked me if I wanted to go to the seminary. It's free! They sponsor you. This seemed like **THE ANSWERS TO MY PRAYERS** and I began my studies at San Carlos Seminary when I was eighteen. I enjoyed my life in the seminary and found it to be an exciting and fun part of my life. **I truly felt that this was where God wanted me to be all along.** But, in my last year of my philosophy degree, my benefactors had stopped paying my tuition fees **for no apparent reason**. As a result, I had to leave the college for a few weeks in search for money to pay for my studies. **With a little luck** from relatives and friends, it was my mom who rescued me by borrowing her entire year's salary in advance in order to pay for my tuition. It was completely selfless and I still thank her for making such a big decision. Finally after five years of studies, **I was fortunate enough** to be able to complete my degree in philosophy at San Carlos Seminary. However in order to become a priest, it was necessary to complete an additional four-year degree in theology. After my search for archdioceses throughout the province that would sponsor me to serve at their dioceses and study for my second degree, **I came up unlucky and it was at this moment that I realized I was not destined to become a priest.**

In Luis's story, he is often not actor, but acted upon. He casts himself in non-agentive semantic roles, as experiencer or affected object in such constructions as "I was fortunate enough" or "I came up unlucky" or "I was not destined to become a priest." The use of adverbs and adverbial phrases that highlight the speaker's lack of control (e.g., "for no apparent reason") also cast the speaker in a non-agentive role (see also Capps and Ochs 1995, 56–58). Nonetheless, the rapid changes of state that his account describes are not seen as random or meaningless: Instead, they are explained by destiny and God's will. Although Linde argues that for middle-class speakers it is psychologically and socially difficult to admit that some important choice in one's life is accidental (1993, 143), Luis responds differently. Fate becomes a way of creating continuity from seemingly random—and negative—events.

In Manila, after working in the export department of the popular department store Rustan's, Luis found a job at an expanding American import/export company. After several years, he was invited to apply for a position at a new office in Saudi Arabia. By that time, his wife's mother and sister had migrated to Canada and issued sponsorship papers for Luis and his family to join them. Now married and expecting a second child, Luis was faced with two options: migrate to Saudi Arabia without his family but with more pay or remain in Manila and hope to get approval for migration into Canada. Luis reports that "throughout my prayers I truly felt my heart telling me to go to Canada." He chose to stay with family.

The first few jobs that Luis had in Canada were unrelated to the work he had done in the Philippines:

(7)
My first Canadian job was at a company called Walbar as a machine operator in Mississauga. At my job at Walbar, each shift we were only required to produce 95 pieces, but even when I took my time I was able to produce up to 105 pieces with the machine. One night, the manager switched me to a new machine, which was differently from the previous one I used, so I got all mixed up with how to use it and by the end of my shift the number of pieces that I produced were deemed damaged and useless. So what did they do? They fired me.

Here, as in middle-class narratives, failures are not seen as linked to individual character (Linde 1993, 132).[7] However, unlike the middle-class narrators, the speaker does not try to solve an obvious discrepancy between jobs that are not intrinsically related by indicating how they are related (Linde 1993, 156). The very fact that there is no attempt to argue that what seems discontinuous really wasn't suggests that Luis does not see himself as presenting a "deficit identity" (Reynolds and Taylor 2004), an identity that must be explained or accounted for. Instead, the attempt to find work, especially professional work, is itself understood as a continuity.

When his wife finally found a stable position, Luis Garcia decided to pursue some community college courses:

(8)
I applied to Centennial College in a computer programming course and studied programming in COBOL and Fortran programs. ... With my computer experience I was hired as a payroll clerk at Guardian and furthered my studies in accounting

and bookkeeping. By 1994, I moved to my present job where I am still working in payroll and accounting. I do not regret my choice in moving to Canada. I worked other places such as Jacuzzi tubs and Allied Moving and Storage Carrier as a mover and also as a sales representative....

In this part of the story, Luis finally seems to become an agent ("I soon applied," "I furthered my studies," "I moved to my present job"). Agency of a certain kind becomes possible after migration, and after finding a certain kind of work. Such structures may seem, disconcertingly, to echo the way that immigration is hegemonically understood and portrayed in Canada, as an unfettered opportunity. However, this way of telling stories may also be understood as socialization into appropriate genre norms for how one talks about finding work in Canada.[8] In Luis's story, as in Marilou's story, the individual is not seen as the sole locus for responsibility, and explanations grounded on preserving family present causal accounts of vocational choices that help establish continuity in the face of apparent discontinuity.

Story 4: "I Ask God Everything"

In Victoria Santos's story about her life, *God* appears to play a role similar to *fate*, *life*, and *luck* in Luis Garcia's story. Unlike many Filipino caregivers now in Canada, Victoria is a career caregiver. Victoria came from a poor family and was the youngest of eight children. Because of her family's poverty, she was unable to attend school regularly, and had to support herself throughout high school as a maid. Her last job before she left for Canada was working for distant relatives as a "helper" where she was in charge of caring for seven children and running the household, including grocery shopping, cleaning, and preparing the household budget.

Victoria's descriptions of her move to Canada, and of the decisions she has made in her work life since then, are not portrayed as her choices. She had applied to work in both Singapore and Canada; when the interviewer asks her how she chose Canada, she replies, "I didn't choose Canada. ...I said 'God, if I cannot find money for the ticket, it means you choose Canada for me.'" In Linde (1993), one narrator used self-distancing in order to explain the choice of a profession that was markedly different from her initial choice of career, arguing that her past and current self were very different. In order to justify her current choice of profession, she absolved herself of responsibility for her past self (156–157). Linde's narrator thus had to use both self and temporal distancing to explain her current state. In Victoria's case, the invocation of God, a separate entity who is guiding Victoria's life, seems to divest her of agency and responsibility but also allows her more continuity of self. It is not her past self and her future self that are distinct; rather, it is God's wishes for her at different moments that are distinct.

Victoria arrived in Canada through the LCP, and has since worked for three different employers. Her first job was with an Anglo family with a very large house who already had another housekeeper. They employed her for three months and then released her, saying she could find more money elsewhere. The second employer was an Anglo woman with three children, including an epileptic child. When Victoria became pregnant, she had to leave, and she found a job with a Filipino family with three children, one of whom was autistic. These employers permitted her to bring her baby to work with her. In these two later families her experience as a caregiver of a child with special needs in the Philippines was, she thought, key. In the last of these families, she was abused. She chooses not to go into much detail, but says that they denied her three months' salary after they offered to adopt her child, and she refused. When the interviewer asked her if she was aware of her rights as an employee, she said that because she is a simple person, she didn't go in for labor rights. Instead, "I told God, I said, 'Oh anyway, we didn't pay rent, we, we ate, so just let it go.'" Although Linde (1993) notes that character traits were not used to describe unsuccessful career choices or 'mistakes,' Victoria uses what can be argued as her positive character traits (such as endurance and faith) to explain how she handled a career catastrophe. Significantly, the divine is not associated with this negative experience.

Where some other narratives seem to use *fate*, *life*, or the *divine* as a bridge between events in a life history in order to make the story seem more coherent, for Victoria the role of the divine is not simply restricted to connectors between events; it is also a part of the event. God is not only the director of events, as he is in Luis's story, but an intimate interlocutor (*I asked God, I told God*).

(9)
Sabi ko kasi, wala akong narrating, kumbaga sa ano, kasi ang akin lang ay (because I said, I didn't achieve anything, because of, well, mine is just) I just ask God, "Ahhh, help." Sabi ko (I said) "Give me a sign Lord. Parang bigyan mo lang ako ng ano, ng lakas, ng (Like, just give me strength). . . . give me strength, OK, and hope all the time. Tapos, kung ano'ng mga problema ko (And then, whatever my problems are), give me sign."

In this excerpt, Victoria denies her own achievements as her own, suggesting they were successful because of God's help; nonetheless, she portrays her agency in the form of desire and her requests (*give me strength, let me pass this second test*). Victoria's narrative illustrates how divine intervention can make a story continuous. Even seeming discontinuities in the narrative and the narrator's lack of agency may be attributed to the active participation of a divine entity, thereby allowing the narrator to distance herself from actions that may be perceived as having insufficient cause. Divine intervention or its absence is also used to explain one's actions, just as personal character was used in Linde's example to explain a choice of profession.

Story 5: "I'm Pretty Sure There's Filipino Lawyers Out There"

All of the stories analyzed thus far have been told by Filipino immigrants to Canada. This story is told by a second-generation Filipino-Canadian.[9] Like several of Linde's interviewees, and in ways that are not used by or perhaps available to some of the earlier narrators, Cherry Ruiz causally explains her present career choice in terms of her character. A twenty-four-year-old pastry-chef apprentice, Cherry Ruiz explains her many years of work in the hospitality and related food-service industry as something that she personally chose because she was skilled in this work. She elaborates on five years spent working at a coffee shop as continuous with her decision to pursue her current apprenticeship:

(10)
Working at the coffee shop helped to meet a lot of interesting people. I worked
with food as well, making sandwiches and serving desserts, making coffee, making
lattes, that's the fun part of the job. More of my interest in it was the people. **I stuck
with it for a long time because I was really good at it and I loved it a lot**. I came
to the decision that I wanted to take up restaurant management, um, hopefully
someday I would work with food.

In her account, a certain degree of coherence with respect to past employment
and present career choice is maintained in two respects: First, her decision to take
up her current trade is framed as continuous with her own interests, talents, and past
involvements in a related sector. Second, this decision comes partly as the result of
a dream to start her own business, and thus has its roots in a long-standing and pre-
existing desire to be an entrepreneur within the industry.

While Cherry's account of how she came to her current career choice wards off
interpretations based on what we consider to be accident, fate, or determinism, her
narrative, like those of a number of the narrators above, employs strategies that do
compel us to question the primacy of *the individual* as the locus of adequate causality. Alongside her initial account, Cherry offers alternative explanations—some
that give prominence to social ties and relations, and others that discuss values and
upbringing as contributing to her chosen path. She says:

(11)
I find it a little bit difficult settling in the career-world in Canada. . . . think Filipinos—
we're just starting to establish ourselves in the Canadian career-world. **I feel that it's
difficult to advance, myself,... because I don't have the influence of any of my
family in a power career-path. I don't see myself as a lawyer, nor do I see my
aunt being a lawyer anytime soon**. We're all just blue-collar, lower-middle-class
to middle-class people trying to make coin.

Where Linde's middle-class informants omitted family connections and
lack of opportunity in their accounts of career choice, Cherry points to structural
factors (*the Canadian career-world*) and family *dis*connections that account for
her current position. Not only does Cherry locate a large part of the influence
externally—the Canadian job market *and* the influence of close kin—but she
has emphasized precisely those external limitations of class that Linde's interviewees did not judge to have significant weight in their own career-related
decisions.

When we examine another passage from her account, the seemingly accidental
is resolved with recourse to her understanding of 'the Filipino family'—a perspective
alert to questions of both class and 'culture':

(12)
My love of being in the kitchen led me to become a pastry chef. . . . That's influenced
by my family, being in the kitchen with my family, their teaching me how to cook,
and making certain Filipino dishes, and just the love of food. The love of food is
because I became fond of bringing people together.

Lest we mistake Cherry for making a purely 'cultural' or class argument about her choices, the very imbrication of cultural values, class, and personal choice is clear from the passage below:

(13)
My family was always hospitable and influenced me to be just as hospitable, and... I join the kindness with the food and that's influenced me to become a pastry chef, a coffee-server, you know, whatever you want to call me. ... **It's always the serving jobs, right? It's not the one to be served, as in the lawyer, you know? (2-second pause) I'm pretty sure there's Filipino lawyers out there. I'm pretty sure there are Filipino doctors, there's probably plenty of them, but, being the first Canadian generation, I don't have (1-second pause) the confidence and the influence to push myself that far along that sort of path.** It ain't my interest anyway HHH.

Culture, class, and personal agency each figure centrally in Cherry Ruiz's decision in a manner that does not permit us to hold one of these as first cause. This both affirms and challenges Linde's original formulation: Cherry, like Linde's interlocutors, is able to find narrative strategies for maintaining coherence through *character* in relating her story of career choice. But rather than discounting the role of others as sources of agency or of class-related constraint in her own decisions, Cherry *emphasizes* these very relations: Close kin are a source of continuity and stability, and family values (such as hospitality) both limit what feels natural as a career choice while allowing for other positive possibilities.

Finally, we may think of the tension between Cherry's different narrative strategies—stressing both internal and external agency—as an expression or narrative embodiment of the very tensions of being a second-generation Filipino Canadian. There is an imperative, on the one hand, to affirm stable character dispositions as prime and causal; there is the need, on the other hand, to confront and acknowledge a relative lack of opportunity and affirm cultural difference. The tension between autonomy and relatedness need not be construed as a problem for coherence, but is itself an expression of Cherry's particular dual position as a second-generation Filipino Canadian. Without resorting to any deterministic claims that link 'culture' to narrative style, and without separating Filipino from North American 'culture' in any essential manner, we might say that the negotiation of multiple perspectives requires that Cherry, likewise, convey these worlds creatively with recourse to more than one narrative form.

Conclusion

Telling stories about their lives places narrators in the paradoxical position of creating coherence out of lived experience, while at the same time reckoning with its impossibility (Ochs and Capps 1996, 29). Elinor Ochs and Lisa Capps argue that these struggles may be particularly salient in cases of mental illness and political repression, but our analyses show that this is also true of economic hardship. Nonetheless, it is important to emphasize that none of these stories are about lives randomly shaped (indeed, the sense that lives are entirely random may be a sign of mental illness, existential angst, or artistic license). Many lean toward a more deterministic rather than individualistic view of life in ways that, interestingly, coincide more with social scientific narratives about how lives are lived than the highly agentive accounts do. Agency, in these stories, is often distributed across social relations with family members or with God.

Different organizations of narratives accord narrators different degrees of responsibility and agency for the narrative, or the actions described within it. The assignment of "responsible agency is seen as an interpretive process that is creative" (Hill and Irvine 1992, 4). The locus of agency and responsibility in the stories analyzed here, as in many other settings, is dialogically constructed (Duranti 1992), but still ranges from a highly individualized sense of responsibility to one linked to economic structures and divine strictures. For the most part, though, the locus of responsibility here, as in the stories of many subalterns (see Hill and Zepeda 1992, 222 on Jewish Americans, African Americans, and Mexican peasants, among others) is not the atomic individual. Indeed, the relative individuality found in narratives may be associated with class (Hill and Zepeda 1992, 225), or at least economic privilege. In the stories analyzed here, agency, continuity, and causality are not always linked as they are in middle-class narratives, nor are they defined in the same way. Although some speakers (especially second-generation immigrants and nurses) describe their choice of career in terms of character, many of the immigrant speakers describe their choice of work as sharply shaped by what their family could offer or by what they could offer to their families. Career choices are "well motivated" in this sense; they are less likely, however, to allude to more psychological traits like temperament, character, and disposition. The immigrant speakers do not seem to hold the same perception of what counts as discontinuity; nonetheless, they draw on strategies for rhetorical continuity that include the need to find any respectable form of work, the desire/need to help family, and/or follow God's will. These are the frames of reference that make these stories coherent ones.

NOTES

1. Other than class and gender, the social identities of the speakers are not named.

2. Other explanations for the problem are also evident in Gumperz's account. Compare Choy's (2003) discussion of the role that scapegoating and racial prejudice played in singling out Filipino nurses for systemic problems in a hospital in Michigan. Although the nurses were originally convicted, massive protests led to a new trial, on the grounds that the testimony of the prosecution witnesses (rather than the nurses) was confusing and inconsistent.

3. A number of recent works have challenged the adequacy of the pre/post 1960s periodization for understanding Filipino migration to the United States (Choy 2003; Espiritu 2003; Lowe 2006); where and how these questions might also apply to Filipino migration to Canada requires more detailed study.

4. Live-in caregivers are given a work visa, and are eligible to apply for permanent residence if they work for twenty-four months in a three-year period as live-in caregivers. Other needed workers are immediately given permanent resident status.

5. We used the following transcription conventions in this chapter:

(2 seconds)	pause in seconds
HHH	laughter
thi-	interrupted utterance
coo:::l	prolonged vowel
CAPS	loud or emphatic speech
Bold	analysts' emphasis

Where speakers use Tagalog, we follow these utterances with an English translation in parentheses.

6. The health-care positions that created the possibility for mobility in the 1960s are now seen by some second-generation Filipinos as a significant constraint. Cristina, a feminist studying to be a counselor working with assaulted women and children, rails against family pressure to work in jobs with well-worn career paths for Filipinos. Cristina is critical of the ways that the gender and ethno-racial segmentation of the workforce leads to the naturalization of certain kinds of careers like nurses and nannies. She yearns for the kind of fictive agency possible for white middle-class native-born narrators, and she wants to tell other Filipinas: "You don't have to be a nurse; you can be whoever you want to be type thing, you know?... Wouldn't it be really great to just [do] something you want to do instead of, you know, wanting to try to do this job just to support your family."

7. Compare also Hill and Zepeda (1992) where responsibility for troubles is distributed in a wide social field rather than being a personal responsibility.

8. Jill Reynolds and Stephanie Taylor (2004, 205), in a study of how narrators talk about being single, also argue for a developmental explanation, with older speakers often presenting younger selves as more passive, more victim than agent.

9. For some of the authors, 'first-generation Filipino' is reserved for those who are born in the Philippines, and then migrate to Canada. For others, however, and in this chapter, this term refers to the children born to Filipino immigrants in Canada.

REFERENCES

Ahearn, Laura. 2001. Language and agency. *Annual Review of Anthropology* 30:109–137.

Anderson, Warwick. 2006. *Colonial pathologies: American tropical medicine, race, and hygiene in the Philippines*. Durham, N.C.: Duke University Press.

Aranas, Marcial Q. 1983. *The Dynamics of Filipino immigrants in Canada*. Edmonton, Alberta, Canada: Coles Printing.

Arat-Koc, Sedef. 2001. *Caregivers break the silence: A participatory action research on the abuse and violence, including the impact of family separation, experienced by women in the live-in caregiver program*. Toronto: Intercede.

Bakan, Abigail, and Daiva Stasiulis. 1997a. Foreign domestic worker policy in Canada and the social boundaries of modern citizenship. In *Not one of the family: Foreign domestic workers in Canada*, ed. Abigail Bakan and Daiva Stasiulis, 29–52. Toronto: University of Toronto Press.

———. 1997b. Introduction. In *Not one of the family: Foreign domestic workers in Canada*, ed. Abigail Bakan and Daiva Stasiulis, 3–28. Toronto: University of Toronto Press.

Blackman, Margaret. 1992. Introduction: The afterlife of the life history. *Journal of Narrative and Life History* 2:1–9.

Briones, Leonor M. 1984. Roots of the present crisis and internal and external forces crucial in the crisis. In *Foreign capital and the Philippine crisis*, ed. Rosalinda Pineda-Ofreneo, 2–7, 25–29. Quezon City: University of the Philippines Press.

Bustamante, Rosalina E. 1984. Filipino Canadians: A growing community. *Polyphony* 6:168–171.

Capps, Lisa, and Elinor Ochs. 1995. *Constructing panic: The discourse of agoraphobia.* Cambridge: Cambridge University Press.

Chen, Anita Beltran. 1998. *From sunbelt to snowbelt: Filipinos in Canada.* Calgary, Alberta, Canada: Canadian Ethnic Studies Association, University of Calgary.

Choy, Catherine Ceniza. 2003. *Empire of care: Nursing and migration in Filipino American history.* Durham, N.C.: Duke University Press.

Cook-Gumperz, Jenny, and John Gumperz. 1997. Narrative explanations: Accounting for past experience in interviews. *Journal of Narrative and Life History* 7:291–298.

Cusipag, Ruben J., and Maria Corazon Buenafe. 1993. *Portrait of Filipino Canadians in Ontario 1960–1990.* Toronto: Kalayaan Medial.

Duranti, Alessandro. 1992. Intentions, self and responsibility: An essay in Samoan ethnopragmatics. In *Responsibility and evidence in oral discourse*, ed. Jane Hill and Judith Irvine, 24–44. Cambridge: Cambridge University Press.

Elvir, Miriam. 1997. The work at home is not recognized: Organizing domestic workers in Montreal. In *Not one of the family: Foreign domestic workers in Canada*, ed. Abigail Bakan and Daiva Stasiulis, 147–156. Toronto: University of Toronto Press.

England, Kim, and Bernadette Stiell. 1997. 'They think you're as stupid as your English is': Constructing foreign domestic workers in Toronto. *Environment and Planning A* 29:195–215.

Espiritu, Yen Le. 1995. *Filipino American lives.* Philadelphia: Temple University Press.

———. 2003. *Homebound: Filipino American lives across cultures, communities and countries.* Berkeley: University of California Press.

Eviota, Elizabeth Uy. 1992. *The political economy of gender: Women and the sexual division of labour in the Philippines.* London: Zed Books.

Ginsburg, Faye. 1989. Interpreting life stories. In *Contested lives: The abortion debate in an American community*, 133–145. Berkeley: University of California Press.

Gumperz, John. 1982. Fact and inference in courtroom testimony. In *Language and social identity*, ed. John Gumperz, 163–194. Cambridge: Cambridge University Press.

Hill, Jane, and Judith Irvine. 1992. Introduction. *Responsibility and evidence in oral discourse*, ed. Jane Hill and Judith Irvine, 1–23. Cambridge: Cambridge University Press.

Hill, Jane, and Ofelia Zepeda. 1992. Mrs. Patricio's trouble: The distribution of responsibility in an account of personal experience. In *Responsibility and evidence in oral discourse*, ed. Jane Hill and Judith Irvine, 197–225. Cambridge: Cambridge University Press.

Kelly, Philip. 2006. Filipinos in Canada: Economic dimensions of immigration and settlement. *Joint Center of excellence for research on immigration and settlement—Toronto* 48:1–37.

Langness, Lewis L., and Gelya Frank. 1981. *Lives: An anthropological approach to biography.* Novat, Calif.: Chandler and Sharp.

Laquian, Eleanor R. 1973. *A study of Filipino immigration to Canada, 1962–1972.* Ottawa: United Council of Filipino Associations in Canada.

Linde, Charlotte. 1993. *Life stories: The creation of coherence.* Oxford: Oxford University Press.

Lowe, Lisa. 2006. Foreword. In *Positively no Filipinos allowed: Building communities and discourse*, ed. Antonio Tiongson, Edgardo Gutierrez, and Ricardo Gutierrez. Philadelphia: Temple University Press.

Macklin, Audrey. 1994. On the inside looking in: Foreign domestic workers in Canada. In *Maid in the market: Women's paid domestic labour*, ed. Wenona Giles and Sedef Arat-Koc, 13–39. Halifax, Nova Scotia: Fernwood Publishing.

McDermott, Ray. 1988. Inarticulateness. In *Linguistics in context: Connecting observation and understanding*, ed. Deborah Tannen, 37–68. Norwood, N.J.: Ablex.

McElhinny, Bonnie. 2005. The international regulation of "love," labor and language: Training programs in language, culture and caregiving for Filipinas in the Philippines and in Canada. In *The American Anthropological Association Annual Conference*, Washington, D.C.

Ochs, Elinor, and Lisa Capps. 1996. Narrating the self. *Annual Review of Anthropology* 25:19–43.

Philippine Women Centre of B.C. 2001. *Filipino nurses doing domestic work in Canada: A stalled development.* Vancouver, British Columbia.

Pratt, Geraldine. 1999. From registered nurse to registered nanny: Discursive geographies of Filipina domestic workers in Vancouver, B.C. *Economic Geography* 75:215–236.

Reynolds, Jill, and Stephanie Taylor. 2004. Narrating singleness: Life stories and deficit identities. *Narrative Inquiry* 15:197–215.

Roberts, Celia, Evelyn Davies, and Tom Jupp. 1992. *Language and discrimination: A study of communication in multi-ethnic workplaces.* London: Longman.

Velasco, Pura. 1997. 'We can still fight back': Organizing domestic workers in Toronto. In *Not one of the family: Foreign domestic workers in Canada*, ed. Abigail Bakan and Daiva Stasiulis, 157–164. Toronto: University of Toronto Press.

Turban Narratives

Discourses of Identification and Difference among Punjabi Sikh Families in Los Angeles

Wendy L. Klein

Asian Indians in the United States encompass a linguistically, religiously, and ethnically diverse group whose population has grown rapidly in the past several decades. Census data indicate that in recent years Indian immigrants have attained high levels of education, professional success, and economic stability.[1] Statistical data, however, fail to illuminate the trajectories, successes, and hardships of specific groups within the Asian Indian population. Sikhs, in particular, face a unique set of challenges in the United States, in regard to maintaining and socializing their beliefs and practices across generations. One prominent symbol of Sikh identity is the *dastaar*, or turban, which is worn most often by men as a sign of their religious affiliation and commitment to Sikh teachings. While the practice of wearing a turban marks Sikhs as visibly different from other Indian Americans, not all Sikh men wear turbans, and the ideological significance of this practice varies among Sikhs today (McLeod 1999). Little research has examined how Sikh experience is diversely constituted and mediated by material practices in everyday life, especially in communities outside of India. This chapter examines how members of eight Punjabi Sikh families in Los Angeles position themselves in relation to other Sikhs, as well as in respect to non-Sikhs, by constructing and indexing discourses about turban practices in open-ended interviews. "Discourse," here, refers to Bronwyn Davies and Rom Harré's (1990, 46) definition of the term as "a multi-faceted public process through which meanings are progressively and dynamically achieved." In participant narratives, the turban becomes an orienting device, positioning one's identity in relation to family, community, and the world at large. Narrative analysis will draw from Elinor Ochs and Lisa Capps's (2001) framework for the study of how organizational, grammatical, and discursive features embedded in speaker's narratives construct systems of moral logic and coherence, which structure their understandings of past experiences, authenticate their current perspectives, and anticipate future scenarios. This study contributes to the new and growing literature in linguistic anthropology that examines the relational production of identity in interaction and in public discourses in which racial or ethnic identities are made relevant (Bucholtz and Hall 2004; Reyes and Lo 2004).

Depending on the location, the term 'Sikh' can simultaneously invoke geo-political, racial, or religious categorizations. In Britain, for example, 'Sikh' refers to a religion, yet for some, it is also synonymous with "Asian" or "Black" (Hall 2002; Maira 2002). Sikhs in Singapore are recognized as a "race" by the government rather than as a multiethnic religious group (Dusenbery 1996). In the United States, the existence of an American Sikh organization (3HO) with primarily Caucasian members informs the local notion of Sikhism as a religion rather than an ethnic or racial category.[2] Rogers Brubaker (2002, 167) suggests that rather than thinking of ethnicities as discrete categories, we need to reconceptualize classifications such as race, nation, and ethnic groups "as political, social, cultural, and psychological processes." Investigating how categories are discursively formulated can provide a deeper understanding of how group affiliation, socialization, conflict, and discrimination are situated in particular social contexts. In the United States, second-generation Sikh American experience is mediated partly through what R. Radhakrishnan (1996) refers to as "ethnic hyphenation," a notion that captures the integrative yet liminal process of negotiating the space between different ethnic experiences in immigrant populations.

The visibility of Sikhs in the United States due to their turbans is constructed as consequential by many of the family members in this study, in regard to their experiences with other Sikhs as well as among non-Sikhs. Narratives highlight participants' experiences of conspicuousness in everyday life, occasions in which they became the focus of attention, and the sense of difference that arose through encounters with others. The multiple perspectives invoked in these narratives reflect George H. Mead's (1934) concept of the objectified self that emerges through viewing oneself from another's standpoint, as well as W. E. B. Du Bois' (1903) notion of "double-consciousness." Yet these narratives move beyond a binary self-other distinction to explore what Homi K. Bhabha (1994, 50) refers to as spaces "*in-between* disavowal and designation," moments of ambivalent interrogation of one's identity that create opportunities for reinterpretation through "narrative agency." Stuart Hall (1996) notes that "identities are thus points of temporary attachment to the subject positions which discursive practices construct for us. ... They are the result of a successful articulation or 'chaining' of the subject into the flow of discourse" (6). As Hall recognizes, however, identities are also shaped through representations constructed by "the Other." In participant narratives, the process of identification also emerges through the discursive accounts of objectification—moments in which individuals contemplate an event or an image through the eyes of another. The production of "othering," discussed within postcolonial perspectives on identity (Bhabha 1994; Radhakrishnan 1996), is particularly relevant to Sikhs in the United States and in a growing number of countries around the world, especially since the events of September 11, 2001.

The narratives analyzed in this study are part of a larger corpus of data collected over a one-year period in the homes of Sikh families and in classes and ceremonies at two local gurdwaras (Sikh temples). The interview methodology employed is "person-centered," an approach in which questions are open-ended and participants are permitted to steer the interview process to a large extent (Levy and Hollan 1998). This format attempts to preempt the interviewer from shaping the participant's talk or nominating the subject of discussion, and encourages participants to discuss issues that are relevant to them. Although the topic of turbans, in particular, was not a focus of my original research agenda, after I began to sift through my data, I found that the number of times the practice of wearing turbans was mentioned by both turbaned and non-turbaned Sikhs was striking. More significant, participants often invoked this practice in ways that were consequential for understanding how they differentiated categories of Sikhs, socialized notions of morality, marked transitions in their lives, and managed the experience of the increased attention they received from non-Sikhs in recent years.

Background on the Punjabi Sikh Community

The majority of Sikhs in the United States trace their ancestry back to the Indian state of Punjab, a predominantly agricultural area and home to the largest population of Sikhs in the world. Sikh historical accounts of life in India make reference to stories of torture, executions, and martyrdom, and emphasize overcoming hardships and persecution by Mughal and Afghan invaders (McLeod 2000). The reputation of Sikhs as warriors gave rise to a military class that served in the British-administered army during colonialism. When India became independent in 1947, the region of Punjab was divided during the partition, and the western part of Punjab became part of the new country of Pakistan, while the eastern area remained in India.[3] In the decades following India's independence, a Sikh separatist group, fueled by a troubled relationship with the Indian government, founded the Khalistan movement, a group that supported the idea of a Sikh homeland. This movement, along with the events of 1984, which included the Indian military storming the Golden Temple in Amritsar, the subsequent assassination of Indira Gandhi by her Sikh bodyguards, and the riots and killings of Sikhs in Delhi that followed, caused divisions among Sikhs and Hindus and created factions within the Sikh community. Recent years, however, have seen moves toward reconciliation among these groups.

The Sikh religion began in the fifteenth century with the life of Guru Nanak, the first of ten gurus who proposed a monotheistic faith that emphasized the equality of all human beings regardless of caste or gender. Guru Nanak's teachings were recorded and elaborated by each of the ten gurus who succeeded him. The *Khalsa*, or religious order, was not founded until the end of the seventeenth century, which some scholars view as the critical period in which Sikh practices were established (Oberoi 1994). Central to Sikh practices is adherence to "the Five Ks," which refers to the five *kakars*, or symbols, of Sikh faith: *kesh* (uncut hair); *kanga* (comb); *kirpan* (sword); *kara* (iron bracelet); and *kachcha* (undergarments). According to W. H. McLeod's (1999) examination of early Sikh texts, the turban was not, originally, a primary Sikh symbol, as compared to the Five Ks, but was used as an effective and hygienic way to cover one's uncut hair, and later became a sign of affiliation, faith, and commitment to the Sikh community. Sikh scholars also discuss the notion that the turban was historically used by Sikhs to distinguish themselves from others during military conflicts (Grewal 1999). The latter explanation was also cited by participants in this study; however, others said it emerged from the belief that hair is God-given, and, therefore, sacred. As the father in one family told me, "Like arms and legs, God gave us hair. We never cut off our arms and legs, so why cut our hair?" While this tradition is not gender-specific, and cutting, plucking, or shaving hair is considered a transgression for both males and females, adherence to these practices varies greatly across the Sikh population. Other turbaned participants in the study pointed out the equalizing effect of the turban; the sense of respect and honor that comes with wearing a turban is shared by all Sikhs, regardless of family, professional, or caste background.

In Los Angeles, the socialization of Sikh teachings and practices occurs in part through family participation in gurdwara activities. Sunday school and summer programs teach *Gurbani* (Sikh script), prayers and hymns from the *Guru Granth Sahib*, musical instruments, history classes, and *dastaarbandi* or turban-tying instruction. In the latter activity, older boys who have uncut hair often serve as the experts to youth who may have short hair and have never worn a turban. In Sikh camp classes, historical accounts, and religious teachings, the turbaned Sikh is presented as the ideal image of a man—the gurus, the gurdwara organizers, and the teachers at the camp wear turbans, and most of the youth with positions of responsibility wear turbans or *patkas*. A *patka* is a cloth that is easy to put on and covers the youth's hair, which is gathered in a bun on the top of their heads. On special occasions, such as weddings and other formal celebrations, young boys often wear turbans. Among Punjabi Sikhs, a few girls wear turbans but most tie back their uncut hair or wear it in braids.[4] While there is no official age at which young men begin to wear turbans on a regular basis, the transition takes place at some point during junior high or high school. This shift, however, is not absolute as many young men continue to wear a *patka* at home and a turban when they leave the home.

Discourses of Differentiation in Relation to Turban Practices

Turbaned and Non-Turbaned Sikhs: Some General Trends

Bhai Harbans Lal (1999, 109–110) notes that according to Sikh scripture, "a Sikh is not to be defined by parental or family lineage, place of birth, geopolitical nationality or caste and creed. To be a Sikh rests on commitment to follow the *Gurmat* (Guru's doctrine) as a path of spiritual and corporal guidance." This broad definition raises the question of what constitutes "commitment to follow the *Gurmat*" in terms of material practices. Sikh scholars refer to a classification system in India in which Sikhs are categorized as *Amrit-dhari* (those who are initiated into the *Khalsa*); *Kes-dhari* (those who do not cut their hair); and *Sahaj-dhari* (those who do not observe the Five Ks but accept Sikh spiritual beliefs).[5] According to these categories, McLeod (1999) contends that the turban should be considered a symbol of the *Khalsa* rather than a pan-Sikh symbol, but Sikh perspectives differ on this point. The Sikh population in Los Angeles is diverse in terms of the number of years spent in the United States, family background and place of origin, socioeconomic status, profession, and level of education. While my sample is small and does not represent the entire Sikh community in Los Angeles, some general trends emerged in my interviews and participant observation in the community. First-generation Sikhs who immigrated most recently from rural areas and regularly attend a gurdwara are more likely to wear turbans, have sons who wear turbans, and express that strict adherence to this practice as well as to the Five Ks constitutes an essential part of being Sikh. Of the first-generation men who have lived in the United States for over thirty years, opinions diverge into four main groups: (1) those who are strict adherents to the Five Ks and wear a turban, and state that these practices are essential; (2) turbaned Sikhs who accept a variety of practices; (3) those who have cut their hair and do not wear turbans but still view themselves as religious; and (4) those who do not follow turban practices and do not consider themselves religious. Among the second generation, a few members fall into the first "strict adherent" category above, and interestingly, these are not necessarily the children of the more recent immigrants or of those who wear turbans. Some of the second generation who are strict adherents were raised in a secular environment and later chose to grow their hair and wear turbans after spending time in India, or when one of their peers did so, or after becoming active in Sikh student organizations in college. In general, however, more second-generation turbaned and non-turbaned Sikhs advocated flexible practices.

First-generation participants in this study linked their practice of wearing a turban to individual faith, family, and community membership, and to an expression of affiliation after the events of 1984,[6] as well as to other events in their lives. Those who removed their turbans upon immigrating discussed the necessity of doing so in order to find employment, a reason that their children also cited when explaining why their fathers no longer wore turbans. In interviews, family members referred to the trend of young men cutting their hair (and no longer wearing turbans) as a point of contention in many Sikh families. Two sets of parents whose sons continue to wear turbans viewed this act as an unforgivable transgression. According to these parents, if their sons decided to no longer wear turbans, they would disown them. Other parents whose sons no longer wear turbans emphasized that while they were disappointed at this shift in practices, they also realized the importance of accepting change as a consequence of their children's upbringing in the United States.

While members of the second generation gave some of the same reasons for wearing turbans—commitment to faith, family, and community affiliation, and post-1984 solidarity—they also discussed other reasons that their parents did not mention. One college student talked about the responsibility he felt toward the younger members of his extended family. For him as well as for some of the other young men, wearing a turban is a way to act as a mentor and a model for younger siblings and cousins to emulate. Other young men said that wearing a turban was less of a display of faith than an expression of individual identity. Some vary in their practices of covering their hair—alternating between a turban, a *patka*, and a hat or baseball cap. Members of the second generation often emphasized the transformative aspect of growing up turbaned and how this experience has shaped them. Both turbaned and non-turbaned second-generation Sikhs discussed the situated nature of material practices across social and geographical contexts. Multiple discourses emerged from the interviews that tied turban practices to different aspects of Sikh identity and everyday experiences. While some of these views were shared across generations, others were more often voiced by one generation in particular. The following sections will outline these perspectives, which fall under three main themes: family and community, transformation, and situated practice.

Turban Ties: Family and Community

According to Sikh parents who immigrated recently and are active in gurdwara activities, it is important for children to be socialized into a sense of affiliation with their family and religious community, as well as prepared for the attention they will receive from non-Sikhs. When I first met Jay and Joti Singh at a local gurdwara, they were getting ready to send their son to a university on the East Coast. Both parents discussed their concerns about their son living on his own and recounted discussions they had with him about public perceptions of Sikhs.

(1) The Singhs reflect on raising their son.[7]

1	Mrs. S.	And he always reminds him that you are not- because
2		being a turbaned Sikh, you are not only a Sikh, you are part of
3		your community. Wherever you will go, (if you will) do anything wrong,
4		because of your- this identity, you will be recognized first. You will do
5		[(xxx) first.
6	Mr. S.	[Yeah, I tell him your photograph got in the newspaper- *why*. There were
7		ten- twenty other students also on that team. Because you have a turban,
8		that is the reason (0.2) your photograph came in the newspaper.
9	Mrs. S.	Always make them conscious that you are part of a community, so, be-
10		before doing anything =
11	Mr. S.	= [Anything.
12	Mrs. S.	= [Don't think only about *your*self. Think about the [pride =
13	Mr. S.	[Think about-
14	Mrs. S.	= of your community.
15	Mr. S.	Yeah.

The Singhs' accounts of their discussions with their son position him, as a turbaned Sikh, as morally accountable not only to them, but to the Sikh community. Charles Taylor (1989, 28) discusses the importance of locating "the self in moral space" as a significant part of establishing identity, and notes, "To know who you are is to be oriented in moral space, a space in which questions arise about what is good or bad, what is worth doing and what not, what has meaning and importance for you and what is trivial and secondary." The turban identifies the wearer as a moral actor whose behavior represents the Sikh community at large. Mrs. Singh cites her husband's repeated exhortations to their son about the responsibilities that distinguish turbaned

Sikhs from non-turbaned Sikhs: (Lines 1–4) "And he always reminds him that you are not- because being a turbaned Sikh, you are not only a Sikh, you are part of your community. Wherever you will go, (if you will) do anything wrong, because of your- this identity, you will be recognized first." Mrs. Singh's imperative in line 9: "Always make them conscious that you are part of a community" invokes the moral obliga- tion of parents to regulate their children's awareness and behavior. With the impera- tive to "make them conscious" along with their reports of their behavior, the Singh parents frame themselves as agents of specific moral and cognitive orientations and display how language can be used to both perform and encode agency (Duranti 2004). Studies in language and interaction (Bergmann 1998; Davies and Harré 1990; Ochs and Capps 2001) have explored how individuals linguistically construct and negotiate moral landscapes in which they situate themselves in relation to others.

For the Singh parents, the turban is a vehicle for differentiation and socializa- tion of category membership. Their claims that their son is "not only a Sikh" but a "turbaned Sikh" confer on him special status as a Sikh whose behavior may be more consequential than that of a non-turbaned Sikh, due to the attention that his turban attracts. Mr. Singh's subsequent utterances in lines 6–8 ground his wife's previous observations in a narrative of an actual past event. He explains the appearance of his son's picture in the local newspaper when the school science team won a champion- ship (lines 7–8): "Because you have a turban, that is the reason (0.2) your photograph came in the newspaper." Mr. Singh constructs the relationship of the turban to the photograph as a causal chain of events, which attributes the appearance of his son in the newspaper to the visibility of his turban. Mr. Singh's conclusion redefines the image of the turbaned Sikh, which is viewed as normative within the Sikh commu- nity, as a curious, markedly different phenomenon outside the community.

Although their son, Jasjit, did not discuss his parents' perspectives on his prac- tices, as it turns out, wearing a turban is critical for his relationship with his family. In another interview, his mother commented that her son knows that if he stops wearing a turban, "he will not be part of this family," which indicates that for Mrs. Singh, the turban not only signals ties to the community but is also a condition of kinship and a reflection of family honor (*izzat*). In another family, the oldest son, Neel, noted that when he was a small child, his hair was kept short, and that the decision to grow his hair came later. One summer when Neel was ten, his cousin, who lived with Neel's family, attended a Sikh summer camp and decided to start growing his hair and wear- ing a turban when he returned home. The cousin's decision initiated a change among the brothers and cousins who now all wear turbans. Neel explained that "when we decided as a family, fine, we're all gonna do it, that's just how it was, we all stuck together." For some families, the collective sense of kin affiliation is embodied in the practice of wearing a turban.

Turban as Transformative

Harpreet, thirteen, is the eldest son in another family and recalls that when he was ten, his parents were approached by one of the teachers at the gurdwara and asked when they thought Harpreet would start wearing a turban (at that time he wore a *patka*). Harpreet's parents viewed this query as the teacher's recognition of him as ready to deepen his religious commitment. In this sense, for some young men and their families, wearing a turban marks a rite of passage and signals a level of maturity in the community. Harpreet has come to associate the turban with becoming closer to God, a step away from the profane and toward the sacred. However, another young man, Jess, views the transformative experience of wearing a turban differently:

(2) Jess discusses growing up turbaned.

1   When your parents tell you that (0.2) you know, this will make you a
2   stronger person, you don't believe it at first. *I* didn't believe it at first.
3   I'm like- *who cares*. But (0.2) it does. It makes- it makes you (have) strong
4   will, strong power, and *tol*erance. To- to take- just- everything. Everything.
5   Racial slurs, um getting up in the morning (0.2) on time, everything.
6   It just gives you a lot of- a lot of strength.

While Harpreet's account points to the transformative aspect of wearing a turban among Sikhs, Jess frames his experience as transformative due to wearing a turban among non-Sikhs. The practice of wearing a turban also leads him to shift his initial position of questioning his parents' perspective to aligning with them in regard to the consequences of growing up with a markedly different appearance. His alternating use of referential indexical pronouns (see Ochs 1990; Silverstein 1976) constructs his stances toward particular discourses about turban practices in different ways. In lines 1–2, Jess first invokes past disbelief toward the parental perspective on the benefits of wearing a turban. His use of the habitual present tense and the second-person pronominal "you" in the first two lines formulates his experience of his parents telling him that wearing a turban will make him "stronger" as a generic practice in Sikh immigrant families. His subsequent phrase, "you don't believe it at first," also generalizes the second-generation reaction to this parental declaration. Jess then personalizes this experience when he switches to the first-person pronoun, marked with a stressed intonation: "*I* didn't believe it at first," which places him in this category of skeptics. He reports that not only did he reject his parent's claim, he dismissed it as unworthy of interest (line 3: I'm like- *who cares*). At this point, Jess repositions himself as in alignment with his parents' belief that wearing a turban is an effective agent of socialization, "But (.) it does. It- it (makes) you have strong will, strong power, and *tol*erance. To- to take- just- everything." Jess's shift back to using the second-person pronominal here generalizes the consequences of growing up turbaned.

Jess's older brother Neel also discussed the experience of wearing a turban as transformative. Neel constructs the role of the turban as an agent that offers him a heightened "theory of mind" with which he can read the thoughts of others:

(3) Neel's perspective on wearing a turban.

1   It really helps me figure out who people are, what they're all about.
2   It's really weird but I know what people are thinking just by their reactions,
3   facial expressions, body language, I know what's going on now because
4   I've seen it so many times.

Neel's comment in line 1, "It really helps me figure out who people are, what they're all about," reveals his view that the turban is a tool that provides him with information about those he encounters. He believes that through his repeated experiences of observing the reactions of others to his appearance, he has learned that certain gestures and facial expressions index specific stances toward him.

Turban as Situated Practice

Mr. Aujla, a turbaned Sikh, came to the United States to study engineering, and he and his wife have been living in the Los Angeles area for over thirty years. The couple has two sons who grew up wearing *patkas* and then turbans and who attended the local gurdwara on a regular basis. Now in their twenties, however, both sons have cut their hair and no longer wear turbans. Raj, the younger son, who decided to cut his hair at the age of twenty-four (the year before my first interview with him), brought up the issue of feeling judged by turbaned Sikhs, which is a sensibility expressed by other non-turbaned men in this study. Raj notes that, "sometimes Sikhs who have uncut hair appear to have some sort of superiority complex among other Sikhs who've cut their hair. It's a really tough part of being a Sikh." In my interviews with Raj, he expressed that he had thought deeply about his religion, and while he embraced certain aspects of Sikhism, he stated that he felt conflicted. He points out: "My parents tried to raise me as a true Sikh but at the same time, they are very open-minded" and added that "there are parts I don't agree with- make no sense to me in my life in my time- for instance, keeping a turban." Raj reports that his cousin, who is a few years older than Raj and is a turbaned Sikh living in India, understood Raj's decision to cut his hair and told him, "You're living in a different world in America- the time, the place, what you're doing." Raj continues, "And he's living in a different time and place and doing different things." Raj's statements construct two models of being Sikh; the "true Sikh," which implies adherence to material practices, and a more flexible model in which Sikh practices are geographically and temporally situated, a view that is validated by his turbaned cousin in India.

Raj's views are shared by a number of second-generation young men and women who were brought up attending gurdwaras and who self-identify as Sikh but see themselves as broadening the definition of what it means to be a Sikh in regard to physical appearance. Raj does, however, recognize that his perspective challenges certain authoritative sources in the Sikh community:

(4) Raj discusses Sikh practices.

1   Our religion says you're supposed to wear a turban and uncut hair-
2   what it says in scripture- but what if I trim my beard- am I still a Sikh?
3   (xxx) If someone says I'm not a Sikh, then good for you, you're entitled
4   to your opinion. In England, they tie their turbans differently, finely trim
5   their beards. I think that's still a Sikh, but a literalist would say no, he's not.

In the above narrative Raj continues to emphasize the contrast between the canonical designation of Sikh practices and the flexible, situated version he alludes to above. His narrative implicitly points to crucial questions for diasporic Sikhs today: Who is considered a Sikh, what are the conditions of membership, and who decides? Raj's hypothetical scenario, "What if I trim my beard- am I still a Sikh?" highlights the problem with appearance-based distinctions, and his declaration that "if someone says I'm not a Sikh, then good for you, you're entitled to your opinion" renders the answer to what constitutes Sikh membership a matter that relies on individual opinion rather than on authoritative perspectives on visible indices. He points out that "in England they tie their turbans differently and finely trim their beards," a practice that would not be acceptable from a 'literalist' standpoint, but Raj declares, "I think that's still a Sikh." Raj's system of logic locates faith within the individual and differentiates between physical appearances and inner epistemological states. His narrative reveals his attempt to reconcile authoritative views with the perspective in which material practices are situated and religious commitment is embodied internally.

Discourses of Differentiation in Response to Non-Sikhs: Monitoring and Visibility Since 9/11

Narratives of Sikh experience also refer to being misunderstood, discriminated against, and harassed by those outside their community. As one of the earliest Asian Indian communities in the United States, Punjabi Sikhs initially came to the United States as agricultural workers on the Pacific coast in the late nineteenth and early twentieth centuries. Studies of farming communities in Central California have documented that Sikhs were routinely referred to as Hindu by the local, non-Indian populations, and were prohibited, along with other Asian immigrants, from owning land until 1946 (Gibson 1988; Leonard 1997). Currently, the Sikh population in the United States is spread out across rural and urban areas and has attained success in a variety of professions. Sikhs, however, have increasingly encountered discriminatory treatment and acts of violent harassment in recent years. Although members of other religious and ethnic groups wear turbans, over 90 percent of those who wear turbans in the United States are Sikh. In 2002, Sikhs were designated as a "vulnerable community" by the U.S. Equal Employment Opportunity Commission (EEOC), which issued several documents that outline workplace rights to "prevent backlash discrimination" since September 11, 2001.[8] The section on the treatment of Sikhs in these documents deals exclusively with their right to wear turbans and the responsibility of employers to respect this practice. While turbaned Sikhs in the United States have experienced discrimination for decades simply for looking different (Gibson 1988; Leonard 1992), many of the more recent acts of harassment have been carried out by those who believe Sikh turbans signal membership in groups that are connected ethnically or politically to terrorist organizations in the Middle East. The first post-9/11 murder that constituted a hate crime was of a Sikh who ran a gas station in Arizona, and was mistaken for a Muslim.[9] To counter the existing confusion and mistaken assumptions about their appearance, Sikhs have established programs to educate law enforcement, interfaith organizations, and secondary school students about their history, beliefs, and practices.[10] There is a significant lack of research that investigates how this treatment has affected notions of identity and everyday practices within these communities.

Among first-generation Sikhs, issues of discriminatory treatment were mentioned most often in relation to procuring employment upon immigrating. Mr. Aujla recounted his experiences with discrimination in job interviews in the 1970s. He never cut his hair, however, and continues to wear a turban. He reported that when he was asked to remove his turban during an interview, he proudly refused and eventually succeeded in getting a job with another company. When he was offered the job, he asked his potential employers to "please judge me by what's in my head, not what's on my head."[11] His recollection of this event displays his awareness that his appearance had an impact on others who might not be able to see beyond his turban. More recently, second-generation turbaned Sikhs have expressed discomfort, fear, and frustration with the treatment that they have sometimes received from non-Sikhs. Accounts of these experiences, as well as discussions of non-Sikh perceptions of Sikhs, surfaced in narratives about their everyday lives.

Post-9/11 Reactions: Recognition, Resemblance,
and the Anticipation of Trouble

Shortly after the events of September 11, 2001, images of those thought responsible for the multiple attacks appeared on television, Internet web sites, and in newspapers and magazines. The images spread rapidly through the media and produced a prototypical image of a 'terrorist' as a dark-skinned, possibly bearded, turbaned male. Priya, the daughter of Sikh immigrants who is in her twenties, talked about her reaction to seeing a photograph of Osama bin Laden on television for the first time just after the reports of the World Trade Center attacks:

(5) Priya's recollections

1	Priya	I- When I *first* saw the picture of what Osama bin Laden looked like-
2		and I- I wasn't- I have to say that I wasn't too familiar with him before
3		nine eleven, before this all came [out.
4	Neel	[Oh I had no idea who he was. =
5	Priya	= U:mm, (0.2) but I guess there were- you know, he was on the map,
6		he was on the radar, but we didn't *know* so: when I *first* saw his picture
7		I *just* wanted to kill myself because I was like Oh my go:d, This *looks*
8		like my da(hh)d- *this* is going to be a pro:blem.

Priya's previous epistemic stance regarding bin Laden (lines 2–3: "I have to say that I wasn't too familiar with him before nine eleven"), with which her husband, Neel, aligns in line 4 ("Oh I had no idea who he was"), is reissued in the first-person plural in line 6 ("he was on the radar but we didn't *know* so:"). Their statements juxtapose an earlier time before their awareness of Osama bin Laden with the shocking moment of recognition when they first encountered his image. Priya's stress on the word 'first' in line 1 (When I *first* saw the picture of Osama bin Laden) introduces this moment as consequential and is repeated later in line 6 ("when I *first* saw his picture"), which is followed by her depiction of her reaction, "I *just* wanted to kill myself." Priya's latter declaration is expressed in a hyperbolic manner, which is indicated in the laugh tokens embedded in her subsequent talk ("This *looks* like my da(hh)d"); however, it also portrays this observation as dramatic. Priya anticipates that her father's similarity in appearance to Osama bin Laden will have grave consequences (line 8: *"this* is going to be a pro:blem").

While Priya continues to contemplate the issue of visual resemblance, she and Neel discuss the close proximity of Punjab to Pakistan and other Islamic countries, and the common cultural roots that run beneath country borders.

(6) Priya discusses differentiation.

```
1      But when I think about Osama bin Laden, and knowing the things
2      I know about our- about my religion, in fact we are different, we're a
3      totally different religion. Our cultures might be, you know, the same,
4      from the east but whatever but- our religion, everything about us is
5      so different except the loo:k- (hh) and that's what- that's what
6      everything is based on here if you don't- if you're ignorant to
7      the culture and the religion and to the beliefs, that's what- that's what
8      we look like so, when I first saw that, I especially had this conversation
9      with my brother that- oh my god- (hh) this is so bad because
10     we look like that you know and you barely- you don't even want
11     to say it because you're saying that you look like a terror(hh)ist,
12     you know, but- similarities are- are great.
```

While Priya is initially struck by the similarity of Osama bin Laden's appearance to Sikhs, she moves on to consider the religious differences: "knowing the things I know about our- about my religion, *in fact* we are different" (lines 1–2). Her pronominal switch in line 2, "the things I know about our- about my religion," is a repair that reveals her attempt to make the distinction between their affiliations clear. The use of "our" could be construed as referring to Osama bin Laden and herself as members of the same religious group, and her shift to "my" religion creates a firm division between the two. A few moments prior to the segment above, Priya had pointed out that a "white person" would not be able to differentiate between the appearance of a Sikh and the image of bin Laden. She declares in lines 4–5, "Everything about us is so different except *the look*," and "that's what everything is based on here." From Priya's perspective, in American society the majority is Caucasian, and ethnic or religious categories are designated by visual appearance only, and in reference to "white" as the unmarked category. Thus, she reasons that to most people who are "ignorant to the culture and the religion and to the beliefs, that's what- that's what we look like" (lines 6–8). Priya points out the difficulty with verbalizing the sense of resemblance and recognition, when she says in lines 10–11, "You don't even want to say it because you're saying that you look like a terror(hh)ist." This latter statement, as well as her previous observation that "this looks like my da(hhd)" are infused with laugh tokens. Gail Jefferson (1984) notes that in "troubles-talk," tellers often laugh in order to display affective "resistance" and to show that they are able to manage the problem. In these segments, however, Priya's laugh tokens also reveal a degree of discomfort and disbelief with what she views as the assumptions that will be made about the appearance and identity of Sikhs. Priya's articulation of the way people are labeled reflects her ideology of ethnicity in the United States, which she views as being based on a visual typology that may be erroneously applied, with hurtful and dangerous consequences.

After 9/11, bin Laden's image became an iconic representation of the "face of terror,"[12] which began to shape the way those with turbans experienced the attention they received in public. Identifying potential criminals based on physical appearance is used in racial profiling, which has increased since 9/11 to categorize individuals as possible terrorists. Profiling constitutes an authoritative coding system in which visual characteristics, such as color, classify individuals and link them to transgressive practices. Employing such a system produces "socially organized ways of seeing" (Goodwin 1994). In the case of turbaned Sikhs post-9/11, the turban as a symbol of deep religious faith and commitment has been reinterpreted by many as representing violence and anti-American sentiment. This juxtaposition reflects Du Bois' (1903, 3) notion of double-consciousness: "this sense of always looking at one's self through the eyes of others." Du Bois' description of double-consciousness involves the idea that one's feelings of self-worth are mediated by the negative projections of others.

The recent stereotyping of turbaned males also stands in direct opposition to the previous, "positive" image of Asian Americans, including Sikhs and other Asian Indians, as a recent addition to the "model minority" (Lessinger 1995; Prashad 2000). Social psychologists (Biernat and Dovidio 2000) point out that stereotypes do not just function as negative judgments about a group but act as "specific semantic associations" that build analogous relationships between categorical types and behaviors. Angela Reyes (this volume) uses the term "widespread typification" to refer to the construction of stereotypes through extensive circulation in public discourse and the media. Reyes demonstrates how Asian American teens position themselves as resisting and rejecting specific stereotypical notions, while invoking others to construct inclusiveness. Sikh reactions to turban stereotyping reveal both of these strategies, including their attempts to distance themselves from the "terrorist image" and differentiate themselves from Muslims in general as well as their attempts to identify with Muslims in terms of their shared burden of enduring the new stereotype of the turbaned male.

Monitoring and Agency: Managing Experiences
of Self as Other

The narratives in this study indicate that the increased attention that Sikhs have received in public places has produced a heightened awareness of difference and "being seen," which involves the dialectical process of experiencing oneself as the object in social encounters. As Mead (1934, 225) noted, an individual's self-perceptions emerge through the process of objectification: "The individual enters as such into his own experience only as an object, not as a subject; and he can enter as an object only on the basis of social relations and interactions, only by means of his experiential transactions with others in an organized social environment." Jean Paul Sartre (1956) also recognized the significance of objectification in his phenomenological perspective on self-consciousness, in which the self emerges from experiencing "the look" of an observer, which requires an individual to undergo objectification. Sikh perspectives construct the gaze of the other as indexing a variety of perspectives ranging from curiosity to suspicion. Jess, an engineering student who is also a musician, is discussing his musical performances when his narrative takes an unexpected turn:

(7) Jess reflects on his experiences in public

1   U : : m, well, (0.2) most of the time wearing a turban and being Sikh is
2   very difficult (0.2) because you have to deal with a lot. Like, for example,
3   if I go to the mall, I can see hundr- hundreds and hundreds of people
4   *look*ing at me- and not only looking at me but looking at me once, twice,
5   and maybe thrice, and I can see that- I can see it all happening.

In his narrative above Jess frames the challenge of 'wearing a turban and being Sikh' as a task that requires enduring the sustained visual attention of others. Erving Goffman (1971, 45–46) notes that the intrusive role of prolonged eye gaze in public space is a violation in human interaction. As the recipients of such stares, turbaned Sikhs must contend with the insinuated projections of others and determine how to manage this attention. Jess's repeated use of the modal constructions, "I can see," in lines 3 and 5, stresses his awareness of being under continual surveillance as well as his ability to easily access this experience in his mind. The numerical intensifiers he uses in line 3, "hundreds and hundreds of people *look*ing at me" and in lines 4–5, "not only looking at me once but looking at me once, twice, and maybe thrice," depict his overwhelming sense of being repeatedly scrutinized by crowds of people. Jess's description evokes the panoptic scenario described by Foucault (1977) and renders his public appearances oppressive as he must continually grapple with the sense of being followed by the gaze of others.

The practice of reflexive monitoring—watching those who are looking at you— is not a gendered experience that surfaced only in interviews with turbaned male Sikhs. Priya, Neel's wife, describes a similar practice in reference to her experiences in public with her husband.

(8) Priya discusses monitoring the reactions of others

1   Yeah, so, for the people around him it's difficult, you're having a good time,
2   but in certain places, you're looking around, you're making sure
3   nobody's doing anything, nobody's- they look and that's fine-
4   you're looking to make sure they're not going to cross that line.

Priya's repetition of the act of "looking"—in line 2, "you're looking around," in line 3, "they look and that's fine," and line 4, "you're looking to make sure they're not going to cross that line"—captures the reflexive dimension of public activity for her when she is with her husband. Priya's "looking" is a specific type of visual practice that involves evaluating the stares received in terms of potential threats: "You're looking around, you're making sure nobody's doing anything." Priya must be able to recognize if and when this focused attention might "cross that line" and lead to verbal or physical assaults. Her use of the habitual present tense and the second-person pronoun "you" constructs this activity as a generic practice that occurs whenever she is with her husband in public "in certain places"—usually areas or establishments where there are large groups of young people. The process of cautiously monitoring the reactions of others requires the ongoing management of visual cues to determine what is occurring in the interactional space between self and other—the "reading" of eye gaze, facial expressions, and body movements.

Jess attributes his experiences of difference as a musician in Los Angeles to world events, and like Priya, discusses the issue of visual appearance and ethnic categorization in the United States. His narrative below describes his perspective on ethnic identities, which has been shaped by his experiences encountering others in clubs or recording studios.

(9) Jess's perspective on "difference"

1	I walk in there and I'm probably nine out of ten times the most *different* person
2	there. I mean it's different *these* days, because, um, like, usually, (0.2)
3	not to be ra:cist or anything but usually when- when you associate different
4	you associate with someone non-white, right, but *no:w*, even *those* people,
5	like Black people, Mexican people, Asian people, they're all the *norm* now and-
6	and what (0.2) especially people with turbans face- especially *this* time
7	in *this* world because you have everything going on in the Middle East,
8	and people who wear turbans there- just- I mean, first of all
9	they don't wear the same turban but no one can really tell, right,
10	and you can't make the difference.

Jess refers to himself as "the most *different* person there," which he goes on to elucidate in his subsequent description of the change in framework for defining ethnic differences. By using specific linguistic forms, such as pronominal or deictic shifters, Jess discursively positions himself vis-à-vis others and maps out temporal and geographical fields of difference. He also draws from indexical terms that include names and membership categories to illustrate relational aspects of social identities (Ochs 1990; Silverstein 1976) and membership categories (Sacks 1992). In lines 3–4, he says, "I mean it's different *these* days," which indicates that a temporal shift has occurred, and that before this shift the categorization of difference referred to "someone non-white." He then states, "But no:w, even *those* people, like Black people, Mexican people, Asian people, they're all the *norm* now." The temporal and spatial indexical terms, "*these* days," "*now*," "*this* time in *this* world," refer to the current time in which everyone except those with turbans are viewed as normative. Since September 11 and the war in Iraq, people with turbans are associated with "everything going on in the Middle East" (line 7). He points out that this is a mistaken assumption since Middle Eastern turbans differ from Sikh turbans, but he realizes that this distinction is difficult to recognize. Table 7.1 maps Jess's use of indexical terms of temporality with the associated categories he references.

From Jess's perspective, the post-9/11 reconstitution of category formations organizes people into two groups: those who fall outside the line of suspicion versus those who resemble the stereotypical image of a terrorist (turbaned male). Jess's distinction of being "most different" aligns with Mr. and Mrs. Singh's assumption that a turbaned Sikh is "recognized first"; however, the Singhs did not contextualize this distinction within a pre- and post-9/11 framework. When Jess speaks subsequently of using this sense of difference to his "advantage," he repositions himself as an agent who has the ability to shift people's focus of attention:

(10) Jess discusses his strategy

1   I use it to my *advantage* because I *know* I'm completely different but
2   I also know I'm somewhat talented and I can impress these people.
3   So- in that- from that standpoint you *have* to use it as an
4   advantage 'cause they're already focused on you, they're already
5   counting against you.

Jess depicts himself as employing the negative assumptions of others to his benefit. He attributes to himself the power and talent to motivate people to look beyond his turban and appreciate his skills. His use of the modal phrase "have to" in lines 3–5 ("you have to use it as an advantage 'cause they're already focused on you, they're already counting against you") frames his actions as morally justified; using difference to his advantage is a critical strategy for overcoming the challenges he faces in a world in which his appearance is consistently evaluated with suspicion. Jess's stance also reflects Goffman's (1967) concept of "impression management" in which the individual adheres to "rules of conduct" that may be related to ethics, law, or ritualistic performance. Goffman discusses how these rules, implicit or explicit, set up contextual expectations and "transform action and inaction into expression and whether the individual abides by the rules or breaks them, something significant is likely to be communicated" (1967, 51). By excelling in his performance, Jess shows his non-Sikh peers that he is able to navigate effectively the shared terrain of musical expression, despite their doubts and low expectations. Jess's narratives reveal his

TABLE 7.1. Jess Defines Difference: Indexical Category Shifts

Time	Pre-9/11: usually		Post-9/11: these days; now; this time; this world	
	'Norm'	'Different'	'Norm'	'Different'
Categories	White	Nonwhite	White, People of Color:	Turbaned:
		Blacks	Previous groups rendered	Sikhs
		Mexicans	normative	Middle
		Asians		Easterners
		(includes Sikhs)		

understanding of the impact of world events on perceptions of ethnic identity and how his insights and experiences have empowered him to overcome the stereotyping he has encountered.

Conclusion

Ideological perspectives on the significance and practice of wearing a turban are variable and reflect the historically situated, dialogically emergent process of identification among Sikhs in Los Angeles. The discursive formulations of Sikh experience among participants in this study reveal ideologies of difference within the Sikh community in relation to Sikhs as well as non-Sikhs. Narrative analysis indicates that discourses of Sikh identity are produced relationally and that parents invoke Sikh material practices to socialize differentiation, kinship, and community, while second-generation perspectives represent a wide range of Sikh identity practices. Parents' narratives reveal their anxieties about the future trajectory of their children's lives as turbaned Sikhs, as well as their ongoing efforts to prepare their children to represent their community and recognize and manage the attention they receive. Several second-generation turbaned Sikhs linked turban practices to family obligation and cohesion, spiritual maturity and leadership within the community, and the development of individual strength of character. Both first- and second-generation Sikhs who once wore turbans and subsequently cut their hair question the relevance of such material practices for the Sikh faith and point out the diverse and situated practices of Sikhs worldwide.

Furthermore, according to second-generation Sikhs in particular, the events of September 11, along with subsequent U.S. involvements in the Middle East, have reshaped ethnic boundaries and necessitated new identity practices in everyday life. The intrusion of media images of turbaned males has led to stereotypes of terrorists who resemble Sikh males and has impacted the daily lives of families who recognize that their appearance may now be viewed with suspicion. Participants referred to the rise in incidents of discrimination and harassment of turbaned Sikhs as precipitating their need to monitor the ongoing attention they receive in public, displaying that it is through interaction with others that people locate and differentiate themselves within social, moral, and affective dimensions of human experience. The practiced ability to anticipate the actions of others by discerning the meaning behind stares, facial expressions, and body movements is invoked as a necessary skill for managing newly constructed categories of difference. At the same time, some Sikhs view the increased attention as a challenge to dispel stereotypes and emphasize the need for individuals in the Sikh community to become agents of change, to transform public misunderstandings about Sikh identity and material practices in the American diaspora.

NOTES

1. U.S. Census Bureau. 2000. Census Brief: The Asian Population: 2000, table 4, p. 9. According to this report, the Asian Indian population in the United States in 2000 was 1.7 million, which reflects an increase of over 100 percent since 1990. Asian Indians are the third largest Asian group in the United States behind the Chinese and Filipino populations.

Priya Agarwal (1991) notes that Asian Indian immigrants with professional skills and educational background were given preferential treatment regarding immigration, which partially accounts for their socioeconomic success.

2. The community of non-Punjabi American Sikhs emerged in the 1970s as followers of the Punjabi teacher Yogi Bhajan, who established the '3HO' (Happy, Healthy, and Holy Organization). Although there are differences among groups in regard to which guru they follow, the American Sikhs adhere to most of the same teachings as the Punjabi Sikhs. Unlike the Punjabi Sikhs, however, they emphasize the importance of yoga in their practice.

3. Further divisions established ostensibly along linguistic lines led to the creation of the predominantly Hindu Haryana and Himachael Pradesh and the Punjabi-speaking state of Punjab.

4. This practice contrasts with non-Punjabi American Sikhs in the Guru Ram Das Ashram community, whose female members all wear turbans. Some Punjabi Sikh women and girls in other parts of California and the United States wear turbans; however, very few female members in the Los Angeles community wear them.

5. This system is complex and also includes other designations that may be based on caste and historical circumstances (see McLeod 1999).

6. The events of 1984, Operation Bluestar in Amritsar, the assassination of Prime Minister Indira Gandhi, and the riots in Delhi that followed, produced fissures in the Sikh community. These events have been cited as critical moments that have shaped Sikh identity in the diaspora (see Tatla 1999).

7. Data are transcribed using a modified version of the system described in Harvey Sacks, Emanuel A. Schegloff, and Gail Jefferson (1974). Transcription conventions:

-	dash indicates a cut-off in sound
[	a left bracket marks the onset of overlapping speech
(0.4)	numbers in parentheses indicate silent pauses in tenths of a second
:	colon indicates elongation of preceding sound
(xxx)	three x's in parentheses indicate indecipherable talk
ital.	words in italics indicate intonational stress
CAPS	capital letters mark increased volume
(hh)	a series of h's in parentheses indicates breathiness or incipient laughter
=	an equal sign indicates the immediate latching of one utterance to the next

8. The U.S. Equal Employment Opportunity Commission, EEOC Provides Answers About Workplace Rights of Muslims, Arabs, South Asians and Sikhs. press release, May 15, 2002. www.eeoc.gov/press/5-15-02.html.

9. Tamar Lewin, "Sikh owner of gas station is fatally shot in rampage." *The New York Times*, Sept. 17, 2001, B16.

10. While attempting to increase awareness about Sikh beliefs and practices, individuals in the Sikh community also emphasize that while they are making an effort to distinguish themselves from Muslims and Arabs, this does not mean that they are in any way superior to these groups.

11. This is a variation of a phrase used by California's first congressman from India, Dalip Singh Saund, who said, "I don't care what a man has on top of his head. All I'm interested in is what he's got inside of it." See Roopinder Singh, Remembering the US Congressman from India. *The Tribune India*, Jan. 12, 2002.

12. Lisa Beyer, "Osama Bin Laden: The face of terror," *Time*, Sept. 24, 2001, 52–59.

REFERENCES

Agarwal, Priya. 1991. Passage from India: Post–1965 Indian immigrants and their children. Palos Verdes, Calif.: Yuvati.

Bergmann, Jörg R. 1998. Introduction: Morality in discourse. *Research on Language and Social Interaction* 31:279–294.

Bhabha, Homi K. 1994. *The location of culture*. New York: Routledge.

Biernat, Monica, and John. F. Dovidio. 2000. Stigma and stereotypes. In *The social psychology of stigma*, ed. Todd F. Heatherton, Robert E. Kleck, Michelle R. Hebl, and Jay G. Hull, 88–113. New York: The Guilford Press.

Brubaker, Rogers. 2002. Ethnicity without groups. *Archive Européennes de Sociologie* 43:163–189.

Bucholtz, Mary, and Kira Hall. 2004. Language and identity. In *A companion to linguistic anthropology*, ed. Alessandro Duranti, 369–394. Malden, Mass.: Blackwell.

Davies, Bronwyn, and Rom Harré. 1990. Positioning: The discursive production of selves. *Journal for the Theory of Social Behaviour* 20:43–63.

Du Bois, W. E. B. 1903. *The souls of black folk: Essays and sketches*. Chicago: A. C. McClurg & Co.

Duranti, Alessandro. 2004. Agency in language. In *A companion to linguistic anthropology*, ed. Alessandro Duranti, 451–473. Malden, Mass.: Blackwell.

Dusenbery, Verne A. 1996. Socializing Sikhs in Singapore: Soliciting the state's support. In *The transmission of Sikh heritage in the diaspora*, ed. Pashaura Singh and N. Gerald Barrier, 113–148. New Delhi: Manohar.

Foucault, Michel. 1977. *Discipline and punish: The birth of the prison*. New York: Vintage Books.

Gibson, Margaret. 1988. *Accommodation without assimilation: Sikh immigrants in an American school*. Ithaca, N.Y.: Cornell University Press.

Goffman, Erving. 1967. *Interaction ritual: Essays on face-to-face behavior*. Chicago: Aldine.

———. 1971. *Relations in public: Microstudies of the public order*. New York: Basic Books.

Goodwin, Charles. 1994. Professional vision. *American Anthropologist* 96:606–633.

Grewal, J. S. 1999. Nabha's *Ham Hindu Nahin*: A declaration of Sikh ethnicity. In *Sikh identity: Continuity and change*, ed. Pashaura Singh and N. Gerald Barrier, 231–254. New Delhi: Manohar.

Hall, Kathleen D. 2002. *Lives in translation: Sikh youth as British citizens*. Philadelphia: University of Pennsylvania Press.

Hall, Stuart. 1996. Introduction. In *Questions of cultural identity*, ed. Stuart Hall and Paul Du Gay, 1–17. London: Sage Publications.

Jefferson, Gail. 1984. On the organization of laughter in talk about troubles. In *Structures of social action: Studies in conversation analysis*, ed. J. Maxwell Atkinson and John Heritage, 346–369. Cambridge: Cambridge University Press.

Lal, Bhai Harbans. 1999. Sahajdharai Sikhs: Their origin and current status within the Panth. In *Sikh identity: Continuity and change*, ed. Pashaura Singh and N. Gerald Barrier, 109–126. New Delhi: Manohar.

Leonard, Karen. I. 1992. *Making ethnic choices: California's Punjabi Mexican Americans*. Philadelphia: Temple University Press.

———. 1997. *South Asian Americans*. Westport, Conn.: Greenwood Press.

Lessinger, Johanna. 1995. *From the Ganges to the Hudson: Indian immigrants in New York City*. Needham Heights, Mass.: Allyn and Bacon.

Levy, Robert I., and Douglas W. Hollan. 1998. Person-centered interviewing and observation in anthropology. In *Handbook of research methods in anthropology*, ed. H. Russell Bernard, 333–364. Walnut Creek, Calif.: Altamira Press.

Maira, Sunaina M. 2002. *Desis in the house: Indian American youth culture in New York City*. Philadelphia: Temple University Press.

McLeod, W. H. 1999. The turban: Symbol of Sikh identity. In *Sikh identity: Continuity and change*, ed. Pashaura Singh and N. Gerald Barrier, 57–68. New Delhi: Manohar.

———. 2000. *Exploring Sikhism: Aspects of Sikh identity, culture, and thought*. Oxford: Oxford University Press.

Mead, George H. 1934. *Mind, self, and society from the standpoint of a social behaviorist*, ed. Charles W. Morris. Chicago: University of Chicago Press.

Oberoi, Harjot S. 1994. *The construction of religious boundaries: Culture, identity and diversity in the Sikh tradition*. Chicago: University of Chicago Press.

Ochs, Elinor. 1990. Indexicality and socialization. In *Cultural psychology: Essays on comparative human development*, ed. James W. Stigler, Robert A. Shweder, and Gilbert Herdt, 287–308. New York: Cambridge University Press.

Ochs, Elinor, and Lisa Capps. 2001. *Living narrative*. Cambridge, Mass.: Harvard University Press.

Prashad, Vijay. 2000. *The karma of brown folk*. Minneapolis: University of Minnesota Press.

Radhakrishnan, R. 1996. *Diasporic meditations: Between home and location*. Minneapolis: University of Minnesota Press.

Reyes, Angela, and Adrienne Lo. 2004. Language, identity and relationality in Asian Pacific America: An introduction. In *Pragmatics*, ed. Adrienne Lo and Angela Reyes, 14:115–125.

Sacks, Harvey 1992. *Lectures on conversation*, ed. Gail Jefferson. Oxford: Blackwell.

Sacks, Harvey, Emanuel A. Schegloff, and Gail Jefferson. 1974. A simplest systematics for the organization of turn-taking for conversation. *Language* 50, 696–735.

Sartre, Jean Paul. 1956. *Being and nothingness: An essay on phenomenological ontology*. New York: Philosophical Library.

Silverstein, Michael. 1976. Shifters, linguistic categories, and cultural description. In *Meaning in anthropology*, ed. Keith Basso and Henry Selby, 11–55. Albuquerque: University of New Mexico Press.

Tatla, Darshan Singh. 1999. *The Sikh diaspora: The search for statehood*. Seattle: University of Washington Press.

Taylor, Charles. 1989. *Sources of the self: The making of the modern identity*. Cambridge, Mass.: Harvard University Press.

8

Constructing Ethnic Identity through Discourse

Self-Categorization among Korean American Camp Counselors

M. Agnes Kang

Recent discussions in the field of discourse analysis have posed the question of whether and when issues of demography or identity become relevant in discourse when not referred to specifically in talk. In a published debate on this issue of "context,"[1] Emanuel A. Schegloff, Margaret Wetherell, and Michael Billig present various perspectives on this issue, using approaches ranging from conversation analysis to critical discourse analysis. One of the main issues discussed in the series of chapters centered on Schegloff's (1997) claim that gender relevance in interaction has to be evidenced by participants' orientations in the talk itself. This claim met with criticism from scholars who found the interpretative limitation too rigid for the study of language and gender. While this theoretical debate continues, with strong advocates on both sides of the issue, situations in which talk *is* focused around identity are also relevant to the notion of context and how speakers create it. After all, what happens when participants *do* talk about identities in discourse? And are there relevant observations to be made beyond the mere topic of discussion when it comes to how such identities are expressed?

In this chapter, I examine the connection between relevant identities (in particular, ethnic identity), the articulation of these identities through discourse, and the ideologies indexed (in the sense of Ochs 1992) by these identities in the interactions of Korean American camp counselors. In particular, I show that a discourse approach to how identities are established and maintained can provide insight into how speakers construct ethnic identity in interaction. In examining ethnic identity, I am not concerned with the participants' cultural heritage, or the fact that all the participants discussed in this chapter are ethnically Korean, but rather in how they identify themselves, or self-categorize, in the course of a discussion in such a way that makes ethnic identity relevant to the interaction. I use *ethnic identity* here to denote a positioning on the part of a speaker within the ethnic category of "Korean." In Richard Jenkins's (1994) terms, I make a distinction between *ethnic category*, or the identity assigned to a group by others, and *ethnic group*, which is an identity established from within. Using this distinction, I hope to show that a more dynamic model of identity formation is needed to address the interactional processes at work in the data analyzed here. Stephen Cornell and Douglas Hartmann (1998, 20–21) discuss the process by which an ethnic group comes into being: "A population or social collectivity may be simply an ethnic category, assigned an ethnic identity by outsiders. Once that identity becomes subjective—that is, once that population sees itself in ethnic terms, perhaps in response to the identity outsiders assign to it—it becomes an ethnic group."

This distinction between ethnic category and ethnic group is useful in articulating the subtle meanings behind the labels "Korean" and "Korean American," among others. In another paper, M. Agnes Kang and Adrienne Lo (2004) discuss the inconsistencies in usage of these ethnic terms among speakers. We found that merely tracing the use of terms like "Korean," "Korean American," or "American" is futile without an attempt at understanding what range of meanings speakers associate with these terms. On one level, the participants of the Korean camp itself, as a recognizable institutional body, may be described as an ethnic category. When the members start to see themselves in terms of ethnicity (as "Korean" counselors or "Korean American" counselors), this is how they constitute their ethnic group. Because subjectivities are expressed variably in discourse, we can trace how different counselors constitute their ethnic identities, or create "ethnic groups," in different ways. In the process of becoming an ethnic group, articulating a Korean identity involves a subjectivity that is accomplished differently by different individuals.

The question of whether there is, in fact, a unified Korean identity established among these participants is also one that will be addressed. In terms of social categories such as "Korean" or "Korean American," what these categories represent is dependent on the particular context and what they are locally opposed to. In this sense, discourse creates, establishes, and transforms boundaries that foreground and background what we think of as our identity (Barth 1969). In the data analyzed here, I demonstrate how participants make ethnic identity relevant to the discussion of the Korean camp through the act of self-categorization. Such an association represents a very distinct kind of identity discourse than what one might find in a different context. The importance of analyzing identity in the local context of specific acts and stances is further explored by Agnes Weiyun He (this volume) with regard to roles and identities in the heritage language classroom. In both contexts, identities are constructed by particular acts and stances that are indexed through specific linguistic practices. Given that the present analysis adopts a modified constructionist approach to the notion of identity, the accomplishment of ethnic identity is located in the discursive performance of this identity; that is, speakers construct, modify, transform, and differentiate identities through the use of language.

Data

The data for this study come from a larger corpus of video data comprising more than eleven hours of meeting interactions that were collected by the author as a participant observer during the summer of 1996. The participants consist of over thirty volunteer camp counselors of a Korean cultural camp in the Bay Area of Northern California (which I will call Camp HPH). During meetings throughout the summer, these ethnically Korean counselors, ranging in age from seventeen to twenty-five, planned and prepared camp activities for more than 100 campers. The meetings were frequent, and the main language used was English. Discussions sometimes centered on ethnic identity issues, especially Korean identity, since the cultural camp offered classes on Korean language, etiquette, and folk music, among others. But when the discussion turned to the purpose or goal of the camp and the counselors' motivations for participating in the camp, issues of ethnic identity were made relevant in a more poignant way that served to establish, challenge, and transform notions of a shared ethnic identity.

In one particularly long and emotionally charged meeting of a diverse group of 1st-, 2nd- and 1.5-generation camp counselors, counselors discuss and debate the goals of the Korean camp, and, by extension, the reasons why each counselor has volunteered to participate. Some counselors seek to share their experiences as Korean Americans with the campers. Many of them have highly individual, personal experiences growing up Korean in American society that they feel they can share with the younger campers. Another strong motivation is the teaching of Korean culture, which is something the camp can provide that is not available in the campers' regular schools. The perceived choice between "heritage" and "mentorship" as the main motivation for participating in the camp is cast as a source of tension that gets mapped onto ideologies of ethnic identity in the course of the meeting. The counselors, through their discursive practices, associate certain motivations, like the emphasis on teaching Korean culture, with notions of being "more Korean" and the emphasis on mentorship with being "more American." The subtle ways in which speakers indexically link ideologies regarding the camp to ethnic identity demonstrate that "being Korean" is anything but stable, homogenous, or fixed.

In a similar study of the later generations of an immigrant community, Anny Bakalian (1993) examines the reconstruction of Armenian American identity. She traces the process from what she calls "being" Armenian to "feeling" Armenian. "Being" Armenian refers to such qualities as sharing a unique language, lifestyle, an identifiable Armenian culture, and Armenian social networks. In contrast, "feeling" Armenian does not necessarily entail any of the above, but rather centers on pride in one's heritage and a strong sense of "peoplehood" (Bakalian 1993, 6). This distinction between "being" and "feeling" may be helpful in thinking about the counselors participating in the Korean camp. The essential aspects of "being" Korean are clearly emphasized at the camp itself, which is evident in the classes taught and the goals of the camp as an institution. However, it is clear that counselors are also orienting to the condition of "feeling" Korean in the way they articulate their own personal goals and motivations. This split in how counselors talk about the experience of identity may also point to the difference between "ethnic category" and "ethnic group" discussed above and suggest ways in which ethnic group formation takes place as discursive performance.

Ideologies of "Korean" Identity

Ideologies of a Shared "Korean" Identity

When considering that this Korean camp is an organization based on the common ethnic background of its participants (all campers and counselors are ethnically Korean), one may ask why counselors may feel the need to self-categorize in terms of ethnicity in an organization that assumes a certain degree of ethnic unity. Part of the reason may lie in the strong ideology of a shared Korean identity that is prevalent in the organization. The idea of a Korean summer camp in itself assumes certain notions about the existence of a "Korean identity." Camp HPH started in the mid-1980s, responding to the lack of resources and opportunities for Korean youth in the area to gather with other Korean youth and learn about Korean history, culture, traditions, and experiences. According to a pamphlet distributed during the counselor meetings, the camp has the following objectives:

- Promotion of a better understanding and awareness of Korean cultural heritage, tradition, and history
- Sharing our bi-cultural experiences and expectations as Korean-Americans with our campers
- Providing an opportunity for campers to get together with other young Korean-Americans like themselves, and experience group activities and responsibilities
- Providing guidance for those in need of strength and encouragement in various individual struggles
- Development of friendship, unity, and pride in being Korean-American
- Have a fun and meaningful time!

The promotion of Korean cultural heritage is one of the primary goals, but the objectives also include reference to a "Korean American" experience and pride. The goals of the camp are also discussed by the camp director, Mark, who points out that Korean children who grow up in "this quote unquote American culture" don't have the opportunity to learn about Korean culture or to see how other Korean people treat one another or to see a Korean cultural performance (see transcript in excerpt 4 below). There is an implicit ideology that all counselors should have the same goals in participating in the camp, just as all counselors, deep down, "should" have a shared sense of ethnic identity. This implicit ideology is apparent in the explicit challenges to these ideas that come up in the course of the meeting. It is apparent that some counselors do not share the view that counselors' motivations should be "the same" or that all counselors share a similar sense of being (or "feeling") "Korean." The resistance to this ideology of "Korean" identity may provide one reason why counselors feel the need to self-categorize in terms of distinct ethnic groups when among a group of counselors of the same heritage or ethnic category.

The specific goals and intentions of the camp become a focus of discussion at some point in the counselors' meeting, and the acceptance of such goals among the participants comes into question when counselors begin to challenge how Korean identity should be presented and taught at the camp. This debate seems to bring to light the diversity within Korean identity that counselors feel should be a part of the preparation and the execution of the camp itself. Even though the sharing of Korean American experience is explicitly stated as one of the objectives of the camp, counselors clearly orient to the teaching of Korean heritage as the perceived primary objective. Among the ways in which the diversity within the counselors is articulated is through the use of "Korean" not as an inclusive term for all the counselors (e.g., as a hypernym or a superordinate category term) but as a term used in opposition with other terms, like "Korean American" or even "American." The expression of ethnic identity by certain counselors serves to counter notions of a shared cultural heritage and index a distinct perspective on the nature of the Korean camp.

Heterogeneous Ideologies: "Heritage" versus "Mentorship"

In the context of these counselor meetings, the term "Korean" acquires a very specific meaning through the practice of self-categorization. These labels of self-classification occur in the course of discussions regarding the reasons for coming and "doing" the camp. While some may be focused on passing on Korean culture and traditions or instilling a sense of Korean pride, others are more interested in sharing their experiences as Korean Americans growing up in American society. Social issues like dealing with one's immigrant parents, interracial dating, and developing one's sense of ethnic identity while growing up among European Americans, among others, motivate some counselors to take part in the youth camp. In the interactions discussed below, the counselors perform their own expressions of ethnic identity by evoking these kinds of oppositions and making associations between their beliefs about what a Korean camp should be and their own sense of ethnic identity. In this way, their views on the camp become a kind of shorthand for the expression of ethnic identity for these counselors, who come to position themselves in the terms of these interactionally specific roles and identities.

For the counselors there are very practical consequences for the associations that are made between social categories of counselors and the goals of the camp itself. Because there are more counselors than spots available at the camp, the camp director must decide who can attend the camp. Some potentially good counselors have had to be cut from the roster, and there has been some criticism over the selection process since many "Korean American" counselors have been let go in favor of some "Korean" counselors who are able to teach Korean culture courses, such as Korean language, etiquette, and folk music. Many of these "Korean" counselors are instructors at the Korean Cultural Center (or KCC) and are also present at the meeting analyzed here. Thus the disagreement as to the main focus of the camp has potentially serious repercussions for how certain decisions are made. Some of the self-designated "more American" counselors clearly feel that Korean American campers need mentors who are able to help them with their identity issues more than they need classes on Korean etiquette. This ideological stance poses problems for the director, who is charged with putting on a cultural camp with all its amenities, while, at the same time, faced with a growing number of eager counselors who may not have this kind of cultural knowledge to pass on to young campers.

Counselors' discussions of the main goal of the camp must be analyzed in light of the very real consequences of such discussions. In particular, counselors who resist classification as "Korean" counselors use the practice of self-categorization to accomplish various acts: (1) to show their resistance to the ideology of an underlying homogeneous "Korean" identity, (2) to stress their own reasons for participating in the camp, which favors "mentorship" over "heritage" as the main goal of the camp, and (3) to suggest that the explicit sharing of individual goals during the course of the counselors' meetings is necessary to the preparation for the camp. The accomplishment of these acts can be seen in the local discursive practices of the counselors who use self-categorization in terms of ethnic identity as a means of classifying themselves as to the kind of counselor they are and the goals they espouse for the camp. In these interactions, the ethnic identity associated with "Korean Americans" or "Americans" (in this particular context) acquires the local meaning of being linked to the importance of mentorship, resisting the perceived alternative choice of "Korean" identity and the associated "heritage" goals of the camp. While Mary Bucholtz (this volume) examines how speakers may use linguistic style as a tool to claim or repudiate a certain identity through "identity performance," the indexical link between linguistic practices and ideological stances and acts that speakers construct may also fall into this category of identity performance. These associations are established, recognized, and used further by participants who come to understand how such associations contribute to the reconstruction of identity through locally accomplished means.

Ethnic Identity through Self-Categorization

In the course of the meeting, several topics were discussed and debated. But one particularly clear structure that emerged from the interaction was the use of self-categorization. Self-categorization in terms of ethnic identity occurred when new speakers expressed a view about the goals of the camp and/or their own motivations for participating in the camp. These views were also often accompanied by statements of individual identity that were used to somehow explain or support their views about the camp and why counselors should participate. Sometimes speakers used specific labels to identify themselves (e.g., "Korean American" or "American") and sometimes they didn't. Although the speakers do not always use these explicit ethnic labels, they do demonstrate that they feel a need to locate themselves in terms of ethnic identity in order to take part in the discussion at hand. Candace West and Sarah Fenstermaker (2002), in a study of a University of California Regents meeting that ended affirmative action policies at the university, use the term "self-categorization" to describe the specification of race category, or race category and sex category, memberships. In their study, they found that speakers identified themselves in terms of gender, race, and social class as a way of seeing themselves as *accountable* (in the sense of Heritage 1984) for their remarks in terms of these category memberships. By introducing oneself as a "woman," or "an African American," a speaker draws attention to her category membership as a means of interpreting her remarks. The camp counselors in the present study similarly used self-categorization as a means of making relational ethnic identities relevant to the discussion of the Korean camp. While these meetings were not as formal or public as the UC Regents meeting, participants still engaged in locational work to situate themselves in the debate regarding the camp's goals and the counselors' motivations.

In the present study, self-categorization is done to specify one's ethnic affiliation. Given that all participants are ethnically Korean, this makes the practice of self-categorization even more interesting. Participants are clearly not stating a fact of heritage, but rather positioning themselves relationally within a field of oppositions that they themselves structure and define. Because the discussion takes place among participants of the same heritage, the relevant oppositions may not be at first obvious. What is interesting to note, however, is that the field of oppositions varies from speaker to speaker, and part of establishing one's "category" involves "laying out" one's specific field of oppositions within which one identifies oneself. While the main debate revolves around the reason for holding this camp, counselors cast their opinions in ethnic identity terms and make the declaration of one's own identity contingent to one's argument; or as West and Fenstermaker might state, counselors are held accountable for their views in terms of their ethnic identity. Consequently, the ideologies regarding the goals of the camp compel one to position oneself in terms of ethnic identity (i.e., how "Korean," "Korean American," or "American" one defines oneself as). In other words, one's motivations for participating in the camp become salient as markers or identifiers of ethnic identity: The reasons for participating, and, by extension, the understanding of the ultimate "goals" of the camp become a touchstone by which one self-categorizes, not just as a counselor, but as a Korean.

In excerpt 1,[2] Ellen self-categorizes as "American," but not without the use of repair and qualifications, demonstrating how contested these identities are. She also lodges a complaint that the counselors have not yet discussed their own ideas about the camp and why they are there, illustrating the importance of explicitly sharing one's identity within the group. Before doing this, however, she explicitly lays out a tripartite field of oppositions using a pronounced list intonation in line 80 within which she later positions herself.

(1) "*Oppa Enni*" 'older brother older sister' [Mentor5; 3:59:87–05:05:00]

69	Ellen:	I have a similar story to Sara why I kept coming to camp and why I always
70		come,
71		you know?
72		and like,
73		I had the exact same revelation she did cause I grew up with a
74		white..crowd,
75		right?
76		**And I think,**
77		**every year that we have like–**
78		**every year that we have camp,**
79		**there's always conflict in what the emphasis is gonna be,**

80	**more Korean, more Korean American, more American,**
81	**you know?**
82	And everyone comes with different ideas,
83	right?
84	And like,
85	right now,
86	I disagree with the *oppa enni*,
87	and I can hang with that,
88	just,
89	you know,
90	whatever,
91	and I'll do it?
92	but it's like,
93	I think we all have different ideas,
94	you know?
95	And like,
96	as she said,
97	no one's discussed the ideas?
98	but it just comes out with our opinions?
99	when we argue like this?
100	you know?
101	and it didn't just come out,
102	we didn't like lay out
103	like,
104	exactly what we're here for.
105	**..And I'm here..more on maybe the American side,**
106	**not American side,**
107	**but more of like a different- a different angle than some other people**
108	**come here for,**
109	you know?
110	And I think that,
111	..that doesn't show unless we argue about like this,
112	but we never..just flat out said,
113	<Q I'm here because,
114	this is what happened to me Q> as she just did right now.

Counselors' self-categorizations typically occur: (1) after laying out a field of oppositions within which they can then situate themselves, and (2) when expressing a view about the goals of the camp and/or their own motivations for participating in the camp. The relevant field of oppositions is given in lines 76–81. While Ellen could have argued that merely stating opinions will only lead to arguments, as she says in lines 93–104, as a means of supporting her point that counselors' ideas about the camp need to be brought out and discussed, she approaches the issue by situating herself in terms of ethnic identity. Ellen aligns herself with "the American side" in lines 105–108, but uses hedges ("maybe"), repair ("I'm here…more on"), and other qualifications ("not American side, / but more of like a different…"). Clearly,

the category of "American" is not a straightforward one and requires some explanation. In the process of trying to distinguish herself from the category of "Korean"
counselor, Ellen struggles to construct a category of "American" that diverges from
a homogeneous "Korean" identity while still including herself as part of the group.
What much of the counselors' talk shows is that not everyone is in agreement as to
the meaning of "Korean" identity and how this concept should be presented at the
camp itself. Ellen's insistence that everyone comes with different ideas (lines 82 and 93)
and with differing perspectives on the need to discuss what these ideas are challenges
the notion that putting on a Korean camp should be straightforward or that everyone
who is ethnically Korean must share the same ideas about identity.

Ellen's talk also explicitly articulates an ideology that says that counselors should
be actively locating themselves and self-categorizing. In lines 69–74, she aligns herself
with another counselor, Sara, who has just shared her story about how she came to
understand her Korean identity after growing up among European American peers.
She then goes on to describe qualities of the camp in lines 76–83, which may at first
seem to be a departure from her previous comments. When she comes to her complaint
that counselors have not discussed their ideas, she returns to self-categorization in lines
105–108, suggesting that her self-classification as "more on maybe the American side"
can serve as an explanation or justification for her views about participating in the camp.

Ellen's talk shows how claiming a "more American" relational identity can also
mean rejecting Korean modes of interaction that embrace social hierarchies, like showing respect for elders through the use of the kinship terms *oppa* 'older brother' and
enni 'older sister.' This linguistic practice is one that is taught at the camp as a part of
learning Korean culture and heritage. By mentioning specifically the practice of using
kinship terms, Ellen also associates a linguistic practice to ideologies of social interaction and hierarchies that she herself does not espouse. For Ellen, being "American" in
this particular context means repudiating Korean culture (here, specifically, in the form
of the use of kinship terms) as her primary emphasis in participating in the camp.

Self-Categorization: "Korean" versus "Korean American" Motivations

Some counselors are even more explicit about the association between ethnic identity
and ideologies about the camp. For Jeff, his reasons for participating in the camp
have to do with being "Korean American" and this self-categorization is used to
explain his motivations for going to the camp.

(2) "Why I am at camp" [Mentor8; 00:20:81–01:42:64]

2	Jeff:	I just want to say,
3		a couple of things,
4		first,
5		you know,
6		why I am at camp.
7		…Um,

8	....to be quite..blunt about it,
9	or,
10	to be quite,
11	you know,
12	simple as can be,
13	I just love kids,
14	and um,
15	..I just wanna,
16	you know,
17	give..what I have..to the kids.
18	I mean um,
19	I think maybe H- HPH's,
20	you know,
21	quote unquote mission statement,
22	I guess is to,
23	spread Korean pride to these kids or–
24	or to,
25	you know,
26	make sure we have these performances,
27	so on and so forth,
28	t- to experience,
29	so the kids can experience Korean things that they haven't experienced
30	before.
31	**..My intentions are–**
32	**are very different.**
33	**Um,**
34	**I think that ma–**
35	**you know,**
36	**by me being there,**
37	**being as a mentor,**
38	**as a Korean American,**
39	**maybe I can instill that pride,**
40	**but my basically- basic intention is just to..be there for them,**
41	**you know,**

Like Ellen in excerpt 1 above, Jeff categorizes himself negatively by declaring himself in terms of what he is not. In stating his reasons for going to the camp, Jeff explicitly denies that the spread of Korean pride or providing experiences of things Korean are his priorities. Instead, he places the mentorship of kids and "just to be there for them" as the main reasons for going to the camp. Here Jeff explicitly classifies himself within the category of "Korean American" in line 38 in opposition to the category of "Korean," which acquires a very specific local meaning of being linked to "pride," "performances," and other "things" "Korean." Jeff's use of the term "Korean American" allows him to distinguish himself from those who would be concerned with spreading Korean pride while positioning himself as a Korean American counselor whose main goal is to serve as a mentor to the campers. The form of his self-categorization reinforces this association between identity and ideology. While his ethnic identity is expressed in line 38 with "as a Korean American," the same phrase, "as an X," is used in the previous line to express his motivation for participating in the camp. In this way, he sets up an explicit link between ethnic identity and ideologies about the camp. Those who see their role as "Korean" counselors are associated with Korean heritage and pride; those who see their role as "Korean American" counselors are associated with the role of a mentor. These are locally defined terms that Jeff lays out, and his self-categorization differs somewhat from Ellen's in excerpt 1. While Ellen defines a tripartite field of oppositions, Jeff assumes an implicit and somewhat binary opposition between "Korean" and "Korean American" identities.

Not all cases of self-categorization are so explicit, however. Jon, like Jeff, places the ideology of mentorship in opposition to the teaching of Korean culture as the main reason why he is going to the camp. He argues that being a member of the Korean Cultural Center (or KCC) shouldn't automatically entitle one to participate in the camp. While he doesn't explicitly identify himself in terms of ethnic identity, like Ellen and Jeff above, Jon does classify himself in terms of what he "knows" in lines 7–16 as a means of understanding his position that mentorship should take precedence over the teaching of Korean culture, and thereby indexing what Jeff would call "Korean American" identity.

(3) "I don't know anything about the KOREAN CULTURE" [Mentor9; 04:43:04–05:36:57]

1	Jon:	You got to be able to understand what this kid wants.
2		What he needs from you.
3		What she needs from you.
4		And if you can't do that,
5		you shouldn't be at the camp.
6		I don't want KCC to take this personally either but,
7		**I don't know how to play the drums,**
8		**but I can play the drums?**
9		**you know?**
10		**I don't know anything about uh uh..the KOREAN CULTURE,**
11		**those traditions and etiquettes,**
12		**but I think I know something about kids.**
13		**I think I know what they need.**
14		**Because I've BEEN there.**
15		**Had those experiences.**
16		**And I can talk to them.**
17		And tha- that's just a- that's just a matter of information.
18		What those things are offering.
19		That's–
20		that's,
21		you know,
22		that's- that's just,
23		you know,

24   a matter of information.
25   If I went to KCC,
26   I could learn the drums.
27   And then I would have that as a resource.
28   That doesn't mean no one else just because they don't know the drums,
29   or they can't speak Korean,
30   or they don't speak English,
31   shouldn't go to camp.
32   You see what I'm saying?

While Jon recognizes that teaching drums is linked to being "Korean," he challenges this association by suggesting that he himself (someone who can't play traditional Korean drums) could go to the cultural center and learn to play. He questions
why this practice must be linked to only one ethnic identity while at the same time
confirming that such an association does in fact exist. He does this by taking a discussion that could have remained general, as it starts off being in lines 1–5, and making it
more personal by introducing his own self-classification as relevant to the discussion.
In doing so, Jon also reiterates the association made by Jeff above between ethnic
identity and ideologies about the goals of the camp. While he does not self-categorize
explicitly in terms of ethnic identity, in the local context, his statement, "I don't know
anything about Korean culture," is understood as performatively equivalent to aligning himself with the Korean Americans. This point illustrates that self-categorization
does not need to be in the explicit form of self-categorization statements in order to be
locally recognized as doing self-categorization, lending more support to the position
that relevance in interaction does not always need to be evidenced explicitly.

What is important to note is that there is no explicit discussion that addresses the
possibility of a "Korean" counselor positioning himself or herself as a mentor. In fact,
all the counselors who self-categorize in the course of this meeting emphasize mentorship and a less "Korean" ethnic identity, which may indicate that the very practice
of self-categorization is perhaps culturally specific. The relatively small group of
counselors who are from KCC and who are able to teach Korean cultural heritage,
for whatever reason, do not participate actively in the discussion, and it is difficult to
glean whether their own self-categorizations would fall in line with particular ideas
about the camp. What this suggests is that, right or not, some counselors conceive of
the goals of the camp as an exclusive choice between emphasizing Korean heritage
and mentorship. And mentorship has been constructed as a value that is removed
from any sense of what Korean heritage is for these counselors. Their choices are
highly personal and often resonate with their own experiences of working through
ethnic identity issues. This has a strong influence on how they see their own roles
as counselors and mentors for the campers who will be attending the camp. In fact,
most of the discussion takes place among counselors who speak out to challenge the
notion of Korean heritage as primary to the camp, suggesting perhaps that the underlying assumption of the importance of Korean heritage does not require reiteration or
confirmation on the part of the counselors. It is only the contrary view, the view that
challenges the homogeneous notion of shared motivations, and by extension, shared
ethnic identity, that seems to require articulation.

Furthermore, there is a conceptualization that cultural heritage is something that is somewhat "transmittable": Culture can be learned in the sense that knowledge (e.g., Korean language, etiquette, customs, arts) can be passed from counselor to camper in the course of this camp. While some may believe this to be true, it is not a position that is ostensibly argued. Instead, the lack of discussion about this kind of understanding indicates that this is an underlying assumption, one that those who see other viable goals for the camp struggle to defy. These counselors are, overall, more vocal, and actively construct the un(der)stated assumption that Korean identity is linked merely to cultural heritage. For these counselors, their self-categorization often takes the oppositional form of "Some think X, I don't" (e.g., Jon in excerpt 3 above).

Counselors also see the practice of self-categorization as a means of explicitly sharing one's sense of identity, which in turn only benefits the counselors in the preparation for the camp. One counselor in particular (Sara) who feels that they have not discussed as a group why everyone is participating in the camp initiates the discussion at the start of this meeting. She finds this to be a sign of a lack of preparation and encourages others to share their "stories" (narratives of ethnic identity formation) and their own reasons for joining the camp. This suggestion is met with various responses, and is eventually implemented, but not without some resistance. Again, the most vocal members are those who seek to defy the understanding that counselors have a shared sense of ethnic identity and that cultural heritage should be a primary goal of the camp. It should be noted, too, that such a belief in the verbal expression of one's ideological positioning is not without cultural significance in itself.

Self-Categorization through the Use of Personal Pronouns

Not all counselors are set on differentiating themselves from a notion of a shared ethnic identity. The camp director, Mark, finds himself somewhat in the middle of this debate and tries what he can to "contain" the formulation of oppositions that may potentially divide the counselors. As director, he seeks to stress the unity among counselors and also defend his own actions (such as his decisions as to who would be cut from the counselor roster). His talk is characterized by a noticeable lack of self-categorization; in fact, Mark is very reluctant to create fields of oppositions, much less classify himself within these fields. He defends the view that the camp is about the teaching of Korean culture, which he opposes to a "quote unquote American culture" in excerpt 4, while at the same time emphasizing that Korean American motivations are equally important.

(4) "This quote unquote American culture" [Mentor3; 7:06:28–9:22:11]

391	Mark:	Uh,
392		lot of these kids that grew up in this uh,
393		this quote unquote American culture,
394		they don't necessarily see..certain aspects..of what Korean culture is
395		about.

396	And I'm not saying that this HPH is–
397	is,
398	uh,
399	uh totally Korean?
400	uh,
401	but that's,
402	I think,
403	what **we** strive to do?
404	For six days out of a year,
405	I think,
406	**we**'re there to,
407	not only interact with the kids but maybe,
408	provide them the opportunity for these kids to see,
409	how other..Korean Americans,
410	or how..uh Koreans?
411	**they** interact to each other–
412	how **they** treat each other?
413	Uh,
414	maybe get to take a look at a performance or a cultural event that they
415	never..had a chance to see?
416	Maybe learn about uh,
417	uh,
418	a Korean history that they never had a chance to learn in..history in their,
419	uh,
420	in their–
421	uh,
422	junior high,
423	in their high school?

Mark uses the term "Korean" in opposition to the "quote unquote American culture" in a way that suggests an opposition of identity. In doing so, he stresses the commonalities among the counselors present. Mark's opposition between "Korean" and "American" is based on the similarities that all campers and counselors share: the experience of growing up "Korean" within mainstream "American" society. His use of "Korean" here, unlike Ellen's, Jeff's, or Jon's above, is based on ancestry regardless of how one behaves or perceives of oneself. For Mark, all the counselors share a common heritage despite their individual reasons for participating in the camp.

Mark also chooses his words carefully to make a distinction between Korean Americans and Koreans, recognizing that some counselors would not consider themselves to be just "Korean." Throughout this excerpt, Mark makes oppositions in a very qualified way, making them and then instantly undercutting them, trying very hard not to create oppositions at all. In lines 396–399, for example, he emphasizes that Camp HPH is not "totally Korean" and then must struggle for the category he wishes to specify in lines 409–410, when talking about the way Koreans interact. He first uses "Korean American," perhaps trying to be more inclusive of those who may not consider themselves exclusively "Korean" in a cultural sense, but then self-repairs with the term "Korean," recognizing that what he really means is the codified social behavior that

Koreans engage in (referring to practices of addressing elders using special terms of address, for example) and not any kind of codified "Korean American" way of interacting. This again associates Korean culture with interactional practices like using kinship terms for older peers, as in excerpt 1 above. The hedging and repair that abound in excerpt 4 indicate the delicate locational work in which Mark engages. While Mark does his best to diffuse any negative opposition between "Korean" and "Korean American" counselors, he also consciously tries to avoid classifying himself in these terms.

His difficulties in articulating the precise social categories in talking about particular groups of people betray the numerous oppositions that can be made between "Korean," "American," and "Korean American." This is clearly seen in his use of personal pronouns. In the course of excerpt 4, Mark switches his use of pronouns, from "we" (referring to the counselors) in lines 403–406 to "they" (referring to "Koreans") in lines 411–412. In a study of national identity through discourse analysis, Ruth Wodak et al. (1999, 35) focuses on the linguistic strategies for constructing ethnicity, including the use of personal pronouns. The power of pronouns is also apparent in this excerpt as Mark encounters a discursive watershed where he must choose a pronoun to refer to the category of people who engage in a certain codified behavior. Whereas he had cast the counselors as part of one group in opposition to "Americans" earlier on, his mention of "Korean American" and "Korean" have introduced problematic categories that force him to choose whether or not to include himself in the category "Korean." By his use of "they" in lines 411–412, Mark constructs his own ethnic identity as "Korean American," perhaps in order to preserve a perceived shared status among the camp counselors. Soon after the end of excerpt 4, Mark returns to the use of "we" to refer to the camp counselors as a group and stress their unity. The use of personal pronouns in the heritage language classroom context is also examined in He's chapter (this volume) to show how "we"/"they" are used to stress unity between the teacher and the students of the Chinese Language School. Both the teacher in the classroom context and Mark in these data use this linguistic resource as a way of constructing a group identity.

Mark's delineation of the field of ethnic identities differs from Ellen's tripartite opposition in excerpt 1. His usage of the term "American," for example, has different connotations than Ellen's usage. He uses "American" in "this quote unquote American culture" as a means of showing how Koreans do not fit into a mainstream American culture, whereas Ellen suggests that counselors like her can also be "American." The different fields of oppositions that Mark and Ellen express illustrate that they are performing different kinds of ethnic identity in their discourse. While Mark contrasts "Koreans" with "Americans," counselors like Ellen express another kind of opposition that they see as relevant to the discussion, namely, the opposition between "Koreans" and "Korean Americans." This difference in oppositions, in addition to the actual performances of self-categorization, serves to index the diverse stances negotiated during this counselors' meeting.

Ethnic Identity and Local Meaning

While the counselors discussed above perform self-categorization in slightly different ways, I would argue that all of them do so as a means of situating themselves in terms of ethnic identity, and, by extension, as counselors who espouse a particular view of the Korean camp. The counselors accomplish this through different levels of explicitness. In a "scale of explicitness," Jeff and Ellen are perhaps the most explicit in their self-categorization as "American" and "Korean American," respectively. Jon positions himself more implicitly, using the locally accomplished association between mentorship and Korean American identity as a means of classifying himself. Because this association is accomplished in the discourse, Jon's self-categorization, though implicit, can clearly be understood as a case of identity performance. Mark is perhaps the most implicit in his self-categorization due to his interest in avoiding explicit oppositional categories in general.

The data analyzed above have shown that counselors participating in this Korean camp have diverse notions of ethnic identity that are performed discursively in interaction. While engaging in talk about the goals of the camp and the motivations for counselors to participate, these views become indexically linked to notions of ethnic identity to the extent that a "Korean American" counselor (as opposed to a "Korean" counselor) can be said to espouse particular beliefs about the goals of the camp and motivations for participating. The fact that the term "Korean" is used in such diverse ways and in opposition to various categories has shown that what the term "Korean" comes to mean can be very specific to the local context. The context in which linguistic practices become associated with particular acts and stances becomes a site for the construction of ideologies that contribute to the various meanings of "Korean." Through the practice of self-categorization, counselors locally construct a sense of ethnic identity that challenges notions of homogeneity within an ethnic category.

An earlier version of this chapter was presented at the 2002 American Anthropological Association Annual Meeting in a panel titled "Rethinking the 'Speech Community' Within and Beyond Asian America," organized by Angela Reyes and Adrienne Lo. I am grateful to Angela, Adrienne, and fellow panelist Elaine Chun for the opportunity to take part in this panel and for their insightful comments on earlier drafts of this chapter.

NOTES

1. Schegloff's article appears in *Discourse and Society* 8. Wetherall's and Billig's articles appear in *Discourse and Society* 9 and 10, respectively, along with responses to these articles by Schegloff.

2. All excerpts are transcribed using the transcription conventions described in John W. Du Bois et al. (1993). Conventions used in the transcripts here include:

Intonation unit	{carriage return}
Truncated intonation unit	–
Truncated word	-
Speaker identity/turn start	:
Rising intonation	?
Continuing intonation	,
Falling intonation	.
Pause (short)	..
Pause (medium)	...
Quotation quality	<Q Q>

Other modified conventions used are:

Speaker emphasis   ALL CAPS
Research emphasis   **bold**

REFERENCES

Bakalian, Anny. 1993. *Armenian-Americans: From being to feeling Armenian*. New Brunswick, N.J.: Transaction.

Barth, Fredrik. 1969. Introduction. In *Ethnic groups and boundaries: The social organization of culture difference*, ed. Frederik Barth, 9–38. Boston: Little, Brown.

Cornell, Stephen, and Douglas Hartmann. 1998. *Ethnicity and race: Making identities in a changing world*. Thousand Oaks, Calif.: Pine Forge Press.

Du Bois, John W., Stephan Schuetze-Coburn, Susanna Cumming, and Danae Paolino. 1993. Outline of discourse transcription. In *Talking data: Transcription and coding in discourse research*, ed. Jane A. Edwards and Martin D. Lampert, 45–90. Hillsdale, N.J.: Lawrence Erlbaum.

Heritage, John. 1984. *Garfinkel and ethnomethodology*. Cambridge: Polity Press.

Jenkins, Richard. 1994. Rethinking ethnicity: Identity, categorization and power. *Ethnic and Racial Studies* 17:197–223.

Kang, M. Agnes, and Adrienne Lo. 2004. Two ways of articulating heterogeneity in Korean American narratives of ethnic identity. *Journal of Asian American Studies* 7:93–116.

Ochs, Elinor. 1992. Indexing gender. In *Rethinking context: Language as an interactive phenomenon*, ed. Alessandro Duranti and Charles Goodwin, 335–359. Cambridge: Cambridge University Press.

Schegloff, Emanuel A. 1997. Whose text? Whose context? *Discourse and Society* 8:165–187.

West, Candace, and Sarah Fenstermaker. 2002. Accountability in action: The accomplishment of gender, race and class in a meeting of the University of California Board of Regents. *Discourse and Society* 13:537–563.

Wodak, Ruth, Rudolf De Cillia, Martin Reisigl, and Karin Liebhart. 1999. *The discursive construction of national identity*, trans. Angelika Hirsch and Richard Mitten. Edinburgh: Edinburgh University Press.

9

Who Is "Japanese" in Hawai'i?

The Discursive Construction of Ethnic Identity

Asuka Suzuki

Who Is "Japanese" in Hawai'i?

We generally rely on categories when referring to a group of people. This is also the case when we talk about the Japanese. The question under consideration in this chapter is how reference to the Japanese in Hawai'i can be understood. According to the U.S. Census Bureau (2000), approximately 17 percent of the total population of Hawai'i is Japanese. At the same time, about 26 percent of the total visitors to Hawai'i are also reported to be Japanese (Hawaii State Department of Business, Economic Development and Tourism 2000).

The category of *Japanese* further comprises multiple categories. For instance, the first group of Japanese immigrants to Hawai'i who arrived around the late 1800s as part of the plantation labor force is often referred to as *Issei* (first-generation Japanese Americans). Their children are subsequently labeled as *Nisei* (second), *Sansei* (third), and *Yonsei* (fourth-generation Japanese Americans).[1] Japanese immigrants who moved to the United States after World War II are often referred to as *Shin Issei* (new Issei).[2] *Okinawan* and *Uchinanchu*[3] are also terms used to refer to persons who originally emigrated from Okinawa, a chain of islands located in the south of Japan. In Hawai'i, people in these categories can also be referred to as *Local* or *Local Japanese*.[4]

Yet how do we know that the meaning of these categories is shared? How are these categories actually being used by members? These questions have seldom been raised in previous work on Japanese American identity, which has been predominantly conducted in the fields of sociology and psychology. Previous research has often treated terms like *Issei* and *Nisei* as descriptors of demographic categories and used them as variables to investigate Japanese American identity (e.g., Johnson 1976; Kendis 1989; Matsumoto et al. 1973; Montero 1980; Stephan 1991, 1992; Stephan and Stephan 1989). Such investigations are often based on the premise that the meaning of these categories is a priori shared between participants and analysts, treating the meaning of each category as stable and clearly delineated. They seldom take into account how the meaning of each category might be emergent and publicly observable in the course of social interaction. Moreover, the relevance of Japanese American identity has often been presupposed; whether it is in effect relevant to the participants has not yet been considered or investigated in its own right.

Discursive Approaches to Categories

In contrast, discursive work on categories (e.g., within the fields of linguistic anthropology, ethnomethodology, and conversation analysis) posits that the meaning of categories is not inherent in the categories themselves, but rather emergent through the ways in which the categories are used (e.g., Hester and Eglin 1997; Sacks 1979). Moreover, in order to understand what particular categories mean to members of a particular social group, it is necessary to understand how the members display to one another what particular categories mean—a phenomenon referred to as intersubjectivity. An analysis of intersubjectivity requires us to examine not only how categories are used but also how they are responded to in an ongoing sequence of interaction (Bilmes 1986, 132). Furthermore, whether a particular category (e.g., ethnicity) is relevant to participants or not is of concern both to the participants as well as to the researchers (e.g., Widdicombe 1998). Hence, categories can only be understood by examining how participants themselves orient to them in interaction (e.g., Schegloff 1997, 2007).

Research on how categories are made relevant and constructed in interaction has examined how reference to people is interactively accomplished between speakers (e.g., Sacks and Schegloff 1979; Schegloff 1996) and how participants deploy categories to accomplish particular positionings that are constructed in interaction (e.g., for ethnic categories see Day 1994, 1998; Hansen 2005; Lo 1999; Moerman 1988; Reyes 2002, 2007, this volume). For instance, Angela Reyes (2007, this volume) examines how Asian Americans of various Asian backgrounds discuss stereotypes of Asians, demonstrating how they choose particular ethnic categories such as *Asian* as a relevant category to associate with stereotypes such as "(their parents) owning stores." In so doing, she explicates how the participants position themselves in relation to stereotypes that are tied to specific categories, which are appreciated or contested by the co-participants at the moment of interaction. Hence, categories are treated not as static constructs, but rather as interactional resources to display, align with, or contest particular social positionings.

Ethnic categories also emerge in relation to attributes that are made relevant to the ethnic categories: social practices (e.g., Reyes 2007, this volume), food (e.g., Moerman 1988), ideology (e.g., Kang, this volume), language (e.g., Day 1998;

Hansen 2005), and place (e.g., Schegloff 1972). For example, when the category *Local Japanese* is used in conjunction with attributes such as a particular language or place and treated as requiring no explanation, participants are displaying that such associations are presumably shared with co-participants.

Moreover, these categories emerge in opposition to one another (e.g., Hausendorf and Kesselheim 2002; Kang, this volume; Lo 1999; Reyes and Lo 2004; Moerman 1988). In analyzing an interaction among three men on a university campus in Los Angeles, Adrienne Lo (1999) demonstrates how a question about the ethnicity of a girl emerges and how the responses to the question frame particular Asian ethnic categories as either "problematic" or "non-problematic." Lo elucidates how the participants' stance toward ethnic categories emerges as non-shared as respondents show non-alignment to one another by displaying "disagreement" (Pomerantz 1984) and by resisting the code-switching practices explicitly demanded in the course of the interaction.

The construction of these categories in opposition is, therefore, contingent on the immediate sequential environments of talk. Participants do not simply index positionings in relation to the categories through metapragmatic comments, but skillfully display their understandings of categories through orienting to prior turns that are consequential for the development of subsequent turns in talk-in-interaction. Therefore, categories do not carry with them self-contained meanings, but rather are interactional resources with which participants accomplish intersubjectivity (Goodwin and Duranti 1992, 27). A detailed analysis of the ways in which categories are employed in ongoing social interaction enables us to see how categories are utilized as (part of) practices that invoke participants' memberships in particular social groups such as ethnic groups (Moerman 1988, 1993; see also Morita, this volume; Song, this volume, for how the (non)use of a particular pronoun or address terms may invoke the users' ethnic identity).

This study examines how people who are often categorized as *Japanese* or *Japanese Americans* in Hawai'i use a variety of categories or references to themselves and others (hereafter I refer to "references to groups of people" as "categories") and how their mutual orientation to the meaning of categories may instantiate their ethnicity. My analysis is mainly concerned with how participants deploy emergent categories to interactively position themselves and co-participants, constructing and negotiating "who-we-know-we-are" at the moment of interaction (Schegloff 1972).

Data

The examples to be analyzed in this study are extracted from the discussion section of a panel presentation titled "Japanese American Contemporary Experiences in Hawai'i," which took place at the Japanese Cultural Center of Hawai'i in March 2003. According to the flyer, the purpose of the event was "to bring together people in the community for a public discussion, particularly from the perspectives of *Yonsei* and to explore such issues as what it means to be Japanese Americans in multiethnic Hawai'i." Though there were three *Yonsei* panelists from Hawai'i, only one of them

(Glen) appears in the present study. There was also a moderator, Michelle, a *Sansei* who was the coordinator of the panel presentations together with James, a *Sansei* who was sitting in the audience. There were approximately sixty audience members (from various ethnic backgrounds) including Naomi, a Japanese national who appears in the transcript.[5]

The forum proceeded in the following order: (1) Michelle talked about the purpose of the forum, and introduced the panelists, her co-coordinator James, and others (e.g., journalists and community leaders), (2) each panelist told personal narratives concerning identity, followed by questions, and (3) a general question-and-answer session was held. The excerpts analyzed below are taken from the final question-and-answer session where audience members were encouraged to participate.

Positioning Oneself and Co-Participants in Relation to Categories through Constructing a Question

This section examines how participants display and contest various categories that are associated with Japanese or Japanese Americans. Specifically, Naomi, one of the audience members, raises a question in which she formulates different subcategories or types of Japanese (Americans). This question is reworked by Michelle, the moderator of the event, as she reformulates the categories in a way that is slightly different from Naomi's construction. In short, there is no clear consensus on what categories are relevant to participants; rather each participant displays a slightly different understanding of and orientation to categories of Japanese (Americans), which they construct through talk. In this section, I demonstrate how participants locate themselves and the co-present participants as members or non-members of particular categories, and how they treat certain categories as requiring explication and exemplification. To this end I first examine how Naomi's categories are reformulated into different categories and grouped together in specific ways by Michelle. Then, I demonstrate how Michelle displays a different orientation to the categories she constructs and how, in so doing, she positions herself as distinct from Naomi.

Michelle's Reformulating and Regrouping Categories into a Question

(1)[6]

1	Naomi:	so: um (.3) you ha:ve (.) ne:w first generation coming from Japan (1.0)
2		and uh: (brought) my question- general question is (.)
3		do <u>yo↑u</u> have a (.3) chance to intera:ct with the:↑m? (1.0)
4		uh: we're from (.) actually from Japa:n ( ) °this time° (.)
5		and have lived here fo:r (.) several yea:rs, (.)
6		and thei::r (.) perceptio↑n (.) is that (.)
7		you're first generation? (.) and Japanese Americans? (.)
8		Nisei Sansei Yonse:i? (.)
9		and then (.) Japanese businessmen that they have business here.

10		they don't intera:ct with each other. (1.0)
11		I was wondering what's your perception about that.
12	Michelle:	so: >the question is about< interaction
13		if there is intera:ction between (.)
14		u:hm I'll say (.) Local Japanese (.) Local Japanese Americans
15		an-and between what we call Shin Isse:i? (.) or more recent immigrants, (.)
16		as well as say tourists or other (.) busi[nesspeople from Japan. (.5)
17	Naomi:	[°business°
18	Michelle:	James, do you have ( )?

Let me first examine how subcategories of Japanese (American) that Naomi uses are understood by investigating the way in which they were treated by Michelle. Various categories emerge in Naomi's turn: *first generation, Japanese American, Nisei, Sansei, Yonsei* and *Japanese businessmen*. Naomi states that "they don't intera:ct with each other" (line 10), thereby displaying that these categories are distinct, yet can be grouped together in specific ways. In order to understand what "they" refers to, it is crucial to understand how these categories are organized into groups.

The first term Naomi introduces is "first generation?" (line 7). As mentioned, the way in which this reference is understood by Michelle can be seen by examining how she treats this term in the following turn. Michelle reformulates Naomi's categories and her question. She says "so: >the question is about< interaction if there is intera:ction between (.) u:hm I'll say (.) Local Japanese (.) Local Japanese Americans an-and between what we call Shin Isse:i? (.) or more recent immigrants, (.) as well as say tourists or other (.) busi[ness people from Japan." The category "first generation?" is therefore treated as "Shin Isse:i? (.) or more recent immigrants" (line 15).

The next term Naomi uses is "Japanese Americans?" (line 7), which is followed by "Nisei Sansei Yonse:i?" (line 8). "Nisei Sansei Yonse:i?" is produced in succession (i.e., without any connectors or pauses in between), which suggests that it is treated as a unified category. The absence of a connector following "Japanese Americans?" seems to indicate that "Nisei Sansei Yonse:i?" is an exemplification of the category "Japanese Americans." These categories are subsequently oriented to as "Local Japanese (.) Local Japanese Americans" (line 14) by Michelle. The last category that Naomi uses, "Japanese businessmen that they have business here" (line 9), contains the deictic "here," which specifies that she is referring to *Japanese businessmen who have business in Hawai'i*. This is oriented to as "tourists or other (.) busi[ness people from Japan" (line 16) by Michelle.

In short, boundaries are created among three categories in Naomi's turn[7]: *first generation, Japanese American/Nisei Sansei Yonsei*, and *Japanese businessmen* (see figure 9.1). The fact that these are depicted as distinct categories is crucial for understanding what "they" refers to in the subsequent utterance: "They don't intera:ct with each other." These three categories are then interpreted as "Shin Isse:i? (.) or more recent immigrants," "Local Japanese (.) Local Japanese Americans," and "tourists or other (.) busi[ness people from Japan" by Michelle, who also depicts them as three separate groups.

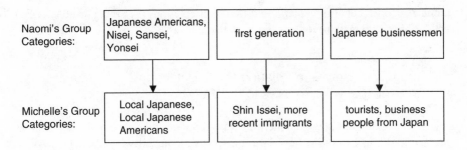

Figure 9.1. Michelle's Reformulation of Naomi's Group Categories

Positioning Self and Other through Category Choice and Different Orientations to Categories

The fact that Michelle is reformulating Naomi's categories can be observed in her use of the pronouns "I" and "we" as in "I'll say" (line 14) and "what we call" (line 15). These pronouns invoke an opposing pronoun "you," delineating a contrast between Michelle and Naomi in terms of the construction of ethnic categories.

For example, Michelle uses the term "Local Japanese (.) Local Japanese Americans" (line 14), in contrast with Naomi's "Japanese Americans? (.) Nisei Sansei Yonse:i?" (lines 7–8).[8] The term *Local* specifies that what is of concern is not simply Japanese Americans but *Japanese Americans in the local community, Hawai'i.* Moreover, the term *Local Japanese Americans* also indicates that Local Japanese are *Americans*, not Japanese nationals. Hence, Michelle orients to these distinctions as meaningful, attending to the specific location (i.e., not the continental United States or Japan, but Hawai'i) and category *Local*.

Next, Michelle uses the category "Shin Isse:i? (.) or more recent immigrants" (line 15) instead of Naomi's category "first generation" (line 7). Michelle marks *Shin Issei* as "non-recognizable" with rising intonation followed by a micro pause (Schegloff 1996, 460). Naomi orients to *first generation, Japanese Americans* and *Nisei Sansei Yonsei* as "non-recognizable" in a similar manner (i.e., with rising intonation followed by a micro pause). Such contrasts therefore seem to invoke different positionings on the part of Michelle and Naomi in relation to the categories: For Naomi, *first generation, Japanese Americans*, and *Nisei Sansei Yonsei* are not shared references with the co-participants while *Shin Issei* is similarly marked as not shared with the audience for Michelle.

The reference *Japanese American* is also treated as "non-shared" by Michelle, however. Specifically, by reformulating Naomi's category *Japanese American* as *Local Japanese (American)*, Michelle constructs herself and the audience as people who share the term *Local Japanese (American)*, while treating Naomi as someone who does not use or identify with this term.

In using different category constructions, therefore, participants display their own positionings as well as co-participants' in relation to the categories. Such different positionings are accomplished not only through choosing different terms for ethnic categories but also by marking different orientations (i.e., recognizable/shared or in need of explanation) to the categories themselves.

Positioning Themselves in Relation to the Categories and Co-Participants: Responses to the Question

This section examines how the emerging question is responded to in the subsequent interaction. First, I examine how James displays alignment with Michelle by way of showing his orientation to her categories (instead of Naomi's), and constructs dichotomous categories by positioning himself as *Local Japanese* in opposition to *Shin Issei*. Then, I look into Michelle's turn; how she aligns with James's dichotomous categories and further emphasizes the division between *Local Japanese* and *Shin Issei*. Last, I analyze Glen's turn; how he presents different category constructions, and thereby contests the dichotomous categories that are reinforced by James and Michelle.

James's Construction of Dichotomous Ethnic Categories: Positioning *Local Japanese* in Opposition to *Shin Issei*

This section examines how James's positionings as *Local Japanese* in opposition to *Shin Issei* emerge. I discuss the following issues: (1) James's construction of dichotomous categories by reducing the three categories into two, (2) James's alignment with Michelle in relation to the ethnic categories, and (3) James's linking of the categories of *Local Japanese* and *Shin Issei* with distinct attributes (e.g., place and language).

(2)

18	Michelle:	James, do you have ( )?
19		James: (1.5) here?=
20	Michelle:	=mhm
21	James:	[( ) there seems to be very limited interaction between uh::
22		[((beep sound))
23	James:	(.3) Local Japane:se and uh::: (.3) what you said Shin Issei here.
24		>Just like that restaurant we tried to go to the other night< (.3)
25		here: (.) it's very to me:
26		uh:: Japane:se uh: (.3) na:tional kind of (.) restaura:nt
27		>everyone was speaking< Japane:se the:re:.
28		>For me: walking into that place
29		I re:ally (.) felt it's not really a Local Japanese restaurant.<
30		( ) a number of them actually opened up here in Moiliili (.3)
31		>for someone who's not familiar with uh Moiliili
32		can go out to a:ll the:se Japanese restaurants.
33		but u:hm Local person would say

34	well this is a Local<ˈhhh Japanese restaurant (.) like uh:: (.) Sekiya:. (.)
35	but uh:m (.) the ones that are re:ally for Japanese na:tionals
36	(I mean) based on how they serve the food too, (.)
37	°they're° different. (.)
38	and uh: (.3) I a↑sked my- one of my students uh::: (.3) from Japa:n
39	studying at uh:: (.) Manoa: (.3)
40	about the Japanese community (1.0)
41	uh: Issei community or stu:de:nts a:nd uh: (.) over he:re: (.) wo:rk (.)
42	a-a:nd (.) do a paper
43	so she identified these places like restaura::nts, ba::rs, uh: (.3)
44	other kinds of social place:s that (.) are basically for Japanese na:tionals.
45	(.3) but uh:: (.3) more Local Japanese young people also at the same age
46	uh::: (.3) don't uh::: (.3) go to them. (.)
47	so there isn't really (a connection at all).

First, James refines Michelle's formulation of three relevant categories of person into two categories. Michelle's "Local Japanese (.) Local Japanese Americans" (line 14) becomes "Local Japane:se" (line 23) in James's turn while Michelle's "Shin Isse:i? (.) or more recent immigrants" (line 15) becomes simply "Shin Issei" (line 23). The category "tourists or other (.) businesspeople from Japan" (line 16) is not mentioned in James's turn, which suggests that he sees this group as less relevant to the question.[9] Thus *Local Japanese* and *Shin Issei* emerge as relevant to his subsequent exemplifications (see figure 9.2).

Like Michelle, James also treats the category *Shin Issei* as a reference that is not shared with the co-participants while orienting to *Local Japanese* as shared.[10] Thus James displays alignment with Michelle not only by selecting categories that are similar to Michelle's but also by displaying positionings that are similar to Michelle in relation to the categories.

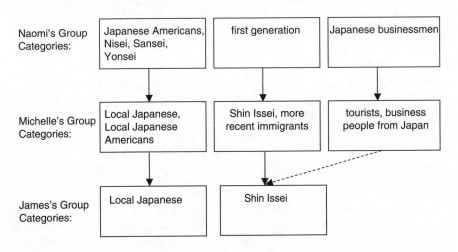

Figure 9.2. Sequential Development of Group Categories from Naomi to Michelle to James

Throughout his turn, James highlights his membership in the category *Local Japanese*. He does so through the way in which he constructs *Local Japanese* as distinct from *Shin Issei*. Specifically, *Shin Issei* is connected to attributes such as a specific language and place: "speaking Japanese" and "Japanese national kind of restaurant"[11] (lines 26–27). Such attributes are treated as the ones for a *non-Local Japanese restaurant* as James produces "I re:ally (.) felt it's not really a Local Japanese restaurant" in line 29. In so doing, James treats the category *Local Japanese* and its invoked or associated attributes such as *non-Japanese speaking* as the "default" or "standard." This construction of the default category and attributes is done in a first-person narrative. James initiates the narrative with "that restaurant we tried to go to the other night" (line 24), and subsequently assigns specific attributes (i.e., "Japanese national kind of restaurant" and "speaking Japanese") to the category *non-Local Japanese* in explaining why he ended up *not* going to the restaurant. The personal accounts are delivered with the use of first-person singular pronouns (e.g., prefacing the introduction of such attributes and the category with "to me:" in line 25 and "for me:" in line 28), thereby further delineating his positioning in the category *Local Japanese*.

James's positioning with *Local Japanese* is also made salient through the way in which he relates categories to specific locations such as "Moiliili" and the *Local Japanese* restaurant "Sekiya" (line 34).[12] James treats these associations as requiring no explication. Such treatment presumes that these locations are recognizable to the audience in terms of not only geography (specified as "here in Moiliili" in line 30)[13] but also cultural meaning (e.g., what type of restaurant Sekiya is, who goes there). By selecting a specific reference *Sekiya* for a *Local Japanese restaurant* (as opposed to a less specified reference "a:ll the:se Japanese restaurants" in "Moiliili" in line 32 for *Japanese national kind of restaurants*), for instance, James invokes his positionings with the category *Local Japanese*.

In short, the dichotomous categories *Local Japanese* and *Shin Issei* emerge as separate and distinct with "very limited interaction" (line 21) between them.[14] This dichotomization is fortified by linking *Shin Issei* to attributes such as "Japanese national kind of restaurant," invoking the nation-state distinction between the categories. Moreover, by situating himself as *Local Japanese* and by constructing *Local Japanese* and its associated items like *Sekiya* as shared between him and the audience (with the possible exception of Naomi), James "highlights" (Goodwin 1997, 124) the positionings of himself, Michelle, and the audience as *Local Japanese*, locating *Shin Issei* and Naomi in the background.

Michelle's Alignment with James with Respect
to the Construction of Dichotomous Ethnic
Categories and Positionings

This section examines how Michelle reinforces the dichotomy between *Local Japanese* and *Shin Issei* by tying her turn to James's turn with a connector "and," thereby co-constructing a sentence with James. In so doing, she displays her alignment with James's construction of the categories, invoking the shared identity of James, the audience, and herself as *Local Japanese*, while framing Naomi as *Shin Issei*.

(3)

48	Michelle:	and one might ask (.) why <u>should</u> there be a connect. (.3)
49		in other wo:rds (.) hhˑhh we don-we don't <u>sha</u>re backgrounds (.)
50		we don'-( ) there may be a blood connect.
51		but uh: as I said earlier >°in my opening remark°<,
52		I think blood connect is is <u>is</u> very <u>te</u>:nuous and a:rbitrary. (.)
53		uh:- <u>an</u>- <u>an</u>d if you're talking about any kind of connection to Ja<u>pa:n</u>,
54		the Ja<u>pa::n</u> that immigrants left was Meiji Japa:n. (.)
55		and Japan has changed tremendously since then.
56		so: if you try to compare Meiji Japan and Heisei Japan,
57		ah: these are almo- these are- these are almost two different countries.
58		(1.0) so: so the question is
59		why <u>should</u> there (.) wh- <u>why assume</u>
60		there would be necessarily a connection between the two.=

Tying to James's turn with a connector "and," Michelle co-constructs a sentence with James, thereby showing her alignment with James and reinforcing the dichotomy between *Local Japanese* and *Shin Issei*. Her utterance "why <u>should</u> there be a connect" (line 48) questions why there should be a connection at all: "we don't <u>sha</u>re backgrounds" (line 49) and "blood connect is is <u>is</u> very <u>te</u>:nuous and a:rbitrary" (line 52).

This dichotomization is further augmented through the association with temporal categories, specifically "Meiji Japan" (line 54 and 56) versus "Heisei Japan" (line 56). Like "formulating place" (Schegloff 1972), the use of these specific temporal terms without explication presumes that the audience shares the knowledge of not only the term itself but also the way in which the term is to be interpreted in this context. For instance, Michelle presumes that her audience not only knows the term *Meiji*, but also understands how the term is associated with the history of Japanese immigrants and how it may be contrasted with *Heisei*, which invokes Japanese nationals in the contemporary era of Japan.[15] These binary references are ultimately associated with "two different countries" (line 57), elaborating the nation-state dichotomy between *Local Japanese* and *Shin Issei*. Thus, such a discrepancy is also increasingly deepened in terms of the participants' positionings mapped onto the categories; namely, James, Michelle, and the audience as *Local Japanese* in opposition to Naomi who is positioned as *Shin Issei* (see figure 9.3).

Michelle's subsequent utterance "<u>why assume</u> there would be necessarily a connection between the two" (lines 59–60) appears to be directed at Naomi who initially brings up the question about "interaction." In so doing, Michelle treats Naomi as presuming that there is "interaction" or a "connection" between *Local Japanese* and *Shin Issei* simply based on shared ethnicity.

Glen's Contestation of Dichotomous Ethnic Category Constructions

In their turns, James and Michelle positioned themselves as *Local Japanese* while strengthening the boundaries between the dichotomous categories *Local Japanese* and *Shin Issei*. In contrast, Glen contests the construction of these categories by

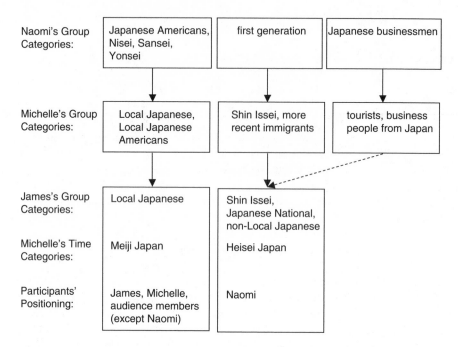

Naomi's Group Categories:	Japanese Americans, Nisei, Sansei, Yonsei	first generation	Japanese businessmen
Michelle's Group Categories:	Local Japanese, Local Japanese Americans	Shin Issei, more recent immigrants	tourists, business people from Japan
James's Group Categories:	Local Japanese	Shin Issei, Japanese National, non-Local Japanese	
Michelle's Time Categories:	Meiji Japan	Heisei Japan	
Participants' Positioning:	James, Michelle, audience members (except Naomi)	Naomi	

Figure 9.3. Participants' Positioning within Group and Time Categories

presenting different ethnic landscapes in his turn, exemplifying them from the perspective of the "Okinawan community" (line 61).[16] In this section, I focus on (1) how Glen contests the dichotomous ethnic categories by presenting different constructions of categories and (2) how the change of category construction also shifts participants' positionings in regard to these categories.

(4)

61	Glen:	=it's kind of an interesting (.) thing with the Okinawan community over
62		here uh: in the sense of community. (.)
63		uh::m (1.0) they're separa- they're separate
64		but they also (.) overlapped in a lot of wa::ys?
65		uh:: (.5) esp-particularly these cultural social practice:s (.)
66		there's a <u>lo:t</u> of overlap
67		in fact the party I'm going to now (.3)
68		uh:m (.5) English speakers are a minority. hhhh
69		but I guess my- my perspective too comes from this (.) this
70		in between places where I can (.) uh:: somewhat bilingua(h):l.
71		hh heh heh heh
72		I can fool people for five minutes here. hhh ((sniff))
73		but uh: (.) uh::m there's: interesting thi:ngs
74		where: in a lot of wa:ys in the Okinawan community (.)

75		a lot of us (.) through::: the clubs and organizations (.)
76		whether it be cultural or social,
77		there's a lo↑t of (.) overlap in that sense. (.3)
78		a:nd-but at the same time too,
79		I guess there's-there's a (.) physica-physical overlap. (.)
80		but of course you have cultural and generational (.3)
81		and someho:w (.3) it's kind of stra:nge
82		because it seems that (.)
83		cultural (.) gap is like (.5) for the younger folks (.3)
84		u:hm they're- they're on side of the fence (.)
85		and then the other side, (.3)
86		the older folks (.) a:nd the folks the Shin Issei, (.3)
87		they kind of understand each other a lot better.
88		there's more of a connection. (.)
89		so the:n for us folks on the other side of fence
90		it's kinda-kinda gro:up the (.) older folks and the Shin Issei
91		all kind of in one package.
92		it's kind of an interesting thing. (.)
93		cause like fo:r a lot of groups I'm involved in,
94		we have older members.
95		(.) uh:m (.) they're- they're the ones that embrace the Shin Issei more.
96		a:nd in fact they'll even go drink coffee with them and stuff
97		and become a part of their ( ) or have yo(h)u. hhh
98		heh [heh.
99	Audience:	[hh heh heh heh heh.
100	Glen:	versus (.) uh:m the younger folks kind of (.)
101		uh:m a little more separated I guess.
102		so: physically:: in an organizational sense (.) we're BO:nded
103		but ah: most of it I think a lot of it is actually linguistic (.) language
104		barrier.
105		luckily uh: Nise:i can still understand a lot of Japane:se (.)
106		versus uh:: most of my peers are fini(h)shing Japanese one o one
107		.hh heh heh.
108	Michelle:	having language is a huge (.) uhm stumbling block
109		to-to the kind of connects that you're-you're °conveying°.
110		are there any questions? (10)

Latching onto Michelle's utterance, Glen orients to the dichotomous categories *Local Japanese* and *Shin Issei* with "they" (line 63), stating that they are "separate" (line 63). However, he also contests this categorization by constructing the two categories as "overlapped" (line 64). Glen provides accounts by positioning himself "in between" (line 70), which is linked with being "somewhat bilingual(h):l"[17] (line 70) as he states "my perspective too comes from this (.) this in between places where I can (.) uh:: somewhat bilingual(h):l" (lines 69–70).[18] The attribute *somewhat bilingual*, which is situated *in between*, thus evokes two oppositional attributes: *English monolingual* and *Japanese monolingual*. *Local Japanese* is now linked to *English monolingual.* The category *Shin Issei* is therefore associated with *Japanese monolingual*, placed in opposition to *Local Japanese* and *English monolingual.*

The introduction of new attributes affects participants' positionings in relation to the ethnic categories. Specifically, James and Michelle, who position themselves as *Local Japanese*, are framed as *English monolingual* by Glen. As a result, Glen positions himself as distinct from James and Michelle in that he is on neither side, but rather "in between places" as *somewhat bilingual.*

However, as he discusses "cultural gaps," Glen adds yet another layer by introducing new categories: "the younger folks" (line 83) and "the older folks" (line 86). These age categories are presented not as overlapping but as separate: *The younger folks* are on one side of the fence while *the older folks* and *Shin Issei* are on the other side. These new categories are related to the earlier ones through the link between *the older folks* and *Shin Issei* who are constructed as "understand[ing] each other a lot better" (line 87), with "more of a connection" (line 88) between them. *The older folks* "embrace the Shin Issei more" (line 95) while they also share social practices such as "go[ing to] drink coffee" together (line 96).[19] Hence, by constructing *the older folks* and *Shin Issei* as distinct from *the younger folks* in terms of their shared social practices, James and Michelle are positioned on the side of *the younger folks* who are constructed as not sharing social practices with *Shin Issei*. At the same time, Glen also positions himself with *the younger folks* as he states "for us folks on the other side of fence it's kinda-kinda gro:up the (.) older folks and the Shin Issei all kind of in one package" (lines 89–91). As a result, as the reference *cultural gaps* emerges, the discrepancy between *the younger folks* and *the older folks/Shin Issei* is made salient, overshadowing the dichotomous categories *Local Japanese* and *Shin Issei* that were constructed by James and Michelle.

In the subsequent part of his utterance, Glen brings the terms "Nise:i" (line 105) into this landscape. Specifically, *the older folks* are associated with *Nisei*, invoking *the younger folks* as *Sansei Yonsei*. As a result, James and Michelle are constructed as both *Sansei Yonsei* and *the younger folks*. While Glen had positioned himself earlier as a member of *the younger folks*, these positionings change yet again as the issue of language becomes relevant with the introduction of "language barrier" (lines 103–104). By invoking his *somewhat bilingual* status, Glen distances himself from the category *the younger folks*, which is constructed as *monolingual English* (or understanding very little Japanese by only finishing Japanese 101 as exemplified in line 106). Thus, as the attribute *speaking Japanese* is made relevant, Glen's positionings shift as demonstrated in figure 9.4.

In sum, Glen contests the dichotomous construction of ethnic categories that are constructed by James and Michelle by presenting different category constructions; that is, ethnic categories are not as clear-cut as James and Michelle have constructed them, but rather are separated or overlapping depending on the specific attributes or references to the particular phenomena that are "highlighted" at the moment of interaction.

As a result, Glen presents ethnic categorizations that are different from the other participants in that he does not comply with the three ethnic categories that are put forth by Naomi (i.e., *first generation, Japanese American/Nisei Sansei Yonsei*, and *Japanese businessmen*), that are constructed simply based on ethnicity and genera-

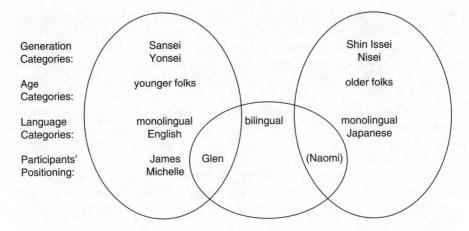

Figure 9.4. Participants' Positioning within Generation, Age, and Language Categories

tion. Nor does he orient to the dichotomous ethnic categories constructed by James and Michelle (e.g., *Local Japanese* and *Shin Issei*). Instead, he remakes new categories based on age (e.g., *the older folks* vs. *the younger folks*) and varying degrees of language competence (e.g., *somewhat bilingual*) that are made relevant to the extent that they may be connected with or separated from *Shin Issei*, thus presenting a more complex and dynamic view of identity.

Conclusion

Previous discursive work on ethnicity has demonstrated how ethnicity is an interactional accomplishment and how it often emerges in topical talk within which attributes such as social practices, food, ideology, language, and place become relevant. This study also shows how ethnicity is instantiated by closely examining how speakers demonstrate their mutual understanding of particular categories as linked with specific attributes. For instance, participants' ethnicity is made salient through the way in which they skillfully deploy ethnic (e.g., *Local Japanese*) and generational (e.g., *Sansei Yonsei*) categories when referring to themselves and co-participants. Such categories are linked to specific attributes such as language (e.g., *non-Japanese speaking*), place (e.g., Local Japanese restaurant like *Sekiya*), and history (e.g., *Meiji Japan*) without providing explication. In so doing, participants are displaying shared knowledge that is historically developed and socially distributed among different members.

Participants in the study, who are often categorized as *Japanese* or *Japanese American*, do not simply consent to using one single term to refer to themselves and co-participants. Rather, participants deploy various categories when referring to themselves and others, artfully aligning with or contesting their co-participants' construction of categories. For instance, alignment or contestation is accomplished not only through selecting either similar or different terms for ethnic categories but also by marking the categories either as recognizable/shared or as in need of explanation.

Moreover, categories are divided (e.g., *Local Japanese* vs. *Shin Issei*), connected (e.g., *the older folks* and *Shin Issei*), or overlapped (e.g., *Local Japanese* and *Shin Issei*) depending on the attributes (e.g., speaking Japanese) or references to the specific phenomena (e.g., cultural gaps) highlighted at the moment of interaction. Such changes also generate shifts in the participants' positionings that are interactively tied to the categories.

Part of what helps position participants in particular categories is the enactment of behaviors that are assigned to the categories. For example, while James and Michelle are positioned as *Local Japanese, the younger folks*, and *Sansei Yonsei*, they also enact the qualities that have been assigned to these categories, namely, not seeing connections with *Shin Issei*, a category that is assigned to Naomi. Likewise, while Glen is positioned as *in between*, he enacts this identity by bringing together and providing points of overlap between the two dichotomous positions of James and Michelle, on the one hand, and Naomi, on the other.

This study further establishes that ethnicity is not concrete or stable, but rather negotiable and contingent on the "immediate exigencies of [its] occasioned occurrence" (Moerman 1993, 92). Ethnicities such as *Japanese* or *Japanese American* thus cannot be a priori presupposed to be constantly relevant to an individual or a group of people. The question "Who is Japanese or Japanese American?" is an open question that should be investigated through the way in which these categories are discursively constructed in social interaction.

NOTES

    1. For example, see Dennis M. Ogawa (1973) for these classifications.

    2. See, e.g., Wayne Muromoto (1992) for the definition of *Shin Issei* (new Issei).

    3. See, e.g., Norman Kaneshiro (2002) for discussion of "Uchinanchu" or "Okinawan" identity in Hawai'i.

    4. Roderick N. Labrador (this volume) states that "Local" is "a racialized identity category composed primarily of the various non-White groups that usually trace their entrance into the islands to the plantation era—namely those of Chinese, Japanese, Okinawan, Filipino, and Korean descent" (p. 291). According to this definition, therefore, recent immigrants and temporary residents, including tourists from Japan and Japanese immigrants to other places besides Hawai'i, would not be included in the category. For further discussion of "Local" identity, see Jonathan Okamura (1992) and Steven Talmy (this volume).

    5. Naomi identified herself as a person from Japan who had lived in Hawai'i for several years (see lines 4–5 in excerpt 1).

    6. Transcription conventions (adapted from Atkinson and Heritage [1984]):

[	point where overlap begins
]	point where overlap terminates
=	(1) turn continues below at the same equal sign, (2) no interval between the two turns and/or between adjacent utterances
(1.5)	intervals between utterances (in seconds)
(.)	very short untimed pause
<u>word</u>	emphasis
wo:rd	elongated vowel or consonant

word-	abrupt cutoff
?	rising intonation, not necessarily a question
!	emphatic tone
,	falling-rising intonation
.	falling intonation
WORD	loud sound relative to surrounding talk
°°	utterances between degree signs are noticeably quieter than surrounding talk
↑↓	marked shifts into higher or lower pitch in the utterances following the arrow
< >	talk surrounded by angle brackets is produced more slowly than surrounding talk
> <	talk surrounded by reversed angle brackets is produced more quickly than surrounding talk
( )	unintelligible speech
(word)	uncertain transcription
.hh	in-breath
hh	out-breath

7. The construction of boundaries is reified not only verbally but also nonverbally through gesture (e.g., see Goodwin 1994, 620), as Naomi's gestures display a distinction between the categories "Japanese businessmen," "first generation," and "Japanese Americans."

8. Note that Michelle changes the sequential order of the categories that Naomi constructed by listing "Local Japanese (.) Local Japanese Americans" (line 14) first. This category was reformulated from Naomi's "Japanese Americans? (.) Nisei Sansei Yonse:i?" (lines 7–8), which was listed second by Naomi (see figure 9.1). This may not be unrelated to the way she subsequently creates the Local Japanese versus non-Local Japanese dichotomy between herself/recipients and Naomi, "highlighting" Local Japanese.

9. James links the category Shin Issei to the new attributes such as "Japanese national kind of restaurant" (line 26) and "Japanese nationals" (lines 35 and 44), thus invoking Shin Issei as equivalent to Japanese nationals. Thus James's category Shin Issei, which he associates with Japanese nationals, may subsume both Michelle's "tourist or other (.) businesspeople from Japan" (line 16) and "Shin Isse:i (.) or more recent immigrants" (line 15).

10. For instance, James specifies that the category "Shin Issei" is used by Michelle (i.e., "what you said" in line 23). However, he does not produce such qualifications of the category "Local Japanese," treating "Local Japanese" as a shared reference among himself and the audience (with the possible exception of Naomi).

11. Notice that James uses an "extreme case formulation" (Pomerantz 1986), "everyone," as in ">everyone is speaking< Japane:se" (line 27) to legitimize his claims about a Japanese national kind of restaurant.

12. Emmanuel A. Schegloff (1972) maintains that formulating locations is recipient-designed as adequate formulation requires mutual recognition of "who-we-know-we-are" and "what-we-are-doing-at-this-point-in-the-conversation" (130). Hence, particular formulation of location invokes the identity of the participants.

13. According to the Hawaii State Department of Business, Economic Development and Tourism (2000), the population of Mo'ili'ili consists of 35.1 percent "Japanese."

14. These dichotomous categories are further delineated by bringing up different kinds of people that are constructed and made relevant to the categories: "Local person" (line 33), "more Local Japanese young people" (line 45) as opposed to "my students from Japan" (line 38).

15. "Meiji" is the name given to the era during the reign of the Meiji emperor, from Sept. 8, 1868, to July 30, 1912. The Meiji era was followed by the Taisho era, the Showa era, and the Heisei era. "Heisei" is the name of the current era in Japan, from Jan. 8, 1989, to the present.

16. Glen's initiation of his talk without being selected as a next speaker as well as the absence of the use of categories such as "Local Japanese" throughout his turn (i.e., the pronoun "they" only subsumes the category) is noteworthy in the sense of "contesting" the category construction that is developed in the prior turns. Note also that "Okinawans" were historically discriminated against by "Japanese" on mainland Japan both before and after their immigration to Hawai'i; as a result, they have their own social organization in Hawai'i (e.g., Kaneshiro 2002; Lebra 1980).

17. Glen's "somewhat bilingual" status is also invoked through his statement, "I can fool people for five minutes here" (line 72).

18. The use of "too" (line 69) may point to Naomi's positioning as "somewhat bilingual."

19. The action of going to drink coffee together makes a meaningful contrast with the prior construction of distinctive ethnic practices (i.e., going to ethnically distinctive restaurants, bars, and other social places). Specifically, "drinking coffee" is not a category-bounded activity in the sense of discrete "ethnic" categorization.

REFERENCES

Atkinson, J. Maxwell, and John Heritage, ed. 1984. *Structures of social action: Studies in conversation analysis*. Cambridge: Cambridge University Press.

Bilmes, Jack. 1986. *Discourse and Behavior*. New York and London: Plenum.

Day, Dennis. 1994. Tang's dilemma and other problems: Ethnification processes at some multi-cultural workplaces. *Pragmatics* 4:315–336.

———. 1998. Being ascribed, and resisting membership of an ethnic group. In *Identities in talk*, ed. Charles Antaki and Sue Widdicombe, 151–170. London: Sage.

Goodwin, Charles. 1994. Professional vision. *American Anthropologist* 96:606–633.

———. 1997. The blackness of black: Color categories as situated practice. In *Discourse, tools, and reasoning*, ed. Lauren B. Resnick, Roger Säljö, Clotilde Pontecorvo, and Barbara Burge, 111–140. Berlin, Heidelberg, New York: Springer.

Goodwin, Charles, and Alessandro Duranti. 1992. Rethinking context: An introduction. In *Rethinking context: Language as an interactive phenomenon*, ed. Alessandro Duranti and Charles Goodwin, 1–42. Cambridge: Cambridge University Press.

Hansen, Alan. D. 2005. A practical task: Ethnicity as a resource in social interaction. *Research on Language and Social Interaction* 38:63–104.

Hausendorf, Heiko, and Wolfgang Kesselheim. 2002. The communicative construction of group identities: A basic mechanism of social categorization. In *Us and others: Social identities across languages, discourses and cultures*, ed. Anna Duszak, 265–289. Amsterdam: John Benjamins.

Hawaii State Department of Business, Economic Development, and Tourism. 2000. Section 7: Recreation and travel. http://www.hawaii.gov/dbedt/dt00/sec07html.

Hester, Stephen, and Peter Eglin. 1997. Membership categorization analysis: An introduction. In *Culture in action*, ed. Stephen Hester and Peter Eglin, 1–23. Washington, D.C.: International Institute for Ethnomethodology and Conversation Analysis and University Press of America.

Johnson, Colleen L. 1976. The principle of generation among the Japanese in Honolulu. *Ethnic Groups* 1:13–35.

Kaneshiro, Norman. 2002. Uchinanchu identity in Hawai'i. In *The Japanese American contemporary experience in Hawai'i*, ed. Jonathan Y. Okamura, 75–94. Honolulu: University of Hawai'i Press.

Kendis, Kaoru O. 1989. *A matter of comfort: Ethnic maintenance and ethnic style among third-generation Japanese Americans*. New York: AMS Press.

Lebra, William. P. 1980. The Okinawans. In *Peoples and cultures of Hawaii*, ed. John F. McDermott, Wen-Shing Tseng, and Thomas W. Maretzki, 111–134. Honolulu: John A. Burns School of Medicine and University of Hawai'i Press.

Lo, Adrienne. 1999. Codeswitching, speech community membership, and the construction of ethnic identity. *Journal of Sociolinguistics* 3:461–479.

Matsumoto, Gary M., Gerald M. Meredith, and Minoru Masuda. 1973. Ethnic identity in three generations of Japanese Americans. *The Journal of Social Psychology* 81:199–207.

Moerman, Michael. 1988. *Talking culture: Ethnography and conversation analysis*. Philadelphia: University of Pennsylvania Press.

———. 1993. Ariadne's thread and Indra's net: Reflections on ethnography, ethnicity, identity, culture, and interaction. *Research on Language and Social Interaction* 26:85–98.

Montero, Darrel. 1980. *Japanese Americans: Changing patterns of ethnic affiliation over three generations*. Boulder, Colo.: Westview Press.

Muromoto, Wayne. 1992. The Shin Issei: The new immigrants from Japan are a mixed lot. *The Hawaii Herald* 13:1 and A–17.

Ogawa, Dennis. M. 1973. *Jan Ken Po: The world of Hawai'i's Japanese Americans*. Honolulu: University of Hawai'i Press.

Okamura, Jonathan. 1992. Why there are no Asian Americans in Hawai'i: The continuing significance of local identity. In *The Ninth National Conference of the Association for Asian American Studies*. San Jose, Calif.

Pomerantz, Anita. 1984. Agreeing and disagreeing with assessments: Some features of preferred/ dispreferred turn shapes. In *Structures of social action: Studies in conversation analysis*, ed. J. Maxwell Atkinson and John Heritage, 57–101. Cambridge: Cambridge University Press.

———. 1986. Extreme case formulations: A way of legitimizing claims. *Human Studies* 9:219–313.

Reyes, Angela. 2002. "Are you losing your culture?": Poetics, indexicality and Asian American identity. *Discourse Studies* 4:183–199.

———. 2007. *Language, identity, and stereotype among Southeast Asian American youth: The other Asian*. Mahwah, N.J.: Lawrence Erlbaum.

Reyes, Angela, and Adrienne Lo. 2004. Language, identity and relationality in Asian Pacific America: An introduction. *Pragmatics* 14:115–125.

Sacks, Harvey. 1979. Hotrodder: A revolutionary category. In *Everyday language: Studies in ethnomethodology*, ed. George Psathas, 7–14. New York: Irvington.

Sacks, Harvey, and Emmanuel A. Schegloff. 1979. Two preferences in the organization of reference to persons in conversation and their interaction. In *Everyday language: Studies in ethnomethodology*, ed. George Psathas, 15–21. New York: Irvington.

Schegloff, Emmanuel A. 1972. Notes on a conversational practice: Formulating place. In *Studies in social interaction*, ed. David Sudnow, 75–119. New York: Free Press.

———. 1996. Some practices for referring to persons in talk-in-interaction: A partial sketch of a systematic. In *Studies in anaphora*, ed. Barbara Fox, 437–485. Amsterdam: John Benjamins.

———. 1997. Whose text? Whose context? *Discourse and Society* 8: 165–187.

———. 2007. A tutorial on membership categorization. *Journal of Pragmatics* 39:462–482.

Stephan, Cookie W. 1991. Ethnic identity among mixed-heritage people in Hawaii. *Symbolic Interaction* 14:261–277.

———. 1992. Mixed-heritage individuals: Ethnic identity and trait characteristics. In *Racially mixed people in America*, ed. Maria P. P. Root, 50–63. Newbury Park: Sage.

Stephan, Cookie W., and Walter G. Stephan. 1989. After intermarriage: Ethnic identity among mixed-heritage Japanese Americans and Hispanics. *Journal of Marriage and the Family* 51:507–519.

U.S. Census Bureau. 2000. *Profile of general demographic characteristics, Hawaii.* http://factfinder.census.gov/servlet/QTTable?_bm=y&-geo_id=04000US15&-qr_name=DEC_2000_SF1_U_DP1&-ds_name=DEC_2000_SF1_U.

Widdicombe, Sue. 1998. Identity as an analysts' and a participants' resource. In *Identities in talk*, ed. Charles Antaki and Sue Widdicombe, 191–206. London: Sage.

10

Communities and Identities

Fraught Categories and Anchoring Resources:
A Commentary

Niko Besnier

The genealogy of the concept "identity" in the social sciences encapsulates the complexities and contradictions that are embedded in the very concept itself. We generally associate the birth of a social scientific understanding of identity with Erik Erikson's pivotal work, *Identity and the Life Cycle* (1959), which sought to capture the insight that, while people go through life facing numerous and diverse challenges, they strive to maintain to themselves and others a sense of continuity and growth, a sense of self that increases in complexity as the challenges become more complex and diverse. At the same time, persons are embedded in social groups, and their sense of identity is also the product, Erikson stressed, of the people around them. Continuity in the context of change, person-internal as well as person-external, the fragile play of divergent forces was embedded in the very concept of identity since its timid appearance in our analytic vocabulary, and militates for an approach to identity as a contingent, interactive, and unfinished project.

Just as fragile and fraught is our notion of "community," which of course goes much further in time than "identity," originating in the social sciences in the visions of Tocqueville, Tönnies, and Durkheim (if not before), and coming to us via a century's worth of anthropological thinking and writing, to late twentieth-century reclaimings of community in some social scientific circles (e.g., Bellah et al. 1985; Lasch 1979). Community and identity bear striking resemblances to each other; equally unstable, the two concepts are the subject of a great deal of romanticization of an idealized past in which social cohesion was made unproblematic by feelings of sameness (Durkheim, and also Marx), as well as an idealized present and future, in which identity politics and the longing for community reify and fetishize them. Just as community is relentlessly portrayed as "unequivocal good, an indicator of a high quality of life, a life of human understanding, caring, selflessness, belonging" (Joseph 2002, vii), identity is a must, and forms the basis, for many, of claims to recognition, pushes for legal protection, and personal feelings of pride and achievement.

The relationship between identity and community, on the one hand, and what they are supposed to oppose, on the other, is fraught. On the one hand, identity politics, based on the construction of sameness and difference, seeks to rectify past and present injustices in the form of oppression, denial of rights, and non-recognition. On the other hand, identity politics is also based on reified notions of authenticity and romanticized understandings of community. At the same time, discourses of community seek to offer a critique of capitalism and of the concomitant inequalities, yet they fail to expose the fact that the very notion of "community" is itself the product of capitalism: Witness the enthusiasm with which the management industry has taken to the notion of "community of practice" (Lave and Wenger 1991); witness how community, just like capitalism, can come to mean inequality and exclusion as readily as it can conjure belonging and cohesion; and witness the propensity with which community is defined in terms of consumption practices, which contribute directly to the expansion of capitalism (Creed 2006). (My favorite examples are letters from banks and other institutions that begin with "Welcome to the So-and-so credit card community.")

The chapters in this section make important contributions to an understanding of these ideological complexities. They demonstrate in vividly empirical ways that a focus on discursive practices can shed light onto how agents negotiate the contradictions inherent in the categories through which they define themselves and are defined by others. Bonnie McElhinny and her collaborators interrogate the continuity across time and contexts that for Erikson constituted the very essence of "identity" and that others (e.g., Linde 1983) treat as fundamental to the act of narrating the self. Highly trained Filipino professionals who migrate to Canada and find themselves, for a variety of ideological and material reasons, confined to low-end service jobs face the task of comprehending the discontinuities and lack of coherence in their life trajectory. Out of this sense-making emerge two projects: an understanding of the self as the product of intersubjectivity, and an understanding of "structure" as constituted by unpredictability and rupture. The argument by Bonnie McElhinny et al. reopens old debates in psychological anthropology about the constitution of the self in different cultural contexts, pitching the atomistic self of the West against the "partibility" of the person "elsewhere" (the term "partibility" is usually associated with Strathern [1988]; see Besnier [1994] and Rumsey [2000], among many other commentaries). Many have commented on the fact that the forms that have come to define the "Western self" are both a product and a constitutive element of a particular position in the capitalist order, namely mainstream male post–World War II middle-classness (e.g., di Leonardo 1991), but many have also demonstrated the extent to which this agentive self, in control of its destiny through rational choices, is fragile, being subject, for example, to the fear or reality of downward mobility, aggravated by the gradual erosion of the welfare state, and by the anxious competitiveness and absence of class consciousness that characterize the middle-class ethos (Ehrenreich 1989; Newman 1988; Ortner 2003).

McElhinny et al. contribute to this critical body of work two important insights. The first is that transnational movement creates new complexities, new forms of downward mobility, and new necessities for self-understanding, which go beyond simple contrasts between the West and the rest, women and men, or middle class and working class. What is particularly interesting in their chapter is the fact that the arguments they make are as much about Filipino stories as they are about white, middle-class, non-immigrant stories that others have analyzed. The second contribution, which they make alongside other chapters in this collection, is that close attention to both text and context can provide a much more nuanced handle on the work of agency than a narrow focus on either text, which characterizes many works in discourse analysis, or context, as is common in psychological anthropology.

Wendy Klein's analysis of "turban narratives" provides important new angles to works on the deployment of the person in discourse, such as socialization and the work of potential and actual oppression by a prejudiced majority. Here again, identity is the product of a complex array of forces, including concerns over morality and continuity, mainstream ignorance and violence, media presentations, and world events such as 9/11. Will Sikh boys' morally laden dastaar wearing make them stand out like sore thumbs in mainstream contexts? Has 9/11 reshuffled the ethnic map of the United States in a way that aligns Sikhs with "the enemy"? The unfinished nature of community formation is particularly evident in this chapter. On the one hand, Sikhs themselves present different views on one of their most visible markers of difference, which begins to encapsulate all the disagreements and divergences over what constitutes identity and community. On the other hand, media representations and mainstream ignorance (and unwillingness to learn) produce undesired and potentially dangerous alignments, placing the high-achieving Sikhs in the undesirable position of having to choose between the most visible marker of their religious and ethnic commitment. High achievement and success, but at what cost?

The camp counselors whom Agnes Kang recorded agonizing over how to locate themselves on an identity map illustrate that the contingency of identity suffuses even the most essentialized contexts, such as that of a summer camp overtly designed to teach kids "their cultural heritage." Arguing over the meaning of labels like "Korean," "Korean American," "American," none of which emerges as stable, they display additional ambivalences, about their roles as camp counselors and what "ethnic" kids need most: a highly reified version of Korean culture or mentoring about how to find their way in multiethnic California. So it is not only identifications that are at stake, but at the same time a host of other issues, which are related to the question of what label they will appropriate for themselves but nevertheless go beyond the confines of the simple question, "What I am going to call myself?" Kang demonstrates the performative nature of identity, which results from performatives like "I am Korean" or "I am American." Like all performatives, if we follow Austin (1962), they are contingent on felicity conditions being satisfied before the act of performance. However, the post-structuralist critique of Austinian performativity modifies the Austinian model in an important way, which is relevant to Kang's analysis: it is not just that felicity conditions are a prerequisite to the success of the performative, but rather than performatives can establish, reinforce, and maintain these conditions, and do so in elusive ways (Butler 1990, 1997). It is this power of performativity, and its complex interconnections with culture and social relations, that Kang's chapter elucidates.

Lastly, Hawai'i, a location that seems to encapsulate all by itself all the complexities and contradictions of the ethnic and indigenous experience: "Who is Japanese in Hawai'i?" Asuka Suzuki asks, and the answer, once again, consists of layers of categories that vary in their composition, their attributes, and the degree to which they mutually overlap or oppose one another. Like the Korean American camp counselors, participants in the debate at the Hawai'i Japanese Cultural Center display configurations of categories that vary from agent to agent: Naomi, Michelle, and James offer different models of the Hawai'i ethnic map, although, as Suzuki demonstrates, these models articulate with one another in a pattern of transformations and permutations. What the participants in the debate also demonstrate is the anchoring mechanism associated with certain key signs: relative language ability, historical moments, restaurants and their target audiences, and so on. These signs, or perhaps particular agents' relationship to these signs, provide signposts that people latch on to in order to make sense of the otherwise shifting terrain that they are faced with.

The four chapters together provide an inspiring model of how to approach ethnicity as a discursively achieved category. They certainly demonstrate how one can talk about ethnicity, community, and identity as socioculturally meaningful categories for both analyst and agent, while foregrounding at the same time the contingent nature of the same categories. They also demonstrate how further work can interrogate these categories in both a more discursive fashion and a more politicized fashion. By "discursive" I mean an expansion of one's analytic focus from labels and key signs (e.g., the Sikh turban, the restaurant for Japanese visitors) to more subtle forms, linguistic and non-linguistic, through which agents understand and construct ethnicity and community—the dispositions that Pierre Bourdieu enshrined in the notion of habitus, the subtle pronoun shifts that Kang comments on, the hesitations and dysfluencies that McElhinny and colleagues picked up on (see also Stromberg 1993), and so on. The chapters also suggest a greater attention paid to the political complexities of identity and community, and the possible ambivalences that they engender. Like the Filipino migrants whom McElhinny and colleagues interviewed, how do agents forge a sense of personhood in a larger context in which inequality and unfairness are part of the constitution of society and community alike? The approaches represented by these analyses have much to offer to future works that take complexity and contingency seriously.

REFERENCES

Austin, J. L. 1962. *How to do things with words*. Oxford: Clarendon Press.
Bellah, Robert N., Richard Madsen, William M. Sullivan, and Ann Swidler. 1985. *Habits of the heart: Individualism and commitment in American life*. Berkeley: University of California Press.
Besnier, Niko. 1994. The evidence from discourse. In *Handbook of Psychological Anthropology*, ed. Philip K. Bock, 197–210. Westport, Conn.: Greenwood Press.
Butler, Judith. 1990. *Gender trouble: Feminism and the subversion of identity*. New York: Routledge.
———. 1997. *Excitable speech: A politics of the performative*. New York: Routledge.

Creed, Gerald W. 2006. Reconsidering community. In *The seductions of community: Emancipations, oppressions, quandaries*, ed. Gerald W. Creed, 3–22. Santa Fe, N.M.: School of American Research Press.

di Leonardo, Micaela. 1991. Habits of the cumbered heart: Ethnic community and women's culture as American invented tradition. In *Golden ages, dark ages: Imagining the past in anthropology and history*, ed. Jay O'Brien and William Roseberry, 234–252. Berkeley: University of California Press.

Ehrenreich, Barbara. 1989. *Fear of falling: The inner life of the middle class*. New York: Pantheon.

Erikson, Erik H. 1959. *Identity and the life cycle: Selected papers*. New York: International Universities Press.

Joseph, Miranda. 2002. *Against the romance of community*. Minneapolis: University of Minnesota Press.

Lasch, Christopher. 1979. *Culture of narcissism: American life in an age of diminishing expectations*. New York: Warner Books.

Lave, Jean, and Etienne Wenger. 1991. *Situated learning: Legitimate peripheral participation*. Cambridge: Cambridge University Press.

Linde, Charlotte. 1983. *Life stories: The creation of coherence*. Oxford: Oxford University Press.

Newman, Katherine S. 1988. *Falling from grace: The experience of downward mobility in the American middle class*. New York: Free Press.

Ortner, Sherry. 2003. *New Jersey dreaming: Capital, culture, and the class of '58*. Durham, N.C.: Duke University Press.

Rumsey, Alan. 2000. Agency, personhood and the "I" of discourse in the Pacific and beyond. *Journal of the Royal Anthropological Institute* 6:101–115.

Strathern, Marilyn. 1988. *The gender of the gift*. Berkeley: University of California Press.

Stromberg, Peter G. 1993. *Language and self-transformation: A study of the Christian conversion narrative*. Cambridge: Cambridge University Press.

III

Languages in Contact

11

Arbitrating Community Norms

The Use of English Me in Japanese Discourse

Emi Morita

Silverstein's Model of Indexical Order

In a series of influential articles on language change, Michael Silverstein advances the notion of sociolinguistic life based on what he calls "indexical order" (2003). In its simplest formulation, indexical order is a concept that allows us to situate what a certain linguistic item means and how it is recognized within the ethno-metapragmatic framework of a given speech community, while remaining in full recognition of the fact that both of these phenomena are in perpetual dialogic co-evolution. What this means in the real-time practice of everyday language use is that linguistic item x habitually indexes referent(s) y in the context of z for a certain social group.

This "normal" use-in-context Silverstein calls the n-th degree indexical order (2003), the algebraic variable indicating, perhaps, the multiply embedded nature of semiotic order. "Within [any] n-th order ethno-metapragmatic perspective," writes Silverstein, the "creative indexical effects [are] the motivated realizations, of performable executions, of an already constituted framework of semiotic value" (2003, 194). Of relevance to this chapter is Silverstein's corollary observation that such an "already constituted framework of semiotic value...presupposes as well a transcendent *and competing* overlay of contextualization possibly *distinct* from the [earlier one]" (2003, 194; emphasis added). He goes on to note that "[there is an] N + 1st order indexicality thus always already *immanent as a competing structure of values* potentially indexed in-and-by a communicative form of the n-th order, depending on the degree and intensity of ideologization" of sociopragmatic use (2003, 194; emphasis added).

Silverstein demonstrates this "immanent structure of competing values" by examining the historical process of linguistic change in the English equivalent of the T/V system—in particular, the socially enacted contest between the second-person address terms *thou/thee* (the "T-form") and *ye/you* (the "Y-" or "V-form") during the seventeenth century (2003, 210–211, see also Silverstein 1985).

Examining Indexical Dialectic Change through Borrowing

Silverstein's analysis of the English language's historical shift into and out of T/V usage is particularly salient to my own investigations into the (currently) transgressive use of borrowed English language *me* in Japanese matrix language talk. For while Silverstein does not examine indexical order in bilingual interaction per se, I argue that the well-documented phenomenon of inter-language borrowing among bilinguals may reveal an indexical order that is not only actively negotiated on the n-th level order, but actively changed on the $n + 1$st level order as well.[1] As Benjamin Bailey (2001) notes, studies of bilingualism "can make visible social negotiation processes that are otherwise veiled" since "alternative frameworks for interpreting experience and constructing social reality that are associated with a code can thus be invoked by a switch into that code" (2001, 238–239). Such "alternative frameworks" are, I believe, precisely what Silverstein is referring to when he speaks of "competing" hierarchies of situated meaning that are simultaneously realized in real time and reorganized over historical time as the dialectic of indexical order.

As a way of contextualizing the discussion, consider the following data fragment:[2]

(1)

Masao:	me *no*	*daigakuseikatsu wa*	gate *nante*	*nai*	*no.*
	me GEN	student-life	TOP gate things like	not-exist	PRT

'During my (<u>me</u>-possessive) student life, there was no such thing like a <u>gate</u>.'

Though it may not be apparent to a non-Japanese speaker, it should be stressed at the onset that use of English language *me* is very marked in Japanese discourse. When we return to this datum later in this discussion, I hope to show how the speaker's use of first-person English *me* here constitutes a challenge to the current $n + 1$st level ideological system in a way that his superficially similar borrowing of the English word *gate* does not.

Using Silverstein's model of nested indexical orders as an analytical tool, this study examines first- and second-generation Japanese Americans' borrowing of the English first-person self-reference term *me* as an example of an emergent—and perpetually transformative—entextualization of possible new community norms. To understand the social cognition involved in this attempt at resetting social parameters through language use, and to fully appreciate its transgressive nature, we turn first to the social and ontological commitments of the existing Japanese person reference system.

Performative Aspects of Indexing the Self in Japanese

The Japanese personal reference system differs radically from English. For while there is only one English term for self—self-subsisting and autonomous "I"—the Japanese language has as many different terms for referring to oneself as there are possible social relations that one might find oneself in. For example, *boku*, *ore*, *wahi*, *atashi*, *watashi*, and *watakushi* are just some of the self-reference terms that a Japanese speaker may need to use in a single day.

I am oversimplifying considerably to give readers a sense of the pragmatics: *Watakushi* is used in very formal situations by both male and female speakers; *watashi* is commonly used by female speakers, while male speakers use it only in certain formal situations; male speakers in casual speech often use *boku* or *ore*, as the latter sounds "rougher" than the former; female speakers may use *atashi* in informal talk but switch to *watashi* in more formal situations, and so on.[3]

Moreover, not only personal pronouns but also kinship terms and occupational terms are used to refer to one's self. For example, a mother may refer to herself as *okaasan* 'mom' or *mama* when talking to her child, but may use *obachan* 'aunty' when she is talking to her child's friend. A few minutes later, she may refer to herself as *oneechan* 'elder sister' when she is talking to her younger sister. If the same speaker is an elementary school teacher, she may use *sensei* 'teacher' when speaking to her students, as in *sensei no ato ni tsuite itte kudasai* 'repeat after teacher (me),' but *watashi* or *watakushi* when conversing with the schoolmaster. In addition, she may refer to herself as *atashi* to a female friend, but as *watashi* to an interlocutor who is just an acquaintance. There are dialectal variations as well. For instance, *washi* is commonly used for "I" in the Kansai dialect, while *ora* is used in the Tohoku dialect. Each term for "I" can index (among other factors) the speaker's gender, age, status, and regional origin; the formality of the context; the intimacy of the relationship between the interlocutors; and the position of the speaker vis-à-vis her immediate interlocutor as well as the larger community.

Choosing a self-reference term can thus be seen as a Japanese speaker's display of her or his understanding of her or his social role at that moment in that context—what Silverstein calls an n-th order indexical deployment into an $n + 1$ sociopragmatic order. Each instance of self- and other- reference is an explicit performance of positioning oneself within the social order in which the n-th level indexes of "self" (now, here, in this context) and "other" (likewise) derive their meaning. When Japanese speakers choose an appropriate (or inappropriate) term to refer to themselves, they explicitly claim a certain stance toward this indexical order.

In addition, Japanese self-reference terms index not only the speaker's shifting social positioning but also her or his positioning of her or his interlocutors, and the relationship she or he wishes to establish with them. In other words, self-reference terms in Japanese are n-th order indexicals that point to the speaker as well as to the speaker's stance toward the interlocutor by defining their relationship within an explicit $n + 1$ order.[4] By comparison, the English language, with only a single first-person singular nominative term "I," can seem "indiscriminate" to Japanese speakers. Yet this single element functions as an all-purpose index for any English-language speaker to refer to oneself in any relationship in any situation at any point. The pronoun "I" thus does not so much eliminate the superordinate $n + 1$ indexical order as it more effectively masks it.

The Non-Appearance of *Me* in Japanese Discourse

The conceptual framework underlying the use of reference terms for the first person is thus radically different in Japanese and in English. It is now clear why the use of English *me* as a self-reference term in Japanese discourse is so marked and how it conflicts with an $n + 1$ level indexical order. First of all, the English term indexes an English-speaking identity. Second, not changing the term depending on the interlocutor and situation and using *me* explicitly indicates the speaker's nonconformity to the prevailing social and linguistic norms of Japan.

The inappropriateness of such behavior has been noted by monolingual Japanese speakers themselves, as is evidenced by the enduring popularity of the famous Japanese comic series *Osomatsukun*, which was written in the 1960s. Iyami, a character in *Osomatsukun*, is an eccentric and somewhat conceited person who was supposed to have spent a long time abroad (specifically, in France). He is repeatedly depicted as a person who always refers to himself as *me* even when he is speaking Japanese to other Japanese in Japan. In the cartoon in figure 11.1, Iyami even adds the wildly inappropriate English address term "Mr." when referring to himself—something that is never done, even with the Japanese equivalent of that term (the suffix *-san*).

The perceived self-absorption and obnoxiousness of "Mr." Iyami's language use suggest that Japanese people in Japan share access to a stereotypical notion that

Figure 11.1. Mr. Iyami: From "Osomatsukun" (Akatsuka 1964/2005). Reprinted with permission of Elsevier and Mouton

Mr. Iyami:	*me ga o-furansu gaeri no dezainaa no mistaa Iyami zansu*
	me SUB HON France return GEN designer GEN mister Iyami am
	'I (<u>me</u>) am Mr. Iyami, a designer coming back from France.'

Japanese who are foolishly proud of how "Westernized" they have become refer to themselves by borrowing the English term *me*. Since the choice of Japanese terms for self must take one's social relationship to other people into perspective, and the use of an all-purpose *me* makes a point of precisely not doing this, deploying *me* as a first-person reference term may be regarded as arrogant, eccentric, or as demeaning of Japanese society.

Although the Japanese language is saturated with foreign loan words, referring to oneself as *me* differs significantly from other English borrowings. In the monolingual speaker's *n*-th level indexical order, it is considered an unambiguous departure from Japanese norms and is thought by many to be characteristic of a certain kind of (perhaps not fully "Japanese") Japanese.

Use of English Me in Japanese American Contexts

In the following data, I want to show how the same indexical item may be undergoing sociolinguistic change in the new indexical order of Japanese speakers living in North America. I examine how *me* is borrowed into Japanese utterances across Japanese American speech communities where members do not share the same semiotic framework. Since the anomalous insertion of an autonomous first-person reference term indexes "a competing structure of values" that is immanent within the present sociolinguistic indexical order (Silverstein 2003, 194), such uses of *me* may be perceived as and also function as challenges to the *n*-th level current ideological system. By contextualizing these dialogic borrowing practices within Silverstein's epistemological framework, I hope to show how the mutually transformative interplay between usage and context may "constitute a major vectorial force in formal linguistic change" (Silverstein 2003, 194).

My data on the everyday borrowing of *me* reveals that this phenomenon is not only contextually motivated but also an effective achievement for the constitution of new *n*-th level community frameworks of semiotic value operating dialectically within—and to some extent, against—the existing *n* +1 order of sociolinguistic indexicality. My emphasis, in particular, will be on the importance of community validation for this semiotic process, which becomes visible by contrasting the different uses of *me* across Japanese American bilingual communities, by different speakers, and in different contexts within the same community.

Japanese Immigrant Talk in North America

Like other ethnic groups, Japanese immigrants or children who are born in the United States to Japanese parents are immersed in two languages, and code-switching and borrowing may occur both in the immigrant generation as well as in later generations. The phenomenon of borrowing *me* that I focus on here occurs when a Japanese-English bilingual speaks Japanese as a matrix language, that is, the syntactic structure and most of the vocabulary are Japanese, and English words or phrases are inserted at the intrautterance level. The excerpt below illustrates such an example. Here we find that Masao, a sixty-four-year-old Japanese American male, refers to himself as *me*.

(2) Conversation between a Japanese American couple (English is in plain text, Japanese in italics)

Masao: *nihon ja kangaerarenai* [*yo.*
           Japan in unthinkable   PRT
           'It is unthinkable in Japan.'

Kyoko: [*nai   ne.*
                                 un(thinkable) PRT
                                 'unthinkable.'

Masao: me *no   daigaku-seikatsu wa*   gate *nante   nai   no.*
           me GEN student-life   TOP gate things like no-exist PRT
           'During my (<u>me</u>-possessive) student life, there was no such thing like a <u>gate</u>.'

           wide open. *ne.*
           wide open PRT
           'It was <u>wide open</u>.'

           Walk in the street middle of night. It's a street.
           'You could <u>walk in the street in the middle of the night. It's a street</u>.'

Masao phrases "my student life" as "me *no daigaku-seikatsu*" in his Japanese sentence. Here the noun phrase consists of the English person pronoun *me* plus the Japanese case particle *no*.[5] Borrowing of frequently used English words in Japanese talk is common among Japanese-English bilinguals in the United States regardless of their length of stay or their proficiency level in English. (As can be seen from the above example, Masao is also fluent in English.) However, borrowing the English first-person pronoun *me* as a self-reference term is usually found only among Japanese American immigrants to the United States and their offspring. English speakers who learn Japanese as a foreign language later in life do not display such behavior. Nor do Japanese students or businesspeople who have been in the United States for relatively short periods of time. In other words, this phenomenon is not a reflection of the speaker's Japanese incompetence, but rather should be seen as a competent speaker's purposeful choice.

It has been noted in the literature on Japanese American bilingualism that many first-generation Japanese Americans characteristically borrow English *me* as a first-person pronoun (e.g., Hiramoto 2006; Nishimura 1986, 1989, 1997; Shindo 1977), as in the following example:

(3)

Hideyo, a seventy-three-year-old Japanese American immigrant, is talking to her brother, Shindo, in the United States. Hideyo and Shindo have not seen each other for fifty-three years, since Hideyo got married and settled in Northern California.

Hideyo: *yuube*   me *tachi de tukuttan yo   tabensai.*
           last night me pl.   by made   PRT eat-IMP
           'Last night we (<u>me</u>-plural) made it. Eat it.'

Shindo: *sushi ya ajituke gohan.*
           sushi and flavored rice
           'Sushi and flavored rice.'

Hideyo: *soo yo,   anta ga   kurun jakee,*
           yes PRT you SUB come because
           'Yes, since you were coming,'

           kodomotachi to   noo, tsukuttan yo,
           children   with PRT made   PRT
           'I made it with my children.'

           maa, tabensai.
           well eat-IMP
           'Well, eat.'
           (Shindo 1977, 175)

In Japan, women in their seventies would normally use *atashi*, *watashi*, a regional dialect equivalent, or a kinship term for self-reference. Yet here we find an *Issei* (first-generation) woman referring to herself as *me* when talking to her monolingual Japanese brother.

In order to contextualize this n-th level phenomenon, we must first examine the $n + 1$ level history of the Japanese in America. In Japan, immigration to other countries became popular around the end of the nineteenth century, with many Japanese leaving to work on Hawai'i's sugarcane plantations and many other Japanese immigrating both to North America and South America. In the United States alone there are currently more than one million Japanese Americans, and these Japanese Americans are often categorized according to their generation, e.g., *Issei* (first generation), *Nisei* (second generation), *Sansei* (third generation), and so on (see Suzuki, this volume).

Issei were born in Japan and the majority of them therefore grew up as monolingual Japanese speakers. Historically, they came to the United States as adults and most were engaged in agriculture.[6] These first-generation Japanese Americans had to learn English in order to deal with daily life with Americans but also formed Japanese American communities (Shindo 1977). Later, during the World War II, many of those same *Issei* experienced life in the relocation camps. Other *Issei* immigrated as the wives of American servicemen. Susan M. Ervin-Tripp reports that English fluency among these *Issei* largely correlated with their "conservatism, identification with America, and acculturation" (Ervin-Tripp 1967, 89).

Of course, just as contemporary *Issei* English language fluency differs considerably among individuals, earlier *Issei* borrowing of English into Japanese discourse most likely also differed both on the individual level and at the level of the region or community. What is interesting to note, however, is that whether the immigrants went to the United States, Hawaiʻi, or Canada, we find the borrowing of *me* as a term for self-reference embedded in their Japanese discourse. Mie Hiramoto (2006), for example, reports that *me* and *you* were prototypical borrowings observed among Japanese immigrants in Hawaiʻi.

The following example is taken from a recording of a conversation by a second-generation (*Nisei*) Japanese Canadian (Nishimura 1989). Born into an English-speaking environment, *Nisei* are usually more fluent in English than in Japanese. They, too, borrow *me* in the place of Japanese first-person reference terms.

(4)

me *wa   sugu   kaette*, lucky.
me TOP immediately return lucky
'I (me) was <u>lucky</u>, because I went home immediately.'

neesan antoki,   Vancouver *de* one week *okuretara…moo*,
sister   that time Vancouver at one week delay if   EMP
'My older sister was late <u>one week</u> in <u>Vancouver</u> at that time, and…really,'

they couldn't move without permit, eh?
they couldn't move without permit, eh?
'<u>They couldn't move without permit, eh</u>?'

soo. she *wa*   took her a month to come home *yo*,   yeah.
so   she TOP took her a month to come home PRT yeah
'Right. It <u>took her a month to come home</u>, you know. <u>Yeah</u>.'

moo, nihonjin wa   minna   watch-*sarete*.
EMP Japanese TOP everyone watch PASS
'Really, Japanese were all <u>watch</u>ed, and…'
(Nishimura 1989, 373)

The speaker switches her matrix sentences back and forth between Japanese and English, but in the first line she starts her Japanese sentence with the English *me* as her first-person pronoun. These examples (and my data also) affirm that such behavior seems to be characteristic of some first- and second-generation Japanese Americans and Japanese Canadians.

Use of English *Me* in the *N* + 1 Sociopragmatic Order

As we have seen, deployment of *me* as a first-person self-referential term is quite marked in Japan, where its valence in the *n* + 1 sociolinguistic pragmatic is negatively appraised. In a homogeneous Japanese-speaking environment it is often regarded as a speakers' explicit assertion of a deviant identity, a deliberate demarcation between "normative" monolingual-Japanese and the Japanese-English bilingual person who borrows.

But such practices may come to seem very different in the bilingual context, as first-generation Japanese immigrants found both the n-th and $n + 1$ level relations of Japanese increasingly in conflict with the demands of American English and its $n + 1$ sociopragmatic order. How did such deviant and "marked" use of self-referencing become an acceptable form of sociolinguistic behavior? As Silverstein notes, real-time evaluation of the use of linguistic items on the n-th level indexical order is done in reference to the $n + 1$ degree order—and this $n + 1$ degree order is not inherent to the language. Rather, it is organic, that is, it may differ from community to community, it may change over time, and it is sustained or changed by the people who use it.

In their first encounters with the English language in its American context, the *Issei* faced a different—and for them as yet unexplicated—theory of $n + 1$ interrelational practice. Here, one did not need to continually reposition oneself anew relative to each new interlocutor; in fact, the resources for doing so were virtually unavailable. To these immigrants, English *me* could have been deployed as an innovative resource for neutralizing overt social differences between fellow Japanese-speaking people, and as a way of assimilating to the downward pressures exerted upon them by an $n + 1$ indexical order where egalitarian display was positively valued and the use of "stratifying" or "differentiating" honorific terms was negatively valued. Since Japanese-English speakers have access to (minimally) two self-standing matrices [i.e., n, $n + 1$, $n + 2 \ldots$] of relational order, one in the Japanese language and another in the English language, when enough of these bilinguals shared the same experience of negotiating these disparate systems, English *me* in Japanese matrix talk lost its strangeness—and, eventually, its Japanese connotations of being arrogant and eccentric.

In addition, the conditions of immigration also impacted language change. Since the first generation of Japanese Americans found themselves in communities with people whom they did not necessarily know before immigrating, choosing which term was appropriate for any given situation was likely difficult. Hiramoto (2006) suggests that pre-World War II Japanese immigrants in Hawai'i borrowed English personal pronouns in part as a strategy to deal with dialectal differences, since regional dialects had different first-person reference terms. The Japanese person reference system makes sense in Japanese society where it is an organic part of everyday social relationships and linguistic history. Once people are cut off from this society, however, such practices may no longer find their use in a new community where such social relationships and history do not exist.

Moreover, the new *me* form appears to have become an $n + 1$st-order register for indexing a specifically Japanese American identity. Using *me* shows one's understanding of the underlying social cognition of the n-th level indexical person reference system in Japanese, as well as the need for compromise within the ideologically competing $n + 1$ social structure of a new speech environment. As predicted under Silverstein's model, a competing set of values that was immanent in these speakers' native Japanese $n + 1$ order appears to have become valorized through n-th level order use, and has, in some cases, become an $n + 1$ sociopragmatic norm for a new community.

Case Study 1: *Me* in the Talk of Japanese American Adults

My data of naturally occurring conversation between Japanese Americans exhibits many instances of such behavior. In these data, a sixty-four-year-old male Japanese American, Masao, constantly refers to himself as *me*. Masao came to the United States in 1955 in his twenties after his college education in Japan. He went to college again in the States and became an American citizen and worked as a pharmacist in a California town. Although his native language is Japanese, he speaks fluent English and in my data he often completely switches to English in his speech.

Masao's wife, Kyoko, came to the United States around the same time as he did but she has been a housewife primarily, and her interaction with native English speakers is limited compared to Masao's. Kyoko says she is not comfortable speaking English, although her comprehension of English is quite advanced. In the data, she often borrows English nouns and phrases, but unlike Masao, she does not produce any entire sentences in English when in a primarily Japanese-speaking environment. When the couple talks to each other, their entire discourse is in Japanese, except for occasional borrowing.

The data are from a videotape of a visit that Masao and Kyoko made to Los Angeles to see their niece, the Japanese-born author of this article, who had been in the United States and speaking English for almost eight years. Here, the couple is meeting the author as an adult for the first time. In the excerpt below, Masao and Kyoko are talking to the author about how often they play golf. The matrix language is Japanese, but some words related to number are borrowed into English. The focus of our analysis is the point where Masao refers to himself as *me*.

(5)

Kyoko: weekly two times *iku no.*
          weekly two times go PRT
          'I go twice a week.'

          e::to toonamento aru   to,
          umm tournament there-is if
          'When there is a tournament,'

          monthly *ni* once a month *toonament aru   no. kurabu no   ne.*
          monthly in once a month tournament there-is PRT club   GEN PRT
          'There is a tournament <u>once a month</u>, in our club.'

          sore ni ikkai iku   desho.
          that to once go   you know
          'I go to that once, you know.'

Masao: *de me to   isshoni iku kara   ne.*
          and me with together go because PRT
          'And you go with <u>me</u>.'

Kyoko: *soo.*
          yes
          'Yes.'

The usual term for a Japanese male person to refer to himself when speaking with his wife is *ore* or *boku*. However, in my data, Masao's self-reference term is always the English *me*. Masao maintains the reference term *me* also when he talks to his Japanese niece.

(6)

Masao: *sooka, Emi   ga   bideo iru   n   dattara* me *ga   doose   ne,*
          I see. (name) SUB video need NR if   me SUB anyway PRT
          'I see. If Emi needed a video, anyway I (<u>me</u>), you know. ...'

Kyoko: *un.*
          yes
          'Yes.'

Masao: *dejitaru no   bideo kau kara.   dakara kore ne.   furui yo.*
          digital   ATT video buy because so   this PRT old   PRT
          'Was going to buy a digital video anyway. This is old, you know?'

          [*Roku-shichi nen   tatteru yo*
          six   seven years spent   PRT
          'It is six to seven years old, you know?'

Kyoko: [*ojisan wa   ne, tansu no   koyashi bakkari katteru no.*
          uncle   TOP PRT closet GEN fertilizer only   buying PRT
          'Your uncle is buying only good-for-nothing things.'

When Masao code-switches to English, he uses "I" for the first-person pronoun as is indicated by the English rules of grammar.

(7)

Masao: Then she uh, completes her, (I don't know,) Master degree and working
          toward (   ) something.

Kyoko: PhD *desho*?
          'PhD isn't it?'

Masao: I don't think PhD yet.

But as observed in other Japanese Americans' borrowing examples, the word that Masao uses to refer to himself when the matrix sentence is in Japanese is *me*.

Likewise, Masao's wife, Kyoko, also refers to herself as *me* when she is talking to Masao.

(8)

Kyoko: *Nakaya-san tteiu hito   to   yoku machigaerunda yo.*
           (name)   QUO person with often mistaken   PRT
           'I'm often mistaken with a person whose name is Nakaya.'

           me no   gorufu no kaato ni Nakaya tte   kaitearu namae ga.
           me GEN golf   of cart   to (name) QUO written name SUB
           'It was written as 'Nakaya' on my (<u>me</u>-possessive) golf cart.'

           Jun Nakaya tte   kaitearu kara.   zenzen.
           (name)   QUO written because not at all
           'Since it says Jun Nakaya, so everyone was clueless.'

           dareno kore, Jun Nakaya tte?
           whose this (name)   QUO
           'Whose is this? Who is Jun Nakaya?'

           hehehehehe.
           'Hehehehehe.'

In the above excerpt, Kyoko refers to herself as *me* when she is facing her husband. Her intended addressee is her husband who—by his lack of any discernible uptake to being addressed as such—displays that he shares the same community norm. Significantly, Kyoko does not refer to herself in the same way when she is talking to the author (who is her niece). In the excerpt below, she first uses the Japanese first-person pronoun *atashi*, then self-repairs and uses the kinship term *obasan* (aunt)—thus taking the niece's point of view, which is a typical Japanese allocentric use of reference terms, that is, taking the youngest person's point of view and referring to oneself and others from that position (Morita 2003, 382; Suzuki 1973, 168–169).

(9)

EM: *nihon de gaaden nanka gaadeningu nante dekiru   toko nai   yo,*
        Japan in garden TOP   gardening   TOP do-POT place not-exist PRT
        'There is no place where you can do such things as gardening in Japan,'

        obasan.
        aunt
        'Aunt.'

Kyoko: *gaaden obasan nanka nihon de gaadenya-san tanondara taihenda kara*
        garden aunt   TOP Japan in gardener   hire-if   serious because
        'Garden-, if I (aunt) hire a gardener in Japan, it will cost too much so,'

atashi ga,   obasan ga   yarunda yo.
I   SUB aunt   SUB do   PRT
'I (atashi), I (aunt) do it myself.'

Here Kyoko's self-repair indicates her sensitivity to the contextually appropriate choice of reference terms. Japanese Americans' borrowing of *me* is therefore not due to the deterioration of competence in Japanese. Rather, such borrowing should be seen as a voluntary and interactively significant act.

Moreover, Masao and Kyoko's borrowing of *me* is produced in and by local contexts, and this local context includes their relationship to their interlocutors. Kyoko's choice of first-person reference term here not only differs at the lexical level, but at the level of $n + 1$st indexical order as well. That is, her choice of kinship term indicates her shifting stance from "Japanese American" to "Japanese niece-aunt relationship" while all the time speaking Japanese to another Japanese person in America. Thus, Japanese Americans must negotiate stance against not only two different levels of indexical order (here, within the traditional Japanese familial relationship and within the relationship of commonality as Japanese migrants to America) but also two different systems of indexical order (i.e., Japanese and Japanese American normativity about both of the above).

Note, too, that although Kyoko shifts her stance, vacillating between the enactment of two different communities' $n + 1$ indexical norms, Masao does not likewise switch his choice of first-person reference term. Given that he is not a blood relative of Kyoko's niece, but only more distantly related through marriage, his more relaxed relations of rights and obligations toward his (not true) niece may be further indexed by the deliberate use of "indiscriminate" *me* in his speech. This suggests that the borrowing of *me* may actually be a useful device for bilinguals to refer to themselves in contexts where the relationship between parties is unclear or has not yet been established.

Since the Japanese person reference system is linked to how people relate to one another and construct their social organization, and since such social organization is embedded in a larger historical as well as geographical context, it may be difficult to apply such a system outside of Japan without an already established social organization outside of the $n + 1$ indexical order that gives such n-th level indexes their "meaning." Thus, we find here an interesting case whereby a certain aspect of a language can become not only unnecessary to code a specific aspect of one's social relations, but can also become an obstacle if it is applied in a society that has not developed the same complex relationships and history. As Silverstein reminds us: "Metapragmatic function, and hence more particularly its explicit, discursive expression in metapragmatic discourse, is ideologically saturated; it relates and, in its discursive mode even describes, explains, or rationalizes the pragmatics of language use (e.g., in terms like 'appropriateness-to-context' and 'effectiveness-in-context') in terms of perhaps more fundamental frameworks" (Silverstein 2003, 196).

Bearing the inherently dialectical nature of this last point in mind, in the next section we will consider a situation where a Japanese American *me* speaker's attempt at deploying an n-th order indexical is frustrated by the invocation of a competing $n + 1$ order indexical framework.

Case Study 2: *Me* in the Talk of a Japanese American
Bilingual Child

I will now consider the case of a Japanese-English bilingual child growing up in a language environment very different from the *Issei* community of Masao and Kyoko. In Emi Morita (2003) I reported on my study of two Japanese-English bilingual children living in the United States. One of the children, Jack, was five years old at the time and only he showed the same borrowing behavior as the first-generation Japanese American adults discussed earlier, that is, when he spoke Japanese, he referred to himself as *me*.[7]

Jack's spontaneous insertion of English lexical or phrasal elements into his Japanese talk can be observed in my data. This seemed to happen especially when he recognized that the Japanese interlocutor was also a bilingual who understood English.

(10)

EM: *Jack-chan wa   nani ga   kirai?*
        (name)   TOP what OBJ dislike
        'What do you dislike?'

Jack: me *wa   hebi   ga   kirai.*
        me TOP snake OBJ dislike
        'I (<u>me</u>) don't like snakes.'

According to his mother, Jack's first Japanese term for himself was "baby-*chan*" and after two months or so, it became *me*. At the time of my observations, he consistently used *me* as a first-person reference term.

Unlike in Masao and Kyoko's Japanese American community, however, where the use of *me* as a term for oneself is common and unmarked, in Jack's peer community environment, this was not the case. Rather, in Jack's Japanese-speaking environment, which consisted primarily of children who were monolingual and recent arrivals from Japan, no co-present Japanese speaker referred to himself or herself using the English reference term *me*. Instead, Jack's peers tended to follow Japanese, rather than Japanese American, norms for self-reference. Whenever I observed Jack playing with other Japanese boys, the boys would refer to themselves with standard Japanese terms for self (first name or *boku*). Although Jack's mother was a fluent bilingual, she also spoke to Jack in Japanese only (e.g., without codeswitching or borrowing) during my observations. Any evidence of borrowing *me* as a first-person pronoun by others appeared to be unavailable in Jack's Japanese-language environment.

It is clear that Jack came up with this particular instance of borrowing simply by use of his own creativity (see Morita 2003 for details). Being caught between two conceptually different reference systems, he incorporated the English person reference system into his Japanese environment when he found it necessary to circumvent the Japanese way of locating oneself in terms of a current unknown social relationship (see Song, this volume). The following excerpt is another example where Jack refers to himself as *me*.

(11)

Jack:

> *Taroo-kun no   okaasan,*
> (name)   GEN mother
> 'Taroo's mom,'

> *Jiroo-kun, saisho hito   ga   tsukutta mono,*
> (name)   first   person SUB made   thing
> 'Jiroo knocked over the building that I (lit: "a person") made,'

> me *ga   tsukutta mono o   boin   tte   tataita.*
> me SUB made   thing OBJ ONO QUO hit
> 'That I (me) made. Like this' (imitating the action of Jiroo)

Jiroo's mom:

> *Jack-chan no hoo ga   oniichan   dakara sa,*
> (name)   than   SUB elder.brother because PRT
> 'Because you (Jack) are the older brother,'

> *Jack-chan Jiroo-chan ni oshiete agete kureru?   nisai   dakara.*
> (name)   (name)   to teach   give   could-you two-year-old because
> 'Can you (Jack) teach Jiroo? Since he is only two years old.'

Jack's motivation for this borrowing can be attributed to several factors. First, the Japanese person address/reference system does not require children to change their self-reference terms as much as it requires adults to do so, since children's roles in Japanese social life are relatively simple and they do not have as many different social roles to linguistically index as adults. Second, and as I have discussed before (Morita 2003), Jack used the English "you" as his second-person reference form in his Japanese-speech environment when he did not know how to refer to his interlocutor. While ingenious, Jack soon changed the term as soon as he figured out the appropriate term, and more often than not, Jack used appropriate Japanese reference terms for other people. For example, when he referred to or addressed his friend Taroo, Jack used "Taroo-kun," and when he addressed or referred to Taroo's mother, he said "Taroo-kun no okaasan (Taroo's mother)." So Jack obviously had the sociocultural $n + 1$ knowledge that using "you" is not the n-th level Japanese social norm. However, his term for self was always *me* regardless of who he was talking to in Japanese (though he used "I" in English conversation). If Jack's strategy was just to simplify the personal reference system, he would have kept using the English second-person pronoun "you" as well.

Similarly, while such borrowing may match local $n + 1$ language ideologies in certain Japanese American communities, this was not the case for Jack. Rather, Jack was actually taking the risk of not being understood by his interlocutors. He regularly borrowed *me* regardless of whether or not the other person appeared to understand English, as illustrated in the example below.

(12) Jack explains to a Japanese six-year-old male child, Isamu, why the other children should not touch his toy railroad track.

Jack: me, me *no   senro dakara.*
           me me GEN track because
           'Because it's my, my (me, me-possessive) track.'

Isamu: *mi: mi: tte?*
           mi: mi: QUO
           'What's "me me"?'

Jack: me, me *no   senro.*
           me me GEN track
           'My, my (me, me-possessive) track.'

Isamu: *mi: tte?*
           mi: QUO
           'What's "me"?'

Here, the fact that Jack used the English n-th level indexical *me* over other pronouns that he knew (such as *boku*) reveals that he recognizes that *boku* and *me* are both availably different options of representing selfhood. Thus, Jack's use of *me* in this context indicates his ability to switch back and forth between two different systems of n-th level indexicality. Here we see the dialectic conflict where Jack's creative use of *me* at the bilingual n-th degree indexical order clashes with its sociopragmatic indexicality on the level of Japanese $n + 1$. Speaking Japanese involves not just the n-th level knowledge of the vocabulary and grammar, but the deft acquisition and deployment of the "knowledge of actual and potential social relations among speakers" as well as of a whole "system of role-dependent dispositions and moral intuitions" (Mühlhäusler and Harré 1990, 114).

As Jack learns. in the example cited above, by "engaging with such indexical semiotic material…observers and/or interactants…reach a sufficiency or cumulativity to make the simplifying abductive leaps from one or another of the dialectically-possible positions…to determine, at least for the moment, what the values of the other cotextual and contextual variables…must have been" (Silverstein 2003, 200). *Me* and *boku* both work equivalently within the conceptual framework of the child bilingual—where they don't work equivalently is in their interaction with the world of other speakers. And it is this latter knowledge that comes to invisibly reshape the prior knowledge.

Thus, the example provides us (and, more important, Jack) with the real-time microsociological evidence that the conflict between n-th and $n + 1$st order indexicality can only be resolved dialectically. It may be resolved as n is indexicalized into the existing order as a challenge, condemned as a mistake, dismissed as a joke, accepted as an alternative, or—eventually—adopted as part of the legitimate new $n + 1$. And the failure of communication depicted above reveals that a minimal amount of community validation is necessary for the process to begin whereby the bottom-up pressures of n-th level indexical practice cause a change in the $n + 1$ indexical order—as had been the case in Masao and Kyoko's community, but not in Jack's community. It is through the tracking of such dialectic evolutionary processes in real-time that we can thus best see "the critical link between the micro-contextual operation of indexical order and the semiotic operation of a macro-social framework in which indexicality is licensed or authorized by processual structures of baptismal essentialization" (Silverstein 2003, 204).

Dialectic Negotiation of Indexical Order

Interestingly, Jack's borrowing of *me* in his Japanese talk eventually ended. Two weeks before his seventh birthday, he finally started referring to himself in Japanese as *boku*, the form that most Japanese boys of his age use. This change happened shortly after he started attending a Japanese afternoon school where most of the students and teachers were native speakers of Japanese. Jack may have gained a better understanding of the Japanese $n + 1$ level's order indexicality of first-person reference through his participation in school. At the same time, he may have been socialized into local Japanese-language ideologies about *me*. If the n-th level identity expressed through *me* was devalued in this new $n + 1$ context, Jack may have ceased trying to maintain his bilingual identity because it was too costly for successful communication. This change in his selection of first-person reference terms indicates that an external factor (such as how marked a particular borrowing is in the environment) may impact language choice across the stages of a bilingual person's development.

Bilingual speakers' choice of terms for self exhibits their identity at least partially, if not largely, through the negotiation of the local community's n-th level and $n + 1$ level indexical orders. As a bilingual's social role as a member of society changes, he or she may need to renegotiate his or her linguistic choice to fit the social norm. Yet whether one does or does not follow the norm, the negotiation process itself fundamentally influences one's social identity.

It is thus not that bilingual children acquire a doubled set of "rules" per se, but rather that they recognize the $n + 1$ social system that n-th level language use relates to, and that they negotiate their own social cognition (of themselves and others) within these respective systems. Thus, Jack's use of *me* was as much a function of the system of social relations that he found himself in as it was a function of the language wherein such relations are expressed.

Yet because these two systems by necessity are in generative dialectic with each other, the dynamics of norm-construction exemplified by Japanese American immigrants' borrowing of *me* reveal that the negotiation of a language is not entirely restricted by the n-th level norm of immediate social consequence—and that whether or not such negotiation succeeds in the moment, it carries potentially challenging consequences for the existing $n + 1$ level order of ideological indexicality as well.

Conclusion

Studies in multilingualism have often argued that the motivation of mixing codes is related to ethnic identity, that is, the code that is mixed is associated with the sociopolitical power of a given language (e.g., Myers-Scotton 1993). Such studies, in other words, examine n-th level indexical phenomena within an $n + 1$ indexical order. It is not surprising, then, that in taking such a unilaterally top-down approach, little explanation is given as to why certain words are often borrowed, while others are rarely borrowed, and why only certain lexical items within a phrase are borrowed, as opposed to mixing an entire phrase. Embedding observed instances of naturally occurring borrowing within Silverstein's dialectical notion of indexical order, this study showed how two adult Japanese immigrants in the United States and an American-born English-Japanese bilingual child, who do not share a common code-speech model, might find good, immediately enactable sociopragmatic reasons to use the English first-person reference term *me* to refer to themselves in a Japanese-language matrix sentence.

Though these Japanese-English bilinguals are of different ages, different generations, different English proficiencies, and live in different environments, I have argued that such socially "dispreferred" behavior is not an idiosyncratic eccentricity on the part of the participants, but rather an ingenious solution of appealing to the ability of the current $n + 1$ order to make available competing norms so as to negotiate inherently ambiguous situations on the n-th level of immediately enacted sociolinguistic order. Given the fact that each speaker has access to two different matrices of n-th level and $n + 1$ level schemes of sociopragmatic order (Japanese and American), bilingualism introduces both exponential difficulties—as well as exponential possibilities—for negotiation and creativity in transgressively (and perhaps transformatively) juxtaposing and resetting the indexes of sociopragmatic order.

In my data, we find not only individuals' creative manipulation of competing $n + 1$ order possibilities but also the groundswell of community usage that may presage the kind of long-term historical "language shift" noted by the elimination of the T/V form in English in the seventeenth century. Whether or not these individually small perturbations in the n-th level order will, indeed, ultimately result in $n + 1$ change, we cannot, of course, predict right now. However, the concept of an interactive hierarchy of ever-evolving semiotic order allows us to see the sense in which *me* simultaneously: (1) becomes a community norm in certain Japanese American communities; (2) is incomprehensible because of insufficient acquaintance with the "competing set of structures" immanent in the present n-th level order; and (3) is comprehensible but looked down upon in Japan. In all of these cases, "the sociocultural reality manifested in-and-by discursive interaction becomes analytically visible, an immanent semiotic fact in such events of self- and other- definition" (Silverstein 2003, 227).

NOTES

1. Borrowing is described by Sarah G. Thomason (2001) as follows: "Most commonly, borrowed items are introduced into a language by native speakers of that language, but of course this is not the only possibility. ... The borrowers do not have to be native speakers. If your native language is English and you also speak Japanese fluently, you could introduce English elements into your version of Japanese as borrowings—not because you failed to master some bit of Japanese grammar, but simply because you wanted to use a particularly convenient English word or phrase or syntactic construction while speaking Japanese. Such introductions could be ephemeral, or they could be permanent parts of your Japanese speech.

You might not want to call the temporary English imports borrowings, but certainly the permanent ones would be, regardless of whether or not any other speakers of Japanese imitated your Japanese usage. And the only difference between the temporary and the permanent importations is social, not strictly linguistic: *once a feature occurs in someone's version of Japanese, even just once, it can and will turn into a borrowing if it becomes frequent and if it is also used by other speakers*" (Thomason 2001, 67–68, emphasis added). I thank Kathy Howard for pointing out that the phenomenon I am discussing in this study is most correctly described as borrowing and not code-mixing, as per Thomason's discussion.

2. Abbreviations used in interlinear gloss:

ATT	attributive form	EMP	emphasis marker	GEN	genitive
HON	honorific	IMP	imperative	NR	nominalizer
OBJ	object marker	ONO	onomatopoeic expression		
PASS	passive	POT	potential form	PRT	interactional particle
QUO	quotative particle	SUB	subject marker	TOP	topic marker

In sentences that are predominantly in Japanese, English words are underlined in the translation.

3. It may be interesting to note that first-person pronouns in Indo-European languages can trace their origin to the Latin *ego*, while the list of usable Japanese first-person pronouns has been changing continually throughout the history of the language. Throughout its past, however, Japanese first-person pronoun reference has always been a system of social practice that explicitly performs dispositiveness toward the other (Suzuki 1973, 4).

4. Note that those times when such double indexicality is done in English—as, for example, when a spouse asks, "Is that how you think you should treat your husband/wife?" instead of "...should treat me?"—the very double indexicality of the usage is marked in a way that is the precise obverse of the Japanese order.

5. Interestingly, all the examples of borrowed first-person pronoun use by Japanese-English bilinguals are uniformly *me* and not *I*—although *I* would be more grammatically equivalent. This phenomenon may be an artifact of the English case system, since, according to Carson T. Schütze and Kenneth Wexler (1996), the default case in English is Accusative or O6. lique (me), not Nominative (I).

6. The earliest *Issei* were allowed to own land (though it usually was barren), but in 1913, the state of California started legally restricting Japanese immigrants' activity in the United States. In 1924, the American government passed new immigration laws and Japanese Americans were prohibited from owning land. Conditions of leasehold changed for the worse, naturalization became impossible, and bringing wives from Japan was also prohibited. At this time, many Japanese Americans were working as tenant farmers under Caucasian Americans.

7. Jack was born in the United States to an American father and a Japanese mother. He was a simultaneous bilingual who was exposed to both Japanese and English from birth. His mother, a native speaker of Japanese, used a one-person-one-language method, that is, she spoke only Japanese to Jack and his monolingual American father spoke only English to Jack. Although he grew up mainly in the United States and attended English monolingual daycare, Jack had abundant exposure to Japanese. For most of the time, Jack had Japanese playmates who lived in the same town and he also had a Japanese babysitter who regularly spent time with him. In addition, he visited his grandparents on his mother's side and other relatives in Japan twice a year for a total of six weeks, and also had relatives who were monolingual Japanese speakers visit his family in the United States in between those trips. On such occasions, he spent a significant amount of time in a Japanese monolingual environment. According to his mother, although Jack had constant exposure to Japanese, when he was playing by himself,

his monologues were always in English. Therefore, she assumed that Jack primarily identified himself as "an English-speaking person." It may also be of some significance that Jack's
parents separated when he was two years and eight months old, and he lived with his Japanese
mother from that point on, though he did visit his English-speaking father on a regular basis.

REFERENCES

Akatsuka, Fujio. [1964] 2005. *Ofuransu gaeri no dezainaa*. [A designer returned from France.]
    Shukan Shonen Sandee. 20. Reprint in *Osomatsukun 6*. Tokyo: Takeshobo Bunko.)
Bailey, Benjamin. 2001. Switching. In *Key terms in language and culture*, ed. Alessandro
    Duranti, 238–240. Malden, Mass.: Blackwell.
Ervin-Tripp, Susan M. 1967. An Issei learns English. *The Journal of Social Issues* 23:78–90.
Hiramoto, Mie. 2006. Dialect contact in Hawai'i: The use of Japanese by plantation immi-
    grants. Manoa: Department of Linguistics. University of Hawai'i.
Morita, Emi. 2003. Children's use of address and reference terms: Language socialization in a
    Japanese-English bilingual environment. *Multilingua* 22:367–395.
Mühlhäusler, Peter, and Rom Harré. 1990. *Pronouns and people: The linguistic construction
    of social and personal identity*. Oxford: Blackwell.
Myers-Scotton, Carol. 1993. *Social motivations for codeswitching: Evidence from Africa.*
    Oxford: Clarendon Press.
Nishimura, Miwa. 1986. Intrasentential code-switching: The case of language assignment. In
    *Language processing in bilinguals: Psycholinguistic and neuropsychological perspec-
    tives*, ed. Jyotsna Vaid, 123–143. Hillsdale, N.J.: Lawrence Erlbaum.
———. 1989. The topic-comment structure in Japanese-English code-switching. *World
    Englishes* 8:365–377.
———. 1997. *Japanese/English code-switching: Syntax and pragmatics*. New York: Peter
    Lang Publishing.
Schütze, Carson T., and Kenneth Wexler. 1996. Subject case licensing and English root infini-
    tive. *Proceedings of the Annual Boston University Conference on Language Development*
    20:670–681.
Shindo, Kaneto. 1977. *Matsuri no koe: Aru Amerika imin no sokuseki*. [Voice of the festival: A
    biography of a Japanese immigrant in America.] Tokyo: Iwanami shinsho.
Silverstein, Michael. 1985. Language and the culture of gender: At the intersection of struc-
    ture, usage, and ideology. In *Semiotic mediation: Sociocultural and psychological
    perspectives*, ed. Elizabeth Mertz and Richard J. Parmentier, 219–259. Orlando, Fla.:
    Academic Press.
———. 2003. Indexical order and the dialectics of sociolinguistic life. *Language and
    Communication* 23:193–229.
Suzuki, Takao. 1973. *Kotoba to bunka* [Language and culture]. Tokyo: Iwanami Shoten.
Thomason, Sarah G. 2001. *Language contact: An introduction*. Edinburgh: Edinburgh
    University Press.

12

Illegitimate Speakers of English

Negotiation of Linguistic Identity among Korean International Students

Joseph Sung-Yul Park

International Graduate Students from a Transnational Perspective

There has been little discussion within Asian American studies about international students pursuing graduate degrees in North America. This is most likely because they are usually not considered to be "Americans" but "foreigners"—not only by mainstream members of society but also by other Asian Americans as well as themselves. Such a view is also reflected in the way international students are treated in academic research beyond Asian American studies. There have been several research topics in which international students studying in North America (of whom Asian nationals form a recognizably large part) figure prominently, such as the "brain drain" (Song 1997), cross-cultural adjustment of international students (Wang, Lin, Pang, and Shen 2007), and linguistic and discursive competence of international teaching assistants (Madden and Myers 1994). We can notice that all of these topics underline the foreignness of these students, rather than their potential membership as Americans and their contribution to the constitution of American society. The underlying assumption that drives these issues, apparently, is that these students "belong" to their "home countries" and should return there as soon as possible, and that their linguistic and cultural backgrounds differ so drastically that they are in a constant struggle to adjust and adapt to life in North America.

But such a perspective can be problematic. Pyong Gap Min (2006) notes that while a larger percentage of students from Asian countries such as Taiwan and South Korea now return to their countries of origin for their careers than they did decades ago, there has been a great increase in the number of students who stay in the United States as permanent residents. This observation suggests that simply identifying international students as foreigners who will eventually return to their countries of origin overlooks an important juncture in the formation of Asian American identities. But more important, imagining these students as passive visitors misses the fact that they are agents who actively construct the meaning of place and belonging in a transnational context. That is, while the status and position of international graduate students depend on various material, institutional, and social constraints of the "host country" and "home country," they may also transcend such boundaries by interpreting and reformulating their transnational experience through the discursive construction of self and the world around them. In fact, the transient status of international graduate students—their possible but unconfirmed future residence in the United States, and their integration into American society via institutions of higher education while maintaining strong transnational ties with their countries of origin—can be made an important point of analysis, rather than an excuse to exclude them from our understanding of Asian Pacific America.

In the context of globalization, the way people cross boundaries of nationhood, race, ethnicity, and gender through language and discourse has become a central issue. Studying how speakers deal with experiences of liminality in that process not only provides us with an account of their adjustment in border contexts but also reveals how language may serve as a creative resource that can index and constitute new identities and positions; that is, the way symbolic resources of language shift in their value as they cross into new contexts and networks of social relationships. Martin F. Manalansan (1995), for example, discusses how swardspeak, a male homosexual argot used among Filipino gay men, "provides a space where Filipino gay immigrants connect traditions and practices of the homeland with those of America, the country of settlement. In other words, swardspeak alleviates the rupture brought about by immigration and resettlement" (253). In this case, swardspeak functions not so much as a "marker" of Filipino gay identity, but as a way of making sense of its speakers' new experiences, as a symbolic field in which they can locate the self and other and give meaning to the relationship between them.

It is through this process that the speaker comes to reposition himself or herself against dominant ideologies of the new social context. As research on language and identity (Bucholtz and Hall 2004) and the chapters in this volume point out, language is an important resource through which oppositions of identities are indexed. Thus, repositioning one's identity involves the reworking of ideologies that link language, ethnicity, race, and nationality, and the transnational speaker must negotiate between the ideologies of one social context and those of another (see Morita, this volume; Song, this volume). Transnational people bring with them symbolic resources from one context, relocating them within new regimes of symbolic power; this shows us how symbolic oppositions in transnational contexts must be seen as constructed through both local systems of oppositions and globally circulated ones.

Looking at international students from a transnational perspective, then, forces us to avoid an essentialist view of how identities are constituted, and to see how relations of oppositions are created through the reworking of existing symbolic relations. In this chapter, I will explore these issues by investigating the construction of linguistic identity by a group of Korean graduate students studying in the United States. The goal of this chapter is not to draw generalizations about the discursive practices of Korean international students, but to understand the process of their identity construction from the perspective of their transnational and transient status. In particular, I will discuss how these people deploy discursive practices and language ideologies from one context into another, thereby making sense of their liminal position in relation to dominant ideologies and stereotypes of society.

Korean Language Ideologies and "Disclaiming English"

Of particular relevance to the discussion of this chapter is the Korean practice of "disclaiming English." As described in detail elsewhere (Park, forthcoming), this refers to a range of practices by which a speaker both (1) denies an association with the identity English indexes in Korean society; and (2) renounces legitimate speakership of the language by acknowledging one's incompetence (a simultaneity that is captured by the dual sense of 'to disclaim'). For instance, many Koreans in Korea often deny that they have good competence in English and use such claims as an excuse for avoiding speaking English publicly; occasions for speaking English are interactionally framed as embarrassing situations through devices such as repair initiators or laughter; and when the topic of English is introduced, speakers commonly relate their experiences of difficulty in using English, as if inability in English is a highly relevant point to raise whenever there is talk about English. In general, Koreans take an interactional stance toward English that treats it as a "difficult language"; they present themselves as having failed to master the language despite many years of formal instruction. This stance is not necessarily an indication of the actual competence of Koreans, for people who are quite competent in English engage in such practices as well. Neither is it a manifestation of humility that is often stereotypically attributed to Koreans, as they do not engage in comparable practices in dealing with other languages—fluent speakers of languages such as Japanese may not openly brag about their competence, but it would be less common to find a Korean fluent in Japanese avoiding an occasion for demonstrating her competence by claiming that it is embarrassing.

Instead, practices of disclaiming English can be seen as a case of strategic ambiguity (Heller 1988; Woolard 1998); they allow the speaker to navigate through the complex terrain of language ideologies in which English is simultaneously a valued resource and a symbol of a foreign, Western culture. English in Korea is seen as highly valuable symbolic capital, due to its status as a language of material opportunity as well as its perceived importance in the global economy. But precisely because of this material value and also because of strong nationalist language ideologies, displaying strong competence in or preference for English is also risky; as I will show below, for instance, openly assuming familiarity with English by pronouncing English words in the midst of Korean utterances with native English pronunciation would be seen as inappropriate, pretentious, or even un-Korean. Engaging in the practices of disclaiming English, then, provides Koreans with a useful means for balancing these ideological pressures. It allows one to profess a distance from English without explicitly engaging in an outright denial of the modern indexicality of the language, negotiating between contesting language ideologies about English.

One consequence of this practice is that Koreans end up constructing themselves as incompetent speakers of English. Through this process, which I call self-deprecation (Park, forthcoming), subjects subordinate themselves within a social or symbolic hierarchy through discourse. Self-deprecation does not merely comment on Koreans' incompetence in English, but links it with issues of power, and as such, may be seen as a subtype of illegitimation (Bucholtz and Hall 2005). Thus, disclaiming English is not really an abrogation of the global hegemony of English, even though it constitutes an effort to distance oneself from English; rather, it must be seen as a practice through which that hegemony is reproduced in a local context.

It is not my claim here that disclaiming English is an exclusive practice of Koreans that uniquely distinguishes them from other groups. Rather, I argue that such practices are an integral element of how Koreans make sense of their relationship with the world, and are thus an important part of how a speaker's identity as a Korean is discursively constructed.[1] Nonetheless, disclaiming English may be seen as a point of contrast for Koreans in Korea and in the United States. Since, for many Asian Americans, English is a native language that they feel they have rightful ownership of and competence in, engagement in self-deprecative practices would be indexical of being "(Korean) Korean" rather than "Korean American"[2] or "American." How do Korean international students studying in the United States, then, align themselves with this practice, given their transient position between Koreans in Korea and Koreans who have long-standing residence in America? The following sections move to a discussion of this question.

"The Person Kept Saying, 'I'm Sorry?'": Disclaiming English among Korean International Students

The following discussion is based on my observation of a group of Korean international students and their spouses in the United States and analysis of recorded interaction among these speakers. My observation and recording of their interactions were made during 1998 and 1999. At that time, these students were in their mid twenties to early thirties, and were studying at various universities in California, pursuing graduate degrees in fields such as engineering and social science. All of them came from Seoul and had finished their undergraduate education there; they also shared a relatively affluent middle-class background. These speakers had known one another since they were college students in Korea, and maintained their connection after coming to the United States, regularly meeting as a group at one another's residences. It is at these casual gatherings that the recordings used in this paper were made.

One might say that these speakers are "typical" international students in the sense that several things about them underline a "foreignness" that is commonly attributed to international students. First, at the time of the recordings, all of the speakers had spent less than two years in the United States. Second, their social life mostly centered around a network of other Koreans, particularly other Korean international students, as opposed to Korean Americans (see Myles and Cheng 2003).

Perhaps most important, they did not see themselves as "Americans"—even though some of them already had clear intentions to remain in the United States after their studies (and eventually secured employment in the United States and became permanent residents). They strongly identified with a Korean national identity—that is, they would self-identify as "Koreans" and not as "Americans"—though at the same time, they had much familiarity with mainstream American lifestyles as well.

Another important aspect that appears to highlight their foreignness is their language use. In their interactions, they would not only communicate with one another in Korean but also frequently adopt interactional practices that are characteristic of Koreans living in Korea. In the interactions that I observed, they engaged in practices of disclaiming English, which, on the surface, seemed to underline their closer connection to widely circulating cultural discourses of Korea rather than those of Asian Americans or mainstream American society.

For instance, their talk about English was commonly framed as talk about one's incompetence in English; that is, they rarely talked about English without, in some way, constructing themselves as incompetent English speakers. This can be illustrated from Example (1) below. Here, the speakers are discussing one type of American experience that involves English: ordering food at drive-through restaurants.[3] At the beginning of this segment shown in (1a), Junho provides a narrative account of his experience at drive-throughs and frames this story as one about his difficulty in comprehending the English of the service staff. His wife Hyeju, as a regular observer of Junho's experience, joins in as a co-teller as well.

(1a) Participants: Junho (m, 28), Hyeju (f, 25), Yongil (m, 31), Seongyeon (f, 26)[4]

36   Junho: *.. na-neun isanghage,*
                 1SG-TOP strangely
                 'Strangely, for me,'

37   *haembeogeo jib-e ga gaj-go wae,*
                 <u>hamburger</u> house-LOC go take-CONN why
                 '(When you) go to a hamburger store,'

38   *.. deulaibeuseulu ga gaj-go wae ileohge,*
                 <u>drive:through</u> go take-CONN why like:this
                 '(When you) go through a drive-through,'

39   *.. jumunha-neun geo iss-[j-anh-a-yo].*
                 order-do-ATTR thing exist-COMPL-NEG-IR-POL
                 'and order, right?'

40   Hyeju: *[geuge] obba-ga isangha-n*
                                      that older:brother-SUB strange-ATTR

                 geo-ji[=],
                 thing-COMM
                 'It's you that is strange.'

41   Junho: [*geu*]*geo-l jal mos*
                         that-OBJ well NEG
                         ha-gess-deu-la-go,
                         do-PRESUM-RETROS-INTROS-ASSR
                         'I can't do that well.'

42   Yongil: @@

((lines omitted))

48   Hyeju: *gajyeo-ga-l geo-nya,*
                         take-go-ATTR thing-IR
                         ' "Are you going to take it (home)?" '

49   *muleo-bo-myeon-eun,*
                         ask-see-COND-TOP
                         'if (the staff) asks,'

50   *na-l chyeoda-<@bw-a@>.*
                         1SG-OBJ look-see-DECL
                         '(Junho) looks at me.'

51   Seongyeon: @@@

Several things underline the fact that this narrative is presented as one about incompetence. Junho's turn (lines 36–39, 41) basically consists of an explicit negative assessment of his ability: "Strangely, I can't do that (drive-through ordering) well." Hyeju's turn (lines 48–50) adds specific details to this assessment—that Junho is unable to respond to an apparently simple question, "Are you going to take it home (or eat in your car)?"⁵ Junho's incompetence is also underlined through the use of unmarked present tense throughout both speakers' turns; by framing the story as something that occurs habitually, the speakers construct Junho's inability as a reflection of his weak English rather than as a singular mistake.

It is important to note that other participants intersubjectively co-produce this framing. This is evidenced from the fact that one of the participants, Geonsu, starts telling a story of his own incompetence at a drive-through a few lines later, as shown in (1b) below.

(1b) Participants: Geonsu (m, 29), Junho (m, 28), Seongyeon (f, 26)

71   Geonsu: …(1.0) *na-neun geugeo-ga himdeul-deo-la-gu.*
                         1SG-TOP that-SUB difficult-RETROS-INTROS-ASSR
                         'As for me, what's difficult is this.'

72   *cha an-eseo meog-eul geo-nya.*
                         car in-LOC eat-ATTR thing-IR
                         ' "Are you going to eat in the car?" '

73   *igeo mul-eo-bo-neunde,*
                     this ask-CONN-see-CIRCUM
                     '(the staff) asks you this,'

74 Junho: *eung geule geugeo.*
                     yes right that.
                     'Yeah, right. That.'

75   .. [X]

76 Geonsu: [*nae*]-*ga han-beon-eun,*
                     1SG-SUB one-CL-TOP
                     'Once, I,'

77   ...(0.8) *oneul-eun geu,*
                     today-TOP that

78   *jom saegdaleuge daedab-eul ha-e-bo-ja geulae-seo,*
                     little differently answer-OBJ do-CONN-see-PROP do: so-PRECED
                     'thought, "maybe I'll answer a little bit differently today," so,'

79 Seongyeon: @@

80 Geonsu: *gajy-eo-ga-gess-da.*
                     take-CONN-go-PRESUM-DECL
                     ' "I will take it (home)" '

81   ... *geugeo-leul nae tta- nae ttan-e-n yeongeo-lo*
                     that-OBJ 1SG:POSS standard 1SG:POSS standard-LOC-TOP
                     hae-ss-geoteun-yo,
                     English-by do-PST-CORREL-POL
                     'I said that in the be- the best of my English.'

82 All: [@@@]

83 Geonsu: [<@*geulae-ss-deo-ni*@>] *geu-jjog-eseo gyesog aim ssoli?*
                     do:so-PST-RETROS-DET that-side-LOC continuously I'm sorry
                     'When I did that, the person kept saying, "I'm sorry?" '

84 All: @@@@

Geonsu makes a connection between his story and Junho's, thereby showing that his story is also one of incompetence. Like Junho, he begins his narrative with a negative assessment: that he has difficulty with the question, 'Are you going to eat in the car?' (lines 71–73). The grammatical construction of this utterance establishes a discursive linkage with Junho's story, as it begins with the contrastive topic marker *-neun* (line 71), which presents Geonsu's difficulty as being parallel with Junho's (i.e., also about difficulties in communicating in English), though contrasting in some respects (i.e., the specific questions with which they have difficulty).[6] This assessment is followed by an account of a specific incident that illustrates Geonsu's incompetence, in which he attempts to communicate with the service staff but fails (lines 76–78, 80–81, 83). Geonsu frames this attempt as carefully produced, but of poor quality, using the phrase *nae ttanen* (which translates roughly as 'in my estimation,' but has a self-condescending connotation)—a formulation that elicits laughter from other participants (line 84). These points demonstrate that the participants share an understanding that focusing on incompetence in English is a relevant stance to take when engaged in talk about English.

Since these practices overlap with what Koreans in Korea commonly do when dealing with English, they seem to highlight the participants' identity as "foreign students," whose cultural allegiance ultimately lies with Korea. Such a perspective, however, would be problematic, for these practices are also used as a way of making sense of their experiences in the United States. That is, practices of disclaiming English are not merely transplanted by the movement of these speakers from Korea to the United States and used as an index of their "Koreanness," but are employed as symbolic resources that help to provide specific meanings for their current social encounters. After all, talking about difficulty of using English in new cultural contexts is something that any linguistically marginalized immigrant group in the United States could engage in. Thus, the participants' practices simultaneously link them with Korean discursive practices and locate them within American society, serving as a resource for the participants to project themselves as cultural subjects positioned at the juncture of both worlds.

This complexity can be further illustrated by the fact that the participants actually present themselves as having significant cultural knowledge regarding the drive-through order routine. In the interaction that follows (1a) and (1b) above, the participants delve into an analysis of the discourse structure of drive-through transactions, listing the things the service staff usually says when taking an order.

(1c) Participants: Hyeju (f, 25), Junho (m, 28), Geonsu (m, 29), Seongyeon (f, 26)

164   Hyeju: *ttak sunseo-ga isseu-nikka [geu-nde]*,
                     exactly order-SUB exist-REASON that-CIRCUM
                     'Since there's a clear sequence,'

165   Junho: [*mwo meog-eul-geo-nya*],
                                        what eat-ATTR-thing-IR
                                        ' "What would you like to eat?" '

166   ... *geu daeum-e mwo*,
                      that ofter-LOC what,
                      'and then,'

167   [*XX-du meog-eul-geo-nya*],
     ?-also eat-ATTR-thing-IR
     '"Would you like XX also?"'

168 Geonsu: [*a hau a yu duing*],
     ah <u>how are you doing</u>
     'Oh, "how are you doing?"'

169   *mwo geuleon geo-buteo ha-ji anh-na*,
     what such thing-from do-COMPL NEG-IR
     'don't they start with that?'

((lines omitted))

182 Junho: *hau mei ai help yu mwo geu daeum-e mwo*,
     <u>how may I help you</u> what that after-LOC what
     '"How may I help you," and then,'

183   …(0.7) geu-ji,
      that-COMM
      'Right?'

184   [*geu daeum-e*],
     that after-LOC
     'and then,'

185 Hyeju: [*geogi-kkaji*]-*neun al-a-deul-eoss-eo.*
     there-until-TOP know-CONN-hear-PST-IE
     '(He/we) got it up until that point.'

186   [@@@@]

187 Seongyeon: [@@@@]

   This extract begins as Hyeju states that there is a given structure to the transaction, implying that it should not be so difficult to successfully place an order (line 164). The participants then attempt to reproduce this structure, listing various things that are said in the ordering sequence (lines 165, 167, 168, and 182) and pointing out that these should be produced in a specific sequential order (line 169). In doing so, the speakers construct themselves as knowledgeable agents who are familiar with the discursive routines of U.S. society. This shows that they place themselves within the cultural context of the United States, invalidating potential claims that they are simply "being Korean" via their practices of disclaiming English.

   However, at the same time, the participants undermine their position as experienced cultural subjects through various practices that highlight their incompetence in English. In line 185, Hyeju produces a commentary '(He/we) got it up until that point' implying that anything more complex than what has been listed so far would be difficult for them to understand. It is worth noting that the subject of this utterance is not specified and is left ambiguous. On the one hand, it could be interpreted as Junho, in which case the utterance forms a continuation of the story Junho and Hyeju were telling in (1a) above (i.e., that Junho has difficulty at a certain point in the ordering routine). But on the other hand, it could also be interpreted as a generic person, in which case the utterance constructs the difficulty as a common, generic experience of all participants. The latter interpretation is supported by the fact that it was not just Junho, but all of the participants, who together jointly produced the list of steps in the process of ordering food.

Geonsu and Junho also adopt a "hyper-Koreanized" style in their pronunciation of the English phrases, *how are you doing* (line 168) and *how may I help you* (line 182); that is, they overemphasize features of Korean phonology to explicitly indicate that their English is "not good."[7] For instance, both phrases are pronounced in a way that emphasizes the syllable-timed rhythm of Korean rather than the stress timing of English. Junho's line 182 is also produced in a slow, monotonous tone, not only making this syllable timing more noticeable but also indicating that it is meant to be heard as disfluent speech. This noticeable effort to make one's speech sound "Korean" shows that this phonological choice should not be seen as a result of involuntary "interference" from Korean, but as a strategic choice in presentation of self (see Song, this volume). For this reason, we may understand it as a way of disclaiming English; it allows one to avoid being seen as a fluent speaker, or more precisely, as a speaker who pretentiously shows off one's English.

The participants' talk about English thus simultaneously points to Korean ways of talking about English and the experiences of people who have immigrated to the United States. While the speakers are deploying practices taken from Korean discourses of English to talk about their experiences in the United States, these practices are adapted to locate them at an ambiguous, thus marginal, position within American society. Korean practices of disclaiming English become a resource through which the speakers' liminal position as transient people is constructed; they are culturally adjusted to U.S. society, yet they do not "belong." As we can see, an important link in the construction of the speakers' ambiguous position is their professed status as illegitimate speakers whose self-described linguistic incompetence is contrasted against mainstream U.S. speakers. In the following section, I move on to a discussion of how this opposition of legitimacy may be constructed.

"I'm Going to Ask an American": Constructing Oppositions of Legitimacy

While the interaction we observed above does not explicitly position the participants by making explicit reference to categories of people, this may also occur, as we can see from the next example. This interaction involves talk about a mutual friend of all of the participants, who lives in Korea but visits the United States often. Prior to the beginning of this interaction, the participants have been gossiping about this person, talking about what he did during his most recent trip to the United States. Extract 2 begins as Junho and Hyeju wonder aloud about what this friend might have been doing in Denver, the destination of his most recent visit (lines 1–2). In doing so, Junho invokes a marked pronunciation of the place name "Denver" (line 5), which elicits some laughter (lines 6–8). Junho and Hyeju then start telling a story that explains the source of this pronunciation: a message the friend left on their answering machine, "Hey, I'm in Denver" (lines 9–18). The speakers then start mocking this pronunciation and laugh together uproariously, and the joking and banter over this topic persist for the next several minutes.

(2) Participants: Junho (m, 28), Hyeju (f, 25), Seongyeon (f, 26), Myeonghui (f, 30)

1	Junho:	...(0.8) *mwo ha-sy-eoss-dae-yo*?
		what do-HON-PST-HEARSAY-POL
		'What did he do?'

2	Hyeju:	.. <@*mwo ha-sy-eoss-dae-yo?*@>
		what do-HON-PST-HEARSAY-POL
		'What did he do?'

| 3 | | @@ |

4	Junho:	*geu-ge gunggeum-ha-deo-la na-neun.*
		that-thing curious-do-RETROS-INTROS 1SG-TOP
		'I was curious about that.'

5		Den[ver]-*e ga*-[<@*seo-neun*@>],
		Denver-LOC go-CONN-TOP
		'Going to Denver (/ tɛnvʊ=r /),'

| 6 | Hyeju: | [@] |

| 7 | | [@@@] |

| 8 | Seongyeon: | [@@@] |

| 9 | Junho: | <@*geu*@>, |
| | | that |

10		[*meseji-leul namgy-eo-nwa-ss-neunde*],
		message-OBJ leave-CONN-put-PST-CIRCUM
		'(He) left us a message (on our answering machine),'

11	Hyeju:	[*wuli* X(*hante-neun*).
		1PL X to-TOP
		'To us (?),'

12		Den]ver-*e*,
		Denver-LOC
		'"In Denver (/ tɛnvʌ=r /),"'

13   [@@@]

14   Seongyeon: [@@@]

15   Junho: [*eo,*
                      hey
                      ' "Hey," '

16   *na yeogi,*]
                      1SG here

17   Denver-*e,*
                      Denver-LOC

18   [*iss-eo*].
                      exist-IE
                      ' "I'm here in Denver (/ tɛnvʊ=r /)" '

19   All: [@]@@@@@@@@@[@@]

20   X: [*geulae-ss-guna,*]
                                          do:so-PST-UNASSIM
                                          'Oh, so he did that.'

21   Junho: [Den<@ver@>]
                      Denver
                      'Denver (/ tɛnvʊ=r /),'

22   Hyeju: [<@(*tto*)@>]
                      also

23   Junho: @ [@@]

24   Hyeju: <@[Denver]-*ga eodi-ya*?@>
                      Denver-SUB where-IE
                      ' "Where is Denver (/ tɛnvʌ=r /)?" '

25   Junho: Denver-*e iss-*[<@*eo*@>]@
                      Denver-LOC exist-IE
                      ' "I'm in Denver (/ tɛnvʊ=r /)." '

26   Hyeju: [Den]ver *ani-gu* Denver-*ga eodi-ya*
                                      Denver NEG-CONN Denver-SUB where-IE
                      <@*ileohge*@>
                      like:this
                      ' "Where is Denver (/ tɛnvʌ=r /), not Denver (/ tɛnbʌ /)?" '
                      'Something like that.'

27   All: @@@@

((lines omitted))

33   Seongyeon: *baleum hwagsil-hae-<@ji-gess-[da]@>.*
                   pronunciation exact-do-INCH-PRESUM-DECL
                   '(Our) pronunciation will become very good.'

34   Hyeju: [Den]ver-*ya*?
                                               Denver-IE
                                               'It's Denver (/ tɛnvʌ=r /)?'

35   [@@@@]

36   Seongyeon: [@@@@]

37   Junho: [Denver-*e*] <@*iss-eo*@>@
                   Denver-LOC exist-IE
                   '"I'm in Denver (/ tɛnvʊ=r /)."'

38   Hyeju: *migug ae-hante ga-seo mul-eo po-l geo-ya*
                   U.S. kid-to go-CONN ask-CONN see-ATTR thing-IE
                   Denver<@-*ya*@>?
                   Denver-IE
                   'I'm going to ask an American: "Is it Denver (/ tɛnvʌ=r /)?"'

39   All: @@@@@@@@@@@

40   Myeonghui: [*maj-eulji-do moleu-ji.*]
                   correct-DUB-also not:know-COMM
                   'Maybe that is right.'

41   Junho: [Denver-*e iss-eo.*]
                   Denver-LOC exist-IE
                   '"I'm in Denver (/ tɛnvʊ=r /)."'

42   Seongyeon: @@

Some discussion of the variant pronunciations of "Denver" is in order. When the word "Denver" is maximally adapted to the Korean phonological system, it is pronounced [tɛnbʌ], as can be seen in line 26. First, voiced stops do not occur in the word initially in Korean, so [d] is replaced with [t]. Second, the sounds [v] and [r] do not occur, so [v] is replaced with [b], while syllabic [r] is replaced with the vowel [ʌ], thus resulting in [tɛnbʌ], the way that this word would usually be spoken in the midst of a Korean utterance. In contrast, the pronunciation Junho and Hyeju attribute to the absent person makes use of [v] and [r], though instead of giving full syllabicity to [r], it contains an epenthetic vowel preceding /r/, [ʌ] for Hyeju, and [ʊ] for Junho. In addition, Hyeju and Junho emphasize the second syllable of the name by lengthening the vowel, producing it with louder volume, and giving it slightly higher pitch. Thus, while the sounds [v] and [r] make the attributed pronunciation closer to the Mainstream American English (MAE) pronunciation of "Denver" than the typical Korean pronunciation, exaggerated prosody that highlights precisely the syllable containing those sounds suggests that Hyeju and Junho are playfully mocking the friend's pronunciation as an overwrought effort to sound like a native MAE speaker.

Junho and Hyeju's performance reflects the stance that the participants hold toward the absent person. First, the participants display a strong critical stance toward the fact that the friend attempted this American pronunciation. This can be seen from Hyeju's utterance in line 26, which can be paraphrased as: "I know where [tɛnbʌ] is, but where is [tɛnvʌ=r]?" Here, she contrasts the Korean pronunciation with the mock-Americanized pronunciation, treating the latter as incomprehensible to her. Her stance implies that this is not simply a matter of pronunciation, but a matter of group identity; roughly, we might translate this stance as "We no longer speak the same language (or belong in the same group) if he speaks like that." In other words, pronouncing "Denver" in a way that is closer to MAE is inappropriate, and even un-Korean, as it potentially indicates an alignment with a non-Korean, or more specifically, (White) American identity, indexed by the mainstream American pronunciation it tries to emulate. Second, it seems that the participants find the mocking pronunciation funny not only because it is pretentious but also because it is perceived to be "incorrect." This assumption can be seen through Hyeju's line 38, "I'm going to ask an American: 'Is it Denver?' (e.g., I'm going to ask if his pronunciation is correct)," which presupposes that the response will most likely be negative.

The specific ways in which the participants display this stance is worth noting, as it shows how the speakers' constructions of their local positioning and the discursive practices that reflect their transnational status intersect in complex ways. On the one hand, this example shows that the participants position themselves as locally grounded subjects who are familiar with the linguistic and cultural norms of the society in which they are now living. Presumably, part of what allows the participants to make this evaluation of their friend's speech as "incorrect" is the fact that they have more familiarity with MAE than he does. Thus, the speakers' common cultural and linguistic experiences as international students appear to be an important basis for the participants' alignment of stance.

On the other hand, the participants almost seem to acknowledge that the friend's pronunciation may actually be a better approximation of mainstream American pronunciation than their own. For example, in line 33, Seongyeon says, "Our pronunciation will become very good," implying that repeated exposure to this pronunciation would help their speech become more native-like. Also, in line 40, Myeonghui says, "Maybe that is right," admitting that it is possible that their friend's pronunciation of "Denver" may indeed be a closer approximation of MAE. In other words, despite their apparent understanding that the absent person's pronunciation would be "incorrect" by the standard of native speakers of MAE, the participants do not make this claim themselves, and position themselves as illegitimate speakers of English who are not capable of making such judgments.

This shows that, although the speakers in this example live in the United States and thus could potentially claim greater knowledge of or familiarity with MAE versus their friend who lives in Korea and is only visiting, they do *not* claim this kind of linguistic authority for themselves. Instead, they downplay and erase their status as culturally knowledgeable subjects through a different kind of opposition that is grounded in the local context. That is, the legitimacy to judge the authenticity of English pronunciation is not simply given up, but relinquished to a specific kind of person—to "an American," who is imagined to embody the competence to make valid judgments regarding whether a pronunciation is "correct" or not. In this case, the legitimate speaker of English is given a concrete image as a white mainstream American. Even though the term *migugae* (literally 'American kid/guy': line 38) is nonspecific with respect to race and ethnicity, the participants used the term primarily to refer to mainstream white Americans that they encountered through their daily life (such as fellow students), rarely for non-white ethnic minorities, and never for Korean Americans. Thus, while the language ideologies and discursive practices that the participants employ are based on discourses of English in Korea, the specific articulation of those ideologies and practices has concrete references in the participants' everyday lives.

This example, then, provides us with another case in which the discursive resource of disclaiming English is not merely a foreign practice that is spatially transposed via the transnational movement of speakers, but a practice that is also embedded within local contexts. In particular, this example underlines how transplantation of discourse practices can place language ideologies from another context within a new network of relationships. The participants, as transnational people, must position themselves amid various oppositional relations that are introduced into their everyday experiences: the opposition between Koreans in Korea and in the United States, between mainstream (white) Americans and Korean Americans, and so on. Through their discursive practices, then, they must negotiate how such oppositions will be linked to the language ideologies that form the basis of those practices. Thus, some oppositions are erased (e.g., Koreans in Korea vs. Korean students in the United States) while others are highlighted (e.g., Korean students in the United States vs. mainstream [white] Americans). In either case, the practice of disclaiming English becomes a mechanism for calibrating the system of oppositions in a transnational context, as the ideology of self-deprecation colors those new relations of difference and identity in terms of legitimacy.

Agency and Structure in the Liminal

This chapter demonstrates how U.S. graduate students from Korea construct their identities through the continual work of repositioning, rather than through channeling fixed, static notions of an ethnic or national essence. I have shown that they drew upon discursive practices and language ideologies that are dominant in Korean society, but rather than merely using them as a marker of their "Koreanness," they deployed them in order to make sense of their positions within U.S. society and culture and to reposition themselves within a network of new relational oppositions. The practices they take from the Korean context serve as resources for negotiating meaningful relations and distinctions: "American" versus "Korean," "native" versus "bad"

English, competent versus incompetent speakers, all of which come to be intercon-
nected by being located within oppositions of legitimacy.

It is important to note the intersection of agency and social structure within this
process. The examples presented above show that the participants play an active role
in the repositioning of their selves. They do not simply take on identities as they are
imposed on them, but present themselves as located within a complex intersection of
social positions—they are culturally adjusted to the United States yet they are non-
belonging; they are critical of pretentious stances toward English yet they relinquish
the legitimacy to evaluate the validity of different Englishes. And this complexity is
constructed through the strategic ambiguity of disclaiming English, which gives the
participants the agency to carefully construct their positions within interactional and
broader social context.

However, at the same time, the construction of the participants as illegitimate
speakers mirrors dominant U.S. language ideologies that view Asians as non-speakers
of English (Tuan 1998; Lo and Reyes, this volume). Disclaiming linguistic legitimacy
and attributing it to mainstream American speakers of English (imagined in a racialized
manner) may have the effect of validating and reproducing the pervasive representation
of Asians as people who do not speak English. Of course this is not an accidental consequence, as the ideology of self-deprecation in Korean society must be seen as a historical
construct that reflects the hegemony of English in Korea and the dependent relationship
between Korea and the United States, which in turn may be influenced by the ways that
Asians are positioned by mainstream U.S. society (see Park, forthcoming).

Understanding the discursive construction of Korean international students'
identities, then, requires considerations on many levels—how they construct systems
of oppositions through micro-level interactional practices; how they make sense of
their everyday life experiences through those practices; how those experiences are
interpreted through the lens of ideologies taken from Korean discourses of English;
and how those discourses link to the dominant ideologies of the United States. In
order to make connections among these levels, focusing on the liminal position of
international students is necessary. While these students are viewed essentially as
"Korean"—by the mainstream U.S. society, by the Asian American community, by
academic researchers, and by themselves—their position can be understood only
with reference to the in-between-ness they hold at the intersection of Korea and
the United States, local groundedness and transnational movements, and locally
and globally circulated ideologies of language and ethnicity. And we would expect
such liminality to be an important element to consider in the study of Asian Pacific
American identities, as the transnational connections of Asian Pacific Americans
become an increasingly critical concern in the age of globalization.

NOTES

1. Given the boom in English-language learning over the past decade (see for instance
Park and Abelmann 2004), it remains to be seen whether disclaiming English will continue to
be a dominant practice among Koreans. Even if younger generations of Koreans move away
from disclaiming English, however, we would predict that this will not simply be a result of
increased opportunities for language learning and transnational movement; such changes will

necessarily involve Koreans' reimagination of their position in the world, which must take place on the political-economic plane of ideology construction as well.

2. See Kang and Lo (2004) for the implications of these terms as they are used in Korean American discourse.

3. There are some drive-throughs in certain upscale areas in Seoul, but in general they are uncommon in Korea and started to appear only very recently.

4. Abbreviations:

ATTR	attributive	ASSR	assertive	CIRCUM	circum-stantial
CL	classifier	COMM	committal	COMPL	complemen-tizer
COND	conditional	CONN	connective	CORREL	correlative
DECL	declarative	DET	determinative	DUB	dubitative
HEARSAY	hearsay	HON	honorific	IE	informal ending
INCH	inchoative	INTROS	introspective	IR	interrogative
LOC	locative	NEG	negative	OBJ	object
POL	polite ending	POSS	possessive	PRECED	precedence
PRESUM	presumptive	PST	past tense	REASON	reason
RETROS	retrospective	SG	singular	SUB	subject
TOP	topic	UNASSIM	unassimilated		

Korean is transcribed according to the Revised Romanization system. Transcription conventions (see Du Bois et al. 1993 for more details):

{*carriage return*}	intonation unit
..	short pause
…	medium pause
…(n.n)	long pause (in seconds)
.	final intonation
,	continuing intonation
?	appeal intonation
=	lengthening
/ /	phonetic transcription
Underline	words spoken in English
@	laughter
<@ @>	laughing quality
X	uncertain syllable
(word)	uncertain hearing
[ ]	speech overlap
(( ))	transcriber comment

5. Take-out customers at the highly popular chain restaurant under discussion are given the option to "eat in the car," in which case food is served in a box rather than in a bag.

6. Incidentally, Geonsu seems to be unaware that the question he has difficulty with is actually the same question that Hyeju reported earlier that Junho is unable to answer, formulated differently (example 1a, line 48). Junho appears to point this out in line 74.

7. Hyper-Koreanized style is comparable to the hyperanglicization found in Mock Spanish (Hill 1993) in that it allows its speaker to distance oneself from a linguistic identity; see Park (forthcoming) for more discussion.

REFERENCES

Bucholtz, Mary, and Kira Hall. 2004. Language and identity. In *A companion to linguistic anthropology*, ed. Alessandro Duranti, 369–394. Malden, Mass.: Blackwell.

———. 2005. Identity and interaction: A sociocultural linguistic approach. *Discourse Studies* 7:585–614.

Du Bois, John W., Stephan Schuetze-Coburn, Susanna Cumming, and Danae Paolino. 1993. Outline of discourse transcription. In *Talking data: Transcription and coding in discourse research*, ed. Jane A. Edwards and Martin D. Lampert, 45–89. Hillsdale, N.J.: Lawrence Erlbaum.

Heller, Monica. 1988. Strategic ambiguity: Code-switching in the management of conflict. In *Codeswitching: Anthropological and sociolinguistic perspectives*, ed. Monica Heller, 77–96. Berlin: Mouton de Gruyter.

Hill, Jane H. 1993. *Hasta la vista, baby*: Anglo Spanish in the American Southwest. *Critique of Anthropology* 13:145–176.

Kang, M. Agnes, and Adrienne Lo. 2004. Two ways of articulating heterogeneity in Korean American narratives of ethnic identity. *Journal of Asian American Studies* 7:93–116.

Madden, Carolyn G., and Cynthia L. Myers, ed. 1994. *Discourse and performance of international teaching assistants*. Alexandria, Va.: TESOL.

Manalansan, Martin F. 1995. "Performing" the Filipino gay experiences in America: Linguistic strategies in a transnational context. In *Beyond the lavender lexicon: Authenticity, imagination, and appropriation in lesbian and gay languages*, ed. William L. Leap, 249–266. Amsterdam: Gordon and Breach.

Min, Pyong Gap. 2006. Asian immigration: History and contemporary trends. In *Asian Americans: Contemporary trends and issues*, 2nd ed., ed. Pyong Gap Min, 7–31. Thousand Oaks, Calif.: Pine Forge Press.

Myles, Johanne, and Liying Cheng. 2003. The social and cultural life of non-native English speaking international graduate students at a Canadian university. *Journal of English for Academic Purposes* 2:247–263.

Park, Joseph Sung-Yul. Forthcoming. *The Local Construction of a Global Language: Ideologies of English in South Korea*. Berlin: Mouton de Gruyter.

Park, So Jin, and Nancy Abelmann. 2004. Class and cosmopolitan striving: Mothers' management of English education in South Korea. *Anthropological Quarterly* 77:645–672.

Song, Hahzoong. 1997. From brain drain to reverse brain drain: Three decades of Korean experience. *Science Technology and Society* 2:317–345.

Tuan, Mia. 1998. *Forever foreigners or honorary whites?: The Asian ethnic experience today*. New Brunswick, N.J.: Rutgers University Press.

Wang, Yu-Wei, Jun-Chih Gisela Lin, Lan-Sze Pang, and Frances C. Shen. 2007. International students from Asia. In *Handbook of Asian American psychology*, 2nd ed., ed. Frederick T. L. Leong, Arpana G. Inman, Angela Ebreo, Lawrence Hsin Yang, Lisa Kinoshita, and Michi Fu, 245–261. Thousand Oaks, Calif.: Sage.

Woolard, Kathryn A. 1998. Simultaneity and bivalency as strategies in bilingualism. *Journal of Linguistic Anthropology* 8:3–29.

13

Bilingual Creativity and Self-Negotiation

Korean American Children's Language Socialization into Korean Address Terms

Juyoung Song

Terms of address convey sociocultural meanings such as social roles, positions, and relationships between interlocutors (Brown and Gilman 1960; Mühlhäusler and Harré 1990). The use and acquisition of these terms depend on a large amount of social knowledge (Hanks 1990). That is, learning to use these terms in a certain community requires not only linguistic knowledge of the lexicon and grammar but also sociocultural knowledge about the structure of social relationships and the notion of personhood that operates in that culture.

Korean American children who are in a Korean-English bilingual environment must negotiate different sociocultural and linguistic norms while navigating different settings. In Korean American community contexts, which include but are not limited to the home, these children are socialized into social relationships associated with the Korean language through interactions with their parents and others while speaking Korean. These bilingual children, however, are also exposed to ideologies about social relationships associated with linguistic practices in English. How bilingual children incorporate these differing ideologies is part of their socialization and also part of their identity construction. This process, though often a challenge for these children due to its complexity, offers much room for creativity. The multiplicity of languages and ideologies that such children are exposed to offer an opportunity for dynamic and often innovative language practices (Bayley and Schecter 2003; Watson-Gegeo 2004).

This chapter explores Korean American children's socialization into Korean terms of address and their creative use of these terms in a Korean-English bilingual environment. I focus on children's construction of the self in interactional negotiations.

The data are drawn from an ethnographic study of a group of five-year-old Korean American children in a Midwestern city in the United States. As residents of a very multiethnic and multilingual neighborhood, the children in this study encounter children from diverse cultural and linguistic backgrounds. Around age five, if not earlier, they begin attending a formal English medium school. At this stage, parents continue to speak Korean primarily while interacting with their children, whereas children begin to use more English. These home interactions become increasingly bilingual, indicating children's gradual transition from primarily Korean-dominant to primarily English-dominant communication. This chapter focuses on two children's interactions in their homes, examining how the children and their caregivers jointly create socialization practices and continually define and redefine their roles in the process.

The results show that parents' language socialization practices play an important role in children's acquisition and use of Korean address terms; children's addressing practices in Korean are mostly mediated through their caregivers. However, the data also indicate children's active participation in the socialization process. The children in this study create unique bilingual practices by (1) "anglicizing" a Korean name and establishing its bivalency, and (2) code-switching into English when pushed to use specific Korean address terms. These bilingual practices are improvised in an attempt to avoid Korean kinship terms that index hierarchy and intimacy with one's interlocutors (Sohn 1981). Children's improvised practices are made possible in part by the context in which more than one language and culture exist. I argue that these novel linguistic practices signify children's negotiation of multiple ideologies in context, and therefore point to bilingual children's ongoing identity construction. Additionally, these practices illuminate the creative potential of children's active participation in the socialization process in a bilingual setting.

Terms of Address and the Self

Terms of address help to constitute social relationships between individuals in a given sociocultural system. For instance, terms of address in Korean index hierarchies between speakers, addressees, and others referred to in discourse. According to local language ideologies, the terms used by a younger or junior person in an interaction define and create a hierarchical relationship with an elder. Through the use of polite forms of address, individuals in junior positions recognize and comply with their roles and act according to the social norms that govern relationships between an older brother (*hyeng*) and a younger brother (*tongsayng*) or between an older married woman (*acwumma*) and a young child. Socially superior persons, in contrast, use names (sometimes with titles or suffixes) to address juniors. Thus, addressing is not only a linguistic practice that referentially denotes persons in discourse but also a social practice that indexes and makes relevant implicit rules and frames for individuals (Hanks 1990). In this sense, Peter Mühlhäusler and Rom Harré (1990, 94) argue that the sociocultural information indexed through address terms (in their case, personal pronouns) locates the speaker "in a moral order of rights and duties of speaking and of acting through speaking." The use of these terms constructs an individual's sociocultural positioning within a given sociocultural world. Therefore, address terms are indexical of social relations and play a significant role in the construction of the self (Ochs 1990).

Address and Reference Terms in Korean

Korean does not have a neutral second-person form such as the English "you,"[1] nor a second-person pronoun that refers to a person regarded as socially superior (Hwang 1990; Lee and Ramsey 2000; Park 2005; Sohn 1999; also see Morita in this volume). Instead, there is extensive use of nominal substitutes such as kinship terms, for example, *nwuna* 'elder sister for a boy,' *enni* 'elder sister for a girl,' *hyeng* 'elder brother for a boy,' and *oppa* 'elder brother for a girl'; social positions, for example, *senpaynim* 'senior at school or work'; titles, for example, *sensayngnim* 'teacher' and *sacangnim* 'president of a firm'; and teknonyms, for example, *X emeni* 'mother of X.' These nominal forms encode social relationships between people in terms of age, social status, kinship, and in- and out-groupness. Some scholars claim that a speaker cannot properly utter a single sentence in Korean without demarcating the social relationship between herself and the addressee or referent (Sohn 1999).

Among adult acquaintances and friends, vague expressions that do not index any hierarchy in terms of age are often seen as distancing. Typically, over the course of a relationship, such address terms are replaced by hierarchically laden ones, indexing increased closeness (Park 2005). For example, when two new graduate students meet for the first time, they typically use polite address terms (usually "full name + *ssi*," a formal suffix) with each other. These formal and symmetrical address terms would be used even in cases where one student is older than the other. As they grow closer, the younger person may begin to address the older one using fictive kinship terms—*enni/nwuna* 'elder sister' or *oppa/hyeng* 'elder brother'—while the older person may address the younger one using first name only or "first name + *ssi*" (which is considered less formal and distancing than "full name + *ssi*"). Though the shift to asymmetrical address terms emphasizes social distance, the use of first names and kinship terms suggests intimacy. In this way, an egalitarian but distant relationship is transformed into a hierarchical but intimate one. However, such a shift does not always occur; sometimes formal address terms are kept to maintain social distance.[2]

Compared to adults, children mark hierarchy in their peer relations more quickly and explicitly. Children do not use "name + *ssi*" to address each other, but use first names to address those who are the same age or younger and fictive kinship terms to address older children. A difference as little as one year (e.g., between a three-year-old and a four-year-old) would conventionally require the younger child to address the older one with a fictive kinship term. Therefore, when children first meet each other, they typically ask each other directly about their ages. In addition, adults provide children's ages and supply appropriate terms to use when introducing them to each other. Consequently, the vast majority of a child's relationships with other children are hierarchical yet intimate and are marked through address terms such as *enni/nwuna* or *oppa/hyeng*.[3]

Thus, using terms that index deference or hierarchy does not necessarily imply distance in Korean (Hwang 1990), similar to Chinese (Blum 1997) and Japanese

(Matsumoto 1988). That is, hierarchy and solidarity are not at opposite ends of the spectrum in Korean culture as Penelope Brown and Stephen C. Levinson (1987) propose in their theory of politeness. Because of the interaction of these two indexical meanings, hierarchy and solidarity, Korean kinship terms play an important role in defining, in the moment, interpersonal relationships among interlocutors and can be strategically deployed to invoke solidarity to relax tension when a conflict occurs (Kang 2003) or to emphasize hierarchy to establish authority.

Language Socialization in a Bilingual Context

From early on, Korean-speaking children learn to shift self-references across contexts, for example, using the humble form of "I" (*ce*) or the plain form of "I" (*na*), as their relations with others change (see Morita's chapter in this volume for similar examples in Japanese). Children must also remember how they are hierarchically situated with respect to their peers and use correct terms of address and reference depending on whom they are speaking to and whom they are speaking about. Thus, children's acquisition of the address system and the acquisition of social and cultural competence (in this case, social relations and self-positioning) are not independent, but intertwined with each other, which is the premise of the language socialization approach to language learning. In this approach, language is viewed as a "system of symbolic resources designed for the production and interpretation of social and intellectual activities" (Ochs 1996, 407). Language in this sense is both the goal of and a tool for socialization. That is, children are socialized to use language and, at the same time, they are socialized through the use of language (Schieffelin and Ochs 1986).

Children, however, do not just imitate the adult world or passively accept cultural resources in the process of socialization but also contribute to the creation of such resources (Bayley and Schecter 2003; Corsaro and Miller 1992; Schieffelin and Ochs 1986). While children are socialized through the resources passed down by previous generations, they create personal meanings out of the particular set of resources to which they are exposed. In this sense, Suzanne Gaskins, Peggy J. Miller, and William A. Corsaro (1992) argue that socialization is not only collective but also individual. Furthermore, children often transform or resist certain value-laden messages (Gaskins, Miller, and Corsaro 1992; He 2003), taking active and selective roles in socialization.

Recent work has considered socialization as not only a developmental process but also as a moment-by-moment practice of identity construction (Langman 2003). In this view, children engage in practices of identity appropriate for their age. Children's practices, for example, are not viewed as just "a trial and error movement" toward adultlike practices, but practices in their own right, as Miki Makihara (2005) discusses in her work on Rapa Nui children's adoption of a new Rapa Nui Spanish style. Juliet Langman (2003) suggests that language socialization is not simply a developmental process leading to adulthood, but rather an ongoing process that defines what it means to be an age-appropriate person in a social group.

Socialization as practice becomes salient especially for bi/multilingual children who are provided with different social norms and values from those of their parents. In a bi/multilingual context, there is no guarantee that adult norms will be the predetermined set of norms by which children are socialized. The social norms that monolingual adults have been socialized into may no longer be valuable to children who are speaking more than one language. Multiple languages and cultures provide these bilingual children with a broader range of selections from which they can make their own choices (Bayley and Schecter 2003). Additionally, the fluidity of context also makes room for creativity in children's socialization processes. As a result, children may not choose one language and its associated culture over the other, but create hybrid practices that belong somewhere in between.

The Current Study

The data in this study are drawn from a one-year ethnographic study of five- to six-year-old Korean-English bilinguals in a Midwestern city in the United States, where Korean neighborhoods are neither concentrated nor visible. The children participate in Korean American networks through Korean schools, churches, and social occasions throughout the city and their participation in these ethnic communities is thus different from children who live in highly concentrated Korean communities (e.g., Shin and Milroy 2000).

The participants were Korean American children with different lengths of residence in the United States and, thus, different levels of proficiency in both Korean and English. The families of these children lived in university-affiliated housing where groups of children would meet and play together every day. I observed these children in their homes, in their school, and at the playground, though the data presented in this chapter draw mainly from interactions observed in the homes. The data for this chapter focus on the linguistic practices of two children, Joonho and Greg, who were both five years old at the beginning of the study.

Joonho came to the United States three months before the beginning of the study to live with his mother, who had been in the United States for three years. He did not have any siblings. At the beginning of my observations, Joonho's mother only allowed him to speak Korean at home in order to maintain and develop his language proficiency. Joonho had also been attending a Sunday Korean language school[4] since arriving in the United States. Although he had only been in the United States for three months, his Korean (both oral and written) was not as highly developed as Greg's, who had been in the United States for four years. Joonho's English was also very limited, especially at the beginning. Thus, his mother tried to create as many opportunities as possible for him to interact in English, while speaking only Korean with him at home. As time went by, however, Joonho's mother enforced Korean less at home, implicitly allowing English.

Greg was born in Korea and came to the United States when he was two years old. He went to an English medium preschool for one year and became a kindergartner at the beginning of the study. He attended a Sunday Korean language school for one year when he was four years old. At the time I conducted my study, Greg and his father went to the community recreation center in their apartment complex and studied Korean reading and writing for an hour almost every day after school. Additionally, Greg and his mother regularly read Korean books together at home. Greg's English proficiency was higher than any other boy in the community and he tested out of ESL at school. Greg's parents spoke only Korean at home except for occasional borrowed English words. When compared with peers in Korea, Greg's Korean proficiency was average, if not advanced, for his age. Although Greg's spoken Korean sometimes sounded a bit awkward according to the other Korean children (it was slower and less colloquial), he was able to elaborate some complex science terms in Korean. Greg himself sometimes code-switched between Korean and English at home. He had one two-year-old brother, who was not speaking much in either Korean or English. Greg had never visited Korea since coming to the United States.

Neither of the families went to a Korean church. The children usually played together with other children at the playground of the apartment complex, where the majority of the residents were international. Joonho and Greg often played with children from Indonesia, Argentina, and South Africa who were in the same age group and went to school with them. When Joonho and Greg were around children from other countries, they spoke English. When there were only Korean American children, they spoke both English and Korean and code-switched frequently.

Language Socialization of Terms of Address in Korean

Before examining how children's addressing practices construct their identity, this section shows how they are socialized to use these terms, mostly through interaction with their parents or other adults. Traditionally, most language socialization research focuses on this process, that is, how young children are socialized into culturally appropriate ways of speaking, presumably acquiring the cultural knowledge underlying language practices and constructing a view of themselves and others (Schieffelin and Ochs 1986).

Typically, adult input plays an important role in socializing children into specific ways of speaking (Schieffelin and Ochs 1986), and previous research has looked in particular at linguistic practices that index cultural affect or social status and roles in relationships (e.g., Andersen 1986; Blum 1997; Clancy 1986, 1989; Morita 2003; Platt 1986). In the case of Korean, adults commonly supply the terms that children should use with others. Since parents are often blamed for their children's improper use of language (in particular, for impoliteness when speaking to elders), parents have a strong interest in ensuring that their children acquire and use socially appropriate terms of address. In this way, adults socialize children into the proper use of these terms and, more important, into the social relationships that they index, both explicitly and implicitly.

Explicit socialization occurs as adults define relationships between children and others and also model children's relationships with others, providing them with proper terms to use. Socialization also occurs implicitly as parents recast children's speech, indirectly correct terms children have used, and narrate around children about roles and relationships.

Defining Relationships for Children

Defining relationships for children commonly occurs when children meet strangers for the first time. The following is an occasion when I (JS) first met Greg, one of the participants, in his home:

(1)'Yes, address her as *imo* 'aunt' '[5]

> 1   JS to Greg: *apulo ettekey pwulullay? Joonhonun imolako pwulununtey.*
> *neto imolako pwulullay?*
> 'How are you going to address me from now on?
> Joonho addresses me as *imo* 'aunt.'
> Would you, too, like to address me as *imo* 'aunt'?'
> 2   Greg's mother to Greg:
> *kulay, imolako pwulle. animyen nwunalako pwulutunci...*
> *acik kyelhon an hayssunika.*
> 'Yes, address her as *imo* 'aunt.' Or, why don't you address
> her as *nwuna* 'elder sister' since she is not married yet.'

In this excerpt, Greg's mother and I explicitly discuss how he should address JS. JS suggests the term *imo* 'aunt' while Greg's mother recommends the term *nwuna* 'elder sister' instead. Here, Greg's mother indicates why these two terms are appropriate by saying "since she is not married yet." She implies that the term *acwumma*, the term that Greg typically uses to address women of JS's age, is not appropriate in this case since *acwumma* is usually reserved for married women. In fact, Greg insisted on using *acwumma* to address JS (which will be discussed in on pages 227–228).

Modeling for Children

In addition to explicitly instructing children about which address terms to use, adults frequently animated children's voices, providing models for them. While modeling terms for second and third persons (from a child's perspective) occurred frequently, modeling terms for the first person (for children to refer to themselves) occurred less often.

In this community, adults commonly referred to themselves with their titles or kinship terms while talking to children. For example, teachers referred to themselves as *sensayngnim* (*sensayng* 'teacher' + *nim* 'respect suffix,' literally 'honorable teacher'). The following excerpt is from a first-grade Korean heritage language classroom in the city.

(2)'Since the teacher [I] didn't see you last week'

> 1   Sicheol to teacher: *nato meli callassnunteyyo.*
> 'I got a haircut too.'
> 2   Teacher to Sicheol: **sensayngnim***i cinancwuey mospwakaciko.*
> 'Since the **teacher** [I] didn't see you last week.'

This example shows how the first-grade teacher at the Korean heritage language school socializes children into the proper term of address by using the term *sensayng-nim* 'teacher' to refer to herself in front of the class. She often used other nominal or verbal honorific suffixes (such as *sensayngnim* + *kkeyse* 'honorable teacher + nominal marker (honorific)' and *hassyesseyo* 'did (honorific) + past + polite speech level') to refer to or describe herself when speaking to students. This kind of self-exalting expression would be considered awkward when speaking to another adult in Korean, since honorific expressions and terms are supposed to be used for others, not for oneself. Here, however, it is used purposefully. By referring to herself as *sensayngnim* in front of her students, the teacher provides a proper term for students to use and at the same time indexes the teacher-student relationship (Mühlhäusler and Harré 1990; Silverstein 1976). In the classroom, particularly in lower grades, teachers seldom used the pronoun "I." The complex social indexicality of such terms is apparent in the fact that parents of children address or refer to teachers with the same honorific term regardless of children's presence, but teachers do not refer to themselves as *sensayngnim* when talking to parents. Instead, they use the first-person humble pronoun *ce* 'I' in these cases.

In much the same fashion, Joonho's mother frequently referred to JS, the researcher, as *imo* 'aunt' when speaking to Joonho:

(3) 'Go and tell *imo*, "*Imo*, please come and eat dinner"'

1	Mother to Joonho:	*Joonhoya, kase imohantey,*
		imo siksa hasile osilako hay.
		'Joonho, go and tell *imo* 'aunt,'
		"*Imo*, please come (HON) and
		eat (HON) dinner (HON)".'
2	Joonho to JS:	*imo, siksa hasile oseyyo.*
		'*Imo*, come (HON) and eat (HON) dinner (HON).'

Here, Joonho's mother refers to JS as *imo* 'aunt' while she is interacting with him. Although the relationship between the mother and JS was close, and she usually called JS by her first name, she always referred to JS as *imo* 'aunt' in front of Joonho and used the honorifics that would be appropriate for Joonho to use in these cases. In so doing, she socialized Joonho into the appropriate terms of address, as well as the social relationships and respect that such terms index.

In fact, Joonho's mother often spoke on behalf of Joonho. For example, when JS asked Joonho what he did over the weekend, his mother responded to JS by speaking for Joonho, from his point of view:

(4) '(I) went to Sicheol *hyeng*'s house'

1	JS:	(to Joonho) *Joonhoya, ecey mwe haysse?*
		'Joonho, what did you do yesterday?'
2	Joonho:	(no response)
3	Joonho's mother:	(to JS and Joonho) *Sicheoli hyenganey cipey kassesseyo.*
		'[I] went to Sicheol *hyeng*'s house.'

4   Joonho's mother: (to Joonho) *kekise caymisskey nolassci, kuchi?*
                          '[You] had fun there, right?'

Here, Joonho's mother spoke to JS in Joonho's voice, using terms like *hyeng* 'elder brother' and verb endings (-"*yo*") that would be appropriate for him to use in this situation. In this way, Joonho's mother provides him with a model for how to speak to JS, thus indirectly socializing him. This kind of child-centered talk is very common in Korean (see Morita 2003 and this volume for discussion of a similar phenomenon in Japanese). Such a shift in the adults' point of view can occur even when a child is not present. For example, a wife can refer to her husband as *appa* 'daddy,' taking her child's perspective when talking to her neighbor (Cho 1982, 3):

(5) daddy = my husband

wuli appan acik an wasseyo.
'Our *appa* 'daddy' hasn't come yet.' [My husband hasn't come home yet.]

Similarly, a grandmother refers to her grown-up son as *apem* 'dad,' taking her grandchild's perspective while talking to her daughter-in-law (Cho 1982, 44):

(6) dad = my son

apem acik an tule wassni?
'Hasn't *apem* 'dad' come in yet?' [Hasn't my son come in yet?]

Here, the dad is neither the speaker nor the listener; he is the father of the speaker's grandchild. The term *apem* 'dad' thus refers to the father from the point of view of the (nonpresent) grandchild. In a similar manner, the parents of the participants in this study referred to the researcher as either *imo* 'aunt' or *sensayngnim* 'teacher' regardless of their children's presence.

Recasting

Parents also frequently repeated and corrected terms that children used while talking to them. In the following example of recasting, Joonho is talking to his mother about the events of the day:

(7) 'Why did Sicheol *hyeng* cry?'

1   Joonho to mother: *onul **Sicheol** pakkeyse wulesse.*
                         'Today, Sicheol cried outside.'
2   Mother to Joonho: ***Sicheol hyeng**a maliya?*
                         ***Sicheol hyeng**aka way wulessnuntey?*
                         'You mean **Sicheol hyeng**? Why did **Sicheol *hyeng*** cry?'
3   Joonho to mother: *waynyahamyen **Sicheol hyeng**i*
                         keympoi kaciko nollyeko hayssnuntey, kaciko kasse.

'Because **Sicheol** *hyeng* wanted
to play with the Game Boy, but
[a friend of his] took it away.'

In the first line, Joonho refers to a boy who is older than him with his first name only. In the next turn the mother recasts this as "Sicheol *hyeng*" or 'Sicheol elder brother.' Following her recasting of his speech, Joonho then refers to the boy as "Sicheol *hyeng*" in the next line.

Narrating Around and About Children

Children were also socialized as overhearers (Miller 1994; Miller et al. 1992). In the following excerpt, Joonho's mother referred to Sicheol as *hyeng* while talking to JS in front of Joonho and Sicheol, who were playing together.

(8) 'Sicheol is a really good *hyeng* to Joonho'

wuli Sicheolinun cham cohun hyengiya. hangsang Joohnolul cal tolpwa cwuntanika. Joonholang kathi issumyen hyeng nolusul thokthokhi hantanika. Joonhoto Sicheolilul cal ttala.
'(Our) Sicheol is a really good *hyeng* to Joonho. (He) always takes good care of him. When (he) is with Joonho, he plays the *hyeng* role well. Joonho also follows Sicheol's lead.'

By referring to Sicheol as *hyeng* 'elder brother' in this example, the mother socializes her son, Joonho, into a hierarchical relationship while defining for the children, who are intended overhearers (Goffman 1981), the kinds of actions and stances that constitute this relationship. In taking on this role of a *hyeng*, Sicheol is expected to take care of Joonho and to be protective of him, while Joonho is expected to be dependent upon Sicheol and respectful toward him.

Children's Negotiation of Self and Bilingual Creativity

When I examined children's practices for address and reference, what I found was that despite parents' socialization efforts, children made their own choices through improvised practices; they did not always comply with their parents' or other adult members' input, but invented new practices as a way to avoid Korean status-charged address terms. In my data, Joonho and Greg pursued different strategies. Joonho would omit *hyeng* 'brother' when referring to Sicheol and also anglicized his name. Greg, on the other hand, avoided using Korean kinship terms by code-switching into English. Such practices reveal children's agency as they pursue their own choices in the negotiation of conflicting beliefs and cultural ideologies. Through such practices, children dynamically transform the socialization process, incorporating often-conflicting norms, ideologies, and expectations. In this sense, children are not the "passive, ready and uniform recipients of socialization" (He 2003, 128) often presumed in traditional language socialization research, but active negotiators of diverse beliefs about cultural norms and linguistic practices.

Omitting the Kinship Term '*Hyeng*' through Anglicizing a Korean Name

Joonho regularly used the Korean kinship term *hyeng* in various contexts to address or refer to other children, including children from other countries, when he first entered school in the United States. As time went by, however, Joonho rarely addressed or referred to one of his closest Korean friends, Sicheol, as "*hyeng*" or "Sicheol *hyeng*." Instead, Joonho addressed or referred to Sicheol by using his first name with an English pronunciation. He would use this anglicized form, which I call {Sicheol}, even in the midst of otherwise entirely Korean utterances.

The differences between these two terms, Sicheol and {Sicheol}, include both phonetic and prosodic features, namely Sicheol [çɪ.tʃəl][6] and {Sicheol} [sɛ́.tʃɔɨ]. The former was pronounced as two distinct syllables [çɪ] and [tʃəl], constituting two Korean characters. Neither syllable was strongly accented, but the second syllable had a higher tone. The latter was pronounced with a strong accent on the first syllable [sɛ]. The pronunciation of {Sicheol} typically occurred with an exaggerated pitch. It is important to note that {Sicheol} was Joonho's own creative hybrid formulation, distinct from the standard Korean pronunciation of this term as well as from the way English speakers usually pronounced Sicheol's name. In school, for example, Sicheol's ESL teacher addressed him as [sɪ.tʃɔɨ]. Joonho's pronunciation of {Sicheol}, in contrast, incorporated elements of both Korean and English phonology. He used this form in English as well as Korean utterances. The following extracts show how Joonho used the anglicized {Sicheol} in Korean utterances:

(9) {Sicheol} as a vocative in Joonho's discourse

Joonho to Sicheol: **{Sicheol}**, *nahako ike kaciko nollay?*
                       'Sicheol, do you want to play with this with me?'

(10) {Sicheol} as a nominal adjective in Joonho's discourse

Joonho to Mother: *emma, na* **{Sicheol}** *cipey kato tway?*
                      'Mom, can I go to Sicheol's house?'

According to Joonho, the anglicized form {Sicheol} was actually an English term. When asked, "Why don't you call Sicheol *hyeng* anymore?" and "Don't you need to address him as *hyeng*?" Joonho told me that {Sicheol} was English and thus he did not have to use the hierarchical kinship term *hyeng*. In this metapragmatic analysis (Agha 1998), Joonho seemed to draw a distinction between different norms attached to two cultural systems. That is, he appeared to believe that using {Sicheol} invoked a different set of norms in the midst of a Korean utterance. Through this hybrid practice of embedding English addressing practices into Korean sentences, Joonho thus performed code-switching.

As Peter Auer (1998) notes, what counts as a code in code-switching depends on the speech community members' point of view. Regardless of whether two codes seem similar to out-group members, when switching produces meaningful effects for bilinguals, the codes should be considered distinct (Auer 1998). In this case, Joonho's anglicization plays an important pragmatic function. By using {Sicheol}, Joonho could address or refer to Sicheol without using the hierarchical kinship term *hyeng*, thus circumventing Korean norms of address through code-switching (Auer 1998). In this sense, Joonho's practice is different from a case of borrowing, which may not have any particular functional effect. The fact that Joonho did not use (1) 'Sicheol' (the Korean first name alone) nor (2) '{Sicheol} + *hyeng*' (English code + *hyeng*) shows that this practice was consistent and not accidental (only 'Sicheol *hyeng*' and '{Sicheol}' were found in my data). In fact, the difference between {Sicheol} and 'Sicheol' was salient both to adults and children in this community. For example, Joonho's mother noticed and mentioned this practice to me several times during the first several months of my observations. In fact, Joonho's mother often corrected the use of {Sicheol} by recasting it (see excerpt 7). However, as time went by, she began to ignore it. Other adults found this practice interesting and some of them also mimicked it. Among Joonho's Korean-speaking peers, {Sicheol} became a shared practice, and a kind of 'we-code' (Gumperz 1982). When I discussed this practice with a group of Sicheol's friends, for example, they had a perspective similar to Joonho's:

(11) '{Sicheol} is an English name'
Insu, Greg, Joonho, and Sicheol are all friends. Insu, Greg, and Joonho are five years old while Sicheol is six years old.

1	JS:	(to Insu and Greg) *nehuytul way Sicheol hyengilako pwuluci anhni?*
		'Why don't you call Sicheol *hyeng* [e.g., elder brother]?'
2	Insu:	*mikwukeysenun* brother *ilako haci anhayo. caki* family *eykeyto* brother *ilako anhhayyo. hankwukey kamyen hyengilako pwuleyo.*
		'In the States, [we] don't call him "<u>brother</u>."'
		Even <u>family</u> members don't use the term "<u>brother</u>" here.
		If I go to Korea, I will call him *hyeng*.'
3	Greg:	*yengelonun* brother *ilako haci anhayo. hankwukeysenun hyengilako pwululkkeyeyyo. kekin hyengiyeyyo.*
		'(We) don't use "<u>brother</u>" in English. I would call him *hyeng* if I were in Korea because he would be a *hyeng* to me [there].'
4	JS:	*kulemyen nanun? nanun yengelo ettehkey pwulle?*
		'Then what about me? How do you address me in English?'
5	Greg:	*e.. Juyoung?* (smiling)
		'Um.. *Juyoung*?'
6	JS:	*e. kuntey ne Juyoung ilako hanpento an pwullesscanha.*
		'Well, you don't address [me] as Juyoung though.'
7	Greg:	*Juyoungen hankwuk ilum. kulayse kulayyo.*
		'Because Juyoung is a Korean name, we don't address you that way.'
8	JS:	*kulemyen Sicheolun?*
		'What about Sicheol?'

9	Greg:	{Sicheol]}...*kuken hankwuk ilum aniyeyyo.*
		'{Sicheol}...That is not a Korean name.'
10	Insu:	{Sicheol} *un yenge.*
		'{Sicheol} is an English name.'
11	JS:	(to Sicheol) *nenun ettehkey sayngkakhay?*
		'What do you think about this?'
12	Sicheol:	It doesn't make sense (raising his voice).
		If I were in Korea, I would be seven years old
		and they were six years old...and...
		kulemyen hyeng icanhayo.[7]
		'Then as you see I am a *hyeng*.'
13	JS:	*kuntey Sicheoli hanpento hwanaykena hancek epscanha.*
		'But you didn't seem to be so upset about their calling you that way.'
14	Sicheol:	*waynyahamyenyo, waynayhamyen hyeng icanhayo.*
		'Because, because I am their *hyeng*.'
15	JS:	*hyengilase chamnunkeya?*
		'Because you are their *hyeng*, you are enduring it?
		[e.g., forgiving them for their mistake?]'
16	Sicheol:	*Yey-ey* (quickly).
		'Yes'
17	Greg:	(to Sicheol) It's okay, {Sicheol}.

This interaction reveals how these children associate different social relationships and practices of terms of address with Korean and English. Insu and Greg link the anglicized form of {Sicheol} to the instantiation of a status-neutral social relationship. At the same time, they note that the creation of such relationships, and indeed, the salience of age itself, is context-dependent: "If I go to Korea I will call him *hyeng*" (line 2), "I would call him *hyeng* if I were in Korea" (line 3), and "If I were in Korea, I would be seven years old" (line 12). It is not that these children do not understand the practice of hierarchical peer relations, but rather that they choose not to create such relationships through the practice of anglicization.

{Sicheol} can be considered a 'bivalent' form, simultaneously Korean and English (Woolard 1998). Kathryn A. Woolard (1998, 7) uses the concept 'bivalency' to describe bilingual words or segments like {Sicheol} that "could 'belong' equally, descriptively and even prescriptively, to both codes." Woolard argues that the significance of bivalency resides in its role in making the boundary between codes less distinct, and in bilinguals' strategic use of such bivalent elements in their interactional negotiations. On the one hand, when embedded in Korean utterances, {Sicheol} may be considered 'Korean with an accent' because of its derivation from a Korean proper name. On the other hand, {Sicheol} can be considered English through the way children in the community use and rationalize it.

The practice of {Sicheol} thus makes the indexical values associated with the address term ambiguous. Through this ambiguity, it blurs "the commitment to indexing any single rights-and-obligations set" attached to each code (Myers-Scotton 1993, 7) and, as a result, enables the children to creatively define what exactly this term entails. In this sense, {Sicheol} is an example of a 'contextualization cue'

(Gumperz 1982) or a change in 'footing' (Goffman 1981), which signals participants' orientations to each other (Auer 1995). By enacting this bivalent term, Joonho
and the other children create hybrid identities that draw from local language ideologies to create new ones (Myers-Scotton 1993; Stroud 1992).

Joonho's hybrid practices are reminiscent of the Japanese American child, discussed by Morita in this volume, who uses the English "you" in Japanese utterances.
A similar practice can be found in Dong-Jae Lee's (1975) study of Korean-English
bilinguals in Hawaii. Lee found that Korean American adults used the English pronoun "you" in Korean sentences to avoid indexing the social relationships associated
with Korean address terms. In all of these cases, bilinguals' use of the English pronoun "you" is a creative response to novel social situations.

Avoiding Korean Kinship Terms through Code-Switching

Greg, who came to the United States four years before my study began, seldom used
Korean kinship terms such as *hyeng* 'elder brother (for a boy)' or *nwuna* 'elder sister
(for a boy)' despite his parents' socialization efforts. He avoided using such terms
through code-switching. The following exemplifies Greg's typical strategy:

(12) 'Greg, address me as *nwuna* 'elder sister' '
Greg (five years old) is asking Misun (eleven years old) whether she would like to play with
him and his friends.

1	Greg to Misun:	*Misun, ne*to *kachi hallay?*
		'Misun, do **you [plain form]** want to play too?'
2	Misun to Greg:	*mwelako? ne? nwuna*lako *pwulle.*
		'What did you say? Did you say '**you**' **[plain form]**?
		Address me as *nwuna* **(elder sister)**.'
3	Greg to Misun:	(switching into English) Do you want to play?

In this example, Greg addresses Misun with her first name and *ne* (the plain form
of 'you') in Korean. Misun, a recent arrival to the United States, sanctions him for
this behavior since usually the first name alone and *ne* are used when an elder person
addresses or refers to a younger person or between same-status, close friends. She
tells Greg to address her as *nwuna* 'elder sister.' In order to avoid using this term,
Greg quickly switches into English and addresses Misun as "you" in English. Misun
told me that Greg never addressed her as *nwuna*, and whenever she pointed this out to
him he would immediately change to English and persist in using English thereafter.
Greg's mother also said that she told Greg to address Misun as *nwuna* on several
occasions, but he would not use the term.

Greg also avoided using other kinship terms that would have located him in a
subordinate relationship vis-à-vis his peers. In this example, he remained silent when
pressed to use the term *hyeng*:

(13) 'Greg, isn't Sicheol your *hyeng* 'elder brother'?
Joonho, Greg, Sicheol, Joonho's mother, and JS were having lunch together at Joonho's.
Joonho and Greg are five years old and Sicheol is six years old.

1	Joonho:	(to his mother) *emma, na namkyeto tway?*
		'Mom, can I leave some food [on my plate]?'
2	Joonho's mother:	(to Joonho) Okay.
3	Joonho:	(to Greg and Sicheol) *aytula, namkyeto toynta*
		'Guys, you don't have to finish everything.'
4	Joonho's mother:	(to Joonho) *mwe, aytulanun?* (.3) *hyengalang*
		Gregun annamkintey.
		'What? Did you say "guys"? *Hyeng* 'elder brother'
		[e.g., Sicheol] and Greg will finish [their food].'
5	Joonho:	(looking at his mother and smiling).
6	Joonho:	*Greg, ne namkilkkeya*
		'Greg, are you going to leave some food [on your plate]?'
7	Joonho's mother:	*Joonhoya neto ta mektunci.*
		'Joonho, then why don't you finish too?'
8	Greg:	(to Joonho) *Sicheolinun…?*
		'What about Sicheol?'
9	Joonho's mother:	**Greg, Sicheoli hyenga aniya?**
		'Greg, isn't Sicheol your *hyeng?'*
10	Greg:	**(no response, keeps looking down and eating his food)**
11	Sicheol:	(to Joonho's mother) *hyenga macayo.*
		'Right. [I am his] *hyeng.'*
12	Greg:	**(still no response, keeps eating)**
13	Joonho's mother:	(looking and smiling at Greg)
14	Joonho:	(to Joonho's mother) *kuntey Gregun tasessaliya.*
		'By the way, Greg is five years old.'

In line 4, Joonho's mother reprimands Joonho for addressing Greg and Sicheol as *aytul*, a third-person plural term typically used by adults to refer to children or by children to refer to other children who are either the same age or younger. She quickly recasts this utterance as "*hyengalang* Greg" or 'elder brother and Greg.' Then Joonho smiles at his mother, perhaps acknowledging his mistake. Greg's response, however, is different from Joonho's. When Joonho's mother sanctions Greg for referring to Sicheol as "Sicheol" and not as "Sicheol *hyeng*" in line 9, Greg becomes silent in lines 10 and 12. His silence here may be interpreted as a form of resistance toward the term, since he never called Sicheol *hyeng* at any point during my study. While Joonho and Sicheol ratify Joonho's mother's understanding of the importance of hierarchical peer relationships by confirming Sicheol's status as a *hyeng* and by noting Greg's age, Greg remains silent through the end of this encounter.

Besides *hyeng* and *nwuna*, Greg also avoided using the kinship term *imo* 'aunt.' When Greg and JS first met, his mother and JS tried to convince him to address JS as *imo* or *nwuna* (see Excerpt 1). However, he did not address JS with either of these terms. Although he had ample opportunity to hear other children addressing JS as *imo* 'aunt' or *sensayngnim* 'teacher,' Greg either omitted such address terms, used my first name alone[8] (see line 5 in Excerpt 11), or used *acwumma*, a polite term similar to English 'ma'am' usually used for married women. Greg's mother and I were surprised at his use of this term, since it is considered inappropriate (and even rude) for unmarried women. Since no other children in this community addressed JS as *acwumma*, Greg's use of this term can be seen as a strategy he devised as his own to avoid using the kinship terms *imo* 'aunt' or *nwuna* 'elder sister.'

As noted earlier, using a kinship term such as *imo* or *nwuna* indexes not only hierarchy but also a family-like close relationship (Sohn 1981). The fact that Greg chose to use *acwumma* (which indexes hierarchy, but can be somewhat distancing) instead of using fictive kin terms such as *imo* or *nwuna* with JS reveals that he may in fact have been resisting the kinship relationship that such terms convey.[9] This became clear when he said in an interview that "these terms, *nwuna* and *hyeng*, are only for family members. You are not my *imo*. So [if I call you *imo*], it will make people confused."[10] Similarly, Greg noted that if he were in Korea, then he would address Sicheol as *hyeng* because Sicheol would be a *hyeng* to him there. Greg's resistance to these address terms stood in contrast to his proper use of honorifics such as polite verb endings. Greg would switch between non-honorific and honorific registers depending on his addressee's age, thus demonstrating that he recognized the salience of age-based hierarchies in Korean. By resisting the extension of such terms to fictive kin as commonly practiced in Korea (see Wang et al. 2005), Greg demonstrates a context-sensitive notion of identity that recognizes the indexical power of address terms to instantiate relationships.

Conclusion

This study explores how Korean American children learned to use terms of address and reference in a bilingual environment. The data reveal that adult input played an important role in children's socialization and that children's use of these terms has mediated through their caregivers. However, children's bilingual practices were not directly imposed by their caregivers. Joonho, for example, created a bivalent form of {Sicheol}, while Greg avoided Korean kinship terms through code-switching. These practices reveal the active role that children play in their socialization process. That is, children do not act according to predetermined adult norms (Langman 2003) but rather create new hybrid practices in collaboration with one another, redefining their social relationships through the dynamic means of language.

Besides adults' input and children's own agency, the notion of context is also important. Here, context is not necessarily physical, but is "constituted by what people are doing and where and when they are doing it" (Erickson and Shultz 1981, 148). What the Korean American parents and their children do in this study differs from what typical Korean parents and children would do in Korea. The nature of a bilingual environment supplies multiple resources for the children (and also their caregivers) to choose from, and the caregivers often adapt and change their socialization practices according to the children's choices. For example, Joonho's mother eventually let Joonho address Sicheol as {Sicheol} and she began to address him that way as well. Greg's mother eventually relented and did not continue to try to get Greg to use kinship terms with others, although she did enforce the use of other honorifics such as polite verb endings. The caregivers' adapted practices and the children's own novel practices together create, define, and redefine the context, which, in turn, influences children's socialization practices recursively. In short, the hybrid, flexible, and fluid nature of the bilingual context plays an important role in the children's socialization processes (Bayley and Schecter 2003).

The practices created by the children in this study are also unique manifestations of an ongoing process of identity construction. Children's linguistic practices select and highlight local ideologies of personhood that index how they view themselves in a particular social relationship. Through code-switching and through the creation of novel linguistic forms, these bilingual children use and avoid address terms that index social values and social relationships, negotiating conflicting ideologies, that are, in turn, part of their construction of the self.

I am deeply grateful to Adrienne Lo and Angela Reyes for their insightful and detailed comments on the various versions of this chapter. I also thank Marcia Farr, Robert Bayley, Donald Winford, and David Bloome for their helpful comments and suggestions.

NOTES

1. Juck-Ryoon Hwang (1990) points out that the term *tangsin* might be the most similar to English "you," but it has very limited usage. Children do not use this term to address or refer to anybody, higher or lower.

2. In a case where adults are supposed to have a close relationship, a younger person's use of "(full) name + *ssi*" can be taken to be offensive. Therefore, the use and meaning of *ssi* are very complex: it can be considered polite toward a social inferior, distancing with a peer, or offensive toward a social superior.

3. Before middle school, Korean kinship terms such as *enni/nwuna* 'elder sister' or *oppa/ hyeng* 'elder brother' are the only terms that children regularly use to address their peers. Whereas in the adult repertoire, kinship terms index intimacy due to their contrast with a wide range of other more formal possible address terms, they may not carry this same meaning, in children's repertoires.

4. There are several Korean language schools in the city, including two Korean language schools and a couple of church-affiliated Korean language programs. The Sunday Korean language school that Joonho and Greg both attended offers two forty-five-minute Korean literacy lessons and one forty-five-minute elective lesson on topics such as Korean culture, music, and sport.

5. Transcription conventions:

Bold	Bold indicates researcher's emphasis or focus of discussion.
brother	Underlined words are English words in Korean sentences.
hyeng	Italics indicates Korean speech.
'you'	Single quotes indicate English translation of Korean speech.
HON	HON represents honorifics (nominal and verbal suffixes).
[ ]	Brackets enclose additional information supplied by the author.
( )	Parentheses enclose comments on the interaction.
(.4)	Pauses are given in tenths of a second.

Korean is transcribed according to the Yale romanization system.

6. These names were transcribed phonetically by four linguists, including one Korean, two native speakers of English, and one Indian speaker of English. There were some individual differences and the versions used in the chapter were the most common transcriptions.

7. In Korea, ages are calculated according to the calendar year and a baby is considered one year old at birth. At the beginning of a new calendar year, everyone's age simultaneously increases by one year. For example, if Sicheol was born in November 2000, then he would be one year old until the end of 2000. On January 1, 2001, he would turn two years old. Thus people are typically one or two years older when they convert their ages into the Korean age system.

8. This use of first name alone to someone more than twenty years older than you would be considered hugely inappropriate in Korea.

9. Greg's avoidance of *imo* or *nwuna* as a form of address for the researcher can be understood as a rejection of the kinship relationship that the terms imply. However, Greg's avoidance of the peer terms *hyeng/nwuna*, I argue, is an attempt to subvert hierarchical peer relations (see note 3). In summary, Korean kinship terms generally index both kinship and hierarchy, but their specific indexical meaning depends on the context, including who is using the term to whom and when, and expected social norms for such a situation.

10. The absence of regular interaction with Korean Americans of different age groups might also have contributed to Greg's reluctance to use these terms.

REFERENCES

Agha, Asif. 1998. Stereotypes and registers of honorific language. *Language in Society* 27:151–193.

Andersen, Elaine S. 1986. The acquisition of register variation by Anglo-American children. In *Language socialization across cultures*, ed. Bambi B. Schieffelin and Elinor Ochs, 153–165. New York: Cambridge University Press.

Auer, Peter. 1995. The pragmatics of code-switching: A sequential approach. In *One speaker, two languages: Cross-disciplinary perspectives on code-switching*, ed. Lesley Milroy and Pieter Muysken, 115–135. New York: Cambridge University Press.

———. 1998. Introduction: Bilingual conversation revisited. In *Code-switching in conversation: Language, interaction and identity*, ed. Peter Auer, 1–24. New York: Routledge.

Bayley, Robert, and Sandra Schecter, ed. 2003. *Language socialization in bilingual and multilingual societies*. Clevedon, UK: Multilingual Matters.

Blum, Susan D. 1997. Naming practices and power of words in China. *Language in Society* 26:357–381.

Brown, Penelope, and Stephen C. Levinson. 1987. *Politeness: Some universals in language usage*. Cambridge: Cambridge University Press.

Brown, Roger, and Albert Gilman. 1960. The pronouns of power and solidarity. In *Style in language*, ed. Thomas A. Sebeok, 253–276. Cambridge, Mass.: MIT Press.

Cho, Choon-Hak. 1982. A study of Korean pragmatics: Deixis and politeness. Honolulu.City: Department of Linguistics, University of Hawaii.

Clancy, Patricia M. 1986. The acquisition of communicative style in Japanese. In *Language socialization across cultures*, ed. Bambi B. Schieffelin and Elinor Ochs, 213–250. New York: Cambridge University Press.

———. 1989. A case study in language socialization: Korean W-H questions. *Discourse Processes* 12:169–192.

Corsaro, William A., and Peggy J. Miller, ed. 1992. *Interpretive approaches to children's socialization*. San Francisco: Jossey-Bass Publishers.

Erickson, Frederick, and Jeffrey Shultz. 1981. When is a context? Some issues and methods in the analysis of social competence. In *Ethnography and language in educational settings*, ed. Judith L. Green and Cynthia Wallat, 147–160. Norwood, N.J.: Ablex.

Gaskins, Suzanne, Peggy J. Miller, and William A. Corsaro. 1992. Theoretical and methodological perspectives in the interpretive study of children. In *Interpretive approaches to children's socialization*, ed. Wiliam A. Corsaro and Peggy J. Miller, 5–24. San Francisco: Jossey-Bass Publishers.

Goffman, Erving. 1981. *Forms of talk*. Oxford: Blackwell.

Gumperz, John. 1982. *Discourse strategies*. New York: Cambridge University Press.

Hanks, William F. 1990. *Referential practice: Language and lived space among the Maya*. Chicago: University of Chicago Press.

He, Agnes W. 2003. Novices and their speech roles in Chinese heritage language classes. In *Language socialization in bilingual and multilingual societies*, ed. Robert Bayley and Sandra Schecter, 128–146. Clevedon, UK: Multilingual Matters.

Hwang, Juck-Ryoon. 1990. 'Deference' versus 'politeness' in Korean speech. *International Journal of the Sociology of Language* 82:41–55.

Kang, Agnes. 2003. Negotiating conflict within the constraints of social hierarchies in Korean American discourse. *Journal of Sociolinguistics* 7:299–329.

Langman, Juliet. 2003. Growing a *Bányavirág* (Rock Crystal) on barren soil: Forming a Hungarian identity in Eastern Slovakia through joint (inter)action. In *Language socialization in bilingual and multilingual societies*, ed. Robert Bayley and Sandra Schecter, 182–199. Clevedon, UK: Multilingual Matters.

Lee, Dong-Jae. 1975. Some problems in learning Korean second person pronouns. In *The Korean language: Its structure and social projection*, ed. Ho-min Sohn. Honolulu: Center for Korean Studies, University of Hawaii.

Lee, Iksop, and Robert Ramsey. 2000. *The Korean language*. Albany: State University of New York Press.

Makihara, Miki. 2005. Rapa Nui ways of speaking Spanish: Language shift and socialization on Easter Island. *Language in Society* 34:727–762.

Matsumoto, Yoshiko. 1988. Reexamination of the universality of face: Politeness phenomena in Japanese. *Journal of Pragmatics* 12:403–426.

Miller, Peggy J. 1994. Narrative practices: Their role in socialization and self-construction. In *The remembering self: Construction and accuracy in the self-narrative*, ed. Ulrich Neisser and Robyn Fivush, 158–179. New York: Cambridge University Press.

Miller, Peggy J., Judy Mintz, Lisa Hoogstra, Heidi Fung, and Randolph Potts. 1992. The narrated self: Young children's construction of self in relation to others in conversational stories of personal experience. *Merrill-Palmer Quarterly* 38:45–67.

Morita, Emi. 2003. Children's use of address and reference terms: Language socialization in a Japanese-English bilingual environment. *Multilingua* 22:367–395.

Mühlhäusler, Peter, and Rom Harré. 1990. *Pronouns and people*. Oxford: Blackwell.

Myers-Scotton, Carol. 1993. *Social motivations for code-switching: Evidence from Africa*. New York: Oxford University Press.

Ochs, Elinor. 1990. Indexicality and socialization. In *Cultural psychology*, ed. James W. Stigler, Richard A. Shweder, and Gilbert Herdt, 287–308. New York: Cambridge University Press.

———. 1996. Linguistic resources for socializing humanity. In *Rethinking linguistic relativity*, ed. Stephen C. Levinson and John Gumperz, 407–437. New York: Cambridge University Press.

Park, Jeong-woon. 2005. Hankwuke hochinge cheykyey [Terms of address in Korean]. In *Hankwuk sahoywa hochinge* [Korean society and terms of address], ed. Han-seok Wang et al., 75–96. Seoul: Yeklak.

Platt, Martha. 1986. Social norms and lexical acquisition: A study of deictic verbs in Samoan child language. In *Language socialization across cultures*, ed. Bambi B. Schieffelin and Elinor Ochs, 127–152. New York: Cambridge University Press.

Schieffelin, Bambi B., and Elinor Ochs, ed. 1986. *Language socialization across cultures*. New York: Cambridge University Press.

Shin, Sarah J., and Lesley Milroy. 2000. Conversational codeswitching among Korean-English bilingual children. *International Journal of Bilingualism* 4:351–383.

Silverstein, Michael. 1976. Shifters, linguistic categories, and cultural description. In *Meaning in anthropology*, ed. Keith H. Basso and Henry A. Selby, 11–55. Albuquerque: University of New Mexico Press.

Sohn, Ho-min. 1981. Power and solidarity in the Korean language. *Papers in Linguistics:* 14:431–452.

———. 1999. *Korean*. London: Routledge.

Stroud, Christopher. 1992. The problem of intention and meaning in code-switching. *Text* 12:127–155.

Wang, Han-seok, Hee-sook Kim, Jeong-woon Park, Seong-chul Kim, Seo-young Chae, Hye-sook Kim, and Jeong-bok Lee. 2005. *Hankwuk sahoywa hochinge* [Korean society and terms of address]. Seoul: Yeklak.

Watson-Gegeo, Karen A. 2004. Mind, language, and epistemology: Toward a language socialization paradigm for SLA. *Modern Language Journal* 88:331–350.

Woolard, Kathryn A. 1998. Simultaneity and bivalency as strategies in bilingualism. *Journal of Linguistic Anthropology* 8:3–29.

14

Phonological and Cultural Innovations in the Speech of Samoans in Southern California

Alessandro Duranti and Jennifer F. Reynolds

I n this chapter we identify a set of phonological innovations in the speech of Samoans living in Southern California and propose an analysis of the cultural implications of such innovations. Starting from an ethnographic understanding of the speech community, we look at bilingual conversation as a cultural practice. By 'cultural practice' we mean an activity that establishes a meaningful connection between the here and now and one or more traditions (Bauman 1992). Such a connection may be at times explicit, like when immigrant speakers quote ways of speaking that are recognizable as uniquely belonging to their "home country," or implicit, like when the logic of linguistic choice or linguistic structure suddenly changes without an immediately apparent reason. We are assuming that in both cases connections are being made, whether or not we can speak of communicative intent.

Like any other kind of ethnographically oriented study of language, in this case as well speakers are not simply seen as producers of utterances to be collected and analyzed but also as social actors, that is, members of communities organized in a variety of social institutions and tied through a set of cultural expectations, beliefs, and moral values about the world (their own actions included) (Duranti 1997a, 3). In this perspective, language use becomes part of a larger set of practices.

We believe that in studying an immigrant community, one must take into consideration not only the culture of its members but also the culture of what they consider their "home" country. In our case, this country is the Samoan archipelago. Despite some important differences between Samoa (formerly Western Samoa, an independent country since 1962) and American Samoa (a U.S. territory), the following cultural traits are common among the island communities globally called "Samoa":

(1) the extended family (`âiga), with its rights and obligations; (2) a hierarchical notion of social relations at all levels of social organization, from the family to the village and beyond, as represented by the *matai* system—*matai* are title holders who act as family heads and family representatives in the village council (*fono*) and other local institutions (Duranti 1994; Ochs 1988; Platt 1986; Shore 1982); (3) a collectivistic view of basic activities and responsibilities with a sharp division of labor according to rank (for titled individuals), age, gender, and skills; (4) a contextually defined notion of person, which includes an anti-individualistic perspective on social responsibility and interpretive practices and a favoring of positional over private identities in more spheres than in Western societies (Duranti 1993; Shore 1982).

After introducing the Samoan community where we carried out our fieldwork and its linguistic repertoire, we will provide some basic information on the type of code switching phenomena we recorded. We will then focus on two phenomena that we analyze as phonological and cultural innovations: (1) the adoption of kinship terms and proper names that violate Samoan phonotactics (i.e., syllable structure and phonological inventory); and (2) the violation of the co-occurrence rules characteristic of a particular phonological register ("bad speech") for Samoan proper names of members of the younger generation. In both cases, we will speculate on the cultural implications of these linguistic phenomena, drawing on our ethnographic experience.

Samoans in Southern California

After World War II, thousands of Samoans left their villages in American Samoa (U.S. territory) and (Western) Samoa (independent since 1962) to migrate to New Zealand, Australia, and the United States (Shankman 1993). Within the United States, Hawaii and California house the largest Samoan communities. Members of Samoan American communities involved in social services estimate that currently more than 90,000 ethnic Samoans live in California and that most of these were born and raised in the United States (Pouesi 1994) (official 1990 U.S. Census estimates are roughly one-third lower).

The data presented in this chapter are drawn from a corpus of over fifty hours of videotaped interactions among children and adults in four Samoan families living in the same neighborhood and attending the same Samoan church in Southern California. The recordings are part of a three-year study (January 1993–December 1995) sponsored by the U.S. Department of Education to examine issues ranging from socialization to problem-solving strategies among families of Samoan descent (Duranti and Ochs 1997). We video-recorded each family four times for several hours, after the children had returned from school. During our visits, we were able to observe and videotape the children as they were involved in a number of activities, including playing, eating, doing homework, taking care of their younger siblings, interacting with their parents and grandparents, and watching television (Duranti 1997b). We also recorded the same children during Sunday school classes and other activities at the local Samoan church (Duranti, Ochs, and Ta`ase 1995).

A common feature of the families in the study is the continuation in the urban environment of the traditional Polynesian extended family structure: In three of the four families, three generations lived under the same roof and there was an under-standing that it is common and socially acceptable for relatives or even close friends to come and live with the family for an indefinite period of time. The extended family structure is also sustained by a continual flow of relatives coming to visit or work for varying lengths of time from Western Samoa, American Samoa, or other Samoan communities in the United States.

Social ties among each family and the larger Samoan community (in the United States and abroad) are mostly organized by the local church, which hosts recurrent collective activities (choir practice, sports events, bingo) as well as elaborate fund-raising events and exchange visits with youth organizations from other congregations in the United States and in the Samoan archipelago. This means that children are continually exposed not only to Samoan cultural practices but also to the Samoan language both within and outside of the home.

Linguistic Repertoire

For Samoans living in the United States, bilingualism itself is not a new practice. In both Samoa and American Samoa there are many adults who can speak English quite fluently due to a variety of factors including the use of English in the schools (secondary education is done in English) and in the media, and to the not uncommon experience of having gone to work in an English-speaking country (New Zealand, Australia, the United States) to augment family income. What changes in the United States are the contexts in which English is used and the range of fluent speakers. On the islands, English is largely restricted to institutional settings like schools and certain work places. Samoan is the preferred code of most (and for many people all) interactions. In the United States, English enters more intimate settings especially through the U.S.-born second generation, whose members are English dominant.

In the four families we studied, both Samoan and English were spoken in the home, but whereas members of the older generations (grandparents, parents) were more likely to speak Samoan, the children preferred English. This difference was accompanied by considerable language loss from generation 1 (parents or grandpar-ents) to generation 2 (the children in our study). Members of generation 1.5 (young adults who came to the United States as teenagers) were among the most balanced bilinguals. We found that even a few years within the same generation make a differ-ence. It is not unusual that within the same family the oldest teenagers and the people in their twenties are often able to speak Samoan rather fluently, whereas the younger children are more likely to have a restricted linguistic repertoire that allows them to understand a number of Samoan recurrent commands and frequently used words but does not allow them to express themselves in a continuous flow of Samoan discourse. This intragenerational difference might be interpreted in a variety of ways. As the number of siblings increases, there is more English spoken in the house and, in this sense, the younger ones are at a disadvantage in terms of exposure to Samoan. On the other hand, it is also possible that children improve their competence in Samoan as they get older. This might be due to the fact that as they grow, they spend more time with older and more fluent Samoan speakers, including adult visitors from the Samoan islands. Furthermore, if they stay within the Samoan community and participate in its religious and cultural activities, there is more pressure on them to know Samoan. We met several people who told us that they (re)learned Samoan as adults, sometimes by going to spend some time in either American Samoa or Western Samoa.

The older fluent speakers of Samoan (generation 1) see the loss of the language by the younger generation as a negative consequence of the migration process. They see themselves and their families as "Samoan"—we never heard anyone refer to themselves as "Samoan American"—and language is seen as an important part of the Samoan cultural heritage, especially given the many public occasions in which Samoan adults are expected to deliver or respond to formal speeches (Duranti 1981, 1994). The church provides a context in which, among other values, knowledge of Samoan is encouraged and rewarded, although the strategies adopted in the religious classes are not always the most effective in terms of second language teaching (see Duranti, Ochs, and Ta`ase 1995). In the church attended by the families in our study, most of the Sunday service is in Samoan, including the hymns and the sermon. On Sunday, the children usually arrive an hour before the service and participate in Sunday school activities. Most of them do not stay for the service. Sunday school teachers speak in English to the children but dedicate a few minutes to Samoan literacy. They might ask the younger children to recite the Samoan alphabet and the older ones to read from the Samoan Bible or explain the meaning of a few Samoan words. Children of all ages are often asked to memorize a few words or verses from the Samoan Bible. These verses often contain words that are too difficult for the children to fully understand or feel comfortable using in other contexts.

We have observed that most of the time children are free to choose the code they speak. For example, when addressed in Samoan by an adult or a sibling, a child can reply in English without fearing negative sanctions. However, there are a few speech activities in which they might be expected to speak in Samoan. These activities include prayers (in the home and in the church) and public performances in the church. For example, during a Christian festivity called "White Sunday" (*Aso Sâ Pa`epa`e*)—an "inversion ritual" in which the adults are expected to honor and even serve the children—the youngest children of each family are expected to memorize and recite verses from the Samoan Bible in front of the entire congregation. These events often cause apprehension and frustration before and during the performance, given the potential for embarrassment if the child is unable to remember the verses or mispronounces some words. More generally, whereas young children spontaneously use Samoan with their older relatives (see below), they are manifestly resentful of being forced to do it. When one of the children in our study was asked by her grandmother to use Samoan to greet on camera one of the researchers who was not present, she first refused and then, when pressured, burst out crying. In our experience, Samoan adults accept limited knowledge of Samoan in everyday interaction but display little tolerance for it during certain public, dramatic performances.

As shown for other immigrant communities in the United States (see Zentella 1997 for Puerto Ricans in New York), Samoans in Los Angeles also alternate—sometimes within the same interaction—among a number of speech varieties in English and in Samoan. English varieties include Standard English (the variety spoken, for example, by Samoan teachers and community workers in their professional settings), Samoan English (a variety of English with Samoan morpho-phonological features, spoken by most first-generation speakers and common in homes), Non-Standard English, which includes features of African American English (especially for second-generation speakers), and two phonological varieties of Samoan: "good speech" (*tautala lelei*) and "bad speech" (*tautala leaga*). Since the alternation between these two varieties will be relevant to our discussion of borrowing practices in Southern California, a brief description of the distinction is here provided.

"Good Speech" and "Bad Speech"

From a phonological point of view, the distinction between "good speech" and "bad speech" can be described as the alternation between the dental-alveolar non-stridents /t/ and /n/ (in "good speech") and their velar counterparts /k/ and /ŋ/ (written 'g' in Samoan standard orthography) (in "bad speech"). In terms of features, this alternation can be defined as the neutralization of the opposition between [+ back] and [– back] (or between Coronal and Dorsal) segments. This neutralization of the opposition results in only a few homonyms (see figure 14.1 for some examples).

The labels "good speech" and "bad speech" are local categories; that is, they are used by Samoans to refer to what are perceived as two distinct ways of speaking, each of which is practiced in and associated with distinct activities (although a considerable amount of shifting occurs within one continuous interaction). "Good speech" is modeled on written Samoan and is strongly associated with literacy activity and Christianity. For example, Samoans always pray in "good speech." Teachers also speak in "good speech" during a lesson and expect their students to do the same. "Bad speech" is, for most speakers, the default variety and is used in the majority

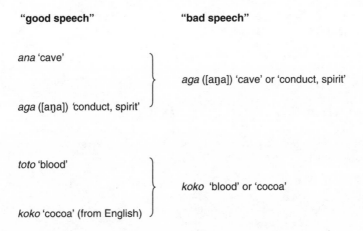

Figure 14.1. Examples of "Good Speech" and "Bad Speech" Pronunciation

of daily interactions, including such traditional activities as speechmaking (Duranti 1981, 1994). In this sense, the labels are misleading to outsiders because despite their literal translation, they do not easily translate into the classic diglossic situation of a "high" (or formal) and a "low" (or "informal") variety. The identification of "bad speech" with "colloquial speech" (e.g., Milner 1966) is hence unfortunate because both "good speech" and "bad speech" exhibit colloquial varieties where we find such features as assimilation, syllable reduction, idiomatic expressions, and tense/aspect markers that are not recorded in dictionaries and grammars (see Ochs 1985).

An ethnographic understanding of this dichotomy suggests that it is one manifestation of a complex relationship Samoans entertain with imported Christian practices, which are "good" by definition, as opposed to traditional ways of being, which may be "bad" from a Christian point of view and yet necessary or perhaps unavoidable from the point of view of (traditional?) Samoan ethos.

In the United States, children of Samoan heritage are exposed to "good speech" much less than Samoan children on the islands given that in two of the most important contexts for socialization to "good speech," namely, the school and the media (radio in particular), the language used is English. Even in the Samoan church activities we observed, English is favored when speaking to children and hence the amount of "good speech" they hear in church is reduced. It is not surprising then that the variety routinely used when code switching from English to Samoan is "bad speech." As we will see, the only consistent violation of this trend is constituted by proper names.

Samoan and English Morphosyntax in Contact

As shown in excerpts 1–4, unlike English, which is predominantly subject-initial, Samoan is predominantly verb-initial. Furthermore, as shown in excerpt 3, case marking is also different. In Samoan, when the subject of transitive clauses (agent NP) appears after the verb, it is marked by the marker *e* (*e kagata* in 3 and *e le ali`i* in 4). It is this feature that makes Samoan an ergative language (see Duranti 1994).[1]

(1) `o   lea `ua ômai   mâlô   Verb + Subject
     Pred this Perf come(Pl) guests
     "now the guests have come"

(2) kigâ ù   lima   Verb + Subject
     hurt my hand
     "my hand hurt(s)"

(3) `â iloa  e   kagaka le `au   o le kîpoki lea   Verb + Agent + Object
     if notice Erg people Art handle of Art teapot this
     'if people notice the handle of this teapot'

(4) gâ la`a fa`aali kou elegi   e le ali`i[2]   Verb + Object + Agent
     DX Fut show your herring Erg Art man
     "the (gentle)man is going to show your herrings"

Verbal morphology also differs in the two languages. Whereas in English verbs inflect by adding suffixes (for example, in the third-person singular form of the present tense [-s] and in the past tense and past participle [-ed]), in Samoan, instead, tense/aspect is encoded with separate particles that precede the verb (for example, `ua in excerpt 1 and la`a in excerpt 4) and person is not marked with inflection, but pre-verbal subject clitic pronouns are possible, as shown in excerpt 5 below.

(5)   `ou ke sau  gâ  `i le fe`au
        I Pres come there on Art errand
        'I come (t)here on an errand'

Ellipsis (zero anaphora) in sentences with finite verbs is not possible in English but common in Samoan, especially with third-person referents (see examples 8, 14, and 16).

In Samoan, only number is marked on some verbs, usually by reduplication of the penultimate syllable: for example, the verb `ai 'eat' (CV-V) becomes `a`ai (CV-CV-V) in the plural (see Mosel and Hovdhaugen 1992). In excerpt 1 above, the verb ômai 'come' is the plural of sau (by suppletion from alu 'go' plus the deictic particle mai). The distinction between verbs and adjectives is difficult to make in Samoan and in general words from almost any class can become verbs, including temporal and local adverbs.

Unlike in English, most nouns in Samoan do not inflect for number, which is instead marked by the article (or its absence). For example, in excerpt 1, mâlô 'guest' is understood as plural due to the absence of the article (and the plural form of the verb ômai instead of sau). The same is true for kagaka in excerpt 3. In Samoan, possessives (or genitives) are marked by a preposition (either o or a) as opposed to the widely used English '-'s' suffix.

Finally, Samoan has a looser connection than English between lexical items and syntactic categories. Not only can many words function as both nouns or verbs (which is common in English as well), but words for numbers and temporal or spatial specification can easily become predicates with the addition of a tense/aspect marker.

As we shall see, when the grammars of English and Samoan come into contact, single word codeswitches and loanwords are typically assimilated to the morphosyntax of the recipient language. This is true of English words inserted in Samoan utterances and of Samoan words inserted in English utterances.

Phonology

At the phonemic level, Samoan has five distinct vowels: /i, e, a, o, u/ and thirteen consonants: /p, t, k, ʔ, m, n, ŋ, f, s, h, v, r, l/. In the variety called "good speech" (see above), the consonants /k/, /h/, and /r/ appear only in borrowings. As we mentioned earlier, in "bad speech," /t/ and /n/ are replaced by /k/ and /ŋ/ (written 'g' in Samoan orthography), respectively.

Unlike English, which allows various kinds of consonant clusters (CCV, VCC), Samoan syllable structure must be (C)V, that is, with no more than one consonant preceding the vowel.

At the phonetic level, only two consonants seem at times to violate the CV rule: /s/ and /n/. For example, the English 'plenty' becomes Samoan [pelenti], and English 'engineer' is usually pronounced [`ensinia] (or [`insinia]) and not [`enisinia] (*pace* Milner 1966, 42), showing a consonant cluster NCV (nasal-consonant-vowel). Another common consonant cluster is the form [ska] from *si+ka* 'positive affect marker (*si*) + first-person singular affective pronoun (*ka*)' (see Ochs 1986).

English initial voiceless stops (/p/, /t/, /k/) are always aspirated when they are at the beginning of a syllable. Aspiration is found in Samoan but not in a consistent manner, and it often seems due to emphasis.

The (C)V syllable structure constraint and the lack of certain English phonemes like the voiced stops /b/, /d/, and /g/ affect all the earlier (and established) borrowings in at least two ways. First, foreign words that have consonant clusters were adapted to Samoan syllable structure by either the introduction of extra vowels or by the deletion of some of the consonants of the borrowed term. For example, 'Australia' became *Ausitalia*, with the introduction of the vowel /i/ to break the /st/ consonant cluster and the reduction of the /tr/ sequence to /t/. All the words that ended in consonants received a final vowel. For example, 'spoon' became *sipuni* and 'teapot' became *tîpoti*. Second, phonemes that are not found in Samoan were transformed to conform to the Samoan phonological inventory. For example, voiced stops become voiceless: The English 'guitar' became *kitala* and 'baby' became *pepe*; vowels were also adapted to the Samoan system but in less predictable ways, especially in nonstressed position. In the communities we observed in Samoa, loanwords also undergo phonological transformation in "bad speech." Thus, table 14.1 displays the phonological variation of a number of established lexical borrowings.

The same kind of phonological variation affects foreign names. Thus, Duranti's first name, 'Alessandro,' in Western Samoa was *Alesana* in "good speech" and *Alesaga* in "bad speech"; his wife's name, 'Elinor,' was *Elenoa* in "good speech" and

TABLE 14.1. Examples of Established English Borrowings in Samoan 'Good Speech' and 'Bad Speech' Pronunciation

English word	Borrowing in "good speech"'	Borrowing in "bad speech"
Australia	Ausitalia	Ausikalia
spoon	sipuni	sipugi [sipuŋi]
knife	naifi	gaifi [ŋaifi]
New Zealand	Niu Sila	Giu Sila [ŋiu sila]
radio	letiô	lekiô
sugar	suka	suka
cement	simâ	simâ
time	taimi	kaimi
tea	tî	kî
teapot	tîpoti	kîpoki

Elegoa in "bad speech." Elinor's son's name, 'David,' was *Tâvita* in "good speech" and *Kâvika* in "bad speech." As we shall see below, in the data collected in Southern California, most of the single-word English code switches and new borrowings do not conform to these rules.

Types of Code-Switching

We found that code-switching (CS) is common in conversational interactions among family members both intersententially (see examples 6–8) and intrasententially (see examples 9–11):

Intersentential CS, across Turns, Different Speakers (Known as "Non-Reciprocal CS" [Gal 1979])

(6) (Family #3; 5/31/93; Father is holding infant and talking to twelve-year-old daughter Fa`a.)

Father:	`o ai lâ ga faia le kou babakyu?[3]	(SAMOAN)
	"who made your barbeque?"	
Fa`a:	our team,	(ENGLISH)

(7) (Family #1; 5/93; A sees camera and asks G about it)

A:	`o le â lale mea lale ola?	(SAMOAN)
	"what is that thing that is on?"	
G:	where?	(ENGLISH)
A:	lale.	(SAMOAN)
	"that." (or "there.")	

Intersentential CS, across Turns, Same Speaker

(8) (Family #1; older brother G talks to twelve-year-old T)

G:	are you gonna- do you wanna eat?	(ENGLISH)
	(pause)	
G:	fia`ai?	(SAMOAN)
	"(are you) hungry?" (lit. 'want-eat')	
T:	((eyebrow flash[4])) yeah yes!	(ENGLISH)

Intrasentential CS

(9) (Family #1; Mother comments on a basketball player)

Mother: I don't think `o   le   sefulu afe   e   lava
                          Pred Art ten   thousand Pres enough
                "I don't think the ten thousand is enough [as a fine]"
                e   kakau   oga suspend kama gâ for a whole season.
                Pres necessary Comp   boy   that
                "(they) should suspend that boy for a whole season."

(10) (Family #2; 6/8/93; Grandmother (Gm) is counting points in a card game)

Gm: *e*   seven Siké-`*ae* nine *a`u.*
        (it) is   but   I/me
        "Sikê has <u>seven</u> (points) and/but I (have) <u>nine</u>."

(11) (Family #4; 10/28/94)

Gm: *ma* Atasau[5] go *kâ`ele.*
        "and Atasau <u>go</u> (take a) shower."

Since the older speakers tend to be Samoan-dominant and the younger ones English-dominant, the role of Samoan versus English in establishing the syntactic frame for CS (what Myers-Scotton [1993] refers to as the "Matrix language") often changes from one turn to the next and only the speakers who are equally (or almost equally) fluent in Samoan and English—a subset of generation 1 and generation 1.5 speakers—engage in the complex intrasentential CS shown in 9–11 above.[6] The rest of the speakers tend to limit their CS to single lexemes (usually nouns or verbs). In our data, probably in part because we tended to follow around young children interacting with adults, most of the intrasentential CSs are single words (we will refer to them as "single-lexeme CSs"). In fact, in many cases, it is not clear whether we should be treating them as CSs or new borrowings; many of them could qualify as "nonce borrowings" (Poplack, Sankoff, and Miller 1988).

Morphological Assimilation

In single-lexeme CSs, there is a considerable amount of morphological assimilation and convergence in both directions. For example, Samoan nouns that appear in the midst of an English utterance may get the English plural marker, as shown in excerpts 12 and 13, which show the non-standard (but colloquially common) English 'there's' with a plural subject:

(12) (Family #2; 6/8/93)

P: but there's *ipu*s in there
                    "dish"

(13) (Family #1; 4/14/93)

G: there's more boxes
        and there's more *koga*s coming
                    "fine mat"

On the other hand, English words in the midst of Samoan utterances usually lose their inflection as they become incorporated into Samoan morphosyntax, as shown in excerpt 14, where the verb 'memorize' appears without the past participle suffix '-d,' and in excerpt 15, where the locative 'at McDonald's' loses the '-'s.'

(14) (Family #2; 5/3/93)

A: 'cause *e   le`i uma-* (.) *ga*   memorize
                     Pres Neg finish   Comp
             "<u>because</u> (it) has not been fully <u>memorized</u>"

(15) (Family #4)

Mo: *mâkou   ui   aku fo`i i* McDonald *e* pick up *mai se-*
             we-excl go-by Dx also to   to   Dx some-
             "we also went by <u>McDonald's</u> to <u>pick up</u> (for us) some-"

Convergence is shown also by the change of syntactic categories undergone by certain English words. For example, a noun like 'football' is used as a verb in excerpt 16 and the verb kî 'turn on' (from English 'key') is made into a noun meaning 'remote control' in excerpt 17.

(16) (Family #1; 12/91)

Mo: *ioe `ae kau   ga   alu e*   football *ma gâ-*
             yes but should Comp go Comp   with those
             "yes but he should go to <u>(play) football</u> with those-"

(17) (Family #2; 5/30/93) (*kî* = 'remote control,' from *kî* 'turn on' < Engl. 'key')

P: give me the other *kî*
                     "remote"

It is to these single-lexeme CSs that we turn our attention in the rest of the article.

Single-Lexeme Code Switches

Single-lexeme code-switches are either single or compound nouns and verbs (in the X-bar notation, they would belong to categories like 'N' and 'V'). As shown above, in our data, single-lexeme forms can be Samoan words in the midst of English stretches of discourse or English words in the midst of Samoan discourse. Sometimes these forms are terms that do not have corresponding terms in the receiving language. For example, the English 'vacuum' in excerpt 18 below has no corresponding Samoan translation.

(18) (Family #2; 6/8/93 Camera 2: uncle A is talking to twelve-year-old P)

A: *fai sau   loa*, (.) *fia*   vacuum *le poku*
      say come then   want   the room
      "tell (her) to hurry up, (.) (I) want (to) <u>vacuum</u> the room"

But other times, the word substitutes for an existing Samoan term (Carol Myers-Scotton [1993] calls these borrowings "core" borrowings because they substitute the "core" vocabulary of the "matrix language") or even an earlier borrowing. We have already seen several examples of this type. For example, in excerpt 10 above, the grandmother uses English numbers instead of Samoan numbers. In excerpt 19 below, the mother uses the English noun 'friends' instead of the Samoan native term *uô*.

(19) (Family #1; 12/91)

Mo: *laga `o lâ e fia eva `oe i au* friends?
       "because you wanted then to go out with your <u>friends</u>?"

In excerpt 20, speaker G uses the English word 'camera' instead of the Samoan term *mea pu`e ata*, literally 'thing take picture' and in 21, he uses the English noun 'rice' despite the availability of the earlier borrowing *araisa*.

(20) (Family #1; 12/91)

G: *va`ai le- va`ai le* camera *ke`i `ua-*
      "watch the- watch the <u>camera</u> in case-"

(21) (Family #1; 12/91)

G: *`ae `â lea* rice?
      "what about this <u>rice</u>?"

Similarly, considerations can be made for Samoan lexemes in the midst of English discourse. In addition to typical Samoan concepts like *koga* 'mat' in excerpt 13 above, we also find words like *ipu* 'dish' in excerpt 12, *meaa`oga* 'homework' (literally 'thing-school') in excerpt 22, and, even more strikingly, *pepa* 'paper' in excerpt 23, which was originally borrowed from English.

(22) (Family #3; 6/7/93; seven-year-old G replies to mother's prohibition to go to her swimming lesson because she needs to do her homework)

G: I'm gonna do all my *meaa`oga* this week.
                          "homework"

(23) (Family #2; 6/8/93; twelve-year-old P finds a piece of paper her mother had been looking for)

P: here's the *pepa*
                "paper"

What is consistent about these single-lexeme CSs is that they are usually mor-
phologically integrated in the surrounding parts of the utterance in which they appear
but exhibit little or no phonological assimilation to the receiving language. In fact,
they tend to be phonological islands, which means that they often violate the phonological rules of the code in the midst of which they are being inserted. For example, we found several cases of isolated English words with consonant clusters in the
midst of Samoan discourse: 'prom,' 'sink,' 'Q-tip,' 'ticket.' These words violate the
Samoan (C)V syllable constraint mentioned above. The contrast between the different treatment given to old and new borrowings is well illustrated in the following segment, in which 1.5-generation speaker G uses in two adjacent utterances the old and
established borrowing *lapisi* (from British English 'rubbish') and the new borrowing
'sink,' with the traditionally unacceptable CVCC structure.

(24) (Family #1; 5/93)

G: then go and- ((points to a plate))
                sasa`a mea lea i le lâpisi
                "pour this stuff in the trash"
                ku`u lou ipu i le sink
                "put your plate in the <u>sink</u>"

Something similar happens to Samoan words inserted in the midst of English
discourse, for example, the frequently used Samoan verb *kâ`ele* 'take a shower,'
which maintains a segment, the glottal stop, which is not part of the English phonological inventory (see example 11 above).

These findings are in some respects consistent with previous studies that have
shown how in their early stages, borrowings are often unassimilated to the phonology of the receiving language (Haugen 1950; Myers-Scotton 1993; Romaine 1989).
Sarah G. Thomason and Terrence Kaufman (1988, 33) also suggested that a distinction must be made between "earlier borrowings" and "later borrowings," with
the former being characteristic of a first-stage contact and limited or nonexistent
bilingualism, and the latter as characteristic of more advanced stages of contact and
a higher level of bilingualism. In our case, as speakers of Samoan descent increase
their contact with English speakers in the United States, the pronunciation of the
English words they insert in their Samoan becomes closer to the pronunciation used
by native speakers of English. However, this hypothesis does not completely square
with the fate of the Samoan words used in the midst of English discourse by second-
generation speakers. Young children who are not fluent bilinguals still preserve the
Samoan pronunciation of Samoan words. It is almost as if bilingualism brings about
a certain respect for the original pronunciation as well as an appreciation of differences,
as represented by the specific pronunciation characteristic of each code. As the adults
seem to accept an increase in the amount of English spoken in the home, children, in turn,
recognize the importance of Samoan by freely importing Samoan words and expressions in

the midst of their English discourse. In so doing, they may be trying to preserve the pronunciation of Samoan words as a partial tribute to their heritage and as a form of ethnic pride. It is common, for example, even for young teenagers who are not fluent in Samoan, to pronounce the words 'Samoa' and 'Samoan' with a long vowel in the first syllable and distinct vocalic segments in the rest of the word ([sa:moa], [sa:moan]) even when they are speaking English.

Phonological Islands

In our data, there are two sets of English single-lexemes that are the most resistant to phonological assimilation to Samoan. They are both sets of commonly used words and, in this sense, they are good candidates for new borrowings. The first are English kinship terms, 'mom' and 'dad' in particular. These two words, used as both address and reference terms, are very common in all of the families we studied. Being CVC, they violate the CV syllable constraint; 'dad' also has the voiced segment (/d/), which is not part of the Samoan phonological inventory.

(25) (Family #2)

A: `a`o fea Mom ma Dad?
        but where   and
        "but where are <u>Mom</u> and <u>Dad</u>?"
L: they just left.

The use of these two terms in the vocabulary of the members of the families we studied is not only a lexical innovation, it is also a cultural innovation. In the interactions recorded in Samoa by Duranti, Ochs, and Platt, children did not use kinship terms in calling their parents. Although there are Samoan words for father (tamâ) and mother (tinâ), these words are used for reference and not for address, and they can also be extended to other members of the family, such as grandparents and other people who take care of or are considered responsible for children.[7] Parents are usually called or referred to by their proper names. This has a number of important implications. First, by calling their mother and father by their names, children are calling their parents as everyone else does. The terms 'mom' and 'dad,' instead, imply that the user is either the person's child or is someone who is momentarily taking the point of view of the child (Hymes 1974, 56; Levinson 1983, 72). Furthermore, since most men over thirty have a matai title and the title becomes the name by which they are addressed, when a Samoan child calls her father by his name, she is calling him by his matai title. Matai titles are de facto public offices associated with a particular lineage that give holders control over one or more plots of land and the right to participate in a range of public activities. All matai titles are ranked with respect to one another. When children call their father by his matai title, they address their father not as their father, but as the person who holds a particular public office, the representative of the extended family vis-à-vis the wider community, which includes the village council (fono), the district, the island, and even the archipelago.

Given these practices on the islands, we cannot help thinking that in the United States, the use of 'mom' and 'dad' might index a new emphasis on the nuclear family and a privileged type of relationship between children and parents. The adoption of American kinship names might signal the recognition of a new set of social and even affective relations within the family.

The second group of phonological islands is constituted by English proper names, which often violate a number of Samoan phonological constraints. Some names are left in their English phonological form even when there are established Samoan equivalents. For example, 'David' was typically converted to *Tâvita* in Samoa in the 1970s and 1980s,[8] but is left unaltered among the Samoans we observed in the United States, even within the context of a Samoan utterance, as shown in example 26. Example 27 shows the same phenomenon with two other English names, Vince and Alice.

(26) (Family #2; 6/8/93 Camera #1)

PM: I don't know
       fai mai e maga`o ia- e maga`o e alaku David `ô.
       "(he) said (he) wants- wants <u>David</u> to go (over) there"

(27) (Family #2; 5/30/93)

L: *fai mai le mea a* Vince
       "<u>Vince</u> said" (lit. "Vince said the thing)
       `*o ai lae ô ma* Alice?
       "who is going with <u>Alice</u>?"

Although the resistance to phonological assimilation of borrowings—including proper names—has been frequently noted in bilingual communities, especially before a borrowing gets established and universally adopted (Poplack, Sankoff, and Miller 1988; Romaine 1989), we want to stress that such a feature is a double innovation for Samoan speakers. First, Samoans traditionally assimilated proper names in the same way in which they assimilated common nouns and verbs. Second, Samoans are known to shift phonological registers with ease, adapting all words to the chosen variety. In the data collected in Samoa in the 1970s and 1980s, not only did speakers adapt proper names to Samoan phonology, they also adapted them to the current phonological variety, changing the /d/ of English 'David' to /t/ in "good speech" and to /k/ in "bad speech" (see table 14.1).

Samoan Proper Names as Phonological Islands

The island-like property discussed above seems to be a general property of names and not just of English proper names. Samoan proper names, especially the names of children, display a similar resistance to phonological assimilation. In our data, many of the Samoan names with a /t/ in "good speech" maintain that segment even when the rest of the utterance they appear in is in "bad speech" and hence contains no /t/

segments. In excerpt 28, for example, the first-person dual pronoun *tâ* is pronounced in "bad speech" (*kâ*), but the name of the youngest boy in the family is left in the "good speech" pronunciation (*Tifo*).

(28) (Family #3; 5/31/93)

Sister: *kâ ô Tifo.*
           we-dual go(Pl)
           "let's go, Tifo."

(29) (Family #1; Mother teases Fitu about a player he is talking about)

Mother: *kama a Fitu.*
           boy of
           "Fitu's friend."

Although the Samoan data shown above could be used to support Michael Clyne's (1967, 1987) claim that for bilinguals proper names are the same in the two codes, there is no evidence of them having what Clyne called a "triggering effect"— that is, an influence on the code or variety used right after the proper name. The use of "good speech" for Samoan proper names does not trigger "good speech" for the rest of the utterance, even when the Samoan proper name with the /t/ segment is at the beginning of the utterance. In excerpt 30, for example, the proper name contains a /t/ while the rest of the turn is in "bad speech," as shown by the fact that the verb *nofo* 'sit' is pronounced *gofo* [ŋofo].[9] In excerpt 31, the same proper name is used in "good speech" at the beginning followed by *kua*, the "bad speech" pronunciation of *tua* 'back.' Similarly, in excerpt 32, the "good speech" pronunciation of the proper name "*Fita*" is followed by an utterance that contains *lokea*, the "bad speech" pronunciation of the verb *lote+a* 'to fiddle around with.'[10]

(30) (Family #3; 3/7/93)

Mo: *Tia, gofo i lalo.*
       "Tia, sit down."

(31) (Family #3; 5/31/93)

Father: *Tia ei, alu i kua alu i fafo o- e- e fai ou siva*
           "Tia, hey, go in the back outside to-to do your dance."

(32) (Family #1; 12/91)

G: *Fita, `aua le lokea le mea.*
      "Fita, don't fiddle around with the thing."

Not all Samoan proper names in our U.S. corpus follow this pattern. We do have cases in which Samoan proper names are adapted to "bad speech" pronunciation.

They are usually names of people who either live on or were born on the islands. In other words, there seems to be a distinction made between names of young children (who were born in the United States or were brought to the United States soon after being born) and the names of everyone else. The names of older people, for example, are more likely to undergo changes in pronunciation depending on the surrounding discourse. More generally, our data suggest that the status of proper names varies within the same immigrant community and that there might be a correlation between the level of phonological assimilation and the level of identification of a particular individual with the home country versus the host country. That there might be an inverse relation between phonological assimilation and openness to change is supported by the fact that the family where the parents use more Samoan than the parents in any of the other families in our study (family #3) is the one in which the pronunciation of proper names is more likely to be adapted to "bad speech." This is consistent with other features that rank the same family as the most conservative, that is, closer to the standards followed on the Samoan islands, in terms of other features of speech and interaction (Reynolds 1995).

Changes in phonological integration of actual or potential borrowings have already been linked to changing attitudes and types of contact situation (Bernstein 1990, cited by Myers-Scotton 1993, 179). One such change in attitudes could be a new way of thinking about the connection between social identity and context. The phonological impermeability of one's name might be an index of a new emphasis on permanence of social identity. A person's name remains the same because it is assumed that that person is also the same across situations and that sameness should be symbolically recognized. This could be an unconscious and yet pervasive effort by the parents to maintain at least one feature of a child's identity steady across situations. It is also possible that it is a way of making it easier for the children to recognize their names. If this were indeed a factor, it would also involve an innovation, given that Elinor Ochs (1982, 1988) showed that in the family interactions recorded in Samoa, adults do not simplify their speech to children.

Conclusion

In this chapter, we have considered some of the features of English and Samoan words used by members of a Samoan American community in Southern California. We relied on previous fieldwork carried out in a (Western) Samoan community by Allesandro Duranti and Elinor Ochs to highlight differences between the ways in which speakers in the two communities deal with foreign words. In particular, we have shown that unlike earlier (and established) borrowings, new borrowings are not adapted to the phonology of the receiving language. This is a trend that has long been noted in the literature on language contact, where some researchers have speculated that lack of phonological assimilation is typical of the first stage of borrowing—that is, before the loanwords become established in the lexicon of the receiving language—and others have posited that it is a phenomenon typical of bilingual communities. In our case, we have suggested that the introduction of certain kinship terms ('mom' and 'dad') and the tendency to preserve across contexts not only the English pronunciation of English words but also the "good speech" pronunciation of Samoan names must be seen as having potentially important cultural implications. In particular, the adoption of kinship terms—as opposed to proper names (and *matai* titles)—in addressing and referring to parents implies a new emphasis on the child's point of view (as opposed to the adults') within the family. This is a new discourse practice in a society in which children are traditionally expected to adapt to adults (Ochs 1982, 1988; Ochs and Schieffelin 1984). The lack of phonological variation found in both English names in general and Samoan names of young children in particular also suggests that Samoan adults in the United States are adopting linguistic strategies that index persons as less contextualized, that is, more permanent entities.

NOTES

1. All the Samoan examples in this section and in table 14.1 are taken from the same transcript of a videotape of a family dinner recorded by A. Duranti and E. Ochs in (then 'Western') Samoa in the summer of 1988.

Abbreviations used in interlinear glosses:

Art:	article	Comp:	complementizer	Dx:	postverbal deictic particle
DX:	preverbal deictic particle			Erg:	ergative marker
Excl:	exclusive	Fut:	Future tense	Neg:	negation
Perf:	perfect aspect	Pred:	predicating particle (which also marks		
			Topic at beginning of utterance)		
Pres:	present tense	Pl:	plural form or marker.		

Transcription conventions:

(.)	micro pause
-	cut off

2. The word *ali`i* is one of the most difficult words to translate in English. It can refer to a 'chief' (as opposed to an orator or talking chief) but it is also used for a commoner of any age. In this example, it conveys a certain degree of respect for the referent. However, bilingual speakers who worked on our project often translated *ali`i* with 'guy,' suggesting that there is also informality associated with its use. Finally, *ali`i* can be used as an address term followed by the name of the addressee or a kinship term, regardless of gender.

3. We found both [babakyu] and [papakyu] in our data.

4. On the use of the eyebrow flash to convey agreement, see Eibl-Eibesfeldt (1972).

5. In changing the names of the children, we have tried to keep features of their phonological structure that might be relevant to our discussion. Unfortunately, in so doing, we have lost the cultural and semantic connotations of the original names and have often created names that do not exist in Samoan.

6. The mother in family #1, who worked as a schoolteacher in the local elementary school and had moved to the United States as an adult, consistently produced the most complex types of CSs in our entire corpus.

7. See Hogbin (1934) on this practice in Ontong Java, a Polynesian outlier.

8. We do not have sufficient information at the moment to know whether these pronunciation practices have been recently altered, nor can we assess whether there are differences in this area between Samoa and American Samoa.

9. For a discussion of this particular expression, see Duranti (1997b).

10. The addition of the suffix -*a* is due to the negative imperative form `*aua*, which requires the nominalization of the following verb.

REFERENCES

Bauman, Richard. 1992. Contextualization, tradition and the dialogue of genres: Icelandic legends of the *Kraftaskáld*. In *Rethinking context: Language as an interactive phenomenon*, ed. Alessandro Duranti and Charles Goodwin, 125–145. Cambridge: Cambridge University Press.

Clyne, Michael. 1967. *Transference and triggering*. The Hague: Martinus Nijhoff.

———. 1987. Constraints on code switching: How universal are they? *Linguistics* 25:739–764.

Duranti, Alessandro. 1981. *The Samoan Fono: A sociolinguistic study*. Pacific Linguistics Monographs, Series B, vol. 80. Canberra: Australian National University, Department of Linguistics, Research School of Pacific Studies.

———. 1993. Intentions, self, and responsibility: An essay in Samoan ethnopragmatics. In *Responsibility and evidence in oral discourse*, ed. Jane H. Hill and Judith T. Irvine, 24–47. Cambridge: Cambridge University Press.

———. 1994. *From grammar to politics: Linguistic anthropology in a Western Samoan village*. Berkeley and Los Angeles: University of California Press.

———. 1997a. *Linguistic anthropology*. Cambridge: Cambridge University Press.

———. 1997b. Indexical speech across Samoan communities. *American Anthropologist* 99:342–354.

Duranti, Alessandro, and Elinor Ochs. 1997. Syncretic literacy in a Samoan American family. In *Discourse, tools, and reasoning: Situated cognition and technologically supported environments*, ed. Lauren Resnick, Roger Saljo, Clotilde Pontecorvo, and Barbara Burge, 169–202. Heidelberg: Springer-Verlag.

Duranti, Alessandro, Elinor Ochs, and Elia K. Ta`ase. 1995. Change and tradition in literacy instruction in a Samoan American community. *Educational Foundations* 9:57–74.

Eibl-Eibesfeldt, Irenäus. 1972. Similarities and differences between cultures in expressive movements. In *Non-verbal communication*, ed. Robert A. Hinde, 297–312. Cambridge: Cambridge University Press.

Gal, Susan. 1979. *Language shift: Social determinants of linguistic change in bilingual Austria*. New York: Academic Press.

Haugen, Einar. 1950. The analysis of linguistic borrowings. *Language* 26:210–231.

Hogbin, Herbert. I. 1934. *Law and order in Polynesia*. New York: Harcourt, Brace.

Hymes, Dell. 1974. *Foundations in sociolinguistics: An ethnographic approach*. Philadelphia: University of Pennsylvania Press.

Levinson, Stephen C. 1983. *Pragmatics*. Cambridge: Cambridge University Press.

Milner, George B. 1966. *Samoan dictionary: Samoan-English English-Samoan*. London: Oxford University Press.

Mosel, Ulrike, and Even Hovdhaugen. 1992. *Samoan reference grammar*. Oslo: Scandinavian University Press/The Institute for Comparative Research in Human Culture.

Myers-Scotton, Carol. 1993. *Duelling languages: Grammatical structure in codeswitching*. Oxford: Clarendon Press.

Ochs, Elinor. 1982. Talking to children in Western Samoa. *Language in Society* 11:77–104.

———. 1985. Variation and error: A sociolinguistic study of language acquisition in Samoa. In *The crosslinguistic study of language acquisition, vol. 2*, ed. Dan. I. Slobin, 783–838. Hillsdale, N.J.: Erlbaum.

———. 1986. From feelings to grammar: A Samoan case study. In *Language socialization across cultures*, ed. Bambi B. Schieffelin and Elinor Ochs, 251–272. New York: Cambridge University Press.

———. 1988. *Culture and language development: Language acquisition and language socialization in a Samoan village*. Cambridge: Cambridge University Press.

Ochs, Elinor, and Bambi B. Schieffelin. 1984. Language acquisition and socialization: Three developmental stories. In *Culture theory: Essays on mind, self, and emotion*, ed. Richard A. Shweder and Robert A. LeVine, 276–320. Cambridge: Cambridge University Press.

Platt, Martha. 1986. Social norms and lexical acquisition: A study of deictic verbs in Samoan child language. In *Language socialization across cultures*, ed. Bambi B. Schieffelin and Elinor Ochs, 127–151. Cambridge: Cambridge University Press.

Poplack, Shana, David Sankoff, and Christopher Miller. 1988. The social correlates and linguistic processes of lexical borrowing and assimilation. *Linguistics* 26:47–104.

Pouesi, Daniel. 1994. *An illustrated history of Samoans in California*. Carson, Calif.: Kin Publications.

Reynolds, Jennifer. 1995. *Tautalaititi and Tags: A study of Samoan American child language socialization as syncretic practice*. Los Angeles: University of California at Los Angeles.

Romaine, Suzanne. 1989. *Bilingualism*. Oxford: Blackwell.

Shankman, Paul. 1993. The Samoan exodus. In *Contemporary Pacific societies: Studies in development and change*, ed. Victoria S. Lockwood, Thomas G. Harding, and Ben J. Wallace, 156–170. Englewood Cliffs, N.J.: Prentice-Hall.

Shore, Bradd. 1982. *Sala'ilua: A Samoan mystery*. New York: Columbia University Press.

Thomason, Sarah G., and Terrence Kaufman. 1988. *Language contact, creolization, and genetic linguistics*. Berkeley and Los Angeles: University of California Press.

Zentella, Ana Celia. 1997. *Growing up bilingual*. Oxford: Blackwell.

15

What Do Bilinguals Do?

A Commentary

Asif Agha

Accounts of the social meaning of bilingualism are only as revealing as the picture of language they invoke. In "codeswitching" accounts, a language is a denotational "code" organized into grammatical units; persons "use" a code when they utter its units; and bilinguals mingle units of one code with units of another. When the mingling of codes is evaluated by criteria of grammatical constituency (whether phonological or lexical constituents are involved; whether forms of mingling cross sentence boundaries; whether constituent-types are deformed or preserved in mingled tokens) the activities of bilinguals can be classified into certain well-known types, such as code-"mixing," "switching," "assimilation," "borrowing," and others. Yet code-centric accounts of "what bilinguals do" reveal very little about the social significance of their doings.

Bilinguals may protest that they mingle in a fuller sense too, as persons do: that they orient to denotational units only in the course of orienting to each other as interactants; that the units through which they orient to each other have social-indexical values additional to their grammatical values; that these social-indexical values are linked to culture-specific models of appropriate conduct which, when juxtaposed with each other within bilingual encounters, are frequently reanalyzed and transformed into new registers of conduct.

The bilingual authors of the accompanying chapters certainly appear to protest in these ways. Through a common focus on geographically transposed populations—immigrants, their children, foreign students—they explore the ways in which the social-indexical values of speech-forms are reevaluated through the reflexive activities of speakers under conditions of linguistic and cultural contact. They are particularly interested in how changes in the "social types" stereotypically indexed by speech are experienced and negotiated by speakers as aspects of their "identities" within bilingual encounters. The issues are best approached by asking how bilingual speech tokens are linked to linguistic and social types in the first place.

Bilingualism is a discursive practice where the *transposition* of speech-tokens across contexts of use (geographical locales, social settings, the "language" co-textually in use) influences their "type"-level construal, both at the level of grammar and social indexicality. It is well known that, in cases of "codemixing," speech tokens routinely occur as phonological or morphosyntactic blends of matrix and source grammatical types; they are partially assimilated to *both* grammatical systems; they exhibit varying degrees of *fidelity-to-type* relative to both systems. Yet the question of whether similar considerations apply to the social indexical values of speech has been less fully explored in the literature. Do bilinguals have "hybrid" social voices in Bakhtin's sense? Which interlocutors recognize these voices? How do they assign them to "social types"? How do persons inhabit or negotiate "social type"-assignments when they produce or encounter speech tokens?

The accompanying chapters show that bilinguals reanalyze not only the grammatical types but also the register models used to interpret transposed speech. The various register distinctions discussed in these chapters—"good versus bad speech" in Samoan (Duranti and Reynolds), registers of Korean address (Song), of self-reference in Japanese (Morita), the register values of disfluent English among Koreans (Park)—all undergo subtle transformations when their associated discursive forms, and the persons who use them, are transposed from their native countries to the United States. The resulting reanalyses yield various figurements of social types, such as contrasts of national belonging (Song), of degrees of foreignness and liminality (Park), of intergenerational difference (Morita), and of the stability versus variability of the self (Duranti and Reynolds). In exploring this range of phenomena, these studies engage with older approaches to bilingualism, including theories of "codeswitching" and "linguistic borrowing," and attempt to move beyond them.

Traditionally, accounts of "codeswitching" have approached bilingualism by taking the denotational-grammatical organization of discourse (viz., phonemic, lexical, and morphosyntactic units) as a point of departure: The idea that bilingual discourse involves two distinct "codes" is simply a way of restating the observation that "two distinct grammatical systems" are in play (Gumperz 1982, 66). The idea that each such code can be identified as having discrete boundaries, that the two codes are neatly bounded off against each other, relies on distinctions "taught in standard grammars" (Gumperz 1982, 99) and hence on Standard Language ideologies that normalize grammatical systems and specify their boundaries. Yet a grammar-centric approach to discourse and a Standard-centric approach to grammar tend to ignore other ideologies of language (such as norms of interaction) that invariably co-exist with ideologies of Standard, and further complicate the construal of utterances. As we move from the grammatical organization of bilingual discourse to its interpersonal organization, the question of just how many codes are involved, and how they can be tracked empirically, becomes problematic. And when the word "code" is used expansively—e.g., to include both norms of denotation and norms of interpersonal conduct—such a usage conflates the grammatical organization of linguistic units with the register appropriateness of using them in particular scenarios of interaction (Agha 2007).

Hence, to speak of bilingual discourse in terms simply of the "switching" or "mixing" of grammatical codes, or of "borrowings" from one discrete code to another, is to lose sight of the logic of type-fidelity through which its interpersonal significance emerges. It is not merely that various codes preexist as fully formed immiscible wholes, waiting to be switched between, mixed with each other, or borrowed as readymades; such a view uncritically accepts the neat partitions that Standard Language ideologies seek to enforce. It is rather that in particular phases or moments of speech production, specific text-segments are foregrounded as fractionally noncongruent with co-textual speech along one or more dimensions of categorial organization (viz., phonemic, lexical, etc.), yielding various kinds of blends and grammatically hybrid forms. Facts of noncongruence mark foregrounded text-segments as interpolations sourced from a language *distinct from* their surrounding co-text. Although such text tokens are merely diacritics of *otherness* to interlocutors acquainted only with the matrix language, they are also typifiable as tokens of a distinct, nameable language for those acquainted with the language from which they are formulated as sourced. And since such tokens occur at some threshold of fidelity-to-type to both matrix and source language, the manner in which bilingual interlocutors *formulate* fidelity-to-type itself constitutes a metacommunicative frame of performance through which the interpersonal significance of type-hybridized speech is negotiated over an extended stretch of multi-party discourse.

We can begin to appreciate the metacommunicative organization of bilingual discursive practice by noting that the practices that Joseph Sung-Yul Park (this volume) calls "disclaiming English" are a special case of what Bauman terms "disclaimers of performance" (Bauman 1992). When Korean speakers "disclaim" English (i.e., claim to lack competence in proper English usage) they formulate a metacommentary that sometimes *explicitly describes* this lack of competence, and sometimes, through utterances that exaggerate the assimilation of English forms to Korean grammatical structure, *implicitly performs* such lack of competence. By drawing a contrast between two degrees of phonological assimilation of the English place-name *Denver* to Korean pronunciation norms, Junho and Hyeju (both Koreans living as foreign students in the United States) draw a contrast between two degrees of cultural assimilation to the United States. In self-identifying with a pronunciation where *Denver* is fully assimilated to Korean phonology, they perform an emblem of non-Americanness; and in formulating the pronunciation of their absent friend as closer to American English phonology, they typify his speech as, by contrast, "an overwrought effort" to assimilate to U.S. cultural norms. We are not dealing with communicative acts that mix or switch between two discrete codes, but with acts whose metacommunicative organization treats the gradient fidelity of text tokens to phonological types as emblematic of degrees of allegiance of speakers to associated cultural identities.

All of the other papers deal with cases that involve—what might more traditionally be called—the "borrowing" of linguistic forms and practices across cultures. The question remains, however, of what exactly "borrowing" is as a linguistic and sociological phenomenon.

The idea that linguistic expressions get "borrowed" from one language to another falsely suggests an analogy with the notion that material possessions can be borrowed from one person by another and thereby undergo a temporary transposition across domains of "use." Just as person A can borrow person B's pencil (or T-shirt or iPod) and use it for a while, so also language community A can borrow linguistic expressions from community B and "use" them for a while. Or so the analogy presents itself. Yet the transposability of linguistic expressions across domains of "use"—particularly in the oral contexts these papers explore—is entirely unlike that of durable commodities.

First, linguistic expressions can be transposed across domains of use and categories of users only through acts of token (re)production. Once manufactured, a pencil can have a complex social life—it can be purchased, possessed, loaned, and borrowed, for instance—without needing to be remanufactured. But linguistic expressions have a social life only insofar as, and as long as, they are reproduced in the utterances of speakers, each event reproducing a token of the type. To speak of *linguistic* borrowing is to speak of recurrent events of token production. Second, since linguistic expressions are category clusters that simultaneously instantiate several dimensions of categorial structure (e.g., phonological, morphosyntactic, deictic, *and* social-indexical category-types), acts of token reproduction are fraught with multiple possibilities of nonfidelity to type. Any linguistic sign-type may be deployed as a text-token in ways that are canonical with respect to one categorial dimension but defective with respect to others. Such *gradations* of categorial assimilation can diagram differences among users, as we have seen, whether implicitly, or through the mediation of explicitly articulated social classifications. Third, whereas person A's act of borrowing a pencil from person B may result in A's using the expropriated item only in the sphere of personal (even effectively "private") use, the kinds of transpositions we call "linguistic borrowings" are typically manifest only in the interpersonal matrix of discursive interaction. Social processes of linguistic borrowing do not merely consist of acts of token reproduction variably anchored in fidelity-to-type, they are tied to interactional frameworks in a variety of ways: Nonfidelity to grammatical type can mediate forms of denotational footing (the symmetric or asymmetric use of denotational units across speaking turns) yielding positive or negative social alignments among interlocutors, whether among individuals in occasion-specific ways, or among social groups through group-differentiating norms of register appropriateness (Agha 2007, 132–142). Only by attending to the interpersonal matrix of acts of language use—analyzed both discursively and metadiscursively—can we begin to approach the question of how such borrowings diagram social roles and relationships, and for whom they do so.

Juyoung Song (this volume) discusses English-to-Korean "borrowings" of address practices where differences in the type-fidelity of transpositions mediate subtle contrasts of interpersonal alignment among interlocutors. In Korean, registers of address normatively draw on a repertoire of nominal expressions larger than in English, and choices among these expressions finely discriminate social relations among interlocutors. Children are socialized to norms of register-appropriate address by caregivers through a variety of metadiscursive practices (including explicit prescription, implicit speech modeling, recasting the child's utterances, using normative forms when the child is within earshot, and others). Korean caregivers dutifully engage in such efforts in the United States, just as in Korea. However, Korean American children engage in only some of these practices, switching in other cases to more culturally hybrid forms that show the influence of English norms (e.g., a more anglicized pronunciation of names, a greater resistance to fictive kinterm usage); and their metapragmatic commentary describes *these usages of Korean as*—interpersonally—*more "American,"* as exhibiting greater type-fidelity to nonhierarchical registers of American address.

Acts of alignment to matrix or source language practices can themselves be construed as having a more or less elaborate *social range* (i.e., the range of identities and social relations indexed by the act); minimally, a speaker's choices may index self as non-in-group vis-à-vis interlocutor; or both speaker and interlocutor may jointly align as a sub-group (e.g., as both non-in-group vis-à-vis a Standard Language community); speech conduct may be linked to standards of proper and improper conduct enforced by sanctions; and explicit role designations and classifications ("bilingual," "trans-national," "foreigner," "cosmopolitan," etc.) may be available to describe specific discursive practices and those who engage in them. In the Japanese case discussed by Emi Morita, the use of English *me* in place of a Japanese first-person pronoun allows speakers a way out of the intricate web of social-indexical contrasts linked to the more elaborate paradigm available in Japanese. But the choice also seems "indiscriminate" or under-differentiating to Japanese interlocutors; and insofar as it avoids Japanese norms of deference and demeanor the usage is potentially indexical of "not-fully-Japanese" identity (despite other signs to the contrary, such as speaker's native competence in all other linguistic and cultural norms). Morita shows that, by contrast, in Japanese American usage, a context where speakers are acquainted not only with two different grammatical codes (English and Japanese) but with two different registers of person reference, and thus with two different n^{th}-order frameworks of appropriate *self*-reference (use of English *me* vs. any of several Japanese pronouns, all differing in social indexicality), the use of English *me* is in the process of being transformed in register valence into "an $n+1^{st}$-order register for indexing a specifically Japanese-American identity."

In sociological terms, cross-linguistic "borrowings" exhibit all of the dimensions of organization linked to officially "monolingual" speech registers (many of which are, of course, differentiated from the rest of the language through borrowings from neighboring languages (Errington 1988; Haviland 1979; Irvine 1998) or from sociolects within the same language (Agha 2007, 136–139, 174–177), and only ideologically stabilized as monolingual varieties). For instance, the social construal of a borrowing can vary in *social domain* (i.e., how many—and what kinds of—persons construe usage in this way; see Agha 2007, chap. 3) and, indeed, can grow or shrink in social domain over time through social processes mediated by the logic of interpersonal footing and alignment in events of language use (Agha 2005). Morita shows that precisely such a logic appears to shape the continued use or non-use of the Japanese American register of English *me* by a Japanese American boy, Jack, who uses this form at age five (even in the face of challenges by individual Japanese kids) but ceases to use the form in favor of Japanese pronouns by age seven, soon after his immersion in a Japanese school (where "Standard Japanese" ideologies lead to more institutionally pervasive forms of nonratification).

Alessandro Duranti and Jennifer F. Reynolds discuss several kinds of speech transpositions. The meaning assigned to some of these is relatively clear, though their interpretation of one subset of their data remains speculative. They note that U.S.-born Samoan American children living in California tend to treat the Samoan words they use in English as phonological islands, uncorrupted by English phonological influence; they appear thereby to pay "partial tribute to their [Samoan] heritage." Conversely, two sets of English lexemes are most resistant to assimilation to Samoan norms: English proper names, which are treated as phonological islands, and the English kinship terms *mom* and *dad*. Tokens of the latter not only violate Samoan phonology, they violate cultural norms of parental address too. In replacing Samoan forms of parental address with *mom* and *dad*, Samoan American children index-ically project a "private" or "nuclear family" alignment to parents; in Samoa, by contrast, children's parental address is formulated as "impersonal" and "societal" through allocentric patterns of address (i.e., addressing parents with proper names and titles, as others do). This, then, is a register of parental address distinctive to Samoan American children, in whose speech habits, its social meaning is clearly transformed by type-fidelity to American interpersonal norms.

The social meaning of a second pattern, which occurs in the speech of Samoan American adults, is not, however, entirely clear. Although adults in Samoa vary the pronunciation of names when they switch across "good" versus "bad" phonolexi-cal registers, some names remain phonologically invariant in the speech of Samoan American parents, particularly names of children born in the United States or brought there soon after birth. Duranti and Reynolds offer two hypotheses: Either this parental practice is designed to make it easier for such children (who are generally English-dominant) to recognize their Samoan names, or the invariant pronunciation of names here indexes a commitment to American models of a contextually invariant "self." This question cannot be resolved without considering further metadiscursive data, since, as we have seen in all of the other studies, the question of the social meaning of transposed speech is susceptible to competing logics of type-fidelity, including fidelity to competing assumptions about the cultural selves of speakers. Bilinguals do not merely transpose speech tokens in ways that foreground their type-hybridity, nor simply acquire "social type" characteristics always already given by register construals of hybrid speech. The activity of negotiating register models for type-hybridized practices with the persons with whom they engage through such practices, is itself a central, ongoing feature of what bilinguals do.

REFERENCES

Agha, Asif. 2005. Voice, footing, enregisterment. *Journal of Linguistic Anthropology* 15:38–59.
———. 2007. *Language and social relations*. Cambridge: Cambridge University Press.
Bauman, Richard. 1992. Disclaimers of performance. In *Responsibility and evidence in oral discourse*, ed. Jane H. Hill and Judith T. Irvine, 182–196. Cambridge: Cambridge University Press.
Errington, J. Joseph. 1988. *Structure and style in Javanese: A semiotic view of linguistic eti-quette*. Philadelphia: University of Pennsylvania Press.
Gumperz, John J. 1982. *Discourse strategies*. Cambridge: Cambridge University Press.
Haviland, John. 1979. How to talk to your brother-in-law in Guugu Yimidhirr. In *Languages and their speakers*, ed. Timothy Shopen, 161–239. Cambridge, Mass.: Winthrop.
Irvine, Judith T. 1998. Ideologies of honorific language. In *Language ideologies: Practice and theory*, ed. Bambi B. Schieffelin, Kathryn A. Woolard, and Paul V. Kroskrity, 51–67. New York: Oxford University Press.

IV

Linguistic Practices in Media Contexts

16

Ideologies of Legitimate Mockery

Margaret Cho's Revoicings of Mock Asian

Elaine W. Chun

In elementary schoolyards across the United States, children of perceived East Asian descent are reminded of their racial otherness when their peers perform ostensibly playful renderings of a 'Chinese accent.' This practice, which I call *Mock Asian* in this chapter, is a discourse that indexes a stereotypical Asian identity. While there is no such language variety called *Asian*, I use the label *Mock Asian* in order to emphasize its racializing nature. Its potential semiotics is similar to that of Mock Spanish, which Jane Hill (1998) identifies as the legitimized use of "disorderly" Spanish by whites in public spaces.

But relative to Mock Spanish, which is found in various public domains from advertisements and greeting cards to political speeches and newscasts (Hill 1998), voicings of Mock Asian are less common, perhaps because of the more overtly racist implications of this practice. Some 'well-meaning' non-Asian adults might utter a *nihao* or *konnichiwa* toward a racial Asian they encounter on the street, but it is less common—at least in public spaces—for them to voice the kind of Mock Asian taunts that children use to overtly mark Asian racial 'difference.' The explicitness with which this language style marks racial otherness, in contrast to the more common incorporation of Mock Spanish into a Mainstream American English (MAE) speaker's "own" linguistic repertoire, may partially account for the relative infrequency of Mock Asian in mainstream American contexts.[1]

Certain contexts outside childhood play, however, do license the circulation of this particular stereotypical discourse. This chapter addresses one of these contexts—namely, the comedy performances of Margaret Cho, a Korean American comedian. By discussing several excerpts from one of her performances, during which she employs Mock Asian, I describe some of the ideologies that legitimate her use of this racializing style. These *ideologies of legitimacy* depend on assumptions about the relationship between communities, the authentication of a speaker's community membership, and the nature of the interpretive frame that has been "keyed" (Goffman 1974). To understand these ideologies beyond the context of her performances, I juxtapose her performance with two controversial Mock Asian incidents that occurred in the United States in recent years. As I will illustrate, the meanings that Cho's linguistic practices convey are multiple and emergent, and her legitimacy to employ Mock Asian is negotiated by both ostensible members and non-members of variously defined communities. Central to this negotiation are the differentials of power to either claim or name those who belong and those who do not.

Rather than attempt to label Cho's practices as exclusively either racist or subversive, I bring attention to the multiple meanings of a linguistic practice that is sometimes controversial. Her Mock Asian depends on and, to some extent, reproduces particular ideological links between race, nation, and language despite the apparent process of ideological subversion, or the *deauthentication* of social and linguistic identities (Coupland 2001a, 2001b). Mary Bucholtz (1999) and Hill (1998) have similarly shown how the appropriation of non-white language by European Americans, known as racial "crossing" (Rampton 1995), may reproduce ideologies that uphold the superiority of whiteness, the stereotypical masculinity of blackness, and the stereotypical moral inferiority of brownness. Yet Cho's use of stereotypical Asian speech is not a straightforward instance of racial crossing, given that she is a comedian who is 'Asian' according to most racial ideologies in the United States. In other words, she engages in racial crossing practices without symbolically crossing racial boundaries herself, performing the speech of a *racialized other* who is not necessarily a *racial other*. Consequently, while Cho's use of Mock Asian may necessarily reproduce mainstream American racializing discourses about Asians, she is able to simultaneously decontextualize and deconstruct these very discourses. I suggest that it is her successful authentication as an Asian American comedian, particularly one who is critical of Asian marginalization in the United States, that legitimizes her use of Mock Asian and that yields an interpretation of her practices primarily as a critique of racist mainstream ideologies.

Margaret Cho's Comedy Performances as a Site for Sociolinguistic Analysis

Humor in interaction has long been of interest in sociolinguistic and linguistic anthropological research, yet humorous performances in the public realm, or comedy performances, have less often been the focus of analysis. Kathryn Woolard's (1987, 1998) examination of Catalan-Castilian codeswitching by a professional comedian in Barcelona and Alexandra Jaffe's (2000) analysis of hybrid forms of Corsican and French used by professional comedians in Corsica are notable exceptions, and both provide important insights for the present analysis (see also Labrador, this volume). Sociolinguists have traditionally been concerned with the analysis of linguistic tokens that are 'authentic' (Bucholtz 2003), both in the sense of their 'natural' and 'every-day' occurrence and their representation of 'core' members of a particular commu-nity (Coupland 2001a). Consequently, stage performances by comedians might be viewed as fundamentally 'inauthentic': the socially marked setting in which they occur is hardly mundane, comedic language practices are highly performative, and a comedian, by nature of how she makes a living, is not likely to be a 'typical' member of the kinds of communities that have been of sociolinguistic interest.

More recently, however, there exists a growing recognition that even every-day uses of language involve performances, projections, or acts of identity (e.g., Bauman and Briggs 1990; Bucholtz [this volume]; Le Page 1980). Studies of how language is stylized by speakers (e.g., Coupland 2001b; Rampton 1995) have placed particular emphasis on the centrality of performance in discourse. While less com-mon than studies of the everyday, studies of performance in popular culture have also drawn the attention of sociolinguistics scholars, such as Rusty Barrett's (1995) examination of style-shifting by African American drag queens performing on stage, Nikolas Coupland's (2001a, 2001b) studies of dialect stylization in radio and televi-sion broadcasts, and Susan Ervin-Tripp's (2001) analysis of style-switching by two African American leaders during the civil rights movement.

As these analyses of performances in popular culture have shown, even highly conscious performances constitute sites for investigating many of the issues that sociolinguists and linguistic anthropologists have generally been interested in. For instance, one of the common goals of this line of research is to understand the ways in which language practices both reflect and reproduce identities. A speaker's iden-tity, or the way in which a speaker positions herself within ideologies that organize the social world, is constituted by her practices, which, in turn, are constituted by her membership in particular communities (Eckert and McConnell-Ginet 1992). I assume in this chapter that performances such as Cho's depend on the same ideolo-gies of community membership and language practice that speakers depend on in their everyday contexts; such congruency is necessary for her audiences to interpret her practices as humorous and, more important, as legitimate.

In addition, like other figures in U.S. popular culture, Cho not only depends on a set of ideologies about practice and identity that she shares with her audience but also contributes to, and sometimes contests, their reproduction in ways that everyday speakers may not be able to. For instance, her performances have been recorded in various media formats (two films on DVD, three CDs, and numerous sound files on the Internet at the time of the present analysis in 2003), she has published an auto-biography (Cho 2001a) that incorporates a large portion of her performed material, her television sitcom *All-American Girl*, which aired for one season in 1994–1995, drew—albeit loosely—from her earlier performances, and her recent tours have gen-erated numerous magazine and newspaper articles. While she is predominantly pop-ular within Asian American and gay and lesbian communities in the United States, revoicings of her practices likely circulate beyond them.

Comedy performances, such as Cho's, then constitute prototypical examples of how verbal texts not only incorporate and rely on various discourses and ideologies but also subsequently become the springboard for new practices and ideological per-spectives. In other words, such performances are characterized by "entextualization"

(Bauman and Briggs 1990) par excellence, whereby the displayed discourse becomes an extractable text. Through this process, texts such as Mock Asian are decontextualized and recontextualized (Bauman and Briggs 1990), providing meanings that move beyond those of the original text. As texts are transported by speakers through different temporal, spatial, and ideological contexts, they may be subject to varying interpretations. A single text can thus have a *multiplicity* of meanings, via both its historical links to past contexts as well as its links to contemporary and competing ideologies. In this chapter, I identify some of the specific ideologies that are present in Cho's performances, in addition to the "voices" (Bakhtin 1981) that she animates and the particular stance, or "footing" (Goffman 1981), that she takes with respect to these voices.

Ideologies of Legitimate Mockery

Implicit in a view of language as a tool for performing identity is the notion that speakers are agents who make choices. These choices are constrained, however, by a speaker's *habitus* (Bourdieu 1977), or embodied dispositions that are both the product of the prior repetition of practices as well as the *source* of subsequent action. Researchers have additionally noted constraints that may exist within interactions, such as the speaker's relationship with her audience (Bell 1984; Giles and Smith 1979), her motivation to establish particular relationships with her interlocutors (Myers-Scotton 1993) or with social groups that she identifies with (Le Page 1980), her access to the groups whose features she seeks to employ, her ability to analyze these features, and her ability to modify her own behavior (Le Page 1980). The identification of such constraints has contributed to the understanding that speakers have agency, but that their choices are influenced by social and linguistic structures.

This chapter addresses another dimension of constraint on language use. Specifically, it focuses on ideologies within mainstream U.S. discourses that define particular voicings of *mock language* (Hill 1998)—namely, Mock Asian—as legitimate. Although I deal with discourses within the United States, the ideologies described here may mirror those found in contexts outside the United States. In addition, although this chapter addresses the specific phenomenon of mock language, the analysis of language, legitimacy, power, and community membership may be generalized to stylization practices more generally. Comparisons of mock language practices to the related practices of cultural appropriation, borrowing, and emulation—along various axes of social identity—will likely lead to a richer analysis of how movements of symbols across social boundaries are interpreted by both members and non-members of particular communities.

While I have referred to these ideologies of legitimacy as "constraints" on language use, I wish to present these ideologies not as predictive of action but as frames for understanding the multiple and emergent meanings of action. Rather than *forecasting* practices, I seek to understand how we *interpret* the meanings of practices, because even practices that defy particular conventional expectations—such as crossing (Rampton 1995)—are socially meaningful. Given the simultaneous existence of competing ideologies that legitimate language practices, a single act is likely to abide by particular constraints, thus being perceived as *legitimate*, while violating others, thus being *illegitimate, but still socially relevant*, acts. In addition, by viewing the relationship between ideology and practice *not* as mechanistically and uni-directionally predictive, I draw attention to the ways in which practices not only reflect ideologies but also reproduce and contest them.

Abercrombie and Shaq: Two Mock Asian Incidents

As useful examples for comparison and as illustrations of the ways in which the ideologies relevant to Cho's Mock Asian extend beyond the immediate context of her performance, I bring to this discussion two recent incidents involving the use of Mock Asian. Both provoked extensive discussion within Asian American communities. The first case ignited in April 2002, when Abercrombie & Fitch, a popular American clothing company for adolescents and young adults, introduced a new line of T-shirts depicting Asians and Asian speech as objects of mockery. One T-shirt read "Wong Brother's Laundry Service: Two Wongs can make it white," referring to the stereotypical association between Asians and the service industry, as well as playing on the stereotypical difficulty for Asians to pronounce the /r/ phoneme of American English. Specifically, by structural parallelism with the saying "Two wrongs don't make a right," *wrong* is contrasted with *Wong* and *right* is contrasted with *white*. These T-shirts generated widespread protest and discussion among Asian Americans on college campuses and in virtual communities across the United States, despite the claim by a company representative that they had been designed to appeal to "Asians" (Strasburg 2002) by being "cheeky, irreverent and funny" (O'Sullivan 2002). However, the vast majority of Asian Americans who chose to publicly voice their opinion on the issue remained critical of the clothing company and supported a nationwide boycott. The day after the protesting began, the company pulled the shirts from its shelves.

The following winter, Shaquille "Shaq" O'Neal, the star center for the Los Angeles Lakers, faced relatively subdued critique for his Mock Asian performance directed toward Yao Ming, a rookie center from Mainland China. Six months after O'Neal appeared on cable television in June 2002 remarking, "Tell Yao Ming, *ching-chong-yang-wah-ah-soh*," a national sports radio program repeatedly played a recording of O'Neal's taunt and "invited listeners and radio commentators to call in jokes making racist fun of Chinese" (Tang 2003). Within days, a series of articles appeared in newspapers and on Internet sites, condemning his actions. As in the Abercrombie & Fitch case, arguments in O'Neal's defense cited the humor that was intended, and O'Neal himself stated, "Those people who know me know I have a sense of humor...I would never seriously say something derogatory to people...I apologize that some people don't have a sense of humor like I do. Because when I did it, the whole room laughed. It's nothing personal. But to say I'm racist against Asians is crazy" (Beck 2003). In addition to his own assertion that he was not racist, his close acquaintances were "quick to point out [that] the NAACP [National Association for the Advancement of Colored People] [had] recently honored O'Neal with its Young Leaders Award" (Ford 2003). As will be discussed below, Shaq's defenders attempted to recontextualize his remarks by pointing to his purported record of commitment to racial justice, validated by the recognition bestowed upon him by an institution that has close historical links with the civil rights movement.

Features of Mock Asian

The two examples discussed above involve the use of Mock Asian features that are widely circulated in mainstream American contexts as stereotypical of Asians attempting to speak English and of Asians speaking an Asian language. Table 16.1 lists other Mock Asian features[2] that, like those employed by O'Neal and Abercrombie & Fitch, explicitly index Asian speech. Mock Asian jokes told by American children (e.g., *How do Chinese people name their kids? They throw spoons down a staircase.*), including Asian American children, are often the vehicle through which knowledge of these features circulates.[3]

The features listed in table 16.1 are often consciously employed and interpreted as prototypical Mock Asian features; they index a stereotypical Asianness that unambiguously mocks Asians, rather than being characteristic of "realistic" impersonations of Asian speech. While professional comedians and actors who perform a 'Chinese accent' sometimes draw from some of the features listed in table 16.1, as professional performers, they also often engage in more subtle linguistic practices that audience members recognize as 'Chinese' or 'Oriental' without necessarily being able to reproduce these features. These comedians and actors commonly use a variety of other Mock Asian features in their revoicings of real and imagined Asians for the purpose of 'sounding Asian.' Speakers' and listeners' knowledge of these practices tend to be less conscious, and thus these practices are less likely the subject of metalinguistic commentary than the prototypical features shown above.

Table 16.2, which has been based on several Mock Asian examples appearing in two of Margaret Cho's performances (*Drunk with Power* [Cho 1996] and *I'm the One that I Want* [Cho 2001b]), provides a general catalog of such features. While some may be unique to Cho's performance style (e.g., particular pitch, amplitude, and tempo modulations), many are present in other comedic performances of Mock Asian, from Mickey Rooney's caricature of a Japanese landlord in the film *Breakfast at Tiffany's* (1961) to Kyle McCulloch's portrayal of a Chinese "houseboy" in the Internet cartoon series *Mr. Wong* (2000).

As I have indicated in the rightmost column of table 16.2, some of the features were employed by Cho to portray the accent of speakers of an unspecified Asian ethnicity (indicated by *A*) or a specific ethnicity (indicated by *C* (Chinese), *J* (Japanese), or *K* (Korean)). I have also specified separately when Cho voiced her mother (indicated by *M*), given that she frequently caricatured her speech, and some of the features she used to do so seemed to be idiosyncratic rather than ethnicity-based.[4] If Cho used the same feature for different speakers of different ethnicities, I have included multiple specifications (e.g., *A, J*).[5] In addition, comedians other than Cho, particularly those who are not as keen to the variations between various Asian accents, may merge these features in their revoicing of an Asian

TABLE 16.1. Prototypical Features of Mock Asian

Description of Mock Asian Feature	Examples and Comments
Phonological Features	
1. Neutralization of the phonemic distinction between /r/ and /w/	[ɹ]→[w] *wrong* pronounced as *wong, right* pronounced as *white*
2. Neutralization of the phonemic distinction between /r/ and /l/	[ɹ] →[l] *fried rice* pronounced as *flied lice* [l]→[ɹ] *Eileen* pronounced as *Irene, like* pronounced as *rike, hello* pronounced as *herro*
3. Alveolarization of voiceless interdental fricative 'th' [θ] to [s]	*thank you* pronounced as *sank you, I think so* pronounced as *I sink so*
4. Nonsensical syllables with the onset 'ch' /t͡ʃ/	**ching-chong, ch**ow
5. Nonsensical syllables with the coda 'ng' /ŋ/	**ching-chong, ting, ping**
6. Alternating high-low intonational contour; one tone for each syllable	H L H L *ching—chong—ching—chong*
7. Epenthetic 'ee' [i] at the end of a closed word	*break-ee, buy-ee, look-ee*
8. Reduplication of word	*pee-pee*; not unique to Mock Asian
Lexical Features	
9. Phrase-final *how*	*ching-chong-**how***
10. *ah-so::* [aso::]:low tone for initial syllable; high-low falling tone for final syllable; final syllable lengthening; backing of /o/; optional interdentalization to [θ] of voiceless alveolar fricative /s/; optional creaky voice at the end of the word.	⌒ *ah—so::: ah—tho:::*
11. *hai-YAH!* [haî:ya] Initial syllable: low-high rising intonation; syllable lengthening Final syllable: high-low falling intonation; explosive, increased amplitude.	Associated with martial arts; final syllable often accompanied by a "karate chop," or a quick, one-handed, downward movement of open-palmed hand (pinky first, palm and back of hand horizontally aligned, fingers extended and parallel to one another)
12. *OOOoooOOh* [o : : : : :]: high pitched; nasal airflow; high-low-high intonation; creaky voice on low tone; backing of /o/ (through exaggerated lip-rounding and lengthening of oral cavity); variations with different vowel qualities exist	Associated with martial arts; usually accompanied by gestures that simulate "kung fu moves"
Syntactic Features	
13. Neutralization of nominative-accusative case distinction for first-person singular pronoun	*Me so horny; me Chinese, me play joke, me put pee-pee in your coke;* not unique to Mock Asian
14. Reduplication of two-word sentence structure	*You breakee, you buyee*
15. Telegraphic speech (absence of grammatical morphemes)	*You breakee, you buyee; Long time no see;* not unique to Mock Asian

TABLE 16.2. Features of Mock Asian in Cho's Performances

Description	Examples	Ethnicity or figure
Phonetic Features		
1. Guttural, pharyngealized voice	I am *no: chi*cken! **YOUR EYE IS TOO BIG!**	A, C, K
2. High pitch	I am *no: chi*cken! **YOUR EYE IS TOO BIG!**	C, K
3. Low pitch	*You are so dykey.*	M
4. Creaky voice	*When I was a little girl…*	K
5. Soft falsetto voice	*When I was young, I was raised on rice and fish.*	K
Phonological Features: Prosodic		
6. Final syllable lengthening	*order number fou::::::r*	A, C, K
7. Emphatic lengthening	*WHY IS YOUR EYE IS SO:: BIG*	A, K
8. Syllable-timed rhythm	*What is your mem ber ship num ber?*	A, C, K
9. Sudden rising and falling intonation	H L H H L H H L *What is your membership number*	C, K
10. Increased amplitude	*YOUR EYE IS TOO BIG!*	A, K
11. Explosive stressed syllables	*My~way~or~the~highway.*	C
12. Increased tempo	*My~way~or~the~highway.*	C
13. Decreased tempo	*When I was a little girl…*	K
Phonological Features: Vowel Quality		
14. Monophthongization	*I don't know* [aɪ̯ doʊ̯n? noʊ̯] → [aɪ̯ don no]	A, C, J, K
15. [ə]→non-reduced vowel	*America* [əmɛɹɪkə] → [amɛɹɪka]	A, J, K
16. [ɪ]→[i]	*chicken* [t͡ʃɪkn̩] → [t͡ʃikʌn]	A, C, J, K
17. [ɛ]→[e]	*forget* [fɔɹgɛt] → [foget]	C, K
18. [æ]→[e]	*have* [hæv] → [hebə]	M
19. [æ]→[ɛ]	*paddy* [pʰæɾi] → [pʰɛdi]	A, J, K
20. [ʊ]→[ʌ]	*world* [wʊɹɫd] → [wʌrl]	M
21. [ʊ]→[u]	*beautiful* [bʲuɾɪfʊɫ] → [bʲuɾiful]	M
22. /o/-backing	*so* [so] → [sɤ]	A, K
23. [ɑ]→[o]	*talk* [tʰɑk] → [tx̂ʰok]	M
24. [ɑ]→[ʌ]	*want* [wɑnt] → [wʌn]	K
25. [ɑ]→[a]	*Mommy* [mɑmi] → [mami]	J, K

Description	Examples	Ethnicity or figure
Phonological Features: Consonant Quality		
26. Interdental alveolarization and de-frication	[ð] → [d]: *this* [ðɪs] → [dɪs]; [θ] → [t]: *with* [wɪθ] → [wɪt]	A, C, J, K
27. Interdentalization: [s] → [θ]	high school [haĩθku]	A
28. Alveolarization: [θ] → [s]	*everything* [ɛvɹɪθɪŋ] → [ɛbrɪsɪŋ]	A, J, K
29. [l]→[ɹ]	*Lowell* [lowɫ] → [ɹowɫ]	A, J
	Godzilla [gədzɪlə] → [gazɪɹa]	
30. Reduced retroflex [ɹ]	really; malaria	K
31. [ɫ]→[w]	*tall* [taɫ] → [taʷ]	A, C
32. [ɫ]→ [ə]	*else* [ɛɫs] → [eəs]	C, K
33. [ɫ]→ [l]	*really*	K
34. Final nasal velarization	*one* [wʌn] → [wʌŋ]	J
35. Non-flapping	*little* [lɪɾɫ] → [lɪtʰl̩]	K
36. Trilled /r/	*Struthers* [stɹʌðəɹz] → [strʌdʌ]	K
37. Increased aspiration	*cool* [kʰuɫ] → [kʰhul]	K
38. Aspiration as uvular frication	*talk* [tʰɑk] → [t͡χʰok]	M
39. Labial de-frication: [v] → [b]	*everywhere* [ɛvɹiwɛɹ] → [ebiwe]	M
40. Bilabial dentalization	*Mommy* [mami] → [m̪am̪i]	M
41. Non-glottalization	*white man* [waĩʔ mæn] → [waĩt mæn]	M
42. De-labialization	*quickly* [kʷɪkli] → [kikli]	K
43. Uvularization of /h/	*hungry* [hʌŋgɹi] → [χʌŋgɹi]	K
44. Gemination	*money* [mʌni]→ [mʌnni]	K
Phonological Features: Syllable Structure		
45. Coda /r/-deletion	*order number four* [ɔɹdəɹ nʌmbəɹ foɹ] → [odə nʌmbə foə]	A, C, J, K
46. Coda /l/-deletion	*Lowell* [lowɫ] → [ɹoː]	A
47. Coda /d/-deletion	*fried rice* [fɹaĩdɹaĩs] → [faĩɹaĩ]	A, C
	Godzilla [gedzɪlə] → [gazɪɹa]	
48. Coda /s/-deletion	*fried rice* [fɹaĩdɹaĩs] → [faĩɹaĩ]	A, C
	like this [laĩk ðɪs] → [laĩk ðɪ]	
49. Coda /z/-deletion	*Struthers* [stɹʌðəɹz] → [stɹʌdʌ]	K
50. /n/-deletion and preceding vowel nasalization	*substitution* [sʌbstətuʃn̩] → [sʌbsətuʃə̃]	C
51. Schwa epenthesis to closed syllable	*if* [ɪf]→ [ifə]; *have* [hæv]→ [hebə]	J, K
52. Glottal stop epenthesis	*with anything else* [wɪθ ɛniθɪŋ ɛɫs] → [wɪt ʔɛniθɪŋ ʔeɫ]	C
53. Onset simplification	*substitution* [sʌbstətuʃn̩] → [sʌbsətuʃə̃]	C
54. Coda simplification	*It's* [ɪts] → [ɪs]	M

(*Continued*)

TABLE 16.2. (Continued)

Description	Examples	Ethnicity or figure
Syntactic Features		
55. Absence of copula	*You ø too tall; You ø gay.*	A, K
56. 3ʳᵈ-person –*s* verbal morpheme deletion	*That **mean** you gay.*	A, K
57. Tense neutralization	*I **grow** up on the rice paddy; I **come** to America.*	J, K
58. Absence of articles	*Because that is ø very good way to lose weight; I want ø eggroll.*	C, K
59. Number neutralization	*Only **gay** screen **call**.*	K
60. Simple negation with 'no'	*I am **no** chicken.*	K
Lexical Features		
61. *Wah* [ħʷaː ː] 'wow!'		M
Discourse Features		
62. Repetition	*Hi, it's Mommy. Hi, it's Mommy. Hi, it's Mommy. Hi, it's Mommy.*	A, J, K
63. Non-contraction	*What do you mean **I am** fucking cock? **I am** not a rooster. **I am** no chicken.*	K
64. 3ʳᵈ-person for self-reference	*Why don't you talk to **Mommy** about it?*	M
65. Miscomprehension	*What do you mean I am fucking cock? I am not a rooster. I am no chicken.*	C, K
66. Abrupt topic change	*Hi, it's Mommy. Hi it's—Don't marry a white man!*	C, K

speaker of any ethnicity. Finally, the audience's interpretation of these features must be considered as well. Interestingly, while Cho often skillfully makes ethnic distinctions in her uses of Mock Asian, those members of her audience who are not familiar with any particular Asian accent potentially interpret these features as indexes of a monolithic racial Asian identity.

Mocking as Social Privilege

While the previous section suggests that different sets of features are typically deployed by different kinds of speakers—for example, a child as opposed to a professional comedian—the public revoicing of Mock Asian features in general is legitimated by similar ideologies. One ideology of legitimacy that permits Mock Asian in some public contexts, such as those described above, licenses those in positions of power to revoice stereotypical discourses of those in less powerful positions.[6] As noted by Hill (1998), such stereotyping language practices not only typically derogate the speakers who are mocked but also simultaneously elevate the personas of those who do the mocking. And like Hill, the many Asian Americans who voiced protest against Abercrombie & Fitch pointed to the racism inherent in those who benefit from this privilege (e.g., Chin 2002). The company's use of Mock Asian on its T-shirts was widely interpreted as a privileged white representation of a relatively powerless racial group. Such an interpretation is likely a consequence of the fact that Abercrombie & Fitch is a U.S. corporation that gears its clothing to a predominantly European American middle- to upper-class market, thus having popular associations with middle-class whiteness.[7] Similarly, critics likely viewed Shaquille O'Neal, while African American, as abusing his privileged status as a famous basketball star and as unquestionably 'American,' in contrast to immigrants from Asia to whom Mock Asian is ideologically linked.[8]

Margaret Cho's Mock Asian might be similarly interpreted. Not unlike uses of Mock Asian by non-Asians, her humor derives at least partially from an implied comical character of Asian Americans who cannot speak English without a 'foreign accent.' In the following example, taken from *Drunk with Power*, a 1996 recording of one of her live performances in a club in San Francisco (Cho 1996), she initially utters "Lowell High School" with an MAE pronunciation and then replaces the pronunciation of "Lowell" with "Rowell" [ɹowɬ]. She uses a Mock Asian style that is marked by a low, guttural voice, monophthongal and backed /o/ vowels, the interdentalization of /s/, a coda-less syllable structure, syllable-timed rhythm, explosive stressed syllables, and an increased tempo for particular strings of words (lines 3, 6, 8, 10).

(1) "Lowell High School"[9]

1   I-I was *raised* in San Francisco. I went to Lowell High School.

2   *((A few cheers from audience))*

3   or uh **_Rowell_** High School.

4   *((Audience laughs))*

5   Such a *hu:ge* Asian population that they dispensed with the L altogether.

6   **Ro—Ro:: I~go~to _Ro:: High~School_**.

      [ɹo ɹoː ː aî go tʰu ɹoː ː haîθku]

      ((Mock Asian style: low guttural "samurai" voice after first word; monophthongization in 'go'; backed /o/ in 'Lowell' and 'go'; [s] to [θ] in 'School'; [l] to [ɹ] in 'Lowell'; coda /l/-deletion in 'Lowell' and 'School'; syllable-timed rhythm; explosive stressed syllables; increased tempo for 'I go to' and 'High School'))

7   *((Audience laughs))*

8   **_Ro::_ High**. *((Low guttural voice))*

9   *((Audience laughs))*

10   **_Ro:_** *((Low guttural voice))*

11   Great school. I was ex*pelled*. *((MAE style))* (Cho 1996)

The paradigmatic shift from MAE phonology (line 1) to one in which the /l/ and /r/ phonemes are confused (line 3) highlights the Mock Asian pronunciation, as do the six repetitions thereafter (lines 6, 8, 10). From the perspective of a linguist who is familiar with the nonnative English spoken by those who speak Japanese natively, Cho's Mock Asian might appear to most closely approximate a 'Japanese accent,' given that neither an /l/ phoneme nor an [l] allophone exists in the Japanese phonemic inventory. Japanese nonnative speakers of English often use a trilled [r] where MAE speakers use either a retroflex /r/ or liquid /l/. While I am suggesting that the replacement of /l/ with /r/ is sometimes characteristic of a 'Japanese accent,' Americans who do not know Japanese or any dialects of Chinese often associate such a stereotype with a 'Chinese accent,' or Mock Asian, which is associated with all racial East Asians. An interpretation of Cho's shift to /r/ as 'Asian' requires the elision of various Asian ethnicities, supporting a mainstream ideology that *all Asians look and therefore sound alike*. The laughter that this use of Mock Asian generates likely results in part from the derisive nature of Mock Asian, which, like Mock Spanish, constructs the imagined speaker as comical.

Semiotics of Mock Asian as a Racializing Discourse

Cho's humorous use of Mock Asian draws from a system of stylistic distinction (Irvine 2001) that indexes and constructs racial and national difference. Throughout her performances, Cho *authenticates* herself as a speaker of MAE—a particularly Californian variety—and *deauthenticates* (Coupland 2001a, 2001b) her use of 'accented English.' While she is not white, she explicitly tells her audience that she was born and "raised in San Francisco" (line 1)—that is, not in Asia—and presents convincing linguistic 'evidence' that MAE, which she uses in linguistically unmarked segments of her performance, is her authentic variety. Cho's audience accepts her use of Mock Asian as her *inauthentic* variety, as shown by its laughter; they undoubtedly 'get' the humorous meaning when she employs the mocking style in contrast to her authentic MAE. In other words, Cho's humor depends on a triadic relationship among language, race, and nation that circulates widely in popular U.S. discourses, though this relationship become contested to a degree within the local context of Cho's performances. As the leftmost diagram (Ideology A) in figure 16.1 shows, MAE (a linguistic variety) indexes both Americanness (nation) and whiteness (race) in widely circulating discourses. Likewise, categories of nation and race are often closely linked, if not overlapping, as indicated by the line that connects them. Yet the next diagram (Ideology B) shows that Cho's use of MAE challenges the one-to-one triadic relationship of Ideology A. This local ideology emerges in contexts in which racial Asians, like Cho, speak MAE.

However, Cho's use of Mock Asian highlights yet another set of widely circulating indexical relations (Ideology C) that complements, and thus reinforces, Ideology A. According to Ideology C, which Cho assumes in her performances, Mock Asian indexes both foreignness and Asianness, remaining consistent with and reinforcing the indexical relations that are present in Ideology A. Importantly, Ideologies A and C, while present as part of the ideological backdrop of many discourses in the United States, emerge as relevant when Cho introduces Mock Asian into the ongoing discourse. I suggest that, as a result of the interactional salience of Ideology C, Ideology

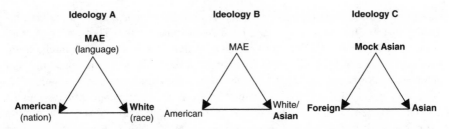

Figure 16.1. Ideologies of Language, Race, and Nation in Cho's Performances of Mock Asian

B becomes both inconsistent and irrelevant. In other words, while Cho's audience may continue to see Cho as simultaneously Asian, American, and a speaker of MAE, her alignment with those who take pleasure in making fun of Asians invokes an interpretive frame that links foreignness with a "Chinese accent" (Ideology C) and, by extension, Americanness with MAE (Ideology A).

In addition, specific categories of race, nation, and language are hierarchially arranged within mainstream ideologies in the United States. Cho's audience sanctions revoicings of the 'Asian accent' as acceptable—as a "strategy of condescension" (Bourdieu 1991)—because it knows that she can speak the more socially acceptable mainstream variety, just as Bourdieu has shown that an educated and urban French mayor, who can speak what is regarded as "good quality" French, may acceptably use the provincial variety of Béarnais. And just as a peasant who speaks only Béarnais would not be praised for using this local variety in a formal speech, a recent Japanese immigrant who uses a Japanese-accented English as her authentic discourse, would typically not be able to elevate her persona merely through her use of such accented English. The legitimacy of an MAE speaker to use Mock Asian—that is, to engage in this practice in public spaces as a means of elevating her persona regardless of her racial identity—parallels uses of Mock Spanish noted by Hill (1998). The legitimated performance of a debased racialized variety by a person who can speak the socially powerful one ultimately maintains the hierarchical relationship between the two racialized varieties.

Thus, while listeners apparently maintain an ideology of pluralistic acceptance of various races into the American landscape, their appreciation of Cho's humor hinges upon the crucial assumption that an acceptable American must speak 'without an accent' from the perspective of MAE speakers. Most recent immigrants would thus be excluded from this category because they are perceived by the mainstream as speaking 'with an accent.' Such immigrants are taken as being not acceptable Americans, but rather acceptable targets of mockery according to this ideology.

The example of O'Neal's Mock Asian provides a useful comparison. As mentioned earlier, his uncontested 'American' identity might, according to some, place him in a position of political privilege relative to immigrants and nonfluent speakers of English who, in legal and everyday contexts in the United States, are often treated as second-class citizens. However, as an African American and speaker of a variety of African American English, he does not have clear links to a racial community that has historically oppressed Asians or immigrants.[11] The subdued nature of the critiques against O'Neal, relative to those against Abercrombie & Fitch, might have derived partly from his racial identity as an African American, absolving him of suspicions of racism, given the history of African Americans in this country.[12-13] Comments in O'Neal's defense that have appeared in newspaper articles suggest not only his membership but also his authentic and representative status within the African American community. For example, newspapers cited that the NAACP, an organization that has historically fought for the civil rights of African Americans, had officially recognized, or authenticated, his representative status in the community just days before the controversy.[14]

Mocking as Self-Deprecation

I have argued above that Cho may perpetuate racial and national hierarchies through her use of Mock Asian. Indeed, some of her critics have argued that her revoicings of Asian stereotypes cater to a racist, European American audience. However, mocking of this sort differs from mainstream 'yellowface' depictions of Asians, given that Cho is Asian herself according to most racial ideologies that link particular phenotypical traits with racial categories. In one part of the performance, she alludes to the fact that her race is written on her body, when she notes that she does not need to pull up the edges of her eyes to stereotypically portray an Asian person whom she has just imitated.

(2) "Doing this with my eyes"

1	I don't know why I'm doing this with my eyes *((While pulling up edges of eyes))*
2	*((Audience laughs loudly))*
3	I don't have to
4	((Audience laughs)) (Cho 1996)

The audience accepts her phenotypical authentication and thus her membership in the Asian racial community, such as when she evokes laughter by performing a *linguistic* authentication of her race in her explicit statement that she is "Asian."

(3) "Well, you see, I'm Asian"

1	You know what? I really lo:ve drinkin? (0.5) I(h)—it's *g(h)rea:t* you know and I never did it that much before? because um (0.5) *((alveolar click))* **well you see I'm Asian?** *((hyperarticulated style, slight breathiness)) ((light alveolar click))*
2	*((Audience laughs lightly))*
3	and uh when we *drink* we get all *red*.
4	((Audience laughs lightly)) (Cho 1996)

Cho's membership within an Asian racial community is obvious to her audience; her overt claim of her membership ("Well, you see I'm Asian" in line 1) is humorous because of its redundancy, and her audience likely recognizes that she keys a humorous frame by her use of alveolar clicks as well as a prosodic shift to a hyperarticulated style. Her use of the third-person pronoun "we" (line 3) to allude to this racial community positions her within this community, privy to knowledge sometimes unknown by out-group members.

According to a commonly held mainstream ideology in the United States, mocking 'one's own' is harmless—not racist—given that 'native' comedians neither are in a position nor would have the intention to oppress their own. In addition, in-group members are often viewed as conveying a more 'truthful' and thus acceptable representation of their own community, as noted by Guy Aoki, the president of an organization that polices Asian American media representations:

> If an Asian-American is making fun of its own community, I think that's accepted because the audience sees some greater truth in it, like Margaret Cho imitating her Korean mother. But if it's someone from outside the community who makes fun of a minority, there's some suspicion there. If Margaret was to make a joke about blacks, people would feel more uncomfortable. (Justin 2002)

But it is also of interest that, in Example 3, by 'having to explain' the 'fact' that Asians cannot drink alcohol without "get[ting] all red" (line 3) she constructs her own community as distinct from—or at least not identical to—the racial community (or communities) of her audience.[15] In other words, just as Cho's self-mockery is sanctioned by mainstream ideologies, so is an out-group's public expression of enjoyment of that mocking.[16] Those who are not members of the community, however, may risk accusations of racism if they engage in the performance of Mock Asian.

A parallel ideological assumption is present in claims that the use of ethnic slurs is acceptable as long as the speaker can claim membership in the specific ethnic group labeled by the slur. Speakers are consequently licensed to mock stereotypical features commonly attributed to a community in which they can authenticate their membership. Cho, who is racially marked as Asian, is thus licensed to publicly use a style that out-group members have historically used to ridicule Asian social and linguistic ineptitude. In particular, those in a higher position on the racial hierarchy—for example, whites—are seen as potentially having the power to reproduce unequal relations of power. This is the operative ideology that restricts white-on-non-white mocking in many public contexts, while non-white-on-white mockery is often deemed as relatively more acceptable.

While such ideological assumptions might be rationalized as a means of censoring racist discourses by out-group members—European Americans in particular—licensing based on in-group membership also problematically elides differences between Asians and Asian Americans of various generational, national, class, gender, and sexual identities. As scholars in Asian American studies have noted, the essentialism that Asians and Asian Americans perpetuate by identifying as 'Asian American,' while often necessary and strategic for political empowerment, risks the erasure of lines of political differences and oppressions within (Lowe 1991). In addition, the ways in which different audiences may have contested definitions of community membership,

and thus may read different social implications into instances of crossing, is an important consideration in understanding the multiple social meanings of Mock Asian. While
Cho is one of the most prominent Asian Americans in the United States, her status as
a 'role model' has been questioned by Asian American community leaders who have
taken offense at her stereotypical portrayals of Asian American cultural and linguistic
practices. Others have disapproved on the basis of her image of defiance against particular expectations of gendered and sexual behavior.[17] One newspaper article reports
that "[s]he was lambasted by the Korean community for presenting a negative image"
(Chonin 1999). Much of the humor of her stage persona depends on rampant car-
nivalesque subversions of mainstream society's physical, linguistic, sexual, and filial
expectations for Asian women. As such, she holds an ambiguous representative status
within the Asian American community as she notes in the following example.

(4) "Controversial within the Korean community"

1   I was very controversial? within the Korean community? I am like the *worst* role
     model in the world. I-I'm sorry that Korea has *me* t(h)o r(h)epresent them.
2   *((Audience laughs lightly))*
3   I-I feel *bad* but I-I can't help being myself? And I-I d—you know—sorry but
     I wou—I would read in *Time* and *Newsweek* when the show was on=I would *read*
     all these Korean *leaders* were saying really mean things about me? And of course
     I didn't try to get their support at all? I was calling them at home? all drunk? from a
     bar? at three in the morning? (going) WHAT THE FUCK IS *WRONG* WITH YOU,
     YOU FUCKIN *COCK*? And um—*((self-quotation in high, guttural voice))*
4   *((Audience laughs))*
5   It's really stupid to call a fifty-year-old Korean man a fuckin cock? because they
     have *no* idea what it is=you know **what do you *mean* I am fucking cock=I am not
     a roo*ster*?=I am *no: chicken!* [wʌt du yu min ai ɛm fʌkɪŋ kɑk ai ɛm nɑɾ ə rustɹ ai
     æm no t͡ʃikʌn] *((Mock Asian style: high pitch, guttural vocal quality; monophthongal
     /o/ in 'no'; [æ]→[ɛ] in 'am'; [ɪ] to[i] and non-reduced [ʌ] in 'chicken' [t͡ʃikʌn];
     syllable-timed rhythm; increased amplitude; absence of article 'a'; simple negation with
     'no' instead of 'not'; absence of contraction 'I'm'; miscomprehension of English))*
6   *((Audience laughs))*
7   Yeah they didn't know
8   *((Audience laughs))*
9   Called me a *racist* which *really pissed* me off.=because I am *many* things but I am
     not racist.(Cho 1996)

In the above sequence, Cho's Mock Asian (line 5) is used in a retelling of an incident in which a Korean American man supposedly responded to her attempt at insult-
ing him. The phonological features that she uses to mark him as a nonnative speaker
of English are consistent with the literal, and thus nonnative, interpretation of the term
cock 'penis' (vulgar slang) (line 5). The particular frantic, guttural vocal quality and
high pitch that she uses, which portray him in a comical light, also mark his discourse
as oppositional to her own. As in example 1, Cho depends on an interpretive frame that
closely links an Asian identity with foreignness and a nonnative variety of English.

Cho's narrative above suggests that one's status as a community representative is negotiated from both inside and outside the represented community. While particular audiences, for example, those who attend her live performances, are likely to accept her representative status with respect to the Asian American community, her membership status is a negotiated project—not a stable reality. Additionally, given the relative lack of power that Asian Americans have historically had in influencing racial ideologies in the United States, community-designated representatives are not necessarily those who eventually represent the community in mainstream cultural production.

Penelope Eckert and Sally McConnell-Ginet (1992) provide the insight that a community of practice, in contrast to the traditional notion of a community, is "defined simultaneously by its membership and by the practice in which that membership engages" (464). However, I additionally suggest that communities are imagined not only by those who have assumed the right to claim membership but also by non-members who have assumed the power to define this membership. Cho's self-identification as a member of an Asian community must thus be seen in the context of competing claims about her membership status.

Yet within the particular bounds of her live performance, typically attended by those who recognize the aesthetic value of her work, Cho's proclaimed racial status as Asian is not problematic. She is thus a legitimate animator of Mock Asian texts who can escape accusations of racism. Even while she may invoke the racializing interpretive frame shown in Ideologies A and C of figure 16.1, this frame coexists with the ideology that Cho, as Asian, would likely simultaneously assume alternative ideologies that do not place Asians like herself in a position of racial inferiority. It is perhaps the ironic tension between these coexisting ideologies that gives rise to her voicings of Mock Asian as humorous.

Legitimacy Through Humor

In addition to Cho's positioning with respect to particular racial communities, the context of *stand-up comedy* contributes to the meanings of her performances. Her practices locate her in a community of stand-up comedians who engage in a similar style of self-deprecating ethnic humor, especially alongside other comedians of color. As in other communities of practice, her practices draw upon those of more seasoned performers, or "masters" (e.g., Richard Pryor), who are the object of emulation for many newcomers, or "apprentices" (Lave and Wenger 1991).

As a genre, stand-up comedy has stylistic features that diverge from but are related to other modes of communication, such as face-to-face interaction. Stand-up comedy is a *performance* in its traditional sense and "consists in the assumption of responsibility to an audience for a display of communicative competence" (Bauman 1977, 11), thus "[calling] forth special attention to and heightened awareness of the act of expression and [giving] license to the audience to regard the act of expression and performer with special intensity" (11). In addition, unlike face-to-face interactions, a single comedian typically stands on an open stage with a microphone and performs while facing her seated audience, who is expected to employ a limited set of responses to the comedian's performance, such as laughter, claps, cheers, whistles, and, occasionally, silence. Such performances are also "keyed" (Goffman 1974) via linguistic cues such as special formulas (e.g., the emcee's introduction, the comedian's greeting, or conventions used in narration), and paralinguistic cues (Bauman 1977, 16), including phonological features of stereotyped styles. By invoking a frame of stand-up comedy, comedians are often sanctioned to break with social conventions of politeness or political correctness that restrict, for example, uses of overtly stereotypical language.

Still, the boundaries between frames—for example, between *nonserious* frames, such as comedy and joking, and more *serious* frames—are not always clear. In Cho's performances, for example, she often shifts between serious narratives and humorous portrayals of characters, but also employs such humorous caricatures in the midst of narrations about serious experiences, such as her struggles with alcohol, eating disorders, and racism. Both O'Neal and Abercrombie & Fitch representatives alluded to this potential ambiguity between serious and nonserious frames, when pointing to their humorous intent, despite the offense taken by some.

The two kinds of frames are also not clearly separable in that they both invoke, and may reproduce, the same set of ideological meanings, such as ideologies about language, race, gender, and community membership. Practices that invoke laughter, and that are thus defined as humorous, can still reproduce hierarchies of race and other social axes, as Hill (1998) has argued. It is for this reason that some Asian Americans have voiced opposition to out-group Mock Asian, even if intended as a "joke" (e.g., Chin 2002). While they may understand that a nonserious frame has been invoked, the ideological assumptions about Asian racial otherness eclipse any humor that might have been intended or achieved.

Ideological Critique by Mocking Mock Asian

It appears then that a context of humor is an ideal space for engaging in ideological work, given that humorous performers have license to break with everyday norms of interaction, such as political correctness, while still drawing from the same ideologies of social organization. Richard Bauman and Charles L. Briggs (1990) have similarly suggested that "play frames not only alter the performative force of utterances but provide settings in which speech and society can be questioned and transformed" (63). On the one hand, such license may allow those in power to reproduce their privilege, as in some cases of Mock Asian and Mock Spanish that construct imagined Asians and Spanish speakers as linguistically comical and socially inferior. On the other hand, a humorous frame sanctions ideological *critique* that might otherwise be unacceptable. In this way, Cho's performances, while necessarily drawing from and, thus, reproducing social hierarchies, simultaneously critique these same ideologies without risking accusations of either 'being a poor sport' or 'being whiny.'

Cho's crossings into a Mock Asian style indeed suggest a highly critical stance toward racist imaginings of the Asian *other* as passive and self-sacrificing. In the following excerpt, she describes an incident in which a tabloid magazine called *The Star* used "fake quotes" (line 3) from her in what she calls a "racist" article about an Asian diet.

(5) "Chow like Cho diet"

1   I was on the cover of *The Star*? once? and it was for this thing called the '*Chow* like *Cho*' diet? (*(Unmarked, MAE style)*)

2   (*(Audience laughs lightly)*)

3   It was *so fuckin racist* because they just *made* this diet up. They didn't con*sult* me. I mean like this *total* diet that they *made up* that they said that I went on? and all these fake quotes from me? (*(Increased tempo; amplitude)*)

4   **When I was young I was raised on rice and fish. So when I get *heavy* I go back to that natural Asian way of eating.** (*(Feminine, calm MAE style: falsetto; decreased tempo; exaggerated and gradual intonational rise and fall)*)

5   You could almost hear the *mandolin* in the *back*ground. (*(Unmarked, MAE style)*)

6   (*(Audience laughs)*)

7   **When I was a little girl? and I grow up on the rice paddy? We don't have any *foo:d* because this was before Sally *Stru*thers. So—**
[wɛn aĩ wʌz əlɪtʰ ḷ gʌɹɬ ænd aĩ gɹowʷ ʌp ɑn də raĩs pʰʰɛdi wi dont hæv ɛni fuːd bikʌz dis wʌz bifo sæli strʌdʌ so]
(*(Mock Asian style: falsetto; creaky voice; decreased tempo; syllable-timed rhythm; monophthongization of /o/ in 'don't,' 'before,' and 'so'; vowel shifts [ə] to [ʌ] in 'girl,' [æ] to [ɛ] in 'paddy,' [ɪ] to [i] in 'this'; de-frication [ð] → [d] in 'this' and 'Struthers'; [ɹ] to trilled [r] in 'Struthers'; aspirated [tʰ] in place of flap in 'little'; increased aspiration in 'paddy'; coda deletion in 'before' and 'Struthers'; past/present neutralization for 'grow' and 'don't')*)

8   (*(Audience laughs)*)

9   **We are *so* hungry all the ti:me. and we have no money and I want to go to the market to buy a chicken head but I have no money eh—so I have to sell my *finger*. But—**
[wi a so χʌngɹi al də taĩm ɛn wi hɛvə no mʌni ɛn aĩ wʌn tʰu go tʰu də mɑɹkɪt tʰu baĩ ə tʃɪkʰn̩ hɛd bʌt aĩ hɛv no mʌnni ɛ so aĩ hɛv tʰu sɛɬ maĩ fiŋgɹ] (*(Similar Mock Asian style and with vowel shift [a] to [a] in 'are,' [æ] to [ɛ] in 'and,' 'have,' [a] to [ʌ] in 'want,' [ɪ] to [i] in 'finger'; monophthongal /o/ in 'go,' 'no,' and 'so'; nonreduced vowel in 'to'; uvularization of /h/ to [χ] in 'hungry'; de-frication [ð] → [d] in 'the'; /n/-gemination in 'money'; aspiration of /k/ in 'chicken'; coda deletion in 'are'; schwa epenthesis in 'have'; tense neutralization in 'are,' 'have,' 'want')*)

10   (*(Audience laughs)*)

11   **I (0.5) I (0.5) was very hungry but I still have *tendency* to put on *weight*.**
[aĩ aĩ wʌz vɛɹi χʌngɹi bʌt aĩ stɪɬ hɛv tʰɛnʌnsi tʰu put ɑn weⁱt] (*(Similar Mock Asian style and with vowel shift [æ] to [ɛ] in 'have,' nonreduced vowel in 'to'; uvularization of /h/ to [χ] in 'hungry'; tense neutralization in 'have'; absence of article 'a')*)

12   (*(Audience laughs)*)

13   **which is why I really hope that I catch malaria (0.3)**
[witʃ iz waĩ aĩ ɹili hop dæt aĩ ketʃ mʌlɛɹiə]
(*(Similar Mock Asian style and with vowel shift [ɪ] to [i] in 'which' and 'is'; reduced retroflex in 'really' and 'malaria'; light /l/ in 'really'; de-frication [ð] → [d] in 'that')*)

14   **because *that is very good* wa:y to *lose* wei:ght *quickly::* (0.4) malaria and *dysentery*.**

[bikʌz dæt ɪz vɛɹi gʊd weʲ tʰu luz weʲt kikli mʌlɛɹiə æn dɪsʌntɛɹi] (*(Cheerful Mock Asian style: falsetto; exaggerated binary high-low tones for 'good way,' lose weight,' 'quickly'; nonreduced vowel in 'to'; [ð]* → *[d] in 'that'; de-labialization in 'quickly'; reduced retroflex in 'very,' 'malaria,' and 'dysentery'; absence of article 'a')*)

15   ((Audience laughs))(Cho 1996)

The "fake quotes," which had been the tabloid's appropriations of Cho's voice, are reappropriated by her in a stereotypically soft feminine style in line 4. Given the nonstereotypically feminine persona that Cho constructs as her own in the rest of the performance, her sudden switch to a soft style aligns herself in opposition to it. While Cho makes explicit in line 3 her critical stance toward the "racist" media representation of her, there exists the possible interpretation that the oppositional footing with respect to the feminine Mock Asian style *simultaneously* (Woolard 1998) positions her against Asianness *in addition to* the specific racist practices of the tabloid. While such hybridity (Jaffe 2000) in positioning is possible, and likely, there is ample evidence suggesting that her use of Mock Asian is primarily a critique of racist imaginings of Asian women and not of these Asian women themselves.

As the narrative continues, the extent of self-sacrifice (first, the selling of her finger, then, the desire for disease in order to lose weight) intensifies as Cho shifts to a Mock Asian style (lines 7, 9, 11, 13, 14). Through this exaggerated style, Cho decontextualizes and critiques stereotypes of Asian women as idealizations of passive, petite, and self-sacrificing femininity. In addition, in line 7, she makes a reference to Sally Struthers, a European American actor who was once a visible spokesperson for Save the Children, a British charity organization that organized sponsorships of Third World children. By mockingly, as opposed to genuinely, voicing her own words as an Asian woman who is grateful to Struthers for saving her family from starvation, she contests a mainstream U.S. ideology that Europeans and European Americans have saved the Third World. In other words, although Cho engages in a Mock Asian style, her comedic recontextualization functions as an ideological critique of mainstream imaginings of Asian women as 'lotus blossoms' that seek to be saved by the West. Her retelling of an incident in which a magazine appropriated her name and Asian identity comments on and deconstructs mainstream ideological links between Asia, femininity, and poverty, particularly perpetuated by the U.S. media.

Although Cho is American, I suggest that her use of a Mock Asian style does not reflect her conception of her Asian self or of other Asian women, but rather comments on racializing mainstream discourses that attempt to ascribe identities to Asian women like herself. It is the Mock Asian text, which suggests an orientalizing Asianness (Said 1978), that she lifts from its racist context and asks her audience to join in objectifying, scrutinizing, and critiquing.

Mock Asian as a Tool for Decentering Whiteness

The example above presents a rather explicit decontextualization and recontextualization of racist discourses about Asians. I wish to argue, however, that even in cases in which Cho does not metalinguistically label particular Mock Asian acts as "racist," an interpretation of Cho's Mock Asian as ideological critique is possible. In the following example from *I'm the One that I Want* (Cho 2001b), Cho uses Mock Asian to describe how "a bunch of Asian people" unapologetically objectify "white people" in their presence.

(6) "Your eye is too big"

1   Although it's difficult to be the only Asian person around a bunch of white people? I
     think it's *wa::y wo:rse*? to be the only white person? around a bunch of Asian people?
2   ((*Audience cheers, claps*))
3   Because we will talk shit about you right to your face?
4   ((*Audience cheers, claps*))
5   **YOUR EYE IS TOO BIG**. [yo aĩ iz tʰu big] ((*Mock Asian style: guttural;
     increased amplitude; syllable-timed rhythm; coda deletion in 'your'; monophthongal
     /o/ in 'your'; vowel shift [ɪ] to [i] in 'is' and 'big'*)) ((*Makes "scrunched up"
     expression: eyes made small; head pulled back; shoulders lifted*))
6   ((*Audience laughs*))
7   **WHY IS YOUR EYE IS SO:: BIG**. [waĩ iz yo aĩ iz so: big] ((*Similar Mock Asian
     style with emphatic lengthening for 'so'; vowel shift [ɪ] to [i] in 'is' and 'big'; de-
     frication [ð] to [d] in 'this'; coda deletion in 'your'; double auxiliary 'is' for question*))
8   ((*Audience laughs, cheers*))
9   **YOUR~EYE~LIKE~THIS~LIKE~THIS~YOUR~EYE~LIKE~THIS~LIKE~T
     HIS WHY~YOUR~EYE~LIKE~*THIS***.
     [yo aĩ laĩk dɪs laĩk dɪs yo aĩ laĩk dɪs laĩk dɪs waĩ yo aĩ laĩk dɪ] ((*Similar Mock
     Asian style with increased tempo; de-frication [ð] to [d] in 'this'; coda deletion
     in 'your' and 'this'; absence of copula 'is'; repetition*)) ((*Confused expression:
     enlarges eyes; ends of mouth point downward; lips never close completely; bends
     torso forward; extends neck; swings face and body from her left to right; points to
     eye on last instance of 'this.'*))
10   ((*Audience laughs, cheers*))
     YOUR EYE IS LIKE *THIS*. [yo aĩ iz laĩk di] ((*Similar Mock Asian style with nor-
     mal tempo; vowel shift [ɪ] to [i] in 'is' and 'this'; de-frication [ð] to [d] in 'this';
     coda deletion in 'your'*)) ((*Maintains forward bow and facial expression with slight
     bobbing motion and tilting of head; points to eye on 'eye is like'*))
11   **ARE YOU GONNA CATCH A FLY WITH YOUR EYE?**
     [ɑ ju gʌnə ketʃ ə flaĩ wis yo aĩ]
     ((*Similar Mock Asian style with vowel shift [ɪ] to [i] in 'with'; de-frication [θ] to [s]
     in 'with'; coda deletion in 'are' and 'your'*))
12   ((*Audience laughs, claps*))
13   ((*Retracts head; makes eyes small*)) **Also you are too tall**. [ɑʷsoʷ ju ɑ tʰu tʰɑʷ]
     ((*Similar Mock Asian style with [ɫ] to [w] in 'also' and 'tall'; coda deletion in 'are'*))
14   ((*Audience laughs*))
15   **YOU TOO TA:::LL** [ju tʰu tʰɑ::ʷ] ((*Similar Mock Asian style with [ɫ] to [w] in 'tall';
     absence of copula 'are'*)) ((*Tilts head back; feigns shouting in upward direction;
     brings right hand to side of mouth to "direct" sound upward on 'tall'*))
16   ((*Keeps head tilted back for seven seconds while audience cheers, whistles, laughs*))
17   **He look like Godzilla** [hi lʊk laĩk gazɪɹa] ((*Similar Mock Asian style with
     non-reduced [a] in 'Go**d**zill**a**'; [l] to [ɹ] in 'Godzilla'; coda /d/ deletion in*

'Godzilla'; third-person –s morpheme deletion in 'look')) ((Brings head back to
normal position; cups right hand around mouth and directs speech to her left side))

18   **GAZIRA:::::** [gazɪɹa ::] ((Raises right arm; turns to right; and runs in place))
(Cho 2001b)

At first glance, the Mock Asian in this example parallels that in example 4.
Specifically, her use of Mock Asian represents the "authentic" variety of a nonnative speaker of English; it does not represent—at least directly—racist imaginings of
Asians as in example 5. Consequently, this excerpt might be subject to an interpretation that parallels that of examples 1 and 4; Cho reproduces a semiotic process of
racialization that links Mock Asian with an inferior Asianness and foreignness as
illustrated in figure 16.1.

In other ways, however, this example is far more complex in its ideological
commentary. If we consider Cho's stance toward the character she revoices, it is
distinct from the one that she takes in example 4. While in the earlier example, she
used Mock Asian to distance herself from a Korean character who had caused her
offense, in this excerpt, she uses it to bring the audience to see "white people" from
the perspective of Asians, who might view them as "too tall" (lines 13, 15) and as
having eyes that are "too big" (line 5). In other words, in examples 1 and 4, Mock
Asian functioned to construct Asians as "foreign"; in example 6, however, it serves
as a tool for conversely *decentering whiteness*.

On the other hand, the argument might be made that the potential for racial
decentering is limited because the particular content of the revoicing is hardly realistic. Given the normative status of white phenotypical characteristics in the media,
racial Asians would not likely claim that whites are either too tall or have eyes that
are too large. Rather, these particular critiques are based on "white" objectifications
of Asian bodies, who are viewed as "too short" and whose eyes are "too small."
Indeed, Cho's revoicing derives some of its humor from its ludicrous nature. *Does
it then fail to decenter whiteness because it indexes racist imaginings of physically
deficient Asians?* I suggest that while such images of Asian bodies as nonnormative
are invoked, they are simultaneously critiqued through their invocation. As discussed
earlier, ideologies that assume that in-group members are not likely to "oppress their
own" and that easily permit ideological critique in contexts of humor encourage an
interpretation of Cho's revoicing as ideological critique; the revoicing of racial objectifications *by* an Asian points to and directs listeners to critique racial objectifications
of Asians. The complex interplay and tension among these ideological processes,
which include the racialization of Asians through Mock Asian, the performance of a
highly unrealistic discourse, the decentering of whiteness, and the sharp ideological
critique, contribute to the excerpt's humor.

Discussion

To the extent that any use of a Mock Asian style articulates with overtly racist usages of
this style, there exists the potential for interpretations that continue to construct Asians
as *other*. Indeed, it is not always clear whether Cho's use of Mock Asian succeeds in

eliciting laughter because it has been decontextualized from racist contexts or because of the direct indexical links to Asians as comical figures. Just as different audience members might interpret Cho's community membership in different ways, they may interpret Cho's Mock Asian as having different ideological meanings (Jaffe 2000).

As mentioned earlier, stand-up comedy, like other genres of verbal art, are characterized by a hyper-awareness of how something is said; "[p]erformance puts the act of speaking on display" (Bauman and Briggs 1990, 73). It is the potential for a performed text to be decontextualized that makes critical and reflexive *metacommentary about* this text a likely interpretation. In particular, the markedness of Mock Asian texts, which are directly linked with racist ideologies of Asian othering and ridiculing, potentiates decontextualization. Given the typical inappropriateness in public contexts of serious statements that overtly suggest racial inferiority, Mock Asian texts, as overtly racist texts, key a nonserious frame. The text is thus "put on display" for an audience. Certainly, decontextualization of these texts does not necessarily entail a critique of them; in some cases, the recontextualization of such texts may function to construct a speaker as having a humorous persona without deconstructing the ideologies to which these texts are linked. In the case of Cho, however, an interpretation of social critique is possible because of factors and ideologies that contextualize her revoicings, including the persona she has constructed as someone who is critical of racism, her overt claim that the texts are racist (example 5, line 3), paralinguistic cues that align her *against* rather than *with* the text, and an ideology of legitimacy that assumes that an in-group member would have neither the intention nor the power to oppress her own community.

On the other hand, analysts of political humor via linguistic recontextualization must be wary of simplistic readings that blindly celebrate its "critique" of oppressive ideologies. As Alexandra Jaffe (2000) suggests, drawing on Judith Irvine's (1996) notion of "leakage," animators of texts cannot escape the fact that "the meanings of the language used do stick to the animator; the words of the character come out of his mouth" (49). In addition, Hill (1998) questions the efficacy of such practices if they remain limited to restricted domains; she suggests that comedy catering to a white middle-class audience is yet another form of "orderly disorder." In the case of Cho, we might ask whether such social critiques are welcomed outside the arena of comedy performances or for audiences that extend beyond "elites in White public space" (Hill 1998, 686). Finally, as I have suggested throughout this chapter, the ideologies that give meaning to these practices are always multiple. The multiplicity of potential meanings of Mock Asian, and language practices in general, presents a challenge for those who seek to understand the relationship between linguistic form and meaning. The meanings of Mock Asian depend on a variety of ideologies about race, nation, community membership, and linguistic legitimacy, which are often simplistic in their organization but complex in their relationship with actual discourse. Numerous ideologies are co-present as potential frames for the interpretation of practices. And practices, while often habitual in their production, are never stable facts about the world that index singular meanings. During the ongoing production and interpretation of practices, whether as live performances or replayings of pre-recordings, certain ideologies become more relevant than others, thus allowing for new meanings to emerge in the context of alternative, potential interpretations.

I sincerely thank Adrienne Lo, Angie Reyes, and Keith Walters for invaluable comments on various versions of this chapter. All remaining shortcomings are my own.

NOTES

1. This is not to say that Mock Spanish is not often racist—and sometimes overtly so. The point being made here is that Mock Asian is often *understood* by Mainstream American English (MAE) speakers and listeners as "more racist" than typical voicings of Mock Spanish.

2. The listed features are based on impressionistic descriptions by Asian and non-Asian students and friends with whom I have discussed the issue of Mock Asian.

3. In addition to the linguistic features listed above, there exist other semiotic resources that index a stereotypical Asian identity in similar ways. These features include (1) gestures, such as a prayer bow, bucktoothed expression, pulling up the end of eyes to create a 'slant-eyed' look, and various martial arts stances; (2) non-linguistic sounds, such as the plinky-plunky musical notes followed by a gong that often 'introduces' Asian characters in American films and (3) scripts or word processing fonts titled, for example, "Wonton," "Chow fun," "Chinese takeaway," "Karate," and "Chinatown"—that attempt to reproduce brushstroke styles associated with Chinese and Japanese calligraphy.

4. I have used the general label "Korean" for features that "Cho's mother" shares with other Korean characters in Cho's revoicings. This categorization is also based on my knowledge of Korean phonology.

5. Cho's intended ethnic portrayal is not always apparent. For example, when she satirizes herself as a subservient girl (example 5), it is not clear whether she is constructing herself as 'Asian' or specifically 'Korean.' In this case, I have assumed the specific ethnic category—that is, 'Korean' and not 'Asian'—because the features that she uses in this particular segment largely overlap with those that she employs for clearly Korean portrayals, such as when she performs her mother's character.

6. Christie Davies (1987) has similarly argued that, cross-culturally, cultures in dominant positions tend to poke fun at those in less dominant ones.

7. In fact, in June 2003, several Latinos and Asian Americans who were once employed by Abercrombie & Fitch sued the company for racial discrimination in its hiring practices. According to the plaintiffs in the lawsuit, the "[Abercrombie & Fitch] look...is overwhelmingly white, judging from the low percentage of minority members who work on the sales floor and from the company's posters and quarterly magazine, which overwhelmingly featured white models" (Kong 2003).

8. As Keith Walters has commented (personal communication), O'Neal's use of Mock Asian also constructs a particular kind of urban masculinity. In addition, his attempt at a playful insult may relate to the verbal practice of "signification" that sociolinguists describe as characteristic of African American discourse.

9. Transcription conventions adapted from Goodwin (1990):

word	Focus of discussion
—	Sudden cut-off
word	Emphasis (pitch, amplitude)
wo:rd	Lengthening
.	Falling contour
?	Rising contour
((comment))	Transcription comments
WORD	Increased volume
(h)	Breathiness, laughter
=	Latching

10. While the indexical link between Asianness and her Americanness becomes less relevant, it does not completely disappear, since the audience still regards Cho as American and Asian.

11. While African Americans are not typically constructed as oppressing Asian immigrants in most mainstream discourses, discourses of racial conflict between African American customers and Korean immigrant storeowners are common (Bailey 1997, 2000).

12. There are likely other reasons not mentioned in this chapter that the public protest against Abercrombie & Fitch was greater than that against O'Neal, including the perception that corporate entities have historically engaged in oppressive practices and the belief that printed images and words on a T-shirt have the potential for circulation that spoken words may not.

13. In contrast to the muted reaction against O'Neal's use of Mock Asian, New York Mets scout Bill Singer was fired in November 2003 after he directed "Mock Chinese" to a Chinese American assistant general manager, Kim Ng, of the Los Angeles Dodgers. It was generally assumed within the mainstream media that his actions were unquestionably racist, likely because of the general recognition of the racial privilege enjoyed by whites like Singer.

14. Discourses that position victims of racism as necessarily nonracists do not remain uncontested in mainstream discourses, as evidenced by writers' references to O'Neal's association with Louis Farrakhan (e.g., Beck 2003; Brown 2003), a Muslim African American leader who was at the center of a controversy in the early 1990s after making anti-Semitic remarks.

15. The audiences at the two shows I attended in Austin, Texas, in 2002 and 2003 appeared ethnically diverse, although more than half of each of the audiences was European American, based on my own impressionistic observations.

16. The possibility of diverse readings of Cho's stereotyped portrayals of Asians became starkly apparent to me at the last show I attended, as I had feelings of both pleasure and discomfort when hearing peals of laughter from non-Asians who seemed to profoundly enjoy her caricatures of Asians and Asian speech. Clearly, my sentiments were partly based on an ideology that restricts out-group members from not only performing but also enjoying Cho's Mock Asian.

17. After the airing of the first episode of *All-American Girl*, a Los Angeles-based Korean American publication listed several quotations by local Korean Americans who disapproved of both Cho and the sitcom in which she appeared. One Korean American explained, "I read an article on Margaret Cho and her show and how it's supposed to be a role model for KAs [Korean Americans]. I would be so disappointed if any kid were to look up to her and want to be so irreverent, rude, and rebellious to her mom. How evil! Not even American kids do that to their parents if they were brought up right" (Whang 1994).

REFERENCES

Bailey, Benjamin.1997. Communication of respect in interethnic service encounters. *Language in Society* 26:327–356.

———. 2000. Communicative behavior and conflict between African-American customers and Korean immigrant retailers in Los Angeles. *Discourse and Society* 11:86–108.

Bakhtin, Mikhail M. 1981. *The dialogic imagination*. Austin: University of Texas Press.

Barrett, Rusty. 1995. The markedness model and style switching: Evidence from African American drag queens. In *SALSA II: Proceedings of the second annual symposium about language and society—Austin*, ed. Pamela Silberman and Jonathan D. Loftin, 40–52. Austin: University of Texas, Department of Linguistics.

Bauman, Richard. 1977. *Verbal art as performance*. Prospect Heights, Ill.: Waveland Press.

Bauman, Richard, and Charles L. Briggs. 1990. Poetics and performance as critical perspectives on language and social life. *Annual Review of Anthropology* 19:59–88.

Beck, Howard. 2003. O'Neal denies charges of racism. *The Daily News of Los Angeles*, January 11.

Bell, Allen. 1984. Language style as audience design. *Language in Society* 13:145–204.

Bourdieu, Pierre. 1977. *Outline of a theory of practice*. Cambridge/New York: Cambridge University Press.

———. 1991. *Language and symbolic power*. Cambridge: Polity Press.

Brown, Tim. 2003. O'Neal issues apology; Laker center says he was only joking in comments about Yao and that his relationship with Louis Farrakhan is his own business. *Los Angeles Times*, January 11.

Bucholtz, Mary. 1999. You da man: Narrating the racial other in the production of white masculinity. *Journal of Sociolinguistics* 3:443–460.

———. 2003. Sociolinguistic nostalgia and the authentication of identity. *Journal of Sociolinguistics* 7:398–416.

Chin, Andrew. 2002. Why Abercrombie and Fitch still doesn't get it. Model minority: A guide to Asian American empowerment, April 23. http://modelminority.com/modules. php?name=News&file=article&sid=21.

Cho, Margaret. 1996. *Drunk with power*. CD. Westlake Village, Calif.: Uproar Entertainment.

———. 2001a. *I'm the one that I want*. New York: Ballantine Books.

———. 2001b. DVD. *I'm the one that I want: Margaret Cho filmed live in concert*, ed. Lionel Coleman. New York: Winstar TV & Video.

Chonin, Neva. 1999. Cho hits comic heights with tales from Hollywood's depths. *The San Francisco Chronicle*, November 15.

Coupland, Nikolas. 2001a. Stylization, authenticity and TV news review. *Discourse Studies* 3:413–442.

———. 2001b. Dialect stylization in radio talk. *Language in Society* 30:345–375.

Davies, Christie. 1987. Language, identity and ethnic jokes about stupidity. *International Journal of the Sociology of Language* 65:39–52.

Eckert, Penelope, and Sally McConnell-Ginet. 1992. Think practically and look locally: Language and gender as community-based practice. *Annual Review of Anthropology* 21:461–490.

Ervin-Tripp, Susan. 2001. Variety, style-shifting, and ideology. In *Style and sociolinguistic variation*, ed. Penelope Eckert and John Rickford, 44–56. Cambridge: Cambridge University Press.

Ford, Chad. 2003. Shaq under fire for Yao-bashing. *ESPN Insider*, January 10. http://insider. espn.go.com/insider/index.

Giles, Howard, and Philip Smith. 1979. Accommodation theory: Optimal levels of convergence. In *Language and social psychology*, ed. Howard Giles and Robert N. St. Clair, 45–65. Baltimore, Md.: University Park Press.

Goffman, Erving. 1974. *Frame analysis: An essay on the organization of experience*. Boston: Northeastern University Press.

———. 1981. *Forms of talk*. Philadelphia: University of Pennsylvania Press.

Goodwin, Marjorie Harness. 1990. *He-said-she-said: Talk as social organization among black children*. Bloomington: Indiana University Press.

Hill, Jane H. 1998. Language, race, and white public space. *American Anthropologist* 100:680–689.

Irvine, Judith T. 1996. Shadow conversations: The indeterminacy of participant roles. In *Natural histories of discourse*, ed. Michael Silverstein and Greg Urban, 131–159. Chicago: University of Chicago Press.

———. 2001. "Style" as distinctiveness: The culture and ideology of linguistic differentiation. In *Style and sociolinguistic variation*, ed. Penelope Eckert and John Rickford, 21–43. Cambridge: Cambridge University Press.

Jaffe, Alexandra. 2000. Comic performance and the articulation of hybrid identity. *Pragmatics* 10:39–59.

Justin, Neal. 2002. Can race be a laughing matter? *Star Tribune*, August 23.

Kong, Deborah. 2003. Abercrombie and Fitch accused of discriminating against minorities. *The Associated Press*, June 17.

Lave, Jean, and Etienne Wenger. 1991. *Situated learning: Legitimate peripheral participation.* Cambridge: Cambridge University Press.

Le Page, Robert B. 1980. 'Projection, focussing, diffusion' or steps towards a sociolinguistic theory of language, illustrated from the sociolinguistic survey of multilingual communities, Stages I: Cayo District, Belize (formerly British Honduras) and II: St. Lucia. *York Papers in Linguistics* 9:9–31.

Lowe, Lisa. 1991. Heterogeneity, hybridity, and multiplicity: Marking Asian American differences. *Diaspora* 1:24–44.

Myers-Scotton, Carol. 1993. *Social motivations for codeswitching: Evidence from Africa.* Oxford: Clarendon Press.

Ochs, Elinor. 1992. Indexing gender. In *Rethinking context: Language as an interactive phenomenon*, ed. Alessandro Duranti and Charles Goodwin, 335–358. Cambridge: Cambridge University Press.

O'Sullivan, Taro. 2002. Asian-American affairs: The two wongs of Abercrombie and Fitch. *Asian Reporter*, April 30.

Rampton, Ben. 1995. *Crossing: Language and ethnicity among adolescents.* London: Longman.

Said, Edward W. 1978. *Orientalism.* New York: Pantheon Books.

Strasburg, Jenny. 2002. Abercrombie and glitch: Asian Americans rip retailer for stereotypes on t-shirts. *The San Francisco Chronicle*, April 18.

Tang, Irwin. 2003. APA community should tell Shaquille O'Neal to 'come down to Chinatown.' *AsianWeek*, January 8.

Whang, Jin. 1994. "All American Girl" premiers negative portrayal of Korean Americans. *Korea Times*, October 4.

Woolard, Kathryn A. 1987. Codeswitching and comedy in Catalonia. *IPrA Papers in Pragmatics* 1:106–122.

———. 1998. Simultaneity and bivalency as strategies in bilingualism. *Journal of Linguistic Anthropology* 8:3–29.

17

"We Can Laugh at Ourselves"

Hawai'i Ethnic Humor, Local Identity, and the Myth of Multiculturalism

Roderick N. Labrador

The typical image of Hawai'i[1] is that of the commoditized touristic scene of white sandy beaches, swaying palm trees, picture-perfect sunsets, and highly sexualized hula girls and surfer boys. In large part, the political, economic, and ideological machinery of global tourism produces and heavily markets this image of Hawai'i as "tropical paradise," a tourist playground for rest and relaxation with warm and inviting "natives" who "hang loose" and happily welcome and serve visitors. A complementary image of Hawai'i depends on its much-celebrated multiculturalism and perceived racial/ethnic harmony; the idea of Hawai'i as "racial paradise" and "the most notable instance of a melting-pot of the modern world" (Park 1938, xiv).[2] This image of groups harmoniously coexisting is derived partially from the fact that there is no numerical majority among the various racial/ethnic groups who have settled in the islands.[3] Because there is no numerical majority, there is a widely held misperception that "everyone is a minority" that serves as "living proof" (Grant and Ogawa 1993) of racial tolerance and cultural intermixture where "peoples of different races and creeds can live together, enriching each other, in harmony and democracy" (Fuchs 1961, 449). In other words, there is a general perception that the various groups have "mixed" together and no single racial/ethnic group is politically and economically dominant despite evidence to the contrary—namely, the history of U.S. colonialism and foreign domination; the displacement, dispossession, and population collapse of Native Hawaiians; the exploitation of Asian workers as sources of cheap labor that facilitated the development of U.S capitalism in Hawai'i and investment in Asia; and the racial and ethnic stratification that positions whites, Japanese, and Chinese as elites, and Native Hawaiians, Filipinos, and Samoans as subordinate (Okamura

1990). Hawai'i as "racial paradise" is also constructed through the widespread promotion of the "Hawai'i Multicultural Model" (Okamura 1998) and its endorsement
of Local,[4] a racialized identity category that indexes a sociopolitically constructed
panethnic formation, as the unmarked normative order (Hill 1998) and the mainstream principle for collective identification. The elevation of the Local as the mainstream disguises differential access to wealth and power and frames multiculturalism
not merely as a political symbol or ideal, but also as *the* ideological underpinning of
everyday social, cultural, political, and economic realities.

   This chapter critiques the idea of Hawai'i as "multicultural paradise" and the
production of Local by examining the popular practice of ethnic humor. Like Elaine
W. Chun (this volume) I use comedy performances as a focus of sociolinguistic analysis. I argue that Hawai'i ethnic humor is both a space for the production of "Local
knowledge(s)" (Chang 1996) and ideologies where identities are constructed and
social order and racial hierarchy enacted. While others have focused on the construction of Local as a non-white panethnic formation (Okamura 1994; Takaki 1983) and
as a sociopolitical identity set in opposition to Native Hawaiians (Fujikane 2000;
Trask 2000), I draw attention to the production of Local as a non-immigrant identity,
especially the ways in which Local comedians appropriate the voice of immigrant
Filipinos through the use of Mock Filipino (or speaking English with a "Filipino
accent"). Mock Filipino is a strategy often employed by Local comedians to differentiate the speakers of Philippine languages from speakers of Pidgin or what most
linguists call Hawai'i Creole English, the lingua franca of Local residents. Audience
members do not necessarily speak or understand Philippine languages, yet many
often recognize individual Filipino words and the shift into Mock Filipino. Although
there are approximately one hundred Philippine languages and the national language
of the Philippines is officially called "Filipino," the language variety mocked by
Local comedians is more of an amalgamation of Ilokano and Tagalog, two of the
most commonly spoken Philippine languages in Hawai'i. Similar to the effects of
Mock Spanish (Hill 1998) and Mock Asian (Chun, this volume), Mock Filipino produces stigmatizing discourses of immigrant Filipinos. Like Mock Asian, public utterances of Mock Filipino in the continental United States are rather rare outside of the
comedy performances of Filipino American comics like Rex Navarrete and Kevin
Camia. In Hawai'i, Mock Filipino seems to have more resonance. Filipinos and non-
Filipinos are more likely to publicly voice a cautionary "*Halla*," an exasperated "*Ay
sus!*" or front a "Filipino accent" in everyday linguistic practice.[5] These public utterances simultaneously point to discourses of tolerance, inclusivity, and acceptance
that reinscribe Hawai'i's mainstream "multiculturalist ideology" (San Juan 2002)
and the marking of immigrant Filipino otherness.

   In this chapter, I examine the linguistic practices in the comedy performances
of Frank DeLima as well as excerpts from *Buckaloose: Shmall Keed Time* (Small
Kid Time), a comedy CD by Da Braddahs, a relatively new but tremendously popular comedy duo in Hawai'i. DeLima, who self-identifies as Portuguese, Hawaiian,
Chinese, English, Spanish, Scottish, Irish, and French, is a pillar of the local comedy
scene and is commonly referred to as the "king of ethnic humor in Hawaii" (Coleman
2003).[6] Da Braddahs is is comprised of of two Hawai'i-born and raised raised comics, James Roaché, who is Filipino and Italian, and Tony Silva, who is Hawaiian,

Chinese, Portuguese, and Irish. In *Buckaloose: Shmall Keed Time*, Da Braddahs follows the template of local comedy established by the pioneering comedy team of Booga Booga in the 1970s and 1980s, who performed jokes based on racial/ethnic stereotypes familiar to Hawai'i audiences (e.g., cheap Chinese, dumb Portuguese), used Pidgin as the primary medium of communication, and included song parodies and character sketches involving wild costumes, racial/ethnic caricatures, and overstated accents. In addition to their comedy CD, Da Braddahs have four self-produced videos and four DVDs, a thirty-minute long television show (called "Da Braddahs and Friends") that airs on local cable TV six nights a week, and they host a live weekly comedy show that depicts "the comic underside of contemporary local living" (Berger 2002, D1). Da Braddahs' character sketches play off of long-standing racial/ethnic stereotypes and a review of *Buckaloose: Shmall Keed Time* notes that the "Chinese, Filipino, 'haole,'[7] and other characters here are staple types" where "the characters and situations are almost all basic Booga/Rap bits that have been used and abused by almost all local comics for the past 20 years" (Berger 1998, D5). Although there are other problematic characters in the videos and on the TV show, like Keoki and Kakio who play on the image of the gay male *kumu hula*[8] and his *alaka'i*,[9] Bush and Bully (the mindless Samoan tree-trimmers), and Pocho and Tanda (two Local boys), here I focus on the Filipino character, Tata Cayatmo, who has a more prominent role in the CD, and his interactions with the Local character, Joe.[10] Da Braddahs' Tata Cayatmo functions as the stereotypical elderly male Filipino immigrant whose linguistic incompetence is positioned against Joe's Pidgin, drawing attention to the use of language in the othering of immigrant Filipinos.

The use of Mock Filipino in Hawai'i ethnic humor is part of broader racializing and stigmatizing discourses. Although media depictions often criminalize and misrepresent Filipinos as prone to violence (Quemuel 1996) as well as focus on "Filipino male sexual violence" (Fujikane 2000), here I focus on discourses that highlight immigrant Filipino linguistic and cultural difference. Local comedians use Mock Filipino as a "strategy of pejoration" (Hill 1993) to construct discourses that place immigrant Filipinos as cultural and linguistic Others, signifying their subordinate position in the social hierarchy and order. Through Mock Filipino, Local comedians construct the linguistic incompetence and subordinate identity of immigrant Filipinos. Although understood as "innocent" and "harmless" joking in which "we can laugh at ourselves," Hawai'i ethnic humor in general and Mock Filipino in particular simultaneously produce stigmatizing and "racially interested" discourses (Hill 1995) that uphold the positive self-image of Locals, especially their membership in Hawai'i's "racial paradise," while lowering that of immigrant Filipinos. The linguistic practice in the comedy performances are thus identity acts that normalize Local and reinforce Hawai'i's myth of multiculturalism while disseminating ideas about language, culture, and identity.

Local Matters and the Myth of Multiculturalism

The idea of "Local" is crucial for understanding ethnic humor and the politics of identity in Hawai'i. Steffi San Buenaventura (1996) suggests that to understand

Hawai'i "is to know the meaning and nuances of 'local' identity and the continuous contradistinctions that are made between the local and the 'non-local' *other*" (38, emphasis in original). Although Local operates in a field of ongoing relational oppositions that form a Local/non-Local binary, it is a racialized identity category composed primarily of the various non-white groups that usually trace their entrance into the islands to the plantation era—namely those of Chinese, Japanese, Okinawan, Filipino, and Korean descent. Local is the label for those who are usually classified as "Asian American" or "Asian Pacific American" in the continental United States. For many Hawai'i residents, particularly those of Asian ancestry, Local is the most salient category for political and cultural identification. Various scholars have focused on the cultural (Grant and Ogawa 1993; Ogawa 1978, 1981; Takaki 1983, 1993), structural (Okamura 1980, 1994, 1998), and political (Fujikane 2000; Trask 2000) to examine the nature and dynamics of Local. A common feature among these various approaches is that each locates the emergence and development of Local in Hawai'i's labor history and the shared experiences among the mainly Asian plantation workers.

A key aspect of the emergence of Local is the development of Pidgin, the language that now serves as the lingua franca of those who identify themselves as Local and is often used as the primary marker of Local-ness. Ronald Takaki (1983) argues that Pidgin was the shared language among the non-white plantation workers and facilitated their shift from "sojourners to settlers" and from individual ethnic groups to an overarching panethnic consolidation. Although "standard English," or mainstream U.S. English, continues to be the language of power and prestige, Pidgin has come to function as the language of Locals, enjoying "covert prestige" as a "badge of honor" (Da Pidgin Coup 1999; see also Lum 1998). It is the primary medium of communication for Local comedians. In addition, Pidgin has come to symbolize Hawai'i's multiculturalism and the ideologies of mixing, acceptance, equality, and assimilation. Pidgin is depicted as a reflection of the islands' history of interracial harmony: "Pidgin is inclusive, a reflection of our historical attitudes and the value placed on getting along and trying to find common ground. It is non-hierarchical, and puts people on an even footing" (Da Pidgin Coup 1999). Pidgin epitomizes the "blending process" associated with the development of Local identity and culture. In this way, Pidgin and Local are inseparable, constituting the symbolic, cultural, and linguistic aspect of multiculturalism in Hawai'i. As Local comedian Frank DeLima puts it: "Hawaii is local. Hawaii is Pidgin" (in Coleman 2003, C4).

Political economic changes in Hawai'i since the mid-1960s, including the development on mass tourism and the Native Hawaiian sovereignty movement, have enhanced the continuing salience of Local. In my analysis I foreground the relationality and situatedness of Local. Depending on the sociohistorical context and actors involved, Local can index racialized bodies ('look Local'), cultural identities ('act Local'), linguistic affiliations ('talk Local'), and political positionings.[11] In this way, the boundaries of Local are constantly changing and continuously policed through processes of self-definition and othering. In the sections that follow, I examine the ways in which racialized imagery and language practices in Local comedy are used to construct Locals and non-Local Filipinos.[12]

Constructing *"Buk Buk"*

Hawai'i ethnic humor is an important site for the practice and performance of Local identity and culture. The history of "Local comedy" can be traced to the 1950s and 1960s when Sterling Mossman, Lucky Luck, and Kent Bowman, aka perpetual senatorial candidate K. K. Ka'umanua (pronounced like "cow manure"), were popular comedic performers (Tonouchi 1999). Mossman, dubbed "Hawai'i's First Comedic Entertainer," was a bandleader who combined singing and telling jokes in his comedy routines. Lucky Luck, known as "Hawai'i's Prince of Comedy," was a popular radio personality with his own variety show and children's television show. Bowman, known as "The King of Pidgin English," recorded a half dozen albums that included his stand-up routines and children's stories told in Pidgin. Arguably, the heyday of Hawai'i ethnic humor was the late 1970s and 1980s. During this period, Andy Bumatai, Mel Cabang, and Booga Booga, the pioneering comedy group of James Kawika Piimauna "Rap" Reiplinger, James Grant Benton, and Ed Ka'ahea, set the stage for subsequent local comedians and established the template for contemporary Hawai'i ethnic humor, often referred to as *"Kanaka*[13] comedy." Race and ethnicity and the production of Local were crucial to the popularity of Booga Booga. Their comedy sketches played up familiar racial/ethnic stereotypes: "Ethnic identity is the key to their ability to generate material which is universally appealing to local audiences: Ka'ahea as the laid back 'token Hawaiian,' Benton the reserved 'Kabuki type,' Reiplinger more indefinably as the hustler—the 'token Portagee,'[14] perhaps" (Smith 1977, 20–21, in Tonouchi 1999). As Naomi Sodetani observes,

> [t]heir whole act was nothing but ethnic jokes and stereotypes: families bickering at home; Hawaiian musicians, busboys, hotel workers having fun while aspiring to be more. They made visible and celebrated a sense of "us-ness" onstage. All spoken in pidgin, not school-mandated 'good English grammar.' (Sodetani 2001, 6)

Booga Booga's *"kanaka* comedy" poked fun at social life in Hawai'i, resonating with the everyday realities of their Local audiences. Although based on problematic racial and ethnic stereotypes, *"kanaka* comedy" and its use of Pidgin, not "school-mandated" English, is integral in the discursive construction of Local and the creation of an "us-ness" among Hawai'i's working-class people. In addition, the comedy group's rise to prominence coincided with the growing legitimization of Pidgin in academic and popular discourse during the 1980s. Furthermore, as Lee Tonouchi suggests, the rise of *"kanaka* comedy" corresponded with the racial/ethnic consciousness-raising of the late 1960s and 1970s and the emergence of "Local nationalism" (Fujikane 1994): "Booga Booga's substantial popularity stems in part from being able to capitalize on dis movement creating separate ethnic identities as well as positing one collective Local identity against da mainland continent" (Tonouchi 1999, 24). The racial/ethnic awareness of this period helped to establish the idea of Local, especially as an identity positioned against "da mainland," producing a Hawai'i/continental U.S. dichotomy. Although the 1990s experienced a lull in the development of *"kanaka* comedy," there has been a recent resurgence with the rise of the next generation of Local comedians, like Lanai and Augie T, Paul Ogata, Greg Hammer, and Da Braddahs.

Filipino jokes are part of the broader "ethnic humor" widely circulated in Local comedy. Filipinos are by no means the only targets of ethnic jokes, but some argue that they bear a disproportionate burden (Quemuel 1996; Revilla 1996). Although there is a wide variety of Filipino jokes, there appear to be two primary types: those that focus on "Filipino vocabulary" (which depend on Mock Filipino) and "Filipino culinary tastes" (specifically dog eating). The Filipino dog-eating jokes are especially prevalent. The following examples are taken from Frank DeLima's *Joke Book* (1991, 68–70):[15]

Did you hear about the new Filipino cookbook?
    101 Ways to Wok Your Dog.
What do Filipinos call a dogcatcher's truck?
    Meals on Wheels.
What's a Filipino's favorite meal?
    Mutt loaf.
What do you call a Filipino family without a dog?
    Vegetarians.
What do you call a Filipino family with one dog?
    A family that doesn't know where its next meal is coming from.
What do you call a Filipino family with five dogs?
    Ranchers.

Filipino dog-eating jokes are widely disseminated, in public and in private. As standards in Local comedy routines (Quemuel 1996), Filipino dog-eating jokes move from light talk in private spheres to public joking (Hill 1993) that is both entertainment and the enactment of social hierarchy and order.

In Local comedy, a dominant Filipino character type is the *manong*,[16] the elderly male immigrant who is Fresh Off the Boat (or FOB) or Just Off the Jet (JOJ), eats dog and goats, speaks with a "heavy Filipino accent," and holds multiple low-wage and low-prestige jobs.[17] The *manong* often stumbles over his words, uses awkward expressions, has long pauses when he talks, and has problems with English pronunciation. What is usually belittled in Filipino jokes is the fresh-off-the-boatness and the linguistic, cultural, social, and ideological characteristics associated with recent immigrants, particularly their perceived "heavy Filipino accent," affinity for bright clothes, alien culinary tastes, and their general cultural incompatibility and incompetence. DeLima's "Filipino Purple Danube,"[18] a song parody using a waltz tempo that mimics the music for the *tinikling*, a traditional Filipino folk dance that uses two bamboo poles, is exemplary. DeLima begins the song with the Ilokano greeting "*Kumustakayo*" ('How are you all?') and immediately jumps into Mock Filipino nonsensical sounds that transform into clucking sounds. The lyrics for the song are as follows:

(1) "Filipino Purple Danube"

01   what's purple and brown, *buk buk, buk buk*
02   what squats on the ground, *buk buk, buk buk*

03   hold knife to your throat, *buk buk, buk buk*
04   and eats billy goat, *buk buk, buk buk*
05   who dance with two poles, *buk buk, buk buk*
06   has hairs on his moles, *buk buk, buk buk*
07   who eats *bagoong*,[19] all day long
08   you are right, it's the *manong*

09   who drives Cadillac, *buk buk, manong*
10   light show on the back, *manong, manong*
11   who wears silver pants, *manong, manong*
12   goes out disco dance, *manong, manong*
13   who greases his hair, *manong, manong*
14   who perfumes the air, *manong, manong*
15   who mixes *opai*[20] with fish eye
16   you are right, it's the P.I.[21]
17   you are right, *salamat*[22]

In the *Silva Anniversary* version of the song above, DeLima substitutes "who greases his hair/who perfumes the air" (lines 13–14) for "who works on Lanai[23]/whose wife is *hapai*"[24] and leaves out the entire third verse that appears in his *Joke Book*. The missing verse is more of the same, referring to Filipinos as "Flips" who participate in cockfighting and wear orange socks to go with their purple shirt and silver pants. (I have been told stories about immigrant Filipinos who intentionally avoid wearing these colors for fear of being ridiculed.) "Filipino Purple Danube" helps to construct the identity category of "*buk buk*"[25] /bʊkbʊk/, which is synonymous with immigrant Filipinos and is the primary marker of linguistic and cultural otherness. DeLima's "Danube" constructs the stereotypical *buk buk* who is dangerous (holds knife to your throat), sexualized (whose wife is *hapai*), wears bright-colored clothes (purple shirt, silver pants, orange socks), conspicuously showy (the entire second verse), and maintains Filipino ethnic signs, primarily culinary tastes (billy goat, *bagoong*, and *opae* with fish eye), cultural behaviors (squats on the ground), and traditions (dance with two poles).[26] This stereotypical image can also be found in Local greeting cards. For instance, a belated birthday card has a picture of a "Filipino" man wearing a bright purple shirt who is accompanied by a black dog, goat, and chicken. The "Filipino" man, aghast, has his hands on his face and the caption exclaims "Ay Sus!" The inside of the card reads, "I porgot yo' bertdey." In order to get the joke in the card, the reader must find both the racialized images as well as the Mock Filipino "funny."

DeLima's stereotypical *buk buk* reappears in the comedy of Da Braddahs. In *Shmall Keed Time*, the Filipino character is Tata Cayatmo. The choice of the name is particularly interesting. In Ilokano, *tata* is a term of address that is used for a male parent or uncle, one generation above the speaker. The word "*cayat*" or "*kayat*"[27] can mean "to want, like, wish, desire, [or] be willing" (Rubino 2000, 267) and *mo* is a second-person informal singular genitive possessive enclitic. The words combined, *cayatmo*, means 'do you want like, wish, desire, or are you willing?' Thus, the name "Tata Cayatmo" can mean 'old man do you like/want" and with the sexual connotations, it can mean something like 'dirty old man.'[28] By all means, Da Braddahs' Tata Cayatmo is *buk buk* and in the context of Filipino representation in Hawai'i, he is an extension of the criminally inclined and sexually predatory men in the Filipino "bachelor societies" of the sugar plantations.[29]

In *Shmall Keed Time*, Tata Cayatmo takes center stage in the song "We Are Filipino," which is sung with a "Filipino accent." The song is the second track in a two-track sequence involving two characters, Joe and Tata Cayatmo. Throughout the CD, the character Joe is the Local "hero," the protagonist in the sketch who meets up with various ethnic characters. Tata Cayatmo is the Filipino character, an older immigrant Filipino man in his fifties. Tata Cayatmo's status as an immigrant is crucial for the setup of the joke. The song is a form of speech play that heavily depends on Mock Filipino for its humor:

(2) "We Are Filipino"

01	ahhhh. I would like to dedicate dis song
02	to all of my fellow countryman
03	from the Filifeens
04	and flease mister DJ
05	can you flease gib me da good reburb
06	like da one on ahhh *Hawai'i Stars*[30]
07	cause I like to be like da good *kadugo*[31]
08	everybody put your hand together
09	and sing wit me the song of my countryman
10	Jim Shapper, gib me the tunes, boy
11	who do you think we are
12	we have to trabel so dam par
13	do you understand my accent?
14	excuse me sir, your change is ahh, fifty cent.
15	*hoy barok*,[32] will you like to try some really fresh *kalamunggay*?[33]
16	*barok, naimas kayatmo*?[34]
	((The sound of chickens crowing in the background))
17	everyday my fighting chicken is getting i-stronger
18	(Joe: Tata, Tata, put the chicken down)

Chorus:

19	we are Filifino
20	we come from the Filifeens
21	we are Filifino
22	trabeling with our pamily
23	we are Filifino
24	my family name is Tangunan
25	we are Filifino
26	my grandfader's your cleaning man
27	we are a *buk buk*, a *suksok*[35]
28	we are a *buk buk*, a *suksok*

29   boy, listen
30   *nataraki la unay dayta, nataraki la unay dayta*
31   *haan nga babait, haan nga babait na babai dayta, nataraki la unay dayta*[36]
32   excuse me, Kalihi[37]
33   everyday my pants are getting i-higher

Chorus:
34   we are Filifino
35   we come from the Filifeens
36   we are Filifino
37   trabeling with more pamily
38   we are Filifino
39   we all squeeze in dat pink house
40   we are Filifino
41   I go PI[38] for one more spouse
42   we are a *buk buk*, a *suksok*
43   we are a *buk buk*, a *suksok*

44   ahhh, my hair does not moob all day
45   because I use goat pomade
46   working at da bus stop
47   we buy our clothes from the Body Shop[39]
48   working 27 more year
49   so I can retarded[40] here
50   da PI channel[41] is da one por me
51   so I can watch it on da big TV
52   everyday my pants are getting i-higher
      ((leafblower sound))
53   (Joe: Tata, get out of the tree. Tata, come down from the tree)

Chorus:
54   we are Filifino
55   we come from the Filifeens
56   we are Filifino ((song fades out...))

Like DeLima's "Danube," "We Are Filipino" tells the listeners what it means to be Filipino in Hawai'i. For those unfamiliar with Filipinos in Hawai'i, the song serves as a brief primer on Filipino speech, culture, history, and socioeconomic status. For example, the song illustrates how Filipinos continue to be heavily concentrated in the more readily available, less prestigious, and lower-paying occupations. When Tata Cayatmo says, "Excuse me sir, your change is, ahh fifty cent" and later, "my grandfader's your cleaning man," he refers to the fact that Filipinos are occupationally concentrated in the new plantations, the hotels and resorts of the tourism industry, as chambermaids, janitors, and gardeners, as well as workers in the retail and service industries. Thus, it is not surprising to find older Filipinos working at fast-food restaurants or as groundskeepers, Tata Cayatmo's occupation. Even though the audience may not understand all of the words in the song, they are familiar with the racialized and classed imagery.

Similar to DeLima's use of *hapai* in "Filipino Purple Danube," Da Braddahs also highlight that Filipinos are *suksok*, a sexually laden Ilokano word that means to insert or penetration. This portrayal of Filipinos continues a tradition of media representations that have depicted Filipinos as a "sex danger," criminally inclined, and prone to violence, which have their origins in the plantation era. In the plantation camps, the image of the Filipino was that of an uncontrollable, dangerous, and sexually predatory male:

> A well-educated professional of Japanese ancestry … remembered the stern warning of his parents that children should not wander too close to the Filipino camps lest something awful should befall them. He also recalled that young girls were told to avoid Filipino men because their mere gaze was said to be sufficient to cause pregnancy. (Teodoro 1981, 55–56)

In the song, the character of Tata Cayatmo takes us back to plantation imagery. The reference to the disreputable woman uttered in Ilokano, "*haan nga babait, haan nga babait. nataraki la unay dayta*/she's not virtuous, she's not virtuous, she's very flashy," and the line, "I go PI for one more spouse" only heightens the sexualization and deviation of Tata Cayatmo and the normalization of Joe.

We also find out in the chorus of the song that Filipinos are largely an immigrant community: "we are Filifino, we come from the Filifeens, we are Filifino, trabeling with more pamily." Since the 1970s Filipinos have constituted the majority of immigrants who arrive annually in Hawai'i. The focus on Filipino immigrants in Local comedy helps to create a social cleavage between Locals and immigrants: "One effect [of these negative stereotypes and jokes] is that we have young Filipinos who are ashamed of being Filipino. Local Filipinos distance themselves from immigrant Filipinos because many of the jokes and stereotypes are based upon immigrant Filipino behaviors, like the accent" (Revilla 1996, 9). In this way, the constant flow of Filipino immigrants and their marked visibility, reproduced in ethnic humor, have led many Local Filipinos to dissociate themselves from their immigrant counterparts, drawing attention to their Local rather than "Philippine" identity (Revilla 1997). Da Braddahs' song elicits laughter because the imagery resonates with their largely Local audience. As Roaché notes, "[P]eople can relate to us and say … 'I have a cousin who's like that'" (in Coleon 2001, F5). In this particular case, "like that" refers to a cousin who is "*buk buk*." The assertion "I have a cousin who's like that" also makes the evaluative claim that "I'm not like my cousin" thereby creating a Local/immigrant dichotomy and constructing immigrant Filipinos as Others.

Mocking Filipino

Eduardo went to UH[42] to learn English. First, he learned vocabulary. The teacher said, "Please use 'tenacious' in a sentence."

> Eduardo thought for a minute, scratched his head. Then he said, "Ebery morning, before I go to school,
> > I bend down and tie my ten-ay-shoos."

The teacher next asked Eduardo to use the word "window" in a sentence.

Eduardo got that right away and said, "Win do we eat?"

Finally, the teacher said, "Please (sic) use the following four words in a sentence: 'deduct ... defense ... defeat ... and detail.'"

Eduardo was quiet for a long time and finally he said, "De duck jumped ober de fence, de feet before de tail."[43]

An important feature in Local comedy is the use of exaggerated accents to differentiate the speech of Locals and non-Locals. Exaggerated accents are a form of speech play that rely on "the manipulation of elements and components of language in relation to one another, in relation to the social and cultural contexts of language use, and against the backdrop of other verbal possibilities in which it is not foregrounded" (Sherzer 2002, 1). In Local comedy, Mock Filipino depends on the intentional disjunctive use of puns, miscommunication, and the manipulation of sound patterns in the formulation of perceived linguistic differences. Furthermore, Mock Filipino and "Filipino vocabulary" jokes (like the example above) depend on phonological and prosodic differences between pidgin (or "standard English," as is the case above) and Tagalog and Ilokano and the ensuing communicative confusion in order for the jokes to be perceived as humorous. For example, in order for the joke above to work, Eduardo's speech must be done in Mock Filipino style. In other words, Eduardo, who is typified as an immigrant Filipino, must speak with a "Filipino accent"; he must "sound" *buk buk*. This "accent" is indicated by certain phonological substitutions: the bilabialization of labiodentals /v/ → /b/ (<every> /ɛvəri/ → /ɛbəri/; <over> /ovər/ → /obər/) and the alveolarization of interdentals /ð/ → /d/ (<the> /ðʌ/ → /dʌ/). In addition, Eduardo confuses syllable stress: <tenacious> /təˈneʃəs/ → /ˈtɛˈneˈʃus/ ('tennis shoes'); <window> /ˈwɪndo/ → /ˈwɪnˈdo/ ('when do'); <deduct> /dəˈdʌkt/ → /ˈdiˈdʌk/ ('the duck'); <defense> /ˈdifɛns/ → /ˈdiˈfɛns/ ('the fence'); <defeat> /dəˈfit/ → /ˈdiˈfit/ ('the feet'); and <detail> /ˈditel/ → /ˈdiˈtel/ ('the tail'). In many "Filipino vocabulary" jokes, the punch line or what elicits laughter is not so much what is said, but *how* it is said (i.e., the pronunciation); that is to say "Filipino" linguistic practices and the speakers associated with them are the objects of derision.

In Local comedy, what is considered humorous about Filipino jokes is that they highlight the different linguistic practices of Locals and immigrant Filipinos and the communicative misunderstandings that arise. In the following excerpts from *Buckaloose: Shmall Keed Time*, mispronunciation leads to linguistic mix-ups and miscommunication between Joe and Tata Cayatmo. Throughout the CD Joe is authenticated as the pidgin speaker and it is his linguistic practices that are privileged. The first excerpt centers on the differences between the words "retired" and "retarded."

(3) "Retarded/Retired"[44]

01   TC: Imagine dis one *kadugu*, twenty sheben more year.
               Imagine this, my friend, twenty-seven more years.

02   J: Rait, rait.
               Right, right.

03 TC: I'm to going to be retarded.
           I'm going to be retarded.

04 J: Nou nou nou nou nou. Yu min ritai:ad.
           No, no, no, no, no.   You mean retired.

05 TC: It is to be working poreber.   [No? What are you sfeaking tired?
           I'll be working forever.   [No! What are you talking about, tired?

06 J: [NO:::U(h)   Not-   Ho?
                                          [No!   Not.   What?

07 TC: My pamily is working two hundred shebenty sheben hours a week
           My family works two hundred seventy-seven hours a week

08 J: Tu handred seventi seven?
           Two hundred seventy-seven?

           ((lines 9–19 are omitted))

20 J: Hau *old* yu Tawtaw Kayats.
           How old are you Tata Kayats?

21 TC: Nga in January I'm going to be making fifty-seven.
           Ahh, in January I'm going to be fifty-seven

22 J: Lem mi si. lem mi si. Faiv seven tu, kaeri da wan
           Lemme see. Lemme see. Five, seven, two, carry the one.

23 TC: Yas.
           Yes.

24 J: Ho- HOU
           Ho!

25 TC: Das da good one. Eighty-pour.
           That's the good one. Eighty-four

26 J: Das eiti for wen u ritaia. E daes nuts maen.
           That's eighty-four when you retire. Hey, that's nuts, man.

27 TC: Eighty-pour. Ay, dat age is ferfect to be ritarted.
           Eighty-four. Hey, that age is perfect to be retarded.

28 J: *Ritaiad*. Tawtaw. *Ritaiad*.
           Retired, Tata. *Retired*.

Here, Joe and Tata Cayatmo are talking about Cayatmo's age, the type and amount of work he does, and when he plans on retiring. In Cayatmo's first turn, Joe acknowledges mutual intelligibility when he says, "right, right" (line 2). In addition to Cayatmo's phonological substitutions (alveolarization of interdentals /ðɪs/ → /dɪs/, and alveo-palatalization of alveolars and bilabialization of labio-dentals /sɛvən/ → /ʃɛbən/ in line 1) what's perceived to be humorous arises in Cayatmo's second turn. He tells Joe that he plans to retire in twenty-seven years when he is eighty-four years old but instead of saying that he is going to be retired, he says "I'm to going to be retarded" in line 3 and again in line 27, "dat age is ferfect to be ritarted." In much the same way that Eduardo's "deduct" becomes "the duck," Cayatmo is not "retired," he's "retarded." Both times Joe picks up on the mispronunciation and corrects Cayatmo (line 4 and line 28), a correction done in pidgin. In line 4 Joe says, "Nou nou nou nou nou. yu min ritai:ad/No, no, no, no, no. You mean retired." Rather than using standard English, Joe uses the r-less pidgin form, "ritaiad." Even with Joe's correction, miscommunication still occurs as Cayatmo misconstrues Joe's "ritaiad" for "tired" and is offended by the insinuation that he's lazy and not hardworking (line 5). Joe repeats this correction in line 28 in a more definitive and emphatic way: "*Ritaiad*. Tawtaw. *Ritaiad./ Retired*, Tata. *Retired*."

Tata Cayatmo's inability to differentiate between "retired" and "retarded" points to his linguistic incompetence, which becomes an explicit point of communicative confusion. Is Cayatmo "retired" or "retarded"? Joe's corrections in line 4 and line 28 help to position Cayatmo as linguistically inferior and Pidgin as the linguistic norm; he speaks neither the overtly prestigious "Standard English" nor the highly regarded Pidgin. Joe's corrections and Cayatmo's inability to pick up on them suggests that perhaps Cayatmo is indeed "retarded," at least linguistically.

In the next excerpt, Cayatmo's linguistic ineptitude is the unambiguous site of misunderstanding. The confusion is over the inconsistency of the phonological substitutions /f/ → /p/ and /p/ → /f/ as Joe wants to clarify who is "fat" and who is "Pat."

(4) "So hard to understand"

01   J: Yur bradas waif Paet Imelda
              Your brother's wife Pat Imelda

02   TC: Yah, she sure is
              Yes, she sure is.

03   J: Shis wat, Paet or Imelda
              She's what, Pat or Imelda?

04   TC: She's Imelda
              She's Imelda.

05   J: Den hus Paet?
             Then who's Pat?

06   TC: Imelda. Imelda is Pat.
             Imelda. Imelda is Pat

07   J: Ou fae:t? Imelda is fae:t. (hhhh)
             Oh, fat. Imelda is fat. ((laughs))

08   TC: Yes Imelda Fat Josefina Kabina Cayatmo. But not now because they are
             diborced.
             Yes, Imelda Fat Josefina Kabina Kayatmo. But not now because
             they are divorced.

09   J: Sou hawd fo andastaend. I get om, I get om. Okei okei. Sou yur pis awr
             efs aend yur efs awr pis end yur bis awr vis aend yur vis awr bis.
             So hard to understand. I get 'em. I get 'em. Okay, okay.
             So your Ps are Fs and your Fs are Ps and your Bs are
             Vs and your Vs are Bs.

10   TC: Pinally, you pigure out my boice.
             Finally, you figure out my voice.

   In their first three turns, Joe and Tata Cayatmo are confused over who exactly
is "Pat" and who is "fat." Although Joe and Tata Cayatmo arrive at some type
of communicative resolution in lines 7–9, Joe expresses his frustration in line 9
when he says, "Sou hawd fo andastaend/So hard to understand." More specifically, for the Pidgin speaker, Philippine languages are "sou hawd fo andastaend/
so hard to understand" because the phonological substitutions make it difficult to
figure out if Imelda is named "Pat" or if she is "fat." Joe's frustrated "sou hawd
fo andastaend/so hard to understand" is an "active distancing" (Hill 1993) from
Tata Cayatmo and speakers of Philippine languages. Joe's arrival at some phonological clarity in line 9 illustrates common linguistic practices of native Filipino
speakers who are second language learners of English, namely the substitution
of consonant sounds (Ramos n.d.): bilabialization of labiodentals /f/ → /p/ (/fæt/
→ /pæt/); /v/ → /b/ (/vɔjs/ → /bɔjs/); and the labiodentalization of bilabials /p/
→ /f/ (/pæt/ → /fæt/) and /b/ → /v/.[45] Cayatmo affirms Joe's understanding of
his pronunciation miscues and phonological substitutions in line 10: "Pinally,
you pigure out my boice/ Finally, you figure out my voice." In the end, the
interactions between Joe and Tata Cayatmo in the excerpts, "retarded/retired"
and "sou hawd fo andastaend/so hard to understand," establish the following sets
of oppositions: Local/immigrant, Local/"Filipino," Pidgin/Mock Filipino, and
insider/outsider. Joe is the young, cool Local while Tata Cayatmo is the flip side,
the elderly Filipino immigrant who is linguistically and culturally the object of
ridicule.

Conclusion

On the Mainland, you can't do ethnic jokes, people get all offended. ... But us local people, we live on an island, we real open, we share everything. We can look at all the dumbness of our lives and talk about it. And that's the beauty of Hawai'i. We can laugh at ourselves.

Augie T[46]

Hawai'i ethnic humor depends on a shared set of assumptions and ideologies about linguistic practice, cultural identity, and Hawai'i society. These "ideologies of legitimacy" (Chun, this volume) hinge on pluralist ideals of racial harmony and the notion that "we can laugh at ourselves." The "we can laugh at ourselves" ideology is understood as a celebration of the islands' racial diversity and cultural differences ("all the dumbness of our lives") and positions the supposed "uniqueness" of Hawai'i against the volatile race relations on the "mainland." Hawai'i is understood as having gone beyond the "melting pot" and "salad bowl" models of race/ethnic relations and is instead an Asian-inspired "chop suey nation." As DeLima explains:

> Here in Hawaii, we laugh at ourselves more than most people do in other places. Hawaii is a chop suey nation—Portagee, Pake, Buddha Head, Sole, Yobo, Kanaka, Haole,[47] all mixed up. Nobody is the majority here. We are all part of at least one minority group. Some of us are part of several minority groups. And we all laugh at ourselves. This is healthy. (DeLima 1991, v)

The "chop suey nation" that DeLima imagines perpetuates the illusion of Hawai'i as a racial paradise (Okamura 1998) where "nobody is the majority," everyone is racially/ethnically "all mixed up," and "we all laugh at ourselves." But who is the "we" that is laughing and who is being laughed at? When "we laugh at ourselves" do "we" acquiesce to the extant structures and systems of white and Local domination while reducing ethnic groups to stigmatizing stereotypes? Or is "laughing at ourselves" a way to maintain the zones of intimacy and friendliness that were initially developed in response to *haole* domination?

For many in Hawai'i, ethnic jokes "represent a powerful link to our past that we hate to lose" (Sodetani 2001, 6). But what is "our past" and who actually is included in "our past"? Are ethnic jokes still the glue that binds the "people of Hawai'i"? Are ethnic jokes nostalgic residues of a much-celebrated originary past that provided the conditions for Native dispossession and displacement and the exploitation of Asian workers? Depictions of Filipinos in Local comedy foreground broader issues of politics and representation, especially who can represent whom and the effects of such representations. Ethnic humor is embedded in a network of social relations and underscored by political contests between and within racial/ethnic groups. Ethnic humor involves questions about who rightfully belongs to the islands, what criteria are used to determine belonging, and, ultimately, who can legitimately laugh at themselves. Who makes the jokes, who is made fun of, and who laughs involves discourses of inclusion and exclusion. Jokes can effectively tell us who belongs and in the process, they construct an order and hierarchy invariably linked to struggles for power.

I am extremely grateful to Adrienne Lo, Angie Reyes, and Christine Quemuel for their extensive editorial comments on earlier versions of this chapter. I would also like to thank Erin Kahunawaika'ala Wright for her help with the pidgin and Hawaiian translations, and Julius Soria for his assistance with the Ilokano and Tagalog.

NOTES

1. Following standard practice, I use the *'okina* (or glottal stop) whenever appropriate, as in "Hawai'i," unless the word appears in a quote or name where it is absent. Also in some cases, I do not use the *'okina* in English-language-derived words, like "Hawaiian."

2. For early work on "the racial melting-pot of the Pacific" see Adams (1937), Lind (1938), and Park (1926, 1937). For more recent discussions of Hawai'i as "multicultural, multiethnic society," see Okamura (1998) and Rosa (2001).

3. The islands' population statistics are sharply different from the rest of the United States. According to the 2004 Hawai'i State Department of Health Survey, Caucasians constitute 26.0 percent of the approximately 1.2 million total population, Japanese 21.6 percent, Native Hawaiians 19.9 percent, Filipinos 15.0 percent, Chinese 5.9 percent, and Other (mostly Pacific Islanders) 11.6 percent.

4. Following convention applied to other racial/ethnic categories such as "Asian American" or "Pacific Islander," here I use the term "Local" with a capital "L." My use of "local" with a lower-case "l" refers to the more general use of the term, which, in this case, points to the relatedness, situatedness, and/or typicality of an object and/or phenomenon to Hawai'i.

5. Outside of Local comedy, examples of Mock Filipino can also be found in local greeting cards (Da Kine Cards) and heard in various morning radio shows in which deejays tell jokes using a "Filipino accent."

6. DeLima began doing "Local comedy" in the late 1970s and since then, his Filipino song parodies (particularly those that include depictions of Filipinos as dog-eaters) have prompted lively public discussion in the Filipino community newspapers. DeLima's critics claim that his song parodies are part of a decades-old stigmatizing discourse that perpetuates lingering negative stereotypes of Filipinos. Supporters of DeLima claimed that his representations are nothing more than part of the Hawai'i tradition of ethnic humor that has a defined target audience and a specific target of ridicule. To this end, the *Hawaii Filipino Chronicle* noted that DeLima "argues that immigrant Filipinos, not local Filipinos, are the ones who object to his jokes" (1995, 5).

7. "Foreigner" in Hawaiian, but refers to "white" in its more racialized contemporary usage.

8. In Hawaiian, *kumu* means 'foundation,' 'source,' 'tree,' or 'teacher.' In this sense, *kumu hula* means 'hula teacher.'

9. In Hawaiian, *alaka'i* means 'leader' or 'to lead.'

10. It is also interesting to note that in their videos and on the TV show, Da Braddahs also have a character named "The Governor," a caricature of the former governor of Hawai'i, Benjamin Cayetano. Cayetano is a Filipino American who by most standards speaks Mainstream American English, but has a "Filipino accent" in the sketches.

11. From a political perspective, Local also points to the islands' history of Native subordination and settler domination. According to Haunani-Kay Trask (2000), Local is the name children of Asian settlers call themselves and it locates Asians outside of the white/ "settler" category, eliding Asian participation in the islands' settler history of foreign domination and Native subordination. In this perspective, the use of Local obscures the history of Hawai'i's indigenous people while asserting a competing claim of rightful belonging to the islands. Local also espouses a "land of immigrants" rhetoric that depends on a multiculturalist ideology and purports an ethos of racial diversity, heterogeneity, tolerance, and harmony.

12. Jonathan Okamura (1994) notes that non-Locals usually include *haole*, immigrants, the military, tourists, and foreign investors.

13. *Kanaka* means 'person' or 'human' in Hawaiian, but in contemporary usage it has come to connote 'Native Hawaiian.'

14. 'Portuguese' in pidgin.

15. For more recent examples, see Paul Ogata's (1998) comedy CD, *Mental Oriental*, especially "Dr. Ay Seuss, parts 1 & 2" which employs Mock Filipino and caricatures the "Filipino" preference for eating black dog.

16. A kin term that means 'older brother' but in Local usage refers to 'older Filipino man.' The Localized pronunciation of the term places the accent on the second syllable rather than the first as it is pronounced in Ilokano.

17. This is often the evidence used in "positive" stereotypes of Filipinos which characterize them as hardworking and industrious.

18. The song originally appears in *Frank DeLima's Joke Book* (1991) as "The Purple Danube." The song lyrics that I transcribe here are taken from a more recent version that appears in DeLima's *Silva Anniversary* (2001).

19. This is equivalent to the Ilokano term, *bugguong*, which is "salted fermented fish or shrimps used to season food" (Rubino 2000, 124) and is known for its pungent odor.

20. In Hawaiian, *opae* are 'small shrimp' (see Simonson et al. 1981).

21. P.I. refers to the Philippine Islands, but is often used alongside terms like *buk buk*, *manong*, and Flip to refer to Filipinos.

22. *Salamat* means 'thank you' in Tagalog.

23. One of the Hawaiian islands that is heavily dependent on the tourism industry and has a large Filipino population.

24. A Hawaiian term that means 'to carry,' but refers to being pregnant.

25. The term "*buk buk*" is derived from a Tagalog term, "*bukbok*," which means 'to rot' and refers to something rotten (Alcantara 1981, 165). In Ilokano, "*bukbok*" is a type of woodworm and also means 'cavity (of teeth)' (Rubino 2000, 125; see also DeLima 1991, 67). The common onomatopoeic explanation for the term "*buk buk*" is that it mimics the clucking sound of chickens, pointing to how Filipinos are closely associated with fighting chickens. Take, for example, the following joke taken from DeLima (1991, 71): "Official Filipino bird: Fighting chicken."

26. Representations of Filipino subordination have their historical origins in the plantation era (Okamura 1996, 3). Despite the large numbers of pre-World War II Filipino immigrants, the community was mostly composed of single men; it was a "bachelor society." At the height of Filipino immigration to Hawai'i, the male to female ratio was 3 to 1 in 1923 and 9 to 1 in 1927 (San Buenaventura 1995).

27. The /k/ is usually preferred in contemporary standard Ilokano orthography.

28. Cayatmo could also be a play on "Cayetano," referring to the former Filipino American governor of Hawai'i.

29. Recent depictions of Filipino male sexual violence also appear in Local literature, particularly in the works of Lois-Ann Yamanaka. For a textual analysis of Yamanaka's most controversial work, *Blu's Hanging*, see Fujikane (2000).

30. For nearly a decade, *Hawai'i Stars* aired weekly on local TV. The half-hour show was a judged karaoke-style singing competition that showcased the singing talents of people from the islands.

31. *Kadugo* is an Ilokano term that can be translated as 'family member' or 'relative.'

32. *Barok* is an Ilokano term that can be translated as 'young man.'

33. *Kalamunggay* is the Tagalog term for a vegetable often used in Filipino dishes. *Marunggay* is the Ilokano equivalent.

34. The Ilokano phrase "*naimas kayatmo*" can be translated as 'It's delicious, do you want some?'

35. In Ilokano, "*suksok*" is loosely translated as 'insertion' or 'penetration.'

36. In Ilokano, this phrase can be loosely translated as 'that girl is not respectable.'

37. A multiethnic, urban, working-class neighborhood on the island of O'ahu that has a high concentration of immigrant Filipino residents.

38. A reference to the Philippines, "PI" = 'Philippine Islands.'

39. This is a local clothing store.

40. I discuss this idea of "retarded/retired" further below.

41. This is a reference to TFC (The Filipino Channel), a twenty-four-hour Philippine-language channel available on cable TV. TFC broadcasts a wide range of programs from the Philippines, including news, entertainment, music, feature films, soap operas, and so on.

42. "UH" refers to the University of Hawai'i.

43. DeLima (1991, 72).

44. Here, I use the Odo orthography to represent pidgin and Mock Filipino (see Odo 1975, 1977; Sakoda and Siegel 2003; Talmy, this volume). Other transcription conventions include:

-	sudden cut-off
italic	Emphasis (pitch, amplitude)
:	Lengthening
.	Falling contour
?	Rising contour
((comments))	Transcriber comments
(h)	Breathiness, laughter
[word	Onset of overlapping talk

45. The /b/ → /v/ labiodentalization does not occur in this particular example, but it is an important feature of Mock Filipino and appears in other parts of the CD.

46. Augie Tulba is a popular Local comedian who is Portuguese, Irish, and Filipino. This quote is taken from an article by Naomi Sodetani (2001, 5) titled "Local Humor and the New World Order," which appears in the *Honolulu Weekly*.

47. These are race/ethnic labels commonly used in pidgin: "Portagee" = Portuguese, "Pake" = Chinese, "Buddha Head" = Japanese, "Sole" = Samoan, "Yobo" = Korean, "Kanaka" = Native Hawaiian, and "Haole" = white.

REFERENCES

Adams, Romanzo. 1937. Intermarriage in Hawaii: A study of mutually conditioned processes of acculturation and amalgamation. New York: Macmillan.

Alcantara, Ruben. 1981. *Sakada: Filipino adaptation in Hawaii*. Washington, D.C.: University Press of America.

Berger, John. 1998. Buckaloose: Da Braddahs. *Honolulu Star-Bulletin*, July 31.

———. 2002. Two wild and crazy guys!: Tony Silva and James Roché [*sic*] may look lolo and act lolo, but they know what they're doing. *Honolulu Star-Bulletin*, June 27.

Chang, Jeff. 1996. Local knowledge(s): Notes on race relations, panethnicity and history in Hawai'i. *Amerasia Journal* 22:1–29.

Coleman, Mark. 2003. Frank DeLima. *Honolulu Star-Bulletin*, March 2.

Coleon, Shayna. 2001. Da Braddahs: Comic pair are gaining fame after a somewhat rough start. *Honolulu Advertiser*, August 15.

Da Braddahs. 1998. *Buckaloose*. CD. Hobo House on the Hill.

Da Pidgin Coup. 1999. Pidgin and education: A position paper. http://www.hawaii.edu/sls/pidgin.html.

DeLima, Frank. 1991. *Frank DeLima's joke book: Having fun with Portagees, Pakes, Buddha Heads, Buk Buks, Blallahs, Soles, Yobos, Haoles, Tidahs, Pit Bulls, and other Hawaiian minorities*. Honolulu: Bess Press.

———. 2001. *Silva anniversary*. CD. Pocholinga Productions.

Fuchs, Lawrence. 1961. *Hawaii pono: A social history*. New York: Harcourt, Brace & World.

Fujikane, Candace. 1994. Between nationalisms: Hawai'i's local nation and its troubled paradise. *Critical Mass: A Journal of Asian American Cultural Criticism* 2:23–57.

———. 2000. Sweeping racism under the rug of "censorship": The controversy of Lois-Ann Yamanaka's *Blu's Hanging. Amerasia Journal* 26:158–194.

Grant, Glen, and Dennis Ogawa. 1993. Living proof: Is Hawai'i the answer? *The ANNALS of the American Academy of Political and Social Science* 530:137–154.

Hawaii Filipino Chronicle. 1995. Filipinos speak out on DeLima jokes. *Hawaii Filipino Chronicle*, January 1.

Hill, Jane H. 1993. Hasta la vista, baby: Anglo Spanish in the American Southwest. *Critique of Anthropology* 13:145–176.

———. 1995. Junk Spanish, covert racism, and the (leaky) boundary between public and private spheres. *Pragmatics* 5:197–212.

———. 1998. Language, race, and white public space. *American Anthropologist* 100:680–689.

Lind, Andrew. 1938. *An Island community: Ecological succession in Hawaii*. Chicago: University of Chicago Press.

Lum, Darrell H. Y. 1998. Local genealogy. What school you went? In *Growing up local: An anthology of poetry and prose from Hawai'i*, ed.

Chock Eric et al., 11–15. Honolulu: Bamboo Ridge Press.

Odo, Carol. 1975. Phonological processes in the English dialect of Hawaii. PhD diss., University of Hawai'i at Manoa.

———. 1977. Phonological representations in Hawaiian English. *University of Hawaii Working Papers in Linguistics* 9:77–85.

Ogata, Paul. 1998. *Mental Oriental*. CD. Tropical Jam Productions.

Ogawa, Dennis. 1978. *Jan ken po: The world of Hawaii's Japanese Americans*, 2nd ed. Honolulu: University of Hawai'i Press.

———. 1981. Dialogue: What is Local? *Hawai'i committee for the humanities news* 2:7.

Okamura, Jonathan. 1980. Aloha kanaka me ke aloha aina: Local culture and society in Hawai'i. *Amerasia Journal* 7:119–137.

———. 1990. Ethnicity and stratification in Hawai'i. *Operation manong resource papers* 1:1–11.

———. 1994. Why there are no Asian Americans in Hawai'i: The continuing significance of local identity. *Social Process in Hawai'i* 35:161–178.

———. 1996. Historical legacies, contemporary challenges, and future visions: The Filipino American community in late twentieth century Hawai'i. In *Pagdiriwang 1996: Legacy and vision of Hawaii's Filipino Americans*, ed. Jonathan Okamura and Roderick Labrador, 1–4. Honolulu: Student Equity, Excellence & Diversity and Center for Southeast Asian Studies, University of Hawai'i at Manoa.

————. 1998. The illusion of paradise: Privileging multiculturalism in Hawai'i. In *Making majorities: Composing the nation in Japan, China, Korea, Fiji, Malaysia, Turkey and the United States*, ed. Dru Gladney, 264–284. Palo Alto, Calif.: Stanford University Press.

Park, Robert. 1926. Our racial frontier in the Pacific. *Survey graphic* 9:192–196.

————. 1937. Introduction. In *Intermarriage in Hawaii: A study of mutually conditioned processes of acculturation and amalgamation*, ed. Romanzo Adams, vii–xiv. New York: Macmillan.

————. 1938. Introduction. In *An island community: Ecological succession in Hawaii*, ed. Andrew Lind, vii–xiv. Chicago: University of Chicago Press.

Quemuel, Christine. 1996. Student apathy or activism: Examining the activism and activities of Filipino student organizations throughout the University of Hawai'i system. In *Pagdiriwang 1996: Legacy and vision of Hawaii's Filipino Americans*, ed. Jonathan Okamura and Roderick Labrador, 17–19. Honolulu: Student Equity, Excellence & Diversity and Center for Southeast Asian Studies, University of Hawai'i at Manoa.

Ramos, Teresita. n.d. Some communication problems of Filipino students.

Revilla, Linda. 1996. Filipino Americans: Issues of identity in Hawai'i. In *Pagdiriwang 1996: Legacy and vision of Hawaii's Filipino Americans*, ed. Jonathan Okamura and Roderick Labrador, 9–12. Honolulu: Student Equity, Excellence & Diversity and Center for Southeast Asian Studies, University of Hawai'i at Manoa.

————. 1997. Filipino American identity: Transcending the crisis. In *Filipino Americans: Transformation and identity*, ed. Maria Root, 95–111. Thousand Oaks, Calif.: Sage Publications.

Rosa, John. 2001. "The coming of the neo-Hawaiian race": Nationalism and metaphors of the melting pot in popular accounts of mixed-race individuals. In *The sum of our parts: Mixed heritage Asian Americans*, ed. Teresa Williams-Leon and Cynthia Nakashima, 49–56. Philadelphia: Temple University Press.

Rubino, Carl. 2000. *Ilocano dictionary and grammar*. Honolulu: University of Hawai'i Press.

Sakoda, Kent, and Jeff Siegel. 2003. *Pidgin grammar: An introduction to the Creole language of Hawai'i*. Honolulu: Bess Press.

San Buenaventura, Steffi. 1995. Filipino immigration to the United States history and legacy. In *The Asian American Encyclopedia*, ed. Franklin Ng, 439–453. New York: Marshall Cavendish.

————. 1996. Hawaii's Filipinos: History and legacy. In *Pagdiriwang 1996: Legacy and vision of Hawaii's Filipino Americans*, ed. Jonathan Okamura and Roderick Labrador, 35–38. Honolulu: Student Equity, Excellence & Diversity and Center for Southeast Asian Studies, University of Hawai'i at Manoa.

San Juan, Epifanio Jr. 2002. *Racism and cultural studies: Critiques of multiculturalist ideology and the politics of difference*. Durham: Duke University Press.

Sherzer, Joel. 2002. *Speech play and verbal art*. Austin: University of Texas Press.

Simonson, Douglas, Ken Sakata, and Pat Sasaki. 1981. *Pidgin to da max*. Honolulu: Bess Press.

Smith, Pam. 1977. Booga Booga: Three mokes with different strokes. *Hawaii Observer* 99:18–23.

Sodetani, Naomi. 2001. Local humor and the new world order. *Honolulu Weekly*, May 30–June 5.

Takaki, Ronald. 1983. *Pau hana: Plantation life and labor in Hawaii, 1835–1920*. Honolulu: University of Hawaii Press.

————. 1993. *Raising cane: The world of plantation Hawaii.* New York: Chelsea House Publishers.

Teodoro, Luis, ed. 1981. *Out of this struggle: The Filipinos in Hawaii.* Honolulu: University Press of Hawaii.

Tonouchi, Lee. 1999. No laugh brah, serious: Pidgin's association wit local comedy. *Hybolics* 1:22–33.

Trask, Haunani-Kay. 2000. Settlers of color and "immigrant" hegemony: "Locals" in Hawai'i. *Amerasia Journal* 26:1–24.

18

Reel to Real

Desi Teens' Linguistic Engagements with Bollywood

Shalini Shankar

Increasingly, scholars have paid attention to the social life of media in diasporic contexts, especially its role in fostering bonds of community and mediating identity while enabling connections to homeland and other diasporic locales. Often a backgrounded theme, language and the linguistic aspects of media consumption can be important dimensions of this process (Spitulnik 1996). Topics of intertextuality, indexicality, bivalency, and, more broadly, identity formation have been sociolinguistically examined in the lives of youth, but seldom with explicit attention to the pervasive role of media in shaping language practices. In this chapter I explore Desi (South Asian American)[1] teens' social and linguistic engagements with "Bollywood" movies. Bollywood, the world's most prolific film industry, produces films that are widely viewed in South Asia and beyond. Once a tongue-in-cheek name used by the English language media in India (Ganti 2004), the term "Bollywood" is now used worldwide to refer to Hindi-language films made in Bombay (renamed Mumbai in 1995). Serving simultaneously as visual culture, a social institution, as well as a linguistic resource for many diasporic youth, Bollywood films have deeply affected the everyday social lives of South Asians in the subcontinent and worldwide. Even Desi teens who may have limited communicative competence in Hindi—the language of most Bollywood films—nonetheless draw linguistically on this rich and multifaceted medium.

Occupying a prime position in many teenagers' worlds, Bollywood films provide a linguistic resource that youth draw on in their everyday speech practices. Richard Bauman and Charles Briggs (1992) examine the notion of "intertextuality" with special regard to genre. Building on work by Mikhail Bakhtin (1981) and Pierre

Bourdieu (1991), they argue that various genres of language are not mutually exclusive, but rather overlap with one another. Bollywood-based language practices are no exception; in fact, they epitomize the idea of intertextuality by toggling between spoken dialogue and fantasy-driven narratives set to song and dance. Likewise, teens engage with Bollywood in ways that enable them to move fluidly through different genres of talk, as well as different levels of reflexivity: from the use of Bollywood dialogue in direct as well as reported speech and the narration of their own lives through the stories of film characters, to the deployment of dialogue, film-specific registers, and song lyrics that index a shared sense of aesthetic tastes and communicative competence. Teens develop evaluative stances through talk as they report on-screen events and use stories and characters to narrate their own lives and dilemmas—a unique speech practice that links reel life to their real lives.

A central aspect of these processes is the notion of voice. Bakhtin's (1981) concept of heteroglossia explores how the same speaker can deploy a number of different types of voices, which can be expressed through register, lexicon, and other types of choices. Indeed, as Webb Keane (1999, 272) articulates, voice can be achieved through a range of linguistic means that "permit speakers to claim, comment on, or disavow different identities and evaluative stances at different moments." This study of Bollywood-based language practices, like Jane Hill's (1995) examination of Mexicanos' use of Don Gabriel's voice, explores how distinct voices and registers are deployed in various speech settings (see also Hill and Irvine 1992).

I examine these topics among Desi teenagers in two diasporic locales: Queens, New York, and Silicon Valley, California. The diversity of religion, nationality, class, and geography underscores both similarities and differences between two South Asian American communities. Discussions of Silicon Valley are part of a larger research project in which I examine the significance of language practices to engagements with material and visual culture, and, more broadly, identity and community formation. I conducted ethnographic and sociolinguistic research for sixteen months in three economically and sociolinguistically diverse schools and community settings in Silicon Valley. In this chapter, I primarily discuss data from Greene High School—which contains both middle-class and upper-middle-class Desi youth, and during the 1999–2000 school year had 2,648 students, of which approximately 15 percent were Desi.

Data presented here include participant observation during film viewings in homes and theater, taped interviews, and spontaneously occurring conversation tape-recorded at lunch and break at school, some of which was done in my absence. Data about Desi teens in Queens were collected during two years as a volunteer at a community-based youth center. Here, I spent approximately three hours per week in an informal atmosphere with primarily middle-class youth from the surrounding neighborhoods. During my eighteen months as a volunteer (1997–1999) I monitored a drop-in space with basketball, where I spoke primarily with boys, and was involved with some girls' and co-ed activities. Data presented here are based on recordings of spontaneously occurring conversations for which I was present, as well as participant-observations during film viewings at the youth center.

Drawing on these data, I examine various verbal repertoires that are based on or incorporate Bollywood language. They include reenacting humorous dialogue for comedic entertainment, inhabiting a particular character's voice, engaging in flirta-

tious dialogue with the opposite sex, and quoting film characters. The indexical properties of film quotes incorporated into conversation rely on the recognition of certain
stylistic registers of speaking typical to Hindi films. As I will discuss, aspects of this
process occur differently according to gender, social class, linguistic background,
as well as place, highlighting some of the similarities and differences between Desi
teens in Queens and Silicon Valley.

Teen Language Use

My examination of Bollywood-based language practices contributes to a growing literature on youth and language. Such inquiries offer insight into how groups actively
constitute themselves around language practices, including multilayered processes
of social network formation (Eckert 1989) and ethnically specific styles (Mendoza-
Denton 1996). There are different ways that teens define and perform Desi identities, and such practices indicate ethnic allegiances (Back 1996; Baumann 1996) and
draw attention to the fluid nature of racial and ethnic meanings across social contexts (Rampton 1995). Religion, social class, gender, and other factors contribute to
how teens relate to and use language with family and community members (Shankar
2003). Teens' language use often closely follows that of their family and community
environments, as I discuss below.

Queens and Silicon Valley are both extremely diverse, linguistically vibrant
places. Desi teens I worked with in Silicon Valley range from first to fourth generation, although most are second generation. They hail from middle-class families
where grandparents labored in peach orchards in Yuba City and parents work on
assembly lines in Silicon Valley, as well as upper-middle-class families where parents
emigrated from South Asia and hold lucrative upper-management jobs at high-tech
companies. The teens at the Queens youth center are primarily from middle-class
families and live in diverse Queens neighborhoods.

In both Silicon Valley and Queens, most teens are bilingual in English and
their heritage language. The most represented group in my Silicon Valley research
is Punjabi-speaking Sikhs, followed by Gujarati-speaking Hindus, and Hindi/Urdu-
speaking Muslims from Pakistan, India, and Fiji. Nearly all Sikh teens are fluent
in Punjabi and speak it with their peers in school. Muslim teens are also fluent in
Bengali, Urdu, or Hindi but their language use at school varies according to class
background. Hindu teens are the least likely to be fluent in their heritage language
and seldom speak it with their peers. These teens represent a number of different
linguistic groups and are often unable to find conversational partners in their heritage language. At the Queens youth center, first-generation teens are more fluent
than second-generation teens in their heritage language and in Hindi, which many of
them studied in school in South Asia before moving to the United States. Most are
Hindi/Urdu or Gujarati speakers, with a number of teens from Guyana and Trinidad
who are less fluent in Hindi but still acquired words, phrases, and songs from film
viewings and their friends at the youth center.

Three types of language practices I observed are code-switching, the process by
which speakers alternate between two or more languages in conversation, (Auer 1998;

Gal 1987; Milroy and Muysken 1995); code-mixing (the use of words and phrases from more than one language during a conversation) (Heller 1999); and the use of Indian-accented English (Rampton 1995; see also Chun, this volume). The latter two occur especially among teens who are less fluent in speaking a particular language variety. Madhu and Neetu, two Punjabi Sikh girls in Silicon Valley, explain that they sometimes speak in Punjabi when they do not want people to understand them. Neetu explains, "We put our 'ings' and 'eds' after every action—I was '*dekh*ing' [looking], I was '*sunn*ing' [listening]. We both have the same level of speaking, so we can use it suddenly if we need to." Such group-specific talk functions as a form of insider language alongside a range of other practices that contribute to the construction and expression of style.

Teens acquire linguistic skills that reflect a wide range of communicative competencies that are linked to different social identities, activities, and practices (see Romaine 1995; Zentella 1997). For example, although many families do not speak Hindi, teens develop varying levels of competence by watching Bollywood films. Although this rarely means they can converse fluently in Hindi, they are able to incorporate dialogues, phrases, and song lyrics from these films into conversation. While most Bollywood films are in Hindi, native speakers of Gujarati, Punjabi, and Bengali as well as Tamil, Telugu, and Malayalam avidly watch them with subtitles. Even within these largely bilingual contexts, it may seem counterintuitive that non-Hindi-speaking teens would watch Hindi-language Bollywood films, a medium for which they require a new set of language skills. Much of the impetus for these practices is peer driven. In Queens, keeping up with other teens at the youth center is important, and even if non-Hindi speakers cannot produce dialogue or utterances themselves, they can at least follow the conversations around them. In Silicon Valley, the resounding popularity of Hindi films among Desi teens makes those who are not familiar with the genre a minority. A closer look at Bollywood and other diasporic media will provide proper context for the examples I discuss in the upcoming sections.

Bollywood Worldwide

In the late 1990s, where discourses of multiculturalism and cultural diversity were an accepted cultural logic, Bollywood films were a key part of living in America for Desi youth. These films were and are popular among communities worldwide (Larkin 1997; Liechty 1995) and watched in Desi diasporic locations such as Fiji (Ray 2000), Great Britain (Gillespie 1995; Hall 2002), and Queens, New York (Shankar 2004). Recent ethnographic work examines "how media are embedded in people's quotidian lives" (Ginsburg et al. 2002, 2) by connecting its consumption to larger processes of nationalism (Abu-Lughod 1995), youth culture (Liechty 2002), and transnationalism (Gillespie 1995). Benedict Anderson (1991) outlines the historical construction of the "imagined community" as a way in which individuals imagine a connection to one another and envision themselves as part of a larger group in the absence of face-to-face contact. This concept has been especially useful in illustrating how media and language are both vital elements of community construction. Using Anderson's concept, Deborah Spitulnik (1996) offers an insightful examination of what she has termed "the social circulation of media discourse." Similar to Spitulnik's discussion of how

Zambians draw on radio show dialogue and personalities by incorporating phrases, types of turn taking, and other verbal styles into their own speech practices, Desi teens engage with Bollywood in ways that increase sociability and connectedness.

Connections between media and diaspora focus on imagination (Appadurai 1996), nostalgia, nationalism (Naficy 1993), and connections to homeland (Kolar-Panov 1996). In this sense, the pervasive influence of Bollywood films, songs, actors, and narratives is undeniable in the Desi diaspora. From watching new releases and following up on film star bios to acquiring Bollywood cell phone ringtones, this media institution has a strong presence in the lives of Silicon Valley and Queens Desi teens. Between multiplexes that screen these films, numerous stores that rent and sell movies and their soundtracks, and ubiquitous Internet sites replete with movie clips and star gossip, most kids participate in Bollywood on some level. Bollywood songs and styles even appear in recent Hollywood films such as *Moulin Rouge*, *Ghost World*, *The Inside Man*, and popular music by Shakira and various hip-hop artists.

Historically, Bollywood films have been made for South Asian audiences, but production has expanded since the 1990s to imagine the diaspora as a key segment of the production process to increase overall marketability (Ganti 2002). Most Desi Bollywood fans began watching films at home with their parents on the VCR, and this trend continues with family DVD and VHS viewing. While new releases used to take months before they were officially released on video, DVD releases are now simultaneous with theater releases and provide viewers with a timely and inexpensive alternative to going to a theater. Films are inexpensively obtained at South Asian grocery stores that also double as movie rental and soundtrack retail centers. Mail-order DVD rentals through services such as Netflix make renting films easier than ever. Both Silicon Valley and Queens have local movie theaters that play the latest releases. Many families tape their DVDs onto videotapes while watching, thereby creating a vast library of titles from which to choose for repeat viewing.

Songs from films are well known and liked among Desi teens and are incorporated into a number of aspects of teen lives. The average film features at least six song sequences that further the narrative structure of the film by celebrating alliances or revealing hidden desires between characters. Outside of the film, songs contribute to the movie's appeal. Especially popular songs are heard in cars, on headphones, and at parties, and are used in teens' own dance productions. They are played repeatedly on DVDs whose menus are programmed for just such repeat viewings. Indeed, film songs are so popular that my 2004 viewing of *Kal Ho Na Ho* at a Mumbai theater was repeatedly embellished by audience members' cell phones ringing loudly with the movie's theme song.

Although teens of various class, linguistic, religious, and geographic backgrounds express avid interest in Bollywood films, how the films are incorporated into everyday talk and social life varies. In the following sections, I will explore various examples of this process.

The Language of Cinematic Appeal

Among Desi teens in Silicon Valley and Queens, Hindi films are as popular as Hollywood films and film knowledge is privileged. A closer look at the nature of these films and elements of their popularity will shed light on this trend. There are many competing visions of modernity in Hindi films, but several recent films made in the 1990s and the first decade of the twenty-first century seem especially relevant to these youth. Bollywood films portray a global youth culture replete with branded products from the United States and Europe. The modern, hip, youth culture and lifestyles portrayed in recent hits *Dil To Pagal Hai* and *Kuch Kuch Hota Hai*, as well as the trend of featuring Desis in London, Los Angeles, and New York have led to films such as *Dilwale Dulhuniya Le Jayenge*, *Pardes*, and *Kal Ho Na Ho*, which center on regions with large Desi diasporic populations. The main characters in these films are young, attractive, and clad in designer clothes popular among Desi teens—including Tommy Hilfiger, Gap, Adidas, and DKNY. Featuring youth as consumers, these films portray a set of leisure activities that is a relatively new addition to youth lives in South Asia, including shopping as a social activity, co-ed basketball, modern dance performances, DJ-ed parties, and cheerleading.

Bollywood films are popular in the diaspora because they portray a global youth culture without losing sight of Desi values. Narratives of good triumphing over evil, maintaining the purity and chastity of women, the sacrificing of individual desires for the larger good of the family, respecting elders, and preserving the sanctity of one's community (see Joshi 2002; Prasad 2001) are crucial to the continued relevance of these films in Desi teen lives. Although the clothing may be skimpier than what many teenage Desi girls are permitted to wear, the characters are often subject to the same sorts of restrictions and obligations as Desi teens in the United States. At the same time, non-Bollywood Desi films, which are primarily in English, such as *Bhaji on the Beach*, *American Desi*, and *Bend It like Beckham*, depict Desis in the diaspora in ways that also resonate with teen viewers. Such films are often coming-of-age stories that explore complex issues around relationships with parents, friendship, and especially romance in various diasporic locales. Although these films are primarily in English, characters do code-switch between English and other South Asian languages—an aspect that teens immediately recognize and appreciate.

Desi teens idolize Bollywood actors and actresses. For girls, popular Bollywood movie actresses such as Aishwarya Rai, Karishma Kapoor, and Preity Zinta are admired Desi counterparts to American teen idols like Britney Spears and Jennifer Lopez. Having Desi role models, many of whom have dark hair and dark eyes, is important to their self-image. Although many of today's Bollywood actresses are exceedingly thin and fair-skinned with light hair and eyes, they are nonetheless South Asian in their looks, speech, mannerisms, and values. Male actors are similarly valued by Desi boys, who are happy to have action heroes they can call their own. Avinash, a Hindi film fan, relates, "I used to be a Shah Rukh Khan fan, but this new guy Hrithik Roshan is off da' hook. He's built, he can act, *and* he can dance." Other youth idolize Hrithik Roshan for his chiseled good looks, muscular physique, and prowess on the dance floor. From adorning girls' notebooks to bedroom walls to screensavers, Hrithik is ubiquitous. Tara, a Gujarati Hindu girl in Silicon Valley, exclaims that Hrithik Roshan is "the best looking guy ever." As we shop for a poster for her to take to college with her, she explains, "for all these White girls know, I can put up the poster and say he's my boyfriend."

Like stars everywhere, these actors and actresses take on larger-than-life personas. Gossiping about the alleged transgressions of some film stars—which include smoking, drinking, drugs, incarceration, and wearing "hootchie" clothing—occurs alongside testimonials of those who can do no wrong. During a visit to her Silicon Valley home, Umber, a middle-class girl, confides her secret ambition to become a Bollywood star and closes her bedroom door to reveal her not so subtle obsession with Bollywood stars personified in a floor-to-ceiling collage of glossy pictures. Umber has transferred schools several times because of her unfortunate knack for getting in trouble. Her solace, however, is Bollywood, and she loves watching the films and singing songs. She explains, "I cut out all these pictures from magazines. This is the second time I changed it. I took them all down and changed them. I used to be really crazed over it but now I don't have [as much] time, but I still like it. Kajol [a popular young actress] is my favorite because her acting was good and I respected her because she didn't dress like a hooch, you know, like most of them do in those movies." Like Umber, numerous other girls bring *filmi* magazines to school, adorn their notebooks with glossy photos they cut out, and keep up with Bollywood on local access television and online.

In addition to how they look, dress, and act, language use is a factor in determining the popularity of an actor or actress. For example, in a discussion of the film *American Desi*, Greene High School students Pinki and Nidhi debate the authenticity of the female lead based on her linguistic skills. Pinki asserts that "Nina" is a believable character because she seems to have some knowledge of Indian culture but is also savvy about her American life. Nidhi raises a strong critique of the character and argues that although "Nina" claims to know all about Indian culture and teach it to others, "She says one line in Hindi and she can't even speak it right!" Other actors and actresses, despite their light skin, hair, and eyes that skew closer to Caucasian rather than average South Asian features, maintain their credibility by being able to speak Hindi fluently. Such critiques underscore the importance of language use in connecting the actors and actresses to the roles they play on-screen.

Quoting Bollywood

Hindi films provide a rich resource for language practices. Through the circulation of films, languages, and cultural forms, themes are selected and reinserted in other social contexts and offer ideological narratives and communicative resources through which youth express themselves (e.g., by adopting dialogue, songs, dances, or styles to be performed). The musical performance genre indexes a certain type of Desi identity. In Queens, for example, a group of teens wrote their own Hindi love song and added a dancehall interlude. Consistent with common Bollywood themes, it depicted a memory about a love lost, and showed flashbacks about how a couple met and courted but ultimately did not end up together. Following Bollywood stylistic conventions, the reel couple only barely held hands. The song lyrics and the style of singing that the students performed drew upon a popular Hindi genre of duets with alternating male and female parts. The intertextual and productive value of these diasporic media are also seen in multicultural day performances in schools (see Shankar 2004) as well as community dance and music performances, both of which incorporate a wide range of popular styles from Hindi films and local popular music. The following discussion explores Bollywood-based talk that occurs during viewing and during other times and places.

During Viewing

Vocally interacting with a Bollywood film is not solely a teen phenomenon. Ethnographic research on film viewing in Indian theaters reports that audiences cheer, hiss, and speak to characters on screen (Srinivas 1998). Diasporic film viewing proves to be no different, as interaction with the screen is a significant component of group viewings. Whether the viewing is on a VCR or DVD at home, or in a local theater in New York or California, audience members often take vocal liberties that would be frowned upon while viewing Hollywood movies. Such verbal practices occur differently during viewings with peers versus with family, and between boys and girls. Among their peers, kids tend to offer uncensored commentary about who is good looking, make risqué jokes, and sing unabashedly. Such was a case during a 1998 screening of *Dil To Pagal Hai* 'The Heart Is Crazy,' at the Queens youth center. The pirated videotape, which did not have subtitles, was played on a color TV in a small lounge. Most of this co-ed audience had seen it on video at least once before, and a few girls said they had seen it as many as five times. The girls sat near one another at the front, with the boys at a slight distance from them.

The opening credits of the film feature a series of shots of couples sitting on a bench, some embracing or kissing. Although there is much embracing, innuendo, and even wet *sari* dances, kissing on the lips is seldom shown. Picking up on this vaguely risqué theme, several of the boys begin hooting and making catcalls. Aamir, a seventeen-year-old Pakistani American boy, jokes, "This is setting a bad example for kids!" Encouraged by laughter from his peers, he quips, "*Kya, unko sharam nehi athe?*" 'Don't they feel ashamed?' The rest of the film ensues with frequent commentary and jokes from the boys and explosions of laughter among the girls. At key moments, teens recite lines of comedic dialogue synchronously with the characters. During the songs, girls and boys sing along loudly to the corresponding male and female parts. At times, a boy and girl would begin to sing to each other, mimicking a reel romantic duet, but would then burst into laughter and quickly turn away.

When teens watch films with parents and family, they also verbally interact with films, albeit in a more restrained manner. When Tara made plans to see a Bollywood film at a Bay Area theater with her parents, she invited me along. Prior to seeing the newly released film *Refugee*, we had to stop at the Indian store to pick up the film's soundtrack. Tara explains, "I need to hear the songs before the movie, at least to get a preview." After visiting one of several Indo-Pak grocery stores, we sit in the strip mall parking lot and preview a few minutes from each song. Wanting to familiarize herself with all the songs before seeing the film, Tara makes fast work of the CD. Her father, who joins us at the theater, has similarly spent part of his workday downloading and listening to song clips from the film *Refugee* and notes the scenes in which they are to be featured. Tara and her father are not the only ones singing along to this new release, suggesting that other viewers had also previewed the songs or come back for repeat viewings. In contrast with the peer viewing in Queens or to other film viewings with Tara's friends, Tara is far less vocal in this screening with her parents. Here, her participation is limited to humming along to songs and commenting on good-looking actors and outfits.

Such interactions with Bollywood films during viewing indicate a more detailed engagement with words, lyrics, and themes than during viewings of Hollywood movies. The type of talk that occurs during the film—especially reciting dramatic dialogue, enacting comedy routines, and singing along with songs—anticipates the incorporation of such verbal practices in talk outside these viewing contexts.

Beyond Contexts of Film Viewing

Enjoying Bollywood films is a participatory activity dependent upon linguistic skills and contextual knowledge that inform shared viewings. Dramatic dialogue, comedic routines, and romantic lyrics stand apart as their own *filmi* registers outside of viewing contexts. Indeed, the affect, intonation, and stylized speech that make Bollywood distinctive are immediately recognizable as such to the trained ear. The juxtaposition of such stylized speech interspersed with everyday Northern California or New York City teenage English can be especially stark. Stylized speech, as Nicholas Coupland (2001) illustrates in his discussion of dialect stylization in radio talk, can be employed in ways that create and cater to a community of listeners that is trained to recognize certain stylized accents and turns of phrase. Likewise, if executed well, a stylized utterance from a Bollywood register can easily create a desired dramatic effect for a receptive audience.

The following is an excerpt from a taped spontaneous conversation during lunch at Greene High School during spring 2001. It features Simran, a middle-class Sikh Punjabi girl and three boys in her clique—Kapil, KB, and Uday—all of whom are Punjabi speakers. The conversation begins with Simran and Uday discussing a film they each saw on video with their families over the weekend. Kapil and KB join them, and Simran changes the topic to inform them that she is tape-recording their conversation for me.

(1) "Doesn't he remind you of that guy?"[2]

Simran:	Whatever you're talking is getting recorded. Remember what Shalini told us yesterday?
Kapil:	Oooooohhhh! Are you serious?
Simran:	It doesn't matter though, 'cause only she's gonna listen to it.
Kapil:	[directly into the tape recorder microphone] *Neehiii! Main tera koon kilaun* 'Nooooo! I'm going to murder you/drink your blood!' [in a *filmi* villain register].
	[Simran, Uday, and KB burst out laughing].
Uday:	It gonna seem like y'all are goin' crazy, ain't it?
Simran:	[laughing, Simran turns to Uday and remarks about Kapil] Doesn't he remind you of that guy [referring to a character in the film she and Uday were discussing earlier]?

In the excerpt above, Kapil employs a *filmi* register that is immediately recognizable to his friends. He creates a comedic moment from being asked to tolerate the tape recorder and masterfully reproduces the affect of an enraged Bollywood psychopath. Rather than using his own voice, he creates a deep, gravelly, drawling utterance associated with a Bollywood villain. Moreover, this performance skillfully conveys Kapil's irritation about the tape recorder and possible homicidal feelings toward the anthropologist that may have been inappropriate to declare directly. Moving from reel to real, Kapil uses this register to create a balance of wit, humor, and social critique.

Reel flirting is another type of dialogue used in real co-ed interactions. For example, conversational code-switching can reveal gender dynamics that resonate with romantic stances taken in film. When boys flirt with girls using subtly suggestive phrases of Punjabi or Hindi by drawing on *filmi* dialogues, girls can playfully yet demurely refuse to engage in such banter and answer back in English. Girls who reply in English in this way are replicating a pattern of linguistic interaction common to Bollywood films and are indexing themselves as being correct, polite, and pure, partly as a put-down to the rowdy, improper male who code-switches. Yet these same girls comfortably code-switch when gossiping among themselves or speaking with relatives, demonstrating that youth are strategic in their code choices.

Especially in the Desi context, where Desi parents place numerous social and parental restrictions on co-ed interaction and dating (Maira 2002), teens use prescripted dialogues of flirting in their own conversations. Bollywood films thus serve as a narrative and linguistic resource through which youth imagine the trajectory of romantic events in their own lives. They see ways in which characters balance the difficult process of exploring flirting, dating, and romance, but ultimately maintain familial and gendered codes of propriety. Teens idolize onscreen couples who are able to overcome religious or ethnic differences, have a "love marriage" rather than an arranged one, and otherwise manage to please their families and act within the social boundaries of their communities without sacrificing true romance.

Unlike their counterparts in American media, who are generally free to engage in social and physical relations with whomever they choose, most Desi teens are not only forbidden to date at all but also to publicly socialize with the opposite sex. Further, the concept of arranged marriage, or its more modern incarnation of being introduced to and being expected to marry someone of one's own religious, linguistic, and caste background is still quite commonplace. At the youth center, Kabeer, a Pakistani Muslim boy, and Sadhna, a Gujarati Hindu girl, have found a way to interact while following the social constraints they are expected to follow. Although they are friends and claim that they are not romantically interested in each other, Sadhna and Kabeer deploy *filmi* flirting sequences in their interaction with each other. In one such instance, Kabeer leans into Sadhna and smoothly asks, "*Kya, maine Robbie ka party main dekhi* [Haven't I seen you before, at Robbie's party?]" "*Main? Really?* [Me? Really?]" Sadhna giggles back, immediately recognizing Kabeer's question as a pick-up line that Raj, the lead character in the popular film *Diliwale Dulhuniya Le Jayenge*, played by Desi heartthrob Shah Rukh Kahn, uses on several swooning girls until he unexpectedly falls for the one who rebuffs his advances. Whether teens follow these rules or quietly break them, there is scant room for discussion of such issues except among trusted friends. Reel couples in Bollywood movies, then, can fill in where real life falls short.

Hindi films offer narrative frameworks and dialogues that can be especially instrumental to teens in similar situations. During the screening of *Dil To Pagal Hai* at the youth center, Aamir tells me his story of unrequited love about an hour into the on-screen love story. He ponders a main premise of the film—that God creates people in pairs and that they find each other—and raises this idea during a scene in which the heroine, "Pooja," talks to her friend who is preparing to have an arranged marriage. Pooja's friend explains to her that it is the duty of Indian women to marry someone their family deems suitable and that *"Pyaar hota hai* [love just happens]" along the way. *"Pyaar hota hai?"* Aamir asks frustratedly. Verbalizing connections between film dialogue and events with his own life, Aamir explains that he used to believe in arranged marriage, until he fell in love. Quoting the film's character Raj (played by Shah Rukh Kahn), he reveals, "I used to be like Shah Rukh, asking *'Mohabbat kya hai?'* 'What is love?' and not believing in it, until I met her. Now I don't think about things the same." During a subsequent scene, featuring an old childhood friend of Pooja's who loves her romantically but whom she only loves platonically, Aamir sighs loudly, signaling that his life once again mirrors that of the reel characters. The particulars of the film's story line—arranged marriage versus love marriage, *pyaar* 'love in a general sense' versus *mohabbat* 'love for a beloved,' and obligation to family—provide a culturally meaningful scheme through which Aamir can make sense of his own plight of familial restrictions and unrequited love. Significant too is the way in which Aamir employs lines of dialogue from the movie into his own speech during the viewing and draws upon characters and quotes in his own narration of self.

Referencing Bollywood and Beyond

The above discussions explore specific references to Bollywood dialogue, register, and quotes. Other language practices, however, also express various types of connectedness and membership. Using Indian-accented English is a popular linguistic choice for nearly all teens, but especially for upper-middle-class teens in Silicon Valley, who occasionally code-mix but rarely code-switch. More often, they use Indian-accented English and words or ways of speaking exclusive to their social group. For many of these teens, referring to language and speaking in Indian-accented English can signify group membership. Ben Rampton (1995) discusses how youth of different ethnicities in the United Kingdom use language to "cross" into groups into which they seek membership. While youth in my study use Indian-accented English within their groups, doing so enables them to amuse one another. They also do so in order to assert differences from their parents, whose accents they are often mimicking.

Accents, as well as other types of references, can only accomplish their intended effect (most often humor and in-group connectedness) if others are able to detect the intended indexical references. Participants must not only have particular types of cultural knowledge, but a well-trained ear to recognize and associate words, phrases, and sounds with their film references. Roland Barthes (1972) and other semioticians have noted that the "connotative" or "second-order value" of an utterance enables a range of interpretations. Such utterances can be "polysemic" or capable of numerous context-sensitive meanings. Even seemingly insignificant utterances can actually be imbued with a wide range of meanings to listeners. Such is the case with the example below, where there is more to a cough than what initially appears.

Indexical References

Accents, words, and even sounds can have indexical value in these closely knit Desi social circles. As the following excerpt illustrates, a seemingly innocent cough, mimicked in the style of actress Madhuri Dixit's coy, flirtatious throat clearing in the immensely popular film *Hum Apke Hain Kaun!* 'Who Am I to You!' leads to rounds of laughter. Pinki taped the recording during a twenty-minute mid-morning break at Greene High School. In the section featured below, she and her four friends, Janvi, Raminder, Renu, and Harbans, transition from discussing a tongue-twisting acronym that one of them invented while studying for a test. Taking turns to see who can recite it the fastest and bursting into laughter each time, they eventually tire of that topic. The transcript begins with Harbans's attempt to move the group on to a new topic.

(2) 'Ahmmm-ahmmm'

Harbans:	Aaaanyway
Janvi:	Aaaannnyywaaayss. Ahm- ahmmmm [throat clearing].
Raminder:	They're like…
Janvi:	Allll rightyyy.
Raminder:	I was teasing my mom yesterday
Janvi:	/ ahmmm-ahmmm. [two distinct coughs rather than one long one]
Renu:	[giggles] ahmmm-ahmmm
Pinki:	/ ahmmm-ahmmm
Janvi:	What is this movie?
Pinki:	ahmmm-ahmmm
Raminder:	It's from *Hum Apke Hain Kaun!* uhooo-uhoo [exactly like the movie].
Pinki:	uhooo-uhoo [in a higher pitch]
Renu:	/ shut up- shut-up! [giggles]
Raminder:	No, she goes: uhooo-uhoo [like the movie].

The conversation continues for several more rounds of coughing and giggling and finally comes to an abrupt halt when Janvi shrieks, "Eeww, Raminder ate an unwrapped piece of gum from her backpack!" and everyone winces in disgust. In the portion of the exchange excerpted above, the girls quickly pick up on an everyday cough and take it as a distinctive verbal cue from a Bollywood film. The reel quote, "uhoo-uhoo" is less of an actual cough and more of a demure, flirtatious noise that Bollywood superstar actress of the 1990s Madhuri Dixit's character makes when interacting with actor Salman Khan's character, her love interest in the film. During their initial humorous, coincidental meeting, she deploys this coy, demure cough in an attempt to mask that she is laughing at him. This distinctive, feminine cough enables the actress to hide her mouth, giggle, and bat her eyelids—all things Madhuri Dixit does especially well. So well, in fact, that the cough soon becomes a hallmark of their romantic interaction and Salman Khan begins to echo the "uhoo-uhoo" cough as a flirtatious response.

The utterance takes on a life of its own that extends far beyond its reel presence. In the above excerpt, an actual, everyday throat clearing and cough by Janvi is recontextualized as a movie quote by the subsequent moves of Raminder, Renu, and Pinki. Only Raminder and Pinki can accurately identify the film and accurately replicate the sound, but their friends know a reference is being made. The indexical value of this utterance enables a particularly humorous situation for those who can identify the cough as a film quote. Moreover, it allows girls who are less comfortable quoting dialogue to participate in the banter, thereby creating a shared source of amusement. This exchange underscores the pervasiveness of quoting Bollywood as a cultural and linguistic practice among these Desi teens.

Bivalent Homophonic Puns

Another teen language practice that relies on insider knowledge is the use of "bivalent homophonic puns."[3] Kathryn Woolard (1998) examines the concept of "bivalency," in which words have meaning in two distinct languages. I use this term in conjunction with homophones—words that are phonetically similar in both languages (or Indian accents of both languages). While such wordplay has been examined in second-language learning (Tarone et al. 1994), I look at it here in relation to everyday talk as well as media-specific language practices. In one instance, Sheetal, a seventeen-year-old Gujarati Hindu girl in Silicon Valley, tells her friends Nandini, Meena, and me about a humorous incident. The joke is a play on the homophones "guy" (the English word for man) and "*gai*" (the Hindi word for cow). Barely able to contain her laughter, Sheetal giggles about how her uncle in Central California had seen a dead cow in his neighbor's backyard and calls his neighbor. In a thick Indian accent, she mimics, "There is a dead *gai* in your backyard!" She then inserts in her regular voice, "Because, you know, the Indian word for cow is *gai*," and switches back into the accent, "There is a dead *gai* in your backyard!" She completes the anecdote by explaining that when her uncle's neighbor starts to become hysterical, he realizes his error and says, "I mean cow! There is a dead cow in your backyard." In Sheetal's telling of the joke, her friends begin laughing as soon as she finishes mimicking her uncle's first line, making her next statement in which she explains the meaning of *gai* superfluous. The joke is effective, then, because her friends immediately recognize the comic value in the bivalent homophonic pun *gai* [guy].

In a media-based instance of this practice from a diasporic film, Harsimran, a sophomore at Greene High School, shares one of his favorite scenes from the film *American Desi* with his friends Uday and Ranvir at lunch. In this scene, a Punjabi man wearing a turban is dancing at a party with a multiracial population. As he raises his arms and shakes his shoulders, he jovially cries out "*Ho! Ho!*" a common Punjabi utterance when dancing. Harsimran imitates the dance while he impersonates the various voices for his friends: "They're all like, '*Ho! Ho!*' [while snapping fingers, dancing with *bhangra* hand gestures]. 'Ho?' [in African American English] 'Who you callin' a fuckin' ho?' Some black lady goes, 'Who you fuckin' callin' ho?'"

Harsimran's reenactment of this movie scene, like Sheetal's telling of the "dead *gai*" joke, is a verbal performance that demands particular kinds of linguistic knowledge, specifically the fact that the Punjabi word *ho* is a homophone with the American slang term "ho," a shortened version of "whore" popularized by African American hip-hop artists. The pun is amusing to Uday, Ranvir, and Harsimran because an African American woman misrecognizes the general shouting of *ho!* to be an insult directed at her. As these two examples indicate, bivalent homophones truly become puns during these contexts of retelling. Their double entendres are only elucidated outside the original context of occurrence. Desi teens engaging in such linguistic practices must possess the bilingual competence to appreciate the pun, making it a significant language practice among these Desi teens.

Conclusion

Bollywood film creates common ground among youth of disparate religious, national, and linguistic communities. Bollywood language practices of quoting dialogue, using *filmi* registers for humor and flirting, and engaging with songs and lyrics create a media-based community. Recent Bollywood films that showcase the lives of the South Asian diaspora portray youth subjectivity to which Desi teens in Queens and Silicon Valley can relate. Bollywood connects teens from different parts of the diaspora and of different linguistic backgrounds by creating shared frames of reference in conversation. Teens from both Silicon Valley and Queens incorporate aspects of Bollywood into their everyday lives and talk, displaying and referencing their shared specialized and insider knowledge. As current Bollywood films increasingly feature diasporic South Asian communities, reel life promises to maintain a steady place in the real linguistic and social practices of Desi teens.

Funding for research and write-up were generously provided by the Social Science Research Council International Migration Program, The Spencer Foundation, and the New York University June E. Esserman Fellowship. Additional support was provided by Binghamton University. I am deeply grateful to Bambi Schieffelin, Faye Ginsburg, Fred Myers, Norma Mendoza-Denton, Tejaswini Ganti, and Jillian Cavanaugh for their insights and suggestions, and to Angela Reyes and Adrienne Lo for their editorial assistance.

NOTES

1. *Desi* is a Hindi word that is used by South Asians living outside the subcontinent to refer to one another.

2. Some lines of the transcript begin with a slash ("/"), which indicates an overlap with the line of speech preceding it. Elongated sounds are indicated by repeated vowels or consonants. Contextual notes about speakers and their utterances are indicated with "[ ]."

3. I am grateful to Norma Mendoza-Denton and Bambi B. Schieffelin for suggesting this term during a conversation in New York, NY, in July 2003.

REFERENCES

Abu-Lughod, Lila. 1995. The objects of soap opera: Egyptian television and the cultural politics of modernity. In *Worlds apart: Modernity through the prism of the local*, ed. Daniel Miller, 190–210. London: Routledge.

Anderson, Benedict. 1991. *Imagined communities*. London: Verso.

Appadurai, Arjun. 1996. *Modernity at large: Cultural dimensions of globalization*. Minneapolis: University of Minnesota Press.

Auer, Peter 1998. *Code-switching in conversation*. London: Routledge.

Back, Les. 1996. *New ethnicities and urban culture*. New York: St. Martin's Press.

Bakhtin, Mikhail. 1981. *The dialogic imagination: Four essays*. Austin: University of Texas Press.

Barthes, Roland. 1972. *Mythologies*. New York: Noonday Press.

Baumann, Gerd. 1996. *Contesting culture: Discourses of identity in multi-ethnic London*. London: Cambridge University Press.

Bauman, Richard, and Charles Briggs. 1992. Genre, intertextuality, and social power. *Journal of Linguistic Anthropology* 2:131–172.

Bourdieu, Pierre. 1991. *Language and symbolic power*. Cambridge, Mass.: Harvard University Press.

Coupland, Nicholas. 2001. Dialect stylization in radio talk. *Language in Society* 30: 345–375.

Eckert, Penelope. 1989. *Jocks and burnouts: Social categories and identity in high school*. New York: Teachers College Press.

Gal, Susan. 1987. Code-switching and consciousness in the European periphery. *American Ethnologist* 14:637–653.

Ganti, Tejaswini. 2002. "And yet my heart is still Indian": The Bombay film industry and the (H)Indianization of Hollywood. In *Media worlds: Anthropology on new terrain*, ed. Faye Ginsburg, Lila Abu-Lughod, and Brian Larkin, 281–300. Berkeley: University of California Press.

———. 2004. *Bollywood: A guidebook to popular Hindi cinema*. New York: Routledge.

Gillespie, Marie. 1995. *Television, ethnicity and cultural change*. London: Routledge.

Ginsburg, Faye, Lila Abu-Lughod, and Brian Larkin, ed. 2002. *Media worlds: Anthropology on new terrain*. Berkeley: University of California Press.

Hall, Kathleen. 2002. *Lives in translation: Sikh youth as British citizens*. Philadelphia: University of Pennsylvania Press.

Heller, Monica. 1999. *Linguistic minorities and modernity: A sociolinguistic ethnography*. New York: Addison Wesley.

Hill, Jane. 1995. The voices of Don Gabriel: Responsibility and self in a modern Mexicano narrative. In *Dialogic emergence of culture*, ed. Dennis Tedlock and Bruce Mannheim, 97–147. Urbana and Chicago: University of Illinois Press.

Hill, Jane, and Judith Irvine, ed. 1992. *Responsibility and evidence in oral discourse*. Cambridge: Cambridge University Press.

Joshi, Lalit. 2002. *Bollywood: Popular Indian cinema*. Delhi: Dakini Books.

Kaur, Raminder and Ajay Sinha, eds. *Bollyworld: Popular Indian Cinema through a Transnational Lens*. London: Sage Publications.

Keane, Webb. 1999. Voice. *Journal of Linguistic Anthropology* 9:271–273.

Kolar-Panov, Donna. 1996. Video and the diasporic imagination of selfhood: A case study of the Croatians in Australia. *Cultural Studies* 10:288–314.

Larkin, Brian. 1997. Indian films, Nigerian lovers: Media and the creation of parallel modernities. *Africa* 67:406–440.

Liechty, Mark. 1995. Media, markets and modernization: Youth identities and the experience of modernity in Katmandu, Nepal. In *Youth cultures: A cross-cultural perspective*, ed. Vered Amit-Talai and Helena Wulff, 166–201. London: Routledge.

———. 2002. *Suitably modern: Making middle-class culture in a new consumer society.* Princeton, N.J.: Princeton University Press.

Maira, Sunaina. 2002. *Desis in the house: Indian American youth culture in New York City.* Philadelphia: Temple University Press.

Mendoza-Denton, Norma. 1996. "Muy macha": Gender and ideology in gang-girls' discourse about makeup. *Ethnos* 61:47–63.

Milroy, Lesley, and Pieter Muysken, ed. 1995. *One speaker, two languages: Cross-disciplinary perspectives on code-switching.* Cambridge: Cambridge University Press.

Naficy, Hamid. 1993. *The making of exile cultures: Iranian television in Los Angeles.* Minneapolis: University of Minnesota Press.

Prasad, Madhav. 2001. *Ideology of the Hindi film: A historical construction.* Delhi: Oxford University Press.

Rampton, Ben. 1995. *Crossing: Language and ethnicity among adolescents.* New York: Longman.

Ray, Manas. 2000. Bollywood down under. In *Floating lives: The media and Asian diasporas*, ed. Stuart Cunningham and John Sinclair, 136–184. Brisbane: University of Queensland Press.

Romaine, Suzanne. 1995. *Bilingualism.* New York: Blackwell.

Shankar, Shalini. 2004. "FOBby or tight?: 'Multicultural Day' and other struggles at two Silicon Valley high schools. In *Local actions: Cultural activism, power and public life*, ed. Melissa Checker and Maggie Fishman, 184–207. New York: Columbia University Press.

———. 2008. *Desi Land: Teen Culture, Class, and Success in Silicon Valley.* Durham: Duke University Press.

Spitulnik, Deborah. 1996. The social circulation of media discourse and the mediation of communities. *Journal of Linguistic Anthropology* 6:161–187.

Srinivas, Lakshmi. 1998. Active viewing: An ethnography of the Indian film audience. *Visual Anthropology* 11:323–353.

Tarone, Elaine, Susan Gass, and Andrew Cohen, ed. 1994. *Research methodology in second-language acquisition.* Mahwah, N.J.: Lawrence Erlbaum.

Woolard, Kathryn. 1998. Simultaneity and bivalency as strategies in bilingualism. *Journal of Linguistic Anthropology* 8:3–29.

Zentella, Ana Celia. 1997. *Growing up bilingual.* Malden, Mass.: Blackwell.

19

Perspective and the Politics of Representation

A Commentary

Susan Gal

The preceding chapters provide an embarrassment of riches for the commentator. The cases are described with a wealth of ethnographic and textual detail. The analyses rightly attend to phenomena at quite different scales: We learn about linguistic utterances and their immediate co-texts of talk, but there is also evidence about broader and broader contexts. The chapters discuss the speech events in which talk occurs, the genres represented, the responses of listeners, the institutional sites at which the talk occurred, the ethnic categories invoked and the discursive field of other social categories within which they gain their meanings, as well as the political economic positions of the speakers. "Asian American" is never analyzed in isolation from contrasting identity labels to which it is culturally opposed. Indeed, each of these three chapters succeeds in describing a complex, regionally and institutionally specific configuration of ethnic, gender, and occupational categories. The "relationality" and localism of ethnic categories is admirably demonstrated.

Furthermore, Elaine W. Chun, Roderick N. Labrador, and Shalini Shankar nicely complicate the usual sociolinguistic paradigm that assumes linguistic forms to be indexical of speakers' identities. Indexicality is fundamental, to be sure. But in the cases presented here, there is no simple relationship between the demographic category to which speakers might be taken to belong (e.g., in a census) and the forms of speech they deploy. Rather, cultural categories of identity and the linguistic forms that index them are seen to be performed, enacted, and evoked, sometimes by speakers who claim them as their "own" and sometimes by others. Mikhail Bakhtin called these the "stylizations" or "typifications" through which speakers regularly and necessarily "ventriloquate" their own social positions and those of others.

Moreover, linguistic forms are differentially keyed or voiced as serious or ironic, parodic, or playful. The linguistic skills required vary a great deal. The authors imply that, depending on the linguistic ideologies in play, a single phonological feature can function to evoke the ethnolinguistic stereotype, or the evocation may require a combination of cues, or even some ability to reproduce and understand whole interactional scenes. Chun, Labrador, and Shankar also take up the possible social consequences of enacting or voicing ethnolinguistic stereotypes in particular ways. This is a more complex notion of "performativity." It is not the same as simply performing an identity, but rather ritually *creates*—in somewhat the same way as the making of a promise does—some new social reality. So, one might ask, when does the use of stereotyped linguistic forms create solidarity? When does it homogenize or denigrate its objects? How might it hide racist attitudes beneath claims of multiculturalism?

Rather than further reiterating the many fine arguments made by the chapters, I would like to use my role as commentator to extend the conversation by considering briefly some of the analytical questions that emerge when the three chapters are read against one another. Let me start with *the politics of representation*, and then discuss mass-mediated *perspectives*.

The chapters propose and discuss labels such as "Mock Asian," "Mock Filipino," and "South Asian American," as well as terms such as "Korean," "Filipino," "Desi," "Indian," "Tamil," and "Local." First, some of these evoke connections to linguistic labels, while others, such as "Desi" and "Local," do not. It would be interesting to know how this is significant from a sociolinguistic perspective. Are there language ideologies at stake here, ones that sometimes focus speakers' attention on linguistic provenance and sometimes erase such linkages? Second, as Chun, Labrador, and Shankar carefully note, some of the labels are used by the speakers described, while others are proposed by the ethnographers for analytical purposes. What are the implications of the "mock" label for analytical purposes? And are they only analytical? Jane Hill's stimulating coinage of "Mock Spanish" remains important and challenging, but also perhaps specific to the position of Spanish and Spanish speakers in the United States. It might be equally useful to examine the very notion and nature of linguistic stereotyping itself—the process that produces "Mock Spanish" among other possible forms—rather than simply extending the term to all practices that typify and evoke social groups through linguistic means. Since stereotypes of groups are always part of a structure of oppositional images within some political context, one would expect linguistic typifications to build on contrasting images and thus to differ in their effects.

As the editors of this book have pointed out, to publish a set of essays on "Asian American" speech is itself a political act aimed at encouraging research about social groups apparently neglected. The terms to be used for analyzing them are therefore not without significance. The labels themselves—whether analytic or "folk"— deserve more serious consideration as part of the agenda of this book, namely the "discursive construction" of "Asian Pacific American identities." The questions to raise include: Who uses the notion of "Asian Pacific American"? How was it created? Is this in part a census or governmental category to which speakers orient? Do some reject it? What are the temporal and spatial erasures and elisions that are the concomitant to the creation of any such category? As in the earlier case of "Italian American" and other white ethnic labels, there are numerous interesting ironies. The country of "Italy" did not exist when many of those retrospectively labeled Italian American first arrived in the United States. Furthermore, no unified Italian identity was available even in Italy until long after the Italian state was unified. Thus the creation of an Italian American identity category was a political process that took place in the United States. The category itself took a while to coalesce, relying not only on mass media but also on the work of advocacy organizations. It was a politics of representation, in keeping with the logic of the civil rights movement of the 1950s and 1960s, and arguably a white response to it. The terms "Latino" or "Hispanic" have been even more contentious. And, as Labrador rightly points out, the categories he discusses are regionally specific.

Thus, one would like to know at what scale of politics—neighborhood, city, regional, national—are any of these labels recruited for interactional or inscriptional use? What are the interactional effects of using one out of the several categories in circulation in a social group? For instance, what are these effects in the case of Shankar's study—Desi versus South Asian American versus Indian versus Tamil. Some categories are strategically or perhaps inadvertently erased, as others come to political prominence. As Shankar notes in passing, these labels are neither transparent nor strictly referential nor stable. Rather, they are likely to be performatives in the following second-order sense: the very use of them in particular contexts marks the user as a certain kind of person within the social group (e.g., pretentious or social climber, politically aware or conservative), just as the parodic use of phonological stereotypes (whether understood as "self" or "other") identifies the speaker in a second-order way as a certain kind of person.

This brings me to a second theme running through these three chapters: They all analyze, in different ways, the use of linguistic stereotypes in mass media and therefore invite some thoughts on questions of perspective. As Chun and Labrador note, and Shankar's chapter demonstrates, in mass mediated forms, it is hard to know who the audiences are, and the uptake by audiences can be quite varied and locally specific. Furthermore, performances that are taped, filmed, or performed in night clubs are doubtless designed for widespread circulation. The constructions of "publics" through the very creation of such tapes and their purchase and use are part of the politics of representation I have just discussed. Mass mediated artifacts can be the means for creating solidarity, either through imitation of forms (as in Desi use of Bollywood films) or through protective alliance (as in the response to Abercrombie & Fitch T-shirts). But analysis of the tapes in itself requires careful attention to perspectives made possible and indeed invited by the process of circulation.

Humor is a fertile site for examining questions of perspective. Theorists as diverse as Charles Peirce, Georg Simmel, Alfred Schutz, and George Herbert Mead long ago noted that social interaction would be impossible without typifications or token-level constructs. Thus, no single label of "racist" versus "subversive" will do for the humor analyzed in these chapters, as the authors are well aware. It is the way such judgments are formed that we should be analyzing, asking how they are arrived at through typifications and keyings as heard by analysts and by various portions and settings among the populations we are analyzing; hence, the relevance of understanding ethnic humor in the United States in terms of a history of in-group/out-group dynamics. Comics who play on ethnic stereotypes often succeed by offering "mainstreamers" or outsiders an insider's glimpse of an ethnic group. The "inside glimpse," no matter how stigmatizing, can mark the movement of the typified category to mainstream status, their presence now publicly speakable. This is often accompanied by the emergence of upwardly mobile populations who gain a measure of authenticity by a distanced association with the stigmatized ethnic category. Think: How charming was the grandmother who sounded like that; but we do not. Comics can succeed not only by subverting mainstream stereotypes (as Chun rightly suggests) but also by offering self-stereotypes to the in-group, allowing a stance for those who identify with the group but can also distance themselves by dint of mobility, education, or simply age. Ethnicity in the United States is often a matter of commodification: the claim to "ownership" of voices, accents, and images that, because of social distance, provide authenticity but not stigma. One can only laud the authors of these chapters for taking up, with such detail and subtlety, these complex and historically embedded processes of signification.

V

Educational Institutions
and Language Acquisition

20

Trading Tongues

Loss of Heritage Languages in the United States

Leanne Hinton

There seems to be a belief in the United States, expressed often by politicians and the man in the street alike, that present-day immigrant families "refuse to learn English." People cite experiences with taxi drivers who have a hard time communicating in English, or get upset at restaurants upon hearing people at another table talking in some other language. They fear that English, and English hegemony, is somehow being endangered.

However, nothing could be further from the truth. According to the 1990 U.S. Census, some 97 percent of the American population knows English "very well" or "well." And as we will see here, young immigrants or children born to immigrants not only learn English well, but often lose their heritage language in the bargain. While there was a time when immigrant families could expect language shift in three generations (first generation monolingual in the heritage language, second generation bilingual, third generation monolingual in English), nowadays there is a much speeded-up shift to English, so fast that children lose the ability to communicate effectively with their own parents.

This chapter is based on a set of about 250 "linguistic autobiographies" I have collected from Asian American college students, done over the last several years in a class at the University of California at Berkeley. The heart of this chapter is the quotes from the autobiographies themselves. In this self-reporting mode, we see the human side of language shift, rather than the political. We will see the hopes parents have for their children to grow up bilingual, and the family difficulties that develop as children instead forget or reject their heritage language as they learn English. We will see also the remorse felt by the students later on over the loss of their heritage language, and their efforts to reclaim it as they get older.

Parental Goals

Immigrant parents have relatives, friends, a lifetime of associations and customs in their home country, and perhaps generations of family history there. They may even intend to return someday. Often, the families see their arrival in the United States not as an abandonment of their old country but rather as a process of making a bridge between the two countries. The language of their country may be the language the family has spoken since time immemorial. Typically, the parents want their children to adapt to the United States, but at the same time retain the knowledge and values of the old country as well:

> Our family was the first one [among our kin] to leave the mainland of South Korea. The day we left for United States, everybody was pretty emotional at the airport, but I remember one single thing my aunt shouted down the airport corridor, "[Korean letters]!" It meant, "Don't forget Korean!" (K-9)[1]

Learning English

The most frequent experience of the students has been that they knew little or no English when they started school in the United States.

> At the age of ten, my family on my mother's side immigrated to America and this is when I learned my second language. Going to school made me feel deaf, mute, and blind. I could understand nothing that was going on around me. (C-6)

> Although I did know some useful phrases, such as, "Could you prease point to the bathroom?" and "Sorry, I don't speake any Engrish," besides those handy phrases, I survived the first few months by utilizing the art of hand gestures and various body language. (K-9)

> I was not able to communicate well at first. Smiling was the best language for me to show other Americans. Whenever I didn't understand, I smiled. I felt stupid, but I didn't look bad. (K-18)

Language Shock

The students entering school without knowing English often undergo shock and depression.

> I started as an eighth grader in a junior high school and soon my burning desire and hope of a brilliant novel life [in America] began to fade away. I faced an unexpected obstacle of miscommunication between my fellow students and teachers. Back in Korea, I and my friends thought that after living in the U.S. for only [a few] months, you would be perfectly fluent in English. ... But soon I found out that several years

of studying English is needed to speak it fluently. Unprepared to meet the dilemma, I was quite depressed and in a condition of despair for the beginning year. ... I used to be very active and popular in my school in Korea and here I was nothing. (K-6)

I got my very first impression of the American culture and language at third grade. I went to an elementary school where there were virtually no Asians and predominately whites. At first, I was excited to see kids with blond hair and pale-colored skin like those people in the movies. However, my excitement didn't last long as I began to realize that there was no way I could communicate with them because I spoke no English at all. I began to dread going to school the few months in America. I was so miserable because all the kids looked at me as if I was a monkey in the zoo. I didn't have any friends at all because nobody spoke Chinese. How I longed to go back to Taiwan and to see familiar faces and to hear my native language being spoken. I never expected so much difficulties in assimilating into a brand new culture with a brand new language. (C-64)

English as a Second Language

Virtually no one who wrote these autobiographies had ever been in a bilingual education program, showing that despite all the controversy about bilingual education in the United States, true bilingual education programs are a rare breed, at least for Asian Americans. For some children, however, ESL (English as a Second Language) classes were available in school.

Thirteen years ago, my family and I escaped from communist Vietnam and arrived at Michigan, USA. At that moment, we found ourselves lost in a new environment where no one spoke Chinese, the only language that we knew. It was a tremendously hard task to communicate with anyone. Fortunately, our church sponsor felt it necessary for my sister, brother, and I to be enrolled in school to learn English, the impossible foreign language then. The administrators gave me a program, English As A Second Language, to aid me in learning English. I was gradually acquainted with this peculiar language, and within one year, my attendance at school allowed me to communicate in English a little. (C-8)

The general impression one gets from the autobiographies is that there is a hodgepodge of approaches to teaching English. Many schools were inadequately prepared for the students who needed to learn English, and some bizarre solutions were offered at times:

When I started kindergarten, I did not know how to speak the English language. I didn't even know my own name in English. (Pretty sad, huh?). ... The only [classes] offered to non-English speakers were ESL for Spanish speakers and Sign Language for the deaf. Since I couldn't be put in the ESL classes, I was taught sign language. That was the only way I knew how to communicate with all the white people who talked so differently than myself. Gradually I began to learn English from my classmates. (K-39)

Television

There are several other sources from which children learn English as well. Chief among these are television and friends. On television:

> For a couple of months [as a newcomer to the United States who spoke no English] I continued my cartoon ritual. Cartoons served as my foothold into English, and I understood more and more as the weeks passed. For a brief, interesting while my vocabulary consisted of words and phrases like "x-ray vision," "transformation," and "radio controlled drones." American television helped me learn English, but more importantly it eased the shock of transition as I struggled to bring American culture into harmony with my Chinese identity. (C-15)

Friends

Friends may play the biggest role of all in helping children learn English.

> One day I found my first true friend in the States. His name was Jason and he was Hispanic. He liked me for who I was, not where I came from. He was not only my best friend but also my teacher. He always invited me to his house and taught me English. I guess if it wasn't for him, I would have really had a hard time adapting to the new language. (K-2)

> When I was in junior high in the United States [having arrived at age fourteen], I hardly had any Korean friends. I had a couple of American friends who I played with all the time. One of them was a deaf person. I learned some of the basic words in sign language, but most of the time I wrote him notes to communicate. Not having Korean friends helped me a lot to learn English fast. I was out of ESL by the end of 8th grade. (K-19)

In the zeal of the incoming children to learn English, sometimes mistakes were made:

> I can still recall that during the first few weeks in my new school, I befriended a group of Vietnamese kids. Because I did not understand what they were saying, and that they looked Asian, I mistakenly assumed that they were ABC's (American-Born-Chinese) who couldn't speak any Chinese. So, in my ignorance, I started to learn from them what I thought was English. (I did wonder why the "English" I was picking up from them sounded different from the one I was simultaneously learning in the classroom.) Not until later on in the semester, when I met a fellow Taiwanese immigrant, did he point out to me that my group of friends were speaking Vietnamese instead of English! (C-43)

Family Involvement in the Child's Learning of English

The family helps the children fight their battle toward English fluency. Siblings play an especially important role in English acquisition.

> I have two older sisters who started school before me, and my oldest sister still has memories of first starting school and not knowing the language. By the time I started

school, it is possible that I had already learned to speak English from my sisters who had learned it at school, because I can't particularly remember being teased for not speaking English when I started preschool. ... Therefore, I am certain that I picked up English before I started formal schooling thanks to the precedent of my two older sisters. (K-26)

... during my early years in L.A., my parents encouraged the use of English at home, both to help me, and to help themselves. Actually, my father didn't need much assistance—he was an English major in college, who actually considered teaching it in Korea. He was, and still is, a nearly perfect bilingual. My mother, on the other hand, was a completely different story. Being an extremely intelligent and proud woman, she didn't like the idea of her being "ignorant" in English. Thus, she watched cartoons and PBS shows like "Sesame Street" and "The Electric Company" with me. We were essentially learning English together. By the second grade, my English skills were proficient enough to enable me to skip the third grade. My parents had a lot to do with it. Even my mother's faculty in English had grown by leaps and bounds. She served at my elementary school as a teacher's aide, for my class in fact. So, she and I would go to school together and spend the whole day in each other's company. Our entire family was slowly, but surely, becoming a bilingual team. (K-23, arrived age six)

Language Rejection

The most important factor in heritage language loss is language rejection by the children themselves. The children are subjected to tough assimilative pressures at school, mainly from their classmates. They are made to feel "different" and "not normal," and their language or their accent is ridiculed. The children begin to develop a strong sense of shame about their language and their heritage culture, and accordingly make every attempt to suppress it.

"Gook."—"Chink."—"Flat-nosed Oriental."—"How do you blindfold a Chinese person?" "You use dental floss."—"Ha, ha, ha..." (Back in the 80s, every Asian was believed to be Chinese.) Taunting and ridiculing, the harsh voices of my worst memories belonged to small elementary children who found diversity just as unfavorable as I did....My sisters and I spent two years attending [school name] that was mainly dominated by Anglo-American students. Our ears burned daily from their words of malicious content, but somehow, this stirred up our motivation to grasp the English language even faster. (K-28)

Peer pressure is the main reason for this language rejection. Children can be heartless teases, and most immigrant children have tales of the cruelty that was aimed at them for being "different." Just a small sample: It was two heartless comments, from a group of small boys in my "white" neighborhood for me to want to deny my language let alone my culture, as well. How was I to react to a racist comment of "Ching chong chooey go back home to where you belong. You can't even speak English right." Sixteen small words which possessed so much strength and contained so much power caused a small, naive child to want to lose her heritage—to lose what made her. (C-2)

It was the Korean language, and "Koreanness" in general, as the ugly monster that kept me from being "normal," isolated me from my peers, and ate away every opportunity to "belong" with people my age. ... I learned to hate hanging out with my family because they reminded me that I wasn't "American." I had learned to hate being a "foreigner" and I saw no reason to speak Korean except to keep my parents content enough to leave me relatively alone. (K-27)

One thing I remember experiencing was that I was always picked on because I couldn't speak English well, but then, I used to let my fists do all the talking. Many of my childhood acts of violence were results of linguistic harassments. (K-9)

My painful road to achieving fluency in English took a few years, during which I sometimes felt alienated from the society around me. I discovered the disrespect, that antipathy, and the hatred that could be directed on a non-English speaking and non-white immigrant. It was then, after countless mockeries from American kids in school and other uncomforting episodes that I became convinced that America, despite the Statue of Liberty, the Constitution's proclamation for equality of all men, and its advertising as a melting pot and a land of freedom and opportunity, was a racist and xenophobic nation. (C-43)

First-Language Attrition

While some students, especially those who came as teenagers, still struggle to perfect their English even at college, most of their worst difficulties with the language are behind them, and they certainly know English well enough to have been admitted to a top American university. For the majority of the students, at this point in their lives they are dominant in English, but find that their heritage language has suffered. This phenomenon of first -language attrition is discussed in almost everyone's writing about their personal language history. Here are a few (out of dozens) statements about language loss.

My family immigrated to the United States on a summer's night of 1980 in search of the American dream. I remember that night clearly because as I stepped foot onto "American soil," I clung to my mother's arms and cried. Years later, my mother told me I wept, "Let's go home, let's go home." That was fourteen years ago; home is now Torrance, California. Korea is now a place I vaguely remember and the Korean language is slowly slipping away from my tongue, day by day. (K-13, arrived age six)

By the end of my first year in the U.S., I spoke English semi-fluently. And by the second year, I was totally "anglicized," with no joy from my parents because at the same time, my Korean speaking and writing ability was slowly deteriorating. (K-10, arrived age eight or nine)

I can still vaguely remember possessing a stunning comprehension of Mandarin before I started school, but now, it has mostly left me. Often, since I have such perfect examples of pronunciation and grammar before me, I can mentally play a wonderful copy of what I want to say; when it comes out of my mouth, though, I can hear a semi-terrible American accent distorting my words. Sometimes I put words in the wrong order, which gives my messages a much different meaning than what I originally intended. (C-12)

The feeling of knowing what to say in one language, but not in the language being spoken, still remains. Now, the situation is often reversed. My proficiency with Hindi today is comparable to my ability in English when I was in second grade. While I can understand almost all levels of spoken Hindi, when I converse with my grandmother, who can only understand Hindi, I often find myself groping for the right words and incorrectly conjugating Hindi verbs; I listen enviously to recordings of myself speaking fluent Hindi as a four-year-old child. Unfortunately, now that I am older, it is much harder to regain the familiarity with speaking Hindi I once took for granted. (I-4)

Passive Knowledge

One typical outcome is that children get to the point where they can understand the home language in a basic way but cannot speak as well as they understand.

My parents and I ventured for a better life in the United States when I was two years old. During the formative years between 5 and 12, I was primarily exposed to English due to my enrollment in school. While English was being imprinted onto my psyche, my parents fluently spoke Tagalog at home. Due to my home life, I strangely was able to understand almost everything my parents spoke in Tagalog but could not speak nor write it. This situation has boggled my mind for years. I have always wondered how I can be exposed to the sound of Tagalog words for so long and not be able to speak a word of it. To this day I still cannot speak nor write in my native language. (P-3)

Mixing Languages

Another typical outcome is that the children speak a mixed language. Mixed Korean and English is often called "Konglish" or "Korenglish," as one student prefers to call it—spin-offs on the first word in this genre, "Spanglish." Chinese-English mixing is sometimes called "Chinglish," and so on.

I spoke only English in school and progressively spoke less and less Chinese at home. I actually started my own language, "Chinglish," which is a mix of Chinese and English. I only spoke this way to my parents and my brother who always laughed whenever I spoke it. My Chinglish started off innocently enough, but more and more English got thrown into my conversations. The reason for this is that I forgot how to say certain words in Chinese and didn't want to bother giving it much thought. (C-23)

The degree to which I am proficient in English is quite high but my command of Tagalog is anything but flawless. I can understand a majority of the vocabulary but putting together phrases and sentences is something I find difficult. The only time I am required to use my knowledge of Tagalog is when I speak with my "Tagalog only" fluent great-grandmother. My communication with her is a comedy in itself since I mix together Tagalog, English, and my own ad-libbed version of sign language. (P-6)

Sometimes, this mixed language actually becomes the main language used at home.

> ... my family and I still speak more English than Hindi at home. We have even developed a sort of "Hinglish," which often consists of a mixture of the two languages. "Mom, is khana (food) ready yet?" (I-3)

> Sadly, I use my Chinese rather sparingly these days. Even with my parents I speak English. Interestingly enough, they use just as much English as Chinese when talking to me (I like to call the mixture "Chinglish"). I think this is an effort (either conscious or unconscious) on their part to reduce the generation gap that has widened because of the cultural gap resulting from having grown up in different countries. (C-33)

> When I communicated with my siblings, I usually used mixture of Korean and English referred to [by] many Korean Americans as "Konglish." I basically felt insecure with both languages that I wasn't fluent with either Korean or English. (K-11)

Illiteracy

Even when children can speak their heritage language, they are usually unable to read and write in their language unless they came over at a late age.

> The problem I face now is that I have difficulty with the Korean language. My reading skills are equivalent to a first grader in Korea, and my writing skills are even worse. In order of what I can do best to what I am worst at would be that my understanding is the best, followed by speaking, then reading, and finally writing. (K-26)

> Even though I can speak one Chinese dialect and understand a little of another, I never learned to read or write the Chinese language. (C-3)

> The languages that I speak are Hindhi and Punjabi at home I speak Punjabi much more fluently and better than Hindhi. Regretfully I cannot write in either language. (I-2)

> Although I am fluent when it comes to speaking Vietnamese, I never had the chance to master its written language. (V-4)

Problems Created by First-Language Attrition

It is clear that this language attrition is accidental and strongly regretted in many cases. Heritage-language attrition creates many problems for the child, who finds himself personally frustrated, unable to communicate effectively with relatives, alienated from peers in the old country, and humiliated in front of visitors to the home.

> Unfortunately, at this point in my life, my lack of versatility in Mandarin is probably one of my greatest regrets. For one thing, while I can communicate with grandparents and relatives, it's not unlike stuttering every few words trying to get a few

simple ideas across. In addition, not having the language at my disposal limits my options for the future, although I plan to take some classes and try to use Mandarin with friends. One of the most significant aspects of my lack of fluency in the language is the fact that China is one of the major players in world politics today, and I have less potential at this point to effect the outcome of the nation. In the end, I realize that I missed a golden opportunity in not learning the language well. (C-36)

I know that I have been extremely fortunate to have been able to learn English so easily, but I have paid a dear price in exchange. I began my English education with the basics, starting in first grade. As a result, I had to end my Chinese education at that time. I have forsaken my own language in order to become "American." I no longer read or write Chinese. I am ashamed and feel as if I am a statistic adding a burden and lowering the status quo of the Asian community as an illiterate of the Chinese language. (C-7)

If there is one regret in my life thus far it would be my inability to speak the language of my parents, grandparents, and ethnicity for that matter, Tagalog. (P-6)

"I believe in immersing the Indians in our civilization and, when we get them under, holding them there until they are thoroughly soaked" [quote of a previous Bureau of Indian Affairs commissioner; Crawford, p. 44]. The problem was that many students drowned in the process. I, too, have been drowned in the process of Americanization and Anglicization. But, unlike the Native Americans, I was not dragged into the water by the throat and submerged. I made the choice myself to plunge into the pool. It was my decision to commit this suicide-of-sorts. (P-8)

Poor Communication between Generations

One of the worst problems that comes about with first-language attrition is its impact on communication in the family.

Trying to speak proper Korean to adults when one can barely speak the language can be extremely embarrassing. My family is very involved in a Korean church, and many times the reverend, elders, and deacons come to visit. When I find myself stuck at home on these unfortunate nights when guests are over, I have to introduce myself and speak to them in Korean. The trouble really begins when they talk to me and ask me questions—I'm usually stuck there in a most awkward position, trying to understand what they are saying, and trying to answer back in the most polite way possible. What usually comes out of my mouth is a mixture of English and informal Korean, which causes all the adults to laugh at me. (K-15)

There are a lot of things that my parents say in Hakka that I do not understand, and my parents, despite having immigrated to the United States some 25 years ago, are not fluent in English. My father understands a little more English than my mother, so sometimes when my mother and I don't understand what the other is trying to say, we have my father translate for us. (C-3)

Even with the Chinese that I can speak, I am limited to the normal yet shallow "everyday" conversations I have with my parents and do not have enough of a vocabulary to have meaningful talks with them. Such was the case just the other night when they asked me what my major at Berkeley was but I did not know the words or phrase for "Biology," much less, "Molecular and Cellular Biology." The best I could manage was "Science" in Chinese and explained the rest in English; I could not communicate to them why I selected this major, what I was going to do with it, and so forth—we ended this discussion by changing the subject. (C-76)

Criticisms from Relatives and Acquaintances

Young people who have lost their first language are also subject to the embarrassment of criticism from other people from their home country.

> I cannot begin to count how many times people have ridiculed my language and my ethnicity by making fun of how spoken Chinese sounds and by mimicking a "Chinese accent" when speaking English. On the other hand I have also experienced linguistic prejudice from Chinese people because I am of Chinese descent but do not speak the language very well and must resort to English when talking to these people. (second-generation student, C-9)

> To [people of my parents' generation] my command of the Korean language showed whether or not I was a true Korean or just a yellow-skinned boy without a cultural identity or pride. And did I resent that attitude. Whenever relatives would visit I'd always get the same show; first the initial looks of surprise, second the question (Don't you know how to speak Korean?), and finally reprimands of shame and pity from anyone and everyone, even my younger, Korean-speaking cousins. The thing that bothered me the most was that I felt I could do so little about my problem. (K-32)

> I have even encountered prejudice from Filipinos because of my linguistic background. Sometimes, even my peers' parents and other elders look down on me for not speaking in a native tongue. (P-1)

People in the home country also feel strongly that people who come to the United States should not forget their heritage.

> When I went to Korea during my summers, I felt proud that I could speak well and easily. In Korea the society used to look up to those who lived in America and could speak English; however, at present they are disappointed by the many youths who have become "Americanized," and have forgotten their heritage. (K-35)

Factors Relating to First-Language Retention and Attrition

There are many factors leading to this loss of heritage language. It is clearly very important for the language to be spoken in the home if it is to be retained, and sometimes parents make the mistake of deciding to teach their children English first so that they will not suffer in school, with the hope of being able to teach the heritage language later. Children will never become bilingual when this strategy is employed.

> My parents took the liberty to teach me English as I grew up, as opposed to Korean like most of my cousins. At the age of five, only after my ear and mind completely operated in English did they then decide that it might be time to mix it up. They tried speaking to me in English in public while speaking to me in Korean at home. Soon they realized, though, that I would never truly be bilingual. (K-32)

Parents deciding to use the heritage language at home is a necessary condition for raising a bilingual child, but it is not sufficient. Many of the families of the students who wrote these autobiographies in fact did choose to use the heritage language at home, and yet still found that their children were losing fluency. With siblings starting to talk to each other and even answer their parents in English, the home language begins to slip away.

> My first memory is learning the correct way of pronounce "Kung Hee Fat Choy," the Cantonese way of saying "Happy New Year," with the intent to charm the socks off the listener and cause him to give me a packet of lucky money. My mother tells me I was a paragon of a baby, usually silent, but when I spoke, I spoke in Chinese. I got along well with all the relatives who visited from Hong Kong (or at least the ones I wanted to get along) with by enchanting them with my baby-talk. This delightful time when I was the perfect Chinese daughter did not last long. Spending time with my older siblings and hearing them speak in English, I soon began to lose my first language. I, in turn, helped speed the deterioration of Chinese in my baby sister. (C-11)

> After graduating from elementary school, I made a lot of new friends. All the friends that I made were English speaking people, so for about six years my main language was English. Only time I spoke Korean was at home because my parents didn't speak any English. … I imagined myself always retaining the Korean language, but to my surprise I almost forgot 50% of the language. (K-2, arrived age eleven)

Two Kinds of Shame

Being an immigrant, looking different, and speaking English with an accent are all sources of shame to children. They become deeply ashamed of their heritage language and cannot bear to speak it in public with their families. At the same time, they are ashamed in front of their relatives and relatives' friends because they do not know their heritage language and culture. They blame themselves for all these problems.

> I wish I can tell you that I'm a fifth generation Chinese American. I wish I can say that my ancestors have been here just as long as your ancestors have, and therefore I am as much an "American" as you are. I wish my Asian Cultures teachers would stop assuming that I am a living Asian History textbook because I'm Chinese. I wish my fellow classmates would quit picking on me because I'm different from them. I wish I can somehow reassure myself that it isn't my fault that I am ignorant of my own culture. But I can't. There is certainly no reason that I can't recall a single event in the Chinese history. There is absolutely no excuse for me to speak Chinese with a horrible accent since I've only lived in the States for a decade. (C-5)

The awareness of being "different" has a profound effect on the immigrant child's feelings about his or her heritage. They also become very self-conscious of their parents' lack of fluency in English (if such is the case).

> The fact that my parents do struggle with English has been at times difficult for me to grow up with. Many times I have even been ashamed of them. ... This is an illustration of the effects of immigrating to a different country, and some of the social "problems" that have to be dealt with. (K-26)

> When I entered [name] Junior High School, my attitude toward the Chinese language changed dramatically, partially because I was no longer protected by the innocence of childhood and partially because [name] was located in a less racially diverse neighborhood. When some of my classmates began to ridicule and throw racist remarks at Chinese people, I began to distance myself away from Chinese culture. I felt ashamed when my parents spoke to me in Cantonese at a supermarket. I got into heated arguments about why only English should be spoken at home. My dad was fluent in English but my mom had this heavy accent and I began to question my mom on why she would not learn English as well as my dad did, even though I knew perfectly well—she did not go to school here like my dad did. I continuously tried to fit in, even if it meant abandoning culture and identity. I was probably most hostile to my background during those years in junior high. (C-45)

> ... I believed in the superiority of American English. Indeed, I even went further as to believe in the superiority of the white man. It is no wonder that I am more fluent in English than I am in my native language, Tagalog. (P-11)

At the University

These students, all at the University of California at the time they wrote their autobiographies, found when they came here a richly diverse student body, with a strong impetus toward learning about their heritage. Campus clubs and nearby church groups allow the students to form bonds with people of a similar background. A large number of the students have found groups of friends of similar ethnic identity and language background, which awakened a new desire to improve their skills in the heritage language. Also, for the first time, most of them were at a school where their languages were taught, so it was their first opportunity (other than heritage language schools, which were generally considered ineffectual) to take classes in their heritage language. Here are a few out of scores of comments by students newly awakened to the pleasures of their heritage language:

> Although my parents saw their goal accomplished when my brother, then I, entered U.C. Berkeley, and though I made my goal of becoming fluent in English, the cost for all of us has been emotionally painful. One of my great goals in college is to get close to my family and show them my support by getting in touch with my native culture and becoming as learned as possible in the Korean language. (K-28)

> After beginning my studies at Cal, a richly diverse campus and community, I began to realize that my "lost" Chinese would have been very handy to me. I joined a Chinese

club, to regain what I "lost" and to retain what I still had left in me, which was not very much. ... The majority of the students in the club spoke Cantonese and thus led me to feel very handicapped since I could not hold a very long conversation without having to revert to English. This was the point at which I told myself that I would try to learn Chinese again. Now if an opportunity is given to me, I will try to utilize what I can of my native language, but obviously, regardless of how "Americanized" or "Chinglish" I sound, I am aware of the necessity to maintain and practice one's own culture. ... I think I found my motivation here at [the university]. (C-62)

Nevertheless, it was only until college that I started to actively seek my true culture; valuing Tagalog came hand in hand. Before this time, I did not know any better; and although I knew I would never let go of my Pilipino heritage, it was not until college that I could tell anyone why. (P-5)

Benefits of Bilingualism

A minority of the Asian American students, despite all odds, have managed through superhuman efforts of their families to grow up bilingual. Those students who have managed to grow up fluent in their heritage language have found that their bilingualism is a great benefit to them. Here is a sample of the dozens of statements about the benefits of bilingualism.

Many times, I do play the role of translator and go-between for my family. For example, even though my father can read and understand simple letters, when he receives documents or little more complex letters in the mail, I attempt to translate it for him....Bilingualism also helped me in other ways. Since I live in an area that is heavily populated with Koreans back at Home, my proficiency in Korean becomes significantly useful. Last summer, I worked in a Korean American community center. The agency deals with many Koreans as well as other ethnic groups. Whenever I received a phone call from someone, either Korean or non-Korean, who was in need of an assistance, I used my language skills to communicate with that person so that I can help in any way possible. (K-11)

Learning Korean can be very beneficial. Speaking two languages is definitely better than speaking one. Also, I have a certain interest in International Business, particularly concerning US and Korean affairs. (K-15)

After the recent L.A. riots, many people were devastated, specifically Korean-American store owners. Many were hopeless and confused as they faced their burnt establishments and the endless insurance reports. Confronted with this unexpected dilemma, hundreds of non-English speaking Koreans sought help from bilingual interpreters. Last year, I had an opportunity to put my bilingual tongue to constructive use. Even with my Konglish, I was able to aid many people in those desperate times. With such great diversity in the U.S. today, multilingualism, with English as one of the languages, is a useful tool in communication. (K-28)

I strongly feel that the more languages you know, the more advantageous it is. For me, I am planning to establish businesses in Burma and Japan. Hopefully, my knowledge of their languages would help me in the future. I think that when we learn a country's language, we also get to understand its culture better, thus, broadening our minds. As a result, we would become more able to communicate and associate with different kinds of people and form many different kinds of friends. Since I feel that the knowledge of a language is so valuable, I will definitely encourage my children to learn as many as possible. (C-54)

Through all nineteen years of my life I never thought that learning Chiou Chou was for acceptance in my family. It was not until I wrote this essay that the thought struck me. From the use of Chiou Chou, the relationship between my family and I has been very close. We usually joke around, tell stories, or share our experiences at dinner time. My acceptance into my family proved to be very rewarding. Because America is a land of prejudices and not everyone is willing to lend a helping hand, one must stick together with one's family to help each other out. For me, I like to learn new languages to be accepted by other groups, but I would never alienate myself from my family. Because learning Chiou Chou has brought my family and I so close together, learning any new language to be accepted by any group can never break us apart. (C-71)

Searching for Identity

Asian American students undergo an intense and poignant effort to reconcile the conflicting forces in their lives and find a comfortable sense of identity. And they see language as a key part of this identity.

About my senior year in high school, I began to realize what a shame it was that I did not know my own native language well enough to even communicate easily with my parents and grandparents. When I thought about it more, I realized I did not even know my own culture that well either. I had totally neglected my own heritage. Thus, I am now in the process of learning my own language and culture again. However, this does not mean I will forsake all the things I am now; I am only seeking a modification. I count my American culture important too. (K-36)

One of my innermost desires is to learn how to speak the language of my heritage. There are several reasons for my passionate desire to learn Tagalog. For one thing, I feel like a complete stranger in my own house; I would like to communicate with my parents without speaking English. Secondly, I would like to be able to communicate with my relatives in "their" language whenever a visit to the Philippines is possible. Thirdly, I would like to be proficient in two languages rather than one. Last but certainly not least, I would like to preserve the language that has been a part of my cultural heritage for years. (P-4)

The loss of one's cultural language symbolized the loss of one's cultural identity. Many Asian Americans pride themselves for successfully turning their kids into "complete" Americans who speak English in flawless American accent. In my perspective, this actually is something that they should be ashamed of. Without doubt, fitting oneself into the mainstream is important; yet retaining one's cultural language is not at all trivial. To me, I will try my best to excel both in English and my mother tongue, Cantonese. (C-26)

Conclusion

The language journey for these college students is far from complete. Most will probably continue to go through different periods of life when their heritage language is more important to them and others when their heritage language is less important. Some will go on to careers where their contacts with the homeland are enhanced or where their heritage language plays a role; others will not. Some will marry people of the same language background; others will not. While almost all the students write that they hope to help their own children grow up bilingual, we know from past experience that second-generation and third-generation Americans are increasingly likely to know very little or nothing of their heritage language, and so the intergenerational struggle so clear in these autobiographies is likely to be repeated between these students and their children, or else the families will "surrender" to English.

The response of some to the points I have made here will be that it is a good thing that language shift is occurring so rapidly, and that America should be comforted by this fact. It is good for our country that immigrants are abandoning their languages, they will say. And, after all, these are successful students, all at the University of California—so if they rejected their language, it seems like it must have done them good. But we need to look at the human cost of what is happening. As this chapter has shown, the first language loss that so many students have experienced has been accompanied by a loss of family intimacy and communication, a sense of bitterness toward a system and people that the students have come to see as racist, and a sense of personal inadequacy. Is this sense of bitterness and alienation good for our country? Our schools, where the prejudice lies that creates this alienation, need to do better in fighting peer discrimination and educating students to be accepting of different ethnic groups. A lesson might be taken from one Asian American student who went to a school that was able to instill respect for cultural diversity among the students; this student remembers positive experiences instead of peer discrimination and ostracism.

> At Independence High School, cultural diversity was cherished. Every year a multicultural assembly and a food fair is held to celebrate and to promote the diverse cultures at Independence as well as to teach students to respect and appreciate cultures different from their own. With respect to the history of race and language in the United States, I was very fortunate in that I did not encounter any discriminations. Prior to the 1980's immigrants and "racially inferior" people were discriminated and denied of opportunities enjoyed by others. All the credits can be attributed to earlier African Americans, Hispanics, and other ethnic groups who had fought a long struggle to win equal rights for everyone. (V-8)

Immigrant families are offering the United States a great resource of bilingual offspring, which the United States is rejecting, not only through the schools but also through political intolerance within the government: Witness the congressional efforts to make English the official language, and the present legislative attacks against bilingual education and other bilingual services. And yet bilingual citizens are increasingly needed, diplomatically and economically. It would appear to be in the interest of the United States to foster and encourage bilingualism, through such programs as strong maintenance-oriented bilingual education programs. Nor should America fear the development of the dual identity that many of these students are attempting to work out. The desire to be an American is not diminished by the desire to maintain a sense of identity with one's ethnic heritage. To end with two final quotes from one of the student autobiographies:

> I do regard multilingualism, or at least bilingualism, as an important part of anyone's lives. I am an American, but we all have our heritage to maintain. Each one of us is filled with a mixture of various cultures and ethnicities; this is what makes America so unique. If we all blend as one, there is nothing to separate our individual lives. There must be something which sets us apart from everyone else, something which allows us to stand out, and this is our ethnicity. We are all Americans, but to me, being an American means that we are all individuals from numerous ethnic backgrounds which have come together to live in peace and harmony. (C-41)

> The lesson that I have learned is the value of language. It identifies the character and heritage of an entire group of people, and serves to bind them together. It is a precious gift that withers away if it is not used. It is often said that a mind is a terrible thing to waste. The same can be said about a language. (C-9)

This chapter has been published under the same title in English Today *(Cambridge: Cambridge University Press, 1999), 15:21–30, and is based on a longer chapter, "Involuntary language loss among immigrants: Asian-American linguistic autobiographies," in* Georgetown University Round Table on Language and Linguistics 1999, *ed. James E. Alatis and Ai-Hui Tan (Washington, D.C.: Georgetown University Press, 2001), 203–252. I thank the publishers for permission to reprint the article.*

NOTE

1. The numbers following the quotations relate to their source autobiographies: thus, C-6 stands for the sixth Chinese autobiography; K = Korea, I = India, P = the Philippines, and V = Vietnam.

21

Forever FOB?

Resisting and Reproducing the Other in High School ESL

Steven Talmy

Public schools in the United States have seen dramatic increases in the number of English as a Second Language (ESL) learners in their classrooms. In the academic year 2001–2002, more than 4.7 million kindergarten–12th grade (K–12) public school students were classified as "limited English proficient" (LEP), the U.S. Department of Education's prescribed term for this population, representing a 95 percent increase since 1991–1992. In contrast, total K–12 enrollment over the same period rose just 12 percent (Christian 2006). In the state of Hawai'i, the number of LEP students has increased over 108 percent since 1989 to nearly 16,000 students, approximately 9 percent of the state's 2005 public school enrollment (Office of the Superintendent 2006). Given the ongoing, decades-long assault on bilingual education in the United States, the majority of LEP students attending U.S. public schools receive English language and occasionally subject matter instruction in a variety of school-based ESL programs. Though these programs are designed to enable "educationally disadvantaged" LEP students to "transition" into "mainstream" classrooms, they come loaded with a range of assumptions about, among much else, second language (L2) learning, the function of ESL programs in relation to the larger school and societal context, and ESL students themselves. The educational policy literature on K–12 ESL students, itself constituted by and constitutive of normalized (language) ideologies concerning immigrants, bi- and multilingualism, and assimilationism, is replete with terms that suggest the deficit-oriented qualities that "ESL" can connote: for example, limited English proficient, educationally disadvantaged, transition, and mainstream. Though perhaps ironic, it should come as no surprise, then, that for many high school L2 English learners, "ESL" is a stigmatizing identity category, with student views toward it ranging from ambivalence to outright hostility (see, e.g., Duff 2002; Harklau, Losey, and Siegal 1999; McKay and Wong 1996; Talmy, forthcoming).

ESL students' perspectives about ESL likely have less to do with the arcane policies mandating and funding K–12 ESL programs, and much more to do with how the assumptions embedded within them play out in everyday classroom life. This chapter, drawn from a two-and-a-half-year critical ethnography (Talmy 2005a) at a multilingual public high school in Hawai'i (Tradewinds High), concerns one such classroom: Ms. Ariel's first-year "ESL-A" class.[1] It focuses on the cultural productions of ESL, examining in particular the outlines of a hegemonic, institutionally sanctioned ESL identity that positioned students labeled "ESL" as cultural and linguistic Others. This Othering worked to reify idealized, stereotypical imaginings of students' pasts over their present circumstances, denying students the possibilities of more complex, hybrid, and shifting affiliations and identities in favor of an enduring, exoticized nostalgia. ESL students at Tradewinds, particularly the "old-timer" (Lave and Wenger 1991), "generation 1.5" (Harklau et al. 1999), or "Local ESL" students derisively referred to this Other as "FOB" ("Fresh Off the Boat"), a noxious label signifying a recently arrived, monumentally uncool, non-English-speaking rube of mythical, and for some, hilarious proportions. Thus, the cultural productions of ESL at Tradewinds not only consisted of an "official" or school-sanctioned ESL identity as it was manifest in school policies, classroom curricula, and instructional practice, but students' creative responses to it as well. As analysis of interaction in Ms. Ariel's class indicates, students resisted being cast as "forever foreigners" (Tuan 1998), or being continually "put back on the boat" (Talmy 2001) and in the process, renegotiated the terms and boundaries of what ESL would signify (i.e., not them). At the same time, these students' actions wound up reinscribing the very assimilationism and language prejudice they had been resisting.

This chapter is organized as follows: First, I introduce central theoretical concepts that inform the chapter, including cultural production, identity markedness, and linguicism. Afterward, I contextualize the study, describing the Tradewinds ESL program, Ms. Ariel's ESL-A class, and one two-week-long activity that was undertaken in it: the pop-up holiday project. I continue by analyzing five extracts of classroom data concerning the pop-up holiday project in which old-timer ESL students resisted being positioned as FOB, first by challenging their teacher, and then by positioning a newcomer classmate as FOB instead. I conclude by considering ways that the reproduction of linguicism might be interrupted.

Cultural Production

The conceptions of subjectivity, agency, and social practice I employ in this chapter are drawn from theories of cultural production (e.g., Lave and Wenger 1991; Levinson and Holland 1996; Willis 1977, 1981). Theories of cultural production bear important associations to a cluster of social, cultural, and economic reproduction theories that concern the ways that hegemonic ideologies, relations, and interests are reproduced, uncontested, through institutions such as schools. A limitation of reproduction theories, however, is the determinism and homogeneity implied by pervasive structural domination. As Paul Willis (1981, 52) argues, reproduction theories provide "no sense of structure being a contested medium [or] outcome of social process"; instead, "agency, struggle, change—those things which...help to produce 'structure' to 'start with'—are banished" from consideration. These theories thus offer little insight into the ways social actors negotiate the conditions of everyday life.

Subjectivity, agency, and "the sense of activity and practice" (Willis 1981, 64) are restored in cultural production, underscoring the idea that cultural and social reproduction are never guaranteed. As Bradley A. Levinson (2001, 326) notes, any reproductive potentiality of schooling "must pass through the dynamics of cultural production, the consequential making of meanings...the implacable agency of students." This allows for "a more nuanced picture of how power operate[s] within schools to shape particular student outcomes" (for additional discussion see Talmy 2005a, 67–94).

Marked and Unmarked Identities

The notion of linguistic markedness applied to identity "describe[s] the process whereby some social categories gain a special, normative status that contrasts with the identities of other groups, which are usually highly recognizable" (Bucholtz and Hall 2004, 372, cf. Barth 1969). Unmarked identity categories are thus "less recognizable as identities" than marked ones because they appear "natural": They are "the norm from which all [other identity categories] diverge." Markedness therefore "implies hierarchy" (Bucholtz and Hall 2004, 372).

At Tradewinds, one such highly recognizable or marked identity was "ESL student." Its unmarked counterpart was "regular" or "mainstream student"; these correspond with a "nonnative speaker" and what Constant Leung, Roxy Harris, and Ben Rampton (1997) have called "the idealised native speaker." As Mary Bucholtz and Kira Hall (2004) note, "[M]arked identities are also ideologically associated with marked language: linguistic structures or practices that differ from the norm." Many of the ESL students at Tradewinds spoke a marked variety of the dominant code; it is what marked them as ESL to begin with. That is, they were identified at Tradewinds by their linguistic "deficiencies," how they "fail[ed] to measure up to an implied or explicit standard" (Bucholtz and Hall 2004, 372).

Linguicism

It has been argued that linguicism, or "language bigotry" (Valdés 1999), is a more sophisticated, socially acceptable form of racism and classism: As openly race- and class-based arguments of superiority and inferiority have waned in government, business, education, and popular discourses, language has served as another criterion, a "proxy," through which inequality can be legitimated and (re)produced (Skutnabb-Kangas and Phillipson 1994). Educational institutions are primary sites for linguicism, since language prejudice can be naturalized by policies as "commonsense" as the medium of instruction for a school—usually the majority language, often with minimal provisions for minority languages or their speakers.

Linguicism at Tradewinds took many forms; in this chapter, I focus on the formation of a "linguicist" identity hierarchy, with a marked "nonnative" English speaker counterposed against an unmarked "native" English speaker. I argue that due to a nationalist language ideology (Woolard 1998) that was in play at the high school, this identity hierarchy came to signify not only "native"/"nonnative" English speaker and mainstream/ESL but also U.S.-American/Other, familiar/exotic, and in-group/out-group (cf. Leung et al. 1997). I argue that the marked variants of these hierarchicalized, dichotomous identities converged in the subject position of FOB.

The ESL-A Class

I observed Ms. Ariel's ESL-A class for sixty-eight hours over a single academic year. Field notes were supplemented by over twenty-six hours of recorded classroom interaction. I also conducted formal, recorded interviews with fourteen students from the class as well as many more informal interviews during class time. In addition, I collected syllabi, assignments, and other documents for analysis.

Ms. Ariel was an ESL-certified teacher in her first year at Tradewinds, though she had considerable ESL teaching experience in public schools and elsewhere. Despite her experience, she maintained that she was "shocked" by circumstances at the high school, particularly the diversity of her classes. Due to administrative policy, student placements into ESL classes at Tradewinds were based not on L2 English proficiency but by the length of time students had been enrolled at the school. Thus, Ms. Ariel's ESL-A class was for LEP students in their first year at Tradewinds, regardless of age, grade level, educational background, or L2 English expertise. The resulting profile of the nearly thirty Asian and Pacific Islander students in this class would serve as a challenge to even the most experienced teacher: 9th and 10th graders (and one 12th grader) from nine different language backgrounds, who, due to varying durations of residence in the United States and notable differences in prior education, differed significantly in their L1 and L2 English proficiencies and literacy abilities. Approximately one-third of the class was Micronesian,[2] most of whom were Chuukese and were considered to have interrupted formal educations; another third consisted of Cantonese- and Mandarin-speaking students from Hong Kong, China, and Taiwan; the rest of the students came from American Samoa, the Philippines, Korea, and Vietnam. Four of the students had lived in the United States for eight years or more, eight had lived in the United States for between two and five years, with the remainder arriving in the United States from one to six months before the start of the school year. About a third of the class, then, could be considered long-term residents of the United States and old-timer ESL students. This same third was also highly proficient in oral L2 English and in their L1s, though the longer-term Chinese and Vietnamese learners reported that their L1 literacy was poor. Another third of the class was near or at very basic levels of oral and written L2 English ability, with two of the Chuukese students unable to write in their L1. The remaining students were at various levels of L2 English expertise between the advanced students and the beginners.

The policy that resulted in these students' placements into the same ESL class signaled the Tradewinds administration's tacit judgment that ESL students were essentially the same, a monolithic category of learners with negligible differences in L1 and L2 proficiencies, educational backgrounds, or needs, who were identified by the simple fact that their L1s were not English. This was also communicated through the ESL program's curriculum. Though each class had a wide range in L2 proficiency levels, little attempt was made to differentiate instruction, that is, to adapt curriculum and instruction to accommodate these differences. Students in nearly all of the ESL classes I observed were given the same books, the same assignments, the same activities, and the same tests, each with the same demands and deadlines. Thus, a common complaint I heard from old-timer and advanced ESL students was that classwork was too easy or that they had completed similar assignments in earlier grades, sometimes repeatedly. The undifferentiated curriculum implied an undifferentiated group of learners, institutionally identified by the hypernym "ESL student."

The Pop-Up Holiday Project

Projects in Ms. Ariel's class generally took two to three weeks of class time to complete. Most involved a considerable amount of artwork, with drawings, collages, and the like counting for one-third to one-half of the project grade; a one- or two-page written summary and an oral report generally counted for the remainder. Over the course of the year, students were asked to complete numerous projects; for my purposes here, I focus on one: the pop-up holiday project.

The pop-up holiday project came toward the middle of the school year. Students were to choose a holiday "from their own country or culture" and write a short summary about it. This would be attached to the back of a "pop-up" scene, a kind of diorama that indexed the holiday somehow, which students were to create with construction paper, crayons, and colored pens. The project was one of scores of assignments in the ESL classes that attempted to promote the significance of and an appreciation for multiculturalism. Yet, despite the best intentions of the ESL teachers, who were working in difficult conditions with minimal administrative, curricular, or instructional support, this turned out to be a narrowly conceptualized multiculturalism, with a comparatively superficial focus on heroes, holidays, and food; a conception of culture as a static corpus of values and beliefs; and a conflation of country, culture, language, nationality, and identity. It was a brand of multiculturalism in which ESL students were repeatedly invoked as stand-ins for "their countries," representative experts on "their cultures."

The two students who figure prominently in the following extracts are Raven and China. At the time the interactions were recorded, Raven, born in Taiwan, was in the 9th grade, and had been living in Hawai'i for eight years. His classmate, China, a 9th-grade-boy from Hong Kong, had lived in Hawai'i for four-and-a-half years. Raven's tan and blond-streaked hair, along with his usual board shorts, T-shirt, and slippers (or "flip-flops") marked him as the avid surfer that he was. China's sport was basketball: He was regularly seen in thick polyester shorts and a T-shirt, the latest pair of Nike Shox, and occasionally a gold medallion around his neck depicting a silhouette of an airborne Michael Jordan. Both boys were highly proficient in oral L2 English and Pidgin (Hawai'i Creole), the Local language of Hawai'i,[3] though China obscured the grammatical and lexical errors he would sometimes make by speaking in fast, staccato bursts. Neither boy's English or Pidgin phonology contained features that might mark him as an L2 learner. Both resented their ESL placement and complained about it regularly; Ms. Ariel responded more than once by "referring" them to a counselor for punishment.

Ascribing FOB

This extract comes from the first day that the pop-up assignment was introduced. Ms. Ariel was standing at the front of the class giving instructions, and as a model was holding her own pop-up depicting *El Día de los Muertos*, the Mexican holiday of The Day of the Dead.[4]

(1) *Can I do Christmas?* (ELA32Wmd3: 899–915)

1	Ms. Ariel:	the assignment for– the assignment for everyone in the class is to
2		pick a holiday from their own country or
3		culture (..) and to research it or if you already know
4		all about it, fine=
5	Raven:	=yeah, Christmas.
6	China:	[New Year!
7	Ms. Ariel:	[you're gonna show us what it looks like with something
8		like this, ((holds up her model Pop-Up)) and you're
9		gonna write about it (.) here. ((points to back of the
10		Pop-Up)) afterwards, we'll share with the class, we're
11		gonna report.
12	China:	(inaudible) (finish by tomorrow.)
13	Eddie*:	can we just <u>write</u> it?
14	Ms. Ariel:	this is what we're doing. this is the assignment.
15	?Ss:	(inaudible)
16	Ms. Ariel:	I have the assignment sheet [right here.
17	Raven:	[((to China))(inaudible)
18		I'm gonna draw Santa Claus [(inaudible)
19	Ms. Ariel:	[and you'll choose one
20		holiday from where you, you come from [and share it
21		with us.
22	China:	[okay. Miss, I'm
23		not gonna argue, I'm just, can I just do Christmas?
24	Ms. Ariel:	the assignment sheet is right there.
25	Raven:	Miss, can I do Christmas? [(inaudible)
26	Ms. Ariel:	[but the requirement is it's
27		from <u>your</u> country.

In her first two turns, Ms. Ariel gives a summary of the instructions for the pop-up project. In doing so, she implies an array of hierarchically associated dualities. "Everyone in the class" is evidently ascribed incumbency in a marked out-group, the members of which are to choose "holiday[s] from their own country or culture" for the pop-up assignment. This out-group implicates a relational corollary, an unmarked in-group, Ms. Ariel's, to which "they" do not belong. This association maps on to the teacher/student relational pair, talked into relevance by the activity of giving instructions, and foregrounded by the pronoun switch in line 3 and directives in lines 7–11. The unique character of the out-group, and of the "countries and cultures" of its members, is signified by Ms. Ariel's choice of *El Día de los Muertos* as a model pop-up project—a holiday that is different, distinctive, and not of the United States; in other words, that is "foreign." Represented schematically, the instructions for the pop-up in these first turns have connoted the relational oppositions represented in figure 21.1, with the marked variants mapping onto the subject position of FOB.

However, it appears there is a tension here that calls into question the implied conflation of (unique) holiday with (exotic) culture with (foreign) country with (FOB) student. Ms. Ariel is from the United States, not Mexico, as the students well know; if she were to follow her own instructions, she might have made a pop-up of, say, the Fourth of July or President's Day. The possibility for multiple or shifting affiliations, for interests and identities that are not determined by race, ethnicity, language, nationality, or place of birth is furthered by her recognition that students may actually need to research the holiday, that is, they may lack an essentialized insider's cultural knowledge and/or may have interests in countries and cultures that are not "theirs."

This ambiguity becomes resolved, however, over the course of the interaction, as Ms. Ariel refuses to ratify Raven's and China's bids of Christmas and New Year's as acceptable holidays for the project. She provides no uptake to their suggestions in lines 5 and 6, and then indirectly rejects them by deferring authority to the "assignment sheet" in lines 16 and 24. Finally, the contrastive ("but") in line 26 signals a negative response to Raven's repeated request to "do Christmas." It becomes clear she is referring to "other" kinds of holidays from "other" kinds of places, with "othered" kinds of students as their representatives; simply put, Christmas and New Year's

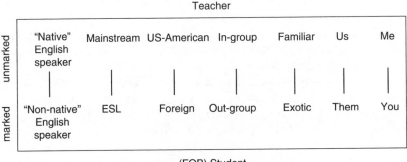

Figure 21.1. Relational Oppositions in the ESL-A Class

belong to her, not "them." This point is reinforced by Ms. Ariel's recognition in lines 3–4 that students might "already know all about" the holiday. Because Christmas and New Year's don't qualify as acceptable choices, though most (if not all) of the students "know about" them, it is clear that what is sought is an exotic holiday that students have some sort of knowledge of, knowledge unavailable to Ms. Ariel or others since they do not "belong" to that culture. In fact, through her use of *El Día de los Muertos* as a model, Ms. Ariel projects *herself* as the sort of Other she envisions for her students. This is hinted at by the switch to the plural pronoun "we" in line 10 ("afterwards, we'll share with the class, we're gonna report") and again in line 14 ("this is what we're doing"). Ms. Ariel's example includes a model pop-up, as well as a model subject position that students are to assume.

Resisting FOB

By offering "Christmas" and "New Year" as viable candidates for a holiday pop-up, China and Raven initiate a challenge either to being positioned as members of a FOB out-group, or to the FOB out-group itself. The timing of Raven's latched "yeah, Christmas" in line 5, combined with his quick, ironic delivery, are likely cues that he knows that Christmas is not the sort of holiday that Ms. Ariel wants students to select. With this utterance he also appears to reject his placement in a FOB out-group and to reposition himself as a member of a different in-group, possibly Ms. Ariel's or, more likely, a Local one he shares with other old-timer ESL students in the class. China immediately takes up Raven's aside with an exuberant "New Year!" However, Ms. Ariel provides no uptake, and until line 22, China and Raven take no further steps to reject the FOB subject position or claim an alternative for themselves.

Ms. Ariel's responses in lines 14, 16, 24, and 26–27 suggest a developing stance of defensiveness: In line 14, after Eddie's protest about the project artwork ("can we just <u>write</u> it?"), she responds to him, and perhaps to Raven and China as well, that the terms of the assignment are not open for negotiation, repeating a form of "this is the assignment" twice before deferring to an external authority (the assignment sheet) in line 16. China appears both to orient to this defensiveness and to try to mollify it with the aligning acceptance in line 22 ("okay."), use of the teacher's address term ("Miss"), and the stake inoculation "I'm not gonna argue." The more aligning interactional tack notwithstanding, China has joined with Raven in proposing Christmas as a legitimate choice of holiday "from where you, you come from," as well as contested his placement in a FOB out-group. An alternative subject position is taking shape here, one that is defined in part by China and Raven through their denotative and interactional resistance to being positioned as FOBs. Ms. Ariel responds in line 24 with another deference of authority to the assignment sheet. Raven then echoes China's request in line 22, to which Ms. Ariel invokes the assignment sheet's newly revealed "requirement" that students must choose holidays from "<u>your</u> country."

China and Raven challenge not only being positioned as members of a FOB out-group in this interaction, but more broadly the conflation of language with culture, nationality, and identity. It could be argued that they are seeking the promise that Ms. Ariel's choice of *El Día de los Muertos* held, however remotely and however briefly, that identity may include, for Raven, Taiwan, and for China, Hong Kong, but also other possibilities beyond those stereotypically associated with race and ethnicity, language, culture, or place of birth.

Approximately half of the class wound up completing the pop-up project. As it turns out, most reported on New Year's, but as it was celebrated in "their" countries. China's presentation was one of several on Chinese New Year's, though he did not do the artwork and his "report" was downloaded from the Internet. Raven was ultimately allowed to "do Christmas," but refused to present his pop-up orally. The inclusion of New Year's and Christmas might be seen as a "victory" of sorts for Raven and China: They succeeded in getting these accepted as holidays "from where you come from." More to the point, however, China and Raven's resistance suggests the formation of an alternative subject position in the ESL-A class, the outlines of which I turn to next.

Reinscribing FOB

In this section, I examine four excerpts from one oral presentation of the pop-up project. Here, I argue that China and Nat*, a 9th-grade boy from the Marshall Islands who had lived in Hawai'i for over eight years, (further) resist being positioned as FOBs by positioning a newcomer classmate as one instead, thereby differentiating themselves from him and defining themselves relationally as non-FOBs. The means by which they accomplish this differs dramatically from those employed by Ms. Ariel above: Here they index their differences from Isaac*, who is presenting on New Year's in Chuuk, by teasing and humiliation, making fun of his lower L2 English ability and his Chuukese heritage. Still, the effect is the same: the reinscription (and redefinition) not only of the FOB subject position, but the relational hierarchies it is part of.

At the time of his presentation, Isaac was a seventeen-year-old sophomore who had come to Hawai'i from Chuuk just weeks before. He was soft-spoken and reserved, and was the only Chuukese boy in the class. His L2 English proficiency allowed him to participate orally in most activities in Ms. Ariel's class, but he had distinct difficulty with academic reading and writing. He regularly wore baggy black jeans that were rolled up at the cuffs, an oversized T-shirt, and old Keds sneakers; his wavy black hair, cut short at the sides, was long on top, pomaded, and pulled into a tight ponytail. He was as different from Raven's surfer image as he was from China's NBA chic and Nat's cultivated hip-hop style.

Isaac's pop-up presentation occurred about two weeks after the pop-up project had been assigned. A few students had already given their presentations, but most of the class hadn't completed the project yet, though it had been due on this day. Ms. Ariel was annoyed about this, as well as by the fact that presentations thus far had averaged about one minute each, despite more than two weeks of class time spent on preparation.

The interaction commenced just before Isaac gave his presentation. He was standing at the front of the class with only his written report; he had not completed the pop-up artwork.

(2) *It's a country again?* (ELA32Wmd5: 1572–1581)

| 1 | Ms. Ariel: | okay. let us know where you're reporting from. |
| 2 | Isaac: | huh? |

3	Ms. Ariel:	where your holiday is from.
4	China:	hwat, its a <u>kan</u>tri [agen.
		what, it's a <u>coun</u>try again?
5	Isaac:	[Chuuk.
6	Ms. Ariel:	country.
7	Isaac:	yeah. Micronesia. uh, Chuuk.
8	Ms. Ariel:	((to the class, nodding)) Micronesia (.) Chuuk.
9	Mona*:	((mimicking voice)) Micronesia (.) Chuuk.
10	Isaac:	[((laugh))
11	Mona:	[((laugh))
12	Chuukese Ss:	[((laugh))
13	China:	((loud, exaggerated laugh))

The frame for the interaction here is keyed by Ms. Ariel in much the same way as it was in extract 1, with reference to a far-off place, distance, the imagery evoked by the phrase "where you're reporting from." The implication is that wherever it is, it isn't "here." Following Ms. Ariel's repair in line 3, but before Isaac has a chance to reply, China interjects with a sarcastic challenge about "it" being a country. China is referring here to an unresolved dispute from an earlier presentation when two Chuukese girls asserted that Chuuk was in fact a country.[5] China had questioned this, the girls had reemphasized it, and with the class looking on, both parties had yielded to Ms. Ariel to arbitrate. Though she had been unsure, Ms. Ariel had sided with the girls, and to China's disbelief, Chuuk's status as a country remained unchanged. China's question here once again challenges Chuuk's status as a country, but more to the point, it challenges Ms. Ariel: The form of the sentence is an exclamatory question ("hwat, its a <u>kan</u>tri agen.") and it is spoken in a loud, deliberate, syllable-timed manner with strong emphasis on the first syllable of "<u>kan</u>tri" and a falling intonational contour, hallmarks of Pidgin (see Sakoda and Siegel 2003, 29–30). The switch to Pidgin further emphasizes the exclamatory nature of the question, and as a variety that tends to be used in more informal domains, it works to compress power disparities between the institutional roles of student and teacher. It also works as a challenge in terms of China's ongoing negotiation of who is and is not FOB: Pidgin is "Local" language; it is hardly something a FOB would or, more precisely, could speak. Thus, the switch to Pidgin also signals in-group membership with other Pidgin speakers in the class: old-timer ESL students such as Nat and Raven who have been living in Hawai'i for years, who may identify more as Local than "foreign," and who resist being cast as FOB. China here not only questions whether Chuuk is a country, but Ms. Ariel's authority, her knowledge, and her power in the classroom; her position, really, to position others as Others.

The confusion about Chuuk serves as an ironic counterpoint to the nationalist language ideology that informs the pop-up project. However, in the context of this class and this assignment, the questionable status of Chuuk and Micronesia leaves the people they are identified/conflated with on an unequal footing with class members who "represent" places that are better known, at least at Tradewinds (China, Taiwan, Korea, the Philippines, etc.). In other words, that there is some question about the status of Chuuk and of Micronesia makes them somehow *less*—less well known;

less worthy, perhaps, of *being* known. Therefore, those students who are identified as Chuukese or Micronesian may be considered somehow less as *people*.[6]

In response to China's question, Ms. Ariel gives a one-word averral that Chuuk is indeed "country." Isaac agrees, but then appears to confuse matters by stating "Micronesia. Uh, Chuuk." Ms. Ariel accepts Isaac's utterance as a confirmation and repeats it for the class. Mona, a Chuukese girl, then revoices the utterance with a higher mimicking pitch, and Isaac and the other Chuukese girls laugh. China joins in, but in an exaggerated manner indexical of mockery.

The interaction continues after the laughter subsides. As Isaac begins his presentation, Nat begins his attempt at rearticulating the attributes of FOB out-group membership.

(3) *Senprade* (ELA32Wmd5: 1582–1597)

14	Isaac:	ready?
15	Ms. Ariel:	we're ready.
16	Isaac:	((reading voice)) in the New Year (.) people walk a– all night and
17		senprade[7] the New Year.
18	?S:	((laugh))
19	Ms. Ariel:	can you try a little louder? [you go out all night?
20	Nat:	[you go out all night eat
21		dinner?
22	Isaac:	((to Ms. Ariel)) yeah.=
23	Isaac:	=((to Nat)) no. senprade [the New Year.
24	?Ss:	[((laugh))
25	Isaac:	they senprade.
26	Nat:	senprade what?
27	Isaac:	the New Year.
28	Nat:	the New Year?
29	?Ss:	((laugh))
30	Nat:	senprade.
31	?Ss:	((laugh))

From Isaac's initial pronunciation of "celebrate" in line 17 up until line 24, student laughter (lines 18 and 24) is comparatively isolated. However, it becomes more widespread once Nat shifts footing and revoices "senprade" twice (lines 25 and 30) in a mock language variety that I call "Mock ESL" (Talmy 2007). Isaac's pronunciation is being singled out for ridicule here as an index of low L2 proficiency, certainly, but Isaac is as well (also see Nat's turn in lines 20–21). What's more, Isaac does not repair the utterance despite Nat's metapragmatic cues, and thus appears unaware there is an apparent trouble-source that might need repair. More significantly, Isaac appears unaware that he is *being teased*. In fact, the public humiliation of lower L2 English proficient students by their more proficient old-timer classmates, particularly over "mistakes" in their L2 oral production such as Isaac's, was a common occurrence in the Tradewinds ESL program. Thus, Nat's Mock ESL revoicings of Isaac's pronunciation position Isaac not only as "limited English proficient" but also as someone who is unfamiliar with this practice. Nat's redefinition of FOB out-group membership has taken shape: Incumbents come from places so exotic they may not even be countries, they speak undeniably "limited" English, they are unfamiliar with the cultures, styles, and practices of the United States and its schools; they are, in short, "fresh off the boat." And it is just what Nat's performative display of difference indicates he is not. Like China and Raven above (and below), Nat is signifying what the school, the ESL program, and the undifferentiated curriculum never did: that there are—that *they are*—different kinds of ESL students.[8]

It is important to point out that there is identity work going on in this exchange beyond that concerning FOB. Nat is Marshallese and Isaac is Chuukese: Both are "Micronesian" in the sense that they come from the region called Micronesia. More specifically, they are "Micronesian" as this identity is locally defined at Tradewinds: an amorphous group of mostly poor, irreconcilably alien Pacific Islanders. In these terms, Nat's public display can be seen as an effort to distinguish himself from Isaac as a non-FOB, and as a non-Chuukese: a "different kind" of Micronesian. In effect, Nat is (re)producing another social hierarchy, this a specifically Micronesian one (cf. Bickel 2002).

Extract 4 continues where extract 3 left off, with Ms. Ariel again prompting Isaac to continue his presentation.

(4) *Yeah, that's all* (ELA32Wmd5: 1598–1610)

32	Ms. Ariel:	what do they do.
33	Isaac:	((reading)) they make noise (.) [and walk–
34	Nat:	[((loud, exaggerated
35		laugh))
36	Isaac:	((laugh; continues reading)) around. dance. and they get gift. they
37		get gift from somebody else.
38	Nat:	((loud, exaggerated laugh))
39	Eddie:	shut up, Nat.
40	Ms. Ariel:	you can get gifts?
41	Isaac:	yes. you have to dance. people dance around and kiss anybody, they
42		dance.
43	Ms. Ariel:	they dance on the beach with anyone they want to?
44	China:	do they have to?
45	Nat:	what if I dance with your grandma.
46	China:	((loud, exaggerated laugh))
47	Isaac:	((half laugh)) yeah, that's all.
48	Eddie:	you're rude.

Nat's overlapped laughter in lines 34–35, just after Isaac says "they make noise," points to an apparent peculiarity of the phrase, and the loud and exaggerated quality of the laughter as well as its duration into line 38, are additional cues that Isaac is being ridiculed (cf. China's laugh in line 13). Eddie, a 9th grader from the Philippines who had lived in Hawai'i for four years, indicates to Nat that the teasing has gone far enough, as he tells him to "shut up" (line 39). But because Ms. Ariel continues to question Isaac (line 40) without validating Eddie's command—or addressing Nat herself—it goes disregarded, and Isaac remains at the front of the room, a target for added derision. China's question in line 44 is an apparent attempt to get in on the action, but it is immediately upstaged by Nat's eye-opening utterance in line 45 about dancing with Isaac's grandmother. China responds with another exaggerated laugh and Isaac, perhaps at last realizing that the interruptions he has endured have been mean-spirited, signals "that's all." Eddie's fitting coda to this segment calls attention to Ms. Ariel's silence regarding the character and quality of Nat's and China's contributions up to now. This is a silence that, unfortunately for Isaac, endures for the remainder of the presentation, even when students' interjections multiply, as they do in the final extract.

(5) *Do they burn themselves?* (ELA32Wmd5: 1611–1641)

49	Ms. Ariel:	what about the fire. [remember you told me about the
50		fire?
51	Raven:	[(inaudible)
52	Isaac.	yeah, yeah.
53	Ms. Ariel:	listen you guys.
54	Isaac:	they make fire around them and (.) they dance (..)
55		around the fire.
56	China:	so, do they burn themselves? ((laugh))
57	Ms. Ariel:	I asked him if anyone ever got burnt, and he said no.
58	China:	that's a lie!
59	?MSs:	[(inaudible)
60	Ms. Ariel:	[they make a ring of fire and they dance around.
61	Raven:	oh, oh, a ring? so they don't dance inside the fire?
62	Isaac:	no.
63	?Ss:	((laugh))
64	Ms. Ariel:	inside or outside.
65	Isaac:	outside.
66	Ms. Ariel:	okay. ((soft laugh)) so–
67	China:	do you dance inside?
68	Nat:	I did! (..) I died once.
69	China:	[((loud, exaggerated laugh))
70	?Ss:	[((laugh))
71	Isaac:	°yeah.°
72	Ms. Ariel:	how long does it last?
73	Isaac:	huh?
74	Ms. Ariel:	how long does it last.
75	?MS:	one day.
76	Isaac:	I don't know.
77	Nat:	twenty-four hours.
78	Ms. Ariel:	is it, is it one day, is it=
79	Isaac:	=no. one week.
80	Ms. Ariel:	one week!

81	?FS:	oh.
82	Ms. Ariel.	oh, so, big party.
83	China:	so, so nomo jab oa samting.
		so, people don't have jobs or what?
84	?Ss:	((laugh))
85	618:	so lai!
		that's a lie!

In this final extract, Raven joins Nat and China, as does 618, a Chinese girl who had lived in the United States for four years (and whose intermediate L2 proficiency made her an occasional target for this sort of teasing herself). China's question in line 56 about whether the Chuukese who dance around fires "burn themselves" is contextualized by the laugh that ensues, yet is ratified as legitimate in Ms. Ariel's line 57 answer. The form of this answer is interesting as she addresses China directly, referring to Isaac in the third person, as if he's not there (also see line 60). In fact, in this turn and in her next (line 60), Ms. Ariel effectively answers *for* Isaac, ventriloquating information that serves as additional resources for Nat, China, and the others to continue their public ridicule. This is evident in line 58, with China's ironic exclamation "that's a lie!" and in line 61, with Raven's absurd clarifying question ("oh, oh, a ring? so they don't dance inside the fire?"). Similar to line 57, Ms. Ariel ratifies Raven's question as information-seeking when she asks Isaac in line 64, "inside or outside." despite the fact that he has already replied in the negative (line 62), and his answer has been followed by student laughter. Ms. Ariel's continued querying of Isaac, her elaborations on his behalf, and her silence on the increasingly overt teasing now come into sharper focus with the ratification of questions clearly aimed at mocking Isaac. Any ambiguity about this point is eliminated in line 66, when Ms. Ariel affirms Isaac's answer and then laughs herself. It appears that Ms. Ariel has aligned herself with Nat and China, perhaps even joined them in the teasing; this clears the way for other students to take part.

The humiliation continues when China asks Isaac about the fire, "do you dance inside?" evoking, as did Raven's question in line 61, racist imagery of fire-walking "savages." Isaac does not have the chance to reply, however, as Nat interjects with "I did! (..) I died once." China laughs loudly in response, and is joined by several other students. Ms. Ariel appears to treat Isaac's soft "yeah." in line 71 as a warrant to continue the questioning, as she pursues further elaboration of the holiday, displaying no orientation toward the derisive actions of China, Nat, and the others.

As represented in figure 21.2, China and Nat have worked together to construct a recursive (Irvine and Gal 2000) hierarchy with a similar but respecified set of oppositions as the one formulated by Ms. Ariel earlier (see figure 21.1): Their Local *me/us* in-group includes Raven, 618, and the students who have been laughing along with them. It excludes Isaac, the other Chuukese students, and those who have not understood what's been said; they are members of a rearticulated *you/them* out-group: the "real" FOBs. In this interaction, China and Nat have usurped Ms. Ariel's power to position and claimed it for themselves. They have appropriated her frame and recast it, posed their own kinds of humbling questions, redefined the character of the FOB out-group, and cast Isaac as its icon. In the process, they have (per)formed alterna-

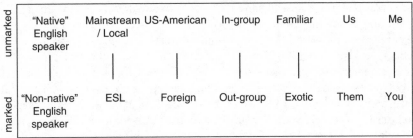

Figure 21.2. Recursive, Respecified Hierarchies in the ESL-A Class

tive identities that index a Local rather than "foreign" affiliation. The differences between these newly (re)defined identities become further articulated as the rest of the interaction plays out. It culminates with another rejoinder from China, again in Pidgin, about Chuukese not having jobs since New Year's is celebrated for a week there, and then 618's strong evaluation, also in Pidgin, of Isaac's answer as a lie (cf. China's line 58 utterance).

The questions and teasing continued rather painfully for nearly a minute more before Ms. Ariel concluded the presentation with a sudden "Okay, I think we should all go there [to Chuuk] for New Year's. Thanks Isaac." This presentation lasted nearly three times as long as the other students', yet during the time that Isaac was in front of the room, he only read two sentences from his paper. The rest of the time was spent contending with the identity performances of Nat and China, with the help of Ms. Ariel, Raven, and other students.

Resisting the Reproduction of Linguicism

China, Raven, and Nat's efforts to reject being Othered, to rearticulate the FOB out-group subject position, and then to relationally define themselves as distinct from it are important forms of resistance. It is resistance in which subjectivity is appropriated in the face of a stigmatizing, institutionally imposed identity category; the reductive conflation of language with culture, country, and personal identity is challenged; and the warm superficiality of a trivializing multiculturalism is subverted. It is resistance that underscores agency and the possibility, or rather the inevitability, of (these adolescents') multiple, complex, and frequently incongruous cultural and linguistic affiliations, of ambiguity and hybridity in identity. Yet it is also resistance that reproduces the same linguicism constituting the FOB subject position that was resisted in the first place. China, Raven, and Nat's redefinition of FOB, at Isaac's expense, signals not a repudiation of the relational hierarchies in Ms. Ariel's class, but these students' perceived place *within* them. In fact, as described above, linguicism serves as an important *resource* for these students' public displays of difference from classmates like Isaac, the "real" ESL students. Without intervention, it appears, linguicism in the Tradewinds ESL program will continue to recruit new subjects and to circulate.

So how to attempt to break the cycle? As Willis (1981, 64) concludes: "The question is less one of bringing in liberation from outside than attempting to drive a wedge between cultural production and reproduction—to preserve the creativity of the articulation of discourses and their radical contents without reproducing the discourses themselves." In other words, how might the radical potential of China, Raven, and Nat's identity work be harnessed to challenge prejudice, rather than used to reinscribe it? Likely starting places for such a "wedge" would be in curriculum and pedagogy, where instead of exoticizing students and reifying romantic notions of their pasts, students could be asked to examine the affiliations and associations of their everyday realities. It could take the form of posing problems (Freire 1993) about the status of particular immigrant groups in the United States, of ESL students in high school, of linguicism as a frequently unexamined form of discrimination, of student resistance, of "FOB," or simply "ESL student" as an identity category itself. It could formulate activities whereby students could take action (e.g., through writing, discussion, drama, or Web-based activities) to change the conditions that allow linguicism and other forms of discrimination to persist. Following Gore (1992, 62), this would be a pedagogy in which "empowerment is constructed as the exercise of power in an attempt to help others to exercise power." In this, it would engage students in creating a participatory pedagogy to begin the processes of interruption that are needed.

Conclusion

At Tradewinds High School, the cultural productions of ESL involved the creation of a FOB out-group subject position as it was relationally defined against an unmarked, "idealized" native English speaker. It involved students who were institutionally categorized as "ESL" being positioned as exoticized Newcomers, cultural and linguistic Others, by an array of national and local institutional policies, school curriculum, and instructional practices, by teachers, and by students themselves. It involved students contesting this positioning and attempting to formulate alternative subjectivities that were consequently defined relationally by a rearticulated FOB subject position, for which a classmate was positioned as an unwitting icon. I have argued that the linguicism that was constitutive of the FOB subject position was the local, recursive projection of a societal linguicism in which "ESL," "nonnative" English speakers, and bi- and multilingualism are denigrated. Finally, I have suggested some possibilities that might work to interrupt the reproduction of linguicism, so that students such as Raven, China, Nat, and Isaac might not be "forever FOB."

The research reported in this chapter was supported by grants from the Spencer Foundation and The International Research Foundation (formerly TESOL International Research Foundation). My thanks to both organizations, and to Diana

Eades, Jo Ann Kadooka, Younhee Kim, and the editors for comments on earlier drafts. The views expressed and any remaining errors are my own.

NOTES

1. The names of the school, the teacher, the students, and the class have been changed. All students selected their own pseudonyms, unless denoted at first mention by an asterisk.

2. At the time of this study, Micronesians were the fastest growing immigrant group in Hawai'i schools, and were the target of an array of discriminatory practices from both students and teachers (see Talmy 2005b).

3. "Local," an identity category in wide circulation in Hawai'i, refers to Asian/Pacific Islanders born and raised in the Islands (see Okamura 1994); central to the production of Local identity is use of Pidgin. In terms of transcription, Pidgin in this chapter is represented using the phonemic Odo orthography (Sakoda and Siegel 2003).

4. Transcript conventions:

word.	(period) falling intonation
word,	(comma) continuing intonation
word?	(question mark) rising intonation
word!	(exclamation point) exclamatory intonation
<u>word</u>	(underline) word stress
word –	(en-dash) abrupt sound stop
(..)	(periods in parentheses) pauses: (.) a short pause, (. .) a longer pause, etc.
[word	(brackets) onset of overlapping talk
[word	
word=	(equal signs) latched speech
=word	
°word°	(degree signs) utterance softer than surrounding talk
(inaudible)	inaudible utterance
(word)	(single parentheses) best guess at a questionable transcription
((word))	(double parentheses) participants' physical movements, characterizations of talk, and vocalizations such as laughter, coughing, etc.
word	(italics, below a transcribed utterance) English gloss of Pidgin
?MS/?FS/?Ss	Unidentified male student, female student, or students, respectively

5. Chuuk is a state (of the Federated States of Micronesia), not a country. A similar issue had arisen with a prior assignment called the Flag Project: There had been confusion among Chuukese students about which flag represented "their country," and they had been unable to find representations of it in classroom reference materials.

6. In fact, a racist "status order" similar to the one John Bickel (2002, 2) reports on was evident at Tradewinds, with "[s]tudents from East Asia often look[ing] down upon Micronesians" (also see Talmy 2005b).

7. "Senprade" is how Isaac spelled "celebrate." He pronounced it [sɛnəpred].

8. It is likely that these students would in fact have preferred to be identified not as "different kinds of ESL students" but as something closer to "students who were 'stuck' in ESL" (see Talmy, forthcoming). That notwithstanding, it is important to acknowledge the power of institutions to sort and label: no matter what these students would have preferred, Tradewinds still classified them as "ESL."

REFERENCES

Barth, Frederik. 1969. Introduction. In *Ethnic groups and boundaries: The social organization of cultural difference*, ed. Frederik Barth, 9–39. Bergen-Oslo: Universitets Forlaget.

Bickel, John. 2002. The Micronesians: The invisible malihini. In *Honolulu Weekly* (honoluluweekly.com/archives/coverstory 2002/2012–2011–2002 Micro/2012–2011–2002 Micro.html).

Bucholtz, Mary, and Kira Hall. 2004. Language and identity. In *A companion to linguistic anthropology*, ed. Alessandro Duranti, 369–394. Malden, Mass.: Blackwell.

Christian, Donna. 2006. Introduction. In *Educating English language learners: A synthesis of research evidence*, ed. Fred Genesee, Kathryn Lindholm-Leary, Bill Saunders, and Donna Christian, 1–13. Cambridge: Cambridge University Press.

Duff, Patricia A. 2002. The discursive co-construction of knowledge, identity, and difference: An ethnography of communication in the high school mainstream. *Applied Linguistics* 23:289–322.

Freire, Paulo. 1993. *Pedagogy of the oppressed*. New York: Continuum. First published 1970 by Seabury Press.

Gore, Jennifer. 1992. What we can do for you! What *can* "we" do for "you"? Struggling over empowerment in critical and feminist pedagogy. In *Feminisms and critical pedagogy*, ed. Carmen Luke and Jennifer Gore, 54–73. New York: Routledge.

Harklau, Linda, Kay M. Losey, and Meryl Siegal, eds. 1999. *Generation 1.5 meets college composition: Issues in the teaching of writing to US-educated learners of ESL*. Mahwah, N.J.: Lawrence Erlbaum.

Irvine, Judith T., and Susan Gal. 2000. Language ideology and linguistic differentiation. In *Regimes of language: Ideologies, polities, and identities*, ed. Paul V. Kroskrity, 35–83. Santa Fe, N.M.: School of American Research Press.

Lave, Jean, and Etienne Wenger. 1991. *Situated learning: Legitimate peripheral participation*. Cambridge: Cambridge University Press.

Leung, Constant, Roxy Harris, and Ben Rampton. 1997. The idealised native speaker, reified ethnicities, and classroom realities. *TESOL Quarterly* 31:543–560.

Levinson, Bradley A. 2001. *We are all equal: Student culture and identity at a Mexican secondary school, 1988–1998*. Durham, N.C.: Duke University Press.

Levinson, Bradley A., and Dorothy C. Holland. 1996. The cultural production of the educated person: An introduction. In *The cultural production of the educated person: Critical ethnographies of schooling and local practice*, ed. Bradley A. Levinson, Douglas E. Foley, and Dorothy C. Holland, 1–54. Albany: State University of New York Press.

McKay, Sandra L., and Sau-Ling C. Wong. 1996. Multiple discourses, multiple identities: Investment and agency in second-language learning among Chinese adolescent immigrant students. *Harvard Educational Review* 66:577–608.

Office of the Superintendent. 2006. *The Superintendent's 16th annual report: 2005*. Honolulu: Hawai'i State Department of Education.

Okamura, Jonathan Y. 1994. Why there are no Asian Americans in Hawai'i: The continuing significance of local identity. *Social Process in Hawaii* 35:161–178.

Sakoda, Kent, and Jeff Siegel. 2003. *Pidgin grammar: An introduction to the creole language of Hawai'i*. Honolulu: Bess Press.

Skutnabb-Kangas, Tove, and Robert Phillipson. 1994. Linguistic human rights, past and present. In *Linguistic human rights: Overcoming linguistic discrimination*, ed. Tove Skutnabb-Kangas and Robert Phillipson, 71–110. New York: Mouton de Gruyter.

Talmy, Steven. 2001. Putting 'em back on the boat: Representational politics in the administration of generation 1.5 students. In *The American Association for Applied Linguistics Annual Conference*, St. Louis, Mo.

———. 2005a. *Lifers and FOBs, rocks and resistance: Generation 1.5, identity, and the cultural productions of ESL in a high school.* Unpublished doctoral dissertation, University of Hawai'i at Mānoa, Honolulu.

———. 2005b. The other Other: Micronesians in a Hawai'i high school. In *Asian and Pacific American education: Learning, socialization, and identity*, ed. Clara C. Park, Russell Endo, and A. Lin Goodwin, 19–49. Greenwich, Conn.: Information Age.

———. 2007. Reproduction and recursivity in high school ESL: A critical analysis of classroom language-in-use. Plenary address to *The 17th International Conference on Pragmatics and Language Learning*, Honolulu.

———. forthcoming. Resisting ESL: Categories and sequence in a critically "motivated" analysis of classroom interaction. In *Talk-in-interaction: Multilingual perspectives*, ed. Gabriele Kasper and Hanh T. Nguyen. Honolulu: University of Hawai'i/National Foreign Language Resource Center.

Tuan, Mia. 1998. *Forever foreigners or honorary whites? The Asian ethnic experience today.* New Brunswick, N.J.: Rutgers University Press.

Valdés, Guadalupe. 1999. Nonnative English speakers: Language bigotry in English mainstream classrooms. *ADFL Bulletin* 31:43–48.

Willis, Paul. 1977. *Learning to labour: How working class kids get working class jobs.* New York: Columbia University Press.

———. 1981. Cultural production is different from cultural reproduction is different from social reproduction is different from reproduction. *Interchange* 12:48–67.

Woolard, Kathryn A. 1998. Introduction: Language ideology as a field of inquiry. In *Language ideologies: Practice and theory*, ed. Bambi B. Schieffelin, Kathryn A. Woolard, and Paul V. Kroskrity, 3–47. New York: Oxford University Press.

22

Sequences, Scripts, and Subject Pronouns in the Construction of Chinese Heritage Identity

Agnes Weiyun He

Language and Identity: A Language Socialization Perspective

Until not long ago research on the relationship between language and identity tended to treat the latter as an a priori given and as an independent constant that could be invoked to account for variations in language use (see He 1995, 1998; Ochs 1993). More recent constructivist approaches including practice theory (Bourdieu 1977), sociohistorical psychology (Vygotsky 1978), conversation analysis/ethnomethodology (Atkinson and Heritage 1984; Drew and Heritage 1992; Garfinkel 1967; Sacks 1992; Sacks et al. 1974), language acquisition and language socialization (to be specified below), and linguistic anthropology of education (Rampton 1995; Wortham and Rymes 2003) have led researchers to examine identity not as a collection of static attributes such as age, occupation, country of birth, skin color, native language, and so forth, but instead as a process of continual emerging and becoming, a process that identifies what a person becomes and achieves through ongoing activities and interactions with other persons and objects (Kang, this volume; Suzuki, this volume).

This chapter specifically draws on work from language socialization, which, as a branch of linguistic anthropology grounded in ethnography, focuses on the process of becoming a culturally competent member through language use in social activities. As formulated by Elinor Ochs and Bambi B. Schieffelin (Ochs 1990, 1996; Ochs and Schieffelin 1984; Schieffelin and Ochs 1986a, 1986b, 1996), language socialization is concerned with: (1) how novices (e.g., children, second language learners) are socialized to be competent members in the target culture through language use, and (2) how novices are socialized to use language. Within the framework of language socialization, identity as part of sociocultural context is constituted by particular stances and acts which in turn are indexed through linguistic forms (Ochs 1990, 1992, 1993). That is to say, from a language socialization perspective, the indexical relationship between linguistic forms and language user's identity is often achieved indirectly. Furthermore, some features of the communicative event bear a direct or indirect relationship to linguistic forms. Social identities of the participants are one of the major sociocultural dimensions along with relationships among participants, affective dispositions (feelings, moods, and attitudes of participants toward some proposition), epistemological dispositions (beliefs or knowledge vis-à-vis some proposition, e.g., the source of participants' knowledge or the degree of certainty of their knowledge), social/speech acts and activities, and genre. Ochs (1990, 1992) argues that among these dimensions *affective and epistemological dispositions* are the two contextual dimensions that are recurrently used to constitute other contextual dimensions. Hence, this two-step indexical relationship can be illustrated in figure 22.1.

Language socialization provides a systematic account of how language relates to identity. It enables us to examine how different displays of and reactions to certain acts and stances construct different identities and relationships. It also allows us to examine the construction of multiple yet compatible/congruent identities, blended and blurred identities in multilingual, multicultural, immigrant contexts (He 1997, 2000, 2006).

linguistic forms → affect/stance → contextual features (identity, activity)

Figure 22.1. Indexical Relationship between Language and Sociocultural Context

The Role of Interaction in Identity Construction

It has been argued, however, that while it is feasible to directly link some linguistic features with some affective or epistemological dispositions (the first step in the indexical relationship in the language socialization model), it appears more challenging to grasp the constitutive relationship between affective or epistemological stances and other contextual features such as social identities and interpersonal relationships (the second step in the language socialization model) (He 2003). In other words, how can we ascertain that it is one specific cultural and situational context (e.g., the participant being a female) and not any other (e.g., the same participant being a teacher) that is invoked by certain affective and epistemological dispositions? To address this concern, we need to ground identity in the *interactional production* of acts and stances.

While many researchers may agree that social identities come to be created through language, few have explicitly acknowledged the role of interaction. Here I would like to highlight and reinforce the dialogical, interactional perspective within language socialization theory and complement it with analytical tools from a parallel perspective, conversation analysis (hereafter CA). I suggest that CA may enrich language socialization's perspective on identity construction in three different ways.

First, CA offers an emergent account of language use and language user, which locates identity work in the context of moment-by-moment interaction. Second, CA directly addresses the problem of identity construction through research on "membership categorization." Third, CA provides rigorous analytical tools to examine the procedures or interactional devices used by the participants to construct identity. One of these devices is "repair organization," which will be the focal point in our data analysis.

CA's Notion of Emergence

From a CA perspective, the encounter between any two parties is first and foremost an activity in which the participants try to make sense of each other's utterances. In other words, the participants take it to be a constant objective in their encounter to achieve a shared understanding of what each person means. Interpersonal and cultural knowledge is revealed and reconstructed from the encounter as interaction between the participants unfolds. The participants' understanding of each other is dialogically based, in the sense that meaning is jointly constructed through interaction between both parties. Such joint construction of meaning is neither objective nor subjective, but intersubjective. It transcends the polarity between an objectivism, which prescribes that there exists some permanent, ahistorical, independent meaning, and an anything goes relativism. The goal of the participants is not to work toward an absolute objectivity but toward an intersubjectivity that is achieved through and mediated by interaction (He 1998).

By interaction, we refer to not only what the participants say to each other in terms of their words (lexicon) and sentence patterns (grammar) but also the speech exchange system that regulates who speaks when for how long and related matters. In any interaction, two or more parties (e.g., teacher and students), through talking to each other, influence each other and react to each other, affectively and cognitively. As interaction, these activities take on an emergent quality as the participants jointly build their discourse moment by moment. Interaction is a vehicle via which intersubjectivity is constantly built and rebuilt, with the potential of shifting from moment to moment. Reciprocally, intersubjectivity provides the basis for interaction; each speaking turn or turn-constructional-unit is oriented to intersubjectivity established thus far.

By considering identity construction as an interactional achievement, we are able to link the language forms and cultural/societal values and preferences, thereby substantiating and operationalizing Language Socialization's theory of indexicality and identity with CA-informed analyses of interactional processes. What this means for language socialization research on identity is that in actual analyses of language use, we need to examine how an intersubjective orientation to contexts (including identity) and other realities is established, maintained, or altered moment by moment. We need to focus on how the participants themselves orient to, manage, and sustain identity in actual, real-time interaction. The specification of identity as part of the context needs to be derived from orientations exhibited by the participants themselves (Schegloff 1992). Hence, for example, in order to claim that some participant's identity as a teacher shapes the way in which language is used, the relevance of that identity must be shown to inhabit the details of the interaction in which the participant takes part.

"Membership Categorization"

The body of research from CA that directly addresses the problem of identity construction can be found in Harvey Sacks's work on "membership categorization," that is, how people do descriptions (Sacks 1992) of participants. Sacks noted that when people use descriptions, they employ categories to label themselves, others, and also objects. These categorizations are "inference-rich" (1992, 40–48) in that when a particular category is used, members of a society rely on their local knowledge of what it means to be labeled with such a category. That is to say, when categories are used and interpreted, participants always tie them to specific characteristics and behaviors that are presumed to be known about the category.

One can thus see that there is a strong parallel between CA's conceptualization of membership categorization and language socialization's perspective on identity construction. They both emphasize the process via which participants' membership or identity is established. CA focuses on not "categories" but *"categorization"*; language socialization stresses the process of *identifying* through affect and stances. Further, they both put forth a two-step inference model with regard to the interpretation of participants' identity/membership. For CA, a specific categorization invokes specific characteristics/behaviors, which, in turn, are tied to a specific membership. For language socialization, specific language forms index specific affective and epistemological stances, which, in turn, index a specific social identity.

Sacks also observed that any feature of a person could be used for membership categorization and that several categories can be applied for the same person (e.g., Chinese, teacher, female, mother). What is of interest is the procedures via which participants select membership categories. Repair organization (Schegloff 1979, 1996; Schegloff et al. 1977) is one such membership categorization device, to which I turn next.

Repair Organization

While all grammatical, lexical, syntactic, and interactional structures can potentially orient to participants' membership categorization or identity construction, repair organization is a particularly effective interactional mechanism for participants to express a stance of affiliation or disaffiliation with each other and, in so doing, to establish, validate, modify, or resist their belonging to one particular membership over another. In the data analysis section below, I will show that it is through interactional mechanisms such as repair that issues of participant identity are expressed and negotiated on a moment-by-moment basis. But first, let us briefly review relevant literature on repair.

When trouble such as mishearing, misunderstanding, or misspeaking in conversation occurs, it is noticed and then corrected, either by the party whose turn contains the source of trouble or by some other party. This sequence of trouble

+ initiation-of-correction + correction is known as a *repair trajectory*. Repair occurs when one party corrects his or her own talk or that of another party and can be accomplished in a number of ways (Schegloff et al. 1977). Of particular relevance to our data are the following:

- *Self-initiated same turn repair* refers to the situation when the current speaker initiates and completes the repair within his/her current turn of talk and before coming to a possible completion of a complete grammatical, lexical, intonational, and pragmatic unit, also known as the turn-constructional-unit (TCU) (Ford and Thompson 1996). It is the earliest position in which repair can be undertaken. The repair is signaled by a number of speech perturbations such as cut-offs, hesitation markers, pauses, and restarts. Emanuel A. Schegloff, Gail Jefferson, and Harvey Sacks (1977) show that this is the most frequent and the most preferred type of repair.
- *Self-initiated repair in transition-relevant-space*. If the speaker of the trouble source does not perform repair during the turn in progress, he/she can repair the utterance in the transition-relevant-place, that is, at the end of a TCU, before another speaker takes a turn.
- *Self-initiated third turn repair*. In this type of repair (Schegloff 1996), a speaker produces a turn and the hearer responds to it without producing any sign of breakdown in intersubjectivity. After the response by the hearer, the speaker uses the next turn to revise his/her previous turn.
- *Self-initiated third-position repair*. While in the third turn repair the hearer provides an appropriate response that does not prompt repair of the speaker's first turn, in third-position repair (Schegloff 1992) it is precisely the hearer's response that engenders the repair. In other words, the hearer's response enables the speaker to notice a problematic understanding of his/her prior turn.
- *Other-initiated self-completed next turn repair* is when repair is initiated by a participant other than the speaker of the trouble-source. When this happens, the repair initiation usually comes in the turn immediately subsequent to the trouble-source turn (known as next turn repair initiation, or NTRI).
- *Other-initiated other-completed repair* occurs when a participant other than the speaker of the trouble-source both initiates and completes the repair. It is usually preceded by discourse markers such as *well* or *uhm* and often takes the form of a candidate understanding with question intonation. This type of repair can theoretically occur in any turn or any position.

Of the types of repair outlined above, the most preferred is self-initiated and self-completed in the same turn as the trouble-source. Other initiation and other completion of repair can index a stance of disaffiliation with the interlocutor; and the farther the distance between the trouble source and the completion of the repair, the greater and the longer the miscommunication.

Identity Work as Link between Interactional
Details and Contextual Concerns

With an interactionally enriched linguistic anthropological approach to language and
identity and a specification of analytical tools from CA, we are now able to posit
that:

1. identity is indexical with specific sets of acts and stances, which, in
   turn, are constructed by specific language forms;
2. identity is dynamic, constantly unfolding along with interaction, and
   thus has the potential to shift and mutate; and
3. identity emerges (at least in part) through others' responses and
   reactions and as such identity construction is intersubjective and
   reciprocal; the construction of one participant's identity also
   simultaneously constructs that of the other.

In what follows, after a brief sketch of the research context, I detail the interactional processes through which the participants' identities come to be constituted,
(re-)enacted, modified, negotiated, or rejected. I focus on the language form of various repair trajectories, examine how they index stances of affiliation or disaffiliation
among the participants, and link these issues with participants' identity/membership
categorization.

Classroom Roles/Identities: The Research Context

Data presented in this chapter were collected in two Chinese heritage language
schools in two different cities in the United States. In these schools, evening or
weekend Chinese language classes are offered for children whose parents come
from China or Taiwan and are pursuing professional careers in the United States.
These children were either born in the United States or came to the United States
with their parents at a very young age. Most of them go to mainstream English-
speaking schools on weekdays. While many of them are bilingual in English and
Chinese in the oral form, some are already English-dominant and few have opportunities to learn how to read and write in Chinese. Their parents send them to these
Chinese language schools to acquire literacy in the heritage language and to affirm
their ethnicity.

Combining elements from family, community, and school, heritage language
schools like these function as an important vehicle for ethnic minority children to
acquire heritage language skills and cultural values (Bradunas and Topping 1988;
Creese and Martin 2006; He 2006; Peyton et al. 2001; Wang 1996). The corpus
includes (1) thirty hours of audio and video recorded class meetings involving four
teachers in four different classes and a total of thirty-five children (aged four and a
half to nine), (2) classroom observations, and (3) interviews with parents, teachers,
and school administrators. Detailed information about the classes can be found in
the appendix.

The next section of the chapter aims to provide an empirical and interactional account of sociocultural identities and interpersonal relationships between the teacher and the students in the Chinese heritage language classroom.

Repair as a Resource for Identity Construction

Scripts and Identity

For complicated social and political reasons, modern Mandarin Chinese is written in two scripts, the traditional (known as *fantizi*), which is typically used in Taiwan, and the simplified (*jiantizi*), which is the official script used in mainland China (see Chen 1999 for a detailed discussion). Analogous to the Balkan situation described by Greenberg (2004), the script used to write the Chinese language is often seen as an integral part of the language and the identity of its speakers. A specific script can act as a political and/or cultural identity marker. While the heritage language schools I observed adopted textbooks published in mainland China (in *jiantizi*), they also provided their students with supplementary reading materials published elsewhere such as Taiwan and Hong Kong. As a principle, the schools I observed accepted any choice made by the instructor or by students who preferred one script to the other. Given the wide range of political, regional, linguistic, and socioeconomic divisions within the communities I studied, bi-script writing has also been part of an attempt to forge a collective identity within an all-encompassing Chinese American cultural framework.

Compounding the subcultural, political, and economic identity factors is the expert-novice role relationship between the teacher and the Chinese heritage language students. Originating in the teachings of Confucius and Mencius 2,000 years ago is the notion of *shi dao zun yan*—the supremacy of the Way of the teacher. The teacher in a traditional Chinese classroom is someone who is the indisputable, unchallenged center and authority of knowledge. The student accordingly is someone who is expected to listen, observe, and follow the teacher's instructions. Below, in data segment (1), I show that the expert-novice relationship between the teacher and the students in Chinese heritage language classes is not a clear-cut case of a representation of an instance of "traditional" classroom practice; instead, it may, in fact, take on a highly emergent quality as the participants ratify, reverse, reject, or make irrelevant their prescribed role identities moment by moment.

The scenario in (1) concerns the choice of script between *jiantizi*, the simplified script, and *fantizi*, the traditional (unsimplified) script. The teacher, who received her education in Mainland China before moving to Taiwan (and then the United States), chooses to use *jiantizi*. Student G5's family is from Taiwan and student G5 prefers *fantizi*.

(1) [TCCDL:953] choice of scripts[1]

((Tc is walking around to check each individual student's writing.))
```
1   Tc:    这个字嗯对吗？
            zhe ge    zi      eh   dui    ma?
            this MSR character PRT correct Q
            Is this character uh correct?
```

2   ((pointing to G5's writing))

3   G5:   嗯::
                en::
                PRT
                Eh

4   Tc: 照书上的写
                zhao   shushang de   xie
                follow book   PRT write
                Write the character exactly as it appears in the book.

5   ((G5 opens the textbook and looks for the character and then opens another book, a storybook; Tc moves on to other students. In a few minutes, Tc returns to G5.))

6   G5:   老师这本书说   [我对了
                laoshi zhe ben shu   shuo   [*wo dui le*
                teacher this MSR book say   I correct PERT
                Teacher, this book says I'm right.

7   ((G5 points at the storybook; Tc looks and then picks up the book.))

8   Tc: [照课本-这是这是什么书-哪里的？
                                [*Zhao keben zhe shi   zhe shi*
                                  follow text   this COP this COP
                shenme shu- nali   de?
                what-Q book where-Q PRT
                Follow the text-What is this is this book- where does it come from?

9   G5:   从图书馆借的
                cong   tushuguan jie   de
                from-LOC library   borrow PRT
                [It is] borrowed from the library. ((The reading room in this Chinese language school.))

10 Tc: 图书馆借   [的？
                tushuguan jie   [*de*
                library   borrow PRT
                Borrowed from the library?

11   [((G5 nods))

12 TC: 这不是简体字》我们学的是简体字《
                zhe bu   shi jiantizi >>women xue de   shi jiantizi<<
                this NEG COP   we   learn PRT COP
                This is not *jiantizi*, what we're learning is *jiantizi*.

13 G5:   陈老师说学繁体字简体字都 ok

            chen laoshi   shuo xue fantizi jiantizi dou   ok
                 teacher say   learn   all-EMP ok
            Teacher Chen says that learning *fantizi* and *jiantizi* are both <u>ok</u>.

14   ((Teacher Chen is the school principal.))

15 Tc: 那-那好.

            na   na   hao.
            then then good.
            Then- okay then.

16   (.2) ((Tc puts down the storybook.))

17 Tc: 让我看你写得对吗.

            rang wo kan ni xie de   dui   ma.
            let   I   see you write PRT correct Q
            Let me see whether you wrote it correctly.

18   ((G5 hands in the storybook to Tc; Tc checks G5's writing against the
            storybook.))

19 Tc: 好

            hao.
            Good.

In terms of sequential organization, Tc (line 1) begins with a question concerning whether a specific character was written correctly, a question to which
G5's answer appears uncertain (line 3). Tc then advises G5 to follow the book
(line 4). G5 consulted two books, first the textbook and then a storybook (line 5),
and finally reported to Tc that the book proved her right (line 6). At this point,
realizing that G5 has mistakenly taken her previous turn (line 4) to mean "follow
any book," Tc initiates and completes a *third position repair* ("follow the textbook," line 8) of her turn in line 4. Immediately subsequent to the third position
repair, Tc also completes a *self-initiated same turn repair* (marked by cut-offs,
restarts, line 8), shifting the focus from the specification of which book G5 should
consult to the questioning of the origin of the storybook. After G5's reply that
the book is from the school reading room (line 9), Tc provides a *next turn repair
initiation* (NTRI) with a partial repeat of G5's previous turn, casting disbelief and
doubt on the legitimacy of the book (line 10). G5, however, affirms that the book
is indeed from the school reading room (line 11); in other words, the NTRI from
Tc in line 10 did not succeed in getting G5 to complete any repair of her (G5's)
previous turn in line 9. Tc subsequently states that the character form present in
the storybook is not permissible (line 12), to which G5 counters by invoking the
school principal (line 13). Tc then reluctantly (indicated by the cut-off) gives in

and revises her assessment of the book (line 15). Finally, Tc asks to check G5's writing (line 17), a request with which G5 complies (line 18). Tc ends with an evaluation of G5's writing (line 19). A schematic representation of the sequential organization follows:

- Tc: question (line 1)➔G5: answer (line 3)
- Tc: directive (line 4)➔G5: response to directive (line 6)➔Tc: third position repair (line 8)
- Tc: question (line 8)➔G5: Answer (line 9)➔Tc: next turn repair initiation (line 10)➔G5: no repair (line 11)
- Tc: assessment (line 12)➔G5: counter-assessment (line 13)➔Tc: revised assessment (line 15)
- Tc: directive (line 17)➔G5: compliance (line 18) ➔Tc: evaluation (line 19)

By attending to interactional details moment by moment, we are able to see that the teacher's expertness and authority is not presupposed to the same degree at all times and is not readily accepted by the student at all times. In this segment, the teacher began being the expert/authority by asking a question (line 1) and issuing a directive (line 4). The student's response to the directive (line 6), however, compelled the teacher to respecify her original directive (line 8). Subsequently, the expert-novice relationship became neutralized, if not reversed. The teacher was not knowledgeable about the origin of the storybook (line 8), whereas the student was (line 9). When the teacher further challenged the student (line 10), the student did not revise her statement (line 11). The student was finally able to strike a balance in the interpersonal relationship when she countered (line 13) the teacher's assessment (line 12) and succeeded in making the teacher agree with her (line 15). In the end, the expert-novice relationship returned to what it was like in the beginning of this episode: the act of examining (line 17) and evaluating (line 19) the student's character writing (though in *fantizi*) and the student's compliance (line 18) reestablished the teacher's expert position. In other words, if the stance of expertness and authority indexes the identity of the teacher, here such a stance is not a static property, but instead an emergent one and the expert-novice relationship is constantly shifting as the interaction unfolds.

Furthermore, the free use of double scripts in Chinese heritage language (CHL) schools presupposes a well-educated language user who is not only familiar with the specific orthographic rules of the scripts but also with their associated cultural, political, and economic connotations. The question is, then, whether the scripts, when adopted into a new textual and cultural environment in the United States, retain their specific connotations for the CHL learners and teachers. Whatever the answer to this question may be, could the adaptation of double scripts be interpreted as a conscious attempt on the part of the teachers and students to construct a layered cultural identity meaningful in, and suitable for, a pluralistic U.S. society? Ultimately, such encounters bring to the foreground the relationship between the scripts that CHL learners and teachers write and the sociocultural identities they imagine in writing and enact in life.

Subject Pronouns and Identities

To examine participants' cultural identity is always a complex inferential and social process. From a Language Socialization perspective, this is because our understandings of which acts and stances constitute resources for constructing particular cultural identities are limited. However, group and cultural identities are particularly relevant and salient in heritage language education. Unlike the case of foreign/second language learning where the learner is clearly a member of his/her "native culture" who is attempting to learn the norms and rules of the "target culture" as enacted and (re)constituted by the target language he/she is learning, the learner of a heritage language appears to have a multifaceted identity as someone who is both similar to and different from members of the target culture since he/she is sociohistorically connected with the target culture and yet experientially displaced from it. Through data segment 2, we may be able to see that with varying language forms—personal pronouns and shifting lexical entailments in various repair trajectories, the students and the teacher present themselves differently and project differential interpersonal alignments with regard to cultural/institutional groups.

(2) [TCCDL:953] choice of subject pronouns

((Tc is organizing the class to set up a writing contest between two groups. *women* = we; *nimen* = you; *tamen* = they))

1   Tc: 好=(.2) 我们现在分成两个组=
            hao(.2) ***women** xianzai fen   cheng liang ge   zu*=
            good we   now   divide PERT two MSR group
            Ok (.2) now let's break into two groups.

2   B3:   =我们比赛?!
            =***women** bisai*?!
            we   compete
            We're going to have a contest?!

3   Ss: [Yeah::

4   Tc: [比赛(.)对(.)看哪组又快又好
            [*bisai* (.) *dui* (.) *kan na   zu   you   kuai you   hao*
            compete yes   see which-Q group CONJ fast CONJ good
            Yes, (.) a contest. (.) Let's see which group is faster and better.

5   G4:   谁-谁谁输谁就买 cookies yeh::
            sh-   shui shui shu shui jiu   mai cookies yeh::
            who-Q who who lose who CONJ buy
            Whoever loses buys <u>cookies</u> (for everybody) yeh::

6   Tc: 买=cookie? 我们学习啊不用吃的

mai cookie? **Women** *xuexi ah   bu   yong chi de*
buy   we   learn PRT NEG   use   eat POS
Buy <u>cookies</u>? We are here to learn. We don't need food.

7   ((Students moving seats to get into groups.))

8   G4:   在学校 Mrs. Colon(.2)叫我们这样
           zai xuexiao Mrs. Colon *jiao* **women** *zhe yang*
           at   school   ask us   this manner
           At school <u>Mrs. Colon</u> (.2) asks us to do like this.

9   Tc: 这里 -这里嗯是中文学校啊我们不-
           *zheli- zheli uh   shi   zhongwen xuexiao ah   **women** bu-*
           here   here PRT COP Chinese   school   PRT   we   NEG
           It's it's uh Chinese School here. We don't-

10   他们这样我们不这样啊
           tamen *zhe yang   **women** bu   zhe yang   ah*
           they   this manner we   NEG this manner PRT
           They do this (but) we don't.

11   ((In the subsequent two–three minutes, the two groups are well into the
           contest. Tc is looking for the next word.))

12   B?:   老师我们赢了有 extra credit 吗？
           laoshi **women** *ying le   you* extra credit *ma*?
           teacher we   win PERT have   Q
           Teacher if we win do we get <u>extra credit</u>?

13   (.4)

14   B3:   我们赢了就加分.
           women *ying le   jiu   jia fen.*
           we   win PERT CONJ add point
           We should receive extra points if (we) win.

15   (.2)

16   Tc: 你们=-=我们不用啊
           nimen- **women** *bu   yong ah*
           you   we   NEG need PRT
           You- we don't need (to receive extra credit).

17   在学校他们给加分吗？
           zai   xuexiao **tamen** *gei   jia fen   ma*?
           at-LOC school they   PRT add point Q
           Do they give (you) extra points at school?

18   Ss: ((inaudible))

19   Tc: 我们不用 -no cookie no extra   [credit ok?
             women bu   yong- no cookie no extra   [credit ok?=
             we   NEG need
             We don't need- <u>no cookie no extra credit ok</u>?

20   B3:   [我们有加分
                                               [***women you jia fen.***
                                               we   have add point
                                               We do have extra points.

21   我们有(.)大家都有.
             women you dajia   dou   you.
             we   have everyone all-EMP have
             We have- everyone gets (extra points).

22   ((A parent entered the classroom to pick up her child early and the
             discussion on whether the writing contest should be associated
             with rewards was interrupted and not brought up again in this
             class meeting.))

TABLE 22.1. References in Data Segment (2)

Line #	Speaker	Pronoun Referent	Activity
1	Tc	we: Ss at CLS	have a writing contest
2	B3	we: Ss at CLS	have a writing contest
6	Tc	we: Ss at CLS	don't need food when learning
8	G4	we: Ss at DTS	have cookies as learning rewards
9	Tc	we: Ss & T at CLS	don't need food/rewards
10	Tc	they: Ss & T at DTS	have/allow cookies as rewards
10	Tc	we: Ss & T at CLS	don't need/allow food/rewards
12	B?	we: Ss at CLS	get extra points?
14	B3	we: Ss at CLS	should get extra points
16	Tc	you: Ss at CLS	
16	Tc	we: Ss at CLS	don't need extra points
17	Tc	they: T at DTS	give extra points?
19	Tc	we: Ss at CLS	don't need cookies or points
20	B3	we: Ss at DTS	get extra points
21	B3	we: all Ss at DTS	get extra points

This table summarizes the use of different pronouns by different speakers. CLS stands for Chinese language school; DTS refers to the regular daytime school the students attend during weekdays.

If we focus on each of the pronouns, "*women* (we)" is used to refer to (1) students at CLS (by both Ss and Tc), (2) students and teachers at CLS (by Tc), (3) students at daytime schools (by Ss), and (4) all students at daytime schools (by Ss). "*Nimen* (you)" is used by Tc to refer to students at CLS (line 16). And "*tamen* (they)" is used by Tc to refer to (1) students and teachers at daytime schools and (2) teachers at daytime schools (lines 10 and 17). Alternatively, if we focus on each of the speakers, the students are self-presented as (1) students at CLS, (2) students at daytime schools, and (3) members of the entire student body at daytime schools. The students are other-presented by Tc as members of CLS only. In other words, while students identify themselves with daytime schools as well as with CLS using "*women* (we)" in all cases, Tc clearly differentiates CLS from daytime schools, marking in each case students and teachers at daytime schools as "*tamen* (they)."

This data segment is also characterized by a number of repair sequences. In line 5, G4 completes a *self-initiated same turn repair*, announcing that whichever team loses the contest will need to buy cookies for everyone. This turn is marked by perturbations in the beginning and the mid-turn code switch from Chinese to English. In line 6, Tc extends an *other-initiated other-completed repair*. She first offers a repair initiation through a partial repeat of G4's previous turn with a question intonation ("Buy cookies?"), which structurally could have functioned as a *next turn repair initiation*. However, without allowing any space for G4 to respond to the repair initiation, Tc continues to complete the repair herself within the same speaking turn, stating that learning should not be associated with food. Hence, interestingly enough, on the one hand, Tc appropriates the English item introduced by G4 ("cookie"), thereby exhibiting her own identification with the students' linguistic membership categorization (i.e., bilingual in Chinese and English). On the other hand, she opts to use the least affiliative repair strategy, that of other-initiated, other-completed repair.

In line 8, G4 argues for the legitimacy of buying cookies by invoking the practices of her daytime school. In lines 9–10, Tc strives (as evidenced by cut-offs and hesitations in the beginning of the turn) to present a counter-argument by differentiating Chinese language school from daytime school. There are two instances of *self-initiated same turn repair* in lines 9–10. The first occurs at the beginning of the turn when Tc is trying to justify why buying cookies is not appropriate. The second instance occurs when she contrasts what is acceptable in CLS with what is acceptable in DTS ("we" versus "they").

In line 16, in reply to a student's question (line 12) whether the winning team will get extra points, Tc produces another *self-initiated same turn repair* (from "you" to "we"), this time shifting from a categorization of students and herself as separate entities to an identification of students and herself as belonging to the same membership.

The last instance of repair occurs in line 19. It is yet another *self-initiated same turn repair*. Unlike other instances of repair of the same type, however, in this instance, the repair is *completed* through code-switching from Chinese to English at the end of a turn-constructional-unit ("We don't need it"). As Tc clearly spoke Chinese much better than English and since she rarely used English in the classroom, code-switching in this case can be seen as evidence for identity adjustment

(Martin-Jones 1998) for Tc, an adjustment from someone who makes a clear distinction between the Chinese speaking "we" and the English speaking "they" to someone who is receptive to ambivalence, duality, and possibly change.

Table 22.2 considers areas where the usage of personal pronouns and sequential organization of this spate of talk converge. It locates the personal pronouns in the trouble source-repair initiation-repair completion sequence.

Table 22.2 shows that where personal references and repair sequences converge, the speaker is exclusively the teacher. As specified above, in each of these instances and accumulatively, the teacher attempts to categorize the students as members of CLSs (as opposed to DTSs) and to align herself with the students.

To sum up, the students' self-presentation appears to be multifaceted and fluid; they categorize themselves as members of simultaneously existing multiple groups and move in and out of groups with ease, aligning themselves with CLS, their daytime school, and/or their teacher at various points in time. The teacher, on the other hand, appears to make every effort (including a successive of self-repairs) to categorize the students solely as members of CLS. In other words, as the participants collaboratively (although differently) define the identity of the students, they at the same time also jointly re-create the identity of the teacher.

Concluding Remarks

In this chapter, I have considered how an interactionally enriched Language Socialization perspective may shed light on the construction of identities in the context of Chinese heritage language classes. I have focused on repair sequences, the choice of scripts, and the use of pronouns in teacher-student interactions that construct various affective stances of certainty or uncertainty, knowledgeability or unknowledgeability, affiliation or disaffiliation, which in turn are constitutive of participant identities of expert/novice, teacher/students, CLS/DTS students, Chinese, American, Chinese American, Taiwanese Chinese American, or Mainland China Chinese American.

TABLE 22.2. Pronouns and Repair Sequence in Data Segment (2)

Line #	Speaker	Pronominal Reference	Location of Reference in Repair Sequence
6	Tc	("buy cookie")	(Trouble source)
		We	Other repair
9	Tc	We	Trouble source
		They	Self-repair
16	Tc	You	Trouble source
		We	Self-repair
19	Tc	We	Trouble source
		(Code-switch)	(Self-repair)

Much remains to be investigated in future studies in terms of the relationship between interaction, identity, and heritage language learning. To learn one's heritage language is in part to (re)establish similarities with members of one's heritage culture or to (re)establish differences from members of mainstream American culture. Theoretically, which acts and stances are constitutive of the shift of learners' (and teacher's) identities that necessarily accompanies and potentially enables language learning? On what grounds could we build a strong connection among change in interactional trajectory, change in acts/stances and thus identity, and change in language ability? Empirically, the robustness of the notion of identity as brought about through interaction needs to be evaluated against the background of classic research on the ethnography of communication (e.g., Gumperz and Gumperz 1982). On the other hand, as fundamental notions such as "speech community" may be in need of further definition considering the dynamics of identity in the postmodern era, contexts such as that of heritage language learning provide possibilities for us to reexamine these notions empirically.

Appendix: The Four Classrooms

Classroom 1

This was a higher-middle level (*bin ban*) class in a range of four proficiency level classes offered in city A, a metropolitan city in the southeastern United States. The students consisted of four girls and nine boys, aged between four and a half and eight. Classes met from 1:30 P.M. to 3:30 P.M. (with a ten-minute break at 2:30) on Sundays on the top floor of a university apartment building. A total of ten hours of lessons in this setting were audiotaped.

The instructor was Teacher Wang (Tw), a forty-five-year-old female with a bachelor's degree in philosophy from a university in China. Prior to coming to the United States, she had taught in elementary schools, middle schools, and universities in the Beijing area. She spoke little English.

Classroom 2

Eight hours of class meetings provided the database for classroom 2, which was beginning-level Chinese, the lowest of the three levels (*xiao ban*) offered in dity C, a university town in the Midwest. There were one girl and two boys in this class, aged between five and six. Classes met from 6:15 P.M. to 7:50 P.M. on Tuesdays on the university campus.

Teacher Zhang (Tz), the instructor, was a thirty-three-year-old female who had recently received a master's degree in educational psychology in China, where she had taught adult students. She was frustrated by the lack of appropriate textbooks for overseas Chinese children and was very interested in learning (new) ways of teaching children.

Classroom 3

Six hours of video- and audio-recorded class meetings provided the database for classroom 3, which was intermediate-level Chinese, the middle of the three levels (*zhong ban*) offered in the same school as classroom 2. There were five girls and two boys in this class, aged between five and nine. Classes met at the same time in the same building as classroom 2.

Teacher Shen (Ts), the instructor, was a twenty-seven-year-old female and a native of Taiwan who had recently received a master's degree in accounting in the United States. She had been teaching in this capacity for two years.

Classroom 4

Six hours of video- and audio-recorded class meetings provided the database for classroom 4, which was advanced-level Chinese, the highest of the three levels (*da ban*) offered in the same setting as classrooms 2 and 3. There were eight girls and four to five boys in this class, aged between five and nine. Classes met at the same time in the same building as classrooms 2 and 3.

Teacher Chao (Tc), the instructor, was a twenty-eight-year-old female and a native of Taiwan who had been in the United States for six years and was taking some computer courses in a local community college. She had experience teaching in a similar Chinese language school in another state and had been teaching in this particular school for two months.

NOTE

    1. Grammatical Gloss:

CONJ	conjunction	COP	copula	EMP	emphatic marker
LOC	locative marker	MSR	measure	NEG	negative marker
PERT	perfective aspect marker			POS	possessive
PRT	sentence, vocative or nominal subordinative particle				
PTP	pre-transitive preposition			Q	question marker

Transcription Symbols:

.	falling intonation
?	rising intonation
[ ]	overlapped talk
-	cut-off
=	latched talk
:	prolonged sound or syllable
(0.0)	silences roughly in seconds and tenths of seconds (measured more according to the relative speech rate of the interaction than according to the actual clock time)
(.)	short, untimed pauses of one-tenth of a second or less
(( ))	additional observation
T:	at the beginning of a stretch of talk, identifies the speaker; T is for teacher (different teachers are represented by different small letters such as Ts or Tz), G for girl, B for boy, Ss for whole class.
> <	fast speech
——	code-switched components

REFERENCES

Atkinson, J. Maxwell, and John Heritage, ed. 1984. *Structures of social action: Studies in conversation analysis*. Cambridge: Cambridge University Press.

Bourdieu, Pierre. 1977. *Outline of a theory of practice*. Cambridge: Cambridge University Press.

Bradunas, Elena, and Brett Topping, ed. 1988. *Ethnic heritage and language schools in America*. Washington, D.C.: Library of Congress.

Chen, Ping. 1999. *Modern Chinese: History and sociolinguistics*. Cambridge: Cambridge University Press.

Creese, Angela, and Peter Martin, ed. 2006. Interaction in complementary school contexts: Developing identities of choice. Special issue, *Language and Education* 20:1.

Drew, Paul, and John Heritage, ed. 1992. *Talk at work*. New York: Cambridge University Press.

Ford, Cecilia, and Sandra Thompson. 1996. Interactional units in conversation: Syntactic, intonational, and pragmatic resources for the management of turns. In *Interaction and grammar*, ed. Elinor Ochs, Emanuel Schegloff, and Sandra Thompson, 134–184. Cambridge: Cambridge University Press.

Garfinkel, Harold. 1967. *Studies in ethnomethodology*. Englewood Cliffs, N.J.: Prentice-Hall.

Greenberg, Robert. 2004. *Language and identity in the Balkans: Serbo-Croatian and its disintegration*. Oxford: Oxford University Press.

Gumperz, John, and Jenny Cook-Gumperz. 1982. Language and the communication of social identity. In *Language and social identity*, ed. John Gumperz, 1–21. Cambridge: Cambridge University Press.

He, Agnes W. 1995. Co-constructing institutional identities: The case of student counselees. *Research on Language and Social Interaction* 28:213–231.

———. 1997. Learning and being: Identity construction in the classroom. *Pragmatics and Language Learning* 8:201–222.

———. 1998. *Reconstructing institutions: Language use in academic counseling encounters*. Greenwich, Conn.: Greenwood.

———. 2000. Grammatical and sequential organization of teachers' directives. *Linguistics and Education* 11:119–140.

———. 2003. Linguistic anthropology and language education. In *Linguistic anthropology of education*, ed. Stanton Wortham and Betsy Rymes, 93–119. Westport, Conn.: Praeger.

———. 2006. Toward an identity theory of the development of Chinese as a heritage language. *The Heritage Language Journal* 4:1. http://www.heritagelanguages.org/.

Martin-Jones, Marilyn. 1998. Teaching and learning bilingually: A survey of recent research. *Working Papers in Urban Language and Literacies*. London: Kings College. http://www.kcl.ac.uk/ depsta/education/ULL/WP10MMJ.doc.pdf.

Ochs, Elinor. 1990. Indexicality and socialization. In *Cultural psychology: Essays on comparative human development*, ed. James W. Stigler, Richard A. Shweder, and Gilbert H. Herdt, 287–308. Cambridge: Cambridge University Press.

———. 1992. Indexing gender. In *Rethinking context*, ed. Alessandro Duranti and Charles Goodwin, 335–358. New York: Cambridge University Press.

———. 1993. Constructing social identity. *Research on Language and Social Interaction* 26:287–306.

———. 1996. Linguistic resources for socializing humanity. In *Rethinking linguistic relativity*, ed. John Gumperz and Stephen C. Levinson, 407–437. Cambridge: Cambridge University Press.

Ochs, Elinor, and Bambi B. Schieffelin. 1984. Language acquisition and socialization: Three developmental stories. In *Culture theory: Essays on mind, self and emotion*, ed. Richard A. Shweder and Robert A. LeVine, 276–320. Cambridge: Cambridge University Press.

Peyton, J. Kreeft, Donald A. Ranard, and Scott McGinnis, ed. 2001. *Heritage languages in America: Preserving a national resource*. McHenry, Ill.: Delta Systems Co., Inc.

Rampton, Ben. 1995. *Crossing: Language and ethnicity among adolescents*. London: Longman.

Sacks, Harvey. 1992. *Lectures on conversation, vol. 1 and 2*, ed. G. Jefferson. Oxford: Blackwell.

Sacks, Harvey, Emanuel A. Schegloff, and Gail Jefferson. 1974. A simplest systematics for the organization of turn-taking for conversation. *Language* 50:696–735.

Schegloff, Emanuel A. 1979. The relevance of repair to syntax-for-conversation. *Syntax and Semantics* 12:261–286.

———. 1992. Repair after next turn: The last structurally provided place for the defense of intersubjectivity in conversation. *American Journal of Sociology* 95:1295–1345.

———. 1996. Third turn repair. In *Towards a social science of language. Papers in honors of William Labov, vol. 2: Social interaction and discourse structures*, ed. Gregory R. Guy, Crawford Feagin, Deborah Schiffrin, and John Baugh, 31–40. Amsterdam: John Benjamins.

Schegloff, Emanuel A., Gail Jefferson, and Harvey Sacks. 1977. The preference for self-repair in the organization of repair in conversation. *Language* 53:361–382.

Schieffelin, Bambi, and Elinor Ochs, ed. 1986a. *Language socialization across cultures*. New York: Cambridge University Press.

———. 1986b. Language socialization. *Annual Review of Anthropology* 15:163–191.

———. 1996. The microgenesis of competence. In *Social interaction, social context, and language*, ed. Dan Slobin, Julie Gerhardt, Amy Kyratzis, and Jiansheng Guo, 251–261. Mahwah, N.J.: Lawrence Erlbaum.

Vygotsky, Lev S. 1978. *Thought and language*. Cambridge, Mass.: MIT Press.

Wang, Xueying, ed. 1996. *A view from within: A case study of Chinese heritage community language schools in the U.S.* Washington, D.C.: National Foreign Language Center.

Wortham, Stanton, and Betsy Rymes, ed. 2003. *Linguistic anthropology of education*. Westport, Conn.: Praeger.

23

The Emergence of Language Identity in Cultural Action

A Commentary

Bonnie Urciuoli

A s analysts, we routinely treat language identity as a kind of ready-made label. Yet as these three chapters—Agnes Weiyun He's "Sequences, Scripts, and Subject Pronouns in the Construction of Chinese Heritage Identity," Leanne Hinton's "Trading Tongues: Loss of Heritage Languages in the United States," and Steven Talmy's "Forever FOB? Resisting and Reproducing the Other in High School ESL"—cumulatively demonstrate, the dimensions of linguistic identity that emerge depend on the linguistic action in which it occurs. He and Talmy examine emergent elements of linguistic identification at moments of interaction, moments at which language per se may or may not be actors' primary consideration. Hinton examines constructions of cultural and linguistic identification in which actors reflect on self-definition in ways that do foreground language as a primary consideration. These perspectives complement each other, providing more nuanced understandings of linguistic identification as a form of markedness in the United States. The issues raised by these three chapters help illustrate how, in the United States, language is so readily intertwined with notions of personhood, and how whiteness operates as a dynamic yet persistent historical concept. Of primary consideration are the sites in which these data are gathered—in each case, sites of education—and what it means to be an American, or a potential American, in those sites.

Language, like culture, is much too readily thought of as a *thing*, an unproblematically bounded entity governing human actions and loyalties. It makes better sense to understand both language and culture as processes in which people participate, processes on which no single person can have a complete perspective. Such processes, anchored in the relative stability of social structures, are at the same time continually played out as elements of actors' everyday reality. To the extent that such processes are not determined, to the extent that actors participate performatively in those processes, both recreating and subtly shifting their structural elements, we can talk about actors' agency. We should also consider the ways in which linguistic and cultural processes form elements of actors' subjectivity. The discursive elements examined in these three chapters, including pronouns, role relations, the use of epithets, and self-descriptive narratives, are manifestations of intersubjective processes in which each participant, acting as *I*, shares some, often much but probably never complete, understanding of their social worlds, each taking a stance and often contesting the stances of others, each tracing a social path through indexical elements that wink in and out of social awareness, each moment of understanding subject to revision in the next. What any one person perceives as a language or a culture emerges partially and contingently from such processes, as we can see in these chapters.

Each of these chapters highlights some aspect of the particular thinginess of language, an objectification particularly linked to and reinforced by the literacy practices of formal education. This is a central theme in He's conversational analysis (CA) of the interactional production of a Chinese literacy-based affirmative ethnic identity. The importance of such ethnic production is particularly salient given the connection of linguistic objectification to the taxonomy of markedness in the United States that governs both constructions of language and ethnicity/race, as Talmy's and Hinton's chapters show. These taxonomies are continually reinforced by public discourses generated not only by education but also by business, media, politics, and law, and are thus routinely reproduced as social facts taken for granted by social actors, particularly those in positions of institutional authority. In this cultural taxonomy, English represents the only unblemished, unproblematic mode of linguistic being; all other forms of linguistic identity index departures from that state. Talmy shows how the stigmatizing nature of the ESL (English as Second Language) label penetrates student classification of each other in a Hawai'i public high school. Hinton's college student autobiographies reveal histories of self-perception in which "lack" of English parallels inadequacies of self.

Since pronouns and the construction of subjectivity and cultural identity are central to these three chapters, let me address the relation of pronouns to the discursive process. As Emile Benveniste argued a half century ago ([1966] 1971a, [1966] 1971b), the construction of subjectivity is one of the fundamental functions of language. Subjectivity is encoded in pronoun systems, in time and space deictics (*here, there, this, that, then, now,* and so on) and in performativity (the capacity for a speaker to bring into being a certain social state, as in the performance of a promise or threat, and of course in less explicit speech acts). Pronominal systems are structured oppositionally: *I* and *we* are intersubjectively linked to *you* and thus index positions and points in the process of discourse. That intersubjective link is opposed to those objects of reference outside the immediate axis of discourse: *he, she, it, they.* The deictic oppositions of *here/there, this/that, then/now,* and so on are anchored in that axis of discourse, which is why the space, time, and social elements they index are so variable. Existing within this complex frame is the system of meanings instantiated through discursive functions. Roman Jakobson (1960) argued that meaning in discourse emerges in a complex of functions, each related to an element of the speech situation, with reference as only one of several such functions. Jakobson further stressed the routine multifunctionality of discourse, a point refined by Michael Silverstein's (1976) distinction between function as conventionally categorized (and often conflated with speaker intention) versus function as actual outcomes. I raise these points, especially about reference, because it is too easy to assume that when speakers engage in acts of reference that that is all they are doing, and that what they refer to exists as a simple label. There is almost certainly more going on performatively, even when, as in Hinton's essay, it looks as though speakers are simply describing themselves. They are constructing stances through which cultural identity emerges, culture in the sense of a shared sense of intelligibility, belonging, way of being in the world. That is not an undifferentiated whole, as we see in these articles, nor does it necessarily correspond to a specific group name. As Greg Urban (1996) has shown, there is no simple, obvious connection between people's use of *we* and a group name; rather, uses of *we* may be variously connected to particular imaginings of shared experience and conditions, imaginings which are discursively produced and which it is the ethnographer's job to account for.

In their microanalyses of interaction, He and Talmy connect pronoun usage to emergent cultural and linguistic identity. As He notes, the advantage of this level of analysis is its capacity to explore ambivalences in identity formation. He does this by focusing on membership categorization and identity construction as points in processes of working out identity. Any given person might define herself or himself according to a range of possible membership categorizations—so what, in a given instance, motivates the foregrounding of language, and how precisely might it be indexed? In He's analysis of Chinese heritage language learners, everyone is operating in a situation in which the value of Chinese literacy is presupposed, and in which everyone is in some respect a cultural insider. So we are looking at relative distances from that position, configured through interpersonal alignments and indexed through personal pronouns—"we" (*women*), "they" (*tamen*), and "you" (*nimen*)—and the repairs in which the teachers sometimes engage. Almost immediately, the deployment of "we" versus "they" and "you" shows the non-isomorphism of the teacher's and students' "we." For the teachers, the central point is that learning is its own reward, which they ground in the authority of their institutional position. But for students, key elements of learning derive from the public school model of instruction, as when they raise the possibility of cookies as a reward for good performance. From the teacher's perspective, not being or being Chinese is indexed not, in this instance, by a contrast of Chinese/English but by the notion of cookies being (or not) an appropriate reward. From the students' perspective, this is not a salient contrast. The several pronoun repairs in which the teacher engages function to rework these splits in categorization, in one instance supported by a code-switch from Chinese to English. Here, much more noticeably than Talmy (below), we see a teacher whose control over her teacher persona is somewhat dependent on her students' ratification. In this instance, being Chinese is indexed by expressions of particular notions of how to be a teacher or student, notions that are not identical for teacher and students. Moreover, the students' sense of identity in the classroom is considerably more fluid than the teacher's, and the teacher does not have full control over how that identity is realized.

Talmy examines the cultural production of otherness via linguistic identity markedness, particularly the ways in which *linguicism* exploits the naturalness of unmarked languages, in this case English. For both students and the school itself, what is labeled *English* or otherwise is less a linguistic construction in a formal sense than a construction of person based on a conflation of linguistic and racial/ethnic elements. At the same time, there is a kind of invisibility as to what linguicism actually is, as evidenced by its "commonsense" status in educational institutions. In this particular school's policy, "not having" English is equated with recentness of enrollment at the high school, independent of other considerations (such as linguistic performance). This markedness is reinforced by an official notion of multiculturalism defined by "heroes, holidays and foods" in which students are assumed to be "natural" experts (critiqued as *culturalism* by Segal and Handler 1995). This produces an institutionally controlled and narrowly acceptable way of being a non-English speaker, which is then available for conflation with the non-official low-status outsider category *FOB*. Talmy tracks pronoun use by teacher and student in relation to discursive function (especially teacher directives and student resistance). Unlike the teachers He describes, Talmy's teacher is much more firmly positioned to define the boundaries of student identity. In her instructions to the class, the teacher sets up a *we* that formally includes her and her students as non-American, but she is also positioned to exit that *we* (and be American) when she chooses while the students cannot, performatively reinforcing their foreignness. They can resist by responding with irony but they have much less leverage than the students in He's study to manage their persona on the classroom stage. The consequences for them are considerably sharper, since they get positioned as low-status outsiders. There is a lot more at stake for them in the construction of subjectivity, given the terrain of markedness in which the contest for one's own agency takes place. Nor does this only exist in teacher-student relations, as we see in students' efforts to reposition themselves by casting another student lower in the hierarchy. This is done through pronoun deployment, the conflation of linguistic limitations, and reference to strange practices, ways of being that don't "fit in" and, above all, identification with a place that may not even be a real country in the students' eyes.

In He's and Talmy's analyses, we see the invocation of linguistic identities mixed with other identity modes. Hinton, by contrast, presents interview selections in which students focus primarily if not entirely on the linguistic lens through which they see themselves. Again, pronoun use is salient, specifically *I*. How (and how much) a narrator perceives herself or himself speaking English or a native language serves as a kind of focusing for that narrator's subjectivity. It is important to note that most narrators describe a cline from full to no linguistic knowledge, describing their own trajectories in terms of gaining or losing. Why should people see themselves and their languages in this way? People are not simply assessing their capacity to communicate, although that is a significant aspect. They are reflecting on the knowledge of their own markedness. In these narratives, we particularly see the conflation of linguistic capacity and marked origin identity, that is, racialization. The issue many narrators address is not simply ethnic (as Chinese, Korean, etc.), but how and why those are seen as "not American" where the baseline for so many routine cultural constructions of being American is racial unmarkedness, or as it is generally termed, whiteness. The structure of feeling in these narratives is typically linear: People routinely describe a polarity with self and family at one end and success in America at the other, often involving generational distance from grandparents and parents, or a cline from alienation and isolation through degrees of nonsociality to full participation. They also describe language as good (clear, complete, literate) or bad (mispronounced, inarticulate, or partial, i.e., "mixed") or describe the zero-sum trade-off between English and one's heritage in terms of its damage to family relations. It is striking that narratives focus far more on individual than community experience of language. Following the line back "up," narrators describe the importance of higher education for regaining linguistic self-respect, or talk about an academically achieved bilingualism in terms of its practical benefits and/or its capacity to validate one's cultural identity. Yet while this regained language shares the same label as the language one may have grown up with, that does not mean that, pragmatically, both are experienced the same way. Certainly when students rediscover heritage language, what it means to them has been reframed in terms of how they come to understand cultural definition.

How the forms of experience and knowledge labeled as a specific language take on symbolic capital is in part a function of the relation of linguistic awareness to educational institutions. In the education process, language is defined and entextualized by standardized literacy practices. Such institutional practices and their long-term effects are so ideologically valued and at the same time naturalized that they are transparent. People take for granted that languages thus represented are language in an unproblematic way, but the simple use of language labels can be deceptive in that they do not necessarily correspond to all the ways in which people actually experience language. The association of language categories with literacy and correctness can overshadow and undervalue the experiential complexities through which linguistic experience becomes part of cultural experience. The chapters discussed here illustrate important dimensions of that experience.

REFERENCES

Benveniste, Emile. [1966] 1971a. The nature of pronouns. In *Problems in general linguistics*, 217–222. Coral Gables: University of Miami Press.
———. [1966] 1971b. Subjectivity in language. In *Problems in general linguistics*, 223–230. Coral Gables: University of Miami Press.
Jakobson, Roman. 1960. Closing statement: Linguistics and poetics. In *Style and language*, ed. Thomas Sebeok, 350–377. Cambridge, Mass.: MIT Press.
Segal, Daniel, and Richard Handler. 1995. U.S. multiculturalism and the concept of culture. *Identities* 1:391–407.
Silverstein, Michael. 1976. Shifters, linguistic categories and cultural description. In *Meaning in anthropology*, ed. Keith Basso and Henry Selby, 11–55. Albuquerque: University of New Mexico Press.
Urban, Greg. 1996. *Metaphysical community: The interplay of the senses and the intellect*. Austin: University of Texas Press.

INDEX